ADMINISTRATIVE SANCTIONS IN THE EUROPEAN UNION

ADMINISTRATIVE SANCTIONS IN THE EUROPEAN UNION

Oswald Jansen (ed.)

intersentia
Cambridge – Antwerp – Portland

Intersentia Publishing Ltd.
Trinity House | Cambridge Business Park | Cowley Road
Cambridge | CB4 0WZ | United Kingdom
Tel.: +44 1223 393 753 | Email: mail@intersentia.co.uk

Distribution for the UK:
NBN International
Airport Business Centre, 10 Thornbury Road
Plymouth, PL6 7 PP
United Kingdom
Tel.: +44 1752 202 301 | Fax: +44 1752 202 331
Email: orders@nbninternational.com

Distribution for the USA and Canada:
International Specialized Book Services
920 NE 58th Ave. Suite 300
Portland, OR 97213
USA
Tel.: +1 800 944 6190 (toll free)
Email: info@isbs.com

Distribution for Austria:
Neuer Wissenschaftlicher Verlag
Argentinierstraße 42/6
1040 Wien
Austria
Tel.: +43 1 535 61 03 24
Email: office@nwv.at

Distribution for other countries:
Intersentia Publishing nv
Groenstraat 31
2640 Mortsel
Belgium
Tel.: +32 3 680 15 50
Email: mail@intersentia.be

Administrative Sanctions in the European Union
Oswald Jansen (ed.)

ISBN 978-1-78068-136-8
D/2013/7849/96
NUR 823

PREFACE

This book is focused on administrative sanctions and offers a thorough overview of the sanctioning systems of 13 EU Member States. The initial idea for this elaborate and challenging project is based on the impression that although sanctioning powers are of great importance in practice both at EU level and nationally, little comparative study has been done on this subject. More importantly, when studying law enforcement one should study both administrative law and criminal law sanctioning systems. In legal scholarship there is clear division between the scholarship in administrative law and the scholarship in criminal law. In the discussion of deterrent administrative sanctions, such as administrative fines (as we will see, in some legal systems remedial measures are not considered sanctions, only punitive measures are) both areas of scholarship should meet, as according to case law of the ECHR and many national constitutional courts, certain criminal law guarantees apply to administrative sanctions that have a punitive aim. The authors that have contributed to this book are both criminal law specialists and administrative law specialists, and they have all managed to address the theme from the perspective of both disciplines. This approach makes this book special.

The project to arrive at this result started with an international meeting of experts on 16 July 2004. Almost all the authors came to Utrecht that day to discuss the subject-matter and design of the project with each other and with colleagues from the Dutch Ministry of Justice and other practitioners interested in administrative sanctions. In the process of finalising this book since then, authors have updated their contributions, many of them even two or more times. They deserve admiration for their patience with the occasionally headache-inducing process to arrive at this result.

The realisation of the research project would not have been possible without the financial support of the Dutch Scientific Council (NWO) and the Dutch Ministry of Justice.

We would like to thank all colleagues and assistants involved for their efforts in publishing their work in most cases in a non-native language. All translators involved, and especially Maris van der Laak, cannot underestimate the value of their work to this book. Special thanks should also be addressed to Lucia van Tellegen and Lionel van den Berg, both students at the law school of Utrecht

University, for their valuable support in finalising this book. And last but not least, we would also like to thank Intersentia for their willingness to publish this book.

We have every confidence that the present book will find its way to everyone who is interested in both administrative law and criminal law, and more precisely in law enforcement and administrative sanctioning.

Utrecht, The Hague,
May 2013
Oswald Jansen

CONTENTS

I. **The Definition of Administrative Sanctions – General Report**
Carlo Enrico PALIERO 1

II. **Country Analysis – Austria**
Frank HÖPFEL and Robert KERT 35

III. **Country Analysis – Belgium**
Johan PUT and Ken ANDRIES 93

IV. **Country Analysis – Finland**
Mikael KOILLINEN 159

V. **Country Analysis – France**
Emmanuel BREEN 195

VI. **Country Analysis – Germany**
Gerhard DANNECKER 213

VII. **Country Analysis – Greece**
George DELLIS 255

VIII. **Country Analysis – Italy**
Alessandro BERNARDI, Ciro GRANDI and Ilaria ZODA 289

IX. **Country Analysis – the Netherlands**
Oswald JANSEN 317

X. **Country Analysis – Portugal**
Pedro CAEIRO and Miguel Ângelo LEMOS 467

XI. **Country Analysis – Romania**
Elena Mihaela FODOR and Corina Cristina BUZDUGAN 497

XII. **Country Analysis – Spain**
Manuel Rebollo Puig, Manuel Izquierdo Carrasco, Lucía Alarcón Sotomayor and Antonio Mª. Bueno Armijo 515

XIII. **Country Analysis – Sweden**
Patricia Blanc-Gonnet Jonason 553

XIV. **Country Analysis – United Kingdom**
John McEldowney. 585

XV. **Administrative Sanctions in EU Law**
Adrienne de Moor-van Vugt 607

DETAILED CONTENTS

Preface v
List of Abbreviations xxiii

I. The Definition of Administrative Sanctions – General Report
Carlo Enrico PALIERO 1

1. Introduction. Different methods for the different purposes of the notion of administrative sanction: *phenomenological* and *typological* tasks 1
2. Method and structure of this general report. 5
3. The legislative frame of reference: indications from EU law and ECHR case law from the point of view of content and function 6
4. Degree of differentiation of the administrative sanction in the strict sense compared with other judicial system reactions 8
   4.1. Compared to criminal sanctions 8
      4.1.1. Countries with a low degree of differentiation 9
      4.1.2. Countries with greater differences 10
      4.1.3. Countries with a low degree of functional differentiation and a high degree of formal differentiation. 11
   4.2. Comparison with other forms of reaction of the public administration to the violation of a precept. 12
      4.2.1. Introduction 12
      4.2.2. Countries with a very high degree of differentiation. 13
      4.2.3. Countries with a high degree of differentiation 15
      4.2.4. Countries with an intermediate level of differentiation 16
      4.2.5. Countries with a low level of differentiation 18
      4.2.6. Countries with a very low degree of differentiation. 19
   4.3. Comparison with disciplinary sanctions 19
5. Internal characteristics of the concept of administrative sanction valid in any given legal system 20
   5.1. The existence of a 'single code' for the category and its relationship with the legality principle 21
      5.1.1. Countries that have a category code. 21
      5.1.2. Countries without a category code 23
   5.2. Typology of sanctions. 26

5.3. Indictment criteria for administrative sanctions (forms and prerequisites of responsibility for the offence) 27
6. Conclusions 30

II. Country Analysis – Austria
Frank HÖPFEL and Robert KERT 35

1. Relation to general fields of law and important general acts 35
1.1. Definition of sanctions and relationship to other measures in the light of the historical development 35
1.2. Administrative sanctions in the Austrian law 38
1.2.1. Administrative penal sanctions 38
1.3. Historical development 44
1.4. Constitutional issues and influence of the European law 45
1.4.1. Division of powers between courts and administrative authorities 45
1.4.2. Relation to constitutional law, administrative law, criminal law and private law 49
1.4.3. Influence of the European law (EC/EU law and ECHR) 50
2. General principles 51
2.1. *Nullum crimen sine lege* 51
2.2. Principles of equality and of proportionality 53
2.3. Legality principle 54
2.4. The rule of law 54
2.5. Principle of fault 55
2.6. Liability of legal persons 56
2.7. *Ne bis in idem* 57
2.8. *Lex mitior* 61
2.9. Inquisitorial principle 61
2.10. Presumption of innocence 62
2.11. *Nemo tenetur* principle 62
3. Rights of defence 63
3.1. Possibilities of protest against the intention of an administrative authority to impose a sanction 63
3.2. Access of the infringer to his dossier 64
4. Organisation of sanctioning powers 64
4.1. Can sanctioning powers be exercised by all administrative authorities and within an administrative authority by any civil servant? 64
4.2. Does it make any difference if this is an independent authority? 65
4.3. Are sanctions to be imposed by judges (administrative, criminal, other), by the public prosecution, by specialised administrative authorities or by any administrative authority? 65

5. Investigation/inspection . . . 67
5.1. Investigative powers of administrative authorities to detect infringements and to examine by whom they have been committed . . . 67
5.1.1. General administrative penal law . . . 67
5.1.2. Competition law . . . 69
5.1.3. Act on Fiscal Offences . . . 70
5.2. Can the investigative powers of an administrative law system be used together with the investigative powers of the criminal law system? . . . 71
5.3. Can the information gathered by the use of criminal powers be used to impose administrative sanctions? . . . 71
5.4. Can the information gathered by the use of administrative powers be used to impose criminal sanctions? . . . 72
6. Legal protection . . . 72
6.1. The system of legal protection in general . . . 72
6.2. Legal remedies . . . 74
6.3. Is it possible to seize a judge with a complaint against a sanction imposed? . . . 76
6.4. Is this judge part of an administrative court, a criminal court or a civil court? . . . 77
6.5. Is it possible for this judge to take provisional measures? . . . 77
6.6. Can sanctions be executed immediately or only after all ways to ask for legal protection have been exhausted? . . . 77
6.7. What possibilities of judicial review does the judge have? . . . 78
6.8. How thorough can this review get (full jurisdiction or less)? . . . 78
6.9. Does this kind of judicial review differ from other administrative decisions? Does it make a difference that certain sanctioning powers allow administrative authorities to weigh interests and have political space or not? How do obligatory sanctions (sanctions that have to be imposed if an infringement has been discovered) fit into this picture? . . . 79
7. National and European/international mutual assistance . . . 80
7.1. Cooperation between national authorities in relation to the imposition of sanctions . . . 80
7.2. Assistance of a foreign EU authority to a national authority . . . 81
7.3. Framework Decision 2005/214/JHA . . . 84
7.4. Agreement between Austria and Germany on legal protection and mutual assistance in fiscal matters . . . 87
8. Actual importance in practice . . . 88
Bibliography . . . 88

III. Country Analysis – Belgium
Johan Put and Ken Andries 93

1. Introduction 93
2. The Belgian constitutional, judicial and administrative system 93
   2.1. Belgium, a federal state 93
      2.1.1. General overview 93
      2.1.2. The division of responsibilities 95
      2.1.3. Responsibilities with regard to administrative and criminal sanctions 96
   2.2. The system of legal protection against sanctions 96
      2.2.1. Constitution 96
      2.2.2. Organisation of judicial powers (*sensu lato*) 97
3. The notion and basic elements of administrative sanctions 117
   3.1. Definition 117
   3.2. Administrative sanctions compared to other measures 118
      3.2.1. Safety measures 118
      3.2.2. Reparation measures 119
      3.2.3. Measures of order 120
      3.2.4. Criminal sanctions 120
      3.2.5. Conditional, obligatory measures 121
   3.3. The different forms of administrative sanctions in Belgium 122
   3.4. Administrative investigation/inspection methods 123
4. Protection against administrative sanctions 124
   4.1. Introduction 124
   4.2. The general principles of proper administration (GPPA) 124
      4.2.1. Scope of application 124
      4.2.2. Classification of the GPPA 125
      4.2.3. The formal GPPA 126
      4.2.4. The material GPPA 133
      4.2.5. The right to information 139
   4.3. The general principles of criminal law (GPCL) 139
      4.3.1. Introduction 139
      4.3.2. Legality 140
      4.3.3. Presumption of innocence and personal nature of the punishment 141
      4.3.4. Reasonable delay 142
      4.3.5. *Nemo tenetur edere contra se* (privilege against self-incrimination) and the right to remain silent 143
      4.3.6. Individualisation of the punishment 145
      4.3.7. *Non bis in idem* 148
      4.3.8. Retroactivity of legislation 151
      4.3.9. Right to a double judicial review 152

5. Conclusions 152
Bibliography 154

IV. Country Analysis – Finland
Mikael KOILLINEN 159

1. Concept of administrative sanctions in Finnish administrative law 159
2. Principles governing the exercise of public powers in the light of the constitution 164
3. General principles of administrative law and sanctions 166
   3.1. A fuller account – general principles concretised in the exercise of sanctioning powers 167
   3.2. The criterion of competence – separation of powers 168
   3.3. The criterion of precision 170
   3.4. The criterion of proportionality 173
   3.5. The prohibition on the abuse of power 174
   3.6. The protection of legitimate expectations 177
   3.7 The reconstructed concept of administrative sanctions in Finnish Administrative Law 178
4. The requirements of protection under the law 180
   4.1. The right to appeal 180
   4.2. Right of access to the dossier 182
   4.3. The right to be heard 183
   4.4. Judicial review of sanctions 186
5. Investigative powers 187
6. European co-operation 191
7. Conclusions 193

V. Country Analysis – France
Emmanuel BREEN 195

1. Introduction 195
2. The conceptual jungle of non-criminal sanctions 196
3. The general principle: a licence to punish 199
   3.1. The Conseil constitutionnel case law 199
   3.2. The Conseil d'Etat case law 201
4. The three layers of administrative sanctions 202
   4.1. Authoritarian use of administrative sanctions 203
   4.2. Diffuse administrative sanctions 204
   4.3. Administrative sanctions as tools for independent agencies 207
5. Guarantees 'à la carte' 208
Bibliography 211

VI. Country Analysis – Germany
Gerhard DANNECKER 213

1. Introductory remarks 213
2. General definition of the term 'sanction' in Germany 214
2.1. Historical background 214
2.2. Definition in German case law 214
2.2.1. Differences between constitutional and general law sanctions 214
2.2.2. General definition of sanctions in the sense of general law . . . 215
2.2.3. Categories of sanctions according to objectives 216
3. Overview of the various provisions on sanctions in Germany 219
3.1. Introduction. 219
3.2. Sanctions under civil law 219
3.3. Sanctions under canon law 220
3.4. Sanctions under public law 221
3.4.1. Introduction 221
3.4.2. Criminal sanctions (general discussion) 221
3.4.3. Non-criminal sanctions under public law (general discussion) 222
3.4.4. Definitions of criminal sanctions versus administrative sanctions 222
3.4.5. The criminal sanction 223
3.4.6. Measures for the reformation of offenders and the prevention of crime 225
3.4.7. Validity of general legal principles within the scope of criminal sanctions 226
4. Administrative sanctions 226
4.1. Introduction. 226
4.2. Categories of administrative sanctions 227
4.2.1. The law governing administrative offences 227
4.2.2. Judicial enforcement measures (*Ordnungsmittel*) 231
4.2.3. Withdrawal/denial of benefits/opportunities 234
4.2.4. Means to enforce administrative acts. 237
4.2.5. Disciplinary measures. 242
4.3. Applicability of criminal law principles to administrative sanctions. 244
4.3.1. Introduction 244
4.3.2. The principle of punishment determined by statutory law ('*nullum crimen, nulla poena sine lege*') 245
4.3.3. The principle of guilt ('*nulla poena sine culpa*') 250
4.3.4. The principle of judicial power exercised by judges, Article 92 GG ('*nulla poena sine judicio*') 252

5. Summary . . . 253

VII. Country Analysis – Greece
George Dellis . . . 255

1. The Greek legal order and the punitive powers of the administration – General overview . . . 255
2. Administrative sanction as a particular field of public action . . . 259
2.1. The evolution of sanctioning administrative functions . . . 259
2.2. Definition and typology of administrative sanctions . . . 260
2.2.1. Administrative sanctions and onerous administrative acts . . . 260
2.2.2. More or less "punitive" sanctions – *stricto* and *lato sensu* administrative sanctions . . . 261
2.2.3. Pecuniary and non-pecuniary sanctions . . . 262
2.2.4. Disciplinary and non-disciplinary sanctions . . . 262
2.2.5. Sub-categories of non-disciplinary sanctions . . . 263
2.2.5.1. Taxation, customs and social security . . . 263
2.2.5.2. Protection of the public order *lato sensu* . . . 263
2.2.5.3. Public regulation . . . 264
2.2.6. Overall evaluation . . . 265
2.3. The institutional aspects of punitive administrative actions . . . 266
2.4. Constitutionality of administrative sanctions as a form of public action . . . 268
3. At the behest of a *jus puniendi*: a special regime for administrative sanctions? . . . 270
3.1. General remarks . . . 270
3.2. The general rules of administrative law in the field of administrative sanctions . . . 272
3.2.1. Legality – Competence . . . 272
3.2.2. Impartiality . . . 272
3.2.3. Right to a prior hearing . . . 273
3.2.4. Reasoning . . . 273
3.2.5. Notification . . . 273
3.2.6. Stay of execution . . . 274
3.2.7. Use of discretion . . . 274
3.3. The (limited) transfer of criminal law principles in the field of administrative sanctions . . . 275
3.3.1. "Repressive due process" . . . 275
3.3.2. Legality in the context of punitive actions . . . 278
3.3.2.1. *Nullum crimen nulla poena sine lege* . . . 278
3.3.2.2. Retroactivity . . . 278
3.3.2.3. Statutes of limitation for the offence. Amnesty. Clemency . . . 279

3.3.3. Responsibility . . . 280
3.3.3.1. Strict liability . . . 280
3.3.3.2. Presumption of innocence . . . 280
3.3.3.3. Choice of the appropriate sanction . . . 281
3.3.3.4. *Non reformatio in peius – non bis in idem* . . . 281
4. Remedies . . . 283
4.1. Administrative recourse . . . 283
4.2. Judicial remedies . . . 283
4.3. Interim relief . . . 285
Selected bibliography . . . 286

VIII. Country Analysis – Italy
Alessandro Bernardi, Ciro Grandi and Ilaria Zoda . . . 289

1. The Italian administrative sanctions system: introductory remarks . . . 289
2. General principles . . . 292
3. The principle of defence . . . 297
4. The organization of the sanctioning powers of the public administration . . . 299
5. The administrative investigation and the powers of inquiry . . . 301
6. The means of judicial protection for individuals against administrative orders . . . 304
7. Cooperation with foreign authorities in administrative matters . . . 306
8. The long-term depenalisation process and the current practical occurrence of administrative sanctions . . . 310

IX. Country Analysis – the Netherlands
Oswald Jansen . . . 317

1. Introduction . . . 317
2. The definition of sanction . . . 318
3. The development of enforcement action (*last onder bestuursdwang*) and the astreinte (*last onder dwangsom*) in the Netherlands . . . 324
4. Development of the administrative fine in the Netherlands . . . 332
5. Relation to general fields of law and important general acts . . . 354
5.1. Introduction: GALA and administrative law . . . 354
5.2. The position of specific legislation in relation to the GALA regulation on administrative fines . . . 356
5.3. A punishable offence or a fineable infringement . . . 370
5.4. The maximum fine . . . 373
5.5. Statutory fine tariff or not . . . 377
5.6. Heavy or light procedure . . . 379
5.7. The current relation to criminal law . . . 381

5.8. The problem of legal unity. 383
5.8.1. Introduction: unity of what? 383
5.8.2. Perpetration of an offence 384
5.8.3. Concurrence and continuous act 388
6. General principles 392
6.1. Introduction. 392
6.2. The principle of legality 394
6.3. The principle of proportionality. 397
6.4. Concurrence of acts and non-cumulation 404
6.5. *Una via* and *ne bis in idem* 405
6.6. No fine on death 412
7. Rights of defence 413
7.1. Introduction. 413
7.2. The presumption of innocence 413
7.3. The right to be informed of the proceeding and its basis. 415
7.4. The right to legal representation and legal aid 418
7.5. The right against self-incrimination and/or the right to remain silent 420
7.5.1. Introduction 420
7.5.2. The right to remain silent, the principle of *nemo tenetur* and the GALA regulation on administrative fines 422
7.6. The right of access to the file. 429
7.7. The right to translation during the proceeding. 430
7.8. The right to be heard 430
7.9. The right to expeditious proceedings 432
7.10. The right to an effective remedy. 433
7.11. The right to a reasoned decision. 434
8. Organization of sanctioning powers 435
9. Investigation/inspection. 437
10. Legal protection 440
10.1. Introduction: the general system 440
10.2. Recent reforms of administrative procedure 441
10.3. Institutional guarantees in the application of criminal law issues by administrative and criminal courts 443
11. National and European/international mutual assistance of administrative sanctions 446
Bibliography 451
Appendix I. The structure of the General Administrative Law Act. 460
Appendix II. Choice between administrative fine and criminal law system 464
Appendix III. The Dutch system of legal protection. 465

X. **Country Analysis – Portugal**
Pedro Caeiro and Miguel Ângelo Lemos . . . 467

1. Introduction . . . 467
2. Administrative sanctions . . . 467
2.1. Elements and types . . . 467
2.1.1. Elements . . . 467
2.1.2. Types . . . 468
2.2. Coimas and other sanctions provided by the Direito de Mera Ordenação Social . . . 470
2.2.1. Historical background . . . 470
2.2.2. Basic features of the Direito de Mera Ordenação Social . . . 471
2.2.3. Coimas . . . 472
2.2.4. Accessory sanctions . . . 473
2.2.5. Fundamental principles of Direito de Mera Ordenação Social . . . 474
2.2.5.1. Principle of legality . . . 474
2.2.5.2. Principle of favourable retroactivity (retroactive application of *lex mitior*) . . . 477
2.2.5.3. Principle of guilt (culpability) . . . 477
2.2.5.4. Societas delinquere potest . . . 477
2.2.5.5. *Non bis in idem* . . . 478
2.2.5.6. Principle of subsidiary applicability of criminal (substantive) law . . . 478
2.2.6. Procedure . . . 479
2.2.6.1. A *sui generis* procedure: the RGCO and criminal procedural law . . . 479
2.2.6.2. Principle of legality . . . 480
2.2.6.3. Gathering of evidence . . . 482
2.2.6.4. Rights of the defence . . . 482
2.2.6.5. Competence to proceed and to apply the sanctions . . . 483
2.2.6.6. Appeals . . . 484
2.3. Other unfavourable administrative measures (police measures *lato sensu*) . . . 485
2.3.1. Definition . . . 485
2.3.2. Examples of police measures . . . 486
2.3.2.1. Measures that are not necessarily connected with an imminent danger to the public interest . . . 486
2.3.2.2. Measures that are intended to avoid or remove an imminent or existing danger to the public interest . . . 487
2.3.3. Fundamental principles of police measures . . . 488
2.3.3.1. Police measures *lato sensu* . . . 488
2.3.3.2. Police measures *stricto sensu* . . . 490

2.4. Some examples of *contra-ordenações* and other unfavourable administrative measures in specific legal areas 491
2.4.1. Urban law (law on building) 491
2.4.2. Protection of the economy and public health 492
2.4.3. Banking law 493
2.4.4. Environmental law 494
3. Conclusion 494
Bibliography 495

XI. Country Analysis – Romania
Elena Mihaela FODOR and Corina Cristina BUZDUGAN 497

1. Introduction: general description of sanctions and the sanction system . . 497
2. General principles and codification 502
3. Sanctioning procedure 509
4. Legal protection 511
Bibliography 514

XII. Country Analysis – Spain
Manuel REBOLLO PUIG, Manuel IZQUIERDO CARRASCO, Lucía ALARCÓN SOTOMAYOR and Antonio Mª. BUENO ARMIJO 515

1. Relation to general fields of law and important general acts 515
1.1. Introduction 515
1.2. The concept of administrative sanction 515
1.3. The concept of administrative infringement 517
1.4. Unfavourable administrative measures that are not administrative sanctions 518
1.4.1. Restraining sanctions 519
1.4.2. Measures to restore the infringed legality 520
1.4.3. The reimbursement of public grants 520
1.4.4. Contractual penalties 520
1.5. General administrative sanctions and disciplinary administrative sanctions 521
1.6. Differences between the statutory regime of administrative sanctions and criminal sanctions 521
1.7. Constitutional and legal system 522
1.8. Content of the sanctions 523
1.9. The material scope of sanctioning administrative law and criminal law 524
2. General principles 526
2.1. The principle of legality 526

2.2. The principle of typology relating to offences and administrative sanctions. 528
2.3. The principle of the proportionality of sanctions 528
2.4. The principle of non-retroactivity of adverse sanctioning rules and retroactivity of favourable sanctioning rules (*lex mitior*). 529
2.5. The principle of guilt 530
2.6. The principle of *non bis in idem*. *530*
2.7. The principle of equality 531
2.8. The principle of the required procedure 532
3. Rights of defence 533
3.1. Enumeration and content of the rights of defence 533
3.1.1. The right to be informed of the charge(s) 534
3.1.2. The right to use relevant means to prove one's innocence 534
3.1.3. The right to refrain from self-incrimination and from pleading guilty 535
3.1.4. The right to the presumption of innocence. 535
3.2. Specific rights of defence in the punitive administrative procedure . 537
3.3. The punitive resolution. Providing the necessary grounds 538
4. Organization of sanctioning powers 539
5. Investigation/ inspection 540
5.1. Powers of investigation and inspection prior to the initiation of a punitive administrative procedure 540
5.2. The sanctioning administrative bodies' powers of investigation and inspection. 541
6. Legal protection. 542
6.1. Judicial control of contentious administrative jurisdiction: a contentious administrative appeal against sanctions 542
6.2. Challenging a sanction before the same public administration: administrative appeals against sanctions 546
6.3. Control by the Constitutional Court: an appeal for legal protection against sanctions and appeals on the ground of unconstitutionality. 547
6.4. Enforcement of sanctions 547
7. National and European/international mutual assistance. 548
7.1. Mutual assistance between the different organs and public administrations in Spain. 548
7.2. Assistance between the Spanish authorities and other Member States of the European Union or other States. 549
8. Actual importance in practice. 550

XIII. Country Analysis – Sweden
Patricia Blanc-Gonnet Jonason 553

1. Definition and typology of sanctions.... 553
   1.1. Definition of sanctions.... 553
   1.2. Typology of sanctions.... 553
      1.2.1. Penal sanctions.... 554
      1.2.2. Civil law sanctions.... 555
      1.2.3. Administrative sanctions.... 555
         1.2.3.1. Revocation of licences and withdrawal of authorization 556
         1.2.3.2. Administrative fees 557
         1.2.3.3. Public law fines.... 560
         1.2.3.4. Disciplinary sanctions according to public law 562
2. The Swedish legal framework regarding the imposition of administrative sanctions 562
   2.1. The legislative power.... 562
   2.2. Principles governing the decision-making power of public authorities 563
      2.2.1. The principle of legality 564
      2.2.2. Freedom from interference (the principle of the independence of public authorities).... 564
      2.2.3. The principles of objectivity and equality 564
      2.2.4. The principle of proportionality 565
   2.3. The Administrative Procedure Act and the Administrative Court Procedure Act 565
      2.3.1. General remarks concerning the Administrative Procedure Act 566
      2.3.2. General remarks about the Administrative Courts Procedure Act.... 567
   2.4. Rights of defence.... 567
      2.4.1. Right of access to the dossier/documents 568
      2.4.2. The right of the party to express his views before the authority takes a decision.... 569
      2.4.3. Right of hearing.... 569
      2.4.4. Right of representation.... 569
      2.4.5. Interpreter.... 570
      2.4.6. Stating the reasons for the decisions.... 570
      2.4.7. Legal aid 571
   2.5. Organization of sanctioning powers 572
      2.5.1. Which authorities have the power to impose administrative sanctions? 572

2.5.2. The division of sanctioning powers within an administrative authority. . . . 573
2.6. Investigation/inspection . . . 574
2.7. Legal protection. . . . 575
2.7.1. Self-correction by the authority which has taken the decision . . . 575
2.7.2. Right of appeal . . . 577
2.7.3. Where can the decision be appealed? . . . 577
2.7.4. What kind of decisions may be appealed against? . . . 579
2.7.5. Leave to appeal . . . 580
2.7.6. Judicial review . . . 580
2.7.7. Legal review . . . 580
2.7.8. Extraordinary remedies in the administrative procedure . . . 581
2.7.9. The ombudsmen. . . . 581
2.8. Can sanctions be executed immediately? . . . 581
3. Topics currently being discussed in Sweden . . . 582
Bibliography . . . 583
Preparatory works . . . 583

XIV. Country Analysis – United Kingdom
John McEldowney. . . . 585

1. Introduction . . . 585
2. The constitutional context of administrative sanctions in the United Kingdom . . . 588
3. Techniques, procedures, and processes in administrative sanctions . . . 593
4. Companies and criminal law. . . . 599
5. Conclusions . . . 603
Select bibliography. . . . 605

XV. Administrative Sanctions in EU Law
Adrienne de Moor-van Vugt . . . 607

1. Introduction . . . 607
2. Enforcement of Union law by way of administrative sanctioning. . . . 608
2.1. The starting point . . . 608
2.2. Filling the gap . . . 609
2.3. A question of competence . . . 610
3. Administrative sanctions . . . 612
3.1. Criminal charge . . . 612
3.2. Definition of sanctions in EC law. . . . 613
4. Principle of legality . . . 615
5. Culpability . . . 617
6. Protection of the individual. . . . 619

6.1. The rights of the defence 619
6.2. The right to silence 622
6.3. Protection against entering business premises or a home 624
7. Judicial protection 626
7.1. Access to justice 626
7.2. Procedural rules 628
7.2.1. Public trial 628
7.2.2. Standing 629
7.2.3. Time limits 630
7.2.4. Legal assistance 630
7.2.5. Burden of proof 631
7.2.6. Full jurisdiction 632
7.2.7. Reasonable time 634
8. Severity of the measure or penalty 635
8.1. Proportionality 635
8.2. Accumulation of sanctions 637
9. Conclusion 639

List of Authors 641

LIST OF ABBREVIATIONS

AACA	Athens' Administrative Court of Appeals
AAI	Autorités administratives indépendantes – independent administrative agencies
AAFDL	Associação Académica da Faculdade de Direito de Lisboa
AB	Administratiefrechtelijke beslissingen – Legal periodical
abbb	algemene beginselen van behoorlijk bestuur
ABRvS	Afdeling bestuursrechtspraak Raad van State – Administrative Jurisdiction Division, Council of State
ACPC	Administrative Court Procedure Code
ACS	Administrative Jurisdictional Section
AFM	Autoriteit Financiële Markten – Authority for the Financial Markets
AG	Advocate-General of the European Court of Justice
AJPA	Administrative Judicial Procedure Act
All ER	All England Reports
AMF	Autorité des marchés financiers – Financial Markets Authority
AmvB	Algemene maatregel van Bestuur – Order in Council
AnwBl.	Anwaltsblatt
AO	Abgabenordnung – German Tax Code
AöR	Archiv des öffentlichen Rechts
APA	Administrative Procedure Act
APC	Administrative Procedure Code
APV	Algemene Plaatselijke Verordening – General municipal by-laws
Arbowet	Arbeidsomstandighedenwet – Working Conditions Act
ASAE	Autoridade de Segurança Alimentar e Económica – Authority for the Safety of Food and Economy
ASL	Aziende Sanitarie Locali – Local health agencies
AVG	Allgemeines Verwaltungsverfahrensgesetz – Code of Administrative Procedure
a.v.v./avv	algemeen verbindend voorschrift – collective binding agreement
Awb	Algemene wet bestuursrecht – Dutch General Administrative Law Act (GALA)

AWBi	Algemene wet op het binnentreden – General Act on Entry into Private homes
Awr	Algemene wet inzake rijksbelastingen – State Taxes Act
BAC	Blood Alcohol Concentration
BayGO	Bayerische Gemeindeordnung
BayPAG	Bayerisches Polizeiaufgabengesetz – Bavarian Police Act
BBBB 1998	Besluit Bestuurlijke Boeten Belastingdienst 1998 – Administrative Fines (Tax and Customs Administration) Decree 1998
BDG	Bundesdisziplinargesetz – Civil Service Disciplinary Act
BGB	Bürgerliches Gesetzbuch
BJagdG	Bundesjagdgesetz – Federal Hunting Act
BlgNR	Beilagen zu den stenographischen Protokollen des Nationalrats (Annexes to the stenographic records of the National Council)
BNB	Beslissingen in Belastingzaken, Nederlandse Belastingrechtspraak – Legal Periodical
BrB	Brottsbalken (1962:700) – Swedish Criminal Code
BVerfG	Bundesverfassungsgericht
B-VG	Bundes-Verfassungsgesetz – Federal Constitution Act
BW	Burgerlijk Wetboek – Dutch Civil Code
BZRG	Bundeszentralregistergesetz – Federal Repository Act
CA	Suomen perustuslaki – Constitution of Finland
CAP	Common Agricultural Policy
Cass.	Cour de cassation – Court of Cassation
CBb	College van Beroep voor het bedrijfsleven – Trade and Industry Appeals Tribunal
CC	Belgian Criminal Court
c.c.p.	Code of Criminal Procedure
CCDRs	Comissões de Coordenação e Desenvolvimento Regional – Commissions of Coordination and Regional Development
CE	Conseil d'État
Charter	Charter of Fundamental Rights of the European Union
CML Rev	Common Market Law Review
CNIL	Commission nationale informatique et libertés – National Commission for Computerised Data and Freedom
COE	Council of Europe
Const.	Italian Constitution
c.civ.p.	Code of Civil Procedure
cf.	confer – compare
c.p.	Código Penal (Criminal Code)

CPC	Criminal Proceedings Code
CPP	Código de Processo Penal – Criminal Procedure Act
Cr. App.R.	Criminal Appeal Reports
CRP	Constituição da República Portuguesa – Portuguese Constitution
CRvB	Centrale Raad van Beroep – Central Appeals Tribunal
CS	Council of State
DC	Déclaration de conformité -
DCC	Dutch Criminal Code – Wetboek van Strafrecht
DCP	Dutch Code of Criminal Procedure – Wetboek van Strafvordering (Sv)
DD	*Delikt en Delinkwent* – Legal periodical
DMOS	Direito de Mera Ordenação Social – Administrative Offences Law
DNB	De Nederlandsche Bank N.V. – Dutch National Bank
DL	Decreto-Lei – Decree-Law
DPC	Dutch Criminal Code – Wetboek van Strafrecht (Sr)
Ds.	*Departementsserien*
DVBI	*Deutsches Verwaltungsblatt*
EEA	Agreement on the European Economic Area
EEEvrD	*Elliniki Epitheorissi Evropaikoou Dikaiou* – Revue hellenique de droit Européen
ECHR	European Convention for the Protection of Human Rights and Fundamental Freedoms
ECtHR	European Court of Human Rights
EC	European Community
E(E)C	European (Economic) Community
ECSC	European Coal and Steel Community
ECJ	European Court of Justice
EFET	National Institution for Food Inspection
e.g.	*exempli gratia* – for example
EGC	The General Court – European Union (formerly known as The Court of First Instance)
EGStGB	Einführungsgesetz zum Strafgesetzbuch – Introductory Law of the Penal Code
EGVG	Einführungsgesetz zu den Verwaltungsverfahrens-gesetzen – Introductory Act for the Acts on Administrative Proceedings
ENDS	Environmental Data Services
etc.	*et cetera*
EU	European Union

EU-JZG	Bundesgesetz über die justizielle Zusammenarbeit in Strafsachen mit den Mitgliedstaaten der Europäischen Union (Federal Act on the judicial cooperation in criminal matters with the Member States of the European Union)
EU-VStVG	Bundesgesetz über die Vollstreckung von Geldstrafen und Geldbußen von Verwaltungsbehörden im Rahmen der Europäischen Union (Federal Act on the execution of financial penalties imposed by administrative authorities of other EU Member States)
EWCW	England and Wales Court of Appeal
FGD	Fundo de Garantia dos Depósitos – Fund for the Guarantee of Deposits
FGG	Gesetz über die Angelegenheiten der freiwilligen Gerichtsbarkeit – German Ex Parte Jurisdiction Act
FIOD-ECD	Fiscale inlichtingen- en opsporingsdienst en Economische controledienst – Fiscal Intelligence and Investigation Service/Economic Investigation Service
FPA	Freedom of Press Act
FSA	Financial Service Authority (of the United Kingdom)
GALA	Algemene wet bestuursrecht – General Administrative Law Act
GastG	Gaststättengesetz – German Licensing Act
Gem.wet	Gemeentewet – Municipalities Act
GewO	Gewerbeordnung – Industrial Code
GG	Grundgesetz – German Constitution
GPCL	General principles of criminal law
GPPA	General principles of proper administration
Gst.	*De Gemeentestem* – Legal periodical
GVG	Gerichtsverfassungsgesetz – German Judicature Act
Gwwd	Gezondheids- en welzijnswet voor dieren – Health and Welfare of Animals Act
HaO	Administrative Court of Hämeenlinna
HAO	Regional Administrative Court of Kuopio
HE	Hallituksen esitykset – Government proposal to parliament for new legislation
HC	Hellenic Constitution
Report HC	Report of the House of Commons of the United Kingdom
HR	Hoge Raad – Supreme Court in the fields of civil, criminal and tax law
Hw	Huisvestingswet – Housing Allocation Act
ib./ibid.	ibidem – in the same passage or page quoted above

ICCPR	International Convention on Civil and Political Rights
i.e.	*id est* – it is/that is more precisely
IGA	Inspecção Geral do Ambiente – General Inspectorate for the Environment
IMOPPI	Instituto dos Mercados das Obras Públicas e Particulares do Imobiliário – Institute for the Market of Public and Private Real Estate Works
IRS	Instituto de Reinserção Social – Institute for the Rehabilitation of Offenders
JAP	Juristische Ausbildung und Praxisvorbereitung
JBl	Juristische Blätter – Legal periodical
JBPlus	Jurisprudentie Bestuursrecht Plus – Legal periodical
JCL	Journal of Criminal Law – Legal periodical
JGG	Jugendgerichtsgesetz – Juvenile Court Act
JM	Jurisprudentie Milieurecht – Legal periodical
JO	Justitieombudsmannen – Parliamentary Ombudsmen
JOR	*Jurisprudentie Onderneming & Recht* – Legal periodical
JöR	*Jahrbuch des öffentlichen Rechts der Gegenwart* – Legal periodical
JUSTICE	United Kingdom section of the International Commission of Jurists
JV	*Jurisprudentie Vreemdelingenrecht* – Legal periodical
KB	King's Bench
KHO	Korkein Hallinto-Oikeus – Supreme Administrative Court of Finland
KM	Komiteanmietintö – Committee Reports
L.	Law
LDJG	Librairie générale de droit et de jurisprudence
LPA	Ley 30/1992, Régimen Jurídico de las Administraciones Públicas y del Procedimiento Administrativo Común – Spanish Act 30/1992 regulating Public Administration, Authorities and Procedures
LSI	*Law & Social Inquiry* – periodical
M&M	*Markt & Mededinging* – Legal periodical
Michigan LR	*Michigan Law Review* – Legal periodical
MLR	*Modern Law Review* – Legal periodical
Msw	Meststoffenwet – Fertilizers Act
Mw	Mededingingswet – Competitive Trading Act
NAO	National Audit Office of the United Kingdom
NbSr	*Nieuwsbrief Strafrecht* – Legal periodical
NJ	*Nederlandse Jurisprudentie* – Legal periodical

NJA	Nytt Juridiskt Arkiv, Avdelning I – Publication of cases from the Swedish Supreme Court
NJV	Nederlandse Juristen Vereniging – Dutch Law Association
NJW	*Neue Juristische Wochenschrift* – Legal periodical
NMa	Nederlandse Mededingingsautoriteit – Dutch Competition Authority
NStZ	*Neue Zeitschrift für Strafrecht* – Legal periodical
NTB	*Nederlands Tijdschrift voor Bestuursrecht* – Legal periodical
NVWA	Nederlandse Voedsel- en Warenautoriteit – Dutch Food and Consumer Product Safety Authority
NZ	Österreichische Notariatszeitung
OGH	Oberster Gerichtshof – Supreme Court in civil and criminal matters
ÖJZ	*Österreichische Juristen-Zeitung*
OLG	Oberlandesgericht – Regional Appelate Court
OM	Openbaar Ministerie – Public Prosecution Service
OPTA	Onafhankelijke Post en Telecom Autoriteit – Independent Post and Telecommunications Authority
öStGB	Österreichisches Strafgesetzbuch 1974 – Austrian Criminal Code
öStPO	Österreichische Strafprozessordnung – Austrian Code of Criminal Procedure
ÖStZ	*Österreichische Steuer-Zeitung*
OWiG	Ordnungswidrigkeitengesetz – Administrative Offenses Act
Paris	Cour d'appel de Paris
PA	Public Administration
PeVL	Perustuslakivaliokunnan Lausunto
PeVM	Perustuslakicaliokunnan Mietintö
PG	Parlementaire Geschiedenis – (Dutch) Parliamentary History
PPS	Public Prosecution Service
PRCC	Public Revenue Collection Code
Publ. Eur. Court H.R	*Publications of the European Court of Human Rights*
R.	Rex or Regina
RÅ	*Regeringsrättens årsbok* – Yearbook of cases from the Swedish Supreme Administrative Court
Rb.	Rechtbank – Regional Court
RF	Regeringsformen – Instrument of Government (Swedish Constitution)

RFDA	*Revue française de droit administratif*
RGCO	Regime Geral de Contra-Ordenações
RGICSF	Regime Geral das Instituições de Crédito e das Sociedades Financeiras – General Legal Framework of Credit Institutions and Financial Corporations
RIW/AWD	Recht der Internationalen Wirtschaft / Außenwirtschaftsdienst des betriebsberaters
RSV	*Rechtspraak Sociale Verzekeringen* – Legal periodical
RZ	*Österreichische Richterzeitung*
SACA	Constitution and Special Act 6 January 1989 concerning the Court of Arbitration
SAC	Korkein Oikeus – Supreme Administrative Court
SARI	Special Act of 8 August 1980 concerning the Reform of the Institutions
SEW	*Tijdschrift voor Europees en economisch recht* – Legal periodical
SFO	Serious Fraud Office
SII	Sistema de Indemnização aos Investidores – System for the Compensation of Investors
SOU	Statens Offentliga Utredningar – Swedish Government Official Reports
SSC	Supreme Special Court
StG	Strafgesetz – Criminal Code
StGB	Strafgesetzbuch – German Criminal Code
StPO	Strafprozeßordnung – German Code of Criminal Procedure – Austrian Code of Criminal Procedure
Strafrecht AT	Strafrecht Allgemeiner Teil
StVG	Straßenverkehrsgesetz – Traffic Law Code
StVollzG	Strafvollzugsgesetz – German Penal Administration Act
SWK	Österreichische Steuer- und Wirtschaftskartei
T&C	*Tekst & Commentaar* – Text and Comments on Dutch Law
TEC	Treaty establishing the European Community
TEU	Treaty on European Union
TFEU	Treaty on the Functioning of the European Union
ToS	*To Syntagma* (The Constitution) – Legal periodical
TOS	*Tijdschrift voor Onderneming en Strafrecht* – Legal periodical
Tw	Telecommunicatiewet – (Dutch) Telecommunications Act
UKUT	United Kingdom Upper Tribunal
UU	Universiteit Utrecht – University of Utrecht
UvA	Universiteit van Amsterdam – University of Amsterdam

UVSs	Unabhängige Verwaltungssenate der Länder – Austrian Independent Administrative Panels of Provinces
UWG	Gesetz gegen den unlauteren Wettbewerb – Act on Unfair Competition
UZwG	Gesetz über den unmittelbaren Zwang – Immediate Coercion Act
VA	Verwaltungsakt – Administrative Act
VAR	Vereniging voor Bestuursrecht – Administrative Law Association
VAR-reeks	*Publicaties Vereniging voor Bestuursrecht* – Legal Periodical
VAT	Value Added Tax
vid. (*infra*)	*vide* (*infra*) – see (below)
VR	*VerkeersRecht* – Legal Periodical
VU	Vrije Universiteit – VU University of Amsterdam
VwGH	Verwaltungsgerichtshof – Administrative Court
VwGO	Verwaltungsgerichtsordnung – Rules of the Administrative Courts
VwVfg	Verwaltungsverfahrensgesetz – Administrative Procedural Law
VwVG	Verwaltungsvollstreckungsgesetz – Administration Enforcement Law
VfGH	Verfassungsgerichtshof – Constitutional Court
VfSlg.	Sammlung der Erkenntnisse und wichtigsten Beschlüsse des Verfassungsgerichtshofes – Collection of the decisions and most important orders of the Austrian Constitutional Court
VStG	Verwaltungsstrafgesetz – Austrian Act on Administrative Criminal Law (in Germany, Vermögenssteuergesetz)
Vw 2000	Vreemdelingenwet 2000 – Aliens Act 2000
VwSlg	Sammlung der Erkenntnisse und Beschlüsse des Verwaltungsgerichtshofes -Collection of the decisions and most important orders of the Austrian Constitutional Court
Wabm	Wet algemene bepalingen milieuhygiëne – Environmental Protection (General Provisions) Act
Wabo	Wet algemene bepalingen omgevingsrecht – Environmental Permitting (General Provisions) Act
Wav	Wet arbeid vreemdelingen – Foreign Nationals (Employment) Act

Wahv	Wet administratiefrechtelijke handhaving verkeersvoorschriften (also: Wet Mulder) – Traffic Regulations (Administrative Enforcement) Act
Wbp	Wet bescherming persoonsgegevens – Personal Data Protection Act
WDO	Wehrdisziplinarordnung – German Military Disciplinary Code
Wed	Wet op de economische delicten – Economic Offences Act
Wet BMTI	Wet boeten, maatregelen, en terug- en invordering sociale zekerheid – (Dutch) Social Security Benefits (Fines, Measures, Recovery and Collection) Act
Wet idbb	Wet introductie dwangsom en bestuurlijke boete – Act on the Introduction of Penalty Payments and Administrative Fines (Financial Legislation) Act
Wet ion	Wet informatie-uitwisseling ondergrondse netten – Underground Grids (Information Exchange) Act
Wet Mulder	Wet administratiefrechtelijke handhaving verkeersvoorschriften (also: Wahv) – Traffic Regulations (Administrative Enforcement) Act
Wft	Wet financieel toezicht – Financial Supervision Act
WGB	Wet gewasbeschermingsmiddelen en biociden – Plant Protection Products and Biocides Act
Wgp	Wet marktordening gezondheidszorg – Health Care (Market Regulation) Act
Whc	Wet handhaving consumentenbescherming – Consumer Protection (Enforcement) Act
Wira	Wet implementatie rechtsbeschermingsrichtlijnen aanbesteden – Improving the Effectiveness of Review Procedures concerning the Award of Public Contracts Directive (Implementation) Act
Wkkp	Wet Kinderopvang en kwaliteitseisen peuterspeelzalen – Childcare Provisions Act and Quality Requirements for Playschools
Wm	Wet milieubeheer – Environmental Management Act
Wr	Wet ruimtevaartactiviteiten – Space Activities Act
Wro	Wet ruimtelijke ordening – Spatial Planning Act
WRV	Weimarer Reichsverfassung – Weimar Reich Constitution
WStG	Wehrstrafgesetz – Military Criminal Code
Wtt	Wet toezicht trustkantoren – Trust Offices (Supervision) Act

Wwft	Wet ter voorkoming van witwassen en financiering van terrorisme – Money Laundering and Terrorist Financing (Prevention) Act
ZfV	*Zeitschrift für Verwaltung* – Legal periodical
ZPO	Zivilprozessordnung – Code of Civil Procedure
ZVR	*Zeitschrift für Verkehrsrecht* – Legal periodical

I. THE DEFINITION OF ADMINISTRATIVE SANCTIONS – GENERAL REPORT

Carlo Enrico PALIERO

1. INTRODUCTION. DIFFERENT METHODS FOR THE DIFFERENT PURPOSES OF THE NOTION OF ADMINISTRATIVE SANCTION: *PHENOMENOLOGICAL* AND *TYPOLOGICAL* TASKS

> "Each country report should contain a description of the measures which are considered to be sanctions under national law, and should also describe other measures if a more restricted definition of sanction is common in national law. Also measures which are a reaction by administrative authorities to an infringement and which have a remedial aim should be described.
> In other words, for the purpose of this project we will use a *broad* (emphasis added) definition of 'sanction'. I have asked Prof. Carlo Enrico Paliero to make a general contribution on the definition of 'sanction', each report should offer him the opportunity to compare the different definitions of 'sanction' and the measures which are considered to be a sanction and which are not, and why."

This in his explanatory notes on the research project Oswald Jansen defined the 'field of observation' within which the various national reports should place the definition of administrative sanction.

Before discussing this issue, we should point out that each national contributor has been asked to make a great effort of conceptualization premised on this methodological basis: attempt to establish a definition of the administrative sanction current in your country using *this* definition of administrative sanction.

The clearly stated objective was to devise a starting method that could describe the field of observation in the broadest possible terms, taking into consideration all the different declinations of the concept of administrative sanction as well as similar or proximate measures.

In other words, contributors had to choose a pre-definition of administrative sanction which could fulfil a phenomenological purpose. The authors of the various national reports were asked to give a definition of administrative sanction suitable for outlining the broadest possible picture. Within this framework they could successively establish whether, where and how stricter or more universal definitions exist for administrative sanctions.

Within the brief of my work also lies the specific *secondary* task of phenomenological definition: comparing the different concepts of administrative sanctions presented by the national reports on the basis of their – *primary* – task of making a phenomenological definition. Associated with this aim there is another, more limited task for definition, which I would define as 'typological': the search for different related or at least comprehensible notions of the administrative sanction. This also with the objective of singling out common aspects of the notion of administrative sanction among the countries considered, and – above all – enhancing communication between the different national administrative sanctions defined typologically.

In other words, there is a methodological difference between my comparison of the definition of administrative sanctions and the method the national contributors have been asked to adopt. And this difference in method is related to a difference in objectives. This is because each task precisely corresponds to a different method of definition of administrative sanction, which in turn ultimately corresponds to a different concept of administrative sanction.

Hence, before beginning this analysis, it is important to clarify what phenomenological and typological definitions coexist in my work with their associated methods of defining the administrative sanction. In other words, my position as the author of this report is that of a *consumer* of the phenomenological approach while it is a *producer* both of phenomenological and typological definitions.

(a) The phenomenological definition seeks to broaden the starting point 'inherited' from the national reports which in turn inherited it from their brief establishing a method common to the whole research project.
(b) In regard to the 'typological' task the search is for a more meaningful final definition.

Sub a) Notion functional to the phenomenological task

In relation to the phenomenological definition we therefore have a broad notion of administrative sanction, *on whose basis the reports were drafted.*

Methodologically, on the basis of this perspective, the concept of administrative sanction is characterized by two elements: the former relating to its content which is disadvantageous for the offender; and the latter functional relating to the violation of a precept. A sanction in terms of its effects, is a measure which takes away rights (ablatory). Its link with the proof of an offence is different compared to typical ablatory measures.

In this perspective, its relationship with the violation of a precept becomes the specific attribute of this sanction and distinguishes it from the other coercitive measures applied by administrations which cannot be considered administrative sanctions.

The fact that its relationship with the violation of a precept can find radically different applications does not contradict the validity of this definition.

Such a relationship between administrative reaction and violation of a precept can indeed relate to very different legal systems. An offence can be committed independently and 'directly' thus become the sole prerequisite justifying the exercise of power. However, it can also be committed 'indirectly', for example, when it only constitutes the criterion determining whether the offender is unsuitable to 'be part' of a certain relationship with the administration. In other words, when an offence constitutes a mere antecedent in the exercise of power by having created an unlawful situation which the administration is called upon to remedy.

Even if it is clear that the multiplicity of relationships impacts fundamentally on the character of the measures applied, in some cases the objective of the administrative sanction is to punish illicit behaviour while in others it restores or preserves substantive interests delegated to the administration independently of any evaluation as to the conduct of the offender. Further, these differences do not impact on the definition of administrative sanction. Instead, they distinguish different categories of administrative sanctions within the concept itself for the purposes of identification (*punitive* sanctions, *restorative* sanctions, *compensatory* sanctions, *sanctions* of expiry and revocation, etc.).

In the light of this perspective, an administrative sanction is in effect any form of reaction by the public administration to the violation of a precept. This wide and generic definition is the most suitable for satisfying the phenomenological objective of the research, reflecting the fragmentary and non-cohesive characteristics characterizing this field. Moreover, this very broad conceptualisation has enabled substantial progress in this discipline in the past, as for example in Italy with the so-called principle of the appropriate administrative sanction.[1] This is the *best starting* point then to establish stricter concepts which are more suitable for other and more specific uses.

Sub b) Functional notion for the typological task

If, however, we modify our perspective and decide to move forward from this starting point, we have to search for a type of sanction suitable for classification as a separate and typical *genus* ('typical' in the strict legal sense). The notion of administrative sanction then has to be based on the *specificity* of this measure

1 Cfr. Paliero-Travi, *La sanzione amministrativa: profili sistematici*, Milan, 1988, 6.

compared to *other* forms of reaction by the public administration to the violation of a precept.

A fundamental point of reference for this orientation in the past has been Zanobini's argument according to which the administrative sanction is primarily a punishment in the technical sense. Therefore, its punitive characteristics mean it cannot be classified with instruments principally directed at preserving or recovering substantive interests damaged by an offence.

This notion of administrative sanction addresses a double need: on the one hand the need for clarity and swiftness in investigation, which suggests establishing a self consistent and meaningful concept, instead of a broader, more heterogeneous and vague one.

On the other, there is the requirement to adhere more concretely to positive law, which obliges enforcers to seek solutions coherent with legislative events.

A systematic conceptualization of administrative sanctions in terms of typologies will therefore have to be based on more meaningful criteria which distinguish this legal device more clearly, both externally from the penal sanction, and internally, from the array of coercitive measures at the disposal of the public administration.

For these purposes it becomes indispensable to steer clear of the temptation to reduce the administrative sanction – insofar as it is punitive – to a merely penal measure.

The specific character of the administrative sanction – whose definition is an indispensable prerequisite for the exact reconstruction of the characteristics of this measure – must therefore be looked for on a different level, and by a different methodology.

Hence, it is not useful to rely exclusively on external aspects, such as the presence of discretionality in the application of a sanction – or for that matter – on intrinsic characteristics such as the content (whether punitive or compensatory) of the sanction itself.

Likewise, I do not believe it is fruitful to systematically reconstruct the administrative sanction on the basis of its objectives eliciting its functions and devising a table detailing its applicable principles. This would confuse the purpose of the sanction with its content, common to any instrument of coercion (whether direct or indirect: anyone forced into hospitalization is no less coerced than someone sentenced to detention), and often even with compensation in civil law.

In my opinion, therefore, a more productive analysis must be based on these two principles:

(a) thorough analysis of positive law;
(b) use of a teleological method, which allows the specific characteristics of the administrative sanction to be inferred from the purposes attributed to it by the legislator.

2. METHOD AND STRUCTURE OF THIS GENERAL REPORT

Consequently, the following comparison will follow this scheme, and seek from point to point, to single out and classify the different national situations with the objective of establishing a single meaningful typology for the administrative sanction and to elaborate a conceptual table for the different notions of the administrative sanctions derived.

More specifically, the two principles enunciated above (analysis of positive law and adoption of a teleological method), will be used to organize the national reports into a series of steps:

(1) in the first place, an overview of the contents and functions of information pertaining to EU law and ECHR law which we can assume to be valid for all the countries considered, for reasons which shall be dealt with in the following;
(2) following this a delimitation *ab externo* (*rectius*: evaluation of the 'degree of differentiation') of the administrative sanction compared to other judicial reactions (criminal punishment, other measures by public administrations, accessory or enforcement measures in general, disciplinary sanctions);
(3) finally, the singling out of characteristics and legal functions of administrative sanctions thereby circumscribed through a series of structural referents indispensable for the construction of a sanctioning system.
In particular:

   (a) The existence of a single code for this category and its relationship with the legality principle;
   (b) The typologies of the sanctions;
   (c) The criteria of indictment (forms and prerequisites of responsibility for the offence).

Instead, when the sanction cannot be defined in this manner, as for example in the UK, a description ensues of the characteristics of this non-definable sanction.

At the end, a paradigm of the different concepts obtained using this method will be presented and organized in three directions. In particular: (1) broadness of the definition; (2) 'normative functionality'; (3) degree of differentiation (principally from the penal sanction) into two aspects: formal and structural.

From these cross-references a series of relationships will emerge, some of which will be evident, but others, perhaps a little less so.

3. THE LEGISLATIVE FRAME OF REFERENCE: INDICATIONS FROM EU LAW AND ECHR CASE LAW FROM THE POINT OF VIEW OF CONTENT AND FUNCTION

The directions from the two European organizations can be assumed as common to all the countries considered. Certainly ECHR law will be analysed because all the countries involved are part of the Council of Europe. But indications will also come from EU law.

Even if the overall European legal context – as stated at the beginning of the de Moor-van Vugt report – "has certainly been favourable to the development of administrative sanctions", the direction of this development has been different for these two organisations. The report continues: "EU law itself has stimulated the introduction of several kinds of administrative sanctions Member States themselves did not have. And the European Court on Human Rights (…) has made it clear that states are allowed to use the instrument of administrative sanctions, as long as they observe the fundamental standards of art. 6 of the European Convention for the Protection of Human Rights and Fundamental Freedoms, when the sanction is of a punitive nature." On this point, there is a fundamental difference between these viewpoints, as aptly summarized by de Moor-van Vugt: "Union law provides for several instruments to impose sanctions, whereas the ECHR makes sure that the protection of the individual is taken care of.".

It becomes opportune, therefore, to analyse indications coming from European Union law separately from those of the Council of Europe, in particular ECHR case law produced by the European Court on Human Rights.

In regard to EU law, one should first of all point out that this legislative system operates on different levels.

On one level, EU law has its own model of administrative sanction, and as such it will be analysed together with all the other national models in our ideal table. On another, EU law impacts on national models, both though its intention to harmonize and by imposing common standards on member states (principle of proportion, rule of law, etc.). On a third level, EU law must respect the standards set by the ECHR, given that on the basis of Art. 6 of the Treaty on European Union the principles contained in this text are considered as general principles of European Union law. Adherence to them is a prerequisite for the validity for all European Union law.

Having said that, it is interesting to note what the de Moor-van Vugt report points out: EU law has no general penal jurisdiction, but has full administrative-punitive competence as was established in the famous case C-240/90 Germany/Commission which is the predecessor to regulation 2988/95. On that occasion a point of equilibrium was set, although this has changed with the enactment of the Lisbon Treaty. According to this, the EU has full prerogatives to promulgate punitive administrative sanctions, which was the basis for the drafting of regulation frame 2988/95. However, it still has no general direct competence in criminal law.

The existence of a potential contradiction between full administrative and criminal law competence in EU law, in the overall argument of this general report means that the system of administrative sanctions in EU law distinguishes itself because of its strongly punitive character, but is also differentiated from criminal law to a great extent. In other words, the indications from EU law have contributed to creating a punitive administrative law which is structurally and functionally different from criminal law. In essence, it is particularly focused on the *dimension of the effectiveness* of administrative penal repression. Nevertheless, as explained in the de Moor-van Vugt report, it is subjected to restraints which guarantee and limit *jus puniendi* as expressed by the ECHR.

Insofar as the Council of Europe is concerned, the ECHR has had a different impact through its independent interpretation of the concept of criminal charge, so that it tends to classify (hence applying the same guarantees to it) not only formally criminal sanctions in this category, but also administrative and disciplinary sanctions with a 'substantially punitive' character. As the de Moor-van Vugt report clearly states:

> "In art. 6 of European Convention on Human Rights (ECHR) citizens are awarded with fundamental rights when they are faced with a *criminal charge*. (...)
> The ECHR has repeatedly stated that this notion must be construed autonomously, without taking into account the categories national systems use. It considers several aspects in order to conclude to applicability of art. 6.
> In the first place, it takes into account the scope of the rules that have been violated. If those provisions cover all citizens, be it in a certain capacity, e.g. as taxpayers, and not a given group with a particular status, this part of the test is satisfied. Secondly, the Court assesses the purpose of the sanction. If it is not intended as pecuniary compensation for damage but essentially as a punishment to deter others from committing an offence, the second stage is passed as well. Thirdly, the sanctions must be imposed under a general rule, the purpose of which is both deterrent and punitive. The last aspect to have a look at is the severity of the sanction. If that is very substantial, this factor also contributes to the conclusion that a criminal charge is at hand. It is also of importance if a financial sanction can be replaced by imprisonment. If, having weighed the various aspects of the case, the Court notes the predominance of those, which have a criminal connotation, art. 6 is applicable. None of those factors are decisive on its own, but taken together and cumulatively they make the 'charge' in issue a 'criminal' one within the meaning of Article 6."

In a nutshell, the ECHR, by privileging the *guarantee* has placed pressure on member states to *amalgamate* criminal law with punitive-administrative law, and at the same time, *differentiate* the administrative sanction as a punishment from other notions of administrative sanctions.

In regard to European directions we therefore note a sort of contradictory movement. Both systems (given that EU law is obliged to comply with the guarantees laid down by the ECHR) have sought to harmonize the level of guarantees. However, the EU law system which is focused on efficacy, has made a greater contribution to differentiating the criminal sanction from the penal administrative sanction (as affirmed explicitly in the Greece report: "The fact that Greece joined the European Communities is also a factor that contributed to the apparition of new fields of regulation whose respect is entrusted to the mechanism of administrative repression due to the absence of criminal offences stemming directly from EC law"). As noted in the de Moor-van Vugt Report, to some extent it has also *connected* punitive administrative sanctions with other administrative measures (using European Union terminology). Instead, the EHRC, which by definition must watch over guarantees, has moved criminal law *closer* to administrative punitive law extending to the latter the guarantees traditionally envisaged for the former. However, it has also separated and made independent the notion of administrative sanction as punishment from other notions of administrative sanctions.

4. DEGREE OF DIFFERENTIATION OF THE ADMINISTRATIVE SANCTION IN THE STRICT SENSE COMPARED WITH OTHER JUDICIAL SYSTEM REACTIONS

4.1. COMPARED TO CRIMINAL SANCTIONS

For the first delimitation *ab externo* in regard to the criminal sanction, which as noted was the object of a wide-ranging study towards the second half of the 1980s (*Les problemes juridiques et pratiques posèes par la difference entre le droit criminel et le droit adminstratif pénal*, published in *Rev. int. dr. pén.*, 1. 1988), we will evaluate here the 'degree of differentiation' between criminal and administrative sanctions and establish whether the *ne bis in idem* principle can be applied.

We can add that no country exhibits total homogeneity between administrative and criminal sanctions. There is a certain degree of differentiation in all countries. Nevertheless, the 'degree of differentiation' varies substantially from country to country.

4.1.1. *Countries with a low degree of differentiation*

In the first place we can single out a group of countries with a relatively low degree of differentiation between criminal and administrative sanctions given the strong conceptual and terminological continuity extant between the criminal and administrative systems. Paradigmatic in this regard is England: "There is no specific statutory regime that applies to all public administration and there is no specific statutory code entitled administrative sanctions. The best that can be done is to fit the category of administrative decision-making into the applicable general law. This may be found both in general administrative law and also in the application of the general criminal law to administrative acts". The UK report subsequently affirms even more cogently: "It must be remembered that in the United Kingdom there has been no equivalent tradition to the system of *droit administratif* (administrative law) and no rigid distinction between public and private law, until relatively recently. The use of the criminal law was often used to underpin the practical working of the licensing system or in certain circumstances through the use of contempt of court powers, where appropriate, the courts had powers to use the criminal law to enforce civil wrongs."

I believe that Sweden can also be classified in this category. Here there is a grey area of sanctions which are difficult to define as criminal sanctions *stricto sensu* (see Swedish report). However, one should also note that in Sweden indirect confirmation of this differentiation comes from the possibility to sanction twice, with both penal and administrative sanctions.

Spain also presents a low degree of differentiation (see Spanish Report: "Although criminal sentences and administrative sanctions are similar, and both Criminal Law and Criminal Procedural Law bear some resemblance to Sanctioning Administrative Law, many differences can also be found") but for a completely different reason. In Spain, the administrative sanction is to some extent codified, despite the fact that this country still maintains constitutional restrictions valid equally for criminal and administrative sanctions (Article 25(1) of the Spanish Constitution states: "No one may be convicted or sentenced for actions or omissions which when committed did not constitute a crime, misdemeanour, or administrative infringement as established by legislation in force at that moment."). This has lead to a reconstruction of the administrative sanction which is excessively parapenal. Compared to other systems it is very close to the structures and functions typical of criminal law (cf. what we will be discussing regarding Italy shortly). Coherent with this configuration is the fact that the Spanish system is founded on the principle of *non bis in idem* between administrative and penal sanctions.

4.1.2. Countries with greater differences

The other European countries can be grouped together as exhibiting a more marked differentiation between administrative and criminal sanctions.

This is the situation in Portugal, Italy, the Netherlands and Germany (see German report): "In principle, it is left to the legislator to classify a sanction as criminal or administrative in nature. (...). What the legislator has to take into consideration is that criminal and administrative offenses have their own basic characteristics. Although no definite borderline can be drawn, 'the constitutional system of values allows to determine with sufficient certainty' which offense belongs to which of those basic elements and which does not. It would be unconstitutional to threaten with a criminal sanction for an offense doubtless belonging to the core of administrative offenses – and vice versa. For, if the legislator ignores these clearly defined constitutional values, offense and legal consequence would not be 'properly coordinated' and thus be in violation of the principles of a constitutional state."

Belgium and Rumania also appear to be in this category as they show a relatively high degree of differentiation. There is, however, the important difference that in Rumania ("In such situations the principle of *non bis in idem* applies, one deed having to be qualified either a contravention or a penal offence, but not both") the *non bis in idem* is always applied, whereas in Belgium, as the consequence of a clear functional distinction "the principle of *non bis in idem* is not necessarily applicable on the accumulation of criminal and administrative sanctions."

Moreover, Rumania exhibits an intermediate degree of differentiation on both the legislative and teleological levels (See Rumanian report: "Features of contraventional sanctions that mirror their penal origin are the division of sanctions into main sanctions – having a punitive character – and complementary sanctions – having a predominantly preventive or reparatory character"). Nonetheless, it is the only country amongst those examined which in terms of content shows very strong continuity between criminal and administrative sanctions (primarily by applying an administrative sanction involving detention). Hence in terms of content, the strong structural and functional differentiation between criminal and administrative sanctions reveals the most classic example of 'labelling fraud'.

The Finnish model takes an intermediate position between Germany and Sweden. Like the Swedish system, it presents an initial (conceptual) differentiation between administrative and penal sanctions tempered by a grey area containing sanctions which are difficult to classify ("Finnish counterpart for German *Ordnungswidrigkeitengesetz* consists only of summary penal fee. However, this penal fee is *considered to be neither an administrative nor even quasi-criminal sanction*, though similarities to *Ordnungswidrigkeitengesetz* do exist. Punishable by a summary penal fee are acts whose realisation represents a punishable misdemeanour, although it affects society to an extent which neither requires nor legitimates the use of more severe punishments. The fundamental difference between *Ordnungswidrigkeitengesetz* and summary penal fee in Finnish system lies within Section 1 of Chapter 6 of Finnish Criminal Code, which clearly categorizes summary penal fees as – not as even quasi criminal but – general *criminal punishment* within the system of criminal law"). However, if in Sweden this grey area is attributable to ambiguity between criminal and penal administrative systems, in Finland the cause appears to be uncertainty between penal administrative law and administrative law as a whole, as we shall see in the next paragraph.

4.1.3. Countries with a low degree of functional differentiation and a high degree of formal differentiation

If we take a more functional perspective in measuring differentiation, the analysis changes. Let us take Italy for example, which shows a high degree of differentiation between criminal and administrative sanctions as emerges from the Italian report. Indeed, this distinction is one of the most refined and rationalised: ("the *stricto sensu* administrative sanction is used in order to attain diversification and other options within the national punitive system; it is normally provided for forms of conducts that are not sufficiently serious to deserve a criminal punishment"). However, this high degree of differentiation and its rationalisation form part of a very close relationship between criminal and punitive administrative sanctions.

The two areas are differentiated, but *they operate in series, not in parallel*: the Italian concept of administrative sanction is directly connected to the objective of depenalisation. This intent is also cited in other reports (see the Greek, UK and Portuguese reports), but only in Italy does it represent the central and *formal* reason for the differentiation between criminal and administrative sanctions within the legal system, as is explained in the Italian report:

> "mechanisms for ameliorating and speeding up the criminal system have been adopted both at procedural and substantial level. (...)
> At substantial level, the legislator has embarked on a depenalisation process, firstly by abolish obsolete offences (decriminalisation); and secondly by replacing criminal sanctions with administrative sanctions (depenalisation *stricto sensu*), according to certain criteria like the seriousness of the offence, the significance of the interest to be protected, the necessity of criminal sanction and the statistical frequency of the violation.
> The latter process (depenalisation *stricto sensu*) was first undertaken in the 1960's, at first by means of sectorial acts and then by means of wide-ranging reforms.

> Nonetheless, the most relevant changes occurred with the enactment of aforementioned law no. 689/1981, which solved the main problem inherent in the ongoing depenalisation process: the lack of a general regulation for administrative sanctions. As is evident, the necessary pre-requisite for the effectiveness of such a process is the availability of certain type of punishment – as an alternative to criminal sanctions – subject to a comprehensive regulation.
> After this act, other reforms followed: (...).
> Eventually, law no. 205/1999, by means of which Parliament has delegated to the Government the power to reform a number of sectors, is worthy of particular attention: besides the wide-ranging scope of its application, this act contains a remarkable set of criteria for deflating the criminal system, each of which fits the peculiarities of the sector concerned.
> Such a comprehensive intervention had to look at general principles for selecting those offences to be depenalised, in order to avoid any possible incoherence: therefore, the Legislator adopted the principles of proportionality and subsidiarity (at a theoretical level) and took into account the statistical frequency of the violation in question (at the empirical level), as guidelines of the reform."

Consequently the degree of differentiation between punitive administrative sanctions and criminal sanctions is quite high, possibly the highest in terms of a formal-rational distinction. However, the difference is much smaller from the substantive viewpoint if we evaluate the structural and functional differences between the criminal sanction and the punitive administrative sanction. From this 'functional' standpoint we can group together three countries: Italy, Germany and Spain (see the relative reports) all endowed with a concept of administrative sanction based on penal law (parapenal model), and hence functionally little different from the criminal sanction.

4.2. COMPARISON WITH OTHER FORMS OF REACTION OF THE PUBLIC ADMINISTRATION TO THE VIOLATION OF A PRECEPT

4.2.1. Introduction

This second level of delimitation is more complex to analyse as the countries involved present a range of solutions that are difficult to classify. Nevertheless, our method of organisation of the material continues in seeking to quantify the degree of differentiation, with the difference that this time it will be evaluated within the administrative field. Here we are firmly taking the typological perspective (see above). The definition of administrative sanction will emerge from the degree of *differentiation* – both normative and functional – of these measures compared to *other* forms of reaction of the public administration to the violation of a precept.

The significance of the definition of administrative sanction which emerges is directly proportional to the degree of differentiation: the clearer the border between administrative sanctions and other forms of reaction by the public administration, the more the definition of administrative sanction will become significant.

First of all, the following three considerations should be made:

(1) In this field it is particularly useful to reiterate what was stated in the introduction: the reports were drafted on the basis of a predefinition of the administrative sanction in the wider sense as specified in the questionnaire. Hence, this term is not helpful in this study because the use of the term 'administrative sanction' in the report may not correspond to the definition expressed by any given national system (on this point the Portuguese report made the following clear affirmation: "There are other administrative measures that affect directly the rights or interests of an individual in an unfavourable manner, although they do not qualify as sanctions. However, as the questionnaire asks for a broad approach on administrative sanctions, our paper will address them as well"). We shall therefore base our analysis exclusively, as mentioned, on the law itself and the teleological approach.

(2) Further, it is generally possible to say that no pure model exists, in other words, neither absolute differentiation nor any differentiation at all.
There are *no* models expressing *absolute differentiation* because all countries are subject to the constitutional and international principles of the rule of law (i.e.: proportion, impartiality, right to a defence) which are applicable to legal systems as a whole, and hence to an even greater extent to the varied reactions by the public administration.
Above all, and this is the most interesting aspect, there are *no* countries having *no differentiation* at all for the fundamental reason that all countries belong to the Council of Europe. They are therefore subject to the process of differentiation as laid down in EHRC case law according to Article 6 ECHR, which imposes respect for certain guarantees *solely* for punitive administrative sanctions belonging to the *matière pénale*.

(3) The question of disciplinary sanctions is another issue and will be dealt with specifically in a subsequent paragraph.

4.2.2. Countries with a very high degree of differentiation

Countries belonging to this category are: Portugal, Germany and to some extent Rumania. Here the degree of differentiation is very high.

In the first place this is because these countries have a concept of punitive administrative sanction which is very well circumscribed and delimited compared to other reactions by the public administration to the violation of a precept. However, as we shall see, this also occurs for the following class of countries with a high degree of differentiation.

What distinguishes these countries and what determines such a high degree of differentiation is that these states do *not* have a general law of administrative action containing principles which are valid for all reactions by the public administration, including the application of sanctions in the strict sense (see the German, Portuguese and Rumanian reports).

Portugal, according to this double cross-reference, is possibly the country having the most differentiated concept of administrative sanction compared to other instruments of the public administration:

> "The Portuguese Constitutional Court (TC) interprets art 165, no 1, c and d, of the Portuguese Constitution (CRP), as allowing *only* for three types of public law sanctions: a) criminal penalties; b) *coimas* and other sanctions imposed by *Direito de Mera Ordenação Social* (Administrative Offences Law, hereafter DMOS); c) and disciplinary sanctions. According to that interpretation, the Constitution provides for a *closed typology* of public law sanctions, and, as a consequence, neither Parliament nor the Government can create *new* types of sanction.
> Therefore, unfavourable administrative measures must comply with the following framework: if they do not qualify as proper sanctions, the legislator is relatively free in creating them, as long as general constitutional principles are respected; if they qualify as proper sanctions, they must belong either to DMOS or to disciplinary law – otherwise, they will violate the Constitution".

Equally, the Portuguese report states further on "it is important to notice that these measures [The other administrative unfavourable measures – police measures *lato sensu* – in Portuguese terminology] do not have a punitive aim and therefore cannot be qualified as sanctions. In fact, even when they affect individual rights, their primary goal is to preserve the public interest against possible harm, irrespective of the allocation of responsibility for the undesired risk, whereas *coimas* and other administrative sanctions aim at the (general and individual) prevention of future offences through the repression of past infringements."

German law takes a similar line and presents a wide range of reactions by the public administration. Therefore, even if the German report on a terminological level offers us a general definition of administrative sanction, one observes a high degree of differentiation due to the unique definitions and disciplinary status of the parapenal model *Ordnungswidrigkeitenrecht* ("the legislative competence referred to as 'criminal law' also include the *Ordnungswidrigkeitenrecht*, or administrative offences law but it does not include the other administrative sanctions. In spite of the similarity, administrative offences law is an entirely separate field of law"). This is associated with the non-assimilability of *Ordnungswidrigkeitenrecht* to other instruments of reaction by the public administration (see the German report, in particular paragraphs 4.2.2: Judicial Enforcement Measures (*Ordnungsmittel*), 4.2.3: Withdrawal/Denial of Benefits/ Opportunities and 4.2.4: Means to Enforce Administrative Acts).

Rumania too presents a *summa divisio*: "Administrative sanctions can be divided into *contraventional sanctions*, considered to be the most important category, and *other administrative sanctions*", where the definition of administrative sanctions is confined to conventional sanctions disciplined by an autonomous and separate legislative corpus: Government Ordinance No. 2/2001 and Government Ordinance No. 55/2002 with successive modifications.

4.2.3. Countries with a high degree of differentiation

A similar structure can be seen in Spain, the Netherlands and Italy. In Spain, despite the absence of a 'strong' model of administrative sanctions like in Portugal with its DMOS, there are constitutional parameters that, as we have seen, clearly differentiate punitive administrative sanctions from other reactions by the public administration. The keystone of this differentiation is the concept of administrative infringement:

> "An administrative sanction can only be imposed if an administrative infringement, in the strict sense of the word, has been committed. An administrative sanction is to a criminal sentence what an administrative infringement is to a crime. All types of non-compliance with the legal system are not to be considered administrative infringement (…) this strict definition of administrative sanction makes it possible to isolate an useful juridical category, since it delimitates the scope of application of a particular juridical regime, different from those governing the remainder of administrative acts. Indeed, only such a strict notion can justify the application of that particular and differentiated juridical regime (…)."

In the Netherlands, the General Administrative Law Act (GALA) provides for a division in punitive administrative sanctions and administrative sanctions with a remedial aim. Although Italy's constitution poses no shared limits between criminal and administrative sanctions (in the strict sense) the latter are highly differentiated from other reactions by the public administration because it lays down principles which are exclusive to them (law No. 689 of 1981).

What makes Italy, the Netherlands and Spain similar and distinguishes them from Germany and Portugal is the existence of a series of principles valid for *all* administrative activity. For Spain, the report explains:

> "The Act regulating Public Administration, Authorities and Procedures (*Régimen Jurídico de las Administraciones Públicas y del Procedimiento Administrativo Común* 30/1992, 26 November) (hereafter, LPA) is the domestic law that establishes the most important general rules on the statutory regime of the Public Administration in Spain. Its title IX deals with "Sanctioning powers" in two chapters: Chapter I is

> entitled "Principles of sanctioning powers" (Articles 127 to 133) and deals with material aspects; Chapter II "Principles of the punitive administrative procedure" (Articles 134 to 138) deals with formal and procedural aspects. This regulation focuses exclusively on principles. It reviews concisely the most salient general aspects, but does not establish general rules about sanctions, liability, aggravating or mitigating circumstances, nor does it classify infringements and sanctions. It provides no more than a framework for offences and sanctions."

In regard to Italy:

> "Firstly, the Italian Constitution provides for a set of fundamental principles and rights related to the PA [Public Administration], which pervade the entire body of legislation on the matter, including the field of sanctioning powers";

secondly:

> "law 7 August 1990 no. 241 (*'Nuove norme in materia di procedimento amministrativo e diritto di accesso ai documenti amministrativi'*) regulates administrative proceeding, which amount to those activities culminating in the adoption of an administrative order (including the sanctioning order). Other relevant acts are: law 6 December 1971 no. 1034 (*'Istituzione dei tribunali amministrativi regionali'*), which establishes the judicial authorities which are competent on the cases involving PA activities, and law 21 July 2000 no. 205 (*'Disposizioni in tema di giustizia amministrativa'*), which lays down a set of instruments for the protection of individual rights affected by an administrative decision."

Similarly, as stated on the first page of the analysis of the Netherlands:

> "One of the interesting features of Dutch administrative law is the availability of a recent codification of general administrative law, the General Administrative Law Act or GALA *(Algemene wet bestuursrecht)*, which not only has general provisions on enforcement action *(last onder bestuursdwang)* and periodic penalty payments *(last onder dwangsom)*, but also on administrative fines *(bestuurlijke boete)*."

4.2.4. Countries with an intermediate level of differentiation

This category encompasses those systems which present no uniform legislation or express definitions of an administrative sanction which can be clearly separated from other coercive instruments of the public administration. In other words, if on the functional and normative level the administrative sanction as punishment is clearly distinguishable in these countries, on the other, its differentiation is confounded by legislative overlap between administrative sanctions and other measures.

Belgium, for example,

> "has not codified its administrative law. There is no 'Administrative Procedure Act' or 'General Administrative Law Code'. There is no coherent legal framework to offer protection against administrative sanctions either. Administrative law in Belgium is instead a fragmentary collection of specific acts, with case law trying to fill in the gaps."

Again:

> "The competent legislator(s) did however create a number of laws to enact certain regulations with a global application. Examples are the Act 'concerning the explicit justification of administrative acts', the 'Government Information Act' and the establishment of ombudsman institutions. There are comprehensive administrative procedure acts in certain legal fields as well, such as the 'charter of the socially insured' in the field of social security law. The administrative sanctions (and sanctioning procedures) themselves are scattered throughout scores of specific acts and the various legal fields. The most notable acts are the Administrative Fines Act in social law, the sanction mechanism of article 119 New Municipalities Act in public law and the Competition Act in economic law."

EU law itself belongs to this category: although the European Union legal system has a legislative framework (Regulation 2988/95), this text is accompanied by legislation relating to competition law. In addition, the text itself does not clearly trace a distinction between sanctions and other measures, as the Report explains:

> "It seems that Union law does not prefer the term 'sanctions' as an umbrella term for labelling the state's reaction to unlawful behaviour. More often we find the terms 'penalty' and 'measure' in the English versions of EU rules. For that matter, the term 'penalty' as used in Regulation 2988/95 is translated in several language versions by an equivalent of the word sanction (French: *Mesures et sanctions administratives*, German: *Verwaltungsrechtliche Maßnahmen und Sanktionen*, Spanish: *Medidas y sanciones administrativas*; Italian: *Misure e sanzioni amministrative*; Dutch: *Administratieve maatregelen en sancties)* which points to the punitive character of a sanction. I have not found an overall term to cover reactions to an offence both of a reparatory and of a punitive nature. This does not seem to justify the use of the term 'sanction' as an umbrella label in my contribution to this book, but in the absence of a better one, it will make do.
>
> The distinction between penalty and measure as such is meaningful. A measure is meant to be of a repairing nature, while the purpose of the penalty is to punish the offender. In Regulation 2988/95 we can find the two types and a list of sanctions, which fall within their scope. These reflect the kinds of sanctions that are usual in Union law."

4.2.5. Countries with a low level of differentiation

This category contains those countries that from the point of view of internal positive law do not set a clear legal definition between administrative sanctions as punishment and other measures. Differentiation is still possible under other terms, so that even at this level, it is not negligible. In the first place, as mentioned, this is due to the influence exercised by the concept of di *matière pénale* in Article 6 ECHR. Secondly, as emerges from the reports, it is because these countries make attempts to differentiate between the two concepts teleologically (see in particular the Finnish example.)

Paradigmatic in this group are Finland and Greece whose reports, beyond their personal styles reflecting their respective authors, highlight a oscillation within these countries between culturally determined concept of punitive administrative sanctions and the practical difficulty of situating such concepts on the plane of positive law.

As the Greek report emphasizes:

> "Neither the texts in force nor the case law of the Council of State have formulated an 'official' definition of administrative sanctions. Nevertheless it seems that Greek law understands those sanctions in a narrow sense. Such legal category includes individual administrative acts inducing a punishment to their addressee, as a consequence of the violation of a norm or an obligation by the same person. From that point of view, they may not be identified with measures of similar nature issued by the courts (civil, criminal or administrative) on the one hand and by bodies of the Administration *lato sensu*, but not governed by public law, on the other. (...)
> In addition, one should not assimilate administrative sanctions in Greece to the vast category of onerous administrative acts. Not every act producing unfavourable effects for the individuals is an administrative sanction. Nevertheless, such separation is not an easy one (...)"

The Finnish report describes this conflict well:

> "The exclusion of summary penalty fee from the sphere of administrative law combined with the silence of APA [Administrative Procedure Act of 1.1.2004] discussed in the beginning leaves concept of administrative sanctions without express statutory support. However, the notion of administrative sanctions based on the *lex specialis* encloses the idea, that they are punitive reactions to illegal acts. Furthermore, if and when they are meant to be punitive, it is also obvious that their legitimation must be based to the deterrent purpose of their existence. The idea of punishment without general deterrent purpose (*Generalprävention*) as justification would be incoherent with *Rechtsstaat* – concept incorporated in Finnish system of public law. (...) However, on the other hand materially criteria discussed above and especially the case-law give support to the wider concept of administrative sanctions. Not only punitive fees and excess fares charged in the case of infringement, but also other negative and restricting administrative acts should sometimes be included

within the notion of sanctions, if they amount to a reaction by administrative authorities against an infringement and can be considered to be a deterrent."

As can clearly be seen, this last paragraph from the Finnish report highlights how both legislative and teleological criteria necessitate a wider definition of administrative sanction. At the same time what emerges on a cultural level is a fairly well defined concept of administrative sanction in the strict sense. Once again the Finnish report brings out this conflict in the "difference between non-accessory sanctions and accessory conditional imposition of a fine can be traced back to the object protected by the deterrence and the nature of that deterrence. Whereas non-accessory sanctions protect the legal order and *a priori* obedience with it *in abstracto*, accessory sanctions are meant to protect authority, efficiency and integrity of administration *in concreto* and *a posteriori*. Similarly, whereas non-accessory sanctions include the notion of *Generalprävention*, accessory sanctions are more likely to have a special deterrent effect (*Spezialprävention*)."

4.2.6. Countries with a very low degree of differentiation

These countries are the UK and Sweden. They both exhibit a wide but fragmented range of administrative sanctions (in the wider sense of the term), but do not express, not even culturally, the concept of administrative sanction as punishment. For these countries it is only thanks to Article 6 of ECHR case law that it becomes possible to make such a distinction. It is interesting to note that these two countries both show a low level of differentiation in this context and from the viewpoint of criminal sanctions.

4.3. COMPARISON WITH DISCIPLINARY SANCTIONS

We shall now dedicate a brief paragraph to a comparison between administrative sanctions and disciplinary sanctions for two reasons.

In the first place because it is well known that ECHR case law does not allow us to trace a clear confine between administrative sanctions belonging to *matière pénale* and to disciplinary sanctions. The combined criteria outlined by the EHRC end up 'cutting in half' disciplinary sanctions. Also belonging to *matière pénale* are disciplinary sanctions if they include the combined criteria indicated by the Court. In particular, this occurs when disciplinary sanctions are considered as being substantially penal in content, for example, in the case of disciplinary sanctions which deprive offenders of personal freedoms (i.e.: disciplinary sanctions for detainees and the military).

In second place, not all reports deal with disciplinary sanctions. This is already significant insofar as it shows how problematic it is to distinguish administrative from disciplinary sanctions. As is obvious, this difficulty results in problems in the area of guarantees.

In Portugal, for example, disciplinary sanctions are subject to the same guarantees as administrative sanctions in the strict sense:

> "The Portuguese Constitutional Court (TC) interprets art 165, no 1, c and d, of the Portuguese Constitution (CRP), as allowing *only* for three types of public law sanctions: a) criminal penalties; b) *coimas* and other sanctions imposed by *Direito de Mera Ordenação Social* (Administrative Offences Law, hereafter DMOS); c) and *disciplinary sanctions*." (Italics added)

Greater difficulties emerge from the Spanish report:

> "There is a distinction between administrative sanctions imposed against any person for his unlawful conduct, and those sanctions imposed against persons more closely linked to the Administration; the latter are considered more serious, as they involve infringement of special duties. For instance, sanctions on civil servants, prisoners, students, and so on when they infringe their duties as such. This second category of sanctions is special in that there is a reduction of formal and material guarantees. The difference could be based on what is called 'disciplinary administrative power' which is distinct from general administrative sanctioning power because it would not be an expression of the same *ius puniendi* of the State; it could also be related to the concept of 'a special binding relationship' (*die besonderen Gewaltverhältlnisse*) inherited from the German legal system. However, the distinction between both types of sanctions or the statutory regimes they conform to is not clear. According to the precedents of the Constitutional Court (hereinafter CC), clear-cut distinctions cannot be established, only differences based on quantity or degree: for instance, both types of sanctions are bound to the principle of legality, although the interpretation of this concept is more flexible when dealing with disciplinary sanctions."

5. INTERNAL CHARACTERISTICS OF THE CONCEPT OF ADMINISTRATIVE SANCTION VALID IN ANY GIVEN LEGAL SYSTEM

As we saw in Paragraph 2, comparison *ab interno* of the concept of administrative sanction will be made by reviewing a series of structural referents.

We shall restate them here:

(1) The existence of a 'single code' for the category and its relationship with the legality principle;
(2) The typology of sanctions;

(3) The criteria of indictment of the sanction (forms and assumptions of responsibility for an illegal act).

5.1. THE EXISTENCE OF A 'SINGLE CODE' FOR THE CATEGORY AND ITS RELATIONSHIP WITH THE LEGALITY PRINCIPLE

The first thing one should say is that the group of countries considered from this viewpoint is split in half. The following countries have a *codex* of administrative sanctions: Rumania, Portugal, Italy, the Netherlands and Germany, to which we can add EU law. In contrast, the other countries are without this code.

5.1.1. Countries that have a category code

In countries with a category code (Germany, Portugal, Italy, the Netherlands and Rumania), the most important common feature, is when the administrative sanction is codified at the same time as a concept of the administrative sanction in the strict sense. In other words, codification introduces the concept of administrative sanction as punishment. Moreover, there is a tendency for a connection to exist between codification and the concept of administrative sanction in the strict sense: where codification occurs there are also sanctions in the strict sense and where there are sanctions in the strict sense there is also codification. This correspondence, however, is only tendential, and not inevitable. In some countries the opposite may occur: this is the case of Spain that adopted a concept in the strict sense without codifying. EU law, vice versa, expresses a codification having the objective of disciplining, under different systems, both 'penal' and 'other measures'.

Among the countries applying a category code we can trace a distinction between Portugal, Germany and Italy on the one hand and Romania on the other. The former all have share the same model, whose matrix, as known, is the German *Ordnungswidrigkeitengesetz* (OWiG, Administrative Offenses Act). Instead, the Rumanian system has a 'category code' (the Government ordinance No. 2/2001), which, as we have seen, has an ambiguous relationship with criminal sanctions. There are great differences in terms of guarantees (see Rumanian Report: "penal offences and their sanctions may be only established by law whereas contraventions and their sanctions may be established by law or supplementary provisions such as Government Decisions, and Decisions of Local and County councils") with many points in common in terms of content.

In this regard, the situation in Portugal with the *Direito de Mera Ordenação Social*, Italy with law No. 689/81, and Germany with its *Ordnungswidrigkeitengesetz* is the exact opposite. These three countries have a *codex* showing strong continuities with criminal sanctions in terms of guarantees, but discontinuities from the point of view of contents.

In all three countries there is a string link between codified administrative sanctions and the law: the legality principle is stated in the introduction of their codes in a manner similar to what is envisaged in these countries for criminal sanctions. It is very similar, *but not identical*: there are mitigations in regard to the principle of criminal legality for different causes and aspects.

As the Italian report reminds us:

> "*The principle of legality* (Article 1), subject to which no one shall be punished with an administrative sanction which is not provided for by the law and no one may be punished as a result of an interpretation which extends the scope of application of a punitive provision by means of analogy. Although this principle, as is well-known, also applies to criminal offences, it has a rather different meaning in criminal law: as regards criminal law, the principle of legality is laid down in the Constitution and it has a more rigorous meaning; in the field of administrative law, the principle is laid down under statutory law and there may be significant derogations therefrom as an administrative offence can be regulated by regional law.".

The Portuguese report is quite analytical on this point and presents us a detailed picture of the differences in legality between the criminal law and legality as specified in the *Direito de Mera Ordenação Social*. Indeed, after having stated clearly that "the principle of legality applicable in DMOS does not have to be *exactly coincident* with the one applicable to criminal law. Some adaptations may be required, either: a) because of their different constitutional framework; b) or for the sake of the coordination of both branches of law; c) or in order to ensure the efficiency of DMOS." The Portuguese report then explains in greater detail what these differences consist in (attenuation of legal reserve, uncertainties in regard to the non-retroactivity principle, mitigation of definiteness).

We can see structural similarities between these models and Regulation 2988/95 CE of EU law. Here too, we see a strong link with legality (in Regulation 2988/95 the principle is expressly mentioned in article 2: "No administrative penalty may be imposed unless a Community act prior to the irregularity has made provision for it. In the event of a subsequent amendment of the provisions, which impose administrative penalties and are contained in Community rules, the less severe provisions shall apply retroactively"). This connection with legality is strengthened by Art. 49 of the Nice Charter, currently integrated into Art. 49 Charter of fundamental rights of the European Union, and envisages a legality principle and proportionality equally valid for criminal offences and penalties.

The EU law report that we have discussed is the only case of a unified *codex* for a category not confined to administrative sanctions in the very strict sense (given that this codex incorporates both 'penalties' and 'measures'). It appears to be connected to this distinction in terms of guarantees because it seems that

> "the principle of legality only applies to the penalties. In the Kõnicke case, however, the Court emphasized that 'penalty, even of a non-criminal nature, cannot be imposed unless it rests on a clear and unambiguous legal basis'. The phrase refers to the forfeiture of a deposit, which might be considered as a 'measure' in terms of Regulation 2988/95, and as a general rule is of a repairing nature. It suggests that a legal basis is necessary for repairing measures as well. However, the forfeiture of a deposit in combination with recovery of sums paid, in reality is a penalty, and that was what the case was about In conclusion, the principle of legality certainly applies to penalties in EU law; however, it is uncertain if it applies to measures as well."

On the other hand, as clearly explained in the analysis of the Netherlands, the Dutch General Administrative Law Act (GALA) provides for a full set of guarantees which are generally related to criminal sanctions and it does not seem to be inspired by the German *Ordnungswidrigkeitengesetz.*

5.1.2. Countries without a category code

We can begin to make to an initial distinction among countries that have a general law that disciplines all the hypotheses of administrative sanction in the wider sense (like any other form of reaction by the public administration when there is a violation of a precept) even though may not have a category code, and those that do not.

- *Countries that have a general law disciplining the different forms of reaction of the public administration to the violation of a precept*

Spain and Finland belong to this category, and to some extent, I believe, Greece. All three present a general normative text albeit with different degrees of application. What is interesting is that beyond these differences, the very existence of such a text guarantees a rather strong link with legality, allowing us to classify these countries together.

In the first place we can discuss Spain, which while not having a unified code of administrative sanction, has a general part containing the principles indicating the overall applicability of sanctioning powers as explained in the report: "The organic Act regulating Public Administration, Authorities and Procedures (*Régimen Jurídico de las Administraciones Públicas y del Procedimiento Administrativo Común* 30/1992, 26 November) (LPA) is the domestic law that establishes the most important general rules on the statutory regime of the Public Administration in Spain. Its title IX deals with "Sanctioning powers" in two chapters: Chapter I is entitled "Principles of sanctioning powers" (Articles 127 to 133) and deals with material aspects; Chapter II "Principles of the punitive administrative procedure" (Articles 134 to 138) deals with formal and procedural aspects. This regulation focuses exclusively on principles. It reviews concisely the most salient general aspects, but does not establish general rules about sanctions, liability, aggravating or mitigating circumstances, nor does it classify infringements and sanctions. It provides no more than a framework for offences and sanctions."

The Spanish solution, while setting general rules, still allows a clear concept of the administrative sanction to emerge (also because of the limits posed by the constitution). Instead in Finland, this concept does not appear. The general Finnish law is not amenable to a precise description of the notion of administrative sanction, as is stated in the introduction to the Finnish report:

> "The cornerstone of the Finnish administrative law, the Administrative Procedure Act (APA) entered into force on 1 January 2004. According to its preparatory works, the intention was to incorporate general and informative statutes governing administrative sanctions. Namely, the predecessor of the current APA, the Administrative Procedure Act from 1982, was completely silent about administrative sanctions. Thus, in section 67 of the new APA it is stated that 'an authority may reinforce a prohibition, obligation or requirement imposed by it by way of a threat of a fine, a threat of compulsory action or a threat of compulsory cessation, or another administrative sanction, as separately provided'.
> However, despite the intentions explicitly expressed in the preparatory works, it must be stated that Section 67 of the APA provides no basis for a positive conceptionalisation of administrative sanctions."

This structural difference between Spain and Finland is less marked when one considers the legality principle. The Spanish report reminds us that this principle informs administrative sanctions as well, whereas Finnish law, by establishing a relationship with legality, distinguishes between administrative sanctions in both the broader and stricter sense:

> "in the field of exercising public powers, one should require legal justification, i.e. statutory support for the existence of discretionary powers in a particular case. Furthermore, goal-rationality on the part of the administration plays a different role here: when exercising public powers against an individual, certain aims and goals are to be derived from the enabling act. In other words, legally speaking, the administration does not use sanctioning powers to pursue public interest, but to apply the law."

In Greek law, the capacity to define administrative law is even more indefinite:

> "Administrative law has been recently codified in part. Except the relevant provisions of the HC, the main procedural rules and guarantees are included in the Administrative Procedure Code (APC – L. 2690/1999). The rules concerning the judicial review of the administrative action may be found in two texts, Presidential decree (p.d.) 18/1989 regarding the Council of State and the Administrative Court Procedure Code (ACPC – L. 2717/1999) regarding the judicial recourse before the 'ordinary' Administrative Courts. Such codification is far from being exhaustive,

> however; except for special written provisions, case law norms in the field of administrative law are shaped and formulated by the decisions of the Council of State, even if, formally speaking, case law is not a source of legal norms within the Greek legal order. There is no special legislation governing the imposition and the regime of administrative punitive sanctions *lato sensu* except for the Public Revenue Collection Code (PRCC – l.d. 356/1974) that deals with the special enforcement proceedings for the collection of public bodies claims against their debtors."

As stated above, the structural differences within Greece are tempered when we move on to evaluate the efficacy of the legality principle:

> "by virtue of the principle of legality, the use of sanctioning powers is not inherent to the administrative functions but has to be attributed *expressis verbis* by a legal provision to a specific administrative authority. The latter is empowered to use such powers only to the extent that the norms governing its action acknowledge specific competence. For instance, an administrative authority is not entitled to inflict a fine exceeding the threshold set by the legislation. Moreover, a law delegating to the administration a broad power to establish by regulatory measures a system of administrative sanctions would be contrary to art. 43 par 2 HC; such measures (decrees or others) would be *ultra vires*, since the delegation would be considered insufficiently described by the legislator. The courts review *ex officio* the legality and competence of sanction even if the issue is not raised by the applicant.".

– *Countries that have no general law disciplining the various forms of reaction by the public administration to the violation of a precept*

We can place the three remaining countries into this category: Belgium, the UK, and Sweden. Here the characterizing data are all in the negative: absence of a code, a general legal framework, or of a conceptualisation of the notion of administrative sanction.

Perhaps the most interesting aspect is the relationship with legality: for these three countries the 'quest for legality' on the basis of Art. 6 of the EHCR was much more intense than for other countries. This in particular is the case for the UK and Belgium (the Swedish report passes some comment on the legality characterizing the national situation).

The aspect that emerges is evident: in the absence of a legal framework of reference for administrative sanctions both in the strict and wider sense, a strong national commitment to the legality principle is lacking. Consequently, the greater the incapacity of internal law to describe the legal confines of a normative context, the greater is the need to outline these confines on the basis of the European legal system.

5.2. TYPOLOGY OF SANCTIONS

Generally speaking the first fact to emerge is the central position of the pecuniary sanction or fine in the whole area considered. Further, the more a country expresses a strict definition of the administrative sanction, the more fines take a central role. In other words, fines are naturally at the heart of administrative sanctions, and their prominence becomes dominance when such fines are defined strictly and meaningfully.

It should be made clear, however, that EU law takes a unique position on this issue: here fines occupy a central role but are not as dominant as in the single countries. As the EU law report states: "The penalties of Article 5 of Regulation 2988/1995 are listed here to show the large variation in types of penalties. They are:

a) payment of an administrative fine;
b) payment of an amount greater than the amounts wrongly received or evaded, plus interest where appropriate; this additional sum shall be determined in accordance with a percentage to be set in the specific rules, and may not exceed the level strictly necessary to constitute a deterrent;
c) total or partial removal of an advantage granted by Community rules, even if the operator wrongly benefited from only a part of that advantage;
d) exclusion from, or withdrawal of, the advantage for a period subsequent to that of the irregularity;
e) temporary withdrawal of the approval or recognition necessary for participation in a Community aid scheme;
f) the loss of a security or deposit provided for the purpose of complying with the conditions laid down by rules or the replenishment of the amount of a security wrongly released;
g) other penalties of a purely economic type, equivalent in nature and scope, provided for in the sector rules adopted by the Council in the light of the specific requirements of the sectors concerned and in compliance with the implementing powers conferred on the Commission by the Council." The reason for this is probably the greater executivity of interdictive sanctions compared to fines within the European Community, given that the former allow for immediate application. This is an advantage when the difficulty of effective execution is greater than on a national level. In addition, it should be remembered that this law has the objective of protecting the financial interests of the European Union, which to a great extent involves protecting community subsidies, and interdictive sanctions are particularly well suited to protecting a funding system.

If we move onto national models we can examine in greater detail what was stated at the beginning of this section.

Administrative fines are absolutely fundamental in Portugal where the DMOS has been built up around a central fine (the *Coimas*) accompanied by accessory sanctions. In Italy, law No. 689/81 makes reference only to administrative fines. A fundamental role is accorded to administrative fines in Germany and in Rumania in regard to which the report states: "the upper limit of the contraventional fine (…) was set at more than the upper limit of the penal fine (…) and, due to the lack of the principle of proportionality (in comparing penal sanctions with their administrative equivalent), the fact that the fine and imprisonment were penal sanctions as well as administrative sanctions and due to the impossibility of suspending administrative sanctions, the possibility existed that a contravention could be punished more severely than a penal offence."

Fines are also fundamental in Spain: "Without doubt, the most usual administrative sanction is a fine, when the offender is made to pay the Administration a sum of money", Finland, as emerges from the initial pages of the Finnish report, and the Netherlands, as shown in paragraph 5.2 of the related report.

The central role accorded to fines is less marked in countries like Belgium and Greece, where, as we have seen, defining the administrative sanction appears to be more problematic. Nevertheless, for these countries, the centrality of fines remains, with this sanction always being present in the various special codes. Sweden too appears to have adopted this position.

Unlike what might be thought, fines also have a central role in the UK. Here, despite what we have observed throughout the course of this general Report, the legal system country has difficulties in defining a concept of administrative sanction (whether strict or broad). Nevertheless, the administrative fine is still the most prominent of the examples considered in the report, probably because fines are at the core of the definition of sanctions inside the UK which is very broad indeed (in that it includes both criminal and civil sanctions).

5.3. INDICTMENT CRITERIA FOR ADMINISTRATIVE SANCTIONS (FORMS AND PREREQUISITES OF RESPONSIBILITY FOR THE OFFENCE)

Here our comparison will follow a slightly different thread: the definition of the administrative sanction will emerge all the more clearly when the *particularities* in the indictment procedures are pointed out.

Before beginning this discussion, a number of caveats should be made.

The differences found until now among definitions of sanctions have an immediate impact in the search for indictment criteria. It is obvious that such a comparison can only be done among those countries that have a typology of administrative sanction that has been defined to some extent. It is not *at all* possible to find indictment criteria for administrative sanctions when they are conceptualised in a fragmentary manner over a number of un-coordinated disciplines, as is the case of Sweden, the UK, Greece, Finland, and Belgium.

Nevertheless, the information that the national reports dedicate to this definition is truly vital: comparison can be effected only on the basis of some themes, in particular: the applicability of administrative sanctions to legal persons and the subjective indictment criteria (guilt or strict liability) for their application. It would also be quite interesting to make comparisons by evaluating proportioning criteria, but this information is not uniformly forthcoming from the reports.

In terms of the first issue we can say that all the countries considered apply administrative sanctions to legal persons. This conclusion in itself is not significant in the context of the argument of this paper which focuses on comparing definitions of administrative sanctions. However, it becomes relevant when applicability to legal persons is *specific* to the administrative sanction, because it helps to define its characteristics.

Hence in Germany, where the report indicates the differences between the criteria for administrative sanctions compared to criminal sanctions: "the legislator has created the Allgemeiner Teil (General Part) of the OWiG by closely following that of the StGB (Sections 1 *et seq.*, OWiG). The only substantial deviations are those defined in Section 14, OWiG, i.e., the principle of Einheitstäterschaft (the monistic model of a perpetrator) and, as defined in Section 30, OWiG, the possibility to impose an administrative fine on legal entities and associations of individuals as an incidental consequence.". In this country the subjective indictment criteria for administrative sanctions is distinguished from criminal law with the differences between the two areas persisting but less clearly:

> "within the scope of OWiG, the term guilt is replaced by the term 'reproachability' (Vorwerfbarkeit), or blame (Section 12, OWiG). This choice of terminology is merely designed to link the reproach of an administrative offense 'with the element of socio-ethical disapproval', an element that is not contained in the reproach itself. In essence, the terms 'reproachable' and 'guilty' have the same meaning. Consequently, although (in view of the lacking moral reproach) guilt in case of an administrative offense is much less significant than in case of a criminal offence, the requirements for its mere presence are the same. In this respect, criminal law rulings are also relevant to rulings under administrative law."

In Portugal we find an identical situation to Germany's, the same relationship and differences to criminal law, also in regard to guilt: "guilt requires acting with intent or negligence, although punishment of negligent offences requires a specific legal provision (art. 8º, nº 1, of the RGCO). Thus, strict liability is not allowed." The same applies to responsibility by corporations and public bodies, which is presented in the Portuguese report by contrasting the criminal and punitive administrative fields: "art. 11 no 1 of the Penal Code states that 'only individuals are liable for criminal offences, unless the law specifically provides for the criminal liability of corporations and legal entities'.

Article 7º of the RGCO follows a different approach, stating that both individuals and legal entities are (always) held liable for *contra-ordenações.*"

Similarly in Rumania, "before 2006 contraventional sanctions may be applied both to natural and legal persons, while penal sanctions may be applied only to natural persons." The Rumanian report then points out how "this difference has disappeared when the Romanian Penal Code was modified by Law No. 278/2006, that introduced penal responsibility for legal persons" pursuing a trend typical in Europe where on the issue of the responsibility of legal persons criminal sanctions follow administrative sanctions in the strict sense.

The Italian report also reminds us that "responsibility exists only in case the offender has acted with intention or recklessness". However, this country's legal system envisages the application of administrative sanctions to legal persons unlike for the criminal law ("The responsibility of legal entities is somewhat peculiar in administrative law, since a criminal offence can only be committed by a natural person under Italian criminal law."). This possibility, however, does not lead to a fully fledged principle of direct responsibility by legal persons for violation of the administrative law but creates a solidarity principle, as the Italian report explains: "Certain categories of individuals or legal persons who have not taken take part in the offence are nevertheless subject to a form of solidarity with the offender as far as the execution of the pecuniary administrative sanction is concerned. Nonetheless, should the fine be paid by one person only, he will have recourse against the author of the illicit act.".

The same position applies to Spain: "Criminal Law states that only natural persons can commit offences and suffer penalties (*societas delinquere non potest*). In contrast, legal persons can commit administrative offences and receive the corresponding sanction (...)However, Criminal Law has been recently amended in order to accept, for the first time, that legal persons can commit offences and suffer penalties (Ley Orgánica 5/2010, de 22 de junio, de Reforma del Código Penal, entered into force on 23 December)." Spain, by virtue of its constitutional constraints on administrative sanctions in the strict sense, has perfectly identical concepts of guilt for its criminal and administrative law: "Administrative sanctions can only be imposed if the improper conduct is committed willingly and with culpability, that is to say, as a result of intent or fault, the same as under Criminal Law. Although the requirement of guilt is not mentioned in the SC [Spanish Constitution], the Constitutional Court has considered it implicit and a fundamental right, so that any law infringing this requirement would be unconstitutional.".

In this perspective the 'negative' proof coming to us through EU law attracts our interest. In this system, the specific indictment criteria cannot be lifted from the criminal law for the obvious reason that the system does not envisage this field. The EU law report consequently highlights the indictment criteria for penalties and other measures. The former "can only be imposed in cases of intent or negligence of the offender" whereas the latter "can be imposed at all times, when an irregularity is found, without the need for culpability.".

6. CONCLUSIONS

To sum up, we have conducted this comparison by reviewing a series of criteria to define the administrative sanction. These criteria are obviously interrelated. For example, to evaluate the degree of functional differentiation between administrative and criminal sanctions one must have a clear idea of the legislative content of the two types of sanction. However, as the opposite is also true, it is only by combining them that one can elicit a current definition of administrative sanction in any given country.

For this reason our conclusion will first present a synopsis in the form of a table giving the distribution of the various models reviewed according to the criteria employed for their definition. We shall then draft a typology of the concept of administrative sanction. Finally we will analyse a series of links between the criteria we examined and the type of concept current in a given country.

First, however, a number of caveats and some clarifications.

The caveat

This table simply reproduces what has been stated in the course of this General Report. Its sole purpose is to present a review of the different criteria considered in the analysis. The table is immediately comprehensible for those reading the report and it was drafted for this purpose. Hence it may not be comprehensible to those who have not read the text of this article.

The clarifications

Not all the countries examined are present in all the rows of the table for the many reasons given above.

The degree of differentiation from criminal sanctions is here presented in two specific rows which distinguish between functional and formal differentiation. It is on the basis of such 'internal' criteria that one can clearly distinguish the two concepts, and we have reviewed these criteria last, so that only now is it possible to clearly distinguish between the two categories. At the same time, as we have seen, it is necessary to keep these areas separate because a low level of functional differentiation is associated with a high level of formal differentiation (as for example in Spain). This leads to a well defined administrative function which is of limited normative functionality because the salient characteristic of the administrative sanction which emerges is actually too similar to the criminal sanction. In contrast, a high degree of functional differentiation associated with a low level of formal differentiation (as for example in Rumania) leads to 'labelling fraud': administrative sanctions substantially become a criminal sanction with less guarantees. This may be practical but not very acceptable from the point of view of the observance of individual rights and hence lacks legitimacy and legitimation.

The evaluation of the legality of the administrative sanction can lead to a misunderstanding which one should immediately dispel: if in certain countries there is an inadequate connection with legality, this does not mean there is a lower level of observance of guarantees. It only means that these guarantees depend more on the international context and overall respect for the legality principle. In other words, it simply means that we do not find a high level of conceptualisation of the legality of the administrative sanction on a given national level (as is the case for Belgium and the UK).

The acronyms denoting countries are derived from their English language name.

Degree of differentiation	**Very high**	**High**	**Middling**	**Little**	**Very little**
Differentiation from criminal sanctions *FORMAL*	(EU)	(It), (P), (NL), (Ger), (B)	(Sp), (Fin), (Gr)	(Rum), (Sw)	(UK)
Differentiation from criminal sanctions *FUNCTIONAL*	(EU)	(P), (Rum), (B)	(Ger), (Gr), (NL)	(It), (Fin), (Sw)	(UK), (Sp)
Differentiation from other administrative sanctions	(P), (Rum), (Ger)	(It), (NL), (Sp)	(B), (EU)	(Fin), (Gr)	(UK), (Sw)
Category 'Code'	(P), (Rum), (Ger), (It), (NL), (EU)	(Sp)	(Fin)	(Gr)	(B), (UK), (Sw)
Legality	(P), (Ger), (It), (Sp), (NL)	(EU), (Fin), (Gr)		(Rum), (Sw)	(B), (UK)
Typology of punishment (centrality of fines)	(It), (P), (Ger)	(Rum), (Sp), (NL), (Fin)	(B), (Gr), (Sv), (UK)	(EU)	
Specificity of indictment criteria		(Rum)	(Por), (Ger)	(It), (Sp)	

At this point we can draft an ideal list on the basis of these criteria and particularly the combinations among them.

These countries present a truly heterogeneous picture and present a wide range of definitions of administrative sanctions.

We have an *ideal* polarity thus:

- On the one hand an *administrative sanction in the very strict sense* which emerges from these following criteria: a high degree of differentiation (formal and functional) both from the criminal and other administrative fields, *combined* with a high degree of *internal* identity and functional-structural specificity of the concept of administrative sanction deriving from, having a category code, specific rules of application, a sanctionary typology typical of the category (which as we have seen is the fine), and the formulation of a strong but specific legality principle;
- On the other, an *administrative sanction in the broadest sense* which emerges when these categories are inverted: a very low degree of differentiation combined with a low level of *internal* identity and functional-structural specificity of the concept of administrative sanction deriving from the non-existence of a category code with specific rules of application or of a sanctionary typology typical of the category and without any formulation of a strong but specific legality principle.

Of course these are two ideal polarities, no country integrates all these conditions solely on the one side or the other, but instead presents them in a more to varying degrees. These polarities are useful in singling out the actual concept of administrative sanction current in any given country.

This is because it is possible to single out trends which can be quite prominent. In particular:

- The more a country occupies positions to the *left* of the table the more this country will present a strict definition of the administrative sanction. Here the case of Portugal is prominent whose model satisfies the maximum number of typical criteria for administrative sanctions in the very strict sense, more than Germany and subsequently Italy;
- Symmetrically, the more one country is on the *right*, the more it will have a broad definition. Here we clearly see the position taken by the UK, followed by Sweden and Greece;
- Consequently, if a country 'moves very horizontally' from left to right according to the different criteria in the table, this will reflect the typology of the administrative sanction. Here the typical examples are Spain, Rumania and the European Union.

The broadness of the concept emerges from the other two parameters I have taken into consideration: *differentiation ab externo* of the notion of administrative sanction, and *internal normative functionality* for the concept of administrative sanction.

These *three* distinct parameters: (1) broadness of the concept of administrative sanctions; (2) 'normative functionality'; (3) degree of differentiation (into two parts: *formal* and *structural*), in the ultimate analysis 'prove' each other.

Some examples:

An inverse proportionality exists between the *broadness* of the notion of administrative sanction and it *normative functionality.*

This relationship is strongly 'conditioned' by the *degree of differentiation both formal and functional*: this relationship is valid only when there is a sufficient differentiation between penal and administrative sanctions. Indeed, if the administrative sanction undergoes an identity crisis in respect of the criminal sanction it no longer needs its own meaningful definition (i.e.: in the UK), because *a priori* it makes no sense to speak of the administrative sanction itself (its functions and hence structure)and hence to make a definition.

Yet, the opposite is of course also true: if the administrative sanction has a very strict definition and to some extent is also codified, but has a low degree of differentiation from the penal sanction (i.e.: as in Spain) it also goes into crisis because by losing an independent structure it also loses functionality.

Contrasting corollary

An administrative sanction with high chances of functionality will be very limited: in other words it becomes a concept of administrative sanction in the very strict sense and this is possible only if it is clearly differentiated.

II. COUNTRY ANALYSIS – AUSTRIA

Frank Höpfel and Robert Kert

1. RELATION TO GENERAL FIELDS OF LAW AND IMPORTANT GENERAL ACTS

1.1. DEFINITION OF SANCTIONS AND RELATIONSHIP TO OTHER MEASURES IN THE LIGHT OF THE HISTORICAL DEVELOPMENT

The term 'sanction' is rarely used in Austrian legal language other than in the general theory of law and of jurisprudence and therefore no general definition exists. In his famous book *Pure Theory of Law*, Hans Kelsen[1] has defined sanction as a certain act towards a person, which in general is perceived as a harm, and which – according to a norm – shall be inflicted on a person, if this person – or another one, who is in a specific relation to him – has behaved in a manner which did not comply with the (social) order. Applied to law, sanctions are established by a normative order to guarantee the effectiveness of the law. If a normative order establishes sanctions, it is supposed that the objective to avoid the harm provided for the case of a violation of a norm, shall constitute a motive to behave according to the norms.[2] Additionally, Kelsen includes positive consequences, foreseen for certain behaviour corresponding to the order, in his concept of 'sanction'.[3] However, this positive understanding of the term sanction has not become common sense.

The classical example for a sanction, which also Kelsen used to give, has been the punishment of a thief. Kelsen's broad definition of the term 'sanction' makes it necessary to distinguish between punitive and non-punitive sanctions.[4] This seems to be the more important distinction, because it depends on the

1 Kelsen, *Reine Rechtslehre*, 2nd ed., 1960, p. 114 *et seq.*; compare Kelsen, *Allgemeine Theorie der Normen*, 1979, p. 108 *et seq.*

2 Kelsen, *Allgemeine Theorie*, p. 111 *et seq.*

3 Kelsen, *Allgemeine Theorie*, pp. 109 and 112.

4 Also Kelsen differs between penalties and civil executions; see Kelsen, *Allgemeine Theorie*, p. 112.

qualification as penalty, whether certain procedural and substantive guarantees must be applied. A 'penalty' *('Strafe')* is defined as an evil which is linked with blame and which is imposed on a specific person by a sovereign act because of a prohibited conduct of that person and on the basis of his/her culpability.[5]

This notion of 'penalty' has reached over the criminal law which today is strictly connected with the administration of justice by independent 'ordinary' courts. In Austrian constitutional legislation the courts became independent only in 1861 by the *Staatsgrundgesetz über die richterliche Gewalt* (State Basic Law on the Power of Judges) when they were separated from all administrative bodies (see Article 94 Federal Constitution Act – *Bundes-Verfassungsgesetz*). This independence is a personal privilege of every professional judge meaning his/her freedom from individual or general administrative instructions *(Weisungen)* as well as the guarantee not to be removed from the post *(Unabsetzbarkeit, Unversetzbarkeit;* see Article 88, para. 2 *Bundes-Verfassungsgesetz*).

Correspondingly, Austrian penal law has developed twofold: the 'hard core' which is supposed to represent a bold blame connected with the registration of a conviction in the criminal records, and which is in the competence of the courts; and a 'light' system of directing certain behaviour by punishments – mainly fines – as part of the vast field of administrative law.

Additionally, in this field of administrative law there is a wide range of other, more or less clearly extra-penal, administrative sanctions. In the light of Kelsen's definition, we need to filter such acts which respond to a certain conduct of a person concerned, from administrative measures which do not require such behaviour. E.g., such measures as the withdrawal of a driver's licence or of a weapon licence can be based either on certain acts or merely on other circumstances, such as bad health. Therefore they have to be thoroughly differentiated according to the rationale of the measure. Within these measures, also all kinds of immediate ('procedureless') emanations of state *imperium*, like the direct use of force (see Act on the Use of Weapons – *Waffengebrauchsgesetz*), must be excluded from our further considerations.

The definition of a punitive sanction is essentially influenced by Articles 6 and 7 of the ECHR. The Convention has the rank of a constitutional law in Austria. Whereas there are differences in the interpretation of the definition of 'civil rights' between the European Court of Human Rights and the Austrian Constitutional

---

5 See for criminal law Kienapfel/Höpfel/Kert, *Grundriss des österreichischen Strafrechts – Allgemeiner Teil*, 14th ed., 2009, p. 4 *et seq.*; Fuchs, *Österreichisches Strafrecht Allgemeiner Teil*, I, 7th ed., 2012, p. 3 *et seq.*; for administrative penal law Thienel/Schulev-Steindl, *Verwaltungsverfahrensrecht*, 5th ed., 2009, p. 390.

Court, there is a far-reaching consensus between these two courts concerning the interpretation of the term 'criminal charge'. According to the Austrian Constitutional Court and in conformity with the European Court of Human Rights, the term of penal law ('criminal charge') in the meaning of Article 6 ECHR must be interpreted autonomously according to its sense and purpose. Even though that a legal provision is part of the criminal law according to the national legal system is taken into account, this is not the only criterion for a qualification of a sanction as 'criminal sanction'. If the concerned provision within the national legislation is not part of the criminal law, the nature of the offence and, finally the nature and the degree of severity of the penalty that the person concerned risked to receive, has to be regarded in the light of the object and purpose of Article 6, to the ordinary meaning of the terms of that Article and to the laws of the Contracting States is considered. Any prison sentences – even when representing disciplinary measures –, are always regarded a 'criminal charge' within the meaning of Article 6 ECHR. The same applies to other penalties, which are similar to the disadvantage of a prison sentence, if according to the nature of the sanction there is no doubt that the character of a punishment is kept on, which is typical for a criminal sanction. Sanctions have this special character of criminal sanctions only if they have the purpose to avenge or to deter.[6] There is no doubt that decisions on administrative penalties are decisions on a 'criminal charge' according to Article 6 ECHR. The question, if disciplinary penalties are a sort of a 'criminal charge', depends on the gravity of the provided sanctions.

The Austrian Constitutional Court consistently assumes a penalty, when the provision has a repressive and preventive sanctioning character and if the sanction is grave *per se*.[7]

In the Austrian legislation, a dividing line is drawn between criminal and administrative penalties because of its relevance to competence. Whereas the jurisdiction in criminal law is in the competence of the courts, administrative penal law is in the competence of administrative authorities. Within the administrative penal law we can distinguish different areas: the 'general' administrative penal law, which is regulated in the *Verwaltungsstrafgesetz* (Act on Administrative Penal Law – VStG); the law of fiscal offences, as far as it is not in the jurisdiction of the courts; the disciplinary law and other administrative penal law which is not executed according to the laws mentioned before.

6 See e.g. Constitutional Court 14 October 1987, VfSlg. 11.506; ECtHR 21 February 1984, GH A 73.

7 See *inter alia* Constitutional Court 14 October 1987, VfSlg 11.506/1987; 26 November 1987, 11.512/1987; 7 December 1987, 11.569/1987; see Grabenwarter/Geppert, 'Die Bedeutung des Art. 6 MRK für die Verhängung von Ordnungs- und Mutwillensstrafen', *JBl* 1996, 159 (166 *et seq.*).

Moreover, as mentioned above, there are administrative measures, *e.g.* the withdrawal of the driving licence, the withdrawal of the trade licence or the exclusion of tenderers from tendering proceedings. These are not administrative penalties and the Act on Administrative Penal Law is not applied. It has not been discussed into depth and researched yet in Austria, if and under which conditions such measures are needed to be classified as 'criminal charge' within the meaning of Article 6 ECHR.[8]

1.2. ADMINISTRATIVE SANCTIONS IN THE AUSTRIAN LAW

1.2.1. Administrative penal sanctions

Imprisonment

The most severe penalty in administrative penal law is imprisonment, which can be provided for not only as an alternative sentence in case, if a fine is not paid, but also as a primary penalty.

A primary imprisonment sentence may only be imposed, if this is explicitly provided for in the concrete administrative provision. The Code of Administrative Penal Law (*Verwaltungsstrafgesetz*) limits the possibility for imposing sentences of imprisonment: It may only be imposed, if this is necessary to defer the offender from another administrative offence (Section 11 VStG). This means that a primary imprisonment sentence may only be imposed due to reasons of special prevention, but not because of reasons of general prevention.[9] The jurisprudence requires that the imposition of an imprisonment sentence is substantiated carefully.

An imprisonment sentence must not be imposed on juveniles under age 16 (Section 58, para. 1 VStG). For other juveniles the imprisonment must not last more than two weeks, if this is necessary due to 'special reasons' at all.

The duration of primary imprisonment sentences must be at the minimum 12 hours. Shorter imprisonment sentences are not admissible. Section 12, para. 1 VStG provides for an upper limit of two weeks. A higher imprisonment sentence may only be imposed due to special aggravating factors and if such imprisonment sentences are provided for in the specific administrative provisions. In

8 See below under 2.2.5.

9 See Raschauer/Wessely, *Verwaltungsstrafrecht*, p. 128 *et seq.*

administrative penal matters, the absolute limit of imprisonment for one and the same offence is six weeks (see *infra* under I.4.1).

Penalties in administrative penal law cannot be conditionally suspended, whereas this is possible in criminal law and in the law of fiscal offences. One reason for this is the fact that there are no criminal records in administrative penal law.

Fines

In practice, the most important penalties in administrative law are fines. Whereas Austrian criminal law provides for a system of day fines, in administrative penal law only minimum and maximum limits exist. As an absolute minimum fine Section 13 VStG provides for €7. Only if the penalty is imposed by a law enforcement agent (organ), it is possible to stay below this limit.

If a fine is imposed, an alternative imprisonment sentence must be determined together with the fine. Therefore in administrative penal law, an imprisonment in default of payment is always connected with a fine, if there are no other provisions in specific laws. This also applies to juveniles under 16. But in this case the imprisonment in default of payment would be executed only after the 16th birthday.[10]

The imprisonment in default of payment must not go beyond the upper limit provided for in the administrative penal provision. If imprisonment is not provided for, the upper limit is two weeks. An imprisonment in default of payment of more than six weeks is not admissible. There is not a fixed conversion key for the determination of the imprisonment in default of payment; therefore it must be determined according to the general rules of determination of penalty. Particularly, it has to be proportional.

Special rules apply for *concursus delictorum:* Whereas for the determination of a penalty in criminal law the absorption principle is applied, the administrative penal law provides for the cumulation of penalties. If one person commits several administrative offences, every offence is punished independently and the penalties are imposed concurrently (Section 22 VStG). This means that several administrative offences of one and the same person are to be prosecuted and punished independently by the authority competent in the very case. An authority dealing with several administrative offences of one person has to total up all single penalties or has to conduct different proceedings for the offences, even in the case that a single conduct fulfils several administrative offences. This

10 Hauer/Leukauf, *Handbuch des österreichischen Verwaltungsverfahrens*, 6th ed., 2009, p. 1732.

can result in very high penalties, which in the political discussions sometimes have been criticised as unreasonable.[11]

Other administrative sanctions

In several administrative acts other administrative sanctions are provided for which are not explicitly seen as penalties and on which the Act on Administrative Penal Law is not applicable, but which can be seen as repressive and punitive measures.

Here are some of the most important measures:

Trade Act (Gewerbeordnung)

According to Section 87, para. 1 of the *Gewerbeordnung* the trade authority has to withdraw the trade licence, if the person carrying on a trade fulfils one of the grounds of exclusion according to Section 13, para. 1 or 2 and if the commitment of the same or similar criminal offences in pursuance of the trade must be expected. Section 13 *Gewerbeordnung* (Trade Act) provides for the exclusion of trades people,

- who have been convicted by a court because of fraudulent bankruptcy, gross negligent bankruptcy, the damage of other creditors or favouritism of a creditor (Sections 156 to 159 *Strafgesetzbuch* – Criminal Code); or
- who have been sentenced to imprisonment of more than three months or who have been convicted by a court to more than 180 daily rates because of another criminal offence, if the conviction has not been set aside (Section 13, para. 1).

Persons can be excluded from the exercise of hotel and restaurant business, if they are convicted because of an offence against the Act on Additive Drugs and the conviction has not been set aside. Persons, who have been punished because of specific fiscal offences according to the Act on Fiscal Offences (*e.g.* smuggling, defrauding of import and export duties, defrauding of monopoly taxes), are excluded from the business, if a fine of more than €726, or if apart from a fine an imprisonment, has been imposed and if not more than five years have passed since the conviction (Section 13, para. 2 *Gewerbeordnung*).

Legal entities are also excluded from trade, if a bankruptcy proceeding has not been opened due to a lack of property to pay the costs of the proceeding. Moreover for certain sorts of trade (*e.g.* insurances) special grounds of exclusion are provided for.

11 See Stadlmayer, 'Ist die Abschaffung des Kumulationsprinzips im Verwaltungsstrafrecht möglich?', *ZVR* 1980, 65.

According to Section 13, para. 7 *Gewerbeordnung* these provisions can be applied on other legal entities than natural persons, if a physical person, who has essential influence on the conduct of the business, fulfils the requirements.[12]

Moreover, the trade authority has to withdraw the trade licence, if

- the tradesman does not have the necessary reliability for the exercise of the trade because of grave infringements of legal provisions and interests to protect, which must be observed when exercising this trade, especially concerning the protection of the reputation of the professional group; protected interests are especially the prevention of illegal employment, of child pornography, of consume of and traffic with drugs, of illegal prostitution and the discrimination of persons on the mere basis because of their race, colour of skin, national and ethnic origin, religious confession or of a handicap;
- the tradesman has been punished because of assistance to the exercise of a trade without the necessary trade licence by another person.

Withdrawal of driving licence according to the Act on Driving Licences (Führerscheingesetz)

If the assumptions for the issuance of a driving licence are not longer fulfilled, the authority either has to withdraw the driving licence or to limit its validity by conditions, limitations or restrictions of place and in time (Section 24 *Führerscheingesetz*). Section 26 *Führerscheingesetz* provides for the withdrawal of the driving licence for four weeks, if a driver drives a car while intoxicated for the first time. Under special aggravating circumstances (*e.g.*, if the driver causes an traffic accident, high blood alcohol level) the withdrawal must be for more than three months. If the blood alcohol level is more than 1.6 promille or if the driver refuses to make an alcohol test, the driving licence must be withdrawn for at least four months. In the case of a blood alcohol level of more than 0.5 promille, but not more than 0.8 promille, the driving licence is withdrawn for at least three weeks, if it is the second offence within twelve months.[13]

The driving licence may only be withdrawn, when the administrative penal proceeding of first instance has been closed by a penal order. If the blood alcohol level is more than 1.2 promille, adherent measures must be ordered besides the withdrawal of the driving licence, *e.g.*, driving education, behavioural training.

In the withdrawal procedure the authorities are obliged to issue a decision on the applications of the parties and appeals without delay, at the latest three

12 See in detail Zellenberg, 'Der Gewerbezugang nach der Gewerberechtsnovelle 1992', *ZfV* 2003/955.

13 See in detail Kaltenegger/Koller, *Entziehung der Lenkberechtigung und Lenkverbot*, 2003, p. 42 *et seq.*

months after entry. In this procedure it is not possible to waive the right to appeal effectively (Section 29 *Führerscheingesetz*).

Holders of foreign driving licences can be deprived of the right to use their driving licences in Austria, if conditions for a withdrawal of a driving licence are fulfilled correspondingly.

Administrative order of dissolution of an association according to the Act on Associations (Vereinsgesetz)

The Act on Associations *(Vereinsgesetz)* provides for – in contrast to the wide rules on denying of the foundation of an association[14] – the dissolution of an association by an administrative order, if the association's activities violate criminal law (Section 29, para. 1 *Vereinsgesetz*).[15] The same provision also allows for the association's dissolution, if the association transgresses its statutory field of activity or is not suitable to the conditions of its legal validity.

Exclusion of tenderers according to the Federal Procurement Act (Bundesvergabegesetz)

Section 51 *Bundesvergabegesetz* (Federal Procurement Act) provides for the exclusion of tenderers from participation in the contract. According to Section 51, para. 1 *Bundesvergabegesetz* the tendering authority must exclude entrepreneurs from participation in the contract, if

- bankruptcy or compensation proceedings have been opened against them (Figure 1);
- they are in liquidation or have stopped their commercial activities (Figure 2);
- the tendering entrepreneurs or, if the tenderers are legal persons or associations, the physical persons, who are working in the business management, have been convicted of an offence concerning their professional conduct by a judgement which has the force of *res judicata* (Figure 3);
- they have committed a grave misconduct in the framework of their professional activity proved by any means which the contracting authorities can justify (Figure 4);
- they have not fulfilled their obligations relating to the payment of social insurance contributions or taxes and duties (Figure 5);
- they are guilty of serious misrepresentation in supplying the information required under the Federal Procurement Act (Figure 6).[16]

---

14 See Section 11 *Vereinsgesetz*.

15 Literally this provision is referring to the association as perpetrator. However, before any corporate criminal liability was introduced into Austrian legislation (see *infra* under II.6), this could only be understood in terms of activities of individual persons attributable to the association.

16 Kert, 'National report of Austria', in: White (ed.), *Procurement and Organised Crime – An EU-wide study*, 2000, p. 83 *et seq.*

Most of the tenderees are not official administrative authorities, but private or semi-public agencies and enterprises, *e.g.*, there are several share companies established for the specific purpose of meeting needs in the general interest without having an industrial or commercial character. Moreover, there are many enterprises which are financed by the state or which belong to the state or to municipalities. Therefore the exclusion of tenderers is not always decided by administrative authorities.

The character of administrative sanctions

The above mentioned administrative sanctions are not regarded as penalties within Austrian legislation, although they have a penal character, if they are imposed because of a misconduct of a person.

There have been discussions in doctrine, whether the withdrawal of driving licences is to be characterised as a pure security measure or a penalty.[17] The purpose of these provisions is to exclude unreliable drivers for a certain time or for ever from taking part in the road traffic. According to the prevailing opinion the withdrawal of the driving licence has no penal character. It is seen mere as an administrative measure.[18] The purpose of the measure is on the one hand the protection of the general public from a single person, on the other hand to protect the person against him/herself.[19] For the people concerned its effects are equal to a penalty. There is no doubt that prevention is an essential purpose of this measure. Therefore in doctrine[20] there have been critical voices seeing it as a problem not to qualify the withdrawal of driving licences as penalties. According to this argument, it contains to essential elements of a penalty, namely special prevention and securing and consequently must be seen as a real penalty.

The Administrative Court, however, does not follow this opinion and does not classify the provisions on the withdrawal of driving licences as penal provisions, but emphasises the objective protection interests of the traffic participants. If only the protection of others is the aim of these provisions, it is a question remains why the *Führerscheingesetz* also provides for the threat of the withdrawal (Section 26, para. 4 last sentence). It is obvious that the purpose of this provision is not the protection of other persons participating in the traffic, but the deterrence of the offender. Therefore to a certain extent these provisions have a penal character.[21]

---

17 See Winkler, 'Führerscheinentzug und gerichtliche Haftstrafe', *JAP* 1996/97, 150; Frank, 'Die Entziehung der Lenkberechtigung – Die fehlende Nebenstrafe', *ZVR* 2000, 326.

18 Compare Administrative Court 10 December 1970, 1361, 1362/70; 20 February 1987, 86/11/0155; Grubmann (ed.), *Das österreichische Kraftfahrrecht*, Vol. II. *Kraftfahrgesetz* (1995, §73 Anm. 1; §66 Anm. 1 und Anm. 37.

19 Grubmann (ed.), *Das österreichische Kraftfahrrecht*, Vol. II. *Kraftfahrgesetz* (1995, §73 Anm. 1.

20 Winkler, *JAP* 1996/97, 158 *et seq.*

21 Winkler, *JAP* 1996/97, 158 *et seq.*

In order to be precise, it is necessary to make a distinction. If a driving licence is withdrawn on health reasons (e.g. someone does not see enough), the withdrawal of the driving licence cannot be classified as penalty. It is essential for a classification as penalty that the offender behaves illegally.

Referring to the withdrawal of the trade licence, the Austrian Administrative Court decided that this was not a penalty, but an administrative measure which is implemented by the trade authority itself.[22]

1.3. HISTORICAL DEVELOPMENT

The punishment of certain infringements by administrative authorities has a quite long tradition in Austria[23]: Already older imperial and regional police acts provided for the punishment of certain minor offences by administrative authorities, not by the courts. The *Josefinisches Strafgesetzbuch* (Criminal Code during Joseph II) and the Code of crimes and severe police offences *(Gesetzbuch über Verbrechen und schwere Polizeiübertretungen)* from 1803 distinguished between criminal offences dealt with by the courts and administrative offences punished by the administrative authorities. These laws tried to make a substantive distinction between judicial and administrative penal law, which resulted in uncertainties.

An important progress was that the Criminal Code *(Strafgesetz* – StG*)* of 1852 did not use such a substantive distinction anymore, but it was only relevant, which authority was competent to deal with the matter. Only offences regulated in the Criminal Code and such offences, which were explicitly referred to the courts, should be criminal offences which were in the competence of the ordinary courts. All other penal offences should fall within the competence of administrative authorities. There were only provisions of singular administrative offences, a general part of an administrative penal law as well as rules of administrative penal procedure were missing.

An important step in the development of the Austrian administrative penal procedure was the creation of an Administrative Court *(Verwaltungsgerichtshof)* in 1875. This was a progressive step towards the consolidation of the rule of law in administrative law which. The Administrative Court had to decide in all cases

---

22 Administrative Court 28 April 1976, VwSlg 9046 A.

23 Concerning the historical development see Wiederin, *Die Zukunft des Verwaltungsstrafverfahrensrechts*, p. 14 *et seq.*

where somebody claimed to be infringed in his/her rights by an illegal decision or order of an administrative authority.[24]

In 1925 the Administrative Penal Code *(Verwaltungsstrafgesetz* – VStG*)*[25] was passed together with other acts on administrative procedure. The *Verwaltungsstrafgesetz* for the first time introduced a written general part of the administrative penal law. It also comprised rules on the administrative penal procedure and the execution of administrative penalties. The statutory definitions of offences are regulated in specific administration laws. Since 1925 the *Verwaltungsstrafgesetz* has been amended several times. Among the most important amendments were the reduction of prison sentences in 1987 and the establishment of the *Unabhängige Verwaltungssenate der Länder* (UVS – Independent Administrative Panels of Provinces).

Although there are provisions of a general part of administrative penal law continued in the *Verwaltungsstrafgesetz*, the objective of the legislator was not to create a completely independent system of rules, but to achieve a certain degree of congruence with criminal law. Therefore many central terms of penal law, such as intent or negligence, are not separately defined. Legislation, jurisprudence and doctrine in criminal law thus have an impact on administrative penal law.[26] On the other hand, important differences between criminal and administrative penal law exist. An example is that in administrative penal law negligent behaviour is normally sufficient for punishment, whereas criminal law in principle requires intent.

1.4. CONSTITUTIONAL ISSUES AND INFLUENCE OF THE EUROPEAN LAW

1.4.1. Division of powers between courts and administrative authorities

Article 94 *Bundes-Verfassungsgesetz* (Federal Constitutional Act) provides for a strict separation of justice and administration in all instances, which is an essential element of the separation of powers in the Austrian legal system. Because of this principle every authority must be clearly classified as a court or an administrative authority. One and the same authority must not be a court and an administrative authority.[27] A sequence of instances from an administrative

---

24 See Barfuß, 'Verrechtlichung des Verwaltungsstrafverfahrens', *AnwBl* 1998, 218.

25 *BGBl.* 1925 No. 275, which was re-announced in 1950 (*BGBl.* 1950 No. 172) and in 1991 (*BGBl.* 1991 No. 52).

26 Thienel/Schulev-Steindl, *Verwaltungsverfahrensrecht*, 5th ed., p. 410; Walter/Mayer, *Verwaltungsverfahrensrecht*, 8th ed., 2003, p. 381.

27 Constitutional Court 15 October 1964, VfSlg. 4455; 19 June 1989, 12.073; 4 December 1991, 12.929.

authority to a court – or *vice versa* – is prohibited.[28] Only a so-called 'successive competence' has been considered constitutional: This condition is given, when after the decision of an administrative authority a court of first instance can be appealed to and the decision of the administrative authority automatically is *ex lege* invalid.[29] The legislator must refer all functions either to the courts or to the administration. Until 1989 this provision was only seen as an organisational division of powers, but not as an obligation of the legislator to attribute particular affairs to the courts while giving others to the competence of the administration (so-called substantive division of powers).[30]

In 1989 the Austrian Constitutional Court[31] ruled that the legislator must attribute certain penal affairs to the competence of courts: According to the opinion to the Constitutional Court, the Austrian Constitution would provide for a three-stage organisational structure of the penal jurisdiction. Relying on a provision in the Federal Constitution (Article 91, para. 2 and 3 *Bundes-Verfassungsgesetz*) on specific competences of jury courts and courts of lay assessors together with the organisational structure (the most severe offences and the political offences falling into the competence of the jury, less severe ones into the competence of the courts of lay assessors, minor crimes into the competence of single and district judges) the Constitutional Court has deduced a principle according to which also the distribution of penal competences between these levels of single judges and any administrative authority can only be understood in relation to their sanctioning powers regardless the legislator's program to label as criminal what is up to the courts and as non-criminal what remains with the administration. The legislator is, according to the Constitutional Court, not free in this question, but has to allocate to the courts (and by that to consider criminal) any act which attracts a serious punishment. If the legislator provides for a severe sanction because of the high social harmfulness of a certain conduct, the legislator is bound by constitutional law to have those crimes in the competence of the criminal courts and not of the administrative authorities. The Constitutional Court deduced from this structure that fines may only be imposed by administration authorities, if the range of these fines is not as high as that of fines imposed by criminal courts. The Constitutional Court did not however set a clear limit on how high the fines in administrative law may be.[32] Within the system of day fines which is a

28 Constitutional Court, VfSlg. 3236; 1 March 1963, 4359; 15 October 1964, 4836; 14 December 1982, 9590.

29 See Mayer, *Das österreichische Bundesverfassungsrecht*, 4th ed., 2007, p. 330 *et seq.*

30 See *inter alia* Winkler, in: Winkler (ed.), *Orientierungen im öffentlichen Leben*, 1979, p. 232 *et seq.*

31 Constitutional Court 27 September 1989, VfSlg 12.151.

32 Critical Miklau, 'Zur Funktion der Geldstrafe – Ist die Höhe der Strafdrohung ein taugliches Abgrenzungskriterium zwischen dem Justiz- und dem Verwaltungsstrafrecht?', *ÖJZ* 1991, 361; Öhlinger, 'Die Geldstrafe im Verwaltungsstrafrecht – Verfassungsrechtliche Grenzen

characteristic element of Austrian criminal law, it could be said that the highest fine possible to be imposed by an Austrian court was about €120,000.[33] Compared with that, in the jurisprudence of the Constitutional Court and in doctrine, the margin for the federal or provincial law makers to provide for administrative fines is drawn at about half of this amount, meaning €60,000.[34]

Whereas there are no explicit limits for pecuniary penalties, there is an explicit substantive division of powers between courts and administrative authorities in connection with imprisonment sentences: In a constitutional reform, a Federal Constitutional Act on the Protection of Personal Freedom *(Bundesverfassungsgesetz über den Schutz der persönlichen Freiheit)* was passed in 1988 and entered into force in 1991, in which the deprivation of liberty as a sanction of administrative penal law in certain limits expressly is acknowledged. This reform was the result of a long discussion about the conformity of administrative penal provisions with Articles 5 and 6 ECHR. According to Article 3 of this Constitutional Act imprisonment by administrative authorities is only permitted for six weeks each or, where a special independent body already has to decide in first instance, up to three months. Imprisonment of more than three months – this is not only applied to primary imprisonment but also to imprisonment in default of paying – can only be imposed by courts and therefore has to fall into criminal law.

Moreover the Federal Constitutional Act on the Protection of Personal Freedom provides that against the imposition of imprisonment an appeal to a fully 'independent authority' and with suspensive effect must be provided for. Independent authorities are tribunals within the meaning of Article 6 ECHR.

The Federal Constitutional Act on the Protection of Personal Freedom was one of the results of a long dispute on the constitutionality and on the legality of imprisonment sentences as administrative penalties and their conformity with Articles 5 and 6 ECHR. It is an important feature of the Austrian legislation that the European Convention of Human Rights (ECHR) together with its protocols is part of the Austrian constitutional law. Therefore the ECHR not only sets an important standard for sanctions in a European context, but also in a national constitutional context. Particularly Articles 5 and 6 of the ECHR have considerable influence on the system of sanctions and on legal guarantees.

At the time of the ratification of the Convention, Austria made a reservation to Article 5 for these forms of imprisonment in the framework of the laws on

gegenüber dem Justizstrafrecht', *ÖJZ* 1991, 217; Burgstaller, in: Korinek/Holoubek (eds.), *Bundesverfassungsrecht*, 1999, Art. 91 B-VG No. 42 *et seq.*

33 In 2009 the upper limit for day fines in criminal law was raised to €5,000, so that the highest fine now is €1.8 million (see *Budgetbegleitgesetz* 2005, *BGBl.* I 2004/136).

34 Compare Thienel/Schulev-Steindl, *Verwaltungsverfahrensrecht*, 5th ed., 393.

administrative procedure. This reservation, however, would only have covered the administrative penal law existing at the time being. According to an established opinion, the reservation only covered punishments foreseen in the very laws on administrative procedure, a part of which is the Administrative Penal Code *(Verwaltungsstrafgesetz)*, which contains a list of general administrative offences such as indecent noise or simple aggression against police.[35] In the light of this opinion the majority of Austrian administrative penal law was not covered by the reservation. These offences are located in the special administrative acts on both federal level and on the level of provinces (*e.g.*, traffic offences, environmental law and construction laws). Therefore, most of the administrative penal provisions were not in conformity with Articles 5 and 6 ECHR, since no independent tribunal was competent to decide in the administrative penal proceeding. Consequently, it was a priority of the efforts of the reform of Austrian constitutional law to base the deprivation of liberty on an entire renewed legal foundation in the Austrian legislation.

As another part of the reform new independent bodies, the so-called *Unabhängige Verwaltungssenate der Länder* (UVS – Independent Administrative Panels of Provinces), were created which are supposed to have the quality of tribunals within the meaning of Articles 5 and 6 ECHR. These *Unabhängige Verwaltungssenate* are composed in a way that renders superior orders impossible and provides for the personal independence of the organs as they are appointed for life time or for a period of at least six years, depending on the special legislation of the provinces. So, they could be called 'administrative judges'. Their jurisdiction covers not only administrative penal law, but also the direct use of force by police as well as certain other acts (as detention for deportation). For administrative penal decisions, these bodies serve as appeals authorities with full review also of the facts.

Nevertheless there are still doubts if it is in conformity with Article 5 ECHR that imprisonment sentences in first instance are imposed by administrative authorities, since Article 5(1)(a) ECHR allows for imprisonment only 'after conviction by a competent court'. This requirement is, however, not fulfilled if an imprisonment sentence imposed by an order of punishment of first instance is executed. The mere possibility of an appeal to the UVSs can hardly satisfy the requirements of Article 5 ECHR, even though the majority of the Austrian doctrine argues for conformity with this regards.[36]

35 Kopetzki, in: Korinek/Holoubek (ed.), *Bundesverfassungsrecht*, Art. 3 PersFrG No. 25.

36 See Berka, *Die Grundrechte*, 1999, p. 234; other opinion Kopetzki, in: Korinek/Holoubek (ed.), *Bundesverfassungsrecht*, Art. 3 PersFrG No. 24; Thienel, *Das Verfahren der Verwaltungssenate*, 2nd ed., 1992, p. 196 *et seq.*

Whereas Article 5 ECHR requires a decision by a court, for a fair trial according to Article 6 ECHR a decision of an independent and impartial tribunal is necessary. This condition is fulfilled by the establishment of the UVSs, which are tribunals in the meaning of Article 6 ECHR.

1.4.2. Relation to constitutional law, administrative law, criminal law and private law

It has already been mentioned above that – according to doctrine and jurisprudence – no essential difference between criminal law and administrative penal law exists. Administrative penal law has the character of penal law in petty cases: an administrative penalty is an evil which is imposed by the state deliberately and knowingly for the purpose to blame the offender to an answer to an unlawful behaviour.[37] Actually, the decision where to allocate a norm remains in the hands of the Parliament, and often discussed in practice in which field a special offence should be situated. For example, some years ago a law was drafted, to deal with the increasing problem of shoplifting. In a draft the Ministry of Justice proposed to attribute the competence to punish shoplifters to the police in a simple and short procedure *in situ*. The fines were supposed to be a source for a fund to support crime victims or for other social purposes. However, the political discussion showed strong scepticism among the commerce. There was concern on how far one could go without diminishing the negative 'grade' characterisation of the behaviour in question. Some years later a 'third way' was found by extending the rules of diversion from juvenile crimes to adults. The Austrian model of diversion implies that the procedure remains in the field of criminal law, but a conviction is avoided through alternative measures which the prosecutor can offer to the suspect. Among others, these measures can consist in a payment of an amount of money. This payment, however, does not have the character of a punishment and does not lead to a criminal record. The same is true for the treatment of traffic offences which result in negligent bodily injury. Plans to take these cases out of the criminal law regime had been developed earlier, not only to save resources for the judiciary, but also to reduce the number of citizens having a criminal record. Also in these cases strong criticism arose arguing that a transfer from criminal to administrative penal law would not adequately honour the protected interest of physical integrity of the individual. This criticism could only be understood on the general background and the general problem of Austrian administrative penal law. While this system is supposed to allow for a simple and non-stigmatising treatment of offenders, it focuses more on the behaviour than on the result and, by doing this, it meets with modern ideas of criminal policy to tackle the attitude of the offender, not the effect of the unlawful act.

---

37 Wiederin, *Die Zukunft des Verwaltungsstrafrechts*, p. 52.

As to the offences with such an effect, negligence causing bodily harm is always regarded as criminal conduct. But with the exception of very serious injuries and death, and of cases of grave guilt (including intoxicated drivers), the criminal traffic offences nowadays are usually handled with the instruments of criminal diversion mentioned above.

In comparison to other countries, the largest part of traffic offences without concrete effects for life and limb does not belong to criminal law. For example, driving without a driving licence or even driving while intoxicated are pure administrative offences. Additionally, at this point it is to be mentioned, that all rules concerning drivers' disqualification are in the hands of the administrative authorities.

If administrative penal law is seen as of form of penal law, it is necessary that the constitutional guarantees applied in criminal law also must apply in administrative penal law. In doctrine this is seen as problem, since criminal guarantees are not always fully implemented in administrative penal law. Administrative penal law sometimes means that legal standards are not as high as in criminal law. There are still relics of a police state in Austrian administrative penal law, as e.g. the inquisitorial principle, the limited remedies (which are not decided by a court) or the limited defence rights.[38]

1.4.3. Influence of the European law (EC/EU law and ECHR)

As mentioned above the European Convention on Human Rights has a far-reaching influence on the Austrian legislation, because the Convention and its protocols have the status of constitutional law.

When ratifying the Convention Austria made – as mentioned *supra* – a reservation to Article 5 ECHR, that the provisions of Article 5 of the Convention should be applied in a way that there shall be no interference with the measures for the deprivation of liberty prescribed in the laws on administrative procedure subject to review by the Administrative Court or the Constitutional Court as provided for in the Austrian Federal Constitution. Referring to Article 6 of the Convention, which later was the reason for organisational and procedural problems of the administrative penal law, no reservation with respect to the administrative penal proceeding was made, since the importance of Article 6 of the Convention for the administrative penal law was not perceived at the time of the ratification.[39] Since also an administrative penal proceeding can be qualified

---

38 See Wiederin, *Die Zukunft des Verwaltungsstrafrechts*, p. 52.

39 It was only a reservation made referring to the criminal law that the provisions of Article 6 of the Convention should be so applied that there should be no prejudice to the principles governing public court hearings laid down in Article 90 of the Federal Constitution Law.

as 'criminal charge' within the meaning of Article 6 ECHR, also the administrative penal proceeding must be in conformity with the provisions of Article 6.[40] At first, the Austrian Constitutional Court and the Administrative Court referred the Austrian reservation on Article 5 also to Article 6.[41] In the last years, the Constitutional Court changed its jurisprudence and referred the reservation only to the organisational guarantees, but not to the procedural guarantees of Article 6. In particular the presumption of innocence was seen as applicable to administrative penal proceedings as well.[42] The European Court of Human Rights at first has limited the reservation to its narrow sense of words.[43] The Austrian Constitutional Court has followed this jurisprudence.[44] In the year 2000 the reservation to Article 6 was found totally invalid by the European Court of Human Rights, since it does not satisfy the requirements of Article 57, para. 2 of the Convention.[45]

The main influence of the EC law on the administrative penal law results from the obligation of the Member States to provide for sanctions for infringements of the EC regulations. The Austrian legislator has qualified most of these infringements as administrative offences and has provided for administrative penal provisions to sanction them. Since the regulations must not be duplicated in the national law, Austrian legislation refers to the EC norms. This leads to a lack of sufficient determination of the penal sanctions.[46] In 2005 the Austrian Constitutional Court saw it as admissible and in conformity with the duty of determination, if a national law refers in general to directly applicable provisions of the EC in the area of transport of goods.[47]

2. GENERAL PRINCIPLES

2.1. *NULLUM CRIMEN SINE LEGE*

The principle *'nullum crimen/nulla poena sine lege'* is laid down for administrative penal offences in Section 1, para. 1 VStG. According to this

40 Frowein/Peukert, *EMRK-Kommentar*, 3rd ed., 2009, p. 182 *et seq.*
41 Constitutional Court 3 July 1965, VfSlg. 5021; 13 October 1970, 6275; 22 June 1977, 8087.
42 See Barfuß, *AnwBl* 1998, 218.
43 See ECtHR 25 August 1993, *Chorherr v. Austria*, Serie A 266-B; 23 October 1995, *Gradinger v. Austria*, Serie A 328-C.
44 Constitutional Court 5 December 1996, VfSlg. 14696.
45 ECtHR 3 October 2000, *Eisenstecken v. Austria*, Appl. No. 29477/95.
46 See Kert, 'Die Sanktionierung von Verstößen gegen Gemeinschaftsrecht durch nationales Strafrecht am Beispiel des Lebensmittelstrafrechts', *JBl* 1999, 87.
47 Constitutional Court 4 March 2005, B 249/04.

provision a conduct may only be punished as administrative offence, if it has fallen under a penalty before its commission.[48]

A constitutional safeguarding – even though limited – can be found in Article 7 of the European Convention on Human Rights (ECHR), which is part of the Austrian constitutional framework.[49] Article 7 ECHR applies to the administrative penal law.[50] If Article 7 ECHR is applied to other administrative sanctions, is not entirely clear. It depends on various factors, in particular on the question who is addressed by the provision (the public or only a limited circle of persons) and on the gravity and intensity of the sanction. The Austrian Administrative Court regarded a surcharge to an illegally obtained compensation for the safety period (*Karenzgeld*) as a penal sanction, but did not decide if Article 7 applied.[51] Some authors assume that the consequences of delay, especially the increase in charges, in fiscal law constitute a penalty in the sense of Article 7 ECHR.[52] According to the Austrian Constitutional Court disciplinary matters have a penal character not only if longer imprisonment penalties, imprisonment in default of payment, or very high fines are provided for, but also if a prohibition to exercise a profession is foreseen, and therefore Article 7 ECHR is applicable.[53]

Whether other administrative measures imposed by administrative authorities are qualified as penalties, must be evaluated not solely according to the national law, but also according to autonomous criteria and. The criteria are: whether the measure is a consequence of a conviction because of a criminal act; the character and purpose of the measure; its qualification in national law; the proceeding in which it is imposed and executed; and the gravity of the measure.[54]

A conduct has only fallen under a penalty, if it is explicitly or at the minimum clearly perceivably declared as punishable at the time it was committed. This assumes that a certain rule or prohibition exists, according to which, in case of defiance a penalty is provided for. The threat of a certain penalty is not necessary in the administrative penal law: If a certain penalty for an administrative offence

---

48 See Raschauer/Wessely, *Verwaltungsstrafrecht*, p. 32.
49 See Nowakowski, in: Foregger/Nowakowski (eds.), *Wiener Kommentar zum Strafgesetzbuch*, 1st ed., 1981, §1, note 2.
50 See Thienel, in: Korinek/Holoubek (eds.), *Österreichisches Bundesverfassungsrecht*, 1999, Article 7, No. 5.
51 Administrative Court (Verwaltungsgerichtshof) 14 November 1995, 95/08/0172.
52 Compare Arnold, 'Zur neuerlichen Neufassung des §9 GebG', *NZ* 1987, 196 (204); Harbich, 'Ausgewählte Themen aus dem Allgemeinen Teil des Finanz- und Justizstrafrechts', *RZ* 1979, 1, 25, 45 (48 f.); Heidinger, 'Rechtsstaat und Rückwirkungsverbot im Steuerrecht', *ÖStZ* 1995, 95.
53 Constitutional Court 14 October 1987, VfSlg 11.506; 30 June 1988, 11.776.
54 ECtHR, Case *Welch*, Serie A No. 307-A (*ÖJZ* 1995, 511).

is not provided for, the subsidiary penalty clause of Article VII *Einführungsgesetz zu den Verwaltungsverfahrensgesetzen* 1991 (EGVG – Introductory Act for the Acts on Administrative Proceeding) applies, which provides for fines up to €218 or – if this is not enough – an imprisonment sentence up to two weeks.

The prohibition of an extension of statutory offences by analogy or extensive interpretation also follows from Section 1, para. 1 VStG: According to the jurisprudence, the interpretation of statutory offences is limited by the utmost possible meaning of the words.[55]

The prohibition of retroaction only applies to substantial administrative penal law. Any retroactive procedural law is not excluded.

2.2. PRINCIPLES OF EQUALITY AND OF PROPORTIONALITY

In its jurisprudence the Austrian Constitutional Court is of the opinion that differentiations, which are not justified by objective reasons, i.e. and which cannot be deduced to differences in the facts, infringe the constitutional right to equality before the law. This principle is enshrined in Article 7 of the Federal Constitution and in Article 2 of the State Basic Law on the General Rights of Citizens of 1867 (*Staatsgrundgesetz über die allgemeinen Rechte der Staatsbürger*).

The principle of equality also applies to administrative penal law. It is infringed, if an administrative authority draws different legal consequences from the same facts.[56] The Austrian Constitutional Court derived from the principle of equality that there must not be an extreme disproportion between the gravity of a penal offence and the severity of the penalty: The level of the penalty must be in a proportionate relation to culpability and to the damage caused by the offence.[57] This is applied in particular to fines[58] and forfeiture.[59] The provision of minimum sentences is admissible, but with respect to the principle of equality they must not be disproportionately high.[60] The principle of equality is also

55 *E.g.* Administrative Court VwSlg. 7181 A/1967; VwGH 7 November 1990, 90/01/0114.

56 See Winkler, *JAP* 1996/97, 163.

57 See Constitutional Court 9 October 1997, VfSlg. 14.973.

58 In its decision VfSlg. 12.151/1989 the Constitutional Court said that it is unconstitutional to provide for a tax evasion a fine of up to thirty times the evaded amount independently from the level of the evaded amount.

59 Constitutional Court 14 December 1983, VfSlg 9901; 14 December 1987, 11.587; the Constitutional Court particularly regarded it as inadmissible, when an administrative regulation provides for the forfeiture without regarding the value of the concerned object. See Grabenwarter, in: Leitner (ed.), *Aktuelles zum Finanzstrafrecht*, 1998, p. 111 (113 *et seq.*).

60 Constitutional Court 16 March 2000, VfSlg. 15.785.

infringed, if an administrative authority encroaches on personal rights without an explicit legal authorisation.[61]

2.3. LEGALITY PRINCIPLE

If there is a suspicion that an administrative offence has been committed, the administrative authority has the obligation to initiate a prosecution. The authority does not have discretion to decide whether it introduces and proceeds with an administrative penal proceeding.[62] This means, the principle of legality applies to administrative penal proceedings. How the authority learns about an offence, is irrelevant for the duty to prosecute.

However, there are exceptions to this duty to initiate a penal proceeding: The authority can refrain from the initiation of the proceeding not only if carrying out of the proceeding seems to be desperate, but also if the expenses which are necessary for the proceeding are disproportionate to the importance of the violation of public interests by the administrative offence (Section 21, para. 1 VStG). The authority can also drop a case, if it is clear that one of the reasons for a withdrawal of prosecution exists.[63]

2.4. THE RULE OF LAW

The rule of law is one of the fundamental principles of the Austrian Constitution. It deemed to be close connection to the democratic principle. The core of the rule of law principle is the principle of legality of administration which is embodied in Article 18, para. 1 *Bundes-Verfassungsgesetz*.[64] It establishes that the administration is strictly bound to follow statutory laws.

But the principle of rule of law today is seen as a more comprehensive idea. It requires the existence of institutions of legal protection to enforce that actions of administration authorities are carried out in accordance with the law. The control of the administration by the Administrative Court and the Constitutional Court is an essential element of the principle of rule of law. Also the duty of the legislation to adhere to the law of higher order and its control by

---

61 See Winkler, *JAP* 1996/97, 163 *et seq.*

62 Administrative Court 22 February 2001, 2001/07/0016; Walter/Mayer, *Verwaltungsverfahrensrecht*, 8th ed., p. 423; Thienel/Schulev-Steindl, *Verwaltungsverfahrensrecht*, 5th ed., p. 464 *et seq.*

63 Administrative Court 25 November 1929, A 527/29.

64 It is common sense that this principle, which literally only addresses the second branch of government (administration), guides the third power (judiciary) as well.

the Constitutional Court today are seen as elements of the rule of law in the Austrian Constitution.[65]

2.5. PRINCIPLE OF FAULT

Administrative penalties can only be imposed if the offender has acted culpably (see Section 5 VStG). According to Section 5, para. 1 VStG in principle intent is not required and negligence is sufficient for the punishment in administrative penal law. This is contrary to the criminal law where intent is necessary, unless it is explicitly provided otherwise. In administrative penal law intent is only required, if the law explicitly requires so. For so-called *'Ungehorsamsdelikte'* (offences of disobedience) Section 5, para. 1 VStG provides for a presumption of negligence: If someone disobeys a legal prohibition or does not obey a rule and the administrative statutory offence does not require an effect or a danger to occur, negligence is presumed without further examinations, unless the offender renders believable that he is not responsible for the taking place of the infringement of the administrative provision.

This presumption only refers to the culpability. The authority must prove that the statutory definition has been fulfilled and that the offender acted unlawfully.[66] But when the authority proves this, negligence is presumed. To prove that s/he has not acted negligently, the offender must – according to jurisprudence – on his/her own initiative present everything which serves for exculpation. It is not enough to simply challenge the charge.[67] But it is not necessary that the accused produces evidence of his/her innocence in the strictest sense, he/she has only to bring about a decision on the probability of his/her innocence (*'glaubhaft machen'*).[68] If during the investigations the authority detects circumstances which exclude the fault of the offender, the authority has to take them into account *ex officio.*

The European Court of Human Rights and the Austrian Constitutional Court have said – with reference to the Austrian reservation to Article 5 ECHR – that the presumption of negligence is compatible with Article 6 ECHR.[69]

---

65 Öhlinger, *Verfassungsrecht*, 8th ed., 2009, p. 59. See also Constitutional Court 11 December 1986, VfSlg. 11.196, 13 October 1992, 13.223.

66 See Walter/Mayer, *Verwaltungsverfahrensrecht*, 8th ed., p. 389.

67 E.g. Administrative Court 4 July 2002, 2000/11/0132.

68 See Administrative Court 30 October 1991, 91/09/0132; Hauer/Leukauf, *Handbuch*, 6th ed., p. 1216 *et seq.*; Walter/Thienel, *Die österreichischen Verwaltungsverfahrensgesetze*, 17th ed., 2008, p. 227.

69 ECtHR 13 October 1993, Appl. No. 19.116/91; Constitutional Court 20 June 1994, VfSlg. 13.790; sceptical Hattenberger, 'Verwaltungsstrafrecht und Arbeitszeitrecht', in: Resch (ed.),

2.6. LIABILITY OF LEGAL PERSONS

In Austrian legislation, at the time being only natural persons can be punished in administrative penal law. Until recently, the introduction of such a corporate liability was regarded as incompatible with the principle *societas delinquere non potest*. Traditional criminal law requires an individual misconduct of a natural person and reacts to a culpable misconduct.[70] The personal reproach for an unlawful act is essential in Austrian law not only within the concept of criminal responsibility, but also for administrative penal responsibility.

Due to various obligations under international and European law concerning the introduction of a liability of legal persons, especially under Articles 3 and 4 of the Second Protocol of the Convention on the Protection of Financial Interests of the European Communities, in 2006 a new law came into force, which introduced a criminal liability of legal persons (*Verbandsverantwortlichkeitsgesetz* – Act on a criminal liability of legal entities).[71] Throughout this new act, organisations can be found responsible for all criminal offences. Requirements for this responsibility are that a decision maker committed a criminal offence or a staff-member has carried out criminalised actions, which have been made possible or considerably easier due to the fact that decision makers failed to apply the due and reasonable care required in the respective circumstances. In both cases, the entity can be held responsible, if the offence was committed for its benefit or if duties of the entity have been neglected by such offence. As penalties, the law provides for fines, which are imposed by criminal courts and are assessed in form of daily rates. The criminal responsibility of the entity does not replace the individual criminal liability of the decision makers or members of staff, but natural persons are punishable besides the entity. At the moment such a liability of organisations is limited to criminal law and it is not being planned so far to introduce a liability of corporations also in administrative penal law.[72] An exception is the administrative fiscal penal law, which does not only provide for a liability of organisations in cases which fall into the jurisdiction of the courts, but also of cases which are in the jurisdiction of administrative fiscal authorities. Most of the provisions of the *Verbandsverantwortlichkeitsgesetz* are also to apply in the administrative fiscal penal law (Section 28a, para. 2 *Finanzstrafgesetz*).[73]

Arbeitszeitrecht – Rechtsgrundlagen und Gestaltungsformen, Sanktionen, Arbeitsteilzeit, 2001, p. 41 (60 *et seq.*); Walter/Mayer, *Verwaltungsverfahrensrecht*, 8th ed., p. 389.

70 Burgstaller, 'Aktuelle Wandlungen im Grundverständnis des Strafrechts', *JBl* 1996, 362 (365).

71 Federal Act on the criminal liability of legal entities *(Bundesgesetz über die Verantwortlichkeit von Verbänden für Straftaten)*, *BGBl* I 2005 No. 151.

72 But see the proposals by Wiederin, *Die Zukunft des Verwaltungsstrafrechts*, 16. Österreichischer Juristentag, Volume III/1, p. 93 *et seq.*

73 See Kert, 'Verbandsverantwortlichkeit und Finanzstrafrecht', in: Leitner (ed.), *Finanzstrafrecht*, 2006, p. 9 (13 et seq.).

Before 2005, legal persons were only indirectly liable under the legal institution of the so-called 'criminal guarantee' (*Kriminelle Bürgschaft*), which can be found in Section 9, para. 7 VStG as well as in some provisions of supplementary criminal law statutes.[74] According to this concept, a legal person can be held liable under civil law for fines, other monetary consequences and costs of the proceedings imposed on natural persons that are representatives of the legal person. This legal person is jointly and severally liable together with the natural person. Since the legal person who is liable for the legal consequences of a punishment is affected by the decision, the legal person has the status of a party in the administrative penal procedure (Section 8 *Allgemeines Verwaltungsverfahrensgesetz*/AVG – Code of Administrative Procedure in connection with Section 24 VStG).[75] Since the legal person is jointly and severally liable, the authority has the choice to execute the pecuniary claims either from the legal person or from the agent.

2.7. *NE BIS IN IDEM*

Like all provisions of the ECHR and its protocols, Article 4 of Protocol No. 7 has the status of constitutional law in Austria. When ratifying the Protocol, Austria made a reservation that Article 4 should only apply to criminal law. This declaration was regarded invalid by the European Court of Human Rights[76] and by the Austrian Constitutional Court.[77] Therefore the principle of *ne bis in idem* does not only apply to criminal procedure, but also applies to administrative penal law.

The dual system of criminal law and administrative penal law, as described above, has led to special problems in the context of the *ne bis in idem* principle within the meaning of Article 4 of Protocol No. 7. The *Verwaltungsstrafgesetz* does not give an explicit priority to criminal law. Therefore it is possible that an offender is punished twice for one and the same conduct, namely under criminal law and under administrative penal law. In the case *Gradinger v. Austria*[78], the European Court of Human Rights ruled that it was an infringement of the Convention, if one person was convicted for the same conduct at first by a court and then by an administrative authority. In the pertinent case, the drunken driver of a car, who caused an accident, was punished according to both criminal

---

74 See Karollus, 'Die Haftung für fremde Geldstrafen und sonstige in Geld bemessene Unrechtsfolgen', Dissertation University of Vienna (1987).

75 Administrative Court 21 November 2000, 99/09/0002; 7 August 2001, 98/02/0235; 20 November 2001, 2000/09/0063.

76 ECtHR 23 October 1995, *Gradinger v. Austria*, Serie A 328-C.

77 Constitutional Court 5 December 1996, VfSlg. 14.696.

78 ECtHR 23 October 1995, *Gradinger v. Austria*, Serie A 328-C.

law and administrative penal law. In Austria, the driving under influence of alcohol *per se* constitutes an administrative offence while being a crime once the driver has hit another person on his or her way. So, when Austrian authorities, one after the other, impose a criminal and an administrative penalty, this is not in line with the prohibition of double jeopardy. Sharing this interpretation of Article 4 of Protocol No. 7, the Constitutional Court declared a *clausula* in the Road Traffic Act (*Straßenverkehrsordnung*) void, which expressly provided for double punishment in cases with intoxicated driving (while in many other situations of *concursus delictorum* the administrative offence is only subsidiary in relation to a criminal offence committed at the same time).

Whereas the preclusion of decisions by criminal courts for later administrative penal proceedings deemed to be quite unproblematic, the preclusion of a criminal prosecution by sanctioning this act as an administrative offence by an administrative authority, which is not conscious of the criminal dimension of the prosecuted act, raises some difficult questions. At a first glance it seems to be obscure, that an administrative decision because of a (relatively) petty offence can exclude the prosecution by a court because of a (relatively) severe criminal act.[79] But in doctrine already after the first decision of the European Court of Human Rights in the case *Gradinger v. Austria* it was pointed out that for the effect of preclusion it is not relevant, if the court or the administrative authority decide first.[80] This consequence was also explicitly drawn by the European Court of Human Rights in the Case *Fischer v. Austria*, where a violation of Article 4 of Protocol No. 7 was found, because after a punishment (due to drunken driving) by an administrative authority a court convicted the driver of the same act (because of negligent homicide in state of drunkenness).

The jurisprudence of the Austrian Supreme Court did not follow the European Court of Human Rights immediately: In the *Fischer* case the Austrian Supreme Court[81] refused to allow an application to renew, according to Section 363a Code of Criminal Procedure, the criminal procedure.[82] The Supreme Court argued that the European Court of Human Rights had not ascertained a violation of the Convention by the decision of a criminal court. Moreover it said, the courts were obliged to respect the national laws and, also if the procedure

79 See e.g. Oberlandesgericht Wien 19 June 1996, 23 Bs 333/96, ZVR 1997, 64 *et seq.*

80 See Grabenwarter, 'Entscheidungsbesprechung', *Juristische Blätter* 1997, 577 (582); Giese, in Grabenwarter/Thienel (eds.), *Kontinuität und Wandel der EMRK*, 1998, p. 113.

81 Supreme Court 22 November 2002, 12 Os 51/01, *Evidenzblatt* 2002/57 = *Juristische Blätter* 2002, 402.

82 Sections 363a to 363c Code of Criminal Procedure were introduced in 1996 into the Austrian Code of Criminal Procedure to have a legal basis to make a new decision after a declaration by the European Court of Human Rights that the European Convention on Human Rights was violated.

was renewed, the charge of a criminal act would not be eliminated. This means that the Supreme Court was of the opinion that the conviction by a court was cogent. This decision was criticised in doctrine, since it did not only disobey the national law, but also did not respect Article 4 of Protocol No. 7. It was argued that this provision contained a directly applicable obstacle for a procedure (*Verfolgungshindernis*).[83]

In a later case, similar to *Fischer*, the Supreme Court[84] quashed a court conviction, which was passed after a punishment by an administrative authority: The administrative authority was not allowed to carry on an administrative penal procedure due to the subsidiarity of the administrative offence, but the administrative penal decision was valid and pursuant to Article 4, para. 2 of Protocol No. 7 another prosecution by a court would be in conflict with it. This obstacle to prosecute would vanish, if the administrative authority would declare its decision invalid and drop the case. Afterwards the criminal procedure would be re-admissible. With this decision the Supreme Court acknowledged the effect of preclusion of administrative penal decisions constitutionally provided for in the Constitution.

In connection with the decision of the European Court of Human Rights in the case *Gradinger* in Austria the problem was perceived that the *Verwaltungsstrafgesetz* – in contrary to the criminal law[85] – provides for the cumulation of penalties, even in cases of ideal concurrence of offences. The Austrian Constitutional Court[86] did not regard these provisions as unconstitutional, since they would only regulate the determination of penalty. The provision would assume the concurrence of several offences and only provides for the consequence of cumulative prosecution. Also the provision of nominal coincidence of offences would not be excluded by Article 4 of Protocol No. 7. Unconstitutional double jeopardy would exist, if someone was prosecuted or punished on the basis of statutory offences which exclude each other because of subsidiarity, speciality or consumption.

The Constitutional Court pointed out that the administrative authority in the case of purely 'seeming concurrence' (*concursus legum*) between an administrative offence and a criminal offence has to follow the provisions of

83 See Thienel/Hauenschild, 'Verfassungsrechtliches "ne bis in idem" und seine Auswirkungen auf das Verhältnis von Justiz- und Verwaltungsstrafverfahren', *JBl* 2004, 69 (71); Reindl, in: Fuchs/Ratz (eds.), *Wiener Kommentar zur Strafprozessordnung*, §363a Figure 8, 2010.

84 Supreme Court 22 August 2002, 15 Os 18/02.

85 See *supra* under I.2.1.2.

86 Constitutional Court 5 December 1996, VfSlg. 14.696/1996; see also 11 March 1998, VfSlg. 15.128/1998.

Section 30, para. 2 and 3 VStG.[87] If an act shall only be prosecuted, in case no other authority or a court is competent, or if the distribution of competences is unclear, the authority has to discontinue the proceeding until this question is decided by the competent authority or by the court. If the authority passed a penal decision *(Straferkenntnis)* before that decision, the penal decision must not be executed. If later arises that the administrative penal procedure should not have been carried out, the administrative authority has to declare the penal decision invalid and drop the case. This however does not solve the problem completely, since it does not cover all problems of double jeopardy arising out of Article 4 of Protocol No. 7: Even if an administrative authority passed a decision without a legal basis, a later conviction by a court is excluded, once the main aspect of the criminal statutory definition has already been dealt with in the administrative proceeding.[88] If a decision of the administrative authority exists, Article 4 of Protocol No. 7 excludes another decision by a court. Yet, according to Section 30 VStG it is the presumption for the annulment of the administrative penal decision that there is a later decision of a court.[89]

Similar problems of *ne bis in idem* have appeared when a person drove a car without permission of the owner, which is a criminal offence (Section 136 *Strafgesetzbuch*), and without a driving licence, which is an administrative offence, or when a dog bites a person due to a mistake of the owner, which is on the one hand an administrative offence and on the other hand an aggravating circumstance of the criminal offence of negligent bodily injury. In the first case, the Austrian Supreme Court decided that it is not in conflict with Article 4 of Protocol No. 7 to impose both an administrative penalty and a criminal penalty.[90]

It has not yet clearly been established in the case law how far Article 4 of Protocol No. 7 also applies to other administrative measures with a punitive character. This problem arises, when for the same conduct a criminal penalty and an administrative measure are imposed. *E.g.*, it is often the case that the driver of a car is punished for a criminal act in connection with driving the car (negligent bodily injury, negligent homicide), and that due to the same behaviour, and based on this conviction, the driving licence is withdrawn. If such administrative sanctions were seen as sanctions with a penal or criminal character, this double sanctioning would be in conflict with the principle of *ne bis in idem*, the same facts having lead to a punishment by a court and by an administrative authority.[91]

---

87 See Constitutional Court 19 June 1998, VfSlg. 15.199.

88 See in detail Thienel/Hauenschild, *JBl* 2004, 80.

89 Thienel/Hauenschild, *JBl* 2004, 164 *et seq.*

90 Oberster Gerichtshof 27 May 2004, 12 Os 27/04, JBl 2004, 739; compare Schwaighofer, 'Überlegungen zur Reichweite des innerstaatlichen "Doppelbestrafungsverbots" nach Art 4 Abs 1 7. ZPMRK', *ÖJZ* 2005/10.

91 See Winkler, *JAP* 1996/97, 161.

Since the prevailing opinion and the jurisprudence do not see these sanctions as penal sanctions, this problem has not yet been discussed intensively in Austria.

2.8. *LEX MITIOR*

In principle, the penalty is determined by the law in force at the time of the offence. But according to Section 1, para. 2 VStG the law in force at the time of the decision of the authority in first instance has priority, if it is more favourable for the offender than the law in force at the time of the offence.

Contrarily to criminal law, where the application of the law in force at the time of the judgement has priority, unless the older law in its entire impact is more favourable for the offender[92], the administrative penal law provides that in the case of a mitigation of the provided penalty between the commission of the offence and the penal decision in first instance the more lenient penalty is to be imposed. This rule also applies to the case that the penal sanction is completely abolished. In this case the offender must not be punished any more.[93] This means that a reduction, as well as an abolishment of the punishment law has retroactive effect in relation to acts committed before the law has come into effect. Changes as to the punishment provision after the decision of first instance, however, during the appeals proceedings, have no relevance for eventual appeals proceedings.[94]

2.9. INQUISITORIAL PRINCIPLE

Whereas the accusatorial principle applies to the criminal procedure, the inquisitorial principle applies in administrative penal procedure.[95] There is no separation between the accusing organ and the organ making the decision. Consequently the penal authority as the only organ in the procedure must prosecute as well as render the decision.

Section 25 VStG explicitly establishes two other principles of administrative penal procedure: As a rule, administrative offences must be prosecuted *ex officio proprio motu*. And the authority is obliged to consider all exonerating and incriminating circumstances equally (principle of **substantive truth**). The administrative penal authority therefore is 'prosecutor, defence lawyer and judge

92 See Höpfel, in: Höpfel/Ratz (eds.), *Wiener Kommentar zum Strafgesetzbuch*, 2nd ed., §61 Figure 2, 2007.

93 See Administrative Court 27 April 1995, 95/11/0012.

94 See Administrative Court 29 October 1991, 91/07/0093; Constitutional Court 14 December 2001, VfSlg. 16.407; Hauer/Leukauf, *Handbuch*, 6th ed., p. 1193.

95 Critical Wiederin, *Die Zukunft des Verwaltungsstrafverfahrens*, p. 102 *et seq.*

in one person'.[96] For the institution of the penal proceedings a formal accusation is not required. According to the jurisprudence of the European Court of Human Rights, this is not in conflict with Article 6 ECHR. In the appeals proceeding the authority that has rendered the decision in first instance has the position of a party and fulfils in this position the role of a prosecuting authority within the meaning of Article 6.[97]

2.10. PRESUMPTION OF INNOCENCE

Since Article 6 of the ECHR applies to the administrative penal procedure, the accused must not be burdened with the onus to prove his/her innocence.[98] The authority must prove the physical and mental elements of an offence – with the exception of the negligence for so-called *'Ungehorsamsdelikten'*.[99] It is not allowed to deduce the guilt of the accused only from his/her missing co-operation.

2.11. *NEMO TENETUR* PRINCIPLE

According to Section 33 VStG the accused cannot be forced to answer the questions he was asked. The imposition of a disciplinary penalty for such a form of non-compliance is forbidden.

As it will be explained below in more detail, it is regarded as a problem of the privilege against self-incrimination that the *Kraftfahrgesetz* (Motor Vehicle Act) obliges the car owner to inform the authorities about who was driving the car at the moment of an administrative offence in order to enable them to identify and prosecute the perpetrator of this offence (Section 103, para. 2).[100] If the car owner does not provide this information, a penalty can be imposed against him/her. This results in the fact that the owner, if he/she has driven the car himself, is obliged to incriminate him/herself. The Austrian Constitutional Court deemed this provision unconstitutional and annulled. It reasoned that it was an infringement of the principle of equality, since the car owner had no right to refuse to testify, which was seen as a problem of the prohibition of self-incrimination and of the accusation principle *(Anklageprinzip)*.[101] After that

96 See Administrative Court 16 October 2001, 2001/09/0071.
97 ECtHR 4 July 2002 *'Weh und Weh'*, 38.544/97.
98 See also Constitutional Court 25 September 1990, B 795/90.
99 See *supra* II.5.
100 See Sprinzel, 'Verfahrensfragen des §103 Abs 2 KFG', *ZVR* 2001, 279.
101 Constitutional Court 3 March 1984, VfSlg. 9950, 8 March 1985, 10.394 and 29 September 1988, 11.829.

decision, however, the Austrian legislator passed a constitutional provision which explicitly says that the rights to refuse to give evidence stand back to the competence of the authorities to ask for such information (Section 103, para. 2 last sentence).

3. RIGHTS OF DEFENCE

3.1. POSSIBILITIES OF PROTEST AGAINST THE INTENTION OF AN ADMINISTRATIVE AUTHORITY TO IMPOSE A SANCTION

Each party of an administrative penal proceeding must be given the opportunity to present and prove all aspects of the case and to take up a position on the results of the official investigations and of the taking of evidence (Section 43, para. 3 AVG).

The right to be heard in the administrative penal procedure is an essential right in administrative penal law, which is particularly emphasised by the Administrative Court. During the investigative stage all parties have the right to present everything which supportive to their point of view. The authority must deal with all arguments of the parties. According to the jurisprudence of the Administrative Court, the parties must be given the opportunity of being heard explicitly,[102] in a formal way[103], and *ex officio*.[104] The Administrative Court sometimes required that the party has the possibility to deliberate and to formulate his/her statement. The opportunity must be given to the parties to present and prove all aspects belonging to the case and to comment on all relevant facts, and on the results of the official investigations (Section 43, para. 3 and 4 AVG). Moreover, parties can call for the production of evidence. The right to be heard does not imply that the party has a claim on holding an oral hearing.

The party must be informed about the results of the taking of evidence (Section 45, para. 3 AVG) and must be allowed to comment on them. For this purpose, a certain time has to be fixed.

The right to be heard also extends to the appeals proceeding (Section 65 AVG). According to the jurisprudence of the Administrative Court[105], an infringement of the right to be heard in the first instance can be cured in the appeals

---

102 Administrative Court 18 January 1971, 1180/70; VwSlgNF 6300 A.

103 VwSlgNF 4557 A; Administrative Court 18 September 2002, 2002/07/0058.

104 VwSlgNF 1227 A; Administrative Court 14 October 1950, 355/46.

105 Administrative Court 20 September 1990, 86/07/0091; 15 December 1987, 84/07/0200; 18 October 2001, 2000/07/0003.

proceeding, if the contested decision explains the results of the investigation proceeding or if the party had the opportunity to give an explanation within the appeals proceeding.[106]

3.2. ACCESS OF THE INFRINGER TO HIS DOSSIER

According to Section 17 AVG, which is also applicable in the administrative penal proceeding, the authority must permit the parties to inspect the files concerning their case. The parties can take copies of the file. If the disclosure would cause the damage of legitimate interests of a party or of third persons or endanger of the tasks of the authority, or if the purpose of the proceeding is deteriorated, the inspection of files can be denied.

4. ORGANISATION OF SANCTIONING POWERS

4.1. CAN SANCTIONING POWERS BE EXERCISED BY ALL ADMINISTRATIVE AUTHORITIES AND WITHIN AN ADMINISTRATIVE AUTHORITY BY ANY CIVIL SERVANT?

In principle, the district administration authorities (*Bezirksverwaltungsbehörden*)[107] are competent to decide in first instance in administrative penal matters (Section 26, para. 1 VStG), which are not allocated by another law to the courts or to a different administrative authority (subsidiary comprehensive jurisdiction). The competence in administrative penal affairs in first instance can also be given to the communities, but this task does not fall into the own scope of activity of the communities.[108]

According to Section 26, para. 2 VStG the *Bundespolizeibehörden* (Federal Police Authorities) have the competence to punish within their field of activity. This is not a subsidiary, but a coercive competence norm. If the *Bundespolizeibehörden* have the competence on a matter within their territorial jurisdiction, they are equally competent in penal matters in first instance. *Bundespolizeibehörden* are established in some communities. E.g., they are competent to deal with administrative traffic offences.

---

106 Critical to this jurisdiction Walter/Mayer, *Verwaltungsverfahrensrecht*, 8th ed., p. 138.

107 District administration authorities are the district offices *(Bezirkshauptmannschaften)*, the mayors of some special towns *(Städte mit eigenem Statut)* and the municipal board Vienna.

108 Constitutional Court 17 October 1979, VfSlg. 8654/1979; Antoniolli/Koja, *Allgemeines Verwaltungsrecht*, 3rd ed., 1986, p. 450.

In administrative fiscal penal law there are special authorities which have jurisdiction, the so-called fiscal offence prosecution authorities *(Finanzstrafbehörden)*. Fiscal offence prosecution authorities of first instance are the tax and customs offices (Section 58 Finanzstrafgesetz).[109]

The competence to impose other administrative sanctions is not regulated in general, but is accorded by the provisions in the concrete acts regulating certain affairs. E.g., the authority, which is competent for traffic affairs, is also competent for the withdrawal of driving licences.

4.2. DOES IT MAKE ANY DIFFERENCE IF THIS IS AN INDEPENDENT AUTHORITY?

In first instance only administrative authorities are competent to decide and they are not independent, but under hierarchical order from another authority.

4.3. ARE SANCTIONS TO BE IMPOSED BY JUDGES (ADMINISTRATIVE, CRIMINAL, OTHER), BY THE PUBLIC PROSECUTION, BY SPECIALISED ADMINISTRATIVE AUTHORITIES OR BY ANY ADMINISTRATIVE AUTHORITY?

In Austria, criminal sanctions are always imposed by judges, but contrarily judges are never competent for the imposition of administrative penalties. Also the public prosecutor does not impose any formal sanctions.

Whether the imposition of penalties is in the hands of the judiciary or of administrative bodies, depends on the positive law. According to Austrian understanding, there is no choice for the legislators. The federal structure of the Republic of Austria brings about, that among the administrative authorities there basically are two distinct systems: 1. The enforcement power is a federal competence *(Bund)*, but the authorities of the provinces *(Länder)* exercise the enforcement of the *Bund* in the provinces. This is called system of *mittelbare Bundesverwaltung*. 2. The *Bund* exercises its function directly *(unmittelbare Bundesverwaltung)*. This, however, in practice is the exception (Article 102 *Bundes-Verfassungsgesetz*).[110] In principle, in first instance administrative penal sanctions can be imposed by any authority. Exceptionally, special competencies are provided for in fiscal matters and asylum matters.

---

109 Leitner/Toifl/Brandl, *Österreichisches Finanzstrafrecht*, p. 532 *et seq.*

110 See Öhlinger, *Verfassungsrecht*, 8th ed., p. 144 *et seq.*; Walter/Mayer/Kucsko-Stadlmayer, *Grundriss des österreichischen Bundesverfassungsrechts*, 10th ed., 2007, p.401 *et seq.*

For administrative penal decisions – other than in fiscal offence matters or asylum matters –, the *Unabhängige Verwaltungssenate der Länder* (UVSs) serve as appeals authorities.[111] In fiscal offence and asylum matters other independent bodies are competent to decide as appeals authorities.

Both tracks, the federal and the provincial administration *(Landes- und Bundesverwaltung)* lead to the same superior control of legality: by the Administrative Court *(Verwaltungsgerichtshof – VwGH)* and, if a constitutional right allegedly has been infringed, the Constitutional Court *(Verfassungsgerichtshof – VfGH).*

In 1997 (in force since 1 January 1998), a special independent appeal body was created to deal with asylum matters, the so-called *Unabhängige Bundesasylsenat* (Independent Federal Asylum Senate). The *Unabhängige Bundesasylsenat* are independent and free from any instructions; their members are appointed for life.

In 2003 – similar to UVSs und *Unabhängigen Bundesasylsenat* – for fiscal administrative matters so-called *Unabhängige Finanzsenate* (Independent Fiscal Senates) were introduced. They replaced the fiscal authorities of the provinces as appeal authorities. The main innovation is that the members of the *Unabhängige Finanzsenate* are completely independent, whereas before 2003 the members of the appeal chambers had been persons who were as civil servants at the fiscal authority bound to instructions, while as deciding members of the appeal chamber they were not bound to any instructions.[112] Another important part of the reform is that now the fiscal office and the taxpayer stand opposite to each other as two parties in the proceeding before the Independent Fiscal Senate. With the fiscal office as sort of an accuser, and the taxpayer as accused a move towards an accusatory system was introduced in these appeals proceedings. Due to the fact that the parties are somehow modelled after the criminal trial procedure, the appeals proceedings in fiscal matters now are 'similar' to a judicial court proceeding.[113]

111 See below.

112 See Glocknitzer, *UFS – unbekanntes Wesen? – Reform. Seit Jahresbeginn gibt es den Unabhängigen Finanzsenat (UFS) – Überblick zu Funktion und Arbeitsweise der neuen Instanz*, persaldo 2003 H 1, 19; Renner, 'Prinzipien der neuen Behörde und des "neuen" Abgabenberufungsverfahrens', *SWK* 2003, 487.

113 Renner, *SWK* 2003, 487.

5. INVESTIGATION/INSPECTION

5.1. INVESTIGATIVE POWERS OF ADMINISTRATIVE AUTHORITIES TO DETECT INFRINGEMENTS AND TO EXAMINE BY WHOM THEY HAVE BEEN COMMITTED

5.1.1. General administrative penal law

According to Section 34 VStG the administrative authority has to clarify the facts of the case and to investigate the identity and the place of residence of the suspected perpetrator, if either his identity or his residence are unknown. The *Verwaltungsstrafgesetz* does not contain more detailed provisions on the measures which the authority can use for the investigations. Particularly, neither house searches nor the mere entering of properties or apartments are provided for. Such measures may not be taken, unless they are foreseen in an express legal provision, as they only may be conducted in conformity with the Act on protection of the domestic right (*Gesetz zum Schutz des Hausrechts – Hausrechtsgesetz*)[114] and with Article 8 ECHR, which both are in the rank of constitutional law.

Section 3 *Hausrechtsgesetz* allows for house searches for the purpose of police and financial supervision. This provision, however, does not give a directly applicable authorisation to conduct a house search. A house search would only be admissible on the basis of a special authorisation in a statutory law. If the legislator does not explicitly give the power for a house search, it is not allowed for administrative authorities to make a house search.[115] For a house search by the police the provision of the Code of Criminal Procedure *(Strafprozessordnung)* applies (Section 5 *Hausrechtsgesetz*). As to house searches by administrative authorities for the purpose of police and financial supervision, it is in dispute, whose authorisation in the concrete case is necessary. Section 5 *Hausrechtsgesetz* refers to the provision of house searches in criminal procedure, where in principle an order by a judge is necessary. Only if danger is ahead, an order of a judge is not required. This opinion was confirmed by the Austrian Constitutional Court in two leading cases, in which it ruled that also for house searches for the purpose of police and financial supervision it is the rule, that only if danger is ahead, an order by a judge is not necessary.[116] In the doctrine, the opposite opinion is dominating. According to this opinion, within the framework of police and financial supervision an order by a judge is only necessary, if this is required for

[114] Gesetz vom 27. Oktober 1862 zum Schutz des Hausrechtes, *RGBl.* 1862 No. 88.

[115] See Wiederin, in: Korinek/Holoubek (eds.), *Österreichisches Bundesverfassungsrecht*, Art. 9 StGG Rz 72.

[116] Constitutional Court 27 June 1949, VfSlg. 1811/1949, 12 October 1971, 6553/1971.

by a law; the legislator can provide such a reservation.[117] A separate question is, whether a house search would have to be ordered by an authority or if an executive organ can make a house search on his/her own responsibility. Whereas the Constitutional Court[118] only would admit this in certain cases which are explicitly listed in the *Hausrechtsgesetz* for house searches in criminal matters, doctrine and administrative practice argue that the legislator is free to decide if the authority or a mere executive organ should conduct the house search. According to the latter opinion, the criteria whether an order is necessary, should be, if a danger is ahead.[119]

The term 'police supervision' ('*polizeiliche Aufsicht*') covers – according to the majority opinion and the jurisprudence – the administrative police as well as the security police.[120] According to the prevailing opinion, activities which serve for the defence of dangers or the preventive or repressive combat against illegal activities are seen as 'police supervision'.

Several administrative provisions authorise administrative authorities and executive organs to conduct house searches: *e.g.*, the *Schieß- und Sprengmittelgesetz* (Shooting and Blasting Agent Act, Section 42), the *Epidemiegesetz* (Act on Epidemics, Section 44), the *Sicherheitspolizeigesetz* (Act on Security Police, Section 39), the *Telekommunikationsgesetz* (Telecommunication Act, Section 87) provide for authorisations of authorities and organs for house searches.[121]

According to Section 35 VStG, the apprehension of persons is admissible in administrative penal matters. The organs of the public security service may arrest persons who have been caught during their act, for the purpose of accompanying them to the authority, if one of the reasons for the arrest is given. The conditions are: (1) the person is unknown to the organ, does not identify him/herself and his/her identity cannot be established otherwise; and (2) there is a reasoned suspicion that the person would evade prosecution or that the person would continue or resume the punishable act in spite of a caution.

The arrested person must soonest be informed about the reasons for the arrest and the accusations against him/her. Every arrested person must be

---

117 Wiederin, in: Korinek/Holoubek (eds.), *Österreichisches Bundesverfassungsrecht*, Art. 9 StGG Rz 73.

118 Constitutional Court 12 October 1971, VfSlg. 6553/1971.

119 See Wiederin, in: Korinek/Holoubek (eds.), *Österreichisches Bundesverfassungsrecht*, Art. 9 StGG Rz 74.

120 Öhlinger, *Verfassungsrecht*, 8th ed., p. 388 *et seq.*

121 See Wiederin, in: Korinek/Holoubek (eds.), *Österreichisches Bundesverfassungsrecht*, Art. 9 StGG Rz 82.

referred to the competent authority immediately or must be dismissed as soon as the reason for the arrest has fallen away. The arrested person must be informed about the reasons of his/her arrest and about the accusations against him/her. The authority must examine the arrested person immediately. One must not be arrested for more than 24 hours.[122]

According to Section 39 VStG objects may be seized to merely secure their forfeiture, but not to secure evidence.

Since there are not as many coercive measures in administrative penal law as in criminal law, in particular, the voluntary participation of the persons concerned is needed for any truth-finding.[123]

Supervision of the telecommunication or other surveillances of persons are not provided for in administrative penal proceedings. Normally, interrogations and observations are the only way in any administrative penal procedure to identify the perpetrator.[124] If the suspected perpetrator is already known, also the formal taking of evidence in an ordinary investigation procedure, *e.g.* the interrogation of witnesses, is possible.

5.1.2. Competition law

In competition law the competition authority has, according to Section 12 *Wettbewerbsgesetz* (Competition Act), the power to conduct a house search, if this is necessary to obtain information concerning business documents. A house search by the competition authority is only admissible on basis of a search warrant by a judge of the Cartel Court. A prerequisite for a house search is a reasoned suspicion of an abuse of a market-dominating position, of infringements of the prohibition on implementing a cartel, or a merger, or of an infringement of Article 81 or 82 EC Treaty, or, finally, an investigation decision by the European Commission due to a suspicion of an offence against competition law.[125]

---

122 See also Article 4, para. 5 Bundesverfassungsgesetz über den Schutz der persönlichen Freiheit.

123 See Bachler, 'Die allgemeine Mitwirkung der Parteien im Verwaltungsverfahren – "Pflicht" oder "Recht"?', *ÖJZ* 1995, 401.

124 Hauer/Leukauf, *Handbuch*, 6th ed., p. 1479 *et seq.*; Walter/Mayer, *Verwaltungsverfahrensrecht*, 8th ed., p. 438.

125 See Höpfel/Kert, 'Country Analysis – Austria', in: Dannecker/Jansen (eds.), *Competition Law Sanctioning in the European Union*, 2004, p. 321.

5.1.3. *Act on Fiscal Offences*

The financial supervision comprises all measures, which are necessary to prevent that duties or goods under customs supervision are withdrawn from the tax and customs proceeding. Beside the preventive activities of organs of the tax, monopoly and customs supervision also the fiscal offence law is comprehended. As far as the fiscal offence law provides for the competence of the criminal courts, for investigative measures as house searches, seizure, etc. the provisions in the code of criminal procedure are applied.

For investigative powers in the framework of an administrative fiscal penal procedure the assumptions are contained in the Act on Fiscal Offences *(Finanzstrafgesetz*, Section 84 *et seq.*).

The *Finanzstrafgesetz* not only provides for a short detention *(Verwahrungshaft)*, but – as single exception in an administrative penal procedure – also for pre-trial detention (Section 86 *et seq.*). It may last two months at the maximum, if the ground of detention is the danger of an escape; in other cases the limit for the detention is one month.

The *Finanzstrafgesetz* permits the seizure of objects which are threatened with forfeiture or which could be used as evidence (Section 89, para. 1). The seizure is possible, independently of who the owner is, and serves to secure the forfeiture or to preserve the evidence. The seizure is only admissible, if there is a concrete suspicion of a specific fiscal offence. It must be ordered in a decision *(Bescheid)* by the competent single fiscal officer. If there is danger ahead, this decree ordering the seizure is not necessary.[126]

According to Section 93 *Finanzstrafgesetz*, house searches may only be carried out, if they are based on a well-founded suspicion that in the house there is a person suspected of a fiscal offence or that there are objects, which are probably forfeited or could be needed as evidence in the fiscal offence procedure. For carrying out the house search an order by the president of the conciliation board *(Spruchsenat)* of the fiscal offence authority, stating the reasons for this measure, is required.[127] If there is danger ahead, the organs of the customs authority, of the public security service and of the tax authority are authorised to carry out a house search.

As for the search of persons, Section 93, para. 3 *Finanzstrafgesetz* allows for such a search, if a high probability exists that the person keeps such things mentioned before or if the searched person is suspected of a fiscal offence.

---

126 See Leitner/Toifl/Brandl, *Österreichisches Finanzstrafrecht*, 3rd ed., p. 624.

127 Leitner/Toifl/Brandl, *Österreichisches Finanzstrafrecht*, 3rd ed., p. 634 *et seq.*

5.2. CAN THE INVESTIGATIVE POWERS OF AN ADMINISTRATIVE LAW SYSTEM BE USED TOGETHER WITH THE INVESTIGATIVE POWERS OF THE CRIMINAL LAW SYSTEM?

There is no rule which would allow for accumulation of such powers, unless investigations have a basis in both tracks.

The prevention of any criminal behaviour, including the detection of such a behaviour until the point of the identification of a particular suspect, is regulated in the *Sicherheitspolizeigesetz* (Act on Security Police). As to this scope only the limited investigative powers of security police are applicable. Since defence of dangers and prevention cannot always be clearly distinguished from clarification and judging of committed offences, in practice police action often fulfils both functions. Therefore, one and the same action can be based on security police and criminal procedural authorisation. According to Section 22, para. 3 *Sicherheitspolizeigesetz*, as soon as a specific person is suspected of a criminal act which as dangerous assault gives reason to investigation by the security police, solely the provisions of the Code of Criminal Procedure apply. However, in the core area of the security police – the defence of dangers – there is no subsidiarity. The *Sicherheitspolizeigesetz* remains the applicable law for cessation of dangerous assaults, even if a specific person is suspected of a criminal act.

5.3. CAN THE INFORMATION GATHERED BY THE USE OF CRIMINAL POWERS BE USED TO IMPOSE ADMINISTRATIVE SANCTIONS?

In Austria, in principle, everything can be used as evidence in administrative penal or in criminal procedure, that is not explicitly forbidden. According to Section 46 AVG everything can be used as evidence, which is appropriate to find out the relevant facts and which are useful for the single case (unlimitedness of evidence). It is admissible to use the results of another procedure in an administrative procedure, especially since the principle of direct taking of evidence is not applied in administrative penal procedure.[128] Therefore, information gathered by the use of criminal powers in principle can be used in the administrative penal procedure.[129] It is nevertheless required that the administrative authority also considers additional motions to hear evidence.[130]

128 See *inter alia* Administrative Court 1 October 1981, 1823/80, 81/16/0093; 15 October 1981, 401, 402/80; 10 December 1985, 84/14/0007; for more details see Walter/Thienel, *Verwaltungsverfahren II*, 2nd ed., p. 742.

129 Administrative Court 23 June 1993, 92/03/0258; 27 January 1995, 94/02/0418.

130 Administrative Court 26 June 1990, 89/11/0245.

According to the Administrative Court the statement of the accused in a criminal procedure on the same case can be used as evidence by the administrative authority within its free evaluation of evidence and because of the unlimitedness of evidence.[131] The authority is obliged to take the evidence collected in a criminal procedure, if the accused person relates to this evidence and if this is necessary for the clarification of the facts.[132] The administrative authority can use the results of court investigations on which the party has already commented on, without giving the party the opportunity for a new statement.[133] According to the Administrative Court even a foreign criminal judgment can be used as evidence.[134] The only limits for the taking of evidence are prohibitions of evidence, which are extremely rare in administrative law.

5.4. CAN THE INFORMATION GATHERED BY THE USE OF ADMINISTRATIVE POWERS BE USED TO IMPOSE CRIMINAL SANCTIONS?

Section 84 of the Code of Criminal Procedure (*Strafprozessordnung* – StPO) does not only allow, but makes it a duty for the administrative authorities to give notice of a suspicion to the public prosecutor. This does not automatically include the transfer of all relevant information to the public prosecutor. The duty to file charges according to Section 84 StPO might cause difficulties in respect of the obligation of discretion of public officials according to Article 22 *Bundesverfassungsgesetz* (B-VG, Federal Constitution Act). The duty to file charges does not totally rule out the obligation of discretion. The unconditional primacy of the duty to file charges applies only to those authorities and their organs whose core function is the clarification and prosecution of criminal offences. All other authorities have to balance the interests of ensuring discretion and the concern of prosecution.[135]

6. LEGAL PROTECTION

6.1. THE SYSTEM OF LEGAL PROTECTION IN GENERAL

The ordinary administrative penal proceeding is terminated by a decision *(Bescheid)*, which contains either the sentence or an admonition, or the stay of

131 Administrative Court 12 October 1983, 83/03/0104.
132 Administrative Court 24 February 1972, 1989/71; 14 December 1978, 155/78.
133 Administrative Court 30 June 1950, VwSlg. 1586 A.
134 Administrative Court 8 October 1990, 90/19/0170.
135 See Schwaighofer, in Höpfel/Fuchs (eds.), *Wiener Kommentar zur StPO*, §84 Figure 34 *et seq.*

the proceeding. Within the ordinary proceedings the authority has to carry on an investigation proceeding, especially a taking of evidence.

Besides this ordinary proceeding, the *Verwaltungsstrafgesetz* provides for abbreviated proceedings. On the one hand the authority can pass a penal decree *(Strafverfügung)*. This is a penal decision *(Strafbescheid)* which is passed without investigation proceedings. Such penal decrees *(Strafverfügungen)* are very important in practice. The competent authority can pass a penal decree *(Strafverfügung)*, if an administrative offence has been notified by a court, by an administrative authority, by an organ of the public supervision or of a military guard due to an own official observations or to a confession given to one of those organs, or if the punishable conduct has been detected by an automatic supervision (*e.g.* radar monitoring in road traffic) (Section 47, para. 1 VStG). In a *Strafverfügung*, a fine up to €365 (and imprisonment in default of payment) can be imposed.

Section 49a VStG provides for an anonymous order *(Anonymverfügung)*, which enables the authority to impose a penalty for petty offences without having found who the offender was. The anonymous order is not a decision *(Bescheid)*, but rather a legal act *sui generis*. It cannot be carried into effect by force, and there is no remedy against an anonymous order: If the penalty is not paid within a certain period of time, the anonymous order becomes obsolete. Then the authority has to identify the offender and introduce a penal proceeding. This construction is seen as constitutionally admissible, since legal protection is guaranteed. The authority competent to decide in first instance, can list certain statutory offences in a regulation, for which anonymous orders can be issued. For this case a certain fine, not exceeding €220, has to be fixed in advance. Other penalties – imprisonment or forfeiture – may not be imposed via anonymous order. If a fine has been determined in advance, the authority is not required to identify the unknown offender and can impose the fine without determining an imprisonment in default of payment, under the condition that the notification is based on an official observation of an organ of the public supervision or an automatic supervision (radar monitoring) and a consideration of the person of the offender is not necessary.

Lastly, it is also possible that organs of the public supervision can impose penalties on their own without identifying the offender (penal decree of an organ – *Organstrafverfügung;* Section 50 VStG). This act cannot be carried into effect by force, and there is no remedy against a penal decree of an organ: if the penalty is not paid, the penal decree of an organ becomes obsolete. The offence must be notified to the authority and an ordinary penal proceeding is carried on. The authority, which is competent to decide in first instance, can authorise specially qualified organs of the public supervision to levy fines because of certain administrative offences which they have officially observed or which were confessed to them. The authority must fix a certain fine up to €36 for this administrative offence. Other penalties are not admissible.

6.2. LEGAL REMEDIES

Depending on the type of decision in first instance, the remedies vary: The ordinary remedy against a penal decision *(Strafbescheid)* is an appeal *(Berufung)*. The ordinary remedy against penal decrees *(Strafverfügung, Organstrafverfügung)* is an objection *(Einspruch)*.

The objection *(Einspruch)* against penal decrees is a remonstrative remedy, on which the administrative authority of first instance decides. According to the wording of Section 49 para. 1 VStG only the accused has the right to remonstrate. But also other parties, especially in the case of forfeiture the person concerned by the forfeiture, or when penalties are imposed on responsible organs, the legal person or undertaking, which is liable for the fine together with the organ, can remonstrate.[136] The objection must be made within two weeks from the issuance of the penal decree. With the objection either the imposed penalty only, or the decision on the costs of the proceedings, or the whole penal decree can be appealed. In the first case, the penal decree stays in force and the authority has to decide on the penalty or the costs. In the second case, the penal decree becomes void, and an ordinary proceeding must be opened; the authority then has to decide by an ordinary decision *(Bescheid),* which is called '*Straferkenntnis*' (sentence). The penalty must not be higher than the penalty in the penal decree (prohibition of *reformatio in peius*). Against this sentence, an appeal to the UVSs is open.[137]

For administrative penal decisions – other than in fiscal offence matters or asylum matters[138] –, the *Unabhängige Verwaltungssenate der Länder* serve as appeals authorities with a competence of full review also of the facts (see Article 129a, para. 1, Figure 1 *Bundesverfassungsgesetz* – Federal Constitution Act).[139] An appeal to the UVSs is possible against substantive as well as against procedural decisions. They decide as single judges, if in the administrative decision of first instance neither an imprisonment nor a fine of more than €2,000 has been imposed. In all other cases they decide in chambers of three. From 1 January 2014 the tasks of the UVS will be taken over by administrative courts of the provinces (*Verwaltungsgerichte der Länder*). On the federal level a federal

136 Walter/Thienel, *Die österreichischen Verwaltungsverfahrensgesetze*, p. 276.

137 See for more details Thienel, *Verwaltungsverfahrensrecht*, 5th ed., p. 484 *et seq.*

138 See below.

139 See Thienel, *Verwaltungsverfahrensrecht*, 5th ed., p. 485 *et seq.*

administrative court (*Verwaltungsgericht des Bundes*) and a federal fiscal court (*Bundesfinanzgericht*) will be established (Article 130 B-VG).

All 'parties' of the administrative penal procedure are legitimated to appeal to the UVSs; i.e. all persons who have the position of a party in the procedure of first instance (Section 51, para. 1 VStG). In the appeal proceedings also the authority which has issued the penal decision that is appealed against has the position of a party. According to a decision of the European Court of Human Rights, in the appeal proceedings the authority of first instance has the function of an accusatorial authority.[140]

The appeal must be filed within two weeks from the issuance of the penal order. An appeal has suspensive effect.

After having exhausted this remedy, the person concerned punished has the right to appeal to the Administrative Court (*Verwaltungsgerichtshof*) or the Constitutional Court (*Verfassungsgerichtshof*). Referring to Article 2 of Protocol No. 7 to the ECHR, Austria made an 'interpretative declaration' that, for the administrative penal law the Administrative Court and the Constitutional Court are considered higher tribunals within the meaning of Article 2. Therefore, in administrative penal law matters the appeal to the Administrative Court must be possible.

The Administrative Court (*Verwaltungsgerichtshof*) is a special court, which serves to control the administration (Article 131 *Bundes-Verfassungsgesetz*). The Administrative Court consists of judges. The control of the Administrative Court is limited to legal questions. It does not review the facts. Therefore it is not a full review of the decision of the administrative authorities. This hinders that the Administrative Court fulfils the requirements of a tribunal within the meaning of Article 6 ECHR.[141] Moreover, the Administrative Court can refuse to deal with an appeal against a decision of an Independent Administrative Panel, if only a small fine has been imposed and the decision does not depend on the solution of a legal question, which is of special importance, especially where the Independent Administrative Panel has deviated from the jurisprudence of the Administrative Court, such a jurisprudence is missing or the legal question to be solved has not been answered homogenously in the jurisprudence of the Administrative Court (Article 131, para. 3 *Bundes-Verfassungsgesetz*).

140 ECtHR 4 July 2002, *Weh and Weh*, 38.544/97.

141 See ECtHR 23 October 1995, 33/1994/480/562, *Gradinger v. Austria*, Serie A No. 328-C = *JBl* 1997, 577.

In fiscal administrative penal law, the ordinary remedies are the appeal (*Berufung*) against judgements (*Erkenntnisse*) of the fiscal offence prosecution authorities, and the remonstrance (*Beschwerde*) against other decisions.[142] Both remedies are ascending remedies which have to be decided by the *Unabhängige Finanzsenate* (Independent Fiscal Senates). In principle, the Independent Fiscal Senates decide in the cases themselves. In fiscal offence matters also the Administrative Court is competent to decide legal questions, once all ordinary remedies have been exhausted.

6.3. IS IT POSSIBLE TO SEIZE A JUDGE WITH A COMPLAINT AGAINST A SANCTION IMPOSED?

In the Austrian system of administrative penal law, until now (2013) it has not been possible to appeal to a court for a full review of the decision of first instance. The *Unabhängigen Verwaltungssenate,* the *Unabhängige Finanzsenate* and the *Unabhängige Asylsenate* do not consist of judges. The members of these senates are independent, but do not have the status of judges. Only where an appellation of the Administrative Court is possible, judges decide on the legality of an imposition of a penalty.

Within a long debate on a comprehensive reform of the Austrian constitution, the introduction of administrative courts of the provinces *(Landesverwaltungsgerichte)* instead of the UVSs had been intensively discussed and on this point a broad political consensus was found. In 2012 administrative courts on the federal level and in the provinces were established, which will start to work on 1 January 2014. These administrative courts will be "real courts" with independent judges. The proceedings before the administrative courts will be of an adversarial structure a contradictory proceeding, opposing the appellant to the administrative authority. Against the decision of the administrative courts (of first instance) an appellation to the Administrative Court will be possible under certain conditions.[143]

In doctrine it was discussed to give the ordinary courts a successive jurisprudence in administrative penal law. This seemed to be a solution which would be in confomity with some European legal acts, e.g. the Framework Decision 2005/214/JHA on the application of mutual recognition of financial

142 See Leitner/Toifl/Brandl, *Österreichisches Finanzstrafrecht*, 3rd ed., p. 429.

143 Concerning the problem see Grabenwarter/Holoubek, 'Demokratie, Rechtsstaat und Kollegialbehörden mit richterlichem Einschlag – Zu den verfassungsrechtlichen Grenzen der Einrichtung von Kollegialbehörden nach Art 20 Abs 2 und Art 133 Z 4 B-VG', *ZfV* 2000/520; referring to the present discussion *Bericht des Ausschusses 9 des Österreich Konvents, Rechtsschutz und Gerichtsbarkeit*, p. 22 *et seq.*

penalties, and which would have practical advantages, since courts would have practical experiences with penal matters. Due to the narrow relationship to the administrative law[144] the political decision preferred specific administrative courts of the provinces.

6.4. IS THIS JUDGE PART OF AN ADMINISTRATIVE COURT, A CRIMINAL COURT OR A CIVIL COURT?

Since until 2013 in Austria no judges could be addressed against an administrative penalty, the question if s/he is part of an administrative, criminal or civil court was not applicable. The UVSs have been administrative authorities within the meaning described above. The judges of the above-mentioned *Verwaltungsgerichte* will be part of administrative courts.

The Administrative Court (*Verwaltungsgerichtshof*) is a special court, which is limited to the legal control of administrative acts (see above).

6.5. IS IT POSSIBLE FOR THIS JUDGE TO TAKE PROVISIONAL MEASURES?

Speaking of the UVSs this institution is only organised for a quasi-judicial control but not to enforce the law, and therefore has no coercive powers at all, in the absence of an adversarial model which would also allow the administrative authority to apply for 'protection'. The same will apply to the above-mentioned administrative courts (*Verwaltungsgerichte*) on the federal and on the provincial level.

6.6. CAN SANCTIONS BE EXECUTED IMMEDIATELY OR ONLY AFTER ALL WAYS TO ASK FOR LEGAL PROTECTION HAVE BEEN EXHAUSTED?

An appeal against a penal decision (*Strafbescheid*) has suspensive effect (Section 64, para. 1 AVG). It is not possible to exclude the suspensive effect in administrative penal proceedings. If a penal decision imposes an imprisonment penalty, the suspensive effect is required by constitutional law (Article 3, para. 3 *Bundesverfassungsgesetz zum Schutz der persönlichen Freiheit*). Therefore sanctions cannot be executed immediately.

144 See the arguments pro and contra at Wiederin, *Die Zukunft des Verwaltungsstrafverfahrens*, p. 113 *et seq.*

Applications (*Beschwerden*) to the Administrative Court (*Verwaltungsgerichtshof*) do not have automatically a suspensive effect by virtue of law. The applicant, however, can make a motion to the Administrative Court that his appeal be adjudged suspensive effect, if this is not in conflict with coercive public interests and if, after considering all affected interests, the execution of the penalty would be a disproportionate disadvantage for the applicant (Section 30, para. 2 *Verwaltungsgerichtshofgesetz* – Act on the Administrative Court).[145]

6.7. WHAT POSSIBILITIES OF JUDICIAL REVIEW DOES THE JUDGE HAVE?

The UVSs always have to decide on the merits of the case. As opposed to other administrative decisions in administrative penal matters they are not supposed to refer the case back to a lower instance. The administrative courts (*Verwaltungsgerichte*) will also decide on the merits of the case in administrative penal matters (Article 130 para. 4 B-VG).

On the basis of an appeal by the accused or an appeal in favour of the accused, the appeals decision must not impose a higher penalty than the contested penal order (prohibition of *reformatio in peius*). Only extra fees can be imposed.

6.8. HOW THOROUGH CAN THIS REVIEW GET (FULL JURISDICTION OR LESS)?

As stated above, the UVSs have full review. They can affirm, change or quash the penal order, or declare the withdrawal of prosecution (Section 45 VStG). It can make an extraordinary mitigation of sentence (Section 20 VStG), pass an admonition instead of a punishment, or refrain from punishment without admonition. It can also, if a party different from the accused has appealed, and a *reformatio in peius* therefore is possible, deliver a penalty instead of refraining from punishment or impose a higher penalty.

The UVSs have full jurisdiction. However, they can only deal with the facts which are the object of the contested penal order, and only to the extent to which the penal order has been contested. If only a separable part of a penal order has been contested, the *Unabhängige Verwaltungssenat* may only adjudicate on the contested part; especially in the case that only the penalty, not the conviction was appealed. In this case the conviction obtains partial legal force.

---

145 See Adamovic/Funk, *Allgemeines Verwaltungsrecht*, 3rd ed., 1987, p. 453; Antoniolli/Koja, *Allgemeines Verwaltungsrecht*, 3rd ed., p. 851.

The *Unabhängige Verwaltungssenat* must not change the administrative offence, which was object of the penal order of the first instance. The power of decision insofar is limited by the offence which the authority of first instance has considered proved (Section 44a, Figure 1 VStG). However, according to jurisprudence it is not an inadmissible change of the legal qualification of an offence, if the offence is subsumed under another penal provision. It is also admissible that the *Unabhängige Verwaltungssenat* corrects mistakes in the conviction of first instance.

The control of the Administrative Court (as well as of the Constitutional Court) is limited to legal questions. Therefore the Administrative Court can only render illegal decisions (*Bescheide*) invalid and refer the case back without deciding in the case itself. The authority then is bound to the legal opinion of the Administrative Court.

6.9. DOES THIS KIND OF JUDICIAL REVIEW DIFFER FROM OTHER ADMINISTRATIVE DECISIONS? DOES IT MAKE A DIFFERENCE THAT CERTAIN SANCTIONING POWERS ALLOW ADMINISTRATIVE AUTHORITIES TO WEIGH INTERESTS AND HAVE POLITICAL SPACE OR NOT? HOW DO OBLIGATORY SANCTIONS (SANCTIONS THAT HAVE TO BE IMPOSED IF AN INFRINGEMENT HAS BEEN DISCOVERED) FIT INTO THIS PICTURE?

The judicial review is limited to the control of the application of law or of a discretionary power (*Ermessensentscheidungen*) within its legal limits. According to the Austrian case law and doctrine, both kinds of decisions are to be judged upon in the light of legality principle (*Legalitätsprinzip*, Articles 18 and 130, para. 2 B-VG). In regard of the latter (discretionary power, *Ermessensentscheidungen)* the review of administrative penal decisions is a paramount example as far as such a decision deals with sentencing powers and similar discretionary decisions. The main purpose of judicial review, in this case, is only to scrutinise the approach, rather than the result, of the authority taken to the Administrative Court. The court, therefore, does not take an own discretionary decision, but only has to find, whether the limits of discretion have been violated, or whether the authority has kept within the so-called sense of the law (see Article 130, para. 2 B-VG: '... *im Sinne des Gesetzes*...'). This constitutional rule has led the Constitutional Court to the view that a law is too vague and therefore unconstitutional, if it does not allow discerning the sense of the law. According to the Austrian system therefore there is no basic difference within legal requirements which call for interpretation, and discretionary rules.[146] But the Constitutional Court makes a difference depending on the subject ruled by the law. Whereas in economic law legal provisions are not supposed be so definite, in penal law or tax law the legal determination must be more precise.

7. NATIONAL AND EUROPEAN/INTERNATIONAL MUTUAL ASSISTANCE

7.1. COOPERATION BETWEEN NATIONAL AUTHORITIES IN RELATION TO THE IMPOSITION OF SANCTIONS

According to Article 22 *Bundes-Verfassungsgesetz* (B-VG) all organs of the federal state, of the provinces and the communities have the duty to mutual cooperation within their legal scope of activity. This duty to mutual assistance exceeds the scopes of the single powers of the state. Therefore this duty is also applied in the relationship between courts and the administration. Mutual assistance may only be demanded within the framework of the legal scope of activity of the requesting as well as the requested organ. An extension of the competencies of the requesting organ is inadmissible. Therefore the requested organ has to examine before giving administrative assistance, if the request of this assistance is covered by the competencies of the requesting organ.[147]

A special problem is the relationship between administrative assistance and official secrecy. Duties to give information within the framework of administrative assistance can be limited by legal provisions, *e.g.* provisions of the Act on Data Protection (*Datenschutzgesetz*). If an administrative organ is bound by official secrecy, information may only be given to another administrative organ, if this organ is also obliged to secrecy. But even in this case, rendering of information may not be admissible, if there are legitimate interests not to give information to another administrative organ. These can either be public interests or interests of a private party (*e.g.* the endangerment of the success of a probation service by passing on of certain information to the police). There is no general priority of administrative assistance over official secrecy. It is always necessary to consider all interests concerned.[148]

---

146 Öhlinger, *Verfassungsrecht*, 8th ed., p. 256 *et seq.*

147 Adamovic/Funk, *Allgemeines Verwaltungsrecht*, 3rd ed., p. 138 *et seq.*; Raschauer, *Allgemeines Verwaltungsrecht*, 3rd ed., 2009, p. 122.

148 Adamovic/Funk, *Allgemeines Verwaltungsrecht*, 3rd ed., p. 140.

7.2. ASSISTANCE OF A FOREIGN EU AUTHORITY TO A NATIONAL AUTHORITY

The mutual cooperation in administrative matters is covered by some international agreements. The main instruments on legal assistance in administrative matters are the European Convention on the Service Abroad of Documents relating to Administrative Matters[149] and the Agreement between the Republic of Austria and the Federal Republic of Germany on the Official and Legal Assistance in Administrative Matters.[150]

Austria signed the European Convention on the Service Abroad of Documents relating to Administrative Matters in 1979 and ratified it on November 24, 1982. It entered into force on 1 March 1983. The Convention at the moment applies in relation to seven other states (Belgium, Estonia, France, Germany, Italy, Luxemburg, Spain). The Convention does not relate to international official assistance as a whole, but only to the service of documents abroad.[151] It obliges the contracting states to afford mutual assistance to each other with regard to the service of documents relating to administrative matters (Article 1, para. 1). Austria declared at the time of its ratification that on the basis of reciprocity the Convention shall also apply to fiscal and criminal matters. The request for service shall be forwarded to the central authority of the requested state (Article 3). The central authorities in Austria are in respect of documents relating to matters concerning refugees, arms and weapons, or police regulations on aliens, for the whole federal territory, the Federal Ministry of the Interior, for all other documents for each of the Federal provinces (*Bundesländer*) the Office of the Province Government. Austria did not designate a forwarding authority to centralise the requests for service emanating from its own authorities and transmit them to the competent central authority abroad. Each authority in Austria has the possibility to contact the central authority of the requested state.[152] The central authority of the requested state shall effect service by means described in its national law for the service of documents in domestic actions upon persons who are within its territory, or by a particular method requested by the requesting authority, unless such a method is incompatible with the law of the requested state. The document may always be served by delivery to an addressee who accepts it voluntarily.

Most important is the agreement between Austria and Germany on mutual assistance in administrative matters which provides for general regulations on assistance in administrative proceedings as well as in administrative penal

149 *BGBl.* 1983/67.

150 Vertrag zwischen der Republik Österreich und der Bundesrepublik Deutschland über Amts- und Rechtshilfe in Verwaltungssachen, *BGBl.* 1990/526.

151 See Walter/Thienel, *Die österreichischen Verwaltungsverfahrensgesetze*, 17th ed., p. 480.

152 See the explanations to the Government Bill, 816 BlgNR 15. GP.

proceedings. According to Article 1, para. 1 the contracting states give administrative and legal assistance in public law proceedings of their administrative authorities, in Austrian administrative penal proceedings and in German administrative fining proceedings (*Bußgeldverfahren*) (if they are not pending in a court), in proceedings at the Administrative Court (*Verwaltungsgerichtshof*) in Austria and German courts of general administrative jurisdiction. Legal assistance is not given in fiscal and customs matters, in external economy affairs and tax consultancy affairs (Article 1, para. 2). For the purpose of administrative assistance between the contracting states, the administrative authorities and the courts of administrative jurisdiction can communicate directly with each other. If the requested authority is not competent to execute the application for legal assistance, it has to forward the request to the competent authority. Administrative and legal assistance is given according to the law of the requested state.

Administrative and legal assistance is not given, if it is not admissible according the legislation of the requested state or if the execution of the application would be appropriate to infringe the sovereignty, security, public order or other essential interests of the requested state (Article 4). The agreement refers to investigation measures, assistance in the execution and to the service of documents. Moreover it contains special provisions for matters of motoring. The contracting states give legal assistance by investigations including taking of evidence, hearing of concerned persons and interrogation of the accused, giving information including information out of the criminal records, sending of documents (Article 5).They also give legal assistance by giving information or sending documents from criminal and fining procedures at the court.

Austria and Germany give administrative aid by the execution of public law pecuniary claims – including the fines of more than €25, which are imposed by Austrian administrative penal decisions or penal decrees or by German administrative authorities, moreover by the withdrawal of documents, which are issued by the requesting state. Imprisonment as penal sanction is excluded (Article 6, para. 1). Since imprisonment sentences are possible according to Austrian administrative penal law, in those cases legal assistance is not given by German authorities. Together with the request for execution the requesting authority has to send a copy of the title of execution or of the penal order, on which the finality must be confirmed by the requesting authority. With respect to the execution, such penal orders are treated like orders by authorities of the requested state.

If there are rejections against the admissibility or the mode of execution, the competent authority of the requested state has to decide. Rejections against the existence, the amount or the executability of the claim to execute must be handled by the requesting authority.

According to Article 10 of the Agreement, documents are directly transmitted by the post according to the provisions applying to the postal service between the contracting states. If the service cannot be made directly by the post or if this is not appropriate, the competent authority in the other contracting state must be requested to arrange the service pursued by the way of administrative assistance.

The special provisions on matters of motoring concern the withdrawal of driving licences and the removal of vehicle documents and registration numbers. A driving licence, which is issued in the other contracting state, is taken away, if the other contracting state requests the execution of a decision on the withdrawal of a driving licence; if the other contracting state requests the transmission of the driving licence for the purpose of registrations by the authority, the right to use the driving licence is deprived. Under similar conditions the removal of vehicle documents and registration numbers in the other contracting state is possible.

Although the agreement between Austria and Germany on mutual assistance in administrative matters exists, in the practice of execution of decisions problems occurred in the other state. From an Austrian point of view, the main problem is that fines cannot be executed in Germany, if the perpetrator of an administrative offence is unknown and must be investigated. In Austria, the *Kraftfahrgesetz* (Motor Vehicle Act) contains a provision which obliges the car owner to give information about the car driver in the moment of the administrative offence to the authorities which enable them to prosecute the perpetrator of the administrative offence (Section 103, para. 2).[153] If the information is not given, this is an administrative offence. In 1985[154] the Austrian Constitutional Court declared this provision unconstitutional and annulled it because of an infringement upon the equality principle, because the car owner has no right to refuse to give evidence, which was seen as a problem of the prohibition of self-incrimination. Consequently, the Austrian legislator passed a new provision in the status of constitutional law which explicitly states that the rights to refuse to give evidence stand back to the competence of the authorities to demand such information (Section 103, para. 2 last sentence). If a German driver, who commits an administrative offence in Austria, is unknown, the German authorities deny giving legal assistance to find the perpetrator, because in Germany the obligation to give information on the identity of the car driver is a violation of the prohibition of self-incrimination. Therefore, if the perpetrator is unknown, it is difficult to execute the administrative fines imposed due to violations of the traffic law despite of the existence of a bilateral treaty.

153 See Sprinzel, 'Verfahrensfragen des §103 Abs 2 KFG', *ZVR* 2001, 279.
154 Constitutional Court 8 March 1985, G 149/84, *ZVR* 1985/137.

Apart from Germany there are no other bilateral treaties on the mutual assistance in administrative matters. Therefore sanctions against foreigners except for Germans, who infringe administrative penal provisions, can only be punished, if they are stopped in Austria or have a residency in Austria or if FD 2005/214/JHA is applicable.

Until now, Austria has not signed and ratified the European Convention on the Obtaining Abroad of Information and Evidence in Administrative Matters from 15 March 1978. The Agreement on Cooperation in Proceedings for Road Traffic Offences and the Enforcement of Financial Penalties imposed in respect thereof[155] has neither been ratified by the Austrian parliament[156], although it would be a helpful instrument for the cooperation between the members of the Schengen Convention in a practically very important field of administrative penal law. Due to the Austrian doctrine the roots for problems in cooperation in administrative penal matters are seen in the considerable differences of legal traffic provisions and the special national provisions on the execution and in the protection of the defence rights of the citizens.[157]

7.3. FRAMEWORK DECISION 2005/214/JHA

On 24 February 2005 the Framework Decision 2005/214/JHA on the application of mutual recognition of financial penalties was passed in the Council.[158] The Framework Decision extends the principle of mutual recognition to financial penalties imposed by judicial or administrative authorities for the purpose of facilitating the enforcement of such penalties in another Member State than the State in which the penalties are imposed. The Framework Decision enables the competent authorities in the issuing state to transmit a decision or a certified copy of it directly to the competent authority in the executing state (Article 4). The competent authorities in the executing state recognise a decision which has been transmitted in accordance with the provisions of the Framework decision without any further formality being required and shall forthwith take all the necessary measures for its execution, unless the competent authority decides to invoke one of the grounds for non-recognition or non-execution provided for in Article 7 of the Framework Decision (Article 6). Article 5 contains a list of

155 OJ 2000 No. L 239, p. 428.

156 Compare Hauptfleisch/Zelenke, 'Die gegenseitige Vollstreckung von Geldstrafen in Europa', *ZVR* 2004/90.

157 Hauptfleisch/Zelenke, *ZVR* 2004/90.

158 Referring to the proposal see Jansen, 'The Systems of International Cooperation in the Administrative and Criminal Matters in Relation to Regulation EC 1/2003', in: Dannecker/Jansen (eds.), *Competition Law Sanctioning in the European Union*, p. 257 (299 *et seq.*).

offences – similar to the Framework decision on the European Arrest Warrant –, where the principle of double criminality shall not be applied.

The Framework Decision 2005/214/JHA was implemented into the Austrian legislation by several legal acts: For decisions of other Member States' courts imposing a financial penalty the implementation was made by introducing a new chapter in a law which contains all regulations on mutual recognition instruments in criminal law, called the *Bundesgesetz über die justizielle Zusammenarbeit in Strafsachen mit den Mitgliedstaaten der Europäischen Union* (EU-JZG; Federal Act on the judicial cooperation in criminal matters with the Member States of the European Union).[159] The implementation in the EU-JZG came into force on 1 July 2007.

At the beginning of the transposition procedure it was not clear, whether the Framework Decision 2005/214 should be transposed for criminal fines and administrative fines together or separately. At first, it was planned to transpose them together in the EU-JZG and give the courts the competence to execute also the administrative fines.[160] It was argued that a separate transposition would be more complicated and would bring the danger that decisions by foreign administrative authorities would be recognised more easily than court decisions in the same affair. The courts would be more appropriate as authorities of legal assistance than administrative authorities. This solution was preferred by the federal provinces *(Bundesländer)* and by the constitutional office of the Federal Chancellery. Nevertheless, for political reasons finally the transposition was carried out separately. As reason it was mentioned that these administrative authorities are penal and law enforcement authorities in administrative penal matters and are used to give legal assistance to foreign authorities.[161]

Therefore, for decisions of other Member States' administrative authorities the Framework Decision was transposed by a specific act, the *Bundesgesetz über die Vollstreckung von Geldstrafen und Geldbußen von Verwaltungsbehörden im Rahmen der Europäischen Union* (*EU-Verwaltungsstrafvollstreckungsgesetz* – EU-VStVG/Federal Act on the execution of financial penalties imposed by administrative authorities of other EU Member States)[162].[163] The EU-VStVG came into force on 1 March 2008.[164]

---

159 *Bundesgesetzblatt* I 2007 No. 38.

160 See Wiederin, *Die Zukunft des Verwaltungsstrafverfahrens*, p. 141 *et seq.*

161 Kert, in: Vernimmen-Van Tiggelen/Surano/Weyembergh (eds.), *The future of mutual recognition in criminal matters in the European Union*, p. 30.

162 *Bundesgesetzblatt* I 2008 No. 3.

163 See Raschauer/Wessely, 'Zum EU-Verwaltungsvollstreckungsgesetz (EU-VStVG)', *ÖJZ* 2008, p. 167 *et seq.*

164 See Kert, 'The implementation and application of mutual recognition instruments in Austria', in: Vernimmen-Van Tiggelen/Surano/Weyembergh (eds.), *The future of mutual recognition in criminal matters in the European Union*, p. 17 (29).

During the legislation process of the EU-VStVG it was discussed, whether decisions of tax and customs authorities should also be included in the scope of the EU-VStVG. Finally, the decisions of these authorities were not taken into the EU-VStVG (see Section 1 EU-VStVG), because in tax and customs law the authorities have a very special position and structure and penalties are imposed by special fiscal penal authorities (*Finanzstrafbehörden*). (Administrative) fines imposed due to fiscal offences therefore do not fall into the scope of application of the EU-VStVG (Section 1 EU-VStVG). To implement the Framework Decision 2005/214 also with regard to fines imposed by tax and customs authorities, in March 2009 an Act to implement the Framework Decision on the application of the principle of mutual recognition to financial penalties in the area of administrative fiscal penal law (*Bundesgesetz zur Durchführung des Rahmenbeschlusses über die Anwendung des Grundsatzes der gegenseitigen Anerkennung von Geldstrafen und Geldbußen im Bereich des verwaltungsbehördlichen Finanzstrafverfahrens – EU-Finanzvollstreckungsgesetz*)[165] was passed.[166]

In the legislation process of the EU-VStVG it was demanded by some experts that the Austrian executing authority has to issue an official notice (*Bescheid*) before executing the fine. Since this would be a new decision by an Austrian authority and therefore contravene the principle of mutual recognition, this idea was not put into law. The EU-VStVG provides for a double-stage proceeding. In a first stage the formal requirements (jurisdiction, admissibility of execution). In the second stage, for which it is provided that before the enforcement of the fine, the executing authority has to demand payment from the punished persons in an informal way and give them the opportunity to pay the amount or to comment to potential grounds for refusal of the execution of the decision.[167] This duty is limited to cases in which the letter can be delivered within Austria (Section 5, para. 5 EU-VStVG).

According to Article 10 of the Framework Decision alternative sanctions, including custodial sanctions, may be applied by the executing State, where it is not possible to enforce a decision. The EU-VStVG does not provide for imprisonment in default of payment. This was quite clear, since this would have caused problems with Article 6 ECHR. It would have been necessary to involve an independent tribunal, which would have caused competence problems between the state and the federal provinces due to the structure of the Austrian administrative penal procedure.

The provisions of dual criminality were transposed as reasons for refusal: The executing authority can refuse the execution of the decision, if the decision refers to an act which is not punishable under Austrian legislation, unless the offence

165 Ministerial draft bill, 232 BlgNR 23. GP p. 1.

166 Kert, in: Vernimmen-Van Tiggelen/Surano/Weyembergh (eds.), *The future of mutual recognition in criminal matters in the European Union*, p. 31.

167 See Raschauer/Wessely, *ÖJZ* 2008, p. 171.

falls into one of the categories listed in the framework decisions' list of offences where a dual criminality is not necessary (Section 5, para. 2, Figure 3 EU-VStVG; Section 52a, para. 1, Figure 3 EU-JZG).[168] These lists are attached to the laws and completely correspond with the list in Article 5, para. 1 Framework Decision. This means that Austria has implemented dual criminality in that way that the lack of dual criminality is a ground of inadmissibility, if the offence does not fall into one of the categories of the list.

In Austrian doctrine it has been doubted, that the Framework Decision obliges other EU Member States to recognise Austrian penal decisions by administrative authorities, since Austrian legislation does not provide for an opportunity to have the case tried by a court having jurisdiction in particular in criminal matters as required in Article 1 Framework Decision 2005/214. Even if the UVSs are seen as tribunals within the meaning of the ECHR and as courts within the meaning of the Framework Decision, they certainly have no genuine jurisdiction in particular in criminal matters. Following this interpretation of Article 1 Framework Decision 2005/214 the requirements of Article 1 Framework Decision 2005/214 are not fulfilled by the Austrian administrative penal law system.[169] The Austrian legislator did not follow this interpretation; it would not be necessary that the court has an original jurisdiction in criminal matters. According to the explanations to the government bill Article 1 Framework Decision 2005/214 only means that the court may also have jurisdiction in other than criminal matters.[170]

7.4. AGREEMENT BETWEEN AUSTRIA AND GERMANY ON LEGAL PROTECTION AND MUTUAL ASSISTANCE IN FISCAL MATTERS

An agreement on legal protection and mutual assistance in fiscal matters[171] between Austria and Germany exists. According to this agreement both states are obliged to give legal assistance in all fiscal matters, in the investigation, determination and appeals proceeding, in the security and in the execution proceeding and in the administrative penal proceeding on the basis of mutuality. Mutual assistance is not given, if the requested state has good reasons for believing that the legal assistance could endanger essential interests of the

168 Compare *Medigovic*, 'Die gegenseitige Anerkennung von vermögensrechlichen Sanktionen innerhalb der EU und ihre Umsetzung im österreichischen Justizstrafrecht', *Juristische Blätter* 2008, p. 69 (75).

169 Wiederin, *Die Zukunft des Verwaltungsstrafverfahrens*, p. 132.

170 Explanations to the Government Bill, 46 BlgNR 23. GP, p. 2; see also Raschauer/Wessely, *ÖJZ* 2008, p. 168.

171 Vertrag zwischen der Republik Österreich und der Bundesrepublik Deutschland über Rechtsschutz und Rechtshilfe in Abgabensachen, *BGBl.* 1955/249.

requested state. Searches, seizures, arrests and the execution of imprisonment sentences are excluded from the mutual assistance.

8. ACTUAL IMPORTANCE IN PRACTICE

In practice fines are the most important sanctions. Primarily imposed imprisonment sentences are rare in administrative penal law. But imprisonment in default of payment is applied quite often, especially if poor people cannot pay for an administrative fine.

Among other administrative sanctions, which are not penalties, the withdrawal of driving licenses, mainly as a consequence of certain behaviour within or outside traffic is of great importance. The withdrawal of other permissions (*e.g.* trade permission) is – in particular in connection with criminal convictions – a sanction which is used by the authorities.

BIBLIOGRAPHY

Adamovic, Ludwig and Funk, Bernd-Christian, *Allgemeines Verwaltungsrecht*, 3rd ed., Vienna – New York, 1987.

Antoniolli, Walter and Koja, Friedrich, *Allgemeines Verwaltungsrecht*, 3rd ed., Vienna 1986.

Arnold, Wolf-Dieter, 'Zur neuerlichen Neufassung des §9 GebG', *NZ* 1987, 196.

Bachler, 'Die allgemeine Mitwirkung der Parteien im Verwaltungsverfahren – "Pflicht" oder "Recht"?', *ÖJZ* 1995, 401.

Barfuß, Walter, 'Verrechtlichung des Verwaltungsstrafverfahrens', *AnwBl* 1998, 218.

Berka, Walter, *Die Grundrechte*, Vienna, 1999.

Burgstaller, Manfred, 'Aktuelle Wandlungen im Grundverständnis des Strafrechts', *JBl* 1996, 362.

Foregger, Egmont and Nowakowski,Friedrich ('ds.), *Wiener Kommentar zum Strafgesetzbuch*, 1st ed., 1981.

Frank, Erich, 'Die Entziehung der Lenkberechtigung – Die fehlende Nebenstrafe', *ZVR* 2000, 326.

Frowein, Jochen and Peukert, Wolfgang, *EMRK-Kommentar*, 3rd ed., Kehl – Straßburg – Arlington, 2009.

Fuchs, Helmut, *Österreichisches Strafrecht Allgemeiner Teil* I, 7th ed., Vienna, 2008.

Fuchs, Helmut and Ratz, Eckart (eds.), *Wiener Kommentar zur Strafprozessordnung*, loose leaf, Vienna, 2003.

Glocknitzer, Harald, *UFS – unbekanntes Wesen? – Reform. Seit Jahresbeginn gibt es den Unabhängigen Finanzsenat (UFS) – Überblick zu Funktion und Arbeitsweise der neuen Instanz*, persaldo 2003 H 1, 19.

Grabenwarter, Christoph, 'Entscheidungsbesprechung', *Juristische Blätter* 1997, 577.

Grabenwarter, Christoph, 'Grundrechtsfragen des Finanzstrafrechts', in: Leitner, Roman (ed.), *Aktuelles zum Finanzstrafrecht – Beiträge zur Finanzstrafrechtlichen Tagung Linz*,1998, Vienna, 1999, p. 111.

Grabenwarter, Christoph and Geppert, Stefan, 'Die Bedeutung des Art 6 MRK für die Verhängung von Ordnungs- und Mutwillensstrafen', *JBl* 1996, 159.

Grabenwarter, Christoph and Holoubek, Michael, 'Demokratie, Rechtsstaat und Kollegialbehörden mit richterlichem Einschlag – Zu den verfassungsrechtlichen Grenzen der Einrichtung von Kollegialbehörden nach Art. 20 Abs 2 und Art 133 Z 4 B-VG', *ZfV* 2000/520.

Giese, Karim, in: Grabenwarter, Christoph and Thienel, Rudolf (eds.), *Kontinuität und Wandel der EMRK*, Vienna,1998.

Grubmann (ed.), *Das österreichische Kraftfahrrecht*, Vol. II. *Kraftfahrgesetz*, Vienna, 1995.

Harbich, 'Ausgewählte Themen aus dem Allgemeinen Teil des Finanz- und Justizstrafrechts', *RZ* 1979, 1, 25, 45

Hattenberger, Doris, 'Verwaltungsstrafrecht und Arbeitszeitrecht', in: Resch, Reinhard (ed.), *Arbeitszeitrecht – Rechtsgrundlagen und Gestaltungsformen, Sanktionen, Arbeitsteilzeit*, Vienna, 2001.

Hauer, Wolfgang and Leukauf, Otto, *Handbuch des österreichischen Verwaltungsverfahrens*, 6th ed., Vienna, 2004, Ergänzungsband 2009.

Hauptfleisch, Hugo and Zelenke, Ursula, 'Die gegenseitige Vollstreckung von Geldstrafen in Europa', *ZVR* 2004/90

Heidinger, Gerald, 'Rechtsstaat und Rückwirkungsverbot im Steuerrecht', *ÖStZ* 1995, 95.

Höpfel, Frank and Kert, Robert, 'Country Analysis – Austria', in: Dannecker and Jansen (eds.), *Competition Law Sanctioning in the European Union*, 2004, p. 321.

Höpfel, Frank and Ratz, Eckart (eds.), *Wiener Kommentar zum Strafgesetzbuch*, 2nd ed., Vienna, 1999.

Jansen, Oswald, 'The Systems of International Cooperation in the Administrative and Criminal Matters in Relation to Regulation EC 1/2003', in: Dannecker, Gerhard and Jansen, Oswald (eds.), *Competition Law Sanctioning in the European Union*, p. 257.

Kaltenegger, Armin and Koller, Thomas, *Entziehung der Lenkberechtigung und Lenkverbot*, Vienna, 2003.

Karollus, 'Die Haftung für fremde Geldstrafen und sonstige in Geld bemessene Unrechtsfolgen', Dissertation University of Vienna, 1987.

Kelsen, Hans, *Allgemeine Theorie der Normen* (edited by Ringhofer, Kurt and Walter, Robert), Vienna, 1979

Kelsen, Hans, *Reine Rechtslehre*, 2nd ed., Vienna, 1960 (Reprint 1992).

Kert, Robert, 'Die Sanktionierung von Verstößen gegen Gemeinschaftsrecht durch nationales Strafrecht am Beispiel des Lebensmittelstrafrechts', *JBl* 1999, 87.

Kert, Robert, 'Verbandsverantwortlichkeit und Finanzstrafrecht', in: Leitner, Roman (ed.), *Finanzstrafrecht 2006*, Vienna, 2007, p. 9.

Kert, Robert, 'National report of Austria', in: White, Simone (ed.), *Procurement and Organised Crime – An EU-wide study*, London, 2000, p. 83.

Kert, Robert, 'The implementation and application of mutual recognition instruments in Austria', in: Vernimmen-Van Tiggelen, Surano and Weyembergh (eds.), *The future of mutual recognition in criminal matters in the European Union*, Brussels, 2009, p. 17.

Kienapfel, Diethelm, Höpfel, Frank, and Kert, Robert, *Grundriss des österreichischen Strafrechts – Allgemeiner Teil*, 14th ed., Vienna, 2013.

Korinek, Karl and Holoubek, Michael (ed.), *Österreichisches Bundesverfassungsrecht. Kommentar* (Loseblattsammlung), Vienna/New York, 1999.

Leitner, Toifl and Brandl, *Österreichisches Finanzstrafrecht*, 3rd ed., 2008.

Mayer, Heinz, *Das österreichische Bundesverfassungsrecht, Manzscher Kurzkommentar*, 4th ed., Vienna, 2007.

Medigovic, Ursula, 'Die gegenseitige Anerkennung von vermögensrechtlichen Sanktionen innerhalb der EU und ihre Umsetzung im österreichischen Justizstrafrecht', *Juristische Blätter* 2008, p. 69.

Miklau, Roland, 'Zur Funktion der Geldstrafe – Ist die Höhe der Strafdrohung ein taugliches Abgrenzungskriterium zwischen dem Justiz- und dem Verwaltungsstrafrecht?', *ÖJZ* 1991, 361.

Öhlinger, Theo, 'Die Geldstrafe im Verwaltungsstrafrecht – Verfassungsrechtliche Grenzen gegenüber dem Justizstrafrecht', *ÖJZ* 1991, 217.

Öhlinger, Theo, *Verfassungsrecht*, 8th ed., Vienna, 2009.

Raschauer, Bernhard, *Allgemeines Verwaltungsrecht*, 3rd ed., Vienna/New York, 2009.

Raschauer, Nicolas and Wessely, Wolfgang, *Verwaltungsstrafrecht – Allgemeiner Teil*, Vienna/Graz, 2005.

Raschauer, Nicolas and Wessely, Wolfgang, 'Zum EU-Verwaltungsvollstreckungsgesetz (EU-VStVG)', *ÖJZ* 2008, p. 167.

Renner, 'Prinzipien der neuen Behörde und des "neuen Abgabenberufungsverfahrens', *SWK* 2003, 487.

Schwaighofer, Klaus, 'Überlegungen zur Reichweite des innerstaatlichen "Doppelbestrafungsverbots" nach Art. 4 Abs 1 7. ZPMRK', *ÖJZ* 2005/10.

Sprinzel, Günter, 'Verfahrensfragen des §103 Abs 2 KFG', *ZVR* 2001, 279.

Stadlmayer, Gabriele, 'Ist die Abschaffung des Kumulationsprinzips im Verwaltungsstrafrecht möglich?', *ZVR* 1980, 65.

Thienel, Rudolf, *Das Verfahren der Verwaltungssenate*, 2nd ed., Vienna, 1992.

Thienel, Rudolf, *Verwaltungsverfahrensrecht*, 5th ed. Vienna, 2009.

Thienel, Rudolf and Hauenschild, Herwig, 'Verfassungsrechtliches "ne bis in idem" und seine Auswirkungen auf das Verhältnis von Justiz- und Verwaltungsstrafverfahren', *JBl* 2004, 69.

Walter, Robert and Mayer, Heinz, *Verwaltungsverfahrensrecht*, 8th ed., Vienna, 2003.

Walter, Robert, Mayer, Heinz and Kucsko-Stadlmayer Gabriele, *Grundriss des österreichischen Bundesverfassungsrecht*, 10th ed., Vienna, 2007.

Walter, Robert and Thienel, Rudolf, *Die österreichischen Verwaltungsverfahrensgesetze*, 17th ed. Vienna, 2008.

Walter, Robert and Thienel, Rudolf, *Die österreichischen Verwaltungsverfahrensgesetze*, Vol. I, 2nd ed., Vienna, 1998.

Walter, Robert and Thienel, Rudolf, *Die österreichischen Verwaltungsverfahrensgesetze*, Vol. II, 2nd ed., Vienna, 2000.

Wiederin, Ewald, *Die Zukunft des Verwaltungsstrafrechts, 16. Österreichischer Juristentag*, Vol. III, Vienna, 2006.

Winkler, Günther, 'Das österreichische Konzept der Gewaltentrennung in Recht und Wirklichkeit', in: Winkler, Günther (ed.), *Orientierungen im öffentlichen Leben*, Vienna, 1979, p. 229.
Winkler, Günther, 'Führerscheinentzug und gerichtliche Haftstrafe - Rechtsfragen der Einrechnung gerichtlicher Haftstrafen in die Dauer einer vorläufigen Entziehung von Fahrzeuglenkerberechtigungen nach §73 und §74 KFG 1967', *JAP* 1996/97, 150.
Zellenberg, Ulrich, 'Der Gewerbezugang nach der Gewerberechtsnovelle 1992', *ZfV* 2003/955.

III. COUNTRY ANALYSIS – BELGIUM

Johan Put and Ken Andries

1. INTRODUCTION

This contribution aims to present a general survey of the Belgian legal system concerning administrative sanctions.

First of all, some general aspects of the Belgian constitutional, judicial and administrative system are outlined, in order to produce a better understanding of the place of administrative sanctions and the systems of legal protection to counter them. Then follows the notion and different forms of administrative sanctions, ending with the legal protection against administrative sanctions. This extensive section deals with the general principles applicable to administrative sanctions, administrative sanction systems and the judicial control on the imposition of administrative sanctions.

2. THE BELGIAN CONSTITUTIONAL, JUDICIAL AND ADMINISTRATIVE SYSTEM

2.1. BELGIUM, A FEDERAL STATE

2.1.1. General overview

Several state reforms (in 1970, 1980–83, 1988–89, 1993–94, 2001 and 2011) have changed Belgium from a unitarian state into the vastly more complex structure of a federal state.[1] The Constitution[2] describes this as follows:

1 See extensively A. Alen, *Handboek van het Belgisch staatsrecht* [*Manual of Belgian public law*], Deurne, Kluwer, 1995, 28–34 and 329; A. Alen and K. Muylle, *Handboek van het Belgisch staatsrecht* [*Manual of Belgian public law*], Mechelen, Kluwer, 2011, 287-301; G. Craenen, *The Institutions of Federal Belgium: an introduction to Belgian public law*, Leuven, Acco, 2001, 175 p.; F. Delpérée, *Le droit constitutionnel de la Belgique* [*The constitutional law of Belgium*], Brussels, Bruylant, 2000, 305–875; M. Uyttendaele, *Précis de droit constitutionnel Belge, regard sur un système institutionnel paradoxal* [*Constitutional law of Belgium, a paradoxical institutional system*], Brussels, Bruylant, 2001, 986 p.

2 Coordinated Belgian Constitution of 17 February 1994.

Art. 1
Belgium is a Federal State made up of communities and regions.

Art. 2
Belgium is made up of three communities: The French Community, the Flemish Community and the German Community.

Art. 3
Belgium is made up of three regions: The Walloon region, the Flemish region and the Brussels region.

Art. 4
Belgium has four linguistic regions: The French-speaking region, the Dutch-speaking region, the bilingual region of Brussels Capital and the German-speaking region. [...]

The Federal State, the Communities and the Regions are on an equal footing.[3] Their distinction lies in the powers and responsibilities with which they have been attributed. The legislation of the Federal State takes the form of an 'Act', that of the Communities and Regions is called a 'decree', except for the Brussels Region where it is called an 'ordinance'.[4]

The balance of power between the different legislators is traditionally ensured through the participation of the local states in a separate federal legislative chamber. This local influence over the federal decision-making process prevents the federal state from unilaterally revising the Constitution.[5] However, the Belgian Senate has only been partially transformed into such a representative organ for the 'defederalised' states.[6] This means that the local states can only exert a limited amount of influence over any revisions to the Constitution. Local states cannot have a constitution of their own either.[7] Instead, a certain level of protection regarding local state responsibilities is offered by so-called 'Special Acts', which are federal acts that require a special majority.[8]

3 P. Peeters, 'The federal structure: kingdom, regions and communities', in: G. Craenen (ed.), *The Institutions of Federal Belgium: an introduction to Belgian public law*, Leuven, Acco, 2001, 63.

4 Based on Article 127 of the Constitution for the Communities and Article 134 for the Regions. The term ordinance is prescribed by Articles 4, 7 and 9 Special Act of 12 January 1989.

5 A. Alen, *Handboek van het Belgisch staatsrecht* [*Manual of Belgian public law*], *o.c.*, 324–325.

6 Articles 67, §1, 3° and 4° Constitution.

7 P. Peeters, 'The federal structure: kingdom, regions and communities', *l.c.*, 65.

8 Article 4, §3 Constitution. The chambers are divided into a Dutch and French language group. A special majority requires a majority of members in both groups to be present and a two-thirds majority in both groups to vote in favour. This method neutralises the risk of a numerically superior group dominating the federal state.

2.1.2. The division of responsibilities

The division of responsibilities between the federal state, the Communities and the Regions has been regulated by the Constitution[9] and in the Special Act of 8 August 1980 concerning the Reform of the Institutions (hereafter: SARI).[10] The responsibilities of the Communities are mainly related to language, culture and assistance to persons, whereas the Regions have been attributed various local and economical responsibilities.[11] The Federal State, while its dominance has been greatly reduced in favour of the Communities and Regions, is still an entity where many crucial responsibilities are centralised, like defence, foreign affairs, social security and the judicial organisation. Moreover, for the moment the residuary responsibilities are still located at the federal level.[12]

The principle behind the attribution of responsibilities in Belgium is that each entity is exclusively competent in a particular matter.[13] Given the way in which the responsibilities have been attributed, conflicts of responsibilities can nonetheless arise. In this view, the theory of implied powers, as implemented by Article 10 SARI, is very important. This article authorises the Communities and Regions to exceed the limit of their attributed responsibilities, provided that the legislation they thereby create is *necessary* for exercising one of their own responsibilities. This implies that there is a sufficiently close link between the explicit 'communitarian' or regional responsibility and the exclusive federal one. The Belgian Constitutional Court[14] imposes two more conditions for the application of Article 10 SARI[15]: 1) the matter must be suitable for a differentiated regulation and 2) the effect on the federal authority can only be marginal.

---

9 Concerning the Communities: Articles 127–133; concerning the Regions: Articles 39 and 134, which authorise the attribution of responsibilities via a Special Act.

10 For Brussels there is the Special Act of 12 January 1989 concerning the Brussels Institutions.

11 A. Alen, *Handboek van het Belgisch staatsrecht* [*Manual of Belgian public law*], *o.c.*, 363–385.

12 This will change when Article 35 of the Constitution will enter into force. From that moment onwards, the Federal State will only be responsible for those matters explicitly enumerated. At present, the entry into force of Article 35 is not expected in the near future.
See also F. Delpérée and A. Alen, 'De residuaire bevoegdheden [the residuary responsibilities]', *Rechtskundig Weekblad* [*Legal Weekly*] 1991-92, 345–349.

13 Court of Arbitration No. 7/85, 20 December 1985, *Belgisch Staatsblad* [*Belgian Bulletin of Acts and Decrees*] 21 January 1986, consideration 6.B.2.
A. Alen, *Handboek van het Belgisch staatsrecht* [*Manual of Belgian public law*], *o.c.*, 340; P. Peeters, 'The federal structure: kingdom, regions and communities', *l.c.*, 63–64.

14 Prior to the Law of 7 May 2007 (*Belgian Bulletin of Acts and Decrees* 8 May 2007) the Constitutional Court was known as the Court of Arbitration. Hereafter references to decisions taken prior to this date will refer to the designation which was applicable at the time.

15 See for example: Court of Arbitration No. 32/92, 23 April 1992, *Belgian Bulletin of Acts and Decrees* 30 May 1992, consideration B.3.6.

The Constitutional Court has the judicial authority to act as an arbiter when any dispute concerning the division of responsibilities arises.[16]

2.1.3. Responsibilities with regard to administrative and criminal sanctions

There has been no explicit attribution of responsibilities regarding the authority to regulate, organise or impose administrative sanctions.[17] Article 11 SARI authorises the Communities and Regions to enact criminal sanctions, within certain parameters[18], but this only applies to (classic) sanctions of criminal law.[19] The Constitutional Court has determined that the attribution of responsibilities to the Communities and Regions also implies an inherent authority to impose sanctions for non-compliance with respect to legislation based on those responsibilities.[20]

Another point of interest is the matter of the division of responsibilities between the legislative and the executive branch. The Constitutional Court has clarified that when the executive branch has been delegated the authority – in accordance with Articles 10, 11, 170 and 172 of the Constitution – to order a particular (fiscal) contribution, the authority to impose an administrative fine for non-compliance has been implicitly delegated as well.[21]

2.2. THE SYSTEM OF LEGAL PROTECTION AGAINST SANCTIONS

2.2.1. Constitution

Article 12, §2 of the Constitution states that no one can be prosecuted except in cases provided for by law, and only in a manner prescribed by law. Article 14 states that no punishment can be created or applied except in pursuance of the law.[22]

---

16 Article 142 Constitution.

17 See J. Put, 'Naar een Kaderwet Administratieve Sancties [Towards a Framework Act on administrative sanctions]', *Rechtskundig Weekblad* [*Legal Weekly*] 2005–06, 321–336.

18 A. Alen, *Handboek van het Belgisch staatsrecht* [*Manual of Belgian public law*], *o.c.*, 354–356.

19 Court of Arbitration No. 127/2000, 6 December 2000, B.13.5. See also Constitutional Court No. 151/2007, 12 December 2007, B.12.4 and Court of Arbitration No. 18/1995, 2 March 1995, B.3.

20 Court of Arbitration No. 125/2002, 10 July 2002, *Belgian Bulletin of Acts and Decrees* 8 November 2002, consideration B.6.1; Court of Arbitration No. 170/2002, 27 November 2002, *Belgian Bulletin of Acts and Decrees* 28 February 2003, consideration B.6.1 and Court of Arbitration No. 18/95, 2 March 1995, *Belgian Bulletin of Acts and Decrees* 11 May 1995, consideration B.2 (administrative fine).

21 Court of Arbitration No. 88/2004, 19 May 2004, consideration B.13.3.

22 In spite of the wording of these articles, which implies the retention of these responsibilities on the federal level, Article 11 SARI and the Court of Arbitration have authorised the Regions and Communities to penalise infractions on their own legislation and to determine the level

These articles are based on the adage *nullum crimen, nulla poena sine lege* and the principle of legality.[23] These articles form the Constitutional basis of the Belgian Penal Code, the Criminal Procedure Code and the various specific criminal acts.

While having been the subject of repeated debate in legal literature, the common view is that these articles are only applicable to criminal and not to administrative sanctions[24], at least not those without a punitive character.[25]

2.2.2. Organisation of judicial powers (sensu lato)

Civil and Political rights (Articles 144–145 Constitution)

Articles 144[26] and 145[27] of the Constitution provide the foundation for the distribution of competences between the 'ordinary' and the 'administrative' courts[28] respectively. The ordinary courts are exclusively competent to hear disputes concerning civil rights, and have – in principle – the competence to deliver judgement on political rights as well. The administrative courts, on the other hand, can – only – be given the competence to decide on political rights.[29] All subjective[30] rights in the Belgian legal system are either civil or political.[31] The Court of Cassation has rejected the notion of a third category of so-called

---

of punishment (A. Alen, *Handboek van het Belgisch staatsrecht* [*Manual of Belgian public law*], *o.c.*, 354).

23 A. Alen, *Handboek van het Belgisch staatsrecht* [*Manual of Belgian public law*], *o.c.*, 354, 570.

24 Regarding Article 14 Constitution: Court of Arbitration Nos. 2/94 and 3/94, 13 January 1994, *Belgian Bulletin of Acts and Decrees* 16 February 1994, considerations B.5.1 to B.5.3 (deciding that decisions to increase a tax (in the form of a fine) are inherent to the legislative authority to implement a tax and are not based on the principle of legality in criminal matters codified in Article 14 of the Constitution (former Article 9)). See J. Put, 'Rechtshandhaving door administratieve sancties in het recht [Law enforcement through administrative sanctions]', *Rechtskundig Weekblad* [*Legal Weekly*] 2001–2002, (1195) 1199.

25 Council of State No. 127.673, 2 February 2004, consideration 5.2.3.2; Council of State No. 134.860, 14 September 2004, consideration 5.3.2. See also *infra* concerning the principle of legality as a General Principle of Criminal Law.

26 Article 144: Courts have exclusive competence with respect to conflicts involving civil rights issues.

27 Article 145: Courts have competence with respect to conflicts involving political rights, save for the exceptions established by law.

28 A. Mast, J. Dujardin, M. Van Damme and J. Vande Lanotte, *Overzicht van het Belgisch administratief recht* [*Overview of Belgian administrative law*], Mechelen, Kluwer, 2002, 798.

29 *Ibid.*, 800.

30 Articles 144 and 145 are only applicable to subjective rights (A. Mast, J. Dujardin, M. Van Damme and J. Vande Lanotte, *o.c.*, 798). Subjective rights are rights where the objective rules in a particular case oblige the administration to take a particular action, without leaving any scope for any discretionary powers (Council of State, No. 13.450, 18 March 1969).

31 A. Mast, J. Dujardin, M. Van Damme and J. Vande Lanotte, *o.c.*, 799; A. Alen, *Handboek van het Belgisch staatsrecht* [*Manual of Belgian public law*], *o.c.*, 240–241; S. Lust, 'Administrative Law in Belgium', in: R. Seerden and F. Stroink (eds.), *Administrative Law of the European Union, its Member States and the United States*, Antwerp, Intersentia, 2007, 37.

'administrative rights', which were meant to fall outside the Constitutional framework.[32]

There is no distinct criterion in Belgian law to determine whether a right is civil or political. Alen states that the following rights are generally accepted to be civil rights: private relations between citizens, decisions concerning detention or imprisonment and the 'most fundamental rights and liberties'.[33] The right to vote (*ius suffragii*), the right to pay taxes (*ius tributi*), the right to join the armed forces (*ius militiae*) and the right to hold office (*ius honorum*) are traditionally seen as political rights.[34] The majority of legal authors and case law hold that the qualification of a right, as either civil or political, is a prerogative of the legislator.[35] As such, the authority to review these qualifications traditionally fell outside the competences of the judiciary. This approach, however, resulted in a circular reasoning: a right is political because the legislator has deemed it to be so, but the judiciary cannot review this decision ... because the legislator deems it to be a political right, resulting in the fact that it falls outside the scope of judicial authority. The Constitutional Court has criticised this *organic*[36] criterion and reserves the right to review the constitutionality of such decisions.[37]

Courts can only be created on the basis of – federal – legislation, according to Article 146 of the Constitution.[38] This article also contains a prohibition on creating 'extraordinary' entities with judicial powers. It aims to prevent tailor-made justice designed to benefit or harm particular individuals: all citizens in a similar situation should be judged in the same type of court.[39]

32 Court of Cassation 21 December 1956, *Pasicrisie* 1957, I, 430, with the opinion of Advocate General G. Van Der Meersch, commentary F. De Visschere; Court of Cassation 31 October 1963, *Pasicrisie* 1964, I, 233.

33 A. Alen, *Handboek van het Belgisch staatsrecht* [*Manual of Belgian public law*], *o.c.*, 239.

34 A. Mast, J. Dujardin, M. Van Damme and J. Vande Lanotte, *o.c.*, 802, footnote 24; S. Lust, *l.c.*, 38.

35 A. Alen, *Handboek van het Belgisch staatsrecht* [*Manual of Belgian public law*], *o.c.*, 239; A. Mast, J. Dujardin, M. Van Damme and J. Vande Lanotte, *o.c.*, 801; P. Peeters, 'The Judiciary', in: G. Craenen (ed.), *The Institutions of Federal Belgium*, Leuven, Acco, 2001, 111.

36 A. Alen, *Handboek van het Belgisch staatsrecht* [*Manual of Belgian public law*], *o.c.*, 239; A. Mast, J. Dujardin, M. Van Damme and J. Vande Lanotte, *o.c.*, 802.

37 Court of Arbitration No. 14/97, 18 March 1997, *Belgian Bulletin of Acts and Decrees* 8 May 1997, considerations B.3 to B.5. C. Berx, *Rechtsbescherming van de burger tegen de overheid* [*Legal protection of the citizen against the government*]', Antwerp, Intersentia, 2000, 96. A decision to attribute certain rights to administrative courts – thereby labelling them as political – might, for example, be discriminatory. This introduces a substantive review.

38 Article 146: 'Under no circumstance may a court or contentious jurisdiction be established, other than on the sole basis of a law. Under no name may a commission or an extraordinary tribunal be created.'

39 A. Mast, J. Dujardin, M. Van Damme and J. Vande Lanotte, *o.c.*, 804.

The Court of Cassation has the authority to settle any dispute relating to the attribution of judicial competences, including conflicts of competence between ordinary and administrative courts.[40]

Organisation of ordinary courts and tribunals[41]

There are four Courts: the Court of Cassation[42], Court of Appeal (Articles 602 to 606 Judicial Code), Court of Assizes and the Labour Court (Article 607 Judicial Code). The term 'court' signifies a higher judicial body. The 'tribunals' are on a lower scale within the hierarchy. On the level of the judicial districts, there are the tribunal of first instance (Articles 568 to 572 Judicial Code)[43], the commerce tribunal (Articles 573 to 576 Judicial Code), the labour tribunal (Articles 578 to 583 Judicial Code)[44], and the district tribunal.[45] The lowest ranked tribunals – on the level of the judicial cantons – are the justice of the peace (Articles 590 to 601 Judicial Code) in civil matters and the police tribunal (Article 601*bis* Judicial Code) in criminal matters.

As explained above, the ordinary courts and tribunals have jurisdiction regarding both civil and political rights, unless the legislator has explicitly attributed jurisdiction concerning a certain political right to an administrative court. The judiciary has the authority to apply the rules of tort liability (Article 1382 Civil Code) on an administration.[46]

Organisation of the administrative courts and tribunals[47]

There is no strict hierarchy of administrative courts in Belgium. They were created whenever the legislator saw the need to do so. Over the years this has led

40 Article 158 Constitution; A. Alen, *Handboek van het Belgisch staatsrecht* [*Manual of Belgian public law*], *o.c.*, 239.

41 Also see P. Peeters, 'The Judiciary', *l.c.*, 111–114.

42 The Court of Cassation is the highest court in Belgium. It can only carry out a procedural review. As it cannot, for example, rectify factual errors it does not meet the requirements of 'full judicial review' required by Article 6.1 ECHR (European Court of Human Rights, judgement in *Le Compte, Van Leuven and De Meyere v. Belgium* of 23 June 1981, *Publ. Eur. Court H.R.* 1981, Series A, No. 43, considerations 33, 51(b) and 60). Its competences can be found in Articles 608 to 615 Judicial Code and Articles 147 and 158 Constitution.

43 Divided into a civil, criminal (also called the correctional tribunal), youth and a criminal sentence execution bench (Article 76 Judicial Code). It is also the appellate body for the two tribunals above, except in certain disputes between merchants (Article 577 Judicial Code).

44 The chairmen of the tribunals of first instance, tribunals of commerce and labour tribunals have specific competencies of their own, such as ordering provisional measures in a case of urgency (Articles 584 to 589 Judicial Code).

45 The district tribunal determines conflicts of jurisdiction (Article 639 Judicial Code).

46 Court of Cassation 5 November 1920, *Pasicrisie* 1920, I, 199.

47 It is always possible to try an – organised or unorganised – appeal within the administration itself in the form of an 'appeal in reconsideration', a 'hierarchic appeal', or an 'appeal to the

to a proliferation of administrative courts, often with their own specific legal proceedings.[48] Legislation concerning common legal rules for all administrative courts is also lacking.[49] Should an appeal against the verdicts of a particular administrative court be possible, the legislator might have designated another administrative court, an ordinary court or the Council of State for this purpose. If no appellate body has been made explicitly competent, an appeal can be lodged with the Council of State.[50]

The Council of State

The Council of State is the supreme administrative court[51] and does not belong to the judiciary in a formal sense.[52] It is divided into two sections: the Legislative and the Administrative Jurisdictional Section.[53] The latter has three relevant competences concerning legal protection against sanctions.

The Administrative Jurisdictional Section has the power to annul administrative acts (14, §1 ACS), a power which ordinary courts and tribunals do not have at their disposal[54] except when they are called to examine the validity of decisions by institutions of the executive branch that impose administrative sanctions. This power to annul is limited to unilateral, binding acts of an administration[55] and is available for administrative decisions which infringe upon substantive procedural requirements or which exceed or misuse power. The validity of the administrative act needs to be assessed in the light of binding norms. Non-binding resolutions, advices or explicatory circulars lack a normative character and cannot lead to an annulment by themselves.[56] The competence of the Council covers both internal (*i.e.* violations of material rules, abuse of power)

---

supervising entity' (S. Lust, *l.c.*, 53; M. Boes, *Administratief recht* [*Administrative law*], Leuven, Acco, 2001, 259–262). These administrative appeals will not have *res judicata effect* (A. Mast, J. Dujardin, M. Van Damme and J. Vande Lanotte, *o.c.*, 769–770; S. Lust, *l.c.*, 35) and have no procedural guarantees other then those applicable by law (M. Boes, *Administratief recht* [*Administrative law*], *o.c.*, 265), but they can take considerations of policy into account (A. Mast, J. Dujardin, M. Van Damme and J. Vande Lanotte, *o.c.*, 743, 769).

48 A. Alen, *Handboek van het Belgisch staatsrecht* [*Manual of Belgian public law*], *o.c.*, 242.

49 P. Peeters, 'The Judiciary', *l.c.*, 114.

50 P. Peeters, 'The Judiciary', *l.c.*, 115; Article 11 Coordinated Acts of 12 January 1973 concerning the Council of State, *Belgian Bulletin of Acts and Decrees* 21 March 1973.

51 *Cf.* Article 160 Constitution.

52 M. Van Damme, 'The Council of State: Institution on the Junction of the Three Traditional Powers of the State', in: J. Vande Lanotte (ed.), *The Principle of Equality: a South African and Belgian Perspective*, Antwerp-Apeldoorn, Maklu, 2001, 74.

53 Article 1 Coordinated Acts of 12 January 1973 concerning the Council of State (hereafter referred to as ACS). The Legislative Section advises the governments and parliaments when drafting legislation. Prior to the Law of 15 September 2006 (which came into force on 1 June 2007) the Administrative Jurisdictional Section was known as the Administrative Section.

54 A. Alen, *Handboek van het Belgisch staatsrecht* [*Manual of Belgian public law*], *o.c.*, 218–219.

55 S. Lust, *l.c.*, 44–45; M. Boes, *Administratief recht* [*Administrative law*], *o.c.*, 303–306.

56 Council of State, Oceane, No. 171.269, 16 May 2007, p. 8–9.

and external (*i.e.* the formalities of the decision) legality.[57] It is generally accepted that the Council of State carries out a full judicial review in this capacity (see *infra*).

The Council can act as a court of cassation as well (14, §2 ACS). It decides on procedural disputes raised against judgements of administrative courts. It cannot re-examine the facts in this capacity. Because of this, the Council of State would not act as a judicial entity with full judicial review in this hypothesis. It would therefore not satisfy the requirements of Article 6 ECHR. The consequence of this is that the administrative tribunals whose decisions are appealed would have to meet the standards of Article 6 ECHR themselves.

The Council occasionally has the power of full jurisdiction (in the internal, Belgian definition of this term – see *infra* regarding Article 6 ECHR) with regard to disputes (16 ACS). In that case it can carry out a full review, without the possibility of a further appeal.[58]

Constitutional Court

The Constitutional Court[59] (previously named the Court of Arbitration[60]) has had a significant impact on the legal system for protection against sanctions.[61] It controls the constitutionality of legislation in the strict, formal sense. The Court cannot review the Constitution itself, nor any administrative decisions or regulations.[62] Determining the constitutionality of the latter is the task of the ordinary courts and the Council of State. The Court decides, by means of judgement, on conflicts of authority and on violations of such articles of the Constitution which the law designates. The Court's frame of reference has been broadened over the years: it can now review the compliance of legislation with all Articles (8–32) of Section II of the Constitution (citizenship, rights and

---

57 P. Peeters, 'The Judiciary', *l.c.*, 117.

58 M. Boes, *Administratieve sancties en art. 6 EVRM in België [Administrative sanctions and art. 6 ECHR in Belgium]*, Zwolle, W.E.J. Tjeenk Willink, 1989, 18–19; S. Lust, *l.c.*, 51. An example is Article 15*ter* of the Act concerning the limitation and the control of election expenses for the election of the federal Chambers, the financing and open bookkeeping of political parties of 4 July 1989.

59 Article 142 Constitution and Special Act 6 January 1989 concerning the Court of Arbitration (hereafter SACA), *Belgian Bulletin of Acts and Decrees* 7 January 1989.

60 The name was changed by the Constitutional Modification of 7 May 2007, *Belgian Bulletin of Acts and Decrees* 8 May 2007. The court is still referred to as the Court of Arbitration for the citation of its rulings prior to this modification.

61 Its case law has, for example, resulted in the introduction of a regulation for applying extenuating circumstances in the Administrative Fines Law (Court of Arbitration No. 40/97 and No. 45/97, 14 July 1997).

62 See A. Alen, *Handboek van het Belgisch staatsrecht [Manual of Belgian public law]*, *o.c.*, 274; P. Peeters, 'The Judiciary', *l.c.*, 128. The Court of Arbitration cannot review the compliance of court decisions with the Constitution either.

liberties) and with Articles 170 (the principle of legality in fiscal matters), 172 (equality in fiscal matters) and 191 (rights of aliens) of the Constitution, along with the rules governing the division of powers of the Federal State, the Communities and the Regions.[63]

The Court has two powers: to annul legislation within a certain time frame – usually six months – after its publication (Articles 1–25 SACA) and to issue preliminary rulings (Articles 26–30 SACA). The cases are brought before the Court by any authority designated by statute by any person who has a justifiable interest or, in a preliminary issue, by any tribunal.

An important aspect of the Court's jurisdiction is the authority to assess the constitutionality of legislation in the light of the constitutional equality principle and the prohibition of unjustifiable discrimination (Articles 10 and 11 Constitution).[64] The Court decided that the concept of administrative sanctioning as such is not discriminatory.[65] The legislator has a discretionary choice to adopt criminal or administrative sanctions for infractions.[66] The Court

---

63 See Article 142 Constitution and the modified Articles 1 and 26 SACA. The Constitutional Court does not have the power to directly examine any violation of general principles or of European or international conventions on human rights or liberties. However, it can take into account these norms for the purpose of determining a discrimination within the meaning of Articles 10 and 11 Constitution or when a provision of such a convention has a scope which is analogous to an article of the Belgian Constitution within the scope of the Court's jurisdiction. The guarantees embodied in those provisions are then inextricably bound up with the constitutional guarantees (e.g. Court of Arbitration No. 158/2004, 20 October 2004, consideration B.5.2, regarding the principle of legality; Constitutional Court No. 2/2008, 17 January 2008, consideration B.4.2, regarding Article 6 ECHR).

64 See e.g. Court of Arbitration No. 155/2002, 6 November 2002 and Court of Arbitration No. 98/2005, 1 June 2005. The cases dealt with differences in the treatment of minors prosecuted either administratively or criminally for misconduct relating to football matches. The Court initially ruled that the differences in procedural guarantees afforded to minors in these procedures resulted in the unconstitutionality of the administrative procedure. The legislator subsequently adapted this procedure, after which the Court concluded that the remaining difference in treatment was constitutional. Compare regarding the treatment of minors under the New Municipalities Act: Court of Arbitration No. 6/2006, 18 January 2006. See also generally: Constitutional Court No. 28/2008, 28 February 2008 (regarding the difference in the statute of limitations concerning the New Municipalities Act).

65 Court of Arbitration No. 40/97 and No. 45/97, 14 July 1997, considerations B.2 and B.3.1; Court of Arbitration No. 178/2006, 29 November 2006, consideration B.3.2; Court of Arbitration No. 67/2007, 26 April 2007, consideration B.6; Constitutional Court No. 42/2009, 11 March 2009, consideration B.5.

66 See also Constitutional Court No. 62/2010, 27 May 2010, considerations B.14-B.16.2 The Flemish Region had enacted a law imposing criminal sanctions on illegal waste dumping. The municipalities could technically adopt administrative sanctions for limited forms of such acts, but they could not do so because of the existence of these criminal sanctions which were applicable regardless of the size of the infringement. The Flemish Region adopted a Decree allowing municipalities to adopt their own regulations and stipulated that the criminal sanctions of the Decree would remain applicable in the absence of measures on the municipal level. The Constitutional Court considered this treatment to be constitutional. The mere difference in treatment between infractions in municipalities that did or did not adopt

adds however that, if an infraction is punishable by both criminal and administrative sanctions, differences in treatment between the two types of procedures can have their constitutionality examined. The legislator can also give administrations the power to initiate criminal procedures without necessarily resulting in an unconstitutional treatment.[67]

Competency of the courts and tribunals to disregard administrative acts taken in violation of legal norms

Based on Article 159 of the Constitution ordinary as well as administrative[68] courts and tribunals have the ability to disregard acts of the executive branch if these are not in conformity with legal norms.[69] The Council of State can also annul administrative acts because of their illegality, for example decisions to impose an administrative sanction without a legal basis.[70] Administrative bodies belonging to the 'active administration' instead of the judiciary *sensu lato* (*i.e.* administrative bodies which do not qualify as administrative courts or tribunals) do not have this competency.[71] Arguments regarding the illegality of an administrative act cannot be addressed by these bodies. The lack of mentioning the illegality in this stage of the proceedings can therefore not be construed as a renunciation. The addressee of the sanction retains the right to raise his grievances regarding the issue by appealing to a court or tribunal.

Originally, only the external legality (competence, procedural requirements) was examined. Nowadays there is less reluctance in both legal doctrine and case law to

administrative sanctions was a legitimate consequence of the division of competencies and could not be considered unconstitutional as such.

67 Court of Arbitration No. 192/2004, 24 November 2004, consideration B.9; Court of Arbitration No. 40/2005, 16 February 2005, consideration B.9. The administration (i.e. not the public prosecution office) had the authority to initiate a criminal prosecution. This entity does not qualify as independent or impartial, however the judge deciding the criminal case is. There was therefore no unjustifiable difference in treatment compared to an ordinary criminal prosecution.

68 A. Mast, J. Dujardin, M. Van Damme and J. Vande Lanotte, *o.c.*, 810–811; A. Alen, *Handboek van het Belgisch staatsrecht* [*Manual of Belgian public law*], *o.c.*, 697–698.

69 It is accepted that Article 159 Constitution is not only applicable to federal legislation, but also to decrees or ordinances of the Communities and Regions (A. Mast, J. Dujardin, M. Van Damme and J. Vande Lanotte, *o.c.*, 811).

70 Council of State, Bielen, No. 99.838, 17 October 2001. The decision in question was the application of a municipal regulation imposing an administrative sanction without basis in the New Municipalities Act (Nieuwe Gemeentewet [New Municipalities Act] of 24 June 1988, *Belgian Bulletin of Acts and Decrees* 3 September 1988. The case at hand dealt with the version of this act prior to the Law of 13 may 1999 concerning administrative sanctions in the municipalities, *Belgian Bulletin of Acts and Decrees* 10 June 1999). See also: Council of State, Profilsteel, No. 63.555, 12 December 1996 (regarding the revocation of an environmental license without a legal basis). See also *infra*, footnote 277.

71 Council of State, Baelden, No. 132.234, 10 June 2004, consideration 2.2.5.

accept a review of internal legality (violations of material rules, abuse of power).[72] Courts and tribunals will normally only review the lawfulness of a decision, without taking policy choices into account.[73] However, a marginal review of the use of discretionary powers can be required to determine the legitimacy of the administrative act in the light of general principles or to remedy abuses of power.[74]

Administrative law

Belgium has not codified its administrative law. There is no 'Administrative Procedure Act' or 'General Administrative Law Code'.[75] There is no coherent legal framework to offer protection against administrative sanctions either.[76] Administrative law in Belgium is instead a fragmentary collection of specific acts, with case law trying to fill in the gaps.[77] To this end, the courts have turned to the general principles of proper administration (and principles of criminal law). These administrative principles are limited by the fact that they cannot be

---

72 A. Mast, J. Dujardin, M. Van Damme and J. Vande Lanotte, *o.c.* 927; A. Alen, *Handboek van het Belgisch staatsrecht* [*Manual of Belgian public law*], *o.c.*, 691–692; S. Lust, *l.c.*, 39.

73 E.g.: Court of Cassation 15 June 2004, *Pasicrisie* 2004, 1035 (regarding a reparation measure); Tribunal of first instance Ghent 23 October 1998, *Tijdschrift voor Milieurecht* [*Periodical of Environmental Law*] 1999, 324 (regarding the validity of a building permit); Correctional tribunal Tongeren 18 December 1998, *Algemeen Juridisch Tijdschrift* [*General Legal Periodical*] 1999-2000, 10, noot L. De Geyter (regarding a reparation measure); A. Mast, J. Dujardin, M. Van Damme and J. Vande Lanotte, *o.c.*, 768–769.

74 Such as the principle of proportionality when imposing a sanction (Court of Arbitration No. 22/99, 24 February 1999, *Belgian Bulletin of Acts and Decrees* 30 April 1999, considerations B.11 and B.12; The Court of Cassation uses the following wording: '[...] that the judge who is asked to review an administrative sanction with a repressive aim in the sense of Article 6 ECHR can review the legality of that sanction; that he can especially review the sanction in light of the imperative demands of international treaties and the internal system of law, including general principles; that this test should especially allow the judge to determine whether an imposed penalty is not disproportional to the infraction, [...]' (Court of Cassation 24 January 2002); Correctional tribunal Dendermonde 13 June 2005, *Tijdschrift voor Gemeenterecht* [*Periodical of Municipality Law*] 2006, 40, note D. Vanheuven and J. Beleyn; A. Alen, *Handboek van het Belgisch staatsrecht* [*Manual of Belgian public law*], *o.c.*, 86 and 693.

75 A proposal concerning a General Administration Act was submitted to Parliament on 26 November 2003 (*Parliamentary Documents of the Chamber of Representatives* 2003–04, No. 496/1), but the proposal expired due to the dissolution of the Belgian Parliament on 2 May 2007.

76 J. Put, 'Rechtshandhaving door administratieve sancties in het recht [Law enforcement through administrative sanctions]', *l.c.*, 1198.

77 *Ibid.*, 1209; S. Lust, *l.c.*, 56.

applied *contra legem*[78], although a certain nuance can be discerned in the Court of Cassation's case law.[79]

The competent legislator(s) did, however, create a number of laws to enact certain regulations with a global application. Examples are the Act 'concerning the explicit justification of administrative acts'[80], the 'Government Information Act'[81] and the establishment of ombudsman institutions.[82] There are

78 Council of State, Laroy Veevoeders, No. 121.935, 30 July 2003, consideration 6.3.2 (the general principle of the right to be heard was not held applicable in a matter where the right of defence was regulated in a specific manner); M. Van Hoecke, 'Algemene Rechtsbeginselen als rechtsbron [General Principles as a source of law]', in: M. Van Hoecke (ed.), *Algemene rechtsbeginselen*, Antwerp, Kluwer, 1991, 4; L. Suetens, 'Algemene beginselen van behoorlijk bestuur: begrip en plaats in de hiërarchie van de normen. Inleidende verkenning [General principles of proper administration: notion and place in the hierarchy of norms. Introductory exploration]', in: I. Opdebeeck (ed.), *Algemene beginselen van behoorlijk bestuur [General Principles of proper administration]*, Antwerp, Kluwer, 1993, No. 10; A. Van Mensel, *Het beginsel van behoorlijk bestuur [The principle of proper administration]*, Ghent, Mys & Breesch, 1997, 21; M. Boes, *Administratief recht [Administrative law]*, *o.c.*, 54; see however S. Lust, *l.c.*, 31–32.

79 See generally: Court of Cassation 1 March 2010, *Rechtskundig Weekblad [Legal Weekly]* 2010–11, 1091 (stating that 'in principle' a citizen cannot invoke the general principle of proper administration of legal certainty *contra legem*. However if the administration invokes the illegality of a decision upon which the citizen bases his claim of legal certainty, the judge must examine to what extent this decision created reasonable expectations. The judge must take the legality of said decision into account in his assessment) and the thorough annotation by W. Vandenbruwaene. See also concerning fiscal matters: V. Scoriels, 'Le principe de la confiance légitime en matière fiscale et la jurisprudence de la Cour de Cassation [The general principle of legal certainty in fiscal matters and the rulings of the Court of Cassation]', *Journal des Tribunaux [Courts Journal]* 2003, 301–310.

80 Act of 29 July 1991 betreffende de uitdrukkelijke motivering van bestuurshandelingen [Formal Justification Act], *Belgian Bulletin of Acts and Decrees* 12 September 1991.

81 Act of 11 April 1994 betreffende de openbaarheid van bestuur [Government Information Act], *Belgian Bulletin of Acts and Decrees* 30 June 1994. Local states have enacted their own legislation in the matter of open government: Decree of 22 December 1994 relatif à la publicité de l'administration [on Government Information], *Belgian Bulletin of Acts and Decrees* 31 December 1994 (French Community); Ordinance of 30 March 1995 relative à la publicité de l'administration [on Government Information], *Belgian Bulletin of Acts and Decrees* 23 December 1995 (Brussels Region); Decree of 30 March 1995 relatif à la publicité de l'administration [on Government Information], *Belgian Bulletin of Acts and Decrees* 28 June 1995 (Walloon Region); Decree of 26 March 2004 betreffende de openbaarheid van bestuur [on Government Information], *Belgian Bulletin of Acts and Decrees* 1 June 2004 (Flemish Community).

82 Act of 22 March betreffende de instelling van de federale ombudsmannen [concerning the establishment of the federal ombudsmen], *Belgian Bulletin of Acts and Decrees* 7 April 1995; Decree of 7 July 1998 betreffende de instelling van de Vlaamse ombudsdienst [concerning the establishment of the Flemish ombudsman institution], *Belgian Bulletin of Acts and Decrees* 24 August 1998 (Flemish Community); Decree of 20 June 2002 portant création du service du médiateur de la Communauté française [concerning the establishment of the French Community ombudsman institution], *Belgian Bulletin of Acts and Decrees* 19 July 2002 (French Community); Decree of 22 December 1994 portant création de l'institution de médiateur de la Région wallonne [concerning the establishment of the Walloon ombudsman institution], *Belgian Bulletin of Acts and Decrees* 19 January 1995.

comprehensive administrative procedure acts in certain legal fields as well, such as the 'charter of the socially insured'[83] in the field of social security law. The administrative sanctions (and sanctioning procedures) themselves are scattered throughout scores of specific acts and the various legal fields. The most notable acts are the Social Criminal Code[84] in social law, the sanction mechanism of Article 119 New Municipalities Act in public law and the Competition Act[85] in economic law.

Administrative law is also influenced by the 'classic' principles of public service in Belgium, which are: flexibility, continuity, and equality of utilisation.[86] When it comes to these principles of public service, the principle of continuity grants the administrations two privileges which are relevant for protection against legal sanctioning.

First of all, the presumption of legality (*privilège du préalable*). All administrative acts are presumed to be legal until a citizen persuades the – ordinary or administrative – judiciary of the contrary.[87] The legal cause of this judicial review can be found in Article 159 of the Constitution, which states that courts and tribunals may only apply administrative decisions insofar as they are in conformity with the law. None of the consequences of an administrative decision will be suspended during this judicial review, unless the law prescribes this[88] or unless a judge grants this suspension. This means that imposed administrative sanctions can be executed, even while a judicial appeal is still pending. We will have to examine how this privilege is influenced by general principles further down, as the administration is not allowed to rely on this principle for imposing sanctions without proper justification or proof.

83 Act of 11 April 1995 concerning the Charter of the socially insured, *Belgian Bulletin of Acts and Decrees* 6 September 1995.

84 Sociaal Strafwetboek [Social Criminal Code] of 6 June 2010, *Belgian Bulletin of Acts and Decrees* 1 July 2010. This code replaces the Act of 30 June 1971 betreffende de administratieve geldboeten [Administrative Fines Act], *Belgian Bulletin of Acts and Decrees* 13 July 1971.

85 Act of 5 August 1991 tot bescherming van de economische mededinging [on the protection of economic competition], *Belgian Bulletin of Acts and Decrees* 11 October 1991 (coordinated on the 1st of July 1999; *Belgian Bulletin of Acts and Decrees* 1 September 1999).

86 M. Boes, *Administratief recht [Administrative law]*, *o.c.*, 107–110.

87 A. Mast, J. Dujardin, M. Van Damme and J. Vande Lanotte, *o.c.*, 7; J. De Staercke, *Algemene beginselen van behoorlijk bestuur en behoorlijk burgerschap. Beginselen van de openbare dienst.* [*General principles of proper administration and proper citizenship. Principles of the public service*], Bruges, Vanden Broele, 2002, 89.

88 Such as Article 3 of the Law concerning social criminal law (Law of 2 June 2010 houdende bepalingen van het sociaal strafrecht, *Belgian Bulletin of Acts and Decrees* 1 July 2010) and Article 121, §6 juncto Article 121, §1, 4° of the Financial Supervision Law (Law of 2 August 2002 betreffende het toezicht op de financiële sector en de financiële diensten, *Belgian Bulletin of Acts and Decrees* 4 September 2002).

Article 159 is not applicable to the executive branch, which means that administrations are not allowed to set aside an act of another administration merely because it seems to be illegitimate, except if the unlawfulness is manifestly present.[89]

Secondly, the direct executable force of an administrative act (*privilège de l'exécution d'office*). Certain administrative acts are directly executable, although this is not an intrinsic element of every administrative act. Constitutional clauses and laws can specify cases in which this privilege is to be applied.[90] This privilege is a strong argument in favour of a well regulated administrative sanctioning procedure, as the addressee of the sanction could be faced with a gap in his legal protection – namely the period between the execution of the decision and the judicial review – if the administrative sanction is directly executable.[91]

The influence of Article 6 ECHR

The European Court of Human Rights has developed an autonomous definition[92] of the term 'criminal charge' in its case law.[93] This means that national legislators or judges cannot rely solely on a formal or organic internal definition of the term

89 Council of State No. 65.971, 22 April 1997, consideration 4.3.2, para. 6; A. Mast, J. Dujardin, M. Van Damme and J. Vande Lanotte, *o.c.*, 815–816; M. Boes, *Administratief recht* [*Administrative law*], *o.c.*, 209. Manifestly unlawful acts are deemed to be non-existent and can therefore never be applied.

90 A. Mast, J. Dujardin, M. Van Damme and J. Vande Lanotte, *o.c.*, 7–9; M. Boes, *Administratief recht* [*Administrative law*], *o.c.*, 210.

91 J. Put, *Administratieve sancties in het socialezekerheidsrecht* [*Administrative sanctions in social security law*] (hereafter: *Administratieve sancties* [*Administrative sanctions*]), Bruges, die Keure, 1998, 546.

92 The mere fact that an administrative sanction has a punitive character in the sense of Article 6 ECHR does not imply however that it has to be classified as a criminal sanction in the internal Belgian legal system. This means that an authorisation of the federal legislator for the Regions to enact criminal sanctions on certain matters does not *a contrario* nullify the authority of the Regions to enact administrative sanctions for these matters. See Court of Arbitration No. 18/95, 2 March 1995, *Belgian Bulletin of Acts and Decrees* 11 May 1995, consideration B.3; Court of Arbitration No. 127/2000, consideration B.13.5. It also explains why the Council of State can have jurisdiction over administrative sanctions in spite of their punitive character within the meaning of Article 6 ECHR (see Court of Cassation, C.09.0019.N, 15 October 2009, *Nieuw Juridisch Weekblad* [*New Legal Review*] 2009, 816; Council of State No. 201.373, 26 February 2010).

93 ECtHR, judgement in *Engel v. the Netherlands* of 8 June 1976, *Publ. Eur. Court H.R.* 1984, Series A, No. 22, considerations 82–83; ECtHR, judgement in *Öztürk v. Germany* of 21 February 1984, *Publ. Eur. Court H.R.* 1984, Series A, No. 73, consideration 53; ECtHR, judgement in *Lutz v. Germany* of 25 August 1987, consideration 54; ECtHR, judgement in Garyfallou AEBE / Greece of 24 September 1997, *Publ. Eur. Court H.R.* 1997, V, 1821, consideration 32. These criteria were further developed in the *Bendenoun* case (ECtHR, judgement in *Bendenoun v. France* of 24 February 1994, *Publ. Eur. Court H.R.* 1994, Series A, No. 284, consideration 47; also see A. Alen, 'Naar een betere rechtsbescherming inzake administratieve geldboeten na de koerswijziging van het Hof van Cassatie in zijn arresten van 5 februari 1999 [Towards a better legal protection concerning administrative fines after the change of course reversal by the Court

'criminal charge' in order to circumvent the requirements of Article 6 ECHR.[94] The ECHR will investigate the internal qualification of the sanction, but can also take into account the nature of the infraction (its general, preventive and repressive nature) and its potential severity. These criteria are not cumulative.[95] As a result a sanction which is qualified as strictly administrative in internal national law nonetheless resorts under Article 6 ECHR if it has a punitive character. Over the years Belgian courts have come to accept the autonomous nature of the definitions in Article 6 ECHR and have attempted to ensure that their rulings are in conformity with ECHR case law.[96] The Court of Cassation initially applied a formal definition, thereby refusing to apply Article 6 ECHR on certain fines which the legislator had classified as administrative.[97] It later recanted its position and has since deferred to the autonomous definition of Article 6 ECHR.[98]

---

of Cassation in its rulings of 5 February 1999]' (hereafter: 'Naar een betere rechtsbescherming [towards a better legal protection]'), *Rechtskundig Weekblad* [*Legal Weekly*] 1999–2000, 630.

94 However, the qualification of a sanction in the light of the ECHR exerts no influence over matters which reside outside the scope of Article 6 ECHR. An example of this is the notion 'criminal charge' with respect to the internal divisions of competency between the different levels of the Belgian state as referred to in Article 11, para. 2 SARI (Court of Arbitration No. 127/2000, 6 December 2000, *Belgian Bulletin of Acts and Decrees* 23 December 2000, consideration B.13.5). This means that legislation concerning criminal sanctions in the internal, formal sense is not necessarily applicable to administrative sanctions with a punitive character. This can result in unconstitutional differences in treatment (see e.g. Constitutional Court No. 86/2007, 20 June 2007, considerations B.6 and B.7.4; Constitutional Court No. 148/2010, 16 December 2010, consideration B.3.3).

95 For an overview of ECtHR case law from a Belgian perspective see A. Alen, 'Naar een betere rechtsbescherming [towards a better legal protection]', *Rechtskundig Weekblad* [*Legal Weekly*] 1999–2000, 630–638; S. Van Drooghenbroeck, 'De vraies sanctions administratives ou des sanctions pénales camouflées? Réflexions à propos de la jurisprudence récente de la Cour européenne des droits de l'Homme [Real administrative sanctions or punitive sanctions in disguise? Reflections regarding the recent case law of the ECtHR]', *Revue de la Faculté de droit de l'Université de Liège* [*Review of the law faculty of the university of Liège*] 2005, 467–490.

96 See e.g.: Constitutional Court No. 148/2010, 16 December 2010, consideration B.3.1; Court of Arbitration No. 14/2007, 14 January 2007, consideration B.3.3; Court of Arbitration No. 77/2001, 7 June 2001, *Belgian Bulletin of Acts and Decrees* 25 September 2001, consideration B.7; Court of Arbitration No. 80/2001, 13 June 2001, *Belgian Bulletin of Acts and Decrees* 11 October 2001, consideration B.7; Court of Arbitration No. 88/2004, 19 May 2004, consideration B.11 and B13.1; see extensively: Council of State No. 127.673, 2 February 2004, consideration 5.2.2.3. Also see A. Mast, J. Dujardin, M. Van Damme and J. Vande Lanotte, *o.c.*, 11; A. Alen, 'Naar een betere rechtsbescherming [towards a better legal protection]', *l.c.*, 638.

97 Cass. 27 September 1991, *Arresten van het Hof van Cassatie* [*Rulings of the Court of Cassation*] 1991–92, 99; see also Cass. 12 January 1995, *Arresten van het Hof van Cassatie* [*Rulings of the Court of Cassation*] 1995, 36.

98 Cass. C.97.0441.N, 5 February 1999, *Arresten van het Hof van Cassatie* [*Rulings of the Court of Cassation*] 1999, 142; Cass. C.98.0398.N, 5 February 1999, *Arresten van het Hof van Cassatie* [*Rulings of the Court of Cassation*] 1999, 155; Court of Cassation 25 May 1999, *Arresten van het Hof van Cassatie* [*Rulings of the Court of Cassation*] 1999, 719; Cass. 24 January 2002, *Arresten van het Hof van Cassatie* [*Rulings of the Court of Cassation*] 2002, 238; Cass. C.04.0390.N, 16 February 2007 *Pasicrisie* 2007, 365; Cass. F.05.0015.N, 16 February 2007, *Pasicrisie* 2007, 369; Cass. 13 February 2009, *Pasicrisie* 2009, 470; Cass. 11 March 2010, *Rechtskundig Weekblad* [*Legal Weekly*] 2010–11, 666. See also Cass. 6 May 2002, *Arresten van*

Limited influence on the administrative sanctioning procedure itself

Due to the case law of the European Court of Human Rights, the impact of Article 6 ECHR has remained rather limited with regard to the administrative sanctioning procedures themselves.[99] The Court accepts that the requirements of Article 6 ECHR need not be met during every phase of the procedure.[100] The administrative procedure as such does not need to live up to the requirements of Article 6, as long as there is a possibility of 'full judicial review' or 'full jurisdiction' afterwards.[101] Belgian case law has adopted the same viewpoint.[102]

Aspects of Article 6 do have some influence on the administrative phase. If the administrative sanctions have a punitive character, the time spent on the administrative handling of the matter could be counted towards determining the reasonable delay.[103] The presumption of innocence should also have an influence at this early stage[104] (*infra*).

Full judicial review in Belgian case law

Administrative sanctions with a punitive character can be imposed by administrative bodies that do not fulfil the requirements of Article 6 ECHR as long as there is a possibility of full judicial review afterwards.[105] The question then becomes what constitutes a full judicial review. This notion can be approached from two angles.

The power to modulate administrative decisions

The first question concerns the scope of the judicial review and the authority of the judge to modulate a sanction which was validly imposed by the

het Hof van Cassatie [*Rulings of the Court of Cassation*] 2002, 1216 (concerning the International Covenant on Civil and Political Rights).

99 J. Put, *Administratieve sancties* [*Administrative sanctions*], *o.c.*, 230.

100 See A. Alen, *Handboek van het Belgisch staatsrecht* [*Manual of Belgian public law*], *o.c.*, 555; J. Put, 'Rechtshandhaving [Law enforcement]', *l.c.*, 1202.

101 A. Mast, J. Dujardin, M. Van Damme and J. Vande Lanotte, *o.c.*, 785; J. Put, *Administratieve sancties*, *o.c.*, 178–180 and 515–535; M. Boes, *Administratieve sancties en art. 6 EVRM in België* [*Administrative sanctions and art. 6 ECHR in Belgium*], *o.c.*, 17–18.

102 See Court of Arbitration No. 72/92, 18 November 1992, *Belgian Bulletin of Acts and Decrees* 16 January 1993, consideration B.4.4; Council of State, No. 201.373, 26 February 2010. J. Put, *Administratieve sancties* [*Administrative sanctions*], *o.c.*, 179–180.

103 In the case of a prior appeal at an administrative court see: M. Boes, *Administratieve sancties en art. 6 EVRM in België* [*Administrative sanctions and art. 6 ECHR in Belgium*], *o.c.*, 25.

104 J. Put, *Administratieve sancties* [*Administrative sanctions*], *o.c.*, 235.

105 ECtHR, No. 6878/75 and 7238/75, judgement in *Le Compte, Van Leuven and De Meyere v. Belgium* of 23 June 1981, consideration 51; ECtHR, No. 47650/99, judgement in *Silvester's Horeca Service v. Belgium* of 4 March 2004, consideration 26.

administration.[106] The Constitutional Court ruled as early as 1992 that a full judicial review is granted when 'nothing which resorted under the authority of the administration remains outside the scope of review of the judge'.[107] The Court of Cassation initially limited the scope of the judicial review to a mere supervision of the administrative decision's legality in cases where the administration enjoyed a discretionary authority to impose sanctions.[108] The Court of Cassation ruled that judges were not allowed to reduce or lift administrative sanctions by founding their ruling on equity or proportionality considerations even though the administration itself could take those factors into account. According to the Court the judges could only review the compatibility of the administrative sanction with the legal framework.[109] Therefore a judge who established that the particular sanction chosen by the administration could legally be imposed under the given circumstances, could not lift or reduce this sentence if he deemed it to be inappropriate or excessive. The reasoning behind this position was that the authority to determine the type and severity of the sanction had been attributed to the administrative and not to the judicial bodies. The Court did rule in 1998 that a judge could fully review everything which resided within the competency of the administration and that it could substitute the administration's decision except where the legislator attributed a discretionary power to the administration.[110]

---

106 Concerning the lower courts and tribunals see *pro*: Labour Court 18 May 2004, *Journal des Tribunaux du Travail [Journal of the Labour Tribunals]* 2005, 242; Labour Court 24 October 1997, *Jurisprudence Liège Mons Bruxelles* 1998, 77; Labour Court Antwerp 16 May 1997, *Chroniques de droit Social [Chronicles of Social Law]* 1997, 406; Labour Court Antwerp (dept. Hasselt) 26 April 1996, *Algemeen Juridisch Tijdschrift [General Legal Journal]* 1996–97, 228, note J. Put; Labour Court Antwerp (dept. Hasselt) 25 January 1996, *Limburgs Rechtsleven [Administration of justice in Limburg]* 1996, 119; Labour Court Antwerp 2 September 1994, *Chroniques de droit Social [Chronicles of Social Law]* 1994, 458; Labour Tribunal Mons 25 October 1989, *Chroniques de droit Social [Chronicles of Social Law]* 1990, 219, note P. Palsterman; *contra*: Labour Court Antwerp 21 September 1992, *Journal des Tribunaux du Travail [Journal of the Labour Tribunals]* 1993, 100; Labour Court Antwerp (dept. Hasselt) 23 November 1989, *Journal des Tribunaux du Travail [Journal of the Labour Tribunals]* 1990, 328 (marginal review only based on the general principles of proper administration).

107 Court of Arbitration No. 72/92, 18 November 1992, *Belgian Bulletin of Acts and Decrees* 16 January 1993, consideration B.4.4 (*'niets van wat onder de beoordelingsbevoegdheid van de ambtenaar valt, ligt buiten de controle van de rechtbank'*).

108 Cass. 27 September 1991, *Arresten van het Hof van Cassatie [Rulings of the Court of Cassation]* 1991–92, 99 (any complaints regarding the administrative sanctions in question had to be filed with the Minister of Finance, who would arguably qualify as neither neutral nor impartial).

109 Court of Cassation 29 September 1997, *Pasicrisie* 1997, No. 371 (fiscal matter); Court of Cassation 22 January 1998, *Bulletin* 1998, 111 (fiscal matter). See also Cass. 10 June 1996, *Bulletin* 1996, 611 (social matter).

110 Cass. 2 February 1998, *Algemeen Juridisch Tijdschrift [General Legal Journal]* 1998–99, 493 (social matter).

The Court further elaborated its vision on full judicial review in the 1999 cases.[111] It acknowledged that a full judicial review requires an examination of the factual and the legal elements.[112] The judge must be able to examine the 'reality' of the sanction and to judge whether the sanction was in accordance with the law, most notably with the applicable legal stipulations, the general principles and the duty of care of the administration. The Court still added however that this competence did not allow the judge to take into account strict equity or opportunity considerations in order to lift or reduce sanctions which were legitimately imposed by the administration.[113] Belgium was held to be in violation of Article 6 of the ECHR by the European Court for Human Rights on the basis of this stance. The ECHR ruled that the addressee of the sanction did not have access to a full judicial review due to the lack of authority to reform the decision of the administrative body on all points.[114]The Constitutional Court for its part had decided that a judge should have the power to modulate[115], lift or reduce[116] sanctions if the administration also enjoyed such power. The Constitutional Court also clarified that if the administration only has the option to either impose an administrative fine or not (without any authority to reduce the fine), the judge can only review the decision to impose the fine as such, without being able to reduce the amount.[117] This line of reasoning leads to the conclusion that the judge would have no authority to modulate the sanction if the law prescribes only one type of sanction of a fixed type and height.[118] In such

111 Cass. C.97.0441.N, 5 February 1999, *Arresten van het Hof van Cassatie* [*Rulings of the Court of Cassation*] 1999, 142; Cass. C.98.0398.N, 5 February 1999, *Arresten van het Hof van Cassatie* [*Rulings of the Court of Cassation*] 1999, 155.

112 See also for the position of the Constitutional Court regarding the introduction of new factual elements during a full judicial review: Constitutional Court No. 45/2010, 29 April 2010, considerations B.5-B.8; Constitutional Court No. 148/2008, 30 October 2008, consideration B.6.6; Constitutional Court No. 81/2008, 27 May 2008, considerations B.29.5 and B.29.6. The possibility of a factual and legal review does not entail an obligation of the judge to conduct new investigations or to take initiative in subjecting elements of the investigation to a debate (Court of Cassation C.09.0227.N, 3 June 2011).

113 The possibility of a proportionality test was hereby indirectly confirmed. The principle of proportionality is after all a general principle (A. Alen, 'Naar een betere rechtsbescherming [towards a better legal protection]', *l.c.*, (630), No. 14, p. 633 and No. 21 p. 635).

114 ECtHR No. 47650/99, 4 March 2004 (*Silvester's Horeca Service v. Belgium*), consideration 27. The Court noted that Belgian case law had since evolved, but that this was not relevant since the matter at hand took place prior to this shift in the case law (consideration 29).

115 Court of Arbitration No. 22/99, 24 February 1999, consideration B.13 (value added tax); Court of Arbitration No. 32/99, 17 March 1999, consideration B.10 (inheritance tax).

116 Court of Arbitration No. 96/02, 12 June 2002, consideration B.4.2 (value added tax). See also Court of Arbitration No. 138/2006, 14 September 2006, consideration B.7.2.

117 Court of Arbitration No. 125/03, 24 September 2003, considerations B.7 and B.8.

118 Court of Arbitration, No. 96/2002, 12 June 2002, consideration B.4.3; Court of Arbitration No. 125/2003, 24 September 2003, consideration B.8; also see Labour Court Brussels 4 February 1999, *Journal des Tribunaux du Travail* [*Journal of the Labour Tribunals*] 2000, 178 (there is no need to appreciate the duration of the exclusion when the sanction has been set at the minimum duration).

cases the examination would be limited to determining whether the conditions for imposing the sanction were met.

The Court of Cassation was able to review its position on this matter in three decisions delivered in 2002[119] and has since confirmed its modified reasoning.[120] The Court explicitly confirmed that the scope of the review included the possibility to examine the proportionality between the imposed sanction and the infraction.[121] It specified that the judge could conduct this examination by taking into account the severity of the infraction, the height of previously imposed sanctions and the manner in which similar cases have been dealt with. The Court added in one of the cases however that the judge was *not* allowed to reduce or lift sanctions 'because of reasons of opportunity and in violation of legal regulations'.[122] The Court has since reiterated this position. It held that the judge can review the proportionality of the decision, but cannot exceed the boundaries imposed by the legislator on the administration merely on the basis of his subjective assessment of what is opportune or reasonable.[123] In other words: the judge does not have the authority to e.g. simply ignore a minimum penalty prescribed by the legislator. If a judge were to deviate from the legal framework of the sanction, he needs to properly motivate this in the light of mandatory norms imposed by international treaties or internal legal norms such as general principles. This position was recently affirmed in another matter dealing with the application of extenuating circumstances.[124]

In short, a judge who is called upon to assess an administrative sanction with a punitive character has an identical term of reference as the administrative body which took the decision. This term of reference encompasses both the extent and the limits of the decision making authority. The position that the full judicial review should be limited to a legality test and a marginal appreciation has been abandoned. A judge is allowed to examine whether the administration could reasonably decide to impose an administrative sanction of a particular magnitude. He *may* particularly take into account the gravity of the infraction, the extent of already imposed sanctions and the manner in which similar cases

119 Court of Cassation C.00.0234.N, C.00.0442.N and C.00.0307.N, 24 January 2002, *Pasiscisie* 2002, 226 and 234; see also Labour Court Ghent (dept. Bruges) 14 February 2003, *Informatieblad R.I.Z.I.V.* [*Social security services newsletter*] 2003, 373.

120 Cass. F.06.0111.N, 12 December 2008, www.juridat.be.

121 Furthermore the Court added that the legality of the decision can also be examined with regard to its reconcilability with compulsory requirements included in international treaties.

122 Court of Cassation C.00.0307.N, 24 January 2002, *Pasicrisie* 2002, 234.

123 Court of Cassation 21 January 2005, *Rechtskundig Weekblad* [*Legal Weekly*] 2005–06, 1015, with the opinion of the Advocate General (concerning extenuating circumstances); Court of Cassation 13 February 2009, *Pasicrisie* 2009, 470.

124 Court of Cassation F.05.0015.N, 16 February 2007, www.juridat.be; see also Court of Cassation C.04.0390.N, 16 February 2007, *Pasicrisie* 2007, 365.

were dealt with. He *must* in any case take into account the extent to which the administration itself was obliged to impose the sanction. He is furthermore *not* allowed to reduce or remit a sanction on the basis of mere opportunity considerations *and* in violation of the applicable legal framework.[125] Therefore a judge cannot take into account e.g. personal considerations regarding the perpetrator if the administration itself does not have a legal basis to do so.[126]

This case law still left some uncertainty as to the extent of the judicial review of the judge. Some legislation concerning administrative sanctioning grants a wide discretion to certain officials in pardoning sanctions legally imposed by the administration.[127] The question then became whether a judge could review the use of this wide power and thereby potentially reduce validly imposed sanctions below their explicitly provided legal thresholds. The case law of the Constitutional Court states that the judge can also review the exercise of these powers, at least if the perpetrator had petitioned their application on his sanction.[128] The Court of Cassation ruled in 2008 that the judge has the authority to review any circumstances which may justify a reduction of an administrative fine below the legally imposed rates.[129] It reiterated this position in 2009.[130] The Court of Cassation has recently given clear guidelines as to how a judge should motivate his decision to reduce or annul a sanction: he should describe the cause of the unreasonableness, should investigate to what extent the administration itself was bound to impose a sanction and should specify the legal basis which would have allowed the administration to deviate from the sanction.[131]

Situations can arise in which the judge must be able to annul or reduce the administrative sanction below the minimum penalty as prescribed by law even

125 See e.g. the standardised formulation of Court of Cassation C.04.0390.N and F.05.0015.N, 16 February 2007, *Pasicrisie* 2007, 365 and 369. This has been reiterated in subsequent rulings as recently as Court of Cassation 11 March 2010, *Rechtskundig Weekblad* [*Legal Weekly*] 2010–11, 666 with the opinion of Advocate General Thijs.

126 See e.g. Court of Cassation 29 June 2009, *Pasicrisie* 2009, 1705. Concerning Article 119, §5 New Municipal Act. This act obliges the administration to determine the gravity of its sanction in the light of the seriousness of the infraction and of its recurrence.

127 For example, Article 9 of the Regency Decision of 18 March 1831 authorises the Minister of Finance to pardon fiscal administrative fines.

128 Constitutional Court No. 79/2008, 15 May 2008, consideration B.8. See also: Court of Arbitration No. 22/99, 24 February 1999, consideration B.13; Court of Arbitration No. 96/02, 12 June 2002, consideration B.4.2; Court of Arbitration No. 138/2006, 14 September 2006, consideration B.6.3-B.7.3.

129 Court of Cassation F.06.0111.N, 12 December 2008, www.juridat.be. Thereby declining to formulate a prejudicial question to the Constitutional Court; see also Court of Cassation F.00.0099.N, 24 January 2002, *Pasicrisie* 2002, 238.

130 Court of Cassation F.06.0107.N, 13 February 2009, *Pasicrisie* 2009, 470.

131 Court of Cassation 11 March 2010, *Rechtskundig Weekblad* [*Legal Weekly*] 2010–11, 666 with the opinion of Advocate General Thijs. See also: Court of Cassation C.07.0507.N, F.06.0108.N, F.06.109.N, 13 February 2009, www. juridat.be.

when the administration has no power to do so. This authority does not directly emanate from the principle of full jurisdiction as such, but from superior international legal norms such as mandatory norms imposed by international treaties or internal legal norms such as general principles of law. In determining the legality of the imposed sanction, the judge needs to determine if it is compatible with the aforementioned legal norms. If he decides that it is incompatible, he needs to carefully motivate this decision in order to avoid it being grounded on a strictly subjective appreciation and mere reasons of oppportunity while being contrary to the applicable legal framework. The Court of Cassation has for exemple ruled that, in principle, a full judicial review regarding the duration of a procedure to impose punitive sanctions within the meaning of Article 6 ECHR requires an examination of the behaviour of the administration and the perpetrator. The principle of proportionality can also justify a reduction of the sentence even if the administration did not possess a margin of appreciation for imposing the sanction.[132]

Another matter in dispute regarding the scope of the review was whether the judge has the authority to substitute the sanction (imposed through a valid decision) chosen by the administration in favour of a *different type of sanction* which he finds more appropriate. If one accepts that the authority of the judge is identical to the authority the administration enjoys[133], it is but a small step to accept that the judge can modify this sanction by replacing it with a different sanction. This requires that the preferred sanction of the judge was also available to the administration itself (and is, in other words, compatible with the applicable legal framework). Both the Constitutional Court and the Court of cassation have affirmed this possibility.[134] The judge can for example substitute an exclusion of the right to unemployment benefits with a mere warning.

The power to substitute annulled administrative decisions

The other angle concerns the power of the judge to actually *substitute his own decision after annulling the decision of the administration.* So far Belgian case law has refused to substitute its own decisions after annulment of the administrative

132 Court of Cassation F.07.0076.N, 12 November 2009, *Pasicrisie* 2009, 2582 (reasonable delay); Court of Cassation F.06.0107.N, 13 February 2009 (proportionality); Court of Cassation F.10.0074.N, 20 May 2011 (proportionality).

133 See Court of Arbitration No. 8/2007, 11 January 2007, consideration B.7.2 and Constitutional Court No. 81/2007, 7 June 2007, consideration B.7.2: it is a general principle of criminal law (in matters of sanctions with a criminal nature) that nothing which falls within the scope of appreciation of the administration, escapes from the review by the judge.

134 Court of Arbitration No. 128/99, 7 December 1999, consideration B.14; Court of Cassation 10 May 2004, *Nieuw Juridisch Weekblad* [*New Legal Review*] 2004, 1055.

decision if caused by the lack of an adequate formal motivation.[135] The justification for this recalcitrance is the respect for the separation of powers. In the context of unemployment benefits it has however been held that, regardless of the lack of any power to substitute, the judiciary is obliged to examine whether the addressee of an annulled decision fulfils the necessary requirements to receive unemployment benefits.[136] If this turns out to be the case, the person must be reinstated in his rights by the judge.

The question whether a full judicial review can be provided by a judge who can merely quash the decision, or whether it *ipso facto* requires a judge with the authority to fully substitute his own decision, is particularly important regarding the Council of State. This administrative court can only annul an administrative decision if it is only susceptible to be contested on the basis of Article 14, §1 ACS (the annulment power of the Council of State). It cannot directly substitute it on this legal basis.

Initial *ECHR* case law has clarified that, at least in civil matters, the full judicial review does not always mandate that the judge reviewing the sanction should be able to directly reform the decision himself.[137] A procedure whereby the judge's authority is limited to quashing the sentence after which a lower administrative body bound by the motives of the annulment[138] may repeat the

135 Court of Cassation 17 December 2001, *Pasicrisie* 2001, 2145, with the opinion of Advocate General Leclercq; Labour Court Mons 24 April 2007, *Jurisprudence Liège Mons Bruxelles* 2007, 1059; Labour Court Liège 14 February 2005, *Jurisprudence Liège Mons Bruxelles* 2006, 200; Labour Court Mons 15 January 2003, *Chroniques de droit social* [*Chronicles of Social Law*] 2003, 395; Labour Court Liège 30 May 2002, *Chroniques de droit social* [*Chronicles of Social Law*] 2002, 497; Labour Court Liège (dept. of Neufchâteau) 24 April 2002, *Journal des Tribunaux du Travail* [*Journal of the Labour Tribunals*] 2002, 447; Labour Court Ghent 4 May 2001, *Journal des Tribunaux du Travail* [*Journal of the Labour Tribunals*] 2002, 33; Labour Court 25 November 1998, *Chroniques de droit Social* [*Chronicles of Social Law*] 1989, 398.

136 Concerning the reinstatement in the right to unemployment benefits after an annulment of the decision to exclude the addressee: Court of Cassation 17 December 2001, *Pasicrisie* 2001, 2145, with the opinion of Advocate General Leclercq; Labour Court Liège 14 February 2005, *Jurisprudence Liège Mons Bruxelles* 2006, 200; Labour Court Brussels 4 February 1999, *Journal des Tribunaux du Travail* [*Journal of the Labour Tribunals*] 2000, 178; see also Court of Cassation 13 March 2000, *Bulletin* 2000, 562; Court of Cassation 12 November 2001, *Pasicrisie* 2001, 1841.

137 ECtHR, judgement in *Kingsley v. United Kingdom* of 7 November 2000, consideration 58. See also S. Van Drooghenbroeck, 'De vraies sanctions administratives ou des sanctions pénales camouflées? Réflexions à propos de la jurisprudence récente de la Cour européenne des droits de l'Homme', *l.c.*, (467) 475–476. See however ECtHR, No. 47650/99, judgement in *Silvester's Horeca Service v. Belgium* of 4 March 2004, consideration 27 (where the court uses the terminology 'reform' rather than quash).

138 This requirement is met concerning Council of State rulings. The administrations are allowed, if they find it necessary, to reach a new decision after an annulment. This decision must however respect the authority of the Council of State's decision to annul the previous decision (Council of State, Reyniers, No. 76.045, 30 September 1998, consideration 2.1.1.4.1). The new decision could have a content identical to the previous one as long as the shortcomings (e.g. lack of motivation) of the previous decision are rectified.

decision making process, can also fulfil the obligations of Article 6 ECHR. The *Constitutional Court* has therefore found that the Council of State can carry out a full judicial review in the context of disputes regarding permits and licenses as it is able to review both the facts and the application of the law as well as to examine the sanction in the light of general principles (including the principle of proportionality).[139] The *Council of State* ruled in 2008, contrary to its previous case law and the position of the Constitutional Court, that only ordinary courts and tribunals could examine administrative sanctions with a punitive character in the sense of Article 6 ECHR.[140] The *Court of Cassation* overturned this judgement in 2009[141], ruling that the Council of State has jurisdiction over such disputes if the legislator did not attribute this competency to the ordinary judiciary. The Council of State can, according to the Court of Cassation, examine whether the administrative decision has a legal basis and whether the perpetrator had the opportunity to have a judge examine the proportionality of the sanction. The Council of State has since conformed its case law. It considers its own assessment on the basis of 14, §1 ACS to constitute a full judicial review as required by Article 6 ECHR, because it can examine the legality, the facts, the motivation as well as the proportionality of the administrative sanction. It is not able to substitute the annulled decision, but the administration to which the matter is referred after annulment is bound by the judgement of the Council of State. If the administrative body takes a new decision on the matter it must respect the content of the annulment judgement.[142]

139 Court of Arbitration No. 14/2007, 17 January 2007; Court of Arbitration No. 6/2006, 18 January 2006, consideration B.14.1; see also Court of Arbitration No. 127/2000, 6 December 2000, B.14.3; Court of Arbitration No. 54/2001, 8 May 2001, consideration B.10.3 (in a disciplinary case). See also regarding full judicial review by the Council of State concerning negative evaluations by an administration of civil servants: Constitutional Court No. 181/2008, 11 December 2008, consideration B.11.

140 Council of State No. 188.455, 4 December 2008.

141 Court of Cassation, C.09.0019.N, 15 October 2009, *Nieuw Juridisch Weekblad* [*New Legal Review*] 2009, 816.

142 Council of State No. 220.330, 16 July 2012; Council of State No. 220.274, 11 July 2012; Council of State No. 220.211, 6 July 2012; Council of State No. 219.322, 10 May 2012; Council of State No. 219.156, 3 May 2012; Council of State, No. 201.373, 26 February 2010. As stated above the Council of State does not exercise a full judicial review when it is acting in its capacity as an administrative court of cassation on the basis of article 14, §2 ACS. This has been confirmed by Council of State jurisprudence (Council of State No. 219.316, 10 May 2012).

3. THE NOTION AND BASIC ELEMENTS OF ADMINISTRATIVE SANCTIONS

3.1. DEFINITION

So far, the Belgian legislator has not defined the term 'administrative sanction'. This lack of a legal definition necessitates a kind of 'gradual qualification process': an inquiry into the scope of application of every norm and every general principle, in order to determine whether or not a particular administrative sanction is affected by it.

As a consequence, it is not possible to give a legal definition that is acceptable to the whole Belgian legal system. Depending upon the norm or principle in question, different concepts, elements and definitions will have to be taken into consideration. That is why it is not possible to determine whether in the Belgian context, for example, the notion of 'administrative sanction' is limited to punitive sanctions or not. For some purposes this will indeed be the case, but for other purposes the punitive character might not be a deciding factor.

However, as will be shown hereunder, a number of definitions have been proposed in legal doctrine, and in most of them the punitive character of the measure is considered to be an important element of the concept of administrative sanctions, and a distinguishing factor from other comparable administrative measures. This fact is of some importance, as it shows the common appreciation of the concept in Belgian doctrine. At the same time it is only of relative importance: these doctrinal definitions mainly aim to define the research subject, and thereby do not have legal consequences.

Some of the definitions proposed by the legal doctrine are[143]:

- 'a legal action of an individual and repressive nature whereby a person or organ, part of the executive branch, acts in non-compliance of a binding legal norm'.[144]
- 'sanctions imposed by the administration without prior interference by a court, whereby a judicial review will only occur *a priori*, either by the Council of State or the ordinary courts and tribunals'.[145]

---

143 For a more complete analysis see J. Put, *Administratieve sancties* [*Administrative sanctions*], *o.c.*, 21–44 and M. Boes, *Administratieve sancties en art. 6 EVRM in België* [*Administrative sanctions and art. 6 ECHR in Belgium*], *o.c.*, 1–4.

144 H. Coremans, 'De administratieve sanctie. Naar een omlijning van het begrip [The administrative sanction. Towards an outline of the concept]', *Rechtskundig Weekblad* [*Legal Weekly*] 1964–1965, 756 (translation).

145 J. Ligot, 'De administratie naar Belgisch recht [The administration according to Belgian law]', *Tijdschrift voor Bestuurswetenschappen en Publiekrecht* [*Journal of public administration and public law*] 1973, 3 (translation).

- 'a harm imposed by the government, with a preventive and repressive aim, to prevent or suppress deviant social behaviour, [which can] be imposed on all members of the mandatory society we call the state'.[146]

Recent legal doctrine refers to the following definition: administrative sanctions are *punitive measures, determined by or in accordance with the law, that are imposed by an administrative body by means of a unilateral, individual administrative act, as a reaction to a prior violation of a legal norm.*[147] The violation of a legal norm is defined as a *culpable, personal action consisting of deliberate behaviour or negligence.*

3.2. ADMINISTRATIVE SANCTIONS COMPARED TO OTHER MEASURES

Legal doctrine generally distinguishes several categories of measures which are similar to administrative sanctions.[148] These are not all sanctions in the strict sense, provided they do not have a punitive character, although the person upon whom they are imposed might perceive them in that way.

3.2.1. Safety measures

In principle safety measures such as the temporary retraction of a driver's license or the prohibition to enter a stadium are not sanctions.[149] The goal of safety measures is to protect the public interest from all kinds of threats. They can be imposed irrespective of fault or responsibility.[150] The aim of the measures will be to contain or resolve the situation, not to sanction a particular individual. Their lack of punitive nature means they are not subject to the requirements of

146 P. Van Orshoven, *Behoorlijke rechtsbedeling bij geschillen over directe rijksbelastingen* [*Proper administration of justice with regard to disputes concerning direct taxes*], Antwerp, Kluwer Rechtswetenschappen, 1987, 81 (translation).

147 Definition proposed in J. Put, *Administratieve sancties* [*Administrative sanctions*], *o.c.*, 21–35 and 103–104. Used in e.g. M. Boes, 'Administratieve sancties [Administrative sanctions]', in: X (ed.), *Sancties en nietigheden* [*Sanctions and nullities*], Ghent, Larcier, 2003, 198 and L. Veny, L. De Geyter and F. Vandendriessche, 'De invoering van gemeentelijke administratieve sancties... of naar een publiekrechtelijke rechtshandhaving op lokaal vlak in België? [The introduction of municipal administrative sanctions... or towards a public law-based legal enforcement on the local level in Belgium?]', *Algemeen Juridisch Tijdschrift* [*General Legal Journal*] 1999–2000, 159.

148 See concerning the difficulties in defining the precise boundaries between measures, sanctions and punishments: J. Put, 'De afbakening van het sanctieconcept [The delimitation of the notion of sanctions]', *Nieuw Juridisch Weekblad* [*New Legal Weekly*] 2002, 80–82.

149 Court of Arbitration No. 105/2001, 13 July 2001, consideration B.2.4; Court of Arbitration No. 154/2004, 22 September 2004, consideration B.1.1; Court of Arbitration No. 156/2004, 22 September 2004, consideration B.4.1; M. Boes, *Administratieve sancties en art. 6 EVRM in België* [*Administrative sanctions and art. 6 ECHR in Belgium*], *o.c.*, 5.

150 *Ibid.*, 5 and M. Boes, 'Administratieve sancties [Administrative sanctions]', *l.c.*, 12.

Article 6 ECHR.[151] Safety measures are often taken in situations of urgency. This means that even certain obligations emanating from the general principles of proper administration, such as the duty to hear, can be sidestepped.

Sanctions, on the other hand, have a repressive aim and can be imposed regardless of any threat to the public interest. They require guilt or negligence. Sanctions can be chosen or modulated in order to reach an appropriate level of punishment and do not have the direct aim of protecting the public.

The mere fact that a safety measure inflicts a measure of 'pain' does not *ipso facto* qualify it as a punishment. However, the mere fact that a measure (also) has a preventive aim does not exclude the possibility that it could qualify as a punishment.[152]

3.2.2. Reparation measures

Like safety measures, the goal of reparation measures is not to punish.[153] Their goal is not to take away or minimise a risk either, but to repair damage that has been inflicted. They can be imposed even though no deliberate breach of a legal norm has occurred. Examples of reparation measures are the revocation of a licence if the requirements are no longer met, or the order to repay a subsidy when the conditions for its receipt were not or are no longer met.[154] Measures, which impose a larger burden on the addressee than the mere reparation of inflicted damage, will be qualified as sanctions and not as reparation measures.[155] Due to the autonomous nature of its definition a reparation

---

151 The Constitutional Court has ruled that this is not discriminatory when compared to the requirements imposed on measures of a punitive nature: Court of Arbitration No. 175/2002, 5 December 2002.

152 Council of State No. 197.212, 23 October 2009, *Tijdschrift voor Bestuurswetenschappen & Publiekrecht [Journal for Administrative Sciences & Public Law]* 2010, 113. A city adopted a regulation (on the basis of Article 135 New Municipalities Act, allowing it to take preventive measures) imposing a street prohibition for certain behaviours. The Council of State determines that the regulation is only applicable to persons who have already committed certain infractions and have been issued warnings. Furthermore the measure turns out to have been embedded in a context of punitive measures. Finally the Council deduces the punitive nature from the escalating durations of the measure in cases of repeated infractions. The Council of State therefore considers the measure to be illegal because Article 119*bis*, §2 New Municipalities Act (which limitatively enumerates the types of administrative sanctions available to municipalities) does not include street prohibitions.

153 M. Boes, *Administratieve sancties en art. 6 EVRM in België [Administrative sanctions and art. 6 ECHR in Belgium]*, *o.c.*, 6.

154 M. Boes, 'Administratieve sancties [Administrative sanctions]', *l.c.*, 205.

155 See J. Put, *Administratieve sancties [Administrative sanctions]*, *o.c.*, 37 and 77. However, the fixed nature of a reparation measure will not necessarily be considered indicative of a sanction with a repressive nature. The Constitutional Court ruled that a 'flat fee solidarity contribution' on behalf of the social security fund was not repressive in nature, but a fixed compensation for the non-payment of previous contributions (Constitutional Court No. 28/2012, 1 March 2012, B.11.1).

measure in the internal legal system could nonetheless be considered a punitive measure in the meaning of Article 6 ECHR.[156]

3.2.3. *Measures of order*

Measures of order are neither sanctions nor disciplinary measures. They are necessary to ensure the efficient functioning of the administration, such as reassigning or transferring a civil servant. They can be combined with disciplinary measures without defying the principle of *non bis in idem*. In principle none of the guarantees attached to disciplinary or administrative sanctioning procedures are applicable to this type of measure.[157] This is not the case if an administration tries to disguise sanctions as measures of order.[158]

3.2.4. *Criminal sanctions*

The distinction between administrative and criminal sanctions is of course crucial. Criminal sanctions have the advantage of the strict set of rules prescribed by criminal procedure and the guarantees contained in criminal acts. Administrative sanctioning procedures, on the other hand, can be influenced by principles emanating from international treaties, the Constitution and from the general principles of criminal law or proper administration, but in the absence of specific legislation this type of protection offers far less legal security. The Constitutional Court has determined that it is not in itself discriminatory to provide two types of procedures (administrative and criminal). But it immediately added that certain principles are applicable to sanctions with a punitive character (*in casu* the fines in labour matters prescribed by the Administrative Fines Act) irrespective of their qualification and that any difference in treatment between the procedures must be based on reasonable grounds.[159]

There are numerous consequences attached to the difference between criminal and administrative sanctions in the Belgian legal system[160]:

---

156 European Court of Human Rights, judgement in Hamer / Belgium of 27 November 2007, considerations 59–60.

157 A. Mast, J. Dujardin, M. Van Damme and J. Vande Lanotte, *o.c.*, 232–233. There is no possibility for an appeal to the Council of State either, except in serious cases such as preventive suspension – often a prelude to disciplinary procedures – in which case the duty to hear is applicable as well (*ibid.*, 233); M. Boes, *Administratief recht* [*Administrative law*], *o.c.*, 181–182.

158 See Council of State No. 50.974, 23 December 1994.

159 Court of Arbitration No. 72/92, 18 November 1992, *Belgian Bulletin of Acts and Decrees* 16 January 1993, consideration B.2.2. and B.4.3 respectively.

160 A. Mast, J. Dujardin, M. Van Damme and J. Vande Lanotte, *o.c.*, 15; J. Put, *Administratieve sancties* [*Administrative sanctions*], *o.c.*, 43.

- The administrative sanction will not be registered on the criminal record.
- The principle of *non bis in idem* is not necessarily applicable to the accumulation of criminal and administrative sanctions. Although recent case law has – in accordance the most recent ECHR case law – applied the 'idem' aspect of the *non bis in idem* principle on the similarity of the facts and not their legal definition, the principle itself is only applicable on the cumulation of sanctions with a punitive character (*infra*).
- Only the administration can reach a settlement with regard to the administrative sanction.
- There is doubt as to whether the right to grant a pardon under Article 110 Constitution is applicable to administrative sanctions.[161] The article does not explicitly restrict its application to criminal sanctions alone.
- Imprisonment for failure to pay an administrative fine is not possible. Article 12, §3 of the Constitution stipulates that only a judge can impose a sanction that entails imprisonment.
- The administrative fine will not expire if the addressee dies.[162]

3.2.5. Conditional, obligatory measures

The question arises whether non discretionary – 'automatic' – measures can qualify as administrative sanctions. These automatic measures do not entail a choice.[163] They are merely a procedural condition for the taking effect or discontinuation of legal consequences prescribed by law or by a judicial decision.[164] The exclusion of a person from unemployment benefits for failing to meet the necessary conditions to qualify for entitlement is for example not considered a sanction[165], whereas exclusions which are imposed as a sanction for providing false statements are.[166] The relevance of the distinction lies in the fact that they are not affected by the guarantees of Article 6 ECHR or the general principles of criminal law if they are not sanctions with a punitive character.

---

161 *Pro*: A. Mast, J. Dujardin, M. Van Damme and J. Vande Lanotte, *o.c.*, 15–16; *contra*: J. Put, *Administratieve sancties* [*Administrative sanctions*], *o.c.*, 43 and L. Huybrechts, *l.c.*, 10–11.

162 L. Huybrechts, *l.c.*, 10.

163 E.g. the dismissal of a civil servant who has lost the right to hold public office because of a criminal conviction. The administration must follow the verdict of the criminal court, irrespective of its own opinion on the matter (Council of State No. 25.397, 29 May 1985).

164 M. Boes, *Administratieve sancties en art 6 EVRM in België* [*Administrative sanctions and art. 6 ECHR in Belgium*], *o.c.*, 3–4.

165 Labour Court Liège 10 November 2003, *Jurisprudence Liège, Mons, Bruxelles* 2004, 430.

166 Labour Court Liège 9 December 2002, *Journal des Tribunaux du Travail* [*Journal of the Labour Tribunals*] 2003, 79; Labour Tribunal Hasselt 2 May 2001, *Rechtskundig Weekblad* [*Legal Weekly*] 2001–02, 956.

3.3. THE DIFFERENT FORMS OF ADMINISTRATIVE SANCTIONS IN BELGIUM

Mast et al. discern four variants of the administrative sanction.[167] A first variant is the administrative sanction 'imposed on persons other than civil servants who cooperate with the government'. Intended here are sanctions which can be imposed on doctors, pharmacists or paramedic professionals involved in the health care system, as well as contractors for public works. Secondly, there are administrative sanctions that could be imposed on consumers of a public service, such as ticket collectors imposing a fine on fare dodging on public transport vehicles. Then there are the quantitatively more prominent 'administrative sanctions imposable for non-compliance with legal or executive regulations' and finally the 'disciplinary measures'.

There is some controversy regarding the classification of disciplinary measures. The problem lies in the fact that, on the one hand, disciplinary measures have all the characteristics of an administrative sanction – violation of the legal order[168], imposed by the administration, punitive aim, unilateral and individual, with a legal basis – whereas, on the other hand, there is a special type of relationship between an administration and its civil servants. Traditionally, the presence of this special type of relationship was not considered to be sufficient to categorise disciplinary measures separately from other types of administrative sanctions.[169] This view has recently been changing.[170]

There are numerous types of administrative sanctions. They could, for example, be: administrative fines; the refusal, postponement, suspension, exclusion or revocation of (the right to) a recognition, authorisation, service, permission or licence; the (temporary or definitive) closure of an institution or company. As mentioned, Article 12, §3 Constitution forbids administrations to impose imprisonment as a sanction. This sanction would require the intervention of a judge.

---

167 A. Mast, J. Dujardin, M. Van Damme and J. Vande Lanotte, *o.c.*, 12–14.

168 Though disciplinary sanctions do not always require an illegal act by a civil servant in a strict sense. It is sufficient that he does not follow orders or disregards guidelines issued to him by his superiors (*ibid.*, 43).

169 M. Boes, *Administratieve sancties en art. 6 EVRM in België* [*Administrative sanctions and art. 6 ECHR in Belgium*], *o.c.*, 5.

170 J. Put, *Administratieve sancties* [*Administrative sanctions*], *o.c.*, 38 and footnote 144. Also see J. Put, 'Rechtshandhaving [Law enforcement]', *l.c.*, 1196.

3.4. ADMINISTRATIVE INVESTIGATION/INSPECTION METHODS

There is no uniform regulation with regard to the investigative competencies of the various administrations. The specific acts containing the administrative sanctions and sanctioning procedures will therefore also need to provide detailed information with respect to the investigative powers. These powers can be wide-ranging[171]:

1° Article 23 of the Competition Act allows the civil servants tasked with the investigation (the Unit of Reporters): to demand information irrespective of who possesses such information; to draft an official report (*'proces-verbaal'*) when establishing infractions; to receive dispositions and written or oral statements; to copy information; to consult experts; and to carry out investigations on location. The reporters can search premises as well, provided that they have a search warrant. During their search they can decide to impound items or seal property for a period of up to 48 hours.

2° Civil servants of the fiscal administration have fewer investigative powers. They can oblige taxpayers to provide information, request copies of digital information and visit locations. They have extensive options with regard to accessing information gathered by other administrations and criminal investigations (Articles 315 to 332 Income Tax Code). Information can be exchanged with fiscal administrations of other member states of the European Union. Provided an agreement has been concluded, the fiscal administration can allow civil servants of another EU member state to collect information on Belgian territory (Article 338).[172]

3° Infractions based on the New Municipalities Act are determined by the police (Article 119*bis*, §6).

4° The infractions contained in the Social Criminal Code can be investigated by civil servants called 'social inspectors', based on the Labour Inspection Act.[173] The social inspectors can investigate locations at any time and without warning, although they are only allowed to access private residences with prior consent from the police tribunal. They have the authority to collect information and interrogate, seal or impound items (Articles 18–52 Social Criminal Code). Similar to the fiscal administration, the social inspectors can access information gathered by other government bodies and can exchange

[171] The police are competent to investigate in all cases where criminal sanctions can be imposed (Article 8 CPC).

[172] For more information on the exchange of information in fiscal matters, see L. Huybrechts, *l.c.*, 308.

[173] This matter was previously regulated by the Act of 16 November 1972 betreffende de arbeidsinspectie [on the labour inspection], *Belgian Bulletin of Acts and Decrees* 6 December 1972, but is now contained in the Social Criminal Code.

intelligence with other member states of the International Labour Organization (Articles 54-57 Social Criminal Code). They can issue warnings prior to drafting an official report as well, preventing the risk of an administrative or criminal sanctioning procedure being initiated (Article 21 Social Criminal Code).

4. PROTECTION AGAINST ADMINISTRATIVE SANCTIONS

4.1. INTRODUCTION

In this chapter the protection against administrative sanctions in the administrative phase and in the subsequent judicial phase is examined. As stated before, there is no coherent legal framework to offer protection against administrative sanctions. Therefore, citizens and judges have to rely upon concurrent dispositions in specific acts, general principles and international conventions (such as Article 6 ECHR). Besides a whole range of provisions in specific administrative sanctioning systems, there are two main sets of principles concerning disputes in relation to administrative sanctions: the general principles of proper administration and the general principles of criminal law. Their applicability and possible consequences will be examined, focussing as much as possible on administrative sanctions, administrative sanctioning systems and the judicial control of the imposition of administrative sanctions.

4.2. THE GENERAL PRINCIPLES OF PROPER ADMINISTRATION (GPPA)

4.2.1. Scope of application

Administrations have to comply with the general principles of proper administration in all their administrative acts (irrespective of any punitive nature).[174] As a consequence, they need to be taken into account when reviewing those acts as well. It is therefore accepted that the GPPA can be enforced in the context of a judicial review.[175] In the traditional view there is only room for the application of the GPPA if a particular legislative act is either silent, needs to be interpreted concerning a particular issue, or provides several alternatives for the administration to choose from. The court, in other words, can scrutinize the administrative acts in the light of the GPPA (only) if the administration had some room for manoeuvre in making its decision. If, on the other hand, a legal

174 E.g. Court of Arbitration No. 14/2007, 14 January 2007, consideration B.4.3.

175 J. Put, *Administratieve sancties [Administrative sanctions]*, *o.c.*, 231.

norm obliges the administration to impose a particular sanction for a particular fact, and that fact has been proven, then the application of the GPPA would be irrelevant. After all, the sanction could not be changed as a result.[176]

Certain authors are of the opinion that at least some general principles can supersede legal norms created by the legislator.[177] Van Oevelen and Popelier make a distinction between a conflict of application and a material conflict.[178] In the first instance the judge would have to review the legality of the administrative act, not of the law itself. But in the second instance there could be a true conflict between the content of a principle and the content of a legal norm. This is where a prohibition of applying the GPPA *contra legem* could come into play.

4.2.2. Classification of the GPPA

There are just about as many different enumerations of general principles as there are attempts in legal doctrine to catalogue them. The 'classic' catalogue by Suetens contained seven principles: fair play, justification, due care, prohibition on the misuse of power, the prohibition of arbitrariness, equality and legal security.[179] The distinction between formal and procedural GPPA has become very widespread over the years.[180] The formal GPPA include: the duty to hear and the right of defence, impartiality, independence, fair play and (formal[181]) justification. The material principles include: (material, substantive) justification, the prohibition on the misuse of power, equality, due care, legal security and reasonableness. The criterion used to differentiate between the two categories is the type of influence which a particular GPPA will have on an administration.[182] Formal GPPA will only influence the formal decision-making process. They add to the quality of this process, but will not (necessarily) influence its outcome. Material principles, on the other hand, will have an intrinsic effect on the decision itself.

---

176 See M. Boes, 'Administratieve sancties [Administrative sanctions]', *l.c.*, 198–200.

177 P. Van Orshoven, 'Non scripta, sed nata lex', in: M. Van Hoecke (ed.), *Algemene rechtsbeginselen* [*General legal principles*], Antwerp, Kluwer, 1991, 76.

178 A. Van Oevelen and P. Popelier, 'De aansprakelijkheid van publiekrechtelijke rechtspersonen voor ondeugdelijke wetgeving [The liability of public law legal entities regarding unsound legislation]', in: X (ed.), *Publiekrecht. De doorwerking van het publiekrecht in het privaatrecht* [*Public law. The continued effect of public law in private law*], Ghent, Mys & Breesch, 1997, 108–113. Also see J. Put, *Administratieve sancties* [*Administrative sanctions*], *o.c.*, 220–224.

179 L. Suetens, *Op de grens van het ideaal denkbare en het praktisch haalbare* [*On the dividing line between the ideal concept and practicability*], Bruges, die Keure, 1997, 375.

180 See e.g. the enumerations in A. Alen, *Handboek van het Belgisch staatsrecht* [*Manual of Belgian public law*], *o.c.*, 693–694; J. Put, *Administratieve sancties* [*Administrative sanctions*], *o.c.*, 237–238; M. Boes, *Administratief recht* [*Administrative law*], *o.c.*, 58–71; S. Lust, *l.c.*, 29–32; J. De Staercke, *o.c.*, XI-XII.

181 *Contra* S. Lust, *l.c.*, 30.

182 M. Boes, *Administratief recht* [*Administrative law*], *o.c.*, 57–58.

4.2.3. The formal GPPA

The duty to hear (*audi alteram partem*)

The duty to hear has been recognised and enforced for a long time by both the Council of State and the Court of Cassation.[183] Its status as a general principle means that it has to be respected even in the absence of specific legal or executive regulations.[184] The duty to hear can be considered as an element of the rights of defence. It is a concrete manifestation of the principle of due care as well.[185] Opdebeeck therefore considers the aim of the duty to hear to be twofold[186]: (1) to safeguard the interests of the addressee (based on the rights of defence) and (2) to avoid administrations taking decisions without all relevant information (based on due care).

The principle of due care entails, amongst other requirements, that the administration does not form an opinion on alleged facts until it has given any implicated persons the opportunity to present their version of the facts. Because of its due care aspect, the duty to hear is applicable to all types of administrative sanctions (with or without a punitive character).

The 'right to be heard' differs in scope and content from the 'right of defence' in the case law of the Council of State. The 'right of defence' has a more narrow field of application – it is only applicable in punitive and disciplinary matters[187] – and imposes more rigid duties on behalf of the administration. The duty to hear, on the other hand, has been given a much broader scope. According to the Council of State, the administration has to observe the duty to hear whenever it considers imposing a serious measure, based on the personal conduct of the addressee, with grave consequences.[188] 'Grave consequences' are those consequences that

---

183 L. Suetens, *o.c.*, 375 referring to W.J. Ganshof van der Meersch, 'Le droit de la défense, principe general de droit. Réflexions sur des arrêts récents [The right of defence, general legal principle]', in: X (ed.), *Mélanges en l'honneur de Jean Dabin* [*Contributions in honour of Jean Dabin*], II, Brussels, Bruylant, 1963, 569–614. The duty to hear is applicable to the addressee of the (potential) measure. There is no general principle obliging the administration to consult with third parties such as lobbying groups (Council of State No. 215.194, 19 September 2011).

184 Council of State No. 190.646, 19 February 2009, consideration 3.5.1; Court of Arbitration No. 139/2006, 14 September 2006, consideration B.9.1.

185 I. Opdebeeck, 'Het recht van verdediging en het recht om zijn standpunt naar voor te brengen [The right of defence and the right to be heard]', in: I. Opdebeeck (ed.), *Algemene beginselen van behoorlijk bestuur* [*General Principles of Proper Administration*], Deurne, Kluwer, 1993, 55.

186 I. Opdebeeck, *l.c.*, 55.

187 Council of State, *Lecluyse*, No. 82.636, 4 October 1999, consideration 2.1.3.1; Council of State No. 211.269, 15 February 2011. See also Council of State No. 220.330, 16 July 2012.

188 Council of State No. 24.651, 18 September 1984, *Rechtskundig Weekblad* [*Legal Weekly*] 1984–85, 946; Council of State, *George*, No. 59.860, 4 June 1996, consideration 2.1.4; Council of

seriously affect the addressee's moral and financial interests.[189] In principle this duty can only arise for administrative decisions with a personal scope (i.e. targeting concrete individuals) and not a regulatory scope (i.e. targeting an abstract category of persons).[190] However the Council of State has ruled that a duty to hear could also arise where the administration seemingly undertakes a regulatory act that in reality has such a restrained scope so that it only targets a few very specific individuals.[191]

The requirements for the duty to hear will be met if the addressee of the sanction was accorded a proper chance to plead his case. This implies a right to access the relevant information, a reasonable timeframe to prepare the defence and a suitable method and channel to communicate his arguments. The Council of State (and the ordinary courts) will judge the requirements of the right to hear according to the particular circumstances of each case. There is no violation of the duty to hear if the addressee had the opportunity to present his view and did not take advantage of it.[192]

The first requirement is that the addressee had the opportunity to be well informed of the essential data on which the administration based its decision.[193] The addressee should be informed of the type and nature of the sanction being considered. This could, for example, be a disciplinary sanction (e.g. suspension, a temporary pay cut), a fine, the revocation of a licence, etc. The administration should also announce on which shortcomings or which facts it plans to base its decision.[194] The Council of State has accepted that the addressee of an administrative sanction (unlike disciplinary measures) need not *a priori* be informed of all facts or grievances. It is sufficient to offer him the opportunity to request access to the information, especially if the administration can

State, *De Brabant*, No. 126.220, 9 December 2003, consideration 3.3.2; Council of State, *Standaert*, No. 131.827, 27 May 2004, consideration 2.I.4. See also Council of State, *Brynaert*, No. 156.078, 8 March 2006 and No. 171.146, 14 May 2007; A. Mast, J. Dujardin, M. Van Damme and J. Vande Lanotte, *o.c.*, 52–53.

189 J. De Staercke, *o.c.*, 36, with a certain nuance in footnote 171.

190 Council of State No. 199.002, 17 December 2009, consideration 55.

191 Council of State No. 171.269, 16 May 2007.

192 Council of State, No. 177.415, 29 November 2007, consideration 2.1.5. The mere fact that the addressee of the sanction had only been in contact with the administration two times during the procedure was held not to be a sufficient reason for the administration to subsequently disregard its duty to offer this individual the possibility of a proper hearing (Council of State No. 210.529, 20 January 2011).

193 Council of State, *De Brabant*, No. 126.220, 9 December 2003, consideration 3.3.2; Court of Arbitration No. 139/2006, 14 September 2006, consideration B.9.1.

194 Council of State, *The box*, No. 50.287, 22 November 1994, consideration 2.1.4; Council of State, *De Brabant*, No. 126.220, 9 December 2003, consideration 3.3.2 and 3.3.4; Council of State No. 190.646, 19 February 2009, consideration 3.5.1.

legitimately assume that the addressee is already acquainted with the essential elements of the case.[195]

The addressee must be given a reasonable time to prepare his case.[196] As the specific requirements of the right to hear (and the other GPPA) can vary from case to case, there is always a degree of uncertainty.[197] For example, a delay of 24 hours to prepare for the hearing will generally be considered too short.[198] But depending on the facts of the matter a delay of two days might already suffice[199], or it may still be too short.[200]

There can also be some uncertainty regarding the manner in which the addressee can present his argumentation. In normal circumstances a written defence will suffice. The administration can, again depending on the circumstances[201], refuse the request for an oral defence. In disciplinary matters the administration which is competent to sanction should itself hear the addressee. A deviation from this principle is possible if it would not be practical for the administration to do this itself.[202] It is not, in the absence of binding norms imposing the contrary, required that the administration who hears the addressee is the same as the administration who actually takes the decision.[203] In general it will usually suffice to have the addressee of the decision heard by a different administrative body, which in turn formulates an advice for the competent administration (e.g. a specialised committee which reports to the minister who is competent to impose the sanction).[204] The assistance of legal counsel in presenting the case is, in theory, always permitted. However, when there is an organised right of defence, this requirement does not need to be met at all stages of the procedure.

---

195 Council of State, Bastiaensen, No. 98.888, 17 September 2001, consideration 2.1.2.3.

196 Court of Arbitration No. 139/2006, 14 September 2006, consideration B.9.1; Council of State, *Brynaert*, No. 156.078, 8 March 2006, No. 171.146, 14 May 2007 and No. 210.529, 20 January 2011.

197 See M. Boes, *Administratief recht* [*Administrative law*], *o.c.*, 55.

198 Council of State No. 23.871, 11 January 1984; Council of State No. 25.350, 23 May 1985; Council of State No. 39.156, 3 April 1992; Council of State No. 39.491, 27 May 1992; Council of State, *Herremans*, No. 61.682, 11 December 1996.

199 Council of State, *Reyniers*, No. 76.045, 30 September 1998, consideration 2.3.3.2.

200 Council of State, *Brynaert*, No. 156.078, 8 March 2006 and No. 171.146, 14 May 2007.

201 E.g. the technical and precise nature of the case: Council of State No. 104.482, 7 March 2002, consideration 2.2. See also Council of State No. 214.399, 4 July 2011. If the more narrow and strict right of defence is applicable, the addressee of the (potential) sanction has the right to an oral defence, unless the applicable law specifically states otherwise (Council of State No. 216.101, 27 October 2011).

202 Council of State, *Delanghe*, No. 125.829, 1 December 2003, consideration 2.3.3.

203 Council of State No. 182.454, 28 April 2008, consideration 4.5.

204 Council of State, George, No. 59.860, 4 June 1996, consideration 2.1.4. See also: Court of Arbitration No. 178/2006, 29 November 2006, B.3.1 and B.5.4. See nonetheless: Pol. Bruges 24 October 2003, *Tijdschrift voor de Vrederechter* [*Journal for the Justice of the Peace*], 2003, 480 (stating that the decision must be taken by the official who heard the perpetrator).

It is sufficient that legal assistance is allowed in the phase of the procedure where it can be exercised in the most efficient manner.[205]

The duty to hear might have a broader scope of application, but it is much more flexible in turn. It can even be disregarded in several situations[206]:

- If the facts upon which the decision is to be based are directly and easily determinable by the administration, no objection can be raised concerning these facts and the administration itself is bound as to the consequences it has to attach to such facts.[207] The right to hear should however be afforded if the facts are not clear or if the administration has a discretionary power to choose whether or not to impose a sanction, to modify the severity of the sanction or to choose between different types of sanctions.[208]
- In case of urgency.[209] If a request for an annulment is lodged, the Council of State can examine whether the situation was sufficiently urgent as to justify side-stepping the duty to hear.[210]
- If the addressee of the decision is unreachable. The addressee must be contactable within a reasonable time frame.

205 I. Opdebeeck, *l.c.*, 74–75; J. De Staercke, *o.c.*, 38.

206 I. Opdebeeck, *l.c.*, 66–69; M. Boes, *Administratief recht* [*Administrative law*], *o.c.*, 59–60.

207 Council of State No. 190.646, 19 February 2009, consideration 3.5.2. However, such a claim by the administration will be thoroughly examined by the Council of State. See for example Council of State No. 198.994, 17 December 2009 (the Council determined that the measure of a permanent closure of the establishment was not as obvious and logical as the administration pictured it to be, thereby determining that the administration should have observed the duty to hear).

208 See for example Council of State, *Devos*, No. 126.049, 4 December 2003. A municipal police regulation stipulated that a market vendor who missed four consecutive market days would see his right to a fixed market stand revoked, except in case of circumstances beyond his control. In that case the market director had to be informed as soon as possible. A market vendor did not attend the market for four consecutive days without alerting the market director and saw his right revoked. He challenged this decision on the basis that he had not been accorded a right to be heard, whereas the municipality argued that they did not have any margin of appreciation in taking the decision. The Council of State however found that there was a certain margin of appreciation, namely whether or not the market vendor was faced with force majeure. It determined that the sanction was linked to the period of absence and not to neglecting to notify the market director. In other words, the sanction could not be applied if there was force majeure, even if the notification requirement was not met. The Council therefore decided that the market vendor should have been accorded a proper right to be heard on the matter. It has been ruled that, even if administration enjoys a wide margin of appreciation, the justification of the decision may be manifestly clear in such a manner that the addressee of the measure need not be heard (Council of State, *Vandekerkhove*, No. 170.195, 19 April 2007, 2.1.2. The addressee had fired an unlicensed automatic weapon in his backyard, upon which the most severe response -a revocation instead of a suspension of the licenses for his other weapons- was chosen without granting him a chance to be heard. Such types of decisions are however more akin to safety measures than sanctions).

209 Council of State No. 196.542, 1 October 2009, consideration 6; Council of State No. 190.646, 19 February 2009, consideration 3.5.4.

210 Council of State No. 67.857, 29 August 1997, consideration 4.3.2.

- When the addressee has already presented his version to the administration on his own initiative[211] or, as seen above, if the administration did not hear the addressee itself but can rely on an advice of the administrative body which did hear the addressee.
- When a decision respecting the duty to hear is later revoked or annulled due to a procedural error (unrelated to the duty to hear), and the administration decides to retake the same decision.[212]
- When the right of defence has been specifically organised regarding a particular matter.[213]

Impartiality (*Nemo iudex in sua causa*) and independence

The principle of impartiality is applicable to administrative tribunals.[214] The question is whether the entities of the 'active' administration (the common administrative bodies) need to respect it. This is definitely the case in disciplinary matters.[215] The Council of State has ultimately ruled that the principle of impartiality is applicable to other administrative matters as well, insofar as it is reconcilable with the nature of the administration, in particular its structure.[216] The latter means that the taking of a decision itself cannot be rendered impossible by the application of the principle of impartiality. If the principle of impartiality is not sufficiently safeguarded in such an instance, protection will need to be sought through the other principles of proper administration (such as due care, proportionality...).[217]

211 Council of State No. 77.153, 24 November 1998, consideration 2.1.4.1; M. Boes criticizes this exception to the duty to hear: it ignores the fact that the addressee should be informed of all useful information and it greatly minimises the procedural aspects (M. Boes, *Administratief recht* [*Administrative law*], *o.c.*, 60). See also Council of State No. 190.646, 19 February 2009, consideration 3.5.4 (hypothesis concerning the duty to inform if the addressee is already aware of the possible decision).

212 Council of State No. 36.481, 22 February 1991. The preparation period can be shortened in such cases as well (Council of State No. 76.045, 30 September 1998, consideration 2.1.1.4.1).

213 Council of State, *Laroy Veevoeders*, No. 121.935, 30 July 2003, consideration 6.3.2.

214 Court of Cassation 14 May 1987, *Pasicrisie* 1987, I, 1067, with the opinion of Advocate General J. Velu; K. Leus, 'De plicht tot onpartijdigheid als beginsel van behoorlijk bestuur [The duty of impartiality as a principle of proper administration]', in: I. Opdebeeck (ed.), *Algemene beginselen behoorlijk bestuur* [*General Principles of Proper Administration*], Antwerp, Kluwer, 1993, 173–175. See concerning the requirements of Article 6 ECHR: Council of State, De Jaeger, No. 102.632, 17 January 2002, consideration 2.2.2.3; Council of State, *Magerman*, No. 102.633, 17 January 2002, consideration 2.1.2.3.

215 K. Leus, *l.c.*, 176–183.

216 Council of State No. 26.116, 28 January 1986, *Journal des Tribunaux* [*Courts Journal*] 1989, 307. Also the Court of Cassation considers the principle of impartiality to be a general principle of law, applicable – as a rule – to organs of the active administration as well: Court of Cassation 9 January 2002, *Pasicrisie* 2002, I, 43, with the opinion of Advocate General J. Spreutels.

217 K. Leus, *l.c.*, 194.

The administrative decision-making bodies should be able to function independently as well.[218] This means that the administration must be structured in a way that allows both the body in its entirety and its individual members to, for example, decide on the imposition of a sanction without any coercion.

Fair play

The acts of an administration lack fair play if it deliberately[219] tries to hinder citizens, through illegitimate means, when they wish to exercise their rights.[220] This includes the withholding of information, delaying tactics, or the taking of rash decisions.[221] The mere fact that the administrative sanction was imposed on the last day of the prescribed term is not in itself a violation of the fair play principle. This 'delay' can even be beneficial to the addressee of the sanction since it offers him a better opportunity to pursue a proper defence and to prepare his business for the negative consequences of the eventual sanction.[222] This GPPA is rarely invoked in the context of administrative sanctions.

Formal justification

Every unilateral decision by the administration of an individual must be based on motives which are not merely present in order to fulfil legal obligations, but which are also pertinent and can account for the decision. This implies two different types of justification: formal and substantive justification. Prior to the Act of 1991 concerning the explicit justification of administrative acts[223], the administration was generally not obliged to include a formal justification.[224] A substantive justification was sufficient, unless a specific act stated otherwise.

The Act of 1991, on the other hand, obliges every administration to include an explicit justification for all its unilateral administrative acts of an individual

218 See A. Van Mensel, *Het beginsel van behoorlijk bestuur* [*The principle of proper administration*], Ghent, Mys & Breesch, 1997, 29.

219 The act must be intentional: A. Mast, J. Dujardin, M. Van Damme and J. Vande Lanotte, *o.c.*, 55; M. Van Damme, 'Goede trouw van burger en bestuur [Good faith on the part of the citizen and the administration]', *Rechtskundig Weekblad* [*Legal Weekly*] 1989–90, 1115; Council of State, Verbelen, No. 59.052, 15 April 1996, consideration 3.2.2.6.

220 M. Boes, *Administratief recht* [*Administrative law*], *o.c.*, 65.

221 L. Suetens, *o.c.*, 382; J. De Staercke, *o.c.*, 34.

222 Council of State, *Laroy Veevoeders*, No. 121.935, 30 July 2003, consideration 6.3.3 (concerning a temporary suspension of the recognition for the production of compound feed).

223 Act of 29 July 1991 betreffende de uitdrukkelijke motivering van bestuurshandelingen [concerning the explicit justification of administrative acts], *Belgian Bulletin of Acts and Decrees* 12 September 1991.

224 See L. Suetens, *o.c.*, 380–381.

nature. The Constitutional Court[225] ruled that by imposing an explicit duty of justification, the law did not intend to affect the organisation and functioning of administrations (*cf.* Article 9 SARI), but to increase the legal protection of citizens. Federal legislation was therefore deemed possible based on federal residuary responsibility.

Article 2 of the 1991 Act demands an explicit justification. The formal justification (only) entails the mentioning of the legal norms applied and the facts pertinent to the case.[226] To determine the notion of 'administration', the 1991 Act refers to Article 14 of the coordinated Acts of 12 January 1973 concerning the Council of State.[227] Administrative acts are defined as unilateral, individual acts aiming to create legal consequences. Sanctions imposed by an administration clearly fit this description.

There are four exceptions to the duty of formal justification. Formal justification is not required if the legal consequences could endanger the external security of the state, disrupt the public order, encroach on the respect of someone's private life, or infringe the duty of confidentiality (Article 4). Urgency is not a proper reason to avoid formal justification (Article 5).

The 1991 Act has the aim of setting a minimum standard concerning the justification of administrative decisions. Article 6 of the 1991 Act ensures this by deviating from the adage *lex specialis derogat legi generali*: in case a specific law does not offer the same level of protection with regard to justification, it will be complemented by the Act of 1991.

The Council of State will relatively easily accept that the duty of formal justification has been met. The justification will be considered sufficient as soon as the decision – even briefly – refers to elements in the administrative file on which it is based. There is no need to elaborate extensively on every piece of information that underlies the decision, provided, of course, that the addressee had the opportunity to access the elements of the file being referred to.[228]

---

225 Court of Arbitration No. 55/2001, 8 May 2001, consideration B.2 to B.5.

226 S. Lust, *l.c.*, 30. See for example: Council of State No. 58.360, 23 February 1996.

227 The problem was that this article did not contain a detailed, conclusive definition of the term either. The Court of Cassation (Court of Cassation 6 September 2002, *Rechtskundig Weekblad* [*Legal Weekly*] 2002–03, 817, note R. Verstegen) seems to have settled the matter by offering the following clarification: institutions founded by the government, or founded by private persons (but recognised by the government) are administrations if their operation is determined and controlled by the government and if they can impose binding decisions on third parties.

228 The government must be able to prove that the addressee was made aware of the existence of a document. Concerning a measure of order: Council of State, *Imbrechts*, No. 129.236, 15 March 2004, consideration 3.4.2.2.

The only way for the administration to prove that its act is formally justified is by including a adequate justification in the decision itself. If no such justification has been expressed in the decision, the administration cannot simply claim the administrative file is sufficient for the purpose of formal justification.[229] On the other hand, administrations are not required to respond to every argument that has been put forward by the addressee. It is sufficient that the grounds of the decision can be deducted from the motives accompanying it.[230] The Council of State can require a more direct response to the arguments of the addressee, though, depending on the circumstances of the case.[231]

The sanctions for neglecting the formal justification are annulment (or non-application on the basis of Article 159 Constitution)[232] and the suspension of the period for appeal. A distinction must be made between the justification of obligatory and discretionary decisions. If the administration is obliged to take a particular decision, the addressee cannot have this decision annulled in case the justification is lacking. He would not have the (required) interest to do so[233]: the annulment would only result in the administration retaking the same decision, without any benefit to the addressee (as he was not harmed by the lack of justification). This is not the case if the administration had a margin of appreciation. Nonetheless, if the addressee was already aware of the motives (e.g. for example through reference to previous or separate documents which leave no room for doubt) he would, depending on the circumstances, lack the necessary interest as well.[234]

4.2.4. The material GPPA

Substantive justification

The other aspect of the principle of justification concerns its material requirements. Formal justification merely requires that motives are included in, or attached to the decision. Should no formal motives have been included, the

229 Article 3 of the Explicit Justification Act; Court of Appeals Ghent 4 March 2003, *Jurisprudence fiscale* [*Fiscal case-law*] 2004, 18. The adequacy of a justification in a particular case is however a matter of fact. A judge can legitimately establish that the justification is sufficient irrespective of a (partial) reference to the administrative file (Cass. 14 April 2003, *Pasicrisie* 2003, 823).

230 Council of State, *St. Clemens*, No. 130.671, 27 April 2004, consideration 2.1.4.1; Council of State, *Vandenbrande*, No. 106.511, 13 May 2002, consideration 2.5.3.

231 E.g. a case concerning disciplinary matters where a heavier sentence than advised was imposed, while an argument concerning extenuating circumstances was discarded without justification: Council of State, *Vanfleteren*, No. 109.992, 3 September 2002, consideration 3.5.

232 See e.g. *supra* footnote 135.

233 Council of State, *Bourdouxhe*, No. 68.265, 24 September 1997.

234 Council of State, *Vandenbrande*, No. 106.511, 13 May 2002, consideration 2.5.3.

decision is illegitimate despite any possible grounds present in the administrative file. In this sense, the requirement of formal justification can be seen as an *addendum* to the material aspect[235], which means that merely respecting the formalities does not suffice. After all, the principle of justification will only be effective if the administration is obliged to base its decisions on pertinent grounds which demonstrate the legitimacy and necessity of its acts.

Therefore Article 3 of the 1991 Act requires the justification to be adequate as well, offering a legal basis for the principle of substantive justification. It demands an accurate and intelligible[236] communication of the factual and legal basis of the decision.

Legal doctrine distinguishes two duties with regard to adequate justification: the duty to ensure that the justification has the capacity to 'carry' the decision, and proportionality.[237] The first duty requires the decision to be supported by its motives. It means that the motives must all be pertinent and avoid vagueness or inconsistency. For example, a justification based on a limited number of grounds will not suffice if it is contradicted by numerous other elements in the administrative file. The motivation should enable the addressee of the sanction to examine whether there is a cause for exercising the methods of legal recourse which are available to him.[238] The duty of proportionality adds some flexibility to the strict requirements of the 1991 Act. It allows for a 'common sense' judgement by the administration with regard to how exhaustive the justification should be. A non-discretionary decision can be motivated by simply referring to the legislation and the facts which provoked the application of this legislation.[239] The more important or discretionary the decision, the more elaborate and thorough the justification should be.[240]

Justification by filling in standard forms or other methods using standard clauses can be acceptable in certain situations (e.g. for an administration that has to take large quantities of non-discretionary decisions). But even with the application of standard forms the justification of the decision must be proportionate, pertinent, individual and intelligible.[241]

---

235 M. Boes, *Administratief recht* [*Administrative law*], *o.c.*, 62.

236 See J. De Staercke, *o.c.*, 20–21.

237 J. Put, *Administratieve sancties* [*Administrative sanctions*], *o.c.*, 338–352.

238 Court of Arbitration No. 14/2007, 14 January 2007, consideration B.4.4.

239 Labour Court Ghent (dept. Bruges) 14 March 2003, *Informatieblad R.I.Z.I.V.* [*Social security services newsletter*] 2003, 373.

240 M. Boes, *Administratief recht* [*Administrative law*], *o.c.*, 64.

241 See M. Boes, 'Motivering van bestuurshandelingen [Justification of administrative acts]', *Recente Arresten van de Raad van State* [*Recent Rulings of the Council of State*] 1994, 119.

If the administration has a certain degree of discretion or freedom in imposing a sanction or in deciding on its amount, the justification will need to be more elaborate. This is because the civil servant will have to take elements such as the legal cause, the facts, the circumstances of the case, the gravity of the infraction, the personal situation of the addressee, *force majeure* and extenuating circumstances into account. He will need to provide a proper justification of their impact on his decision accordingly. It should be noted that, if an administration is required to take multiple decisions the regarding the same facts, the justification must be adequate for all decisions involved. A justification which is sufficient for decisions which were non-discretionary may not suffice for decisions for which the administration enjoyed a margin of appreciation.[242]

Often the civil servant will be able to choose or modulate the penalty. Justification is required for those aspects as well. It should be noted that the decision to impose a penalty and the decision concerning the severity of the penalty can be justified and reviewed separately. It is possible that the decision was justified, but that the administration imposed a higher fine than the minimum without proper justification. The imposition of a penalty is for example not carried by the justification that it amounts to the 'average penalty', without the justification that the facts of the matter were of an average severity. In such cases the decision does not need to be considered as completely void (which would be the consequence if the entire decision were unjustified) if the imposition of the sanction in itself is properly justified. The penalty could simply be reduced to the minimum penalty.[243] Conversely, the imposition of the minimum penalty does not justify why any sanction was necessary, which results in a lack of justification if the administration had the option of not imposing a sanction.[244]

Due care

The principle of due care has both a procedural and a material aspect. The administration should respect all procedural requirements of the decision-making process or regarding the execution of the decision (formal due care), and the decision should be proper and correct with appropriate consideration for the interests of those affected by it (material due care).[245]

242 Labour Court Mons 16 April 1999, *Journal des Tribunaux du Travail* [*Journal of the Labour Tribunals*] 2000, 176.

243 Labour Court Brussels 18 November 1998, *Chroniques de droit sociale* [*Chronicles of Social Law*] 1999, 268; J. Put, *Administratieve sancties* [*Administrative sanctions*], *o.c.*, 346–348.

244 Labour Court Liège 28 April 1999, *Jurisprudence Liège, Mons, Bruxelles* 1999, 1582.

245 W. Lambrechts, 'Het zorgvuldigheidsbeginsel [The principle of due care]', in: I. Opdebeeck (ed.), *Algemene beginselen van behoorlijk bestuur* [*General Principles of Proper Administration*], Antwerp, Kluwer, 1993, 30–31.

This principle goes through several phases. An administration should initiate its decision-making process with 'due preparation', which entails the diligent gathering of information. This can occur by, for example, allowing the potential addressee of a sanction to exercise his right of defence[246], or by seeking expert advice in technical matters.[247] All the members of a decision-making body should examine all the available information as well. This phase then has to lead to 'due decision making' and ultimately result in a 'timely' decision.[248]

Both the Council of State and the ordinary courts and tribunals attach great importance to the fact-finding aspect of the due care principle. The administration must have convincing evidence before it decides to impose sanctions. It cannot simply rely on the direct executable force or the presumption of legality to reverse the burden of proof.[249]

According to the Constitutional Court, the principle of due care mandates the civil servant which hears the perpetrator to draft a written report and that the civil servant who takes the decision to impose a sanction consults this this report.[250]

Reasonableness

The administration must take the principle of reasonableness into account when exercising a discretionary power.[251] It is also known as the prohibition of arbitrariness or the principle of proportionality.[252] It allows a judge to marginally review the (discretionary) decision of an administration. The judge, in other words, is not able to repeat the decision-making process of the civil servant, but to review it and to determine its legitimacy.[253] If a decision is not manifestly unreasonable, then the judge must refrain from imposing his own judgement.[254] See however the influence of Article 6 ECHR on the examination by the judiciary of administrative sanctions with a punitive character discussed above.

---

246 Thereby illustrating the close link between the principle of due care and other principles such as the duty to hear.

247 W. Lambrechts, *l.c.*, 34–36.

248 *Ibid.*, 41–44.

249 J. Put, *Administratieve sancties [Administrative sanctions]*, *o.c.*, 249.

250 Court of Arbitration No. 178/2006, 29 November 2006, B.5.4.

251 If it is obliged to take a particular decision then this principle is not applicable (M. Boes, 'Het redelijkheidsbeginsel [the principle of proportionality]', *l.c.*, 92, 115).

252 L. Suetens, *o.c.*, 386.

253 A. Mast, J. Dujardin, M. Van Damme and J. Vande Lanotte, *o.c.*, 56.

254 See for example Council of State No. 133.216, 28 June 2004, consideration 3.3.3.

Reasonable delay

The principle of reasonable delay was originally considered to be part of the principles of legal security and due care, but has evolved into a principle with an autonomous application.[255] The obligation it entails – to reach a decision within a reasonable timeframe – is of course one of the requirements embedded in Article 6 ECHR as well. Article 6 deals with the reasonable delay in (civil and) criminal proceedings and should be applied to administrative sanctions with a punitive character from that perspective.[256] In its capacity of GPPA, however, it is applicable to the administrative decision-making process. The principle of reasonable delay is accepted by the Council of State as a general principle and is, as such, applicable to the administrative courts even when Article 6 ECHR does not apply.[257] The Council considers the reasonable term requirement to be applicable in disciplinary and other types of administrative proceedings as well[258], even in the absence of binding time limits.[259]

There is no strict criterion by which to determine whether or not a delay has become unreasonable. This will have to be evaluated on a case by case basis. The nature and complexity of the dispute, the behaviour of the addressee, the severity of the potential sanction and the behaviour of the authorities all need to be taken into account by the judge.[260]

An important aspect of determining whether the delay is reasonable is establishing the starting and ending point of the (administrative) decision-making process. These are not necessarily identical to the starting and ending point of the reasonable time prescribed by Article 6 ECHR, which only needs to be taken into account for administrative sanctions with a punitive character. The starting point with regard to the reasonable administrative delay is the date on which the decision-making process was either initiated, or should have been initiated. For administrative sanctions this is the moment when the

---

255 M. Van Damme, 'Het rechtszekerheids- en vertrouwensbeginsel [The principles of legal certainty and legitimate expectations]', in: I. Opdebeeck (ed.), *Algemene beginselen van behoorlijk bestuur* [*General Principles of Proper Administration*], Antwerp, Kluwer, 1993, 121.

256 See e.g.: Court of Cassation F.07.0076.N, 12 November 2009, *Pasicrisie* 2009, 2582; Labour Tribunal Antwerp, 5 September 1996 *Rechtskundig Weekblad* [*Legal Weekly*] 1997–98, 304.

257 Council of State, *De Vare*, No. 133.273, 29 June 2004, consideration 2.1.2.1; Council of State, *Waeterschoot*, No. 154.424, 2 February 2006, consideration 2.1.2.

258 J. Put, *Administratieve sancties* [*Administrative sanctions*], *o.c.*, 307.

259 Council of State, *Mahieu*, No. 130209, 9 April 2004, consideration III, B, 2.

260 See concerning the severity of the sanction: Council of State 29 June 2006, No. 160.796; Council of State 12 November 2002, No. 112.461. Administrative difficulties in themselves are not a justification for exceeding the reasonable delay. It is the duty of the executive branch to enable the administrations to handle cases within an appropriate timeframe (Council of State, *Mahieu*, No. 130209, 9 April 2004, consideration III, B, 2; see also Council of State No. 111.745, 22 October 2002).

administration is informed about the facts eligible for the imposition of administrative sanctions.[261] The end of the period to be taken into consideration for the administrative version of the reasonable delay is the moment when the administrative decision is reported to its addressee. It makes sense that the administration is not held responsible for infringing the administrative version of the reasonable delay principle, if delays are incurred by the judiciary after a timely administrative decision. Delays incurred by the administration could be relevant for determining whether the reasonable delay as required by Article 6 ECHR has been respected with regard to administrative sanctions with a punitive character.

If a decision (e.g. concerning a sanction) was not taken within a reasonable time, the Council of State will have but one option: to annul the decision. After this annulment, the administration could re-examine the case and decide whether or not a new decision should be taken[262], while taking into account the unreasonable delay in the evaluation of the case.[263]

Legal certainty

The principle of legal certainty entails that a citizen should be able to have his legitimate expectations respected by administrative decisions.[264] It mandates that an administration does not, in the absence of an objective and reasonable justification, infringe upon the interest of its legal subjects in being able to reasonable predict the consequences of their actions. The Court of Cassation considers this principle to entail that a citizen must be able to place his trust in the public services and must be able to count on their respect for rules and the

261 Court of Appeal Brussels 13 December 2011, *Bank en Financieel Recht* [Banking and Finance Law] 2012, 212. This court makes a clear distinction between the objective component of the reasonable delay, i.e. the duty of the administration to swiftly carry out its investigation and decide on whether or not to pursue an administrative sanctioning procedure, and the subjective component, i.e. the right of the addressee of the potential sanction to receive a decision within a reasonable delay.

262 Council of State, *Swerts*, No. 111.745, 22 October 2002, final consideration.

263 Council of State, *Waeterschoot*, No. 154.424, 2 February 2006, consideration 2.1.2.

264 See e.g. Labour Tribunal Antwerp, 5 September 1996, *Rechtskundig Weekblad* [*Legal Weekly*] 1997–98, 304; Tribunal of First Instance Liège 23 June 2005, *Jurisprudence Fiscale* [*Fiscal Jurisprudence*] 2006, 287 (the fiscal administration is obliged on the basis of this principle to follow its own instructions); Council of State No. 177.645, 6 December 2007, consideration 10 (suspension of a decision to revoke a license for which the license holder qualified under Belgian law which was motivated by a reference to a more detailed foreign legal norm); Council of State No. 134.860, 14 September 2004, consideration 4.4.2 (also mentioning the general principle restricting the use measures with a retroactive operation). See also: Council of State No. 199.002, 17 December 2009, consideration 57. See also Council of State No. 199.002, 17 December 2009, consideration 57 (the provision of building permits for certain activities on particular locations did not as such imply a legitimate expectation to be able to continue those activities there that would trump a subsequent legitimate municipal prohibition).

adoption of steadfast policies that are unambiguous for the legal subjects.[265] Administrative acts, even those not imposing sanctions of a criminal nature within the meaning of Article 6 ECHR, which impose burdens with retroactive effect need to be justified by special circumstances related to a public interest. The administration is obliged to prove the necessity or even indispensability of such a measure for achieving that goal.[266]

4.2.5. The right to information

The right to (actively) access information or to be (passively) informed are not GPPA themselves, but are often necessitated by principles such as legal certainty and due care.[267] For example, proper justification requires the addressee to be aware of any elements in the file being referred to, exercising the right to be heard implies knowing what one needs to defend oneself against, etc. Therefore information (and access thereto) is an important aid in the legal protection against administrative acts.

There is a difference between the passive and active type of publicity. Passive publicity is the right to consult the administrations' documents upon request. This has been embedded in Article 32 of the Constitution. Active publicity is the requirement of the government to inform citizens of certain types of information on its own initiative. Both the passive and active types of publicity have been regulated in the Government Information Act of 1994.[268] Article 2, 4° of this Act states that every document through which an administrative act of an individual nature (such as the imposition of a sanction) is notified to its addressee, must indicate the possible methods of appeal, the entities where the appeal can be lodged, along with the necessary formalities and terms. If this information is lacking, the period for lodging an appeal does not commence.

4.3. THE GENERAL PRINCIPLES OF CRIMINAL LAW (GPCL)

4.3.1. Introduction

The Criminal Code (CC), the Criminal Proceedings Code (CPC), and the various specific acts (such as the Act concerning suspension, delay and

---

265 Court of Cassation 1 March 2010, *Rechtskundig Weekblad* [*Legal Weekly*] 2010 11, 1091.

266 Council of State No. 134.860, 14 September 2004, consideration 4.4.2.

267 The old right to access information based on the duty to hear now only plays a marginal role after the Government Information Act.

268 Unlike the Explicit Justification Act of 1991, there was no residuary federal power to exclusively legislate on the topic. Therefore the regional entities have implemented similar legislation regarding the publicity of information related to their own responsibilities. See footnote 72.

probation[269]) are, in principle, only applicable to proceedings qualified as 'criminal' according to internal law.[270] Administrative sanctions and administrative sanctioning procedures technically fall outside their scope of application. However, by means of two sets of reasoning, some classic criminal principles and legal concepts can be invoked in disputes concerning administrative sanctions.[271]

First of all, the guarantees laid down in international treaties such as Article 6 ECHR and Article 14 ICCPR are applicable to all kinds of sanctions with a punitive character. In this respect, national case law has abandoned the formal criterion of internal qualification to determine whether or not a sanction has a criminal character in favour of the material approach developed by the European Court of Human Rights.

Secondly, other principles or legal concepts can be considered as part of internal criminal law. These 'internal GPCL' are, in principle, only applicable to criminal procedures in the strict, internal sense. Here the Constitutional Court has played a significant role in expanding the protection offered by some of these internal GPCL to certain administrative procedures as well.[272] The Court ruled that the rights and freedoms safeguarded by Articles 10 (equality) and 11 (non-discrimination) of the Constitution, include the guarantees emanating from general principles and that 'insofar as these principles apply to the legislator, they are applicable independently of the qualification as criminal or non-criminal, which the legislator could attribute to the measures it prescribes'.[273] The Court can therefore examine, on a case by case basis, whether a particular difference in treatment between a criminal and administrative sanctioning procedure is based on reasonable grounds.

4.3.2. Legality[274]

In the past it was assumed that Article 14 of the Constitution only applied to sanctions qualified as 'criminal'.[275] However, more recent legal doctrine is of the

---

269 Act of 29 June 1964 concerning suspension, delay and probation, *Belgian Bulletin of Acts and Decrees* 17 July 1964.

270 Constitutional Court No. 119/2009, 16 July 2009, B.6.2.

271 Constitutional Court No. 148/2010, 16 December 2010, consideration B.3.1 and B.3.3; Constitutional Court No. 119/2009, 16 July 2009, B.6.3; J. PUT, 'Rechtshandhaving [Law enforcement]', *l.c.*, 1206–1207.

272 Court of Arbitration No. 4/2001, 25 January 2001, *Belgian Bulletin of Acts and Decrees* 10 February 2001 (concerning a disciplinary procedure). See A. Alen, 'Administratieve geldboetes: hun internationale en internrechtelijke kwalificatie [Administrative fines: their international and internal legal qualification]' (hereafter: *Liber Amicorum G. Baeteman)*, in: X (ed.), *Liber Amicorum G. Baeteman*, Deurne, Kluwer, 1997, 406.

273 Court of Arbitration No. 72/92, 18 November 1992, *Rechtskundig Weekblad* [*Legal Weekly*] 1992–93, 673, consideration B.2.2. See also Court of Arbitration No. 76/99, 30 June 1999, *Belgian Bulletin of Acts and Decrees* 24 November 1999, consideration B.4.2.

274 The principle of legality has been embedded in Articles 12 and 14 of the Constitution, Article 7 ECHR and Article 15 ICCPR.

275 See *supra* title 2.2.1.

opinion that the principle of legality should apply to administrative sanctions with a punitive aim as well.[276] This means that such administrative sanctions need to have a legal foundation. This legal foundation needs to detail, for example, the circumstances in which an administrative sanction can be imposed, the types of these sanctions and their degree of severity. Recent case law has confirmed that the principle of legality applies to administrative sanctions with a punitive aim.[277]

4.3.3. *Presumption of innocence and personal nature of the punishment*

The *presumption of innocence* is a general GPCL and also included in Article 6 ECHR and Article 14 ICCPR. Because of that, it is applicable to all administrative sanctions with a punitive character. The burden of proof for an infraction lies with the administration.[278] This is illustrated by the Constitutional Court's ruling of 18 November 1992[279] concerning the former Administrative Fines Act in labour matters (now regulated by the Social Criminal Code). In its original version, this Act instituted a form of administrative settlement. The administration could 'propose' a certain fine to the infringer of certain social Acts. If the infringer did not accept, the administration had to take the initiative and commence a procedure with the Labour Tribunal. An amended version reversed this approach: the administration could impose a fine, upon which the addressee would have to lodge an appeal with the Labour Tribunal if he wanted to dispute the administration's decision. The Constitutional Court refused to accept the argument that this violated the presumption of innocence by stating that: 'It is the administration's task to prove the facts committed by the alleged infringer, not just when it imposes the fine, but also when its decision is appealed. [By forcing the addressee to initiate any appeal] the legislator did not intend to abandon the presumption of innocence'.[280] Presumptions of guilt are possible if they meet the standards determined by ECHR case law.[281]

---

276 A. Alen, *Liber Amicorum G. Baeteman*, *l.c.* 403; M. Boes, *Administratieve sancties en art. 6 EVRM in België [Administrative sanctions and art. 6 ECHR in Belgium]*, *o.c.*, 28; J. Put, *Administratieve sancties [Administrative sanctions]*, *o.c.*, 33.

277 See also *supra*, footnote 70; Council of State No. 127.673, 2 February 2004, consideration 5.2.3.2; Council of State No. 134.860, 14 September 2004, consideration 5.3.2; Labour Tribunal Brussels 21 September 2005, *Tijdschrift voor Vreemdelingenrecht [Journal for Immigration Law]* 2006, 53. See also Labour Court Ghent (dept. Bruges) 20 February 2003, *Informatieblad R.I.Z.I.V. [Social security services newsletter]* 2003, 366.

278 For a disciplinary sanction see: Court of Arbitration No. 4/2001, 25 January 2001, *Belgian Bulletin of Acts and Decrees* 10 February 2001, consideration B.5.5.

279 See A. Alen, *Liber Amicorum G. Baeteman*, *l.c.*, 406–410; Court of Arbitration No. 72/92, 18 November 1992.

280 Court of Arbitration No. 72/92, 18 November 1992, consideration B.3.

281 J. Put, *Administratieve sancties [Administrative sanctions]*, *o.c.*, 252.

According to the persistent opinion the Legislative Section of the Council of State[282], the presumption of innocence and the more general concern to provide an effective legal recourse for criminal prosecutions within the meaning of Article 6 ECHR may require that the execution of the administrative sanction remains suspended until the addressee of the sanction has had the opportunity to have a judge exercise his full judicial review. The *Constitutional Court* for its part decided however that neither the Belgian Constitution nor any international norm (e.g. Article 13 ECHR) requires the legislator to generally link an appeal with a suspension of the administrative decision, except as to the extent necessary to prevent the execution of measures in violation of the ECHR and of which the consequences would potentially be irreversible. However if the legislator voluntarily decides to implement such suspensions in a piecemeal fashion, this may not result in unconstitutional discriminations.[283]

Administrative sanctions with a punitive character, due to their internal classification as administrative instead of criminal, do not directly resort under the scope of Article 86 Criminal Code or Article 20 of the Preliminary Title to the Criminal Proceedings Code. These articles stipulate that criminal sanctions or criminal proceedings expire upon the death of the perpetrator. They are in other words the legal basis for the *personal nature of punishments*. The Constitutional Court ruled that this results in an unconstitutional treatment based on Article 6 ECHR, and the GPCL's of the personal nature of punishments and the presumption of innocence for heirs who are faced with administrative sanctions with a punitive character incurred by their predecessor that would not expire upon the death of said predecessor and for which they were not allowed to prove that they themselves had not committed the infraction (Article 132 Succession Tax Code).[284]

4.3.4. Reasonable delay

The Court of Cassation has ruled, in conformity with ECHR case law, that the guarantees of Article 6 need to be respected as soon as a person is faced with an accusation that entails a threat of criminal prosecution (by analogy one could extend this to the threat of an administrative procedure which could lead to sanctions of a punitive nature), causing him to take measures to organise his

---

282 E.g.: Advice of the Council of State No. 33.239/2, 2 May 2002, *Parliamentary Proceedings of the Chamber of Representatives* session 2001–02, 1843/1, 291; Advice of the Council of State No. 39.536, 24 January 2006, *Parliamentary Proceedings of the Flemish Parliament*, session 2005–06, 824/1, 70. Also see the many references cited there.

283 Constitutional Court No. 81/2008, 27 May 2008, consideration B.36.3.

284 Constitutional Court No. 119/2009, 16 July 2009, considerations B.6.3 and B.6.4.

defence.[285] In this context the official report (termed *'proces-verbaal'* in Dutch and *'procès-verbal'* in French) drafted by a social inspector was not considered to be an accusation.[286]

The Constitutional Court has issued a ruling regarding the sanction attached to decisions which exceed the reasonable time frame.[287] It ruled that the regulation for exceeding the reasonable delay in criminal matters (Article 21*ter* of the preliminary title to the CPC) is not applicable to the administrative sanctions contained in the former Administrative Fines Act (which had a punitive character), but that judges are nonetheless obliged to respect the principle of reasonable delay and the requirements of Article 6 ECHR. This means that a judge, when reviewing the imposition of an administrative sanction with a punitive character, is allowed to determine the starting point of the reasonable delay and the consequences of an unreasonable delay independently of Article 21*ter.*

4.3.5. Nemo tenetur edere contra se (privilege against self-incrimination) and the right to remain silent

According to European case law the administrative phase need not fulfil the requirements of Article 6 ECHR if there is the possibility of a review with full jurisdiction (*supra*). This approach could potentially conflict with the requirements of the right to remain silent and the right against self-incrimination.

Certain Belgian acts impose a duty to provide information in order to facilitate government supervision in fiscal or social matters, and this can be enforced with sanctions.[288] Belgian case law has ruled that the subject of an inquiry is not obliged to cooperate if he has been accused, if there is an intention to accuse him or if he is clearly suspected of infractions which may lead to the imposition of criminal

---

285 Court of Cassation 20 March 2000, *Arresten van het Hof van Cassatie* [*Rulings of the Court of Cassation*] 2000, 191. It should be noted that the Court of Cassation ruled in 1991 that the starting date of the reasonable delay is not necessarily the starting date of the administrative investigation (Court of Cassation 29 October 1991, *Rechtskundig Weekblad* [*Legal Weekly*] 1991–92, 712). It required a threat of (*in casu* criminal) prosecution which had a serious effect on the personal condition of the suspect because it obliged him to take measures to ensure his defence against the type of accusations under the scope of the ECHR.

286 See critically: W. Gekiere, 'Zwijgen of meewerken. Over de houding van de 'beschuldigde' tijdens sanctieprocedures in het socialezekerheidsrecht [To remain silent or to cooperate. On the position of the 'accused' during sanctioning procedures in social security law]', *Tijdschrift voor Sociaal Recht* [*Journal of Social Law*] 2002, 297–301.

287 Court of Arbitration No. 148/2004, 15 September 2004, considerations B.4. to B.6.

288 *Cf.* Article 1*bis* §1, 3°, a) Administrative Fines Act.

sanctions or administrative sanctions with a punitive character.[289] A person is for example not obliged to respond to a request for information after he has been informed there are indications he committed fiscal fraud which could lead to criminal or administrative sanctions of a punitive nature.

The right to remain silent and against self-incrimination is however not absolute. It does not affect the power of the administration to examine potentially self incriminating records which a person is legally obliged to keep.[290] Hence the Court of Cassation did not consider the legal duty to hand over documents to be a violation of the *nemo tenetur* principle (nor of the presumption of innocence) in itself, even if those documents could lead to the proof of criminal acts.[291] The fact that the administration would point out the potential criminal or administrative sanctions associated with the refusal to cooperate with an ordinary administrative control (without specific suspicions) does not as such imply an intention to initiate a criminal prosecution.[292]

The privilege against self-incrimination does not prohibit the use of compulsory powers to obtain information outside the context of criminal proceedings in itself.[293] In order to determine whether the *nemo tenetur* principle has been violated the judge can examine whether there was use of compulsion during the

---

289 Court of Appeal Liège, *Fiscale Jurisprudentie* [*Fiscal Jurisprudence*] 2010, 1160; Court of Appeal Liège 3 December 2008, *Revue Générale du Contentieux Fiscal* [*General Review of Fiscal Disputes*] 2009, 250; Tribunal of First Instance Liège 30 November 2004, *Tijdschrift voor Fiscaal Recht* [*Journal for Fiscal Law*] 2005, 590, note B. Coopman; Tribunal of first instance Mons 12 January 2005, *Tijdschrift voor Fiscaal Recht* [*Journal for Fiscal Law*] 2006, 948; Correctional tribunal Liège 14 April 2005, *Fiscale Jurisprudentie* [*Fiscal Jurisprudence*] 2005, 757. See also European Court of Human Rights judgement in *Shannon v. United Kingdom* of 4 January 2006, considerations 33–41.

290 Court of Appeal Antwerp 11 October 2001, *Tijdschrift voor Strafrecht* [*Journal for criminal law*] 2003, 297.

291 Court of Cassation 6 June 2000, *Pas.* 2000, I, 343. The ECHR has judged in the past that the right to remain silent does not affect information which exists independently of the will of the person involved (ECtHR judgement in *Saunders v. United Kingdom* of 17 December 1996, *Rep. Eur. Court H.R.* 1996, Series IV, 2044; W. Gekiere, *l.c.*, 290–295), at least provided it is known to exist as opposed to being suspected to exist (ECtHR, *Funke v. France*, 25 February 1993, consideration 44). See also (in a disciplinary case) concerning the legal duty to keep and produce certain records: Court of Cassation 3 June 2005, *Pasicrisie* 2005, I, 1206.

292 See Tribunal of First Instance Mons 12 January 2005, *Jurisprudence Fiscal* [*Fiscal Jurisprudence*] 2005, 965.

293 ECtHR judgement in *Weh v. Austria* of 8 April 2004, consideration 44. See also ECtHR judgement in *Saunders v. United Kingdom* of 17 December 1996, *Rep. Eur. Court H.R.* 1996, Series IV, 2044 ('accordingly the Court's sole concern in the present case is with the use made of the relevant statements at the applicant's criminal trial') and European Court of Human rights judgement of *J.B. v. Switzerland* of 3 May 2001, consideration 63 ('the Court is called upon to examine whether or not the imposition of a fine on the applicant for having failed to provide certain information complied with the requirements of the Convention. It follows that the Court is not deciding in the present case the issue whether a State can oblige a taxpayer to give information for the sole purpose of securing a correct tax assessment').

investigation by the fiscal administration and whether such evidence procured through coercion was used during the criminal trial.[294]

The Court of Cassation has also ruled that the *nemo tenetur* principle is only activated once a criminal prosecution is started. It was therefore held not to apply to an administrative procedure which was merely aimed at determining facts, and in which the person being interrogated was not a suspect and did not live under threat of prosecutions. Such a person could legally be obliged to assist the investigation, but was not obliged to make self incriminating statements.[295]

The Court of Appeal of Liège has decided that the notion "accusation in criminal matters" contained in the ECHR has an autonomous meaning, namely "the official notification, by an authorized government, of the reproach of having committed a punishable infraction". In the light of this definition it determined that a request for information aimed at a taxpayer warning him of a suspicion of having committed an infraction qualifies as such an accusation. The taxpayer could therefore invoke his right to remain silent and could not be sanctioned for not answering the request for information.[296]

4.3.6. *Individualisation of the punishment*

The individualisation of the punishment allows a criminal court judge to regulate the sentence according to the severity of the infraction and the individual circumstances of the person concerned. It concerns, more specifically, the ability of a criminal court judge to take into account extenuating circumstances, to defer the judgement, to suspend the sentence or to impose probation as a sentence. The legislator can, excluding manifestly unreasonable measures, freely determine repressive policies. This includes – in principle – the prerogative to deny the courts any margin of appreciation when imposing a

294 See Court of Cassation 13 January 1999, *Pasicrisie* 1999, I, 28; Court of Appeal Liège 2 March 2006, *Fiscale Koerier* [*Fiscal Courier*] 2006, 532, note W. Defoor. See also ECtHR, *Chambaz v. Switzerland*, 5 April 2012, considerations 50-58. ECHR case law has developed a test for the application of compulsion. It consists of three criterions: firstly the nature and degree of compulsion used to obtain the evidence is taken into account, secondly the presence of relevant safeguards in the procedure and thirdly the use to which the material was put (ECtHR, *Jalloh v. Germany*, 11 July 2006, consideration 117 (this judgment includes the additional criterion of the weight of the public interest in the investigation, but this has not been repeated in the subsequent *O'Halloran* and *Francis* case, possibly to avoid conflicts with absolute norms such as the prohibition of torture). The compulsion might for example be acceptable if the required information is limited in scope and the sanction for refusal is moderate and non-custodial.

295 Court of Cassation P.11.0113.N, 29 November 2011.

296 Court of Appeal Liège No. 02/4393/A, 9 February 2012, *Revue Générale du Contentieux Fiscal* [*General Review of Fiscal Litigation*] 2012, 465.

particular sanction.[297] The Constitutional Court clarified that in its view Article 6 ECHR does not require that administrative sanctions with a punitive character should benefit from the exact same options the legislator provides to extenuate criminal punishments in the internal, formal sense. As previously mentioned the mere fact that a legislator opts for a different type of sanctioning mechanism is not discriminatory in itself.[298] The Court will only examine whether a specific difference in treatment is constitutional or not. The legislator does need to maintain the overall consistency of his repressive procedures as manifest inconsistencies can result in unjustified discriminations. For example, the choice of the legislator to provide substantial administrative fines without the possibility of reduction results in an unconstitutional treatment that cannot be justified by the desire to maintain the dissuasive effect of these sanctions, when the criminal fines contained in the same law (which are technically a more severe type of sanction) are susceptible to mitigation to amounts far lower than those of the administrative fines.[299]

The Constitutional Court's ruling of 14 July 1997[300] concluded that the absence of a system of *extenuating circumstances* in the former Administrative Fines Act constituted an unreasonable difference in treatment between persons prosecuted through the criminal or the administrative procedure respectively. This prompted the legislator to introduce such a system.[301] In another case, the Court decided however that differences in the potential severity of the penalty due to the applications of extenuating circumstances on criminal fines were not disproportionate because the administrative fine would otherwise risk losing its dissuasive nature.[302] This was considered to be the case if the amount of the administrative fine is set at the same height as the minimum criminal fine, or if it is very low in itself. On the other hand, in a recent (criminal) case the Constitutional Court found that the total absence of a possibility for the judge to lower a fine of a high amount due to extenuating circumstances was contrary to the principle of non-discrimination, combined with Article 6 ECHR.[303] The Constitutional Court has found an unconstitutional difference in treatment between persons being prosecuted for illegal gangmaster activities by the administration in the Labour Tribunal and the persons being prosecuted for the same facts in a criminal procedure in the Correctional Tribunal. The

---

297 Constitutional Court No. 93/2008, 26 June 2008, B.15.3.

298 Constitutional Court No. 42/2009, 11 March 2009, considerations B.4 and B.5.

299 Constitutional Court No. 42/2009, 11 March 2009, considerations B.20 and B.21.

300 Court of Arbitration No. 40/97 and No. 45/97, 14 July 1997. The Court came to the same conclusion in (a.o.) Court of Arbitration No. 128/99, 7 December 1999 and Constitutional Court No. 86/2007, 20 June 2007.

301 Article 1*ter* of the former Administrative Fines Act. See Article 115 Social Criminal Code.

302 Court of Arbitration No. 127/2000, 6 December 2000, considerations B.11.2 to B.11.6; see also Court of Arbitration No. 153/2001, 28 November 2001, consideration B.8.3.

303 Constitutional Court No. 81/2007, 7 June 2007.

administrative sanctions with a punitive character imposable in the administrative proceeding do not – due to their administrative (i.e. *not* criminal) nature as defined by the internal legal system – qualify for the application of extenuating circumstances as regulated in Article 85 of the Criminal Code, whereas a person prosecuted in the criminal proceeding can benefit from this article.[304]

For a long time the Constitutional Court did not consider the absence of mechanisms such as *suspension, delay or probation* in administrative procedures to be an unreasonable difference in treatment. In the context of administrative fines it ruled that these types of measures had a narrow link with criminal sanctions (in a strict sense) because they intended to mitigate or prevent the negative consequences caused by criminal convictions. Administrative fines, on the other hand, are exclusively monetary, do not have a degrading character, are not included in a criminal record, and do not pose a risk to the rehabilitation of the convicted person. Therefore, the application of mechanisms to mitigate or prevent their consequences was not considered to be necessary.[305]

The Constitutional Court partially reversed its case law in this matter with a ruling on 16 June 2004. The Court was asked to examine whether the absence of the option to suspend the verdict or delay the execution, with respect to the sanctions contained in the former Administrative Fines Act, was discriminatory compared to criminal sanctions (to which the aforementioned Act of 1964 is applicable). It determined that the origin of a possible discrimination lay in the fact that the addressee of the sanction could not choose to be prosecuted through either the criminal or administrative procedure. This meant that he was faced with different guarantees and rights irrespective of his own will. The question was then whether this difference in treatment was based on reasonable grounds. The Court still decided that it was reasonable not to apply a mechanism *suspending the delivery of the verdict*, because this measure was too narrowly linked with the criminal procedure.[306] After all, a judge reviewing an administrative fine does not impose the fine itself, he merely reviews the administrative decision which imposed it. Suspension of the verdict specifically aims to avoid certain consequences of a particular criminal punishment, as mentioned above.

---

304 Constitutional Court No. 86/2007, 20 June 2007, consideration B.8.

305 Court of Arbitration Nos. 40/97 and 45/97, 14 July 1997, consideration B.6.2; Court of Arbitration No. 153/2001, 28 November 2001, consideration B.9.

306 Court of Arbitration No. 105/2004, 16 June 2004, consideration B.6.3; see also Constitutional Court No. 13/2013, 21 February 2013.

The Court held a different view however regarding the option of *delaying the execution* of the judgement or administrative act respectively.[307] This measure intends to mitigate the consequences of the execution of the punishment, which makes it compatible with administrative sanctions (as the legislator had already demonstrated by introducing it in procedures other than the former Administrative Fines Act). The absence of an option to delay the execution of the administrative punishment was considered discriminatory because the threat of a postponed execution of the punishment could be useful to discourage recidivism in criminal as well as administrative types of procedures. The Court's standard formulation in these cases is that 'when, as in this case, the perpetrator of the same fact can be referred to either the Correctional Tribunal or receive an administrative sanction against which he can lodge an appeal with a non-criminal tribunal, the Court rules that in principle there should be a parallelism between the options to individualise the punishment'.[308]

4.3.7. Non bis in idem

In Belgian law the principle of *non bis in idem* – as a GPCL and partially laid down in the Criminal Proceedings Code – is applicable when a person is prosecuted for the same facts.[309] In other words, it is the material behaviour which is the criterion for the *non bis in idem* principle, not the legal qualification of the facts. This results in a broad scope for the principle. If there is a prosecution for multiple infractions, the judge has the competence to determine whether those infractions have been caused by one or by several different facts.[310] The principle tends, however, to have a weak influence on the outcome of a second procedure in that it does not necessarily preclude a second prosecution, but is only a factor in determining the exact magnitude of the sanction.[311]

The *Court of Cassation* ruled that the *non bis in idem* principle of Article 14 paragraph 7 ICCPR does not prohibit the legislator from providing both criminal and administrative sanctions for the same offence, even if the administrative

307 Court of Arbitration No. 105/2004, 16 June 2004 (consideration B.7.1); Constitutional Court No. 86/2007, 20 June 2007 (considerations B.10.1 and B.10.2). See also concerning the Value Added Tax Code: Constitutional Court No. 157/2008, 6 November 2008, B.4.1-B.5.3; concerning a sanction regarding social benefits: Constitutional Court No. 148/2010, 16 December 2010, consideration B.4.3 and B.4.4.

308 See Constitutional Court No. 148/2010, 16 December 2010, consideration B.4.2 and the references to previous Court rulings cited there (Cases Nos. 40/97, 45/97, 128/99, 86/2007 and 157/2008).

309 See extensively J. Put, 'Bis, sed non in idem', *Rechtskundig Weekblad* [*Legal Weekly*] 2001–02, (937), 938–940.

310 Court of Cassation 25 November 1987, *Arresten van het Hof van Cassatie* [*Rulings of the Court of Cassation*] 1987–88, 185.

311 J. Put, 'Bis, sed non in idem', *Rechtskundig Weekblad* [*Legal Weekly*] 2001–02, (937), 943–948.

sanction has a criminal nature in the sense of Article 6 ECHR. It added that a judge, when reviewing the imposition of the administrative sanction, has the authority to take previously imposed criminal sanctions into account.[312] In this specific context, the *non bis in idem* principle would therefore have a wide application as it is potentially applicable to facts or sanctions irrespective of their legal qualification, but it also has a more limited scope as it would only mitigate (and not necessarily fully preclude) sanctions imposed by a subsequent procedure depending on a concrete assessment of the judge.[313] Nonetheless some hierarchically lower courts were resisting this analysis by ruling that Article 14 ICCPR does exclude the cumulation of multiple sanctions of a punitive nature.[314]

Until recently, there was few *Constitutional Court* case law[315] clarifying whether or not the *non bis in idem* principle is applicable when a particular fact is eligible for prosecution through both an administrative and a criminal procedure. This is not really surprising, as in many sanctioning systems the legislator has explicitly adopted a type of '*una via*' approach, compelling the public prosecutor or the administration to make a choice between criminal or administrative sanctioning procedures. The choice for a certain type of procedure subsequently excludes the possibility to resort to the other type of procedure. This is for example the case with regard to the Social Criminal Code[316] and the New Municipalities Act.[317] Recently this approach has also been introduced in the domain of fiscal law.[318]

---

312 Court of Cassation 5 February 1999, *Arresten van het Hof van Cassatie* [*Rulings of the Court of Cassation*] 1999, 67; Court of Cassation 12 January 2001, *Arresten van het Hof van Cassatie* [*Rulings of the Court of Cassation*] 2001, 66; Court of Cassation C.00.0234.N, C.00.0442.N, 24 January 2002, *Pasicrisie* 2002, 226.

313 See J. Put, 'Bis, sed non in idem', *Rechtskundig Weekblad* [*Legal Weekly*] 2001–02, (937), 946.

314 Court of Appeal Brussels 3 April 2008, *Fiscale Koerier* [*Fiscal Courrier*] 2008, 521, annotated by A. Kiekens.

315 See nonetheless: Court of Arbitration No. 127/2000, 6 December 2000, considerations B.12.1–12.4 (the legislator may provide several types of sanctions, the judge has the task of examining whether the *non bis in idem* principle is being violated).

316 The public prosecutor has preference in deciding whether or not to initiate criminal proceedings. Only after he decides not to do so can the administration impose an administrative sanction (articles 71 and 72 Social Criminal Code).

317 Article 119bis, §7-§8bis New Municipalities Act (also granting the initiative to the public prosecutor).

318 Law of 20 September 2012 tot instelling van het "una via"-principe in de vervolging van overtredingen van de fiscale wetgeving en tot verhoging van de fiscale penale boetes [*Law to institute the 'una via' principle in the prosecution of fiscal infractions and to increase the fiscal criminal fines*], *Belgian Bulletin of Acts and Decrees* 20 October 2012.
For example, prior to the aforementioned law the first words of article 449 Income Tax Code (which imposes a criminal sanction) were "Notwithstanding the administrative sanctions […]". This part has been dropped from the article. Concurrently the maximum amount of the criminal fine imposed by this article was increased from 125,000 EUR to 500,000 EUR.

A ruling of 26 April 2007 concludes that the *non bis in idem* principle prohibits the imposition of successively (in two sets of proceedings) an administrative fine of a criminal nature and a criminal sanction, based upon an act resulting in multiple infractions containing the same essential elements[319] The applicable legislation in this case allowed the imposition of an administrative fine on the addressee on the one hand, while on the other hand, even after payment of the administrative fine, maintaining the possibility of criminal prosecutions. The Court compares this legislation to other legal norms which do exclude criminal prosecution after the imposition of an administrative fine. The Court establishes that both the administrative and the criminal component of the applicable legislation in the matter at hand target the same behaviour of the addressee and that the essential elements of both infractions are identical. It therefore decides to apply the *non bis in idem* principle as a general principle of law and deems the difference in treatment to be unconstitutional.[320] In a case concerning fiscal administrative sanctions the Constitutional Court did not consider the essential elements of the infractions to be identical because the was a difference in their moral element: only one of them required a fraudulent design or intent to cause damages.[321]

ECHR[322] case law has clarified that the *idem* aspect of the *non bis in idem* adage prohibits the prosecution for – or trial of – a second offence in so far as it *arises from identical facts or facts which are substantially the same.*[323] *Prima facie* this was incompatible with the case law of *Constitutional Court*, as it examined the principle of *non bis in idem* in the light of the similarities between the legal definition of the infractions rather than the facts, e.g. denying to apply the

319 Constitutional Court No. 67/2007, 26 April 2007, referring to the ECtHR Cases *Fischer* (29 May 2001) and *Hauser-Sporn* (7 December 2006). The Court explicitly considers that it limits its ruling to the situation of a same behaviour leading to successive administrative and criminal sanctions, which means it does not consider the hypothesis of a same offence leading to different sanctions under different qualifications, nor the hypothesis of the application of different sanctions within the scope of only one proceeding.

320 Constitutional Court No. 67/2007, 26 April 2007, considerations B.9.2-B.12.

321 Constitutional Court No. 91/2008, 18 June 2008, consideration B.17.

322 See also Article 4, Protocol No. 7 to the ECHR. It should be noted that this protocol has only entered into force in Belgian law on the 1st of July 2012 (Act of 6 March 2007, *Belgian Bulletin of Acts and Decrees* 22 June 2012).

323 ECtHR No. 14939/03, judgement in Sergey *Zolotukhin v. Russia* of 10 February 2009, considerations 70–78; ECtHR No. 13079/03, judgement in *Ruotsalainen v. Finland*, 16 June 2009, considerations 48–57 (concerning the application of the principle on the combination of criminal and administrative sanctioning procedures. See for lower case law mentioning this ECHR clarification: Labour Court Brussels 11 August 2010, *Journal des Tribunaux du Travail* [*Journal of the Labour Tribunals*] 2011, 27; Correctional Tribunal Verviers 18 May 2009, *Jurisprudence de Liège, Mons et Bruxelles* [*Case law of Liège, Mons and Brussels*] 2009, 1565. See also based on *non bis in idem* as a general principle, without specific reference to the ECHR: Correctional Tribunal 27 January 2010, *Journal des Tribunaux* [*Courts Journal*] 2010, 425.

principle if the criminal and administrative sanctions require a different element of intent.[324] The ECHR on the other hand has even explicitly mentioned that a mere difference in the required element of intent does not exclude the application of the principle.[325] In its most recent case concerning the principle *non bis in idem* the Constitutional Court diligently cited the recent ECHR case law on the matter. It concluded however that the *non bis in idem* principle was not applicable in the case at hand, which only dealt with the combination of a tax and an administrative sanction. The Court concluded that the principle was not applicable here (even regardless of the punitive character of the administrative sanction) because the tax itself could not, in the Court's opinion, be qualified as a form of punishment.[326] The Constitutional Court therefore has not yet had the occasion to express its opinion after the Zolotukhin judgement of the ECHR, but it is very likely that it will comply with the ECHR case law given the references that it has already included in its decisions. The wording of some *Court of Cassation* decisions seemed compatible with the ECHR rulings. In 2010 the Court of Cassation decided that the application of the *non bis in idem* principle requires a new prosecution for the *same facts* as the previously decided case (which resembles the formulation of the ECHR), and also stressed that the previous case and the second prosecution must target the same person.[327]

In recent cases the Court of Cassation accepted that, confronted with a 'final' sanction of a criminal nature (whether strictly criminal, administrative or disciplinary), a second procedure is precluded.[328] The Court also stated that the point of reference is '(essentially) the same facts', but nonetheless considered the facts as not being similar when the infractions require a different element of intent[329], which is difficult to reconcile with the rulings of the ECHR.

4.3.8. *Retroactivity of legislation*

If the administrative sanction has a punitive character there cannot be a more severe sentence imposed than the one applicable at the time the facts were committed. A more lenient treatment will be retroactively applied to past

324 *Cf.* Constitutional Court No. 91/2008, 18 June 2008, consideration B.17.

325 ECtHR No. 13079/03, judgement in *Ruotsalainen v. Finland*, 16 June 2009, consideration 56.

326 Constitutional Court No. 91/2010, 29 July 2010, consideration B.4.5. It can be noted that the Court examined in previous case law whether a particular tax had the nature of a repressive sanction (Constitutional Court No. 106/2008, 17 July 2008, considerations B.19.1–B.19.4). See also Constitutional Court No. 28/2012, 1 March 2012 and Constitutional Court No. 112/2012, 20 September 2012.

327 Court of Cassation F.09.0067.N, 12 November 2010, www.juridat.be.

328 Court of Cassation P.11.1349.F, 21 December 2011; see also Court of Cassation P.11.0894.N, 3 January 2012.

329 Court of Cassation P.11.0199.F, 25 May 2011.

events.[330] This is not the case for administrative sanctions *without* a punitive character, for which the legislation applicable at the time will be applied.[331]

4.3.9. Right to a double judicial review

Article 14.5 ICCPR and Article 2 Protocol No. 7 to the ECHR[332] grant everyone convicted of a crime the right to have his conviction and sentence reviewed by a higher judge according to law. This right is also accepted as a GPCL.[333] It is not, however, a general principle applicable to all domains of the law.[334] The Court of Cassation has ruled that this right can be applicable to disputes concerning other domains of the law, such as tax legislation, provided that the prosecutions lead or could lead to a criminal sanction within the meaning of Article 14.5 ICCPR.[335] The Council of State has ruled that since this right requires a double *judicial* review, it is not applicable to administrations which are not judicial bodies within the meaning of article 6 ECHR.[336]

5. CONCLUSIONS

The lack of a legal definition of the concept of 'administrative sanctions' and the uncertainty surrounding the applicability and/or consequences of a number of rules of international law and general principles of law at first sight result in a rather negative assessment of the actual law enforcement system by way of administrative sanctions in the Belgian legal system. However, the judge-made law – at all levels, but especially the rulings of the Constitutional Court and the influence of the European Court of Human Rights – can claim great credit for having gradually given shape to the legal protection against administrative sanctioning, albeit necessarily fragmented and within certain limits.

---

330 Labour Court Antwerp, 20 November 2001, *Chroniques de droit social* [*Chronicles of Social Law*] 2003, 381; Labour Tribunal Antwerp 28 June 2001, *Chroniques de droit social* [*Chronicles of Social Law*] 2002, 196. This rule is contained in international treaties (Article 15 ICCPR) and internal legislation (Article 2 of the Penal Code). The Constitutional Court (Court of Arbitration No. 76/99, 30 June 1999, consideration B.4.3), the Court of Cassation (Court of Cassation 18 February 2002, *Pasicrisie* 2002, 491) and the Council of State (Council of State No. 168.119, 22 February 2007, consideration 2.4.5) consider this rule a general principle as well.

331 Court of Cassation 18 February 2002, *Pasicrisie* 2002, 491; Court of Cassation 14 March 2005, *Chroniques de droit social* [*Chronicles of Social Law*] 2005, 518; Labour Court Antwerp 16 January 2003, *Chroniques de droit social* [*Chronicles of Social Law*] 2003, 391.

332 This Protocol has entered into force under Belgian law on the 1st of July 2012 (Act of 6 March 2007, *Belgian Bulletin of Acts and Decrees* 22 June 2012).

333 See e.g. Court of Arbitration No. 61/2002, 28 March 2002, B.5,.

334 Court of Arbitration No. 107/2001, 13 July 2001, consideration B.5; Court of Arbitration No. 61/2002, 28 March 2002, B.5.

335 Court of Cassation F.08.0001.N, 15 October 2009, *Rechtskundig Weekblad* [*Legal Weekly*] 2010–11, 198.

336 Council of State No. 219.156, 3 May 2012.

The case law construction of 'full jurisdiction', the applicability of the general principles of criminal law to punitive administrative sanctions and the finding that certain principles or legal concepts of internal criminal law should also apply to administrative sanctions – on pain of violation of the non-discrimination principle – are the most notable developments of the last few decades in the field of the balance of power in the state structure. One could call it almost an – enlightened – seizure of power, a repositioning of the judicial power in a society in which the government and the administration have become more and more dominant. These principles being acquired, the case law still has to clarify the contours and consequences.

Now, it is time for the legislator to make a move, and to counter the proliferation of disparate administrative sanctioning systems and the ongoing legal uncertainty.

The evolution of administrative enforcement systems give little hope to those who question the system as such, who are in favour of a return to 'pure' criminal enforcement by judges. The advantages of administrative handling, from the viewpoint of the legislator and the administration, are too important, and the faith in effective and efficient criminal enforcement too limited.

Probably more realistic is the call for a framework legislation on administrative sanctions. There are already some forerunners of such regulations: the Social Criminal Code in social law, or the framework on administrative sanctions by local authorities in the New Municipalities Act. Now, further steps in this direction have to be taken. Based upon the judgements in European and internal case law, doctrinal views and proposals and examples in certain fields of internal law and in a number of countries, an Administrative Sanctions Code – comparable to the Criminal Code – has to be elaborated. In this Code the following should at least be integrated: the definition and different forms of administrative sanctions; the essential guarantees during the administrative procedure; the specific elements of judicial control; and the relationship between administrative and other enforcement systems. This Code would function as an overall framework which is applicable to all specific administrative sanctioning systems. In this way, and subject to the condition that the specificity of administrative law enforcement is properly taken into consideration, a balance could be reached between legal protection and efficiency.[337]

[337] See F. Moderne, 'Le pouvoir de sanction administrative en confluant du droit interne et des droits européens [The power of administrative sanctions at the crossroads between internal and European law]', *Revue française de droit administratif* [*French review of administrative law*] 1997, 1.

BIBLIOGRAPHY

Alen, A., 'Naar een betere rechtsbescherming inzake administratieve geldboeten na de koerswijziging van het Hof van Cassatie in zijn arresten van 5 februari 1999 [Towards a better legal protection concerning administrative fines after the change of course by the Court of Cassation in its rulings of 5 February 1999]', *Rechtskundig Weekblad* [*Legal Weekly*] 1999–2000, 630–638.

Alen, A., *Handboek van het Belgisch staatsrecht* [*Manual of Belgian public law*], Deurne, Kluwer, 1995, 889 p.

Alen, A., 'Administratieve geldboetes: hun internationale en internrechtelijke kwalificatie [Administrative fines: their international and internal legal qualification]', in: X (ed.), *Liber Amicorum G. Baeteman*, Deurne, Kluwer, 1997, 369–422.

Andersen, R., Déom, D. and Renders, D. (eds.), *Les sanctions administratives* [*Administrative sanctions*], Brussels, Bruylant, 2007, 728 p.

Ankaert, E., Put, J., Adriaanse, P.C., Barkhuysen, T. and Van Emmerik, M.L., *Europeesrechtelijke eisen bij de toepassing van bestuurlijke punitieve sancties* [*European standards concerning punitive administrative sanctions*], Preadvies voor de Vereniging voor de vergelijkende studie van het recht van België en Nederland [Preliminary advice for the Association for the comparative study of the laws of Belgium and the Netherlands], Alphen a/d Rijn, Kluwer, 2006, 157 p.

Berx, C., *Rechtsbescherming van de burger tegen de overheid* [*Legal protection of the citizen against the government*], Antwerp, Intersentia, 2000, 649 p.

Boes, M., 'Administratieve sancties [Administrative sanctions]', in: X (ed.), *Sancties en nietigheden* [*Sanctions and nullities*], Ghent, Larcier, 2003, 197–226.

Boes, M., 'Het redelijkheidsbeginsel [The principle of proportionality]', in: Opdebeeck, I. (ed.), *Algemene beginselen van behoorlijk bestuur* [*General principles of proper administration*], Antwerp, Kluwer, 1993, 187–116.

Boes, M., 'Motivering van bestuurshandelingen [Justification of administrative acts]', *Recente Arresten van de Raad van State* [*Recent Rulings of the Council of State*] 1994, 117–120.

Boes, M., *Administratief recht* [*Administrative law*], Leuven, Acco, 2001, 322 p.

Boes, M., *Administratieve sancties en art. 6 EVRM in België* [*Administrative sanctions and art. 6 ECHR in Belgium*], Zwolle, W.E.J. Tjeenk Willink, 1989, 36 p.

Boone, I. and Van Haegenborgh, G., 'Administratieve sancties [Administrative sanctions]', in: X, *Jaarverslag van het Hof van Cassatie van België 2004* [*Annual report of the Belgian Court of Cassation 2004*], Brussels, Court of Cassation, 2005, 185–255 (www.juridat.be/cass/cass_nl/2004/cass2004_nl_light.pdf).

Bouhon, F., 'Réflexions autour de la qualification pénale des amendes fiscales [Reflections concerning the criminal qualification of fiscal fines]', *Journal des Tribunaux* [*Courts Journal*] 2009, 681–691.

Boullart, S., 'De ene volle rechtsmacht is de andere niet: over volle en minder volle rechtsmacht [The one full judicial review is not like the other: on full and less full judicial review]', *Publiekrechtelijke Kronieken - Chroniques de Droit Public* [*Public Law Chronicles*] 2007, 246–273.

Braekmans, P., *Administratieve geldboeten in het sociale handhavingsrecht* [*Administrative fines in social enforcement law*], Diegem, Ced.Samsom, 2000, 223 p.

Coremans, H., 'De administratieve sanctie. Naar een omlijning van het begrip [The administrative sanction. Towards an outline of the concept]', *Rechtskundig Weekblad* [*Legal Weekly*] 1964–1965, 753–763.

Craenen, G., *The Institutions of Federal Belgium: an introduction to Belgian public law*, Leuven, Acco, 2001, 175 p.

De Staercke, J., *Algemene beginselen van behoorlijk bestuur en behoorlijk burgerschap. Beginselen van de openbare dienst* [*General principles of proper administration and proper citizenship. Principles of the public service*], Bruges, Uitgeverij Vanden Broele, 2002, 140 p.

Delpérée, F. and Alen, A., 'De residuaire bevoegdheden [The residuary responsibilities]', *Rechtskundig Weekblad* [*Legal Weekly*] 1991–92, 345–356.

Delpérée, F., *Le droit constitutionnel de la Belgique* [*The constitutional law of Belgium*], Brussels, Bruylant, 2000, 1048 p.

Dumont, H., Jadoul, P. and Van Drooghenbroeck, S. (eds.), *La protection juridictionnelle du citoyen face à l'administration*, la Charte, Brussels, 2007, 576 p.

Gekiere, W., 'Zwijgen of meewerken. Over de houding van de "beschuldigde" tijdens sanctieprocedures in het socialezekerheidsrecht [To remain silent or to cooperate. On the position of the 'accused' during sanctioning procedures in social security law]', *Tijdschrift voor Sociaal Recht* [*Journal of Social Law*] 2002, 279–313.

Huybrechts, L., 'Fiscaal strafrecht [Fiscal criminal law]', in: X (ed.), *Algemene Praktische Rechtsverzameling* [*General Practical Law Collection*], Mechelen, Kluwer, 2002, 317 p.

Lambrechts, W., 'Het zorgvuldigheidsbeginsel [The principle of due care]', in: Opdebeeck, I. (ed.), *Algemene beginselen van behoorlijk bestuur* [*General principles of proper administration*], Antwerp, Kluwer, 1993, 27–50.

Lavrysen, L. and De Geyter, L., 'De rechtspraak van het Grondwettelijk Hof ten aanzien van de gemeentelijke administratieve sancties [The case law of the Constitutional Court concerning municipal administrative sanctions]', in: *Liber Amicorum R. Andersen*, Brussels, Bruylant, 2009, 325–341.

Leus, K., 'De plicht tot onpartijdigheid als beginsel van behoorlijk bestuur [The duty of impartiality as a principle of proper administration]', in: Opdebeeck, I. (ed.), *Algemene beginselen behoorlijk bestuur* [*General Principles of Proper Administration*], Antwerp, Kluwer, 1993, 169–194.

Ligot, J., 'De administratie naar Belgisch recht [The administration according to Belgian law]', *Tijdschrift voor Bestuurswetenschappen en Publiekrecht* [*Journal of public administration and public law*] 1973, 3–22.

Lust, S., 'Administrative Law in Belgium', in: R. Seerden and F. Stroink (eds.), *Administrative Law of the European Union, its Member States and the United States*, Antwerp, Intersentia, 2002, 5–58.

Lust, A. and Lust, S., 'Het grondrecht op een rechter met volle rechtsmacht en de stedenbouwkundige herstelvordering [The fundamental right to a judge with full judicial review and the urban planning reparation measure]', in *Liber Amicorum L. Dupont*, Leuven, Universitaire Pers, 2005, 869–904.

Mast, A., Dujardin, J., Van Damme, M. and Vande Lanotte J., *Overzicht van het Belgisch administratief recht* [*Overview of Belgian administrative law*], Mechelen, Kluwer, 2002, 1130 p.

Masset, A., 'De vraies sanctions administratives ou des sanctions pénales camouflées? Réflexions en droit interne belge [Real administrative sanctions or punitive sanctions in disguise? Reflections regarding internal Belgian law]', *Revue de la Faculté de droit de l'Université de Liège* [*Review of the law faculty of the university of Liège*] 2005, 441–466.

Maus, M., 'Kritische bemerkingen bij de arresten van het Hof van Cassatie van 5 februari 1999 inzake de fiscaal-administratieve sancties [Critical remarks concerning the Court of Cassation's rulings of 5 February 1999]', *Algemeen Juridisch Tijdschrift* [*General legal Journal*] 1998–99, 981–988.

Nudelhole, S. and Kirkpatrick, J., 'Le contrôle judiciaire des amendes fiscales et le principe de proportionalité [The judicial review of fiscal fines and the principle of proportionality]', (note under Court of cassation 5 February 1999), *Revue Critique de Jurisprudence Belge* [*Critical review of Belgian case law*] 2002, 594–652.

Opdebeeck, I., 'Het recht van verdediging en het recht om zijn standpunt naar voor te brengen [The right of defence and the right to be heard]', in: Opdebeeck, I. (ed.), *Algemene beginselen van behoorlijk bestuur* [*General principles of proper administration*], Antwerp, Kluwer, 1993, 51–86.

Peeters, P., 'The federal structure: kingdom, regions and communities', in: Craenen, G. (ed.), *The Institutions of Federal Belgium: an introduction to Belgian public law*, Leuven, Acco, 2001, 55–71.

Peeters, P., 'The Judiciary', in: Craenen, G. (ed.), *The Institutions of Federal Belgium*, Leuven, Acco, 2001, 109–133.

Put, J., 'Administratieve boeten, verzachtende omstandigheden en volle rechtsmacht: contradicties in de rechtspraak van het Arbitragehof? [Administrative fines, extenuating circumstances and full jurisdiction: contradictions in Court of Arbitration case law?]', *Tijdschrift voor Bestuurswetenschappen en Publiekrecht* [*Journal of public administration and public law*] 2002, 675–683.

Put, J., 'Bis, sed non in idem', *Rechtskundig Weekblad* [*Legal Weekly*] 2001–02, 937–949.

Put, J., 'Naar een Kaderwet Administratieve Sancties [Towards a Framework Act on Administrative Sanctions]', *Rechtskundig Weekblad* [*Legal Weekly*] 2005–06, 321–336.

Put, J., 'De afbakening van het sanctieconcept [The delimitation of the notion of sanctions', *Nieuw Juridisch Weekblad* [*New Legal Weekly*] 2002, 80–82.

Put, J., 'Rechtshandhaving door administratieve sancties in het recht [Law enforcement through administrative sanctions]', *Rechtskundig Weekblad* [*Legal Weekly*] 2001–02, 1195–1209.

Put, J., *Administratieve sancties in het socialezekerheidsrecht* [*Administrative sanctions in social security law*], Bruges, die Keure, 1998, 605.

Scoriels, V., 'Le principe de la confiance légitime en matière fiscale et la jurisprudence de la Cour de Cassation [The general principle of legal certainty in fiscal matters and the rulings of the Court of Cassation]', *Journal des Tribunaux* [*Courts Journal*] 2003, 301–310.

Sepulchre, V., *Droits de l'homme et libertés fondamentales en droit fiscal* [*Human rights and basic freedoms in fiscal law*], Brussels, Larcier, 2005, 531 p.

Smet, F., 'Rechterlijke controle op administratieve sancties: is de motivering van de evenredigheidstoetsing de sleutel? [Judicial review concerning administrative sanctions: is the motivation of the proportionality examination the key?]' (note under Court of Cassation F.06.0107.N 13 February 2009), *Tijdschrift voor Fiscaal Recht* [*Journal for Fiscal Law*] 2009, 903–909.

Suetens, L., *Op de grens van het ideaal denkbare en het praktisch haalbare* [*On the dividing line between the ideal concept and practicability*], Bruges, die Keure, 1997, 532 p.

Uyttendaele, M., *Précis de droit constitutionnel Belge, regard sur un système institutionnel paradoxal* [*Constitutional law of Belgium, a paradoxical institutional system*], Brussels, Bruylant, 2001, 986 p.

Van Damme, M., 'Goede trouw van burger en bestuur [Good faith on the part of the citizen and administration]', *Rechtskundig Weekblad* [*Legal Weekly*] 1989–90, 1105–1119.

Van Damme, M., 'Het rechtszekerheids- en vertrouwensbeginsel [The principles of legal certainty and legitimate expectations]', in: Opdebeeck, I. (ed.), *Algemene beginselen van behoorlijk bestuur* [*General principles of proper administration*], Antwerp, Kluwer, 1993, 117–168.

Van Damme, M., 'The Council of State: Institution on the Junction of the Three Traditional Powers of the State', in: Vande Lanotte, J. (ed.), *The Principle of Equality: a South African and Belgian Perspective*, Antwerp, Maklu, 2001, 71–88.

Van Drooghenbroeck, S. 'De vraies sanctions administratives ou des sanctions pénales camouflées? Réflexions à propos de la jurisprudence récente de la Cour européenne des droits de l'Homme' [Real administrative sanctions or punitive sanctions in disguise? Reflections regarding the recent case law of the ECHR], *Revue de la Faculté de droit de l'Université de Liège* [*Review of the law faculty of the University of Liège*] 2005, 467–490.

Van Mensel, A., *Het beginsel van behoorlijk bestuur* [*The principle of proper administration*], Ghent, Mys & Breesch, 1997, 189 p.

Van Oevelen, A. and Populier, P., 'De aansprakelijkheid van publiekrechtelijke rechtspersonen voor ondeugdelijke wetgeving [The liability of public law legal entities regarding unsound legislation]', in: X (ed.), *Publiekrecht. De doorwerking van het publiekrecht in het privaatrecht* [*Public law. The continued effect of public law in private law*], Ghent, Mys & Breesch, 1997, 75–128.

Van Orshoven, P., *Behoorlijke rechtsbedeling bij geschillen over directe rijksbelastingen* [*Proper administration of justice with regard to disputes concerning direct taxes*], Antwerp, Kluwer rechtswetenschappen, 1987, 588.

Van Orshoven, P., 'Non scripta, sed nata lex', in: Vanhoecke, M. (ed.), *Algemene rechtsbeginselen* [*General legal principles*], Antwerp, Kluwer, 1991, 59–80.

Veny, L., De Geyter, L. and Vandendriessche, F., 'De invoering van gemeentelijke administratieve sancties… of naar een publiekrechtelijke rechtshandhaving op lokaal vlak in België? [The introduction of municipal administrative sanctions… or towards a public law-based legal enforcement on the local level in Belgium?], *Algemeen Juridisch Tijdschrift* [*General Legal Journal*] 1999–2000, 157–173.

Verougstraete, I., Leclercq, J.-F., Lecroart, P. and Lierman, S. (eds.), *Jaarverslag van het Hof van Cassatie van België* [*Annual report of the Belgian Court of Cassation*], 2004, 185–255.

Constitutional Court / Court of Arbitration rulings can be consulted at www.courconstitutionnelle.be.

Court of Cassation rulings can be consulted at http://jure.juridat.just.fgov.be.

Council of State rulings can be consulted at www.raadvst-consetat.be.

A 'crossroads bank' for all publicly funded databases concerning Belgian legislation, parliamentary proceedings and case law can be found at www.belgiumlex.be.

IV. COUNTRY ANALYSIS – FINLAND

Mikael KOILLINEN

1. CONCEPT OF ADMINISTRATIVE SANCTIONS IN FINNISH ADMINISTRATIVE LAW

The statutory cornerstone of the Finnish administrative law, Administrative Procedure Act (APA)[1] entered into force on 1 January 2004. According to its preparatory works, the intention was to incorporate general and informative statutes governing administrative sanctions.[2] Namely, the predecessor of the current APA, the Administrative Procedure Act from 1982, was completely silent about administrative sanctions. Thus, in section 67 of the new APA it is stated that "an authority may reinforce a prohibition, obligation or requirement imposed by it by way of a threat of a fine, a threat of compulsory action or a threat of compulsory cessation, or another administrative sanction, as separately provided".

However, despite the intentions explicitly expressed in the preparatory works, the Section 67 of the APA provides no basis for a positive conceptionalization of administrative sanctions. Firstly, the *ratio legis* of the statute is only informative and referential. The statute enables an authority with no external competence whatsoever to impose means enacted within it; the competence to exercise these powers is to be provided separately. Secondly, the wording of the section ignores the core element of administrative sanctions: Section 67 applies only to *accessory means for reinforcing* primary obligations laid down by the administration. The wording of section 67 does not apply to non-accessory administrative sanctions, which are punitive measures exercised by an authority due to an infringement.

So the exercise of sanctioning powers within the administration takes place mainly on the basis of material regulations on certain matters, in accordance with standard procedural regulations and within the organisational context

1 The APA is available in English (although unofficial translation, it is provided by the Ministry of Justice): www.finlex.fi/en/laki/kaannokset/2003/en20030434.pdf.

2 See HE 72/2002vp, p. 129. (HE stands for a government proposal to parliament for new legislation).

of "normal" administrative organization. No general statute concerning administrative sanctions exists.

At least two different definitions of the term sanction can be identified. The wider concept accommodates a wide variety of detrimental legal consequences ("*hallinnollinen seuraamus*"[3]) laid down due to infringement or dereliction of the law or other public law duty.[4] The narrow concept contains only punitive monetary fees. If one concentrates only to narrow concept of sanctions, in general textbooks on administrative or criminal law[5] traditionally there were usually only three examples of administrative sanctions mentioned; namely parking tickets, the fee to be paid by vehicles carrying an excess load and public transport penalty fares. However, in legislation an administrative fine is nowadays not so unfamiliar[6] – especially in legislation relevant to the EU law. In addition, in the public discourse some emphasis has been placed on the competition infringement fine in the field of competition law. Recently also the tax surcharges have gained attraction due to the *ne bis in idem* – case law of the ECHR.

The lack of general legislation and general legal literature concerning administrative sanctions is partly due to the fact that the Finnish counterpart of the German *Ordnungswidrigkeitengesetz* consists only of a summary penal fee. However, this penal fee is *neither considered to be an administrative nor even a quasi-criminal sanction*, although similarities to the *Ordnungswidrigkeitengesetz* do exist. Punishable by a summary penal fee are acts whose realization represents a punishable misdemeanour, although it affects society to an extent that neither requires nor legitimates the use of more severe punishments. The fundamental difference between the *Ordnungswidrigkeitengesetz* and the summary penal fee in the Finnish system lies in Section 1 of Chapter 6 of the Finnish Criminal Code, which clearly categorizes summary penal fees as – not as even-quasi criminal but – general *criminal punishment* within the system of criminal law. Usually it is stated, that this arrangement is due to the better guarantees of the legal protection and procedural protection of the rule of law within the field of criminal law compared to the guarantees laid in the administrative law.[7]

---

3 It must be noted, that even the translation of the APA provided by the Ministry of Justice seems to focus perhaps too strictly on sanctions in narrow sense: the Finnish wording refers to "seuraamus".

4 Kulla, Heikki: Sanktionluonteiset hallintoasiat: tunnusmerkkejä ja rajausperusteista. In Juhlakirja Pentti Arajärvi 1948 – 2/6 – 2008, p. 248.

5 See, for example, Tapio Lappi-Seppälä, Rikosten seuraamukset (2000), 481.

6 See Kiiski, Kimmo Ilmari: Hallinnollinen sanktiointi. 2011, p. 97–120.

7 Kiiski, Kimmo Ilmari: Hallinnollinen sanktiointi. 2011.

This point has some merits. The Finnish Supreme Administrative (SAC) court has recently argued in SAC 2009:83 explicitly that the burden of proof can be set in the field of the administrative law lower than it is in the field of criminal law. SAC argued, that due to the fact that the chapter 51 of Administrative Judicial Procedure Act provided court powers to evaluate evidence freely and because the case law of the ECJ did not contradict, SAC was more free to evaluate facts than the criminal court would be in criminal matter, although the administrative fines under judicial review amounted to over 82 million euro. However, legitimate generalisation of this judgment has some limits, due to the fact that it was question of competition law; a nation-wide cartel among corporations.

Finnish legal literature within the field of administrative law has been traditionally silent on administrative sanctions. In addition to a few monographs concentrating mainly on accessory means of reinforcement of primary obligations, there were only a few references concentrating on non-accessory administrative sanctions in general textbooks on administrative law,[8] but no comprehensive analysis of this issue exists. However, *Olli Mäenpää* has recently made some references to administrative criminal procedure, which contain procedures for exercise of sanctioning powers, and *Heikki Kulla* has discussed the characteristics of administrative sanctions under the conceptual umbrella provided by the article 6 of ECHR.[9] The exact scope of application of administrative criminal procedure remains still somewhat undefined.

Within the field of criminal law, *Kimmo Kiiski* has recently published a doctoral thesis concerning the division between criminal and administrative sanctions.[10] In addition, recent judgment of the European Court of Human Rights (Ruotsalainen v. Finland 16.06.2009) and Supreme Court's judgments adopting interpretation concerning application of the *ne bis in idem* between criminal sanction and punitive administrative measures within the field of taxation has raised discussion on the topic,[11] but mainly from the perspective of criminal procedure. The discussion has concentrated to the question, whether criminal punishment can be sentenced after adopting administrative measures identified as sanctions by criteria adopted in the case-law of European Court of Human Rights. Traditionally the principle of double jeopardy (*ne bis in idem*) is not

8 Mäenpää, Olli, Hallinto-oikeus (2003), 425–6. The book by of Aaro Ahtee concentrating on administrative deprivation of liberty ("Hallinto-oikeudellinen vapaudenriisto", 1950) should however be mentioned. Due to its age it is mostly of historical value.

9 Mäenpää, Olli: Hallintoprosessioikeus 2. ed., 2007, s. 193–195, Kulla, Heikki: Sanktionluonteiset hallintoasiat: tunnusmerkkejä ja rajausperusteista. In Juhlakirja Pentti Arajärvi 1948 – 2/6 – 2008, p. 325–336.

10 Kiiski, Kimmo Ilmari: Hallinnollinen sanktiointi. 2011.

11 See for example Vuorenpää, Mikko: Veropetos, veronkorotus ja kielto käsitellä samaa asiaa kahdesti – EIT Jukka Ruotsalainen vs. Suomi 16.6.2009, in Lakimies 2010/1 s. 94 and Vuorenpää, Mikko: KKO 2010:45 ja KKO 2010:46 – Veronkorotus, veropetos ja kielto käsitellä samaa asiaa kahdesti. Osa 2. in Lakimies 2010/6 s. 1113.

considered to be applicable to the relationship between administrative and criminal sanctions. Although they are *usually* imposed as alternatives to each other, no normative legal prohibition against double jeopardy exists. According to section 7 of chapter 6 of the Penal Code, other consequences relating from the offence *may* be taken into account in order to mitigate the punishment imposed on the offender. However, the current discussion, which abandons this orthodoxy, concentrates mainly on interpretation of the ECHR and it's ramifications to the *criminal* sanctions, and thus detailed analysis is somewhat unprofitable here.

The predominant doctrine in the administrative law can be divided into two core notions. Formally, non-accessory administrative sanctions are defined as being punitive and reactive in relation to the infringement. They are punitive measures outside the criminal justice system and are applied by an authority other than a court of law. However, no *clear-cut* division has been identified either between administrative sanctions and administrative measures establishing burdens, obligations or restrictions on an individual due to infringement, nor between punitive sanctions and accessory threats for the reinforcement of primary obligations or other means for restoring legality.

Due to the vagueness of the Finnish doctrine concerning administrative sanctions, it must be pointed out also, that no established delimited criteria for identifying administrative sanctions exist. For example, certain withdrawals of licences, which are based to the illegal conduct of license holder, are sometimes seen as sanctions, sometimes not.[12] There is some case-law supporting narrow concept. For example, in SAC 2011:15 it was reasoned, that revocation of trade licences are not to be understand as sanctions or detrimental legal consequences. According to SAC, they constitute only a supervisory administrative action. Within this narrow context, the contents of terminology referring to administrative consequences ("hallinnollinen seuraamus") become also thinner and are identified as synonym for sanction.[13] However, there are also some case-law, especially later analysed SAC 2004:15[14] which supports wider concept. There is also some statutory support for wider concept including for example revocations of permits. For example, the rubric of the section in later analyzed Alcohol Act refers to "*Seuraamukset rikkomuksista*", which is translated in [unofficial] translation with terms "*Sanctions for offences*".[15] However, literally

12 Mäenpää, Olli, Olli, Hallinto-oikeus 2003, p 426, Mäenpää, Olli: Hallintoprosessioikeus. 2007, p. 194.

13 Kiiski, Kimmo Ilmari: Hallinnollinen sanktiointi. 2011, p. 29.

14 See below section 3.3.

15 Translation of Alcohol Act provided by Ministry of Social Affairs and Health, available at www.finlex.fi/en/laki/kaannokset/1994/en19941143.

more accurate translation would be "*Consequences for misdemeanours*": the contents of section are punitive. Section 22 enables the licensing authority to issue the licence holder an admonition or a written warning, set conditions necessary for the supervision of serving of alcoholic beverages or without compensation restrict the licence which it has granted by limiting the serving hours, the serving area, the kinds of alcoholic beverages to be served, or without compensation withdraw the licence it has granted either for a certain period or permanently, if the Alcohol Act or the provisions or regulations issued in virtue of it have been violated in the business.

Furthermore, some scholars tend to identify administrative acts, which are of punitive nature on the basis of the case law concerning the article 6 of ECHR and by supplementing this approach by views from national legal order.[16] The problem of this approach lies within the nature of ECHR as sort of *minimal* guarantees. Because of this, approaches consisting mainly on these minimal guarantees tend to lead to casuistic approach. Sanctions are identified only where the European Court of Human Rights states them to exist and only with ramifications *in casu* stated explicitly in the judgment of the court. For example, few years ago Jussila v. Finland (23.11.2006) the Court found that, although the tax surcharges in the case were part of the fiscal regime, they were imposed by a rule whose purpose was deterrent and punitive, and the offence was therefore "criminal", within the meaning of Article 6. Although *Jussila* case was adopted in Finnish case-law[17], no comprehensive analysis concerning the scope of application of the deterrent and punitive administrative sanctions were made and/or no legislative changes were adopted. The *ne bis in idem* judgment Ruotsalainen v. Finland (16.6.2009) entered a structural vacuum again.

Due to this, a broad definition of administrative sanction is adopted in this paper, as the questionnaire for this project suggests. In other words, this paper will try to identify a possible variety of administrative measures, which have the nature of sanctions regardless of their *a priori* classification in Finnish administrative law. However, due to the questionnaire and task of this project, instead of concentrating to the interpretation of article 6 of ECHR, emphasis will be laid to the nature of administrative action in question: is it a reaction of an authority to person's infringement?

---

16 See Kulla, Heikki: Sanktionluonteiset hallintoasiat: tunnusmerkkejä ja rajausperusteista. In Juhlakirja Pentti Arajärvi 1948 – 2/6 – 2008, p. 325–336.

17 See SAC 2007:67 and SAC 2007:68.

2. PRINCIPLES GOVERNING THE EXERCISE OF PUBLIC POWERS IN THE LIGHT OF THE CONSTITUTION

The traditional and prevailing doctrine on administrative sanctions places them under the general requirements of *the rule of law* or *legality* in administration instead of the requirement of legality in criminal law.[18] Thus there are also no general requirements concerning questions relevant to all sanctions adopted in criminal law: for example, the presence of the guilt principle has no uniform concept among administrative sanctions; it varies from statute to another.[19] However, some scholars argue, that the guarantees of due process and legality within criminal law should also be applied when exercising administrative sanctioning powers. For example, *Olli Mäenpää* refers to legality and presumption of innocence based on CA 8 and the privilege against self-incrimination, which are applicable *mutatis mutandis* also to administrative sanctions.[20]

Section 2 of the Finnish Constitution lays down two fundamental criteria for the exercise of public powers. First of all, the first sentence of section 2(3) confirms the existence of the *so-called "Rechtsstaatliche Gesetzesvorbehalt"* by requiring that the executive powers of an administrative body must be expressly based on the law and be justified on the grounds laid down in that law ("*The exercise of public powers shall be based on an Act*"). In others words; Section 2(3) denies that the authority has general competence to carry out its duties: competence must always be derived from the law. This requirement applies to the exercise of public or official authority, i.e. when an authority takes decisions or any other actions that affect the rights or obligations of an individual.[21] Exercise of sanctioning powers falls evidently in the scope of application of this requirement.[22] Th The term "Act" is to be understood here as an Act of Parliament. Furthermore, the constitution lays down certain criteria for the precision of an enabling act in question.

For example, in SAC 2010:34 a decision, which was made according to the regulation made by authority without explicit support of the Act of Parliament was overturn. The law in question allowed raised fees in cases where construction project has been already started without license, but prescribed that those should be based on the expenses of the authority. According to SAC, the fact that fee in question was charged

18 See for example PeVL 32/2005, PeVL 55/2005. PeVL stands for opinion of the Constitutional Committee of Parliament; a form of judicial *pre*view of the constitutionality of legislation in the law-making process. Although performed by parliament, this *a priori* control has traditionally had essential status in Finnish constitution.

19 Kiiski, Kimmo Ilmari: Hallinnollinen sanktiointi. 2011, p. 29.

20 Mäenpää, Olli: Hallintolaki ja hyvän hallinnon takeet. 2012, s. 210.

21 See also Mäenpää, Olli: Hallinto-oikeus (2003), p. 405.

22 PeVL 55/2005vp.

always as triplicate despite expensens, if construction has already been started without permission, made it *punitative.*

Second, conformity with the law in Section 2(3) means conforming to the legal order. In all public activity the whole legal order, including statutory sources and legal principles, must be observed. Although it is obvious that the legal order required to be observed here does not exclude constitution, some limitations concerning the administration might exist. Namely Section 106 prescribes an obligation to give primacy to the provision in the Constitution if, in a matter being tried by a *court of law*, the application of an Act would evidently be in conflict with the Constitution. Noteworthy is the fact that the wording of the section only mentions courts remaining silent as regards the administrative authorities.[23] It has been argued that Section 106 should be interpreted *a contrario* and thus even those Parliamentary Acts evidently in conflict with the Constitution would bind the administration.[24] On the other hand, it has been emphasized that individuals must be able to rely on the non-infringement of their basic rights by the authorities, and that conformity with the law includes the constitution as [*even a statutory*] law.[25]

For example, according to Section 9 of the CA, everyone has the right to leave the country. Limitations on this right may be provided by a specific Act, if they are necessary for the purpose of *safeguarding legal proceedings* or *for the enforcement of penalties* or *for national defence.* In 1995, the same wording was adopted in Section 7 of the 1919 CA. When the old Passport Act (L 22.8.1986/642)[26] was enacted, it was determined that a passport may be refused if it is reasonable to expect that a person will commit a crime utilizing his/her passport (Section 9). Respectively it was also possible to withdraw person's passport if, after the issuing of the passport, certain facts emerge that would have prohibited its issuance (Section 14). Withdrawals subject to the conditions in this section are considered to be both a precautionary measure and an administrative sanction.[27]

However, in the decision of the Regional Administrative Court of Uusimaa (LO 12.12.1995 T: 1557/2) the court argued that these restrictions must be interpreted in the light of Section 7 of the 1919 CA. The merits of the case concerned whether the police were empowered to withdraw a person's passport if it was reasonable to assume that that person would leave the country in order to avoid a criminal sentence imposed by a Finnish court and in order to continue his criminal activities. The court stated that, according to Section 7 of the 1919 CA, even a reasonable expectation of a

23 This problem is also not addressed in the official *travaux préparatoires* of the constitution.

24 See, for example, Karapuu, Heikki, Perusoikeudet kansallisten normien hierkiassa, in Lakimies 6–7/1999, 875–6.

25 See Mäenpää Olli: Hallinto-oikeus 2003, 406.

26 New Passport Act (21.7.2006/671) has already entered into force.

27 Mäenpää, Olli, Hallintosanktio, in Encyclopaedia Iuridica Fennica V (1997), 227.

person's criminal conduct *in the future* was neither acceptable nor a legal ground for withdrawing a passport – or even for refusal in the first place, albeit the Passport Act clearly states this.[28]

3. GENERAL PRINCIPLES OF ADMINISTRATIVE LAW AND SANCTIONS

As pointed out in the opinion of the Constitutional Law Committee of Parliament 74/2002 vp, formal legality is – although necessary –, not sufficient guarantee of the rule of law. The general principles of administrative law influences also exercise of sanctioning powers.

Traditionally, the Finnish doctrine of administrative law has included – in addition to conformity with the law discussed above – four general principles which restrict the discretionary powers of an administrative authority. They originated in French and German administrative law, from where they were adopted by the Finnish system, mainly due to the decades of research carried out by Prof. V. Merikoski. Due to the limited space and scope of this contribution, there is no point in thoroughly examining them *per se*. Furthermore, one could argue with sufficient certainty that these principles of equality, objectivity, proportionality and the prohibition of abuse of power are somewhat familiar to every legal academic in Europe.

In present-day administrative law the scope of application of these principles is wide. Whereas traditional principles were only applicable as restrictions on *discretion*, the constitutional connection with basic rights has evolved this scope to all forms of administrative action – from *discretionary powers* to the *syllogical application of the law* and everything in between. This paradigmatic shift has also been expressly laid down in APA Section 6:

> Section 6 – Legal principles of administration
> An authority shall treat its on an equal footing and exercise its competence only for purposes that are acceptable under the law. The acts of the authority shall be impartial and proportionate to their objective. They shall protect legitimate expectations based on the legal system.

[28] After this case-law, Passport Act was revised in 1998 (L 14/1998), partly so as to be in conformity with the constitution. (See HE 182/1997, p. 1).

3.1. A FULLER ACCOUNT – GENERAL PRINCIPLES CONCRETISED IN THE EXERCISE OF SANCTIONING POWERS

The prevailing understanding of the concept of administration sees it as a society-oriented and future-oriented action, which uses legal norms only as a means to achieve specific ends. In other words, a strict separation between the logics of decision-making in a court of law and decision-making in the administration is deemed to exist. This division has been dichotomized into the models of syllogical and practical decision-making.

The *prima facie* dichotomous nature of decision-making has survived practically intact *also within* the theory of discretionary powers in administration. There are respectively two models of decision making: the *syllogical model,* i.e. the *consideration of legal matters* and the *practical model,* i.e. *expediency considerations (considering matters of policy).* Nowadays the existence of this division as a clear-cut dichotomy is considered controversial[29]; according to current theory one should rather talk about a sliding scale which has a pure syllogical application of the law at one end, and pure objective rationality at the other. However, in the field of exercising public powers, one should require legal justification, *i.e.* statutory support for the existence of discretionary powers in a particular case. Furthermore, goal-rationality on the part of the administration plays a different role here: when exercising public powers against an individual, certain aims and goals are to be derived from the enabling act. In other words, legally speaking, the administration does not use sanctioning powers to pursue the public interest of the future, but to apply the law in order to evaluate past.

From this development of the discretionary powers it follows that decision-making in the case of sanctions against individuals should be seen as the application of the law according to the syllogical model. In practice, this means that an authority may only impose administrative sanctions against an individual if certain conditions are met.

1. The *Criterion of competence.* An authority must have the necessary competence to impose sanctions, and this competence must have been derived from an Act of Parliament.
2. The *Criterion of precision.* The Act of Parliament in question must contain precise and definite provisions concerning essential elements of the punishable acts. The minimum requirement here is to enact principles governing the obligations of private individuals with such precision that the individual in question can foresee – with sufficient confidence – how the sanctioning powers will be exercised in his/her particular case.

29 See, for example, Mäenpää Olli, Hallinto-oikeus. 2003, p. 353.

3. The *Criterion of proportionality*. Use of sanctioning powers must be a last resort; sanctions are means which are only available if other, less intrusive, means are not possible. The use sanctioning powers must – at least in principle – be effective: if it is obvious that the aim prescribed by the law cannot be attained even with the use of sanctions, then these sanctioning powers cannot be exercised. And, furthermore, there must be a reasonable balance between the content of the sanction and the aim prescribed by the law.
4. The *Criterion of the prohibition of abuse of power*. Sanctioning powers must only be used to protect those interests laid down in the in enabling law; pursuing other purposes by means of sanctions is forbidden.
5. The *Criterion of the protection of legitimate expectations*. The use of sanctioning powers cannot infringe individuals' legitimate expectations based on the legal system.

3.2. THE CRITERION OF COMPETENCE – SEPARATION OF POWERS

Section 3 of the Finnish Constitutions reads as follows.

> *Section 3, subsection 3 – Parliamentarism and the separation of powers*
> ...
> The judicial powers are exercised by independent courts of law, with the Supreme Court and the Supreme Administrative Court as the highest instances.

According to the Finnish Constitution, sanctioning powers are to be used by courts of law. Traditionally, this separation had been considered to be somewhat rigid,[30] and enabling some body other than the courts to be able to make use of sanctioning powers required special arrangements.

> For example, the already revised Law on Parking Fines (3.4.1970/248), which enabled the police or the municipal authorities to impose administrative fines for parking violations, was enacted as an exception to the Constitution which required 2/3-majority in parliament. According to the government's proposal[31], reasons for the use of this procedure were related to the fact that a parking fine could neither be categorized as criminal punishment, nor as a state tax and also not as a charge to be levied under the official functions mentioned in Section 62 of the 1919 CA (Section 81 of the CA). In addition it was noted that a fine was in this case imposed on the owner of a vehicle, who was not necessarily the person who had committed the parking violation. These arguments (*inter alia*) led the government to the conclusion that the *constitutional protection of property* required the bill to be passed through the qualified procedure for enacting exceptions to the Constitution, although the opinion of the Constitutional Committee was not sought.

30 See, for example, PeVL 1/1982vp, p. 8.
31 HE 130/1970vp, p. 13–14.

The Constitutional Committee has previously emphasized that if administrative sanctions are intended to be used as a punishment, they are materially alike[32], and that imposing a specific penalty, regardless of the procedure or the legal consequences, constitutes the exercise of judicial powers.[33] Although formally rigid, in practice the doctrine of separation of powers has proved to be somewhat flexible. Despite the separation of powers, enabling a body other than the courts to have sanctioning powers has been considered possible, at least when the sanctions only consist of diminutive monetary consequences for the transgressor.[34] In recent years, the doctrine has evolved more and more flexible. Nowadays administrative sanctioning powers are so customary, that the problems connected to separation of powers have vanished, allthough some scholars still use the doctrine of separation of powers as a critical yardstick for adminitsrative sanctions.[35] For example nowadays administrative sanctions even in monetary form are seen so well-established in "case-law" of the Constitutional Committee, that the conformity to the legality in CA 2.3 is enough to set questions arising from separation of powers aside.[36]

> Committee usually argues, that punitive monetary fee should be identified as *de facto* criminal punishment. (PeVL 17/2012vp, PeVL 9/2012 vp, p. 2/I, PeVL 55/2005 vp, p. 2/I ja PeVL 32/2005 vp, p. 2/II). According to established line of argumentation, the committee also requires, that the general basis for competence for exercise of sanctioning powers must be enacted by the parliamentary law, due to the fact that exercise of sanctioning powers constitute an exercise of public powers mentioned in PL 2.3 §. In addition to that, committee usually states that although the guarantees of legality in the field of the criminal law are not directly applicable to administrative sanctions, the general requirement of precision cannot be set aside. (PeVL 9/2012 vp, p. 2/II, PeVL 57/2010 vp, p. 2/II ja PeVL 71/2002 vp, p. 5/I).

However, the flexibility of the doctrine has led also to the separation of doctrines of criminal and administrative sanctions. For example, even somewhat ambiguous and reverse burden of proof has been evaluated to be in conformity to constitution, because the bill in question – amendment containing administrative penalty fee to Act on the Prevention of Pollution from Ships – had acceptable aims connected to everyone's responsibility of the environment mentioned in CA 20 and were to be carried out by administrative authority bound to general framework laid down in APA.[37] Despite the flexibility adopted in the law-making process, some sensitivity can be identified from the case-law

32 PeVL 3/1977vp, p. 1.
33 PeVL 1/1982vp, p. 8.
34 PeVL 1/1982vp,. p. 4 *e contrario*.
35 Kiiski, Kimmo Ilmari: Hallinnollinen sanktiointi. 2011, p. 153–169.
36 PeVL 55/2005vp.
37 PeVL 32/2005 vp, see also PeVL 4/2004 vp.

of the administrative courts in the form of constitutional control of the precision of an Act enabling authority to exercise sanctioning powers.

3.3. THE CRITERION OF PRECISION

The requirement of precision is emphasized when exercising sanctioning powers against individuals. An illustrative example from the practice of the courts is the interpretation of the old, already overridden Law on Licensed Passenger Traffic (15.2.1991/343), which mainly regulates scheduled public transport and taxis. According to sections 5.1 and 6a of the Law, it was forbidden to carry any passengers in a private vehicle against a charge without a licence.[38] A licence to drive a taxi could be granted to any person who fulfils the criteria laid down in section 9b. Furthermore, section 10 of the Law enabled the licensing authority to stipulate certain terms relating to the location where the licence can be used, *i.e.* where the person in question is allowed to ply his/her trade.

First of all, it should be noted that the Act on Licensed Passenger Traffic was enacted before the constitutional reforms, and thus its compatibility with the current constitutional protection of basic rights was never reviewed by the Constitutional Committee. However, Section 18 of the CA grants a person the fundamental freedom to earn his or her livelihood by the employment, occupation or commercial activity of his or her choice, and thus the requirement to obtain a licence for a certain activity and administrative sanctions relating to this freedom is considered to be a restriction on this freedom. This question has arisen on many occasions in case law. Maybe the most comprehensive example is the decision of the Regional Administrative Court of Hämeenlinna (HaO 15.6.2000 T:00/403/4), which deserves further examination.

> The Law on Licensed Passenger Traffic also prescribed that a licence to operate licensed passenger vehicles can be cancelled if the operations are exercised in a manner, which is contrary to the conditions of the licence. In this case, the entrepreneur had not acted in compliance with the terms of the licence, which restricted passenger traffic routes. However, the authority only became aware of this when the entrepreneur appealed against another decision by the authority in question. Because of this breach, the Provincial State Office temporarily withdrew the licence. The Regional Administrative Court considered this as administrative sanction to be too severe.
>
> The Court argued that the decision by the Provincial State Office concerning passenger traffic routes in the area and the provisions of the Law on Licensed Passenger Traffic concerning the legal relevance of terms relating to specific routes were open to various interpretations. The entrepreneur would have had difficulties in

38 According to sections 5.1 and 6, some exceptions do exist.

> foreseeing, that the Provincial State Office could possibly have exercised its sanctioning powers in this manner.
>
> In summing up the Court stated that in these circumstances *the rights and obligations* of the entrepreneur could not have been understood by *the entrepreneur himself with sufficient certainty and without undue difficulty,* even though they were formally laid down in an Act and other statutes derived emanating therefrom, and thus the requirements of parliamentary legislation, i.e. precision and definition, had not been fulfilled. Furthermore, the court emphasized the fact that operating a taxi is, as such, a *prima facie* legal means of earning one's living, and thus restrictions thereto also meant restrictions on the constitutional guarantee of freedom to engage in commercial activities and the protection of property. As a consequence of these rights, the Court stated that the gaps in the statutes could not be resolved by an interpretation, which was detrimental to the entrepreneur. At the end of the day, the Court overturned the withdrawal of the licence.[39]

In SAC 2008:41 authority had withdrawn a certificate required to work as charger with detonators for six months, when the charger has been sentenced to a criminal fine due to the breach of safety at work. Authority had ruled that the charger no longer fulfilled preconditions prescibed by the law and government decree. The Supreme Administrative Court overturned decisions. Act and government decree in question did not prescribe in detail the conditions under which the person's suitability for chargers task was considered. The withdrawal was justified exclusively by reference to the criminal punishment. Taking into account the employment history of charger as well as chargers ability to exercise his/her profession, and the fact that the conditions for cancellation of certificate were prescribed only with a very general suitability clause in the law, the preconditions for the cancellation was not met.[40]

Whereas the arguments of above case were based on the criterion of precision connected to the constitutional protection of property and the freedom to engage in commercial activities, the Supreme Administrative Court has sometimes based argumentation more straightforwardly on the implications of legality in criminal law, as protected under section 8 of the CA. This solution has raised some discussion in the literature; some see the expansion of legality in criminal law at least justifiable and reasoned,[41] naturally dissenting justified opinions exists too.[42]

---

39 This decision was reviewed by the Supreme Administrative Court, which upheld the court's decision.

40 See, however very recent and contradicting SAC 2010:82.

41 See, for example Tapani, Jussi – Tolvanen, Matti: Rikosoikeuden yleinen osa – Vastuuoppi s. 137 (Helsinki 2008) and Koillinen, Mikael: Seuraamusjärjestelmien leikkauspisteessä – nulla poena sine lege certa s. 83–107, in Timo Ahonen (ed.): Oikeussosiologiaa ja kriminologiaa, Juhlajulkaisu Ahti Laitinen (Turku 2006).

42 See, for example Kimmo Ilmari Kiiski: Kohti rationaalisempaa rankaisemista. Lakimies 1/2009 s. 34–58.

In the Supreme Administrative Court (SAC 2004:15) the court argued that legality under criminal law – as protected in section 8 of the CA – prevented the Law on Estate Agencies and Businesses Letting Real Property (L 15.12.2000/1075) from being interpreted in such a way that it automatically prevented a person from practising as an estate agent if he had committed a punishable crime during a certain period of time. This case did not formally concern administrative sanctions as such, but certain similarities can be discerned. The case focused on the question whether legality in criminal law also prevented the imposition of punishments other than criminal sanctions as a legal consequence of having committed a crime, if there was no statute regulating these consequences when the crime was committed. The Law on Estate Agencies and Businesses Letting Real Property, which lays down certain criteria for the suitability of estate agents including the above-mentioned requirement of not having a criminal record, entered into force on 1.3.2001. The criminal conviction dated from 28.8.1998. The original crimes had been committed in 1996. According to the Provincial State Office, this conviction prohibited the person in question from being registered as an estate agent.

The solution adopted by the Supreme Administrative Court was somewhat ambiguous and twofold. First of all, the court emphasized that the general requirement of predictability, *derived from the constitutional protection of legality in criminal law*, prevented this kind of connection: the person in question, who had been convicted in 1998 for crimes committed in 1996, could have had no possibility to foresee that, in 2001, a bill would be passed, which would impose on him – in addition to a criminal conviction – additional sanctions. Thus section 5 of the Law in question could not be applied due to its wording, which clearly and unconditionally tied the evaluation of a person's suitability to a 5-year time-limit. The ambiguousness of the case rests in the final argument presented in the case. Although the SAC emphasized the general requirement of predictability, it stated that a person's criminal record can be taken into account subject to the discretion mentioned in Section 5.3 of the Law in question, which contains no precise or definite criteria for suitability. Because this appeal was decided partly on cassation, no further criteria for discretion were laid down by the SAC.

However, the rigid rule of the criterion of precision based on the constitution and developed by the Constitutional Committee, has gained a variable degree of force in the case law. Fluctuating examples of case law could be identified. For example, in the decision of the Regional Administrative Court of Kuopio (HAO 9.8.2000 T: 01243/00/5500) a licence to drive a taxi was revoked because the driver in question had lost his suitability to act as a taxi driver partly because he had sworn in front of three passengers.

3.4. THE CRITERION OF PROPORTIONALITY

Traditionally, the principle of proportionality has meant a limitation to the administrative body's discretionary powers. Its essence was the requirement of a balance between means and ends: the severity of an administrative act was proportional to the objective pursued thereby. A more recent approach, which has been influenced by German *Verhältnismäßigkeit,* EU law and the ECHR, is based on three criteria embodied in proportionality when restricting basic rights.[43] Each of these criteria should be seriously taken into account when deciding on a sanction or restrictive or otherwise negative administrative action.

Firstly, proportionality requires the administrative act to be appropriate and effective. Second, the requirement of necessity provides that the exercise of public authority should only be used restrictively. This requirement is incorporates the notion of *Übermaßverbot*: if some other comparably efficient and less restrictive means to achieve the intended objective exists, they must be used instead of the more restrictive means.[44] Some scholars also suggest, that the *ultima ratio* principle of criminal law should apply also to administrative sanctions, while others emphasizes, that the criminal sanction should be in fact the *ultima ratio* compared to administrative sanction. However, as *Kiiski* suggests, neither position has realized in legislative practices. The requirement of *Übermaßverbot* has however been crystallized in established case law of courts. The predominant legal literature provides that, before the exercise of sanctioning powers with more or even the most severe sanctions allowed by the law, more lenient means should first be applied.

> For example, in the Taxi case of the Regional Administrative Court of Hämeenlinna discussed above, the court argued – in addition to arguments concerning precision and definition – that the Provincial State Office could have used public powers, which were more lenient. In this case the court argued that the principle of proportionality required the use of caution. Only if caution has no effect on the conduct of the person in question is it possible – at least in principle – to revoke that person's licence.

Thirdly, the criterion of proportionality includes traditional balance between means and ends (*proportionality in the narrow sense*). Emphasis must be places on the strengthened constitutional weight of this requirement. Whereas this requirement traditionally played a role in restricting discretionary powers, nowadays this reconstitutionalized requirement has sometimes even set aside a clear and precise legal provision.

---

43 PeVM 25/1994vp, p. 5.

44 See Viljanen, Veli-Pekka: perusoikeuksien rajoitusedellytykset. 2001, p.212.

The Supreme Administrative Court decided (SAC 1999:33) that an obligation to pay all one's taxes as laid down in the taxation law may breach the principle of proportionality. This case was based on the wording of the Motor Vehicle Taxation Act (L 29.12.1994/1482), which lays down liability to pay full tax on a car if the car in question is foreign and is driven on a Finnish territory by a person who has his/her permanent domicile in Finland, even though the car in question is owned by a foreign citizen. The tax in question can increase up to tens of thousands of euros. In this case, the Finnish citizen Y drove a foreign car owned by his companion X on one occasion only. According to the Finnish Customs Service, this conduct led to the car having to be taxed in full as the car in question had been imported into Finland. This tax, including VAT and a *punitive tax increase,* amounted to 87,000 FMK (about €15,000). The SAC decided that liability to pay the full tax was in breach of the principle of proportionality – despite the clear and precise wording of the Motor Vehicle Taxation Act. At the end of the day the court stated that the obligation to pay full taxes was not reasonable considering the temporary and minor use to be made of the vehicle in question.

Furthermore, the state's authorized representative appealed against the decision of the SAC by means of an extraordinary appeal.[45] The SAC dismissed the appeal, this time arguing more explicitly concerning the constitutional balance to be struck between a *person's conduct and the consequences deriving therefrom*. According to the SAC, the constitutional protection of property requires that in an individual case a person's actions and their consequences must be reasonably balanced – even despite the clear wording of a particular Act.

3.5. THE PROHIBITION ON THE ABUSE OF POWER

The classic definition of the prohibition on the abuse of power in Finnish doctrine as a restriction on discretionary powers traditionally argued that even if the administration is formally competent to perform a certain task, this task cannot be performed in order to achieve objectives other than those deriving from the tasks and competence of the administrative body. Section 6 of the APA requires that an authority shall exercise its competences only for those purposes that are acceptable under the law. Very illustrative example concerning abuse of power and exercise of sanctioning powers can be found within the scope of application of the legislation regulating alcohol.

The Alcohol Act (1143/1994) lays down certain conditions for making, importing, selling and serving alcohol in Finland. According to section 1 of the Act, the purpose of this Act is to "prevent detrimental societal, social and health effects *caused by*

45 This method of appeal is available after the decision has become final or on grounds specifically provided by the law, see the Administrative Judicial Procedure Act (L 586/1996) Chapter 11.

alcoholic substances by *controlling the consumption of alcohol*". Furthermore, according to section 21 the serving of alcoholic beverages can only take place on licensed premises, *a serving licence*, having been granted by the Authority. Section 21 further provides that a serving licence may be permanently or temporarily issued to a person who is considered to have the necessary *qualifications* and is *sufficiently reliable to carry out this activity*. Furthermore, the serving of alcoholic beverages may only take place in premises that are approved by the licensing authority as being *adequate both as regards location and the serving facilities*. Section 21 of the Alcohol Act enables the Authority to refuse a licence to serve alcoholic beverages if *the authority considers this necessary in order to achieve the purpose of this Act*. Before discussing the sanctioning powers granted by the Act, it is useful to point out two decisions by the SAC which illustrate the problem of interpreting the Act in question.

In SAC 1997:57 the court argued that the traditional doctrine, which gave the Authority wide discretion as to whether a new restaurant in the area was necessary, was no longer valid. The SAC stated, that the interpretation of the Alcohol Act and especially certain provisions on licences contained therein must be based on a friendly interpretation of *constitutional rights* in order to ensure that the constitutional guarantees of the freedom to engage in commercial activities are restricted as little as possible, and that these powers are only exercised within the limits of the *ratio legis* explicitly laid down in section 1.

In addition, in SAC 1997:58 the court argued that a serving licence could not be refused only on the basis that the idea of an 'erotic' restaurant was not suitable. The Court argued that this could only be an acceptable reason for refusal when it was directly connected with the prevention of detrimental societal, social and health effects caused by the consumption of alcoholic substances. In other words, the SAC stated that there was no connection between staging an erotic show and the consumption of alcoholic beverages, and thus it could not be a ground for refusal.

The sanctioning powers within the scope of the Alcohol Act are laid down in section 22, which enables authority to issue the licensee with an admonition and a written warning, or, *without compensation to restrict the licence* which it has granted by limiting the opening hours, the serving area, the kinds of alcoholic beverages to be served, or even to *withdraw a licence which it has granted either for a certain period of time or permanently*, if (amongst other things):

1) The Alcohol Act or the provisions, regulations or restrictions issued by virtue thereof have been violated on the licensed premises, or
2) the licensee is considered no longer to fulfil the conditions for having the licence or to have become unreliable.
3) a disturbance or other breach of peace has taken place on the licensed premises.

The question which now arises is how should these restrictions to or the withdrawal of a licence be evaluated? The Constitutional Committee has on many occasions, and urged in a well-established line of interpretation, argued that in order to pass a bill without the qualified procedure for enacting exceptions to the Constitution, the bill must protect proportionality by recognizing that sanction-like restrictions or withdrawals are more severe than refusing the licence in the first place.[46] The underlying notion is that the withdrawal of a licence interrupts the already established legal position of a person, and thus the constitutional protection of property and especially the protection of legitimate expectations requires a greater degree of protection than a person's rights in abstract when the application for a licence is refused. However, two lines of argumentation have been sometimes adopted by the SAC which can be seen inconsistent with this constitutional requirement.

First of all, despite emphasising the *ratio legis* discussed above, the SAC has always considered the *non-payment of taxes* to be a *prima facie* sufficient ground for the withdrawal of a licence to sell alcohol.[47] If provisions laying down certain conditions for licensees and their business activities must be interpreted as narrowly as possible and only in the light of the *ratio legis*, it is difficult to see the connection between paying taxes and the prevention of detrimental societal, social and health effects by means of controlling *the consumption* of alcohol. The idea is that the licensing system in the field of selling alcohol only exists to prevent the harm mentioned in section 1, and, according to the prohibition on the abuse of power, it shall not be used to ensure tax income for the state. So whether the licensee has lost his/her reliability to sell alcohol (section 22) should be evaluated *also within the limits of the ratio legis*. In this light, an acceptable reason could be, for example, crimes related to alcohol or the selling of alcohol to minors. Nobody would argue that it would be legitimate to prohibit a person from running a bookstore as a result of an *administrative sanction* when he had lost his ability to pay taxes. The only legally justifiable difference between a bookstore and licensed premises seems to be the *ratio legis* in section 1.

Also in the SAC 2004:1 court back-pedalled even further from its earlier cases. On this occasion the court stated that it was not in breach of the prohibition on the abuse of power to revoke a licence because the restaurant owner had neglected to supervise that customers were not offering their sexual services for a fee. Evidence against restaurant owner was not required, it was merely accepted that he could not have been oblivious to the conduct of his customers, and he had not intervened. Furthermore, even though this kind of conduct *was not forbidden* by the law, the Authority argued that such conduct contravened *public morality* and thus did not fulfil the requirement of adequate business operations provided in section 21. The SAC approved this line of argumentation, complemented by the provision on disturbance or other breach of the peace mentioned in section 22, and stated that the

46 PeVL 8/2006 vp.

47 See, for example, KHO 23.8.2000 T:1697 and KHO 19.5.2000 T:927.

sale of sexual services by the customers and the *sale of alcohol by the restaurant owner* had occurred on the same premises, and they *"might"* therefore have had a connection. Thus – according to the SAC – these are not separate questions, and the withdrawal of the licence by the Authority was not in breach of either the law or the prohibition on the abuse of power.

3.6. THE PROTECTION OF LEGITIMATE EXPECTATIONS

The protection of legitimate expectations was established in Finnish administrative law in the late 1990s. After a lively debate[48], it was incorporated in Section 6 of the APA. However, even before the new APA the Constitutional Committee had emphasized that the protection of legitimate expectations was a part of the constitutional protection offered to a person against the public authorities and the legislator.

The core idea of legitimate expectations can be crystallized in a requirement, that stipulates that everyone is allowed rely on the lawfulness and correctness of the administration. For example, if the administration has given advice[49], the protection of legitimate expectations means that a person should not be punished for following that advice, even if the advice proves to be false or misleading.[50] Also according to Finnish criminal law (Chapter 4 Section 2 of the Penal Code) an offender is exempt from criminal liability if he/she believes his/her action to be lawful and this mistake is deemed to be manifestly excusable due to the misleading or erroneous publication of the law; the particular obtuseness of the contents of the law; erroneous advice by an authority; or another comparable reason.[51] Although it is possible to argue *a fortiori* or *ex analogi*, that this rule should be applied to sanctions imposed outside the Penal Code's scope of application, *i.e.* to administrative sanctions, it is more reasonable to assume, that the requirements discussed above would lead to the same outcome.

48 Seppo Laakso: Oikeudellisesta sääntelystä ja päätöksenteosta. 1991, p. 217-, Outi Suviranta, The Principle of Legitimate Expectations in Finnish Administrative Law. Reply to Questionnare IV.D.2. Offprint of Finnish National Reports to the XVth Congress of the International Academy of Comparative Law (1998).

49 Section 8 of the APA does not differentiate between advice on material matters and advice on procedural matters.

50 See Mäenpää Olli, Hallinto-oikeus, 2003 p. 393–4.

51 See also Tapio Lappi-Seppälä, Rikosoikeuden yleisiä oppeja koskeva uudistus, Lakimies 1/2004, 8.

3.7 THE RECONSTRUCTED CONCEPT OF ADMINISTRATIVE SANCTIONS IN FINNISH ADMINISTRATIVE LAW

The exclusion of the summary penalty fee from the sphere of administrative law, combined with the silence of the APA discussed at the beginning, leaves the concept of administrative sanctions without express statutory support. However, they seem to be punitive reactions to acts or derelictions against the law or other public law duty. Furthermore, if and when they are meant to be punitive, it seems also reasonable that their legitimation must be based on the deterrent purpose of their existence. The idea of punishment without a general deterrent purpose as its justification would be inconsistent with the principle of the *Rechtsstaat* – a concept which has been incorporated into the Finnish system of public law. The general principles discussed above point in the same direction. They ensure the connection between administrative sanctions and deterrence by binding the use of sanctioning powers to legislation. In addition, this legislation has to be materially and formally in compliance with the Constitution in order to oblige persons to act according to the material rules contained therein.

However, on the other hand, the material criteria discussed above and especially the case law tend to provide support to the wider concept of administrative sanctions. Not only punitive fees and excess fares charged in the case of infringement, but also other negative and restrictive administrative acts should sometimes be included within the notion of sanctions, if they amount to a reaction by the administrative authorities against an infringement and can be considered to be a deterrent. For example, in addition to punitive revocations of various licences, other measures in the grey area between precautionary measures and measures protecting the original legality of one's legal position amounting to an administrative act and administrative sanctions can be seen as – at least partly – measures which have *features in common with sanctions.* As discussed above, the same applies to punitive tax increases. After all, all these measures have one common purpose: to ensure that a person fulfils his/her obligations prior to applying sanctions, and thus to have a general deterrent purpose, and thus should be connected to same kind of legal protection.

Finally, some measures laid down in the Act on the Conditional Imposition of a Fine (14.12.1990/1113)[52] have common features with administrative

[52] According to the Ministry of Justice, this Act is currently subject to major reform. However, no official document relating to this reform has yet been published.

sanctions,[53] although they are typically identified as non-punitive legal consequences.[54] These *accessory means of reinforcement* mentioned for reference purposes also in Section 67 of the APA consist of the conditional imposition of a fine, the threat that a legal measure will be ordered at the defaulter's expense if the contravening conduct does not cease, and the threat of interrupting certain operations. Whilst the latter two threats of coercive means are only meant to ensure the proper enforcement of administrative obligations without a punitive character, it is obvious that imposition of a conditionally imposed fine has not only a deterrent but also a reactive character. Namely, according to the Act on the Conditional Imposition of a Fine, a fixed or ascending and periodic fine may be imposed conditionally in order to reinforce a primary obligation if this is provided for by an Act concerning a primary obligation.

However, the difference between non-accessory sanctions and an accessory conditional imposition of a fine can be traced back to the objective protected by the deterrence and the nature of that deterrence. Whereas non-accessory sanctions protect the legal order and *a priori* obedience with it *in abstracto*, accessory sanctions are meant to protect the authority, efficiency and integrity of the administration *in concreto* and *a posteriori*. Similarly, whereas non-accessory sanctions include the notion of *Generalprävention*, accessory sanctions are more likely to have a special deterrent effect: for example, the "conditionality" of the conditional imposition of a fine only makes it effective in relation to a dereliction of a primary obligation in a particular case.[55]

> However, it must be stated that the conditional imposition of a fine is a twofold process: in the first stage, the competent authority *threatens* to impose a fine. Only thereafter, in a second stage, is it possible to actually impose the fine if the person in question has not fulfilled his/her obligation without an acceptable reason and the decision taken in the first stage has become final. The partially punitive character of the conditional imposition of a fine is only connected with this latter stage of the process. However, both stages result in a decision which can be appealed to the administrative courts. The principle of proportionality plays an important role here: the SAC has even *ex officio* made certain threats more equitable (SAC 1978 A II 95).

53 See also Kulla, Heikki: Sanktionluonteiset hallintoasiat: tunnusmerkkejä ja rajausperusteista. In Juhlakirja Pentti Arajärvi 1948 – 2/6 – 2008, p. 325.

54 Mäenpää, Olli: Hallintolaki ja hyvän hallinnon takeet. 2012, p. 37.

55 See also Mäenpää, Olli: Hallinto-oikeus. 2003, p. 416, which describes the conditional imposition of a fine as an indirect coercive measure.

4. THE REQUIREMENTS OF PROTECTION UNDER THE LAW

4.1. THE RIGHT TO APPEAL

Section 21 of the Finnish Constitution reads as follows:

> Protection under the law
> Everyone has the right to have his or her case dealt with appropriately and without undue delay by a legally competent court of law or other authority, as well as to have a decision pertaining to his or her rights or obligations reviewed by a court of law or other independent organ for the administration of justice.
> Provisions concerning the publicity of proceedings, the right to be heard, the right to receive a reasoned decision and the right of appeal, as well as the other guarantees of a fair trial and good governance shall be laid down in an Act of Parliament.

The section is twofold. The first subsection guarantees every person a subjective right to a fair trial and appropriate procedures. The material content of this requirement is closely connected to article 6 of the ECHR, but has a wider scope of application. Although the scope of application of article 6 ECHR has been extended by interpretation and applies to some extent to matters of public law, it is noteworthy that section 21 of the Finnish CA does not share the restrictive wording of *civil* rights and obligations. The first subsection guarantees a subjective right to have a decision pertaining to one's rights or obligations reviewed by a court of law, when the act in question concerns a person's rights or obligations.[56]

An administrative act consisting of sanctions against a person as a result of that person not adhering to an *obligation* indisputably fulfils the criteria laid down in the first subsection. Thus everyone has a constitutional subjective right to appeal against sanctions. Even the legislator is bound by this requirement, and it has a very narrow margin of appreciation when enacting prohibitions against appeal procedures. In the recent "case law" of the Constitutional Committee, this right has gained significant importance. For example, when the government proposed a prohibition against an appeal in a matter concerning the claim for recovery of subsidies paid to employers for employing unemployed persons[57], the Constitutional Committee required that, in order to pass the bill without a qualified procedure for enacting amendments or exceptions to the Constitution, the prohibition against an appeal had to be removed from the bill.[58] This

---

56 The "unofficial translation" of section 21 of the Constitution cited above has been provided by the Ministry of Justice.
57 HE 115/2002 vp.
58 PeVL 46/2002 vp.

subjective right has also led the courts setting aside an illegitimate prohibition against an appeal.[59]

The second subsection of section 21 of the CA is intended to provide *complementary* guarantees for due process and good administration. Thus its wording is not exhaustive. Provisions concerning the publicity of proceedings, the right to be heard, the right to receive a reasoned decision and the right of appeal are to be laid down in an Act of Parliament, but only to the extent not already covered in the first subsection. Thus the wording of "the right of appeal" which is to be guaranteed by an Act and is not to be considered as a constitutional subjective right does not include decisions concerning rights and obligations, but decisions based on wide the discretionary powers of an administrative body.[60] The core element of subsection 2 is allowing the legislator to regulate matters enacted therein by means of an Act and in coherence with the constitutional criteria discussed earlier.

The right to appeal against an administrative sanction is defined on the basis of the first subsection. The procedure and organization of the appeal process is defined on the basis of the second subsection. There is neither a specific organization nor a general specific procedure concerning the exercise of sanctioning powers or appeals against such sanctions, so these matters are resolved within the framework laid down by the APA and the Administrative Judicial Procedure Act (AJPA). There is only few particular statutes concerning administrative sanctions in APA and AJPA. Section 67 of APA is already mentioned numerous times above. In addition to that, in 2009 added section 53a of AJPA stipulates, that the amount of monetary punitive can be reduced or it can be even completely removed, if the process in matter has taken so long time, that it is in breach of a requirement of a reasonable time of the fair trial. Furthermore, according to section 52(2), in case of a tie, the chairman of the court shall have the casting vote; however, in case of a tied vote in a disciplinary matter, a matter relating to a penal fee and a matter relating to the execution of a threat of a fine, a fine or another special sanction imposed to safeguard the progress of the procedure, the result that is more lenient to the person concerned shall prevail.

59 See, for example, SAC 1998:16 (*e contrario*), where the court argued that the prohibition against an appeal was in fact applicable, because the merits of the case *did not* concern any rights or obligations mentioned in section 16a of the CA 1919 (Section 21 of the CA) and art. 6(1) ECHR.

60 Also this division has been rationalised in the recent *"case-law"* of the Constitutional Committee. The Committee has noted that a discretion is never a purely extrajudicial question, and that discretionary powers *per se* cannot remove the right of appeal. Only when the discretion in a matter is a pure expediency discretion and there are no statutory guidelines whatsoever concerning the matter in question is a prohibition against an appeal possibly acceptable. Otherwise, the Committee has stated, "on the grounds derived from the Constitution" a prohibition must be removed. See, for example, PeVL 55/2002 vp.

These statutes are however subsidiary. Material, organizational and procedural Acts concerning the sanctions in question have precedence thereover (Section 5 of the APA and section 3 of the AJPA). Despite this precedence of the *lex specialis*, the established procedure requires these exceptions to the *lex generalis* to be interpreted in the light of due process provided in these general Acts as a reflection of the Section 21 of the CA.

The basic solution adopted in the AJPA is to provide any person to whom a decision is addressed or whose right, obligation or interest is directly affected by a decision with a right to challenge that decision by means of an appeal (Section 6.1). According to the rule of admissibility (Section 5), any measure by which a case has been resolved or dismissed may be challenged by means of an appeal. The court structure consists of two instances. Appeals against a decision of an authority, which is subordinate to the Council of State, lie to a Regional Administrative Court (Section 7); appeals against a decision of the Council of State or a Ministry and some other as laid down in the *lex specialis* are heard before in the Supreme Administrative Court. With the exception of appeals challenging the decisions of the Council of State or a Ministry or appeals against the decisions of a municipal authority as laid down in The Municipalities Act (365/1995), where an appeal can only be based to the illegality of the decision, an appeal can – at least in theory – be based on both the illegality and/or the expediency of the decision.

The principal rule is that administrative decisions are usually enforceable after becoming final. However, some exceptions do exist. State taxes and charges are usually enforceable after decision without finality. The constitutional law committee has however sometimes required, that monetary fees as administrative sanctions cannot be enforceable before becoming final.[61] Outside the scope of monetary sanctions, for example, Section 51.3 of the Alcohol Act prescribes that a decision to revoke a licence is immediately enforceable, despite the decision being challenged on appeal, unless the appellate authority states otherwise. In practice, the courts tend to deny enforcement by means of a with writ of execution issued in an accelerated process before considering the merits of the case.

4.2. RIGHT OF ACCESS TO THE DOSSIER

The complementary nature of Section 21.2 of the CA also applies to the publicity of proceedings with respect to the dossier. Namely, according to subsection 2 of section 12 of the CA,

61 PeVL 4/2004 vp.

> [d]ocuments and recordings in the possession of the authorities are public, unless their publication has for compelling reasons been specifically restricted by an Act. Everyone has the right of access to public documents and recordings.

This basic right of access to information may be invoked by anyone – regardless of the purpose for which that right is exercised. If an official has denied access, the individual who has requested access can demand that the authority in question produces a formal decision, and this decision can be challenged by means of an appeal to the administrative court.

However, this right can naturally be restricted by an Act of Parliament, which lays down certain criteria for secrecy and non-disclosure. These criteria of secrecy are subject to a very narrow interpretation, unless the protection of other basic rights requires wider interpretation.[62] Albeit that there is restricted access to some information (as provided, for compelling reasons, under section 24 of the Act on the Openness of Government Activities (Access Act, L 621/1999) or under other Acts) according to section 11 of the Access Act a petitioner, an appellant and any other person whose right, interest or obligation in a matter is concerned, shall also have the right of access, to be granted by the authority which is considering or has considered the matter, to the contents of a document which is not in the public domain, if such a document may influence or may have influenced the consideration of his/her case. In other words, secret, confidential and draft documents may also be subject to access by the parties.

This latter form of publicity involving the parties to a matter is not unconditional; it, too, can be restricted on the grounds laid down in section 11. Although the wording of these restrictions may seem to leave a wide margin of appreciation (for example, *"a very important public interest"*), the connection with Sections 12 and 21 of the CA requires them to be interpreted and construed very narrowly. The justification for this wider publicity for the parties to a matter lies partly in the right to be heard.[63]

4.3. THE RIGHT TO BE HEARD

The right to be heard (*audi alteram partem*) can be based on both subsections of Section 21 of the CA. This requirement can be seen as a fundamental cornerstone of *due process and fair procedures*: in order to fulfil everyone's right to have his or her case dealt with appropriately by an authority [other than a court] (Section 21(1)), a party must be given an opportunity to express his/her opinion on the

---

62 See Heikki Kulla, Hallintomenettelyn perusteet (2008), 328–338.

63 See also Mäenpää, Olli: Hallinto-oikeus. 2003, p. 423.

merits and facts of the case. According to certain guarantees laid down in Section 21(2), the right to be heard has been embodied in legislation regulating administrative procedures and the administrative judicial procedure.

Section 34(1) of the APA reads as follows:

> *Hearing a party*
> Before the matter is decided, a party shall be reserved an opportunity to express an opinion on the matter and to submit an explanation on the demands and information which may have an effect on its decision.

Section 34(1) of the AJPA reads as follows:

> *Hearing the parties*
> Before the resolution of the matter, the parties shall be reserved an opportunity to comment on the demands of other parties and on evidence that may affect the resolution of the matter.

Both Acts impose restrictions on the right to be heard.

Due to the constitutional character of the right to be heard, these restrictions are to be narrowly construed and interpreted.[64] In this light it is difficult to envisage a situation where sanctioning powers could be exercised before reserving an opportunity to express an opinion on the matter. Additionally, in order to exercise this right effectively, the authority must provide the party in question with all the relevant information.[65]

> Some sanctioning procedures necessarily mean that the right to be heard is factually unavoidable. For example, the fine for a vehicle with an excess load (Act on Fines for Excess Loads of Vehicles 14.1.1982/51) can only be imposed, when the excess load is observed directly on the road during transportation (Section 1.3). In practice this occurs during stop checks by police and customs offices. However, due to the fact that this sanction is imposed against the *owner of the vehicle*, which is not necessarily the same person as the person who is driving, it is also expressly laid down that the *person liable for the payment of the fine* must be given an opportunity to express an opinion on the matter in written form within a two-week time-limit (Section 12).

Hearing of the party is usually arranged in written form. However, in administrative procedure, an authority must reserve a party the opportunity to submit information orally, if requested and if this is necessary for purposes of clarification of the matter and if written procedure would cause unreasonable

64 See Mäenpää, Olli: Hallinto-oikeus. 2003, p. 422.
65 See Mäenpää, Olli: Hallinto-oikeus. 2003, p. 421.

inconvenience to the party. On the request of a party, an authority *may* reserve an opportunity for the oral submission of information necessary for the clarification of the matter also in events other than that. In administrative *judicial* procedure, in order to establish the facts of a case, administrative court shall arrange an oral hearing, if a private party so requests. The same applies to the Supreme Administrative Court where it is considering an appeal against the decision of an administrative authority. However, according to section 37 of the AJPA, the oral hearing requested by a party need not be conducted if the claim is dismissed without considering its merits or immediately rejected or if an oral hearing is manifestly unnecessary in view of the nature of the matter or for another reason. Despite this restriction, it has been emphasized, that the right to oral hearing should be conducted when the case concerns administrative sanctions.[66] Also the Parliamentary Ombudsman of Finland has recently noted in his decision EOA 736/2006 that consideration of an appeal relating to a tax increase constitutes determination of a criminal charge in the meaning of Article 6 of the ECHR, and that the complainant's right to a fair trial would have required the arrangement of the oral hearing that the complainant had demanded.

In the Jussila v. Finland The European Court of Human Rights it was question of denying oral hearing in administrative judicial procedure. The court found that, although the tax surcharges in the case were part of the fiscal regime, they were imposed by a rule whose purpose was deterrent and punitive. The offence was therefore "criminal", within the meaning of Article 6 of ECHR and Article 6 was thus applicable in the applicant's case. The Finnish Administrative Court, which had taken the measure of inviting written observations from the tax inspector and after that a statement from an expert chosen by the applicant, found that in the circumstances an oral hearing was manifestly unnecessary, as the information provided by the applicant himself formed a sufficient factual basis for the consideration of the case. The Court further observed that the applicant was not denied the possibility of requesting an oral hearing, although it was for the courts to decide whether a hearing was necessary. The Administrative Court gave such consideration with reasons. The Court also noted the minor sum of money at stake. Since the applicant was given ample opportunity to put forward his case in writing and to comment on the submissions of the tax authority, the Court found that the requirements of fairness were complied with and did not, in the particular circumstances of the case, necessitate an oral hearing. There had, therefore, been no violation of Article 6 §1. The line of argumentation based on article 6 of ECHR is adopted in SAC 2007:67 and SAC 2007:68.

66 Mäenpää, Olli: Hallintoprosessioikeus. 2007, p. 194.

4.4. JUDICIAL REVIEW OF SANCTIONS

Some elements of the judicial review have already been discussed above from the point of view of the appellant. Although it was stated that neither the specific organization of the administration nor the courts in the field of sanctioning powers are no different from the general organization of the administration and the administrative courts, some complementary remarks from the courts' point of view must be made.

The standard system of administrative courts arranged in two instances (Regional Administrative Courts and the Supreme Administrative Court) does have some exceptions connected not only to Section 7 of the AJPA discussed above, but also to various solutions adopted in the *lex specialis* governing the exercise of sanctioning powers. For example, in the field of social security law appeals are lodged with the Insurance Court and, generally, no further to appeal against the decision of the Insurance Court to the SAC are available. Under the Competition Act (27.5.1992/480), a case involving the imposition of a fine for a competition infringement is heard by the Market Court, but only subject to a proposal by the Finnish Competition Authority/Insurance Supervision Authority, as the Market Court has no competence to impose this fine itself. This decision can be appealed to the SAC (with certain exceptions). In matters concerning taxation, leave to appeal to the SAC is required.

Regardless of the instance, the administrative courts usually have full powers to review the matter.[67] Minor exceptions referred to earlier have no relevance in this matter, because – on the grounds of general principles – the exercise of sanctioning powers must be based on the express provisions of an Act.

Although it is usually stated that the general or ordinary appeal is of a *reformatory* type and that the municipal appeal is only *cassatory* in nature, this division is somewhat relative. In both cases the court can either affirm or overrule the decision which is the subject of the appeal; the difference lies in the fact that in the reformatory type of appeal the court is not only allowed to overturn, but also to substitute the contents of the challenged decision with a new contents. The principle of *reformatio in peius* limits the possibility to alter the decision against private appellant.[68]

In addition, in the reformatory type of appeal the court's role is more active at the investigatory stage whereas in the municipal cassatory process the court's

---

67 Mäenpää, Olli: Hallintoprosessioikeus. 2007, p. 531.

68 Mäenpää, Olli: Hallintoprosessioikeus. 2007, p. 485–6.

role remains more passive and adversarial.[69] According to Section 51(1) of the AJPA, the "appellate authority shall in its decision resolve all the demands made in the matter. It shall review all evidence available and determine on which grounds the resolution can be based." In addition, section 33(2) prescribes that "the appellate authority shall on its own initiative obtain evidence in so far as the impartiality and fairness of the procedure and the nature of the case so require." However, even the reformatory type of appeal tends to lead to cassation only. For example, in SAC 2004:15 discussed earlier, the SAC overturned the decision, but still returned the decision to the authority, although it had the possibility to take a detailed stand on the case as a whole.

5. INVESTIGATIVE POWERS

Part of the legal protection guaranteed in section 21 of the CA is at the original decision agreed upon within the authorities. The APA regulates procedural questions relating to administrative bodies in general. As mentioned before, the exercise of sanctioning powers takes place mainly within the normal procedure and in the normal organization of the administration, so only a few complementary remarks concerning sanctioning powers are here necessary.

The exercise of sanctioning powers is typically initiated by an authority. Thus the duty of clarification lies with the authority in question.[70] Namely, according to Section 31 of the APA, an authority shall ensure that a matter is adequately and appropriately clarified, by obtaining the necessary information and accounts in order to reach a decision on the matter. A party is only obliged to provide information, which forms the grounds for its request or application, and a party shall also otherwise contribute to the clarification of a matter filed by him/her. For the exercise of sanctioning powers this means that nobody is obliged to provide the authority in question with any information which may be harmful to the provider without an express obligation to do so as laid down in the *lex specialis*.

> Naturally, there are numerous statutes, which oblige a person to provide certain information and other clarification. The prevailing view is, that statutory obligations to give information to authority are not problematic.[71] However, there are some limits to these statutes within the constitutional framework. First of all, when clarification refers to information, which is protected by the constitutional right to privacy, this obligation must be based on a specific Act, which expressly and precisely

69 Mäenpää, Olli: Hallintoprosessioikeus. 2007, p. 459.

70 See Eija Siitari-Vanne, Todistustaakasta hallintolainkäytön eri asiaryhmissä, in Defensor Legis 3/1998.

71 Mäenpää, Olli: Hallintolaki ja hyvän hallinnon takeet. 2012, p. 207.

prescribes the type of information, which is subject to this obligation.[72] Second, the "type" of information must be restricted as narrowly as possible: an authority only has the right to obtain that information which is necessary for it to reach a decision on the matter. Third, it is doubtful whether information obtained without a person's genuine consent can be used for purposes other than those laid down in the enabling Act. For example, it is somewhat disputable whether the material collected during an administrative inspection for the purpose of clarifying the administrative matter in question can be used against the person who is the subject of this obligation during criminal proceedings or when exercising administrative sanctioning powers.[73] It has been discussed whether the privilege against self-incrimination derived from art. 6(1) ECHR[74] and section 7 of the CA prohibits this kind of use[75], but no case law on this matter exists. Furthermore, the constitutional committee has sometimes required, that everyone's right not to incriminate oneself based on section 21 of CA (see PeVL 19/2000 vp, p. 4/II and PeVL 28/2001 vp, p. 7/II) should be enacted in the statutory legislation. Committee has referred to the functional model, which can be found, for example under the present Act of Procedures on the Field of Agricultural Subsidies (18.12.1992/1336). The section 8 of Act defines bounds of the statutory obligation to disclose information required: "Obligation to provide information does not apply to a matter in which he or she is legally entitled to refuse to give evidence, other than on the grounds that it is matter of business or trade secret."

This division of the duty of clarification is also relevant to the division of norms and facts. Whereas the duty to clarify facts can rest upon a party, the duty to clarify norms always rests upon the within authority in question (*jura novit curia*).[76] Despite these divisions, it must be emphasized that the ultimate duty of clarification always rests with the authority. To sum up, it is the duty of the authority to clarify and prove that both legal and factual prerequisites for the sanction exist.

The investigative powers of the administrative authorities to prove infringements in the field of administrative sanctions are constitutionally limited, however. Namely, according to section 10 of the CA, everyone's private life, honour and the sanctity of the home are guaranteed. But, according to subsection 3, measures encroaching upon the sanctity of the home, and which are necessary for the purpose of guaranteeing basic rights and liberties or for the investigation of a crime, may be determined by an Act of Parliament. Traditionally this has meant, that it is not possible – even under an ordinary parliamentary Act – to

---

72 PeVL 15/2002, p. 2–3.

73 Mäenpää, Olli: Hallintolaki ja hyvän hallinnon takeet. 2012, p. 207.

74 Funke v. France, (25.2.1993, A 256-A).

75 See Ari-Matti Nuutila, Saako rikoksella saadut varat salata verotuksessa, in Turun Yliopiston oikeustieteellinen tiedekunta 40 vuotta, Timo Ahonen (ed.) (2001), p. 157 ff.

76 See Kulla, Heikki: Hallintomenettelyn perusteet. 2008., p. 156.

enable an administrative authority with investigatory powers to search a house for the purpose of an investigation leading only to administrative sanctions.

Although the scope of the sanctity of the home is wider than a person's private home, the qualified criteria for restricting the sanctity of the home are at their strongest concerning a private home and its immediate surroundings: according to the *government's proposal*, all measures of investigation encroaching upon this sphere are only allowed for the purpose of *guaranteeing basic rights and liberties or for the investigation of a crime*. As an exception to constitutional rights this criterion containing a *numerus clausus* list of acceptable reasons for these measures is narrowly interpreted and construed.[77]

> However, according to section 20a of the Act on Competition Restrictions (480/1992), the Market Court can, upon an application by the Commission, grant an authorization to inspect premises protected by the sanctity of the home. Authorization must be sought in advance and can only be granted if the Commission of the European Communities has, pursuant to Article 21 of Council Regulation (EC) No. 1/2003, ordered an inspection to be conducted on the premises. In addition, the Market Court may prohibit an inspection if it would be arbitrary or excessive. Although, even with these additional criteria, this measure appears to be in conflict with section 10.3 of the CA, it should be emphasized that this regulation seems to rely at least partly on the supremacy of EU law over national legislation.[78]

In concreto these measures are governed by the Coercive Measures Act and the Police Act which both safeguard the prerequisites for the qualified criteria for restriction of the sanctity of the home. However, exercise of the sanctioning powers outside the criminal law system is left outside the scope of application of these laws.

Different criteria apply when a person is subjected to a bodily search. In addition to the right to private life as protected in section 10, according to section 7 of the CA, the personal integrity of the individual shall not be violated. Because no qualified criteria for restricting this right exist in the wording of the CA, the restrictability of these rights is evaluated within the framework of the seven general criteria for the restriction of basic rights. A bodily search requires express legislation granting this competence; no general statute is applicable to the exercise of sanctioning powers in this respect. For example, according to Section 14 of the Customs Act (29.12.1994/1466), a bodily search may be carried out when passing through customs if this is necessary in order to perform a task relating to the functions of the customs authorities. The information obtained in this

---

77 See 309/1993vp. However, the Constitutional Committee has back-pedalled on this requirement on quite a few occasions. For example. in PeVL 12/2002vp (p. 3–4) it was accepted that unpaid taxes could be recovered from the home of the taxpayer, notwithstanding that the requirements laid down in subsection 3 had not been fulfilled.

78 See, however, PeVL 7/2004vp.

investigation may lead to punitive customs duties having to be paid (Section 31). It is noteworthy that the Customs Act also provides the competence to search premises, but expressly excludes premises, which are solely used for the purpose of accommodation *i.e.* domestic premises protected by section 10 of the CA.

In general sections 38–40 of the APA regulate the methods of investigation. According to section 38, an authority may view locations and premises if this is necessary to the matter. According to subsection 3, such viewing shall not take place in domestic premises, unless this is otherwise specifically provided under a certain Act.

Section 39 of the APA regulates the procedure to be followed in the case of *inspections*. This procedural legislation does not bestow an authority with the competence to carry out inspections, the competence must rather be derived from the *lex specialis*. However, according to the *government's proposal* even this procedural regulation only applies to inspections carried out in order to investigate a pending administrative matter.[79] This therefore excludes inspections carried out *in abstracto*.

> For example, the Act on the Protection of Floral Health (18.7.2003/702) enables The Plant Production Inspection Centre to carry out inspections on agricultural premises; an inspection can only be carried out within the sphere protected under section 10 CA if it is necessary and it is reasonable to suspect that a crime has been or is being committed (Section 20 of the Act). The information gathered during an inspection outside domestic premises can lead to the imposition of an administrative sanction; according to Section 31, the compensation paid due to the economic hardship caused by coercive plant protection can be denied, if the injured party has, for example, acted in breach of the Act or otherwise contributed to the existence of the hardship.

Section 40 of the APA regulates oral evidence. *For some specific reason*, in administrative matter witnesses may be heard under oath and the parties may be heard under affirmation of truth. The parties immediately concerned by the matter shall be given an opportunity to be present when a witness or a party is being heard. They have the right to put questions to the person being heard and to express their opinion concerning the testimony. Judicial assistance for obtaining testimony is given by an Administrative Court.

[79] HE 72/2002, p.102.

6. EUROPEAN CO-OPERATION

Section 10 §of the APA, which is the general statute regulating interauthority co-operation and executive assistance reads as follows:

> Section 10 – Interauthority co-operation
> (1) An authority shall provide the requested assistance, within its competence and as required by the nature of the matter, to another authority for taking care of an administrative matter; it should also otherwise promote interauthority co-operation.
> (2) Executive assistance between authorities is subject to separate provisions.

According to the *government's proposal*, the aim of the first subsection was not only to make the administration more effective from the point of view of actually administering the country, but also from the point of view of the parties concerned: the emphasized co-operation was meant to simplify and to speed up procedures.[80] Subsection 1 has an independent objective both to enable and oblige the authority in question to indulge in interauthority co-operation. However, whereas this obligation to co-operate is mainly restricted to the exchange of information, the executive assistance mentioned in the subsection consists of the exercise of public powers. According to the *government's proposal*, the executive assistance mentioned is to be understood as assistance in the so-called actual exercise of public powers or functions, *i.e.* informal procedures, which consists of actual execution.[81] It should be noted that the subsection only has a reference function, i.e. it does not given an authority certain powers of executive assistance. These powers are to be provided separately.

The wording of section 10 of the APA remains silent as to the possible scope of application concerning mutual assistance beyond Finnish territory. In general, it has been argued that the general duty to act in good faith established in article 10 of the Treaty establishing the European Community both obliges and enables national authorities to co-operate with the authorities of other member states. This duty could justify a wide interpretation of section 10, but no comprehensive analysis on this matter exists. Thus the obligation to co-operate with an authority of another member state is directly related in Finnish doctrine to the article of the EC Treaty mentioned above.

However, when the imposition of a sanction falls within the scope of the council directive on mutual assistance for the recovery of claims relating to certain levies, duties, taxes and other measures (76/308/EEC), and the imposition consists of administrative sanctions as defined in subsection (h) of article 2, the

80 HE 72/2002vp, p. 65–66.
81 HE 72/2002vp, p. 67.

executive assistance in the recovery of financial sanctions is carried out within the framework laid down in the Act on Mutual Executive Assistance for the Recovery of Claims Relating to Certain Levies, Duties and Taxes (L 1221/1994). The Act enables certain Finnish authorities to provide executive assistance to an authority of another member state in order to recover claims mentioned in the directive (Section 1 of the Act). According to section 3, this executive assistance consists of exchanging information, providing notification and the actual recovery, as well as precautionary measures to ensure the recovery of a claim provided in the Directive.

> The competence to exchange information with a foreign authority is naturally restricted by confidentiality obligations laid down in the Act on the Openness of Government Activities (621/1999). Section 30, which regulates the granting of access to secret information to the authority of a foreign state or to an international institution, provides that, in addition to the specific statutory provisions on the matter, an authority may grant access to a confidential official document to an authority of a foreign state or to an international institution, if an international agreement binding on Finland contains a provision on such co-operation between the Finnish and foreign authorities, or if there is a provision to this effect in a Finnish Act, and if the Finnish authority in charge of the co-operation could have access to the document under this Act.

However, the Council Framework Decision 2005/214/JHA of 24 February 2005 on the application of the principle of mutual recognition to financial penalties has been incorporated to Finnish legal system with parliamentary act which entered force in 22.3.2007. The scope of application of the act covers also administrative financial penalties. However, due to the fact that council framework decision provides, that the person concerned had to had an opportunity to have the case tried by a court having jurisdiction in particular *in criminal matters,* and nature of the act as incorporative blanket act, the *government's proposal* suggests that mainly the punitive fee for oil emissions of ships falls into the scope of application of this act.[82] It is separately pointed out, that monetary administrative sanctions discussed above are not tried by court having jurisdiction in criminal matters, and thus are not penalties mentioned in the framework decision.[83] One must also keep in mind, that the summary penalty fee, the Finnish counterpart of the German *Ordnungswidrigkeitengesetz* belongs to the criminal legal system in Finland.[84] Thus the scope of application of the Council Framework Decision in the field of the administrative sanctions remains very narrow in Finland.

---

82 HE 142/2006vp, p. 11.

83 Ibid.

84 See above 1.1.

7. CONCLUSIONS

Albeit the picture of the Finnish system for the exercise of sanctioning powers within the sphere of the administration still remains far from complete, some elements of the reconstruction of its general framework can be discerned above. However, many relevant questions are left without answers. This is partly due to the nature and extent of this article, but is also the result of silence on the part of the legal literature in a small country, which has only a limited number of legal academics – and an even more limited number of legal academics concentrating on administrative law. Thus the literature available on a particular subject is usually very limited. This lack of sources is usually compensated by the fruits of foreign research with methods of comparative law or/and international and EC-law. However, this particular task of describing the Finnish system of administrative sanctions as part of a multinational project has limited this possibility. Replacing the silence of Finnish legal doctrine with the polyphony of foreign legal science in order to describe the Finnish system to foreign lawyers seems somewhat irrational.

The same silence can be heard from the legislator. No general legislation concerning explicitly administrative sanctions, either material or procedural, exists. For example, co-operation between national authorities and an EU authority remains generally unregulated; only separate provisions in material legislation exist. Although the system seems to work in practice – at least superficially – with only the *lex specialis*, from the constitutional point of view the legal position is far from acceptable. A lack of general legislation inevitably leaves gaps. Furthermore, the *lex specialis* approach inevitably leads to *non-coherence* in the legal system. Instead of legitimate use of administrative sanctions as means to decriminalize misdemeanour[85], this kind of expansion has something else to pursue: It leads to the paradigm where the authorities are able to use sanctioning powers instead of relying on criminal law, because the lack of general legislation and the non-coherence between material and procedural protection provided in the Constitution leads the legislator to conclude that administrative sanctioning is the preferable choice in relation to criminal law *due to its flexibility and the limited legal protection provided by administrative law.*[86]

The most recent phase in this flexibility has been the emergence of *private* exercise of sanctioning powers. The Finnish Supreme Court has accepted in verdict KKO 2010:23 the possibility of exercise on sanctioning powers in the field

85 See, for example Tolvanen, Matti: Hallinnolliset maksut vähäisten tieliikenteen rikkomusten sanktioina. Lakimies 2/2002, s. 194–218.

86 See, for example PeVL 32/2005 vp, s. 2.

of parking fees based on implied contract between the driver of the vehicle and landowner. Afterwards, government has proposed a bill, which confirms existence of this construction: the first version of this bill was seen unconstitutional by the Constitutional Committee due to section 124 of CA, which prohibited privatisation of administrative sanctions.[87] However, the legislative process is still in unfinished. In these circumstances, call made by *Kimmo Ilmari Kiiski* for comprehensive re-evaluation of Finnish system of sanctions seems to be justified.[88]

87 PeVL 57/2010 vp.

88 See Kiiski, Kimmo Ilmari, Hallinnollinen Sanktiointi, 2011, p. 194.

V. COUNTRY ANALYSIS – FRANCE

Emmanuel Breen

1. INTRODUCTION

Administrative sanctions are deeply rooted in the French legal tradition: in 1995, a study by the Conseil d'Etat (the supreme administrative court) listed no less than 500 types of infringements punishable by administrative sanctions in domains as diverse as culture and communication, tax, market regulation, employment, education, health, social security, sports, the environment or public transportation ...[1] Indeed, the enforcement of most technical legislations relies, to some degree, on administrative sanctions, and in certain key sectors of French national life, such as financial markets, competition law, tax assessment and collection, illegal immigration and employment, enforcement hinges in practice on administrative sanctions – generally considered as a flexible and efficient substitute for criminal penalties. Despite several landmark studies[2], the phenomenon remains, however, somewhat underestimated in general presentations of the French legal system, which tend to overlook this aspect of French enforcement procedures, as well as, more generally, the importance of the punitive powers of the Executive Branch. But, as we have tried to explain elsewhere[3], the variable but overall high degree of involvement of the Government and governmental agencies in the investigation *and punishment* of unlawful forms of conduct is coherent with the French *jacobin* tradition of a centralised and powerful bureaucracy and the remanence of the revolutionary distrust of the Judicial Branch.

Criminal law in France constitutes a major political issue and criminal procedural law is characterised by an ongoing process of legislative reform. By contrast, administrative sanctions are more discreet and follow a less exposed although no less important path: they prosper quickly in a relative disorder, outside the ambit of codified legislation and are, for most of their legal regime,

1 Conseil d'Etat (1995), p. 85–174.

2 Mourgeon (1967), Delmas-Marty, Teitgen-Colly (1992), Moderne (1993), Dellis (1997), Degoffe (2000).

3 Breen (2003).

dependent on the case law of the Conseil d'Etat and the Conseil constitutionnel (the constitutional court), not to mention the central role of the ECHR.

This non-codified legal framework induces specific definition issues (I). After addressing them, we will turn to general principles (II), the typology of administrative sanctions (III) and, last but not least, guarantees (IV).

2. THE CONCEPTUAL JUNGLE OF NON-CRIMINAL SANCTIONS

There are no unambiguous official statutory or case law definitions of French terms such as '*sanction*' (sanction), '*punition*' (punishment), '*peine*' (penalty) or '*sanction administrative*' (administrative sanction). Hence, questions of definition have been much debated in this field and no clear-cut consensus emerges. Rather than engaging the reader in this complex debate, let us here simply expose the definitions that we use when we write or teach on the topic and which we will retain in this paper.

The matter may first be approached negatively, as being concerned with the kinds of sanctions that are not '*pénal*' (criminal). If by '*pénal*', one means the sanctions that are pronounced by a special type of courts ('*tribunal de police*', '*tribunal correctionnel*' and '*cour d'assise*', as far as adults are concerned) pursuant to the procedural rules set in the '*Code de procédure pénale*' (criminal procedure code) one gets a purely negative but clear definition of what is commonly referred to in France as '*sanctions extra-pénales*' or '*sanctions non pénales*' (non-criminal sanctions).[4] All these sanctions share a certain number of basic substantive and procedural rules inspired by criminal law but not formally included in the scope of criminal law, by the application of the general philosophy governing the *Öztürk* ECtHR case, which is largely shared by the French superior courts.[5]

In a more positive way, how can one define '*sanctions administratives*' (administrative sanctions)?

Obviously, administrative sanctions are non-criminal sanctions of a certain type, besides private sanctions such as may be imposed in work relationships, disciplinary sanctions against public servants, restitutive or preventive measures, etc. But where should the lines be drawn and what terms should be applied to each type of reality? One may not emphasise too much on the fact that the legal

4 See e.g. the title of Degoffe (2000).
5 ECtHR 21 February 1984, Öztürk v. Federal Republic of Germany.

vocabulary and scholarship is not fully coherent and that the following definitions are no more than a personal effort to understand and clarify the current situation.

We suggest that the term '*sanction*' (sanction) be used in a broad sense as referring to *ex-post* responses of the institutions to unlawful conduct consisting of inflicting a form of suffering of one kind or another on the infringer. Sanctions thus differ from ex-ante measures designed to prevent the infringement (known in France as measures of '*police administrative*") and from positive incentives designed to reward conforming behaviour. Many border-line cases in France have involved the distinction between sanctions and *police administrative*, for example in the case of the withdrawal of an administrative authorisation. The criterion retained by the courts is the predominant motive for the withdrawal: if this motive consists of preventing further infringements and protecting public order or third party interests, the measure is not considered as constituting a sanction. This exercise in administrative second-guessing is of course particularly difficult and in practice leaves great leeway for the courts.

We submit, in addition, that, in French law, the terms '*peine*' (penalty), '*punition*' (punishment) or '*répression*' (punishment) are synonymous or very closely linked and refer to a certain kind of sanction. This interpretation is based, principally, on the case law of the Conseil constitutionnel, which uses the notion of '*sanction ayant le caractère d'une punition*' (sanction of a punitive nature), which clearly implies that certain sanctions may be adequately referred to by using the terms 'peine', 'punition' or 'répression' and that some may not.[6] Among non-punitive sanctions, one may classically shelve indemnification, restitutive and corrective measures, as well as the cancellation of contracts and unilateral acts.

The general implicit idea behind the distinction, in French case law, of punitive and non-punitive sanctions is, in our opinion, that punitive sanctions aim principally at inflicting on the infringer a form of suffering or an inconvenience that is justified by the mere fact that the law has been broken and that the sanctions are proportional to the seriousness of the breach.[7] From a certain point of view, this is a definition by deterrence, but in the French context, approaches in more symbolical terms of retribution for the crime are not to be excluded, albeit less frequently so in the context of administrative sanctions.

6 See e.g. recently Cons. const. No. 2006-535 DC, 30 mars 2006, Loi pour l'égalité des chances, cons. No. 36.

7 Breen (2003), p. 9.

Although this may seem a bit confusing for the outsider, the term '*sanctions administratives*' should generally, in a French law context, be understood as meaning '*sanctions administratives* punitives' and thus refers to the same reality as the term '*répression administrative*' (administrative punishment): we shall use it in this sense in this paper, thus leaving aside non-punitive administrative sanctions or measures.

One should keep in mind, however, that the importance of the distinction in French law between sanctions and other measures such as *police administrative*, on the one hand, and between punitive and other sanctions, on the other, should be relativised: defence rights during the course of the administrative procedure are quite well protected for all negative personal decisions taken by the Government, irrespective of their punitive nature, especially since the passing of law no. 2000–321 of 12 April 2000 concerning the rights of citizens in their relationships with the administrative authorities.[8] However, the entitlement to the full scope of the rights associated with the ECHR Article 6, §1 concept of 'fair trial' and its French equivalents (such as, for example, the right to a public hearing or to a full review by an impartial and independent court), as well as to certain substantive rules inspired by criminal law (such as, for example, the principle *nullum crimen, nulla poena, sine lege*) is dependent on the punitive nature of the sanction, which hence has not lost its legal operational nature.

A final definitional issue concerns the status of '*sanctions disciplinaires*' (disciplinary sanctions). Punitive sanctions pronounced by the Government against its agents or against certain specific groups of persons placed under the strict control of the Government (such as, for example, pupils or detainees) are generally referred to as '*sanctions disciplinaires*' rather than '*sanctions administratives*'. Broadly speaking, disciplinary (punitive) sanctions are considered, in a French law context, as being mainly concerned with the 'inner life' of the administrative institution and thus affected by numerous specific aspects (such as the restriction on the right to a judicial review for certain sanctions against pupils, prisoners and the military, or the specific guarantees provided for civil servants and other public agents such as, for example, the consultation of the representative of the agents during the course of the disciplinary procedure). On the contrary, 'sanctions administratives' are rather considered as concerning the relationships of the administrative entities and the outside world and as a substitute for criminal procedures put at the disposal of the Government in its enforcement function. Given the high level of the

8 Article 24 provides, in particular, subject to certain exceptions, that the recipient of a negative individual administrative decision has a right to be heard by the administration and to communicate in writing his observations before the decision is taken. A right to be assisted or represented by counsel is also guaranteed.

specificity of disciplinary sanctions, we tend, as do others, to exclude them from the scope of our studies on administrative sanctions. However, disciplinary sanctions are punitive sanctions imposed by the Government and it would be far from absurd to include them in the definition of '*sanctions administratives*'.

To sum up these initial remarks, '*sanctions administratives*' are, for the purpose of this paper, defined as *punitive sanctions, other than disciplinary sanctions, imposed by administrative entities.* The following will only be concerned with this type of sanctions.

3. THE GENERAL PRINCIPLE: A LICENCE TO PUNISH

As comparative literature evidences, no contemporary democracy has significantly contained administrative sanctions by limiting the right of the Government to impose punitive sanctions in certain constitutionally defined situations or matters.[9] France is no exception and the Conseil d'Etat as well as the Conseil constitutionnel case law is globally coherent with the general idea behind the policy initiated by the ECHR in 1984: the Government may freely substitute administrative sanctions for criminal penalties, as long as, by doing so, it does not deprive individuals of their basic traditional substantive and procedural guarantees protecting anybody charged with a 'criminal' offence.[10]

3.1. THE CONSEIL CONSTITUTIONNEL CASE LAW

The same year as the ECtHR *Öztürk* judgement, the Conseil constitutionnel expressed a certain uneasiness towards administrative sanctions and was generally considered by commentators as willing to limit, in principle, the possibility of the Government to resort to administrative sanctions. In a decision on 10 and 11 October 1984, it had determined that given the fact that freedom of communication was not liable to be restricted by means of prior administrative authorisation, the Government was not allowed to institute administrative sanctions that would submit freedom of communication to a limitation equivalent to a regime of administrative authorisation.[11] Many had understood, at the time, that the Conseil constitutionnel would prohibit administrative sanctions in certain cases in order to protect certain freedoms from excessive administrative control.

9 Moderne (1993), p. 169.
10 Ref. *Öztürk*.
11 No. 84–181 DC, cons. on Articles 19 and 20 of the deferred law.

In a decision on 17 January 1989, the Conseil constitutionnel seemed prepared to abandon most of its pretensions to contain administrative sanctions, but its decision could still be read by containment advocates as limiting the technique to independent administrative agencies (*autorités administratives indépendantes*, or *AAI*). A few months later, the Conseil constitutionnel clarified its position and decided in principle to admit, administrative sanctions, as long as basic constitutional guarantees were preserved:

> 'Neither separation of powers nor any other constitutional principle or rule opposes the right of an administrative entity, acting by means of the public power prerogative ("*prérogatives de puissance publique*"), to wield a punitive power, as long as: (i) the incurred penalty is exclusive of any kind of detention; (ii) constitutional rights and freedoms are preserved, during the punitive process, by adequate statutory rules ("*par la loi*")'.[12]

This judgement has since been confirmed on many occasions and is still the basis of the constitutional recognition and supervision of administrative sanctions.

By referring to the 'public power prerogative', the Conseil constitutionnel sides with a scholarly current that considers administrative sanctions as one among other aspects of the general powers put at the disposal of the Government for the achievement of its law enforcement function.[13]

Although since 28 July 1989 the Conseil constitutionnel case law has been coherent with the general spirit of the ECHR case law, there is a special twist to the Conseil constitutionnel does not as clearly as the ECHR distinguish between an 'administrative phase' during which the guarantees associated with the 'criminal' nature of the matter may be alleviated and a 'judicial phase' of full jurisdictional control before a court where all guarantees are observed. The approach of the Conseil constitutionnel is more of a global nature: the entire process (the administrative decision and judicial review) is supposed to be in accordance with criminal constitutional guarantees. This tends to impose certain constraints during the administrative as well as the phase such as, in particular, respecting the principles set in Articles 7 to 9 of the 1789 Declaration of Human Rights (which has full constitutional effect under the Vth Republic): the principle of legality, of non-retroactivity (except for more favourable legislation), the presumption of innocence and the rights of defence. However,

---

12 Cons. const. 28 July 1989, cons. No. 6.

13 Munch (1947). By contrast, many other authors have tried to root the power of the Government to impost sanctions in cases in which there is a pre-existing legal link between the individual and the administrative entity (for example, the individual benefits from the public services or is using public premises), thus trying to derive administrative sanctions from disciplinary or contractual sanctions (see e.g. Mourgeon (1967), p. 59).

the interpretation of these guarantees by the Conseil constitutionnel is more flexible in matters of administrative sanctions than in criminal law *stricto sensu*.[14]

3.2. THE CONSEIL D'ETAT CASE LAW

The Conseil d'Etat has taken a comparable stance. From a legal point of view, it occupies a secondary position, because the interpretations by the Conseil constitutionnel prevail, but from a historical and practical perspective the Conseil d'Etat sets the leading case law: the Conseil constitutionnel often follows, without saying so, the Conseil d'Etat in administrative law matters. This is the case in administrative sanctions.

The Conseil d'Etat has long accepted both the general principle of administrative sanctions, without limiting their domain or legitimity, and has submitted these sanctions to substantial and procedural guarantees inspired by criminal law, but less stringently in many respects. The landmark case here is *Dme Veuve Trompier-Gravier*, a 1944 case, in which the Conseil d'Etat determined that the revocation of an authorisation to occupy the public domain amounted to a sanction and that the administrative procedure leading to this sanction was to respect *the audi alteram partem* principle (*principe du contradictoire*):

> 'Considering that it is beyond doubt that the contested decision, by which the Préfet de la Seine has revoked the authorisation granted to the widow Madame Trompier-Gravier to sell newspapers in a newsstand on bd Saint-Denis in Paris, was motivated by a wrongdoing allegedly committed by the plaintiff;
> Considering that given the characteristics of the said authorisation revocation, in the above-mentioned circumstances, and the seriousness of the sanction, this measure could not legally be pronounced unless Madame Trompier-Gravier had been given the opportunity to discuss the charges instigated against her (...) [administrative decision nullified]'.[15]

The fact that the Conseil d'Etat did not in principle oppose administrative sanctions and neither did it limit them to specific matters or situations has been mainly implicit for many years. In a recent judgement, however, it has been explicitly decided that 'when the administrative authority is competent to set rules to organise a profession, it is also competent to enact administrative sanctions that, by their aim and nature, are linked to this regulation'.[16] The '*commissaire du gouvernement*' – a member of the court who expresses an independent opinion on

---

14 See *infra*.

15 CE Sect. 5 May 1944: *Grands arrêts de la jurisprudence administrative*, 15th edition, No. 56.

16 CE Ass. 7 July 2004, *Min. de l'intérieur v. M. Benkerrou*, *Droit administratif* November 2004, note Breen.

the case – made explicit in his '*conclusions*' on this case the philosophy of administrative sanctions that has often guided the Conseil d'Etat: 'the power to punish is part of the remit of the Government because it constitutes the necessary corollary of its prerogatives (…) [It is] inherent in the administrative activity'.[17] As a consequence, the Conseil d'Etat decided, after wavering for many years, that 'when applied to administrative sanctions, the principle *nullum crimen, nulla poena sine lege* (…) implies that sanctions must be provided for and enumerated in an instrument; but that – as is also the case in criminal law – this instrument does not have, in all cases, to be of a statutory nature (*une loi*)'.[18] A few years later, the Conseil d'Etat clarified the cases in which administrative sanctions may be created only by statute ("*une loi*") and the cases in which a by-law ("*un règlement*") is a sufficent expression of the *nullem crimen, nulla poena* principle. The nature of the instrument that creates the administrative sanction depends on the nature of the instrument which defines the obligation the sanction is associated to. If, according to the French Constitution, the obligation must be defined by a statute, then only a statute can create the administrative sanction designed to punish the obligation infringement.[19][20] Anyhow, in both cases, the limit set on the use of administrative sanctions is only procedural and no substantive restriction on the use of the technique has been determined.

This policy of openness to administrative sanctions has accompanied an impressive development of administrative sanctions over time, in a variety of historical and political contexts.

4. THE THREE LAYERS OF ADMINISTRATIVE SANCTIONS

Administrative sanctions in France may be said to have proved to be useful instruments of the Government in at least three types of political configurations. Hence, today, the 'geology' of administrative sanctions reveals three superimposed layers of sanctions, very different in their inspiration.

17 Mathias Guyomar, conclusions, unpublished.

18 CE Ass. 7 July 2004, *Min. de l'intérieur v. M. Benkerrou*, cited above.

19 CE, 18 July 2008, No. 300304, *Fédération de l'hospitalisation privée*.

20 See also below, in the case of the revocation of an administrative authorisation to exercise a profession.

4.1. AUTHORITARIAN USE OF ADMINISTRATIVE SANCTIONS

A *first layer* corresponds to what may be qualified as an *authoritarian* use of administrative sanctions. Here, these sanctions are used by the Government as a means of eschewing potentially burdensome and subversive courts and judicial procedures. This is part of the ancient legacy of French administrative law, and corresponds to the core functions of public powers, such as, for example, tax assessment and collection. Administrative penalties have been applied since before the French Revolution, concurrent with criminal penalties, to pursue tax law compliance, especially as far as indirect taxes were concerned.[21] Nowadays, what is commonly referred to as '*sanctions fiscales*' (tax penalties) are a very vivid sector of administrative sanctions.[22] They have long lost their purely authoritative outlook and have been included in the general effort to democratise and appease relationships between the taxpayer and the Government.[23] They remain, however, very much a deterrent and range, for the more general case of a failure to produce timely and accurate statements of income, from 10% to 80% of the considered taxation.[24]

A few more recent types of administrative sanctions may be assimilated to this historical bedrock of administrative sanctions, because they share the same motives: increasing the powers of the central Government on a key issue. For example, a 1992 Act introduced, in view of reinforcing the arsenal to combat illegal immigration, an administrative penalty pronounced by the Interior Minister against sea or air transportation companies of €5,000 for each non-EU passenger disembarking on French territory without the proper travel or immigration documents.[25] In the same general context, the *Agence nationale de l'accueil des étrangers et des migrations* (National agency for the reception of foreigners and migration) is empowered to demand a 'special contribution',

21 See. e.g. Marion (1914).

22 See e.g. Lambert (2006).

23 A movement launched in 1986 by the report by M. Aicardi, 'L'amélioration des rapports entre les citoyens et les administrations fiscales et douanières' and summarised today, in particular, in the 'Taxpayer charter' (*Charte du contribuable*) (www2.impots.gouv.fr/documentation/charte_contrib/index.htm – last visited on 7 June 2007).

24 Code général des impôts, Articles 1728 and 1729. These penalties should be distinguished from the legal late payment interest rates (0.4% per month – see Code général des impôts, Article 1727) which are not considered by the Conseil d'Etat to constitute a sanction, as long as the legal interest is not set at a level which is manifestly disproportionate to the market interest (CE Ass., Avis, 12 April 2002, Sté anonyme Financière Labeyrie, No. 239693, publié au *Recueil Lebon*).

25 Law No. 92-1990 of 26 February 1992, codified in Articles L.625-1 to L.625-6 of Code de l'entrée et du séjour des étrangers et du droit d'asile (CESEDA). See e.g. Haïm (2001) and Ducarouge (2001).

which the Conseil d'Etat has deemed to be a punitive sanction against companies employing illegal foreign workers.[26]

4.2. DIFFUSE ADMINISTRATIVE SANCTIONS

A *second layer* of administrative sanctions has accompanied the establishment and the development in France of a strong network of administrative regulations, especially in the context of the welfare state that has become the predominant model since the end of World War II. This kind of sanction may be called, after Pr Franck Moderne, *diffuse administrative sanctions*: they are often not instituted by a special instrument and tend to be considered as the necessary accessory to the normative powers of the Government, to its powers of control and authorisation (*police administrative*) or to its role as a provider of public services and benefits.[27] This stratum constitutes the most important part, in quantitative terms, of administrative sanctions in France: they have been empirically instituted by practice as a result of the impossibility of the criminal system and courts to catch up with increasingly developed, complex and evolutive administrative regulations involved in the strong level of involvement by the Government in social and economic life. This is still a dynamic area of administrative sanctions: for example, in 2000 a new sanction of this type was introduced, with the specific aspect that it is pronounced by a Government representative (*préfet*) against urban municipalities that do not provide for the construction of enough council housing.[28]

More often than not, this type of sanction does not consist of the institution of a positive, self-standing punishment, but of the explicit or implicit use of administrative prerogatives with a punitive intention.

One classical and multiform example is the revocation of an authorisation, in the context of the use by the Government of its powers of '*police administrative*' (preventive protection of legality and public order by means of authorisations and interdictions, as opposed to '*police judiciaire*', which is concerned with the investigation of actual offences). A revocation of an authorisation is considered, under French administrative law, as capable of being justified by three distinct types of reasons.

---

26 Code du travail, Article 341-7.

27 Moderne (1993), p. 30.

28 Law No. 2000-1208 of 13 December 2000, codified in Article L. 302-5 et seq. of the Code of construction and housing (*Code de la construction et de l'habitation*).

The revocation may be deemed necessary by the administrative authority because the continuation of the activity subject to the administrative authorisation would be likely to provoke disorder and illegal conduct. For example, the fact that a *café* was the usual place of gathering for known criminals and that a fake passport and a gun were found on the premises justified, in the judgement of the Conseil d'Etat, the revoking of the authorisation to sell alcohol in this *café* as a means of protecting public order and preventing future offences.[29] A similar example may be taken from the case of the revocation of an authorisation to work in a casino after some irregularities had been found, but not as a means of sanctioning such irregularities.

The revocation of an authorisation may also be the consequence of the fact that its holder has ceased to meet a condition which was set for obtaining such authorisation, for example a condition pertaining to nationality, physical ability or a financial guarantee. The Conseil d'Etat considers that the Government is always entitled to revoke an authorisation in such cases.[30]

Last but not least, the revocation may be an easy means for the Government to react in a punitive way against an infringement, without resorting to the burdensome and more court-controlled criminal procedure. The examples are numerous and this is a part of administrative sanctions that is very dynamic and difficult to precisely circumscribe given the general tendency of administrative authorities to use their authorisation powers in this repressive manner. It has, in addition, remained unclear for a long time whether the Government was entitled to resort to this kind of sanction without a prior formal statutory or other provision. This stemmed from the fact that the question of the applicability of the general principle of criminal law *nullum crimen, nulla poena sine lege* was not unequivocally settled by the Conseil constitutionnel and the Conseil d'Etat. In practice, this uncertainty meant that there was no firm resistance to the extension of this type of sanction and that more often than not the attribution of a power of authorisation to an administrative entity implicitly induced a new case of an administrative sanction. The question is not fully settled today, but the *Benkerrou* case made it clear that, as far as authorisations to carry out a professional activity were concerned, sanctions (including the revocation of the

29 CE 19 juin 1992, *SARL 'Le bistrot aixois'*, no. 126413, *Recueil Lebon*, p. 706. But in other cases the revocation of the right to sell alcohol may be intended by the administrative authority as a sanction. Article L.3332–15 of the Public Health Code (*Code de la santé publique*) now explicitly distinguishes three cases of revocation: (i) revocation as an administrative sanction for non-compliance with the sale of alcohol regulations or other staturoty regulations; (ii) revocation as an act of *police administrative* designed to prevent breaches of public order; (iii) revocation as the (administrative) sanctioning of a criminal offence.

30 CE Ass. 7 July 2004, No. 255136, *Ministère de l'intérieur v. M. Benkerrou*, *Droit administratif* November 2004, p. 27, comm. 155, note Breen.

authorisation) could only be legally imposed pursuant to a prior legal instrument instituting the principle of the sanction, but that this instrument could only be of an administrative nature (*nature réglementaire*) and that a statute (*une loi*) as such was not required.[31]

Many of the preceding considerations are applicable to another important type of diffuse administrative sanction: exclusion from a social benefit. As for authorisation, the exclusion of a benefit may in certain cases *not* be treated as a sanction, which is in particular of course the case when the beneficiary ceases to meet the legal prerequirements. But in other cases, the fact that a beneficiary fails to observe certain laws and regulations may lead to the suspension of the benefit. This is, in theory at least, a particularly powerful enforcement means, but also a very controversial one since it uses the social protection of the less well-off part of the population as a means of enhanced policing and institutional control. The nature of the link between the benefit and the obligation enforced by means of excluding a benefit strongly impacts the political and legal viability of the sanction: if the obligation and the benefit are strongly linked, the sanction may be presented and perceived as constituting only a slight deviation from the largely admissible idea that a benefit may be suspended or terminated if the beneficiary ceases to meet the conditions set for obtaining that benefit. But a loose definition of these conditions or the use of the benefits to enforce unrelated or indirectly related obligations amounts to subjecting the less well-off part of the population to additional sanctions.

This type of sanction had been limited to making child-related benefits (*allocations familiales*) conditional upon parents respecting their parental obligations, such as, in particular, the obligation to have under-16s attend school (or follow home education), but the situation has recently evolved. Instituted by the Decree (*Ordonnance*) of 6 January 1959, and limited to school attendance, the benefits exclusion has been increasingly challenged in the last few years, both concerning its perceived discriminatory nature and – paradoxically – its relative inefficiency.[32] This sanction was suppressed by law (*loi*) no. 2004–1 of 2 January 2004, only to be reintroduced in a pseudo-contractual form by Law no. 2006–396 of 31 March 2006, codified in Article L. 222–4–1 of the Code on Social Action and Families (*Code de l'action social et des familles*) and Article L. 552–3 of the Social Security Code (*Code de la sécurité sociale*). Interestingly, this new scheme both gives the benefits exclusion a more social aspect – by linking it to a 'contract of parental responsibility' designed to remotivate parents and help

31 CE Ass., 7 July 2004, No. 255136, *Ministère de l'intérieur v. M. Benkerrou* cited above.

32 See. e.g. A. Rozan, J. Damon, L. Hontarrède, 'Sanctions et actions de prévention des CAF en matière d'absentéisme scolaire, L'e-ssentiel' (publication électronique de la Caisse nationale des allocations familiales), No. 9, February 2003, www.caf.fr/web/WebCnaf.nsf/VueLien/E-SSENTIEL09?opendocument (last visited 13 June 2007).

them to fulfil their duties – and extends the range of obligations liable to trigger the benefits exclusion. As the 1959 sanctions were limited to the failure of the parents to ensure that their children attend school, the 2006 mechanism is applicable in the case of: (i) pupil absenteeism; (ii) a child disrupting school life; (iii) 'any other difficulty linked to the inadequacy of parental authority'. This administrative sanction has thus become close to a general means, for the Government and Local authorities, to try and control lower-class schoolchildren through financial pressure on their parents. What we have classified as a 'diffuse administrative sanction' may now also be seen as comprising an authoritarian aspect.

4.3. ADMINISTRATIVE SANCTIONS AS TOOLS FOR INDEPENDENT AGENCIES

Ironically, a third layer of administrative sanctions is constituted by sanctions created from the mid-1980s onwards within the framework of a new set of liberal policies that have constituted, in France as well as in the UK, although less drastically, an effort to end a period of unlimited extension of the welfare state and to curtail the role of the Government in the economy and society. Formerly an instrument of Government power (in an authoritarian or diffuse manner), administrative sanctions have also been used as a way to enhance the credibility of newly-founded independent agencies (*autorités administratives indépendantes*, or AAIs) meant to limit central Government power.

Hence, most AAIs have been granted punitive powers, even in cases where their US model did not hold these powers in the name of the separation of powers.[33] AAIs, once created, have actively lobbied, often successfully, in order to be granted such powers, or to convince Parliament to reinforce them: the idea has prevailed in France that cooperation between the AAIs and the civil or criminal courts and with the criminal prosecution service (*ministère public*) was not a sufficient deterrent and would not ensure a proper level of the enforcement of the policies for which AAIs were responsible. This is, again, an illustration of the link between the development of administrative sanctions in France and the *jacobin* tradition of the relative weakness and distrust of the judiciary.

The main AAIs exerting punitive powers are:

- *Commission nationale de l'informatique et des libertés* (National Commission for Data Processing and Freedoms) (1978, granted punitive powers in 2004)

33 See e.g. the case of the Securities and Exchange Commission (SEC).

- *Autorité des marchés financiers* (Financial Markets Authority), formerly the Commission des opérations de bourse (created in 1967, granted punitive powers in 1989)
- *Conseil de la concurrence* (Competition Council) (1986)
- *Conseil supérieur de l'audiovisuel* (Superior Council for Radio and Television) (1989)
- *Commission de contrôle des assurances* (Insurance Control Commission) (1989)
- *Autorité de régulation des communications électroniques et de la poste* (Electronic and Postal Communication Regulatory Authority), formerly Autorité de régulation des télécommunications (1996)
- *Agence française de lutte contre le dopage* (French Agency against Doping), formerly Conseil de prévention et de lutte contre le dopage (1999)
- *Autorité de contrôle des nuisances sonores aéroportuaires* (Airport Noise Pollution Control Authority) (1999)
- *Commission de régulation de l'énergie* (Energy Regulatory Commission) (2000)

As explained below, the Conseil d'Etat has often subjected these entities to stricter procedural guarantees than those applicable to other administrative authorities wielding punitive powers: this is an aspect of the 'a la carte' nature of the guarantees.

5. GUARANTEES 'À LA CARTE'

The Conseil d'Etat has shown, over the years, a great willingness to take into account the diversity of contexts in which administrative sanctions are used and has been reluctant to impose in a too general and abstract way a set of substantive and procedural guarantees. If all the traditional constitutional and European guarantees of criminal law have been transposed in the field of administrative sanctions, the degree of transposition – i.e. the level of intensity of the guarantees – is very variable and depends a great deal on a case by case judgement by the Conseil d'Etat in which pragmatic considerations play a decisive role. In particular the Conseil d'Etat ponders, often implicitly, on the potential disruptive effects of a reinforcement of the level of guarantees and adapts – often without saying so – the guarantees to the level of sophistication, funding and efficiency of the various administrative entities that are endowed with punitive powers.

Three main criteria may, however, help in drawing lines on this somewhat impressionist landscape.

First, not all administrative sanctions are considered by the Conseil d'Etat as having to be submitted to the fair trial regime instituted by Article 6 of the ECHR. However, sanctions that remain outside the scope of Article 6 ECHR are submitted to a certain level of guarantees pursuant to 'general principles of administrative law' (*principes généraux du droit*) – a set of legal principles designed by the Conseil d'Etat without any direct statutory or other basis. But, generally speaking, the protection granted under Article 6 ECHR is stronger than that of the general principles.

In one instance, for example, a warning issued by the National Commission for Computerised Data and Freedom (*Commission nationale informatique et libertés* or CNIL) was challenged due to the lack of procedural guarantees. The Conseil d'Etat decided that although Article 6 ECHR was not applicable to this case, because the warning was not issued by a 'court' but by an administrative entity[34], the administrative procedure should, nonetheless, have been subject to the general principles of impartiality and defence rights. However, these principles did not prohibit, in this case, the Commission's *rapporteur* who had investigated the case from participating in the decision on the same case.[35]

More generally, when Article 6 ECHR is not applicable, sanction decisions, like all individual negative administrative decisions, must be reasoned and the person concerned must have been given the opportunity to present prior written and, upon his/her demand, oral observations.[36]

A second criterion draws a line within the group of sanctions that fall within the scope of Article 6 ECHR. For some of these sanctions – generally those pronounced by independent agencies (*autorités administratives indépendantes* or AAIs) – some of the Article 6 guarantees are applicable during the administrative procedure leading to the sanction decision. For other sanctions, the Article 6 guarantees only apply during the judicial review procedure.[37] Generally speaking, the Conseil d'Etat accepts a certain degree of relaxation of the fair trial guarantees during the administrative phase, as long as the sanctioned person retains an effective right to a full review of the facts and the law by an impartial and independent court. However, the degree of relaxation varies according to the type of sanction. For some sanctions, the Conseil d'Etat considers that although

34 However, see below the examples of cases in which Article 6 ECHR is applicable to administrative procedures, pursuant to the *Didier* case law.

35 Conseil d'Etat, Assemblée, 3 December 1999, *Caisse de credit mutuel de Bain-Tresboeuf*, nos. 197060, 197061.

36 Law no. 2000-321 of 12 April 2000, Article 24 and law no. 79-587 of 11 July 1979, Article 1.

37 A full judicial review is in itself a guarantee: ECtHR 21 February 1984, *Öztürk v. Federal Republic of Germany*; 26 September 1995, *Diennet v. France*; 23 October 1995, *Umlauft v. Austria*.

these administrative entities are not 'courts' under French law, they should be considered as such for the purpose of the application of Article 6 ECHR and that most of the corresponding guarantees should be applicable from the beginning of the 'administrative' procedure and not only during a judicial review.[38]

The typical example of this anticipation of fair trial guarantees may be taken from the Financial Markets Authority (*Autorité des marchés financiers* or AMF). AMF sanctions are administrative sanctions imposed by an independent entity within the AMF called the 'Sanctions Commission' (*Commission des sanctions*), in order to better separate investigation, prosecution and sanctioning functions. Most, but not all, Article 6 ECHR guarantees are applicable to the Sanctions Commission procedure, as recently confirmed and made explicit by the Conseil d'Etat:

> 'When deciding upon sanctions enacted in the Monetary and Financial Code (Code monétaire et financier), (...) the AMF Sanctions Commission must be regarded as deciding upon a 'criminal charge' within the meaning of [Article 6 of ECHR]. Given the fact that [its decisions] are subject to a full judicial review by the Conseil d'Etat, a failure to grant all procedural guarantees provided by Article 6 §3 of ECHR does not, in all cases, violate the right to a fair trial. However – and although (...) the AMF Sanctions Commission is not a court under national law – the rights of defence as restated by Article 6 §1 and made explicit by art. 6 §3 (...) are to be granted from the start of the procedure in order to ensure a fair trial and debate. (...) But the right to the free assistance of a lawyer [is not applicable to the Sanctions Commissions because it] is specific to judicial proceedings.'39

A third difference in the regime concerns the sole '*nulla poena sine lege*' principle. In its *Benkerrou* case, the Conseil d'Etat decided that no new sanction could be created without a legal instrument as its basis. But the Conseil d'Etat has made clear that in some cases an Act of Parliament (*une loi*) would be necessary and that in others a mere by-law (*un règlement*) would be sufficient. This distinction between two types of administrative sanctions is very clear as to the applicable legal regime: (i) in some cases the administrative authority has the power to confer upon itself the power to impose certain sanctions; (ii) in other cases the administrative authority has to convince a majority of Parliament that it should increase its punitive power. In its *Fédération de l'hospitalisation privée* case, the Conseil d'Etat ruled that, in order to determine which regime is to be applied, one must refer to the Constitution. If only Parliament can create the obligation, an act of Parliament is required to create the administrative sanction. Otherwise, a by-law is sufficient.[40]

38 Conseil d'Etat, Assemblée, 3 December 1999, *Didier*, no. 207434.
39 Conseil d'Etat, Section, 27 October 2006, *M. Eric B.*, no. 276069 (emphasis added).
40 CE, 18 July 2008, No. 300304, *Fédération de l'hospitalisation privée*.

BIBLIOGRAPHY

Actualité juridique Droit administratif, special issue, 'Les sanctions administratives, actualités et perspectives', 20 October 2001, 151 pp.

Breen, E. (2003), *Gouverner et punir*, Paris, PUF, coll. 'Les voies du droit', 226 pp.

Conseil d'Etat (1995), *Les pouvoirs de l'administration dans le domaine des sanctions*, Paris, La documentation française, coll. 'Les études du Conseil d'Etat', 197 pp.

Degoffe, M. (2000), *Droit de la sanction non pénale*, Paris, Economica, 375 pp.

Dellis, G. (1997), *Droit pénal et droit administratif (l'influence des principes du droit pénal sur le droit administratif répressif)*, Paris, LGDJ, coll. 'Bibliothèque de droit public', 464 pp.

Delmas-Marty, M. and C. Teitgen-Colly (1992), *Punir sans juger? (De la répression administrative au droit administratif pénal)*, Paris, Economica, 191 pp.

Ducarouge, F., 'Le transport international de voyageurs: le cas des amendes administratives infligées aux transporteurs', in: *Actualité juridique Droit administratif*, special issue, 'Les sanctions administratives, actualités et perspectives', 20 October 2001, p. 65.

V. Haïm (2001), 'Un exemple de sanction administrative: l'amende infligée à une entreprise débarquant en France un étranger démuni du titre requis', *Revue française de droit administratif*, p. 823.

Lambert, T. (dir.), *Les sanctions administratives fiscales: aspects de droit comparé*, Paris, L'Harmattan, coll. Finances publiques, 2006.

Marion, M. (1914), *Histoire financière de la France depuis 1715*, Paris, Rousseau.

Moderne, F. (1993), *Sanctions administratives et justice constitutionnelle (contribution à l'étude du jus puniendi de l'Etat dans les démocraties contemporaines)*, Paris, Economica, 341 p.

Mourgeon, J. (1967), *La répression administrative*, Paris, LGDJ, coll. 'Bibliothèque de droit public', 643 pp.

Munch, J.P. (1947), *La sanction administrative*, thèse dact. Paris, 232 pp.

VI. COUNTRY ANALYSIS – GERMANY

Gerhard DANNECKER

1. INTRODUCTORY REMARKS

In the past, administrative sanctions – compared to 'classical' criminal law – were largely neglected by legal scholars in Germany.[1] This is quite surprising, not only because administrative sanctions play a significant role in practice.[2] Let us recall that this category includes the majority of traffic violations (*cf.* Section 49, StVG, or the Traffic Law Code).[3] Moreover, German law distinguishes strictly between criminal sanctions[4] and administrative sanctions[5] since the middle of the 20th century. After all, it was as early as 1952 that the first *Ordnungswidrigkeitengesetz* (OWiG), or Administrative Offences Act, was enacted.[6] This law, defining administrative offences, contains what seems to be the most essential part of administrative sanctions.[7] Before going into detail on administrative sanctions as subject of this study, a general definition of the term 'sanction' is given, followed by a breakdown of the various types of sanctions based on their individual objectives, which in turn is followed by an overview of the various definitions of sanction in German law. Then specific administrative sanctions will be introduced. A discussion about the legal principles applying to them will follow.

---

1 Wolff, Bachof, Stober and Kluth, *Verwaltungsrecht 1*, 12th ed., 2007, §65 at para. 1; Winter, *NStZ* 1990, p. 373.

2 Jescheck and Weigend, *Strafrecht Allgemeiner Teil*, 5th ed., 1996, p. 60; Pache, *Der Schutz der finanziellen Interessen der Europäischen Gemeinschaften*, 1994, p. 214.

3 Baumann, Weber and Mitsch, *Strafrecht Allgemeiner Teil*, 11th ed., 2003, §4 at para. 15; Jescheck and Weigend, *Strafrecht Allgemeiner Teil*, p. 57 *et seq.*

4 See 3.4.5.

5 See 4.2.

6 Göhler, Gürtler and Seitz, *Ordnungswidrigkeitengesetz*, 15th ed., 2009, Introduction at para. 8; Bohnert, *Jura* 1984, p. 18.

7 Bohnert, *Jura* 1984, p. 18, 19; Böse, *Strafen und Sanktionen im europäischen Gemeinschaftsrecht*, 1996, p. 37.

2. GENERAL DEFINITION OF THE TERM 'SANCTION' IN GERMANY

2.1. HISTORICAL BACKGROUND

The term 'sanction' originated from the Latin word '*sancire*', which means 'to sanctify'.[8] Sanction as a legal term was first introduced in Roman law as part of criminal law[9] and the so-called '*sanctio legis*' was the concluding provision of law. This final provision, with a threat of legal detriment in cases of contravention, established the binding force of a law.[10] Thus, a sanction was to express the inviolability (rooted in sacral law) of a law.[11]

2.2. DEFINITION IN GERMAN CASE LAW

German jurisprudence distinguishes between two fundamentally different definitions of the term sanction,[12] but neither of them has been adopted under the German law.[13] One category is sanctions in a constitutional sense, the other is sanctions in the sense of law theory (of applied law). Each category has its own meaning and the respective prerequisites are totally different as well.

2.2.1. Differences between constitutional and general law sanctions

Category one, constitutional-type sanctions, has its roots in the historical term of '*sanctio legis*'.[14] As already explained, the concluding provision in Roman law was to express the binding force of a law. Nearly the same applies to the constitutional-type sanction under German law, which is defined as the transition from a bill to binding law.[15] Thus, a constitutional sanction is synonym to the enactment of a statutory law.[16] Statutory law is enacted by a

8 Mommsen, *Römisches Strafrecht*, 1899, p. 901, fn. 5; Kindhäuser, Artikel 'Sanktion', in: *Staatslexikon*, 7th ed., 1988, p. 999.

9 Kindhäuser, Artikel 'Sanktion', in: *Staatslexikon*, p. 999; Mommsen, *Römisches Strafrecht*, p. 901.

10 Böse, *Strafen und Sanktionen im europäischen Gemeinschaftsrecht*, pp. 46–47; Mommsen, *Römisches Strafrecht*, p. 901, fn. 5.

11 Mommsen, *Römisches Strafrecht*, pp. 882 *et seq.*; Kindhäuser, Artikel 'Sanktion', in: *Staatslexikon*, p. 999.

12 Kindhäuser, Artikel 'Sanktion', in: *Staatslexikon*, pp. 998–999.

13 Wolff, Bachof, Stober and Kluth, *Verwaltungsrecht 1*, §65, at para. 3 *et seq.*; Baumann, Weber and Mitsch, *Strafrecht Allgemeiner Teil*, §33, at para. 1.

14 See 2.1.

15 Arndt, *Die Verfassung des Deutschen Reiches*, 3rd ed., 1927, Article 5, S. 65; Kindhäuser, Artikel 'Sanktion', in: *Staatslexikon*, p. 998, 999.

16 Anschütz, *Die Verfassung des Deutschen Reiches*, 14th ed., 1933, pp. 365–366; Kindhäuser, Artikel 'Sanktion', in: *Staatslexikon*, pp. 998 *et seq.*

legislative act in accordance with Article 77 I 1 of the *Grundgesetz* (GG), the [German] Constitution, or Basic Law, which encompasses two components: firstly, determining the contents of the law, i.e., what is to be turned into law; and secondly, determining its sanction which causes the defined text (admittedly, regardless of Articles 78 and 82/I of the GG) to become law.[17] By this formal act according to Article 77 I 1 of the GG the bill gets legal force and becomes binding law.[18]

After all, the abidance and enforcement of norms largely depends on violators having to put up with a legal detriment.[19] Such detriment is what general law theory calls sanctions.[20] The following study will exclusively deal with this category of sanctions.

Of course, there are also so-called 'positive' sanctions that reward persons who comply with certain standards,[21] e.g. the reward for the finder in civil law. In view of its very minor importance,[22] this type of sanction will not be discussed here. In other words, any sanctions mentioned in the following text are meant to be (negative) sanctions in the sense of general law theory.

2.2.2. General definition of sanctions in the sense of general law

Law scholars in Germany are far from using 'sanction' as a standard term.[23] Hence, it is difficult to distinguish between instruments that can be summed up under sanctions and those that cannot be.

This is the reason why the following text focuses on explaining the definitions of the term 'sanctions' as they are used under German law and on working out the various meanings of the word.

For this, it is essential to distinguish between two different approaches to define the term sanction. It is generally accepted that sanctions do include legal instruments that impose an additional burden with a deterring effect on the person concerned.[24] Moreover, there are other measures that are made to ensure

---

17 Schmidt, Bleibtreu, Hofmann, Hopfauf and Sannwald, *Grundgesetz Kommentar*, 12th ed., 2011, Article 77, at para. 11.

18 Maunz and Dürig, Maunz, *Grundgesetz Kommentar IV*, 1999, Article 77, at para. 3; Arndt, *Die Verfassung des Deutschen Reiches*, Article. 5, p. 65.

19 Pache, *Der Schutz der finanziellen Interessen der europäischen Gemeinschaften*, p. 191; Böse, *Strafen und Sanktionen im europäischen Gemeinschaftsrecht*, p. 47; critical: Röhl, *Rechtssoziologie*, 1987, p. 206.

20 Wolff, Bachof, Stober and Kluth, *Verwaltungsrecht 1*, §65, at para. 3; Kindhäuser, Artikel 'Sanktion', in: *Staatslexikon*, pp. 998–999.

21 Böse, *Strafen und Sanktionen im europäischen Gemeinschaftsrecht*, p. 47, fn. 3; Röhl, *Allgemeine Rechtslehre*, 3rd ed., 2008, pp. 218 *et seq.*

22 Röhl, *Rechtssoziologie*, p. 205; Pache, *Der Schutz der finanziellen Interessen der Europäischen Gemeinschaften*, p. 188.

23 Wolff, Bachof, Stober and Kluth, *Verwaltungsrecht 1*, §65, at para. 3.

24 Pache, *Der Schutz der finanziellen Interessen der Europäischen Gemeinschaften*, p. 188; Heine, in: Dannecker (ed.), *Lebensmittelstrafrecht und Verwaltungssanktionen in der EU*, 1994, p. 25.

that certain obligations are met or a legal condition is restored. Among those are, above all, steps to remove or withhold an advantage or a possibility granted by law under certain circumstances (such as the suspension of a driving licence according to Section 4 III/1 No. 3, *Straßenverkehrsgesetz* – StVG, or Road Traffic Act) if the required conditions are not met or are only met by improper fictitious or evasive acts[25] (e.g., Section 42, *Abgabenordnung* – AO, or Tax Code). In cases like this, the measure does not go beyond suspending or withholding an advantage or a possibility.[26]

Whether such legal instruments should be classified as sanctions or not is controversial. Advocates of a narrow definition of the term sanction reject a wider definition, arguing that some cases are more likely to lack the prerequisites for exercising a right.[27] They point out that such narrowly defined sanctions are nothing but repressive measures that are punitive in character.[28] The prevailing view does not support this opinion, however. As already explained,[29] the idea and purpose of a sanction is to ensure[30] adherence to certain rules. Consequently, another definition of sanction needs to be used as a basis, a definition that also encompasses non-repressive legal detriments (withdrawals etc.). After all, they also represent a negative reaction to illegal behaviour[31] (*cf.* Section 4/II, StVG) of the person concerned[32] and are thus designed to urge individuals as subject to law to behave properly. In summary, sanctions are all (legal) measures in reaction to non-standard behaviour, designed to show the person as subject of law that his/her misbehaviour cannot be tolerated.[33]

This (wider) definition of sanctions is the basis of the following study.

2.2.3. Categories of sanctions according to objectives

The next step is to categorise the various types of sanctions by objectives, one obvious of possible criterions.

---

25 Götz, *Bekämpfung der Subventionserschleichung*, 1974, pp. 46 *et seq.*; Heine, in: Dannecker (ed.), *Lebensmittelstrafrecht und Verwaltungssanktionen in der EU*, p. 24.

26 Götz, *Bekämpfung der Subventionserschleichung*, p. 49.

27 Heine, in: Dannecker (ed.), *Lebensmittelstrafrecht und Verwaltungssanktionen in der EU*, p. 24.

28 Böse, *Strafen und Sanktionen im europäischen Gemeinschaftsrecht*, p. 53.

29 See 2.2.1.

30 Bernsdorf, *Wörterbuch der Soziologie*, 2nd ed., 1969, 'Sanktion', pp. 906 *et seq.*; Pache, *Der Schutz der finanziellen Interessen der Europäischen Gemeinschaften*, p. 191.

31 Hentschel and Dauer, *StVG-Kommentar*, 41st ed., 2011, §4, at para. 3.

32 Wolff, Bachof, Stober and Kluth, *Verwaltungsrecht 1*, §65, at para. 5; Röhl, *Allgemeine Rechtslehre*, pp. 219 *et seq.*

33 Spittler, *Norm und Sanktion*, 1967, pp. 23 *et seq.*; Wolff, Bachof, Stober and Kluth, *Verwaltungsrecht 1*, §65, at para. 5.

Remedial Sanctions

The first category is remedial sanctions. This category includes all measures which are of compensating nature and aimed at restoration or compensation.[34] In other words, such reactions are meant to restore the legal status quo ante[35], what serves to remedy illegal encroachments or effects. By offenders paying damages or being forced to perform, the victim is to be set into the same situation that he/she would have been in if the offender had behaved properly.[36]

Ranking among these, for example, is the claim for damages under civil law according to Sections 823/I and 249 *et seq.*, BGB (*Bürgerliches Gesetzbuch*, or German Civil Code), if the offender has damaged someone else's property.

Repressive Sanctions

Repressive sanctions are another category. Their object is retribution in response to an offence by doing harm to the perpetrator.[37] Such action is meant to balance the victim's and the observer's sense of justice[38], thus to restore the legal order.[39] The classical instrument, maybe the only one, of repressive sanctions is (criminal) punishment.[40]

Preventive Sanctions

Finally, as a third category, there are preventive sanctions.[41] Their goal is also to express disapproval of an offence[42] by way of a legal detriment; however, their primary objective is to stop a continuing or to prevent a future offence.[43] Although repressive measures are also designed to prevent further misbehaviour (so-called negative general prevention),[44] preventive and repressive sanctions differ with regard to the basis on which they are imposed.

---

34 Böse, *Strafen und Sanktionen im europäischen Gemeinschaftsrecht*, pp. 47–48; Durkheim, *Über die Teilung der sozialen Arbeit*, 1977, pp. 109–110.

35 Röhl, *Rechtssoziologie*, p. 206; Böse, *Strafen und Sanktionen im europäischen Gemeinschaftsrecht*, p. 47.

36 Röhl, *Allgemeine Rechtslehre*, p. 219.

37 Durkheim, *Über die Teilung der sozialen Arbeit*, p. 109; Raiser, *Rechtssoziologie*, 1987, p. 239.

38 Röhl, *Allgemeine Rechtslehre*, p. 219.

39 Wessels and Beulke, *Strafrecht Allgemeiner Teil*, 41st ed., 2011, at para. 12a.

40 Otto, *Allgemeine Strafrechtslehre*, 7th ed., 2004, §1, at para. 48 *et seq.*; Durkheim, *Über die Teilung der sozialen Arbeit*, p. 109.

41 Lackner and Kühl, *Strafgesetzbuch*, 27th ed., 2011, §61, at para. 2.

42 Röhl, *Rechtssoziologie*, pp. 206–207.

43 Fischer, *Strafgesetzbuch*, 59th ed., 2012, vor §61, at para. 1; Böse, *Strafen und Sanktionen im europäischen Gemeinschaftsrecht*, p. 48.

44 Jescheck and Weigend, *Strafrecht Allgemeiner Teil*, p. 5; Otto, *Allgemeine Strafrechtslehre*, §1, at para. 68.

Repressive sanctions are exclusively seen as a result of the normative judgement of the offender's behaviour.[45] By contrast, preventive sanctions are exclusively imposed[46] as a result of the offence, in view of the offender's danger as indicated by his/her violation. Thus, a prerequisite for this type of sanction is the fear that further offences may be committed, i.e., there is a 'risk of recidivism'.[47] Hence, preventive measures are not primarily the result of an offence. Instead, they are imposed prospectively, so to speak, to keep the offender from committing another illegal act.[48] This category includes sanctions like public security and correction measures (Sections 61 seq., *Strafgesetzbuch*, StGB, or German Penal Code).

Summary

Remedial, repressive, and preventive sanctions are distinguished by their objectives. As will be discussed later, such differentiation also has an impact on the specific applicable principles of law.[49] Nevertheless, it should be mentioned here that any concrete measure may bring about other unintended effects in addition to their real objective.[50] A claim for damages, exclusively with the goal of restitution, for instance, usually gives the person concerned the feeling of a repressive measure.[51] Consequently, such a reaction always involves a preventive effect[52] because (general) prevention (inevitably) results from repression.[53] Prevention and retribution, contrary to formerly held absolute penal theories,[54] are not conflicting; they rather form a unity (so-called *Vereinigungstheorien*, or merger theories).[55]

The aforesaid leads to the conclusion that we must make a clear distinction between the actual objective and the actual effect of a sanction[56] because the

45 Schönke, Schröder, Stree and Kinzig, *Strafgesetzbuch*, 28th ed., 2010, Vorbem §§38 ff., at para. 3; Otto, *Allgemeine Strafrechtslehre*, §1, at paras. 51 *et seq.*

46 Jescheck and Weigend, *Strafrecht Allgemeiner Teil*, p. 67; Schönke and Schröder, Stree and Kinzig, *Strafgesetzbuch*, Vorbem §§38 ff., at para. 3.

47 Fischer, *Strafgesetzbuch*, vor §61, at para. 3; Lackner and Kühl, *Strafgesetzbuch*, §61, at para. 2.

48 Götz, *Allgemeines Polizei- und Ordnungsrecht*, 14th ed., 2008, p. 164; Schönke, Schröder, Stree and Kinzig, *Strafgesetzbuch*, Vorbem §§61 ff., at paras. 8 *et seq.*

49 See 4.2.

50 Röhl, *Allgemeine Rechtslehre*, p. 219.

51 Jescheck and Weigend, *Strafrecht Allgemeiner Teil*, p. 748; Röhl, *Allgemeine Rechtslehre*, p. 219.

52 Röhl, *Rechtssoziologie*, p. 206, 207.

53 Jescheck and Weigend, *Strafrecht Allgemeiner Teil*, p. 4; Röhl, *Allgemeine Rechtslehre*, p. 219.

54 Roxin, *Strafrecht Allgemeiner Teil I*, 4th ed., 2006, §3, at paras. 2 *et seq.*; Otto, *Allgemeine Strafrechtslehre*, §1, at paras. 71 *et seq.*

55 Wessels and Beulke, *Strafrecht Allgemeiner Teil*, at para. 12a; Jescheck and Weigend, *Strafrecht Allgemeiner Teil*, p. 4.

56 Jescheck and Weigend, *Strafrecht Allgemeiner Teil*, p. 748; Röhl, *Allgemeine Rechtslehre*, p. 219.

standard for the applicability of general legal principles to a sanction cannot be anything but the (immediate) objective of a sanction.[57]

3. OVERVIEW OF THE VARIOUS PROVISIONS ON SANCTIONS IN GERMANY

After discussing the various objectives of a sanction, next step is to give an overview of the sanctions provided in the various fields of law.

3.1. INTRODUCTION

German law provides for a multitude of sanctions.[58] This multitude seems to be necessary because, for one thing, the goal of our legal system is to enforce laws.[59] Also, it must react appropriately to each of the various types of misbehaviour (*cf.* Article 20 III, GG).

The definition of the term sanction alone[60] shows that sanctions must by no means be limited to penal actions. In this sense, sanctions could very well be claims for damages under civil law[61] or administrative reactions to non-standard behaviour.

The following overview is limited to the most important provisions concerning sanctions in the various fields of law. This will be followed by a detailed definition and study of administrative sanctions that are the actual subject of this country analysis.

3.2. SANCTIONS UNDER CIVIL LAW[62]

Unlike sanctions under public law[63], which will be discussed later, the so-called sanctions under civil law belong to the *Ebene der Gleichordnung* (level of equal status).[64] They serve to protect and enforce claims of civil parties against each other.[65] Even though the term 'sanction under civil law' suggests so, no real 'penalty' is imposed.[66] In Germany, the term 'penalty' is exclusively used for the

57 BVerfGE 20, p. 331; Röhl, *Allgemeine Rechtslehre*, p. 219.
58 Fliedner, *AöR* 1974, pp. 242–243.
59 Pache, *Der Schutz der finanziellen Interessen der Europäischen Gemeinschaften*, p. 188.
60 See 2.2.2.
61 §§249 *et seq.* BGB.
62 In detail: Jescheck and Weigend, *Strafrecht Allgemeiner Teil*, p. 15.
63 See 3.4. *et seq.*
64 Maurach and Zipf, *Strafrecht Allgemeiner Teil*, Teilband 1, 8th ed., 1992, p. 12.
65 Jescheck and Weigend, *Strafrecht Allgemeiner Teil*, p. 15.
66 Maurach and Zipf, *Strafrecht Allgemeiner Teil*, Teilband 1, p. 12.

punishment of criminal offences[67] (Article 5 EGStGB, or Introductory Law of the Penal Code). Therefore, the term '*strafähnliche Ahndung*' (quasi-criminal sanction) is used[68] in Germany for other repressive sanctions that are not regarded as criminal sanctions.

Sanctions under civil law belong to neither of these two categories (criminal and quasi-criminal sanctions). Typical examples of non-criminal sanctions to be mentioned here are penalties for a breach of contract – according to Sections 339 *et seq.*, BGB – and for *Vereinsstrafen*, or violations of the laws on associations.[69] Note must also be taken of internal disciplinary measures taken in companies[70] and the very narrowly defined and accepted parental disciplinary authority according to Sections 1626 and 1631, BGB.[71] Eventually, it is a controversial question whether or not a claim for damages for pain and suffering according to Section 253 II, BGB, can be considered to be a sanction under civil law.[72]

3.3. SANCTIONS UNDER CANON LAW

Like sanctions under civil law, sanctions under canon law serve non-public purposes. They have two primary functions: the first reason, they are to contribute to settling the internal affairs of a church[73]; the second reason, they are designed to promote the salvation of the person concerned.[74]

The individual offences range from the renunciation of a religious faith (apostasy) to offences against life.[75] Church sanctions are differentiated accordingly, but almost all of them provide for the suspension or withdrawal of rights, qualifications or claims.[76] However, no church sanction will ever involve excommunication,[77] thus leaving the 'sinner's' tax liability untouched.

From a secular point of view, a church's authorisation to impose penalties is derived from the German *Grundgesetz* (GG). Specifically, ecclesiastical

---

67 See 3.4.2.

68 Sachs and Degenhart, *Grundgesetz Kommentar*, 6th ed., 2011, Article 103, at para. 60.

69 Meyer-Cording, *NJW* 1966, p. 225, 226; Maurach and Zipf, *Strafrecht Allgemeiner Teil*, Teilband 1, p. 12.

70 Maurach and Zipf, *Strafrecht Allgemeiner Teil*, Teilband 1, p. 12.

71 Fischer, *Strafgesetzbuch*, §223, at para. 17; critical: Wessels and Beulke, *Strafrecht Allgemeiner Teil*, at para. 387.

72 Deutsch, *JuS* 1969, p. 203; Hirsch, 'Zur Abgrenzung von Strafrecht und Zivilrecht', in: *FS für Engisch*, 1969, p. 304 *et seq.*; critical: Jescheck and Weigend, *Strafrecht Allgemeiner Teil*, p. 15.

73 Listl and Schmitz, *Handbuch des katholischen Kirchenrechts*, 2nd ed., 1999; Rees, p. 1121.

74 Listl, Müller and Schmitz, *Grundriß des nachkonziliaren Kirchenrechts*, 1980, Strigl, pp. 748 *et seq.*; Jescheck and Weigend, *Strafrecht Allgemeiner Teil*, p. 15.

75 Listl and Schmitz, *Handbuch des katholischen Kirchenrechts*, Rees, pp. 1138 *et seq.*

76 Listl, Müller and Schmitz, *Grundriß des nachkonziliaren Kirchenrechts*, Strigl, pp. 754 *et seq.*

77 Listl and Schmitz, *Handbuch des katholischen Kirchenrechts*, Rees, p. 1121; Listl, Müller and Schmitz, *Grundriß des nachkonziliaren Kirchenrechts*, Strigl, pp. 756 *et seq.*

jurisdiction is granted by Article 140, GG, in conjunction with Article 137 III, *Weimarer Reichsverfassung* (Weimar Reich Constitution) (WRV).[78]

3.4. SANCTIONS UNDER PUBLIC LAW

3.4.1. Introduction

As already indicated, sanctions under public law do not belong to the 'level of equal status'. Instead, the directing authority and the person affected by the measure face each other as superordinates and subordinates.[79] Within the scope of sanctions under public law one has to distinguish strictly between sanctions within and those beyond criminal law.[80] After all, only criminal sanctions are entered in the penal register[81] (*cf.* Sections 3 and 4, BZRG, or *Bundeszentralregistergesetz* – Federal Repository Act) while this distinction has an impact on the individually applicable principles of law – as will be discussed in detail later.[82]

3.4.2. Criminal sanctions (general discussion)

The system of criminal sanctions has a dualistic character, i.e., it essentially reflects two categories of legal consequences for criminal offences:[83] One category is 'classical' punishment in the retributive sense, while measures taken to reform the offender and to protect the public are the second category of legal consequences.[84] Despite their different objectives,[85] these two categories of sanctions originally assume that an illegal act according to Section 11 I 5, StGB has been committed.[86] In other words, it is essential that a perpetrator has actually committed an offence.[87] Penal law exclusively deals with criminal offences[88] which require a punishable crime and the necessity for punishment.[89]

78 Sachs and Detterbeck, *Grundgesetz Kommentar*, Article 92, at para. 28; Dreier and Morlok, *Grundgesetz Kommentar III*, 2nd ed., 2008, Article 140 at paras. 40 *et seq.*

79 Maurach and Zipf, *Strafrecht Allgemeiner Teil*, Teilband 1, pp. 11–12.

80 In detail: Maurach and Zipf, *Strafrecht Allgemeiner Teil*, Teilband 1, p. 2.

81 Maurach and Zipf, *Strafrecht Allgemeiner Teil*, Teilband 1, p. 19.

82 See 4.2.

83 Schönke, Schröder, Stree and Kinzig, *Strafgesetzbuch*, Vorbem §§38 ff., at paras. 3 *et seq.*; Fischer, *Strafgesetzbuch*, vor §38, at para. 4.

84 Müller-Dietz, *Grundfragen des strafrechtlichen Sanktionensystems*, 1979, p. 67.

85 C, III, 4 *et seq.*

86 Fischer, *Strafgesetzbuch*, vor §61, at para. 2.

87 Baumann, Weber and Mitsch, *Strafrecht Allgemeiner Teil*, §33, at para. 5; Schönke, Schröder, Eser and Hecker, *Strafgesetzbuch*, §11, at paras. 36 *et seq.*

88 Schönke, Schröder, Stree and Kinzig, *Strafgesetzbuch*, Vorbem §§38 ff., at paras. 36 *et seq.*

89 Wessels and Beulke, *Strafrecht Allgemeiner Teil*, at para. 11; Otto, *Allgemeine Strafrechtslehre*, §1, at paras. 48 *et seq.*

It is this distinction that is the decisive criterion to draw a clear dividing line between criminal sanctions, on the one hand, and non-criminal sanctions under public law, on the other.

3.4.3. *Non-criminal sanctions under public law (general discussion)*

The second pillar of the public sanction system involves non-criminal sanctions. They include all provisions under public law that the state uses as reaction to deviating behaviour and which are not covered by legal consequences under criminal law.[90] Legal consequences imposed by administrative bodies are called administrative sanctions.[91] They are the actual subject of this study and will be analysed in full detail in a separate section below.[92] Before going into detail on administrative sanctions, criminal sanctions as opposed to administrative sanctions are to be defined, followed by a description of criminal sanctions.

3.4.4. *Definitions of criminal sanctions versus administrative sanctions*

Characteristic of criminal sanctions is the special socio-ethical condemnation of both the offence and the offender.[93] By contrast, administrative sanctions lack this high degree of culpability with regard to the committed offence,[94] which would justify such severe socio-ethical condemnation. In comparison with the acts described in criminal offences, the acts described in administrative sanctions come closer to what is socially adequate.[95]

In principle, it is left to the legislator[96] to classify a sanction as criminal or administrative in nature. Wherever the legislator threatens punishment for any particular behaviour, the type of sanction is a criminal sanction[97] (Article 5 EGStGB). Otherwise, if the legislator calls for a fine, for instance, an administrative sanction would be the consequence (*cf.* Section 1 I, OWiG).[98]

The legislator has to take into consideration that criminal and administrative offences have their own basic characteristics.[99] Although no definite borderline can be drawn, 'the constitutional system of values allows one to determine with

90 See 3.4.5.
91 Wolff, Bachof, Stober and Kluth, *Verwaltungsrecht 1*, §65, at para. 3; Böse, *Strafen und Sanktionen im europäischen Gemeinschaftsrecht*, p. 37.
92 See 4.
93 Maurach and Zipf, *Strafrecht Allgemeiner Teil*, Teilband 1, p. 18.
94 LK, Häger, *StGB*, vor §38 at para. 74; Jescheck and Weigend, *Strafrecht Allgemeiner Teil*, p. 59.
95 Jakobs, *Strafrecht Allgemeiner Teil*, 2nd ed., 1991, p. 50.
96 BVerfGE 51, p. 74; Maurach and Zipf, *Strafrecht Allgemeiner Teil*, Teilband 1, p. 16.
97 Göhler, Gürtler and Seitz, *Ordnungswidrigkeitengesetz*, Introduction at para. 9.
98 Jakobs, *Strafrecht Allgemeiner Teil*, p. 53; Maurach and Zipf, *Strafrecht Allgemeiner Teil*, Teilband 1, p. 16.
99 Jescheck and Weigend, *Strafrecht Allgemeiner Teil*, p. 59; Göhler and Gürtler, *Ordnungswidrigkeitengesetz*, vor §1, at para. 6.

sufficient certainty' which offence belongs to which of those basic elements and which does not.[100] It would be unconstitutional to threaten a criminal sanction for an offence which doubtlessly belongs to the core of administrative offences – and vice versa.[101] For, if the legislator ignored these clearly defined constitutional values, offence and legal consequence would not be 'properly coordinated' and thus be in violation of the principles of a constitutional state.[102]

Consequently, the legislator's hands are tied whenever an offence reaches a certain degree of socio-ethical culpability or, vice versa, does not go beyond a certain degree of culpability.[103] In borderline cases, beyond these unequivocal evaluations, the legislator may, however, make a clear and binding distinction 'in individual cases, taking into consideration the concrete historical situation'.[104] In such cases, the legal consequence is not inferred from the offence; instead, the substance of the offence is determined by the legal consequence.[105]

Prevailing opinion thus favours a mixture of qualitative-quantitative reasoning[106] when it comes to drawing a line between criminal and administrative sanctions. Within the range of basic characteristics of each type of sanction, a qualitative, i.e., characteristic difference is assumed,[107] while in borderline cases the criminal and administrative sanctions can only quantitatively be defined, i.e. gradually,[108] depending on the seriousness of the offence.[109]

3.4.5. The criminal sanction

Criminal sanctions[110] are undoubtedly the state's most severe type of punishment. In view of its far-reaching consequences for the person concerned,

---

100 BVerfGE 27, pp. 28 *et seq.*; Maurach and Zipf, *Strafrecht Allgemeiner Teil*, Teilband 1, p. 16.

101 Wolff, Bachof, Stober and Kluth, *Verwaltungsrecht 1*, §65, at para. 33; Baumann, Weber and Mitsch, *Strafrecht Allgemeiner Teil*, §4, at para. 16.

102 BVerfGE 27, p. 29; Appel, *Verfassung und Strafe*, 1998, p. 109; Schönke, Schröder, Stree and Kinzig, *Strafgesetzbuch*, Vorbem §§38 ff., at para. 37.

103 Baumann, Weber and Mitsch, *Strafrecht Allgemeiner Teil*, §4, at para. 16; Maurach and Zipf, *Strafrecht Allgemeiner Teil*, Teilband 1, p. 17.

104 BVerfGE 27, p. 30; Maurach and Zipf, *Strafrecht Allgemeiner Teil*, Teilband 1, p. 16.

105 Bohnert, *Jura* 1984, p. 20; Wolff, Bachof, Stober and Kluth, *Verwaltungsrecht 1*, §65, at para. 44.

106 Roxin, *Strafrecht Allgemeiner Teil I*, §2, at paras. 60 *et seq.*; Böse, *Strafen und Sanktionen im europäischen Gemeinschaftsrecht*, p. 39.

107 Jakobs, *Strafrecht Allgemeiner Teil*, p. 55; Roxin, *Strafrecht Allgemeiner Teil I*, §2, at paras. 60 *et seq.*

108 Baumann, Weber and Mitsch, *Strafrecht Allgemeiner Teil*, §4, at para. 16; Jescheck and Weigend, *Strafrecht Allgemeiner Teil*, p. 59.

109 Maurach and Zipf, *Strafrecht Allgemeiner Teil*, Teilband 1, p. 17; Pache, *Der Schutz der finanziellen Interessen der Europäischen Gemeinschaften*, p. 217.

110 Jescheck and Weigend, *Strafrecht Allgemeiner Teil*, p. 2; Maurach and Zipf, *Strafrecht Allgemeiner Teil*, Teilband 1, p. 5.

it is also the most important means to maintain legal order.[111] The criminal sanction presents itself as an evil imposed as a just compensation for a committed illegal and culpable act, and it expresses public disapproval[112] of both the act and the offender.[113] From that point of view it pursues repressive as well as preventive goals.[114] Although this is not the only opinion held, it is the prevailing one,[115] and the legislator has adopted it – a fact that is expressed in various provisions. According to Section 46 I 1, StGB, for instance, guilt is the basis for determining a penalty for the offender. Hence, this norm takes into account the concept of repression.[116] By contrast, Section 46 I 2, StGB contains aspects of the offender's rehabilitation,[117] i.e., special prevention.[118] In addition, another preventive aspect referred to as '*Verteidigung der Rechtsordnung*' (defence of the legal system), within the meaning of Section 47 I, StGB, has gained access into the law[119] because this provision is designed to prevent further offences (so-called *Generalprävention*, or general prevention).[120] Consequently, under the law, the preventive character of criminal sanctions applies to both the offender (*Spezialprävention*, or special prevention) and the general public (*Generalprävention*).[121]

The individual types of offences that call for a criminal sanction are codified in the StGB and in the supplementary penal provisions.[122] The main sanctions provided for by law are imprisonment (Section 38, StGB), a fine (Section 40, StGB), and – for the military – detention (Section 9, *WStG*, or Military Criminal Code).[123] By contrast, the suspension of a person's driver license according to Section 44, StGB, and the fines levied on property, as defined in Section 43a, StGB, are additional penalties in that they can or could only be imposed in

---

111 Fliedner, *AöR* 1974, p. 275.

112 See 3.4.2.

113 Otto, *Allgemeine Strafrechtslehre*, §1, at para. 8; Jescheck and Weigend, *Strafrecht Allgemeiner Teil*, p. 13.

114 BVerfGE 95, p. 140; Wessels and Beulke, *Strafrecht Allgemeiner Teil*, at para. 12a; Roxin, *Strafrecht Allgemeiner Teil I*, §3, at paras. 33 *et seq.*

115 Lackner and Kühl, *Strafgesetzbuch*, §46, at paras. 2 *et seq.*; Roxin, *Strafrecht Allgemeiner Teil I*, §3, at paras. 33 *et seq.*

116 Fischer, *Strafgesetzbuch*, §46, at paras. 5 *et seq.*; Wessels and Beulke, *Strafrecht Allgemeiner Teil*, at para. 12a.

117 Lackner and Kühl, *Strafgesetzbuch*, §46, at para. 27; Otto, *Allgemeine Strafrechtslehre*, §1, at para. 70.

118 Maurach and Zipf, *Strafrecht Allgemeiner Teil*, Teilband 1, p. 82.

119 Wessels and Beulke, *Strafrecht Allgemeiner Teil*, at para. 12a; Fischer, *Strafgesetzbuch*, §46, at paras. 10 *et seq.*

120 Fischer, *Strafgesetzbuch*, §46, at para. 2a; Otto, *Allgemeine Strafrechtslehre*, §1, at paras. 67 *et seq.*

121 Wessels and Beulke, *Strafrecht Allgemeiner Teil*, at para. 12a; Maurach and Zipf, *Strafrecht Allgemeiner Teil*, Teilband 1, p. 82.

122 Otto, *Allgemeine Strafrechtslehre*, §1, at paras. 3 *et seq.*; Maurach and Zipf, *Strafrecht Allgemeiner Teil*, Teilband 1, p. 5, 6.

123 Schönke, Schröder, Stree and Kinzig, *Strafgesetzbuch*, Vorbem §§38 ff., at para. 29.

addition to a principal punishment.[124] According to a decision of the *Bundesverfassungsgericht* (Federal Constitutional Court) the provision of Section 43a, StGB, is unconstitutional anyway and is thus null and void.[125]

3.4.6. *Measures for the reformation of offenders and the prevention of crime*

The second pillar of the criminal sanction system is composed of, as mentioned earlier, measures for the prevention of crime and for the reformation of offenders.[126] These measures are purely preventive in character[127] and are not retribution for a culpable offence. Their sole purpose is the protection of the general public against a dangerous perpetrator by aiming to reform or to detain him, thus keeping him from committing another offence.[128] That is why they, unlike criminal sanctions, are not linked to the question of guilt. Instead, they are linked to the offender's danger to society and are thus exclusively future-oriented.[129] Consequently, the commitment of an illegal act within the meaning of Section 11 I No. 5, StGB, is only the reason[130] for ordering a measure to be taken, while the legal basis for such an order is the danger posed by the perpetrator[131] as expressed by his offence (cf. Section 62, StGB). The requirement of a measure is determined within the framework of a negative risk evaluation concerning the perpetrator's future misconduct.[132]

Although, as already discussed, punishment and other measures than punishment require different prerequisites for application – i.e. guilt on the one hand and danger to the public on the other – they definitely do not exclude each other. On the contrary, it is quite possible for both of them to be imposed jointly and simultaneously.[133] This is normally done when the penalty for the guilt appears insufficient to ward off a certain danger.[134] This shows that the extent of a measure is exclusively determined by the public need for protection from a dangerous perpetrator.[135]

---

124 Fischer, *Strafgesetzbuch*, §44, at para. 2; Schönke, Schröder, Stree and Kinzig, *Strafgesetzbuch*, Vorbem §§38 ff., at paras. 30.

125 BVerfGE 105, p. 135 *et seq.*

126 Lackner and Kühl, *Strafgesetzbuch*, §61, at para. 2.

127 Otto, *Allgemeine Strafrechtslehre*, §1, at paras. 12 *et seq.*; Schönke, Schröder, Stree and Kinzig, *Strafgesetzbuch*, Vorbem §§38 ff., at para. 22.

128 Fischer, *Strafgesetzbuch*, vor §61, at para. 1.

129 Wessels and Beulke, *Strafrecht Allgemeiner Teil*, at para. 396; Lackner and Kühl, *Strafgesetzbuch*, §61, at para. 4.

130 Fischer, *Strafgesetzbuch*, vor §61, at para. 2.

131 Jescheck and Weigend, *Strafrecht Allgemeiner Teil*, p. 83; Schönke and Schröder, Stree and Kinzig, *Strafgesetzbuch*, Vorbem §§38 ff., at para. 22.

132 Lackner and Kühl, *Strafgesetzbuch*, §61, at para. 4; Fischer, *Strafgesetzbuch*, vor §61, at para. 3.

133 Bruns, *GA* 1959, p. 195; Roxin, *Strafrecht Allgemeiner Teil I*, §1, at para. 3.

134 Fischer, *Strafgesetzbuch*, vor §61, at para.1; Roxin, *Strafrecht Allgemeiner Teil I*, §3, at para. 63.

135 Schönke, Schröder, Stree and Kinzig, *Strafgesetzbuch*, Vorbem §§38 ff., at para. 22.

More details on the requirements for ordering measures are to be found in Sections 61 *et seq.*, StGB. Section 61, StGB contains a catalogue-like listing of measures for reformation and the prevention of crime provided for by the [German] Penal Code.[136] Further measures are contained in the supplementary penal provisions such as, for instance, in Section 41, *BJagdG* (Federal Hunting Act), and Section 20, *TierschutzG* (Prevention of Cruelty to Animals Act).

3.4.7. Validity of general legal principles within the scope of criminal sanctions

Criminal sanctions have just been discussed with due brevity. For lack of space, no further details concerning related legal principles applying to them can be given here, except the brief hint that the governing legal principles applying to criminal sanctions result from various provisions of the *Grundgesetz*, the [German] Penal Code, and the regulations provided by the judiciary and criminal procedural law.

Incidentally, it should be noted at this point that a detailed explanation of some fundamental legal principles of the German legal system will be given following the descriptions of administrative sanctions. There the applicability of these legal principles to administrative sanctions is explained[137], how they distinguish themselves from criminal sanctions and what criminal and administrative sanctions have in common.

4. ADMINISTRATIVE SANCTIONS

4.1. INTRODUCTION

Now that a general overview of sanctions under German law has been given, it is necessary to illustrate the scope of applicability and the function of administrative sanctions as the primary subject of this study.

First of all, we must keep in mind that the law provides for a multitude of such sanctions and, moreover, the meanings of the individual sanctions differ considerably.[138] Related provisions range from interest levied for tax evasion to claims for return according to the *Filmförderungsgesetz* (Film Development Act).[139]

Thus, only instances of the most important categories of such provisions and linked applicable procedures are to be examined, followed by a detailed

---

136 Schönke, Schröder, Stree and Kinzig, *Strafgesetzbuch*, §61, at para. 1; critical: Fischer, *Strafgesetzbuch*, §61, at para. 1.

137 See 4.2.

138 Fliedner, *AöR* 1974, p. 242 *et seq.*

139 Götz, *Bekämpfung der Subventionserschleichung*, p. 47; Fliedner, *AöR* 1974, p. 243.

comment on the legal principles applying in each individual case – which requires prior clarification of the individual sanction's character.

4.2. CATEGORIES OF ADMINISTRATIVE SANCTIONS

4.2.1. The law governing administrative offences

General information

The law governing administrative offences undoubtedly includes the essential part of administrative sanctions in Germany and is very similar to the law governing criminal offences.[140] This similarity is, for example, expressed in Article 74 I no. 1 GG.[141] The legislative competence referred to as 'criminal law' also includes the *Ordnungswidrigkeitenrecht*, or administrative offences law, but it does not include the other administrative sanctions.[142] In spite of the similarity, administrative offences law is an entirely separate field of law.[143]

The *OWiG* (Administrative Offences Act) defines only some of the administrative offences (*cf.* Sections 111 *et seq.* OWiG),[144] while most of the administrative sanctions are scattered over a multitude of various laws and regulations.[145] Nevertheless, the rules of the OWiG (Section 2 OWiG) must be adhered to in order to respond to illegal acts. To this extent, the OWiG contains the key and general regulations for all administrative offences according to federal and state laws.[146]

The legislator has created the *Allgemeiner Teil* (General Part) of the OWiG closely following that the structure of the StGB (Sections 1 *et seq.*, OWiG).[147] The only substantial deviations are those defined in Section 14 OWiG, i.e., the principle of *Einheitstäterschaft* (the monistic model of a perpetrator) and, as defined in Section 30 OWiG, the possibility to impose an administrative fine[148] on legal entities and associations of individuals as an incidental consequence.

---

140 Lemke, *Ordnungswidrigkeitengesetz*, 2nd ed., 2005, Introduction, at para. 12.

141 Waldhoff, in: Hoffmann-Riem, Schmidt-Aßmann and Voßkuhle, *Grundlagen des Verwaltungsrechts*, Bd. III, 2009, §46 at para 192.

142 BVerfGE 27, p. 32, 33; Jarass and Pieroth, *Grundgesetz Kommentar*, 11th ed., 2011, Article 74, at paras. 5 *et seq.*

143 Jescheck and Weigend, *Strafrecht Allgemeiner Teil*, p. 59; Lemke, *Ordnungswidrigkeitengesetz*, Introduction, at paras. 11, 12.

144 Göhler and Gürtler, *Ordnungswidrigkeitengesetz*, vor §111, at para. 2; Lemke, *Ordnungswidrigkeitengesetz*, vor §111, at para. 1.

145 Baumann, Weber and Mitsch, *Strafrecht Allgemeiner Teil*, §4, at para. 13.

146 Göhler and Gürtler, *Ordnungswidrigkeitengesetz*, vor §1, at para. 1.

147 Dannecker, *Entsanktionierung des Lebensmittelrechts*, 1996, p. 36; Jakobs, *Strafrecht Allgemeiner Teil*, p. 53.

148 Tiedemann, *NJW* 1988, p. 1169; Jakobs, *Strafrecht Allgemeiner Teil*, p. 53; Waldhoff, in: Hofmann-Riehm, Schmidt-Aßmann and Voßkuhle, *Grundlagen des Verwaltungsrechts*, Bd.

The main legal consequence provided by law is the administrative fine[149] (Section 17 OWiG). Also of importance are the withdrawal of items linked with an offence (Section 22 OWiG) and imposing a driving ban (Section 25 StVG, or Road Traffic Act). The latter two reactions have the character of an incidental consequence. Therefore, as a matter of principle, they can only be imposed in conjunction with an administrative fine.[150]

In cases of minor administrative offences, the competent authority may also admonish the perpetrator and, if this is found to be insufficient, impose an admonition fine. However, a prerequisite for this is that the person concerned, having been advised of his right of refusal, agrees and pays on the spot or within a week (Section 56 OWiG). If the suspect disagrees or does not make payment in due time, such admonition is invalid,[151] which means that monetary fine proceedings may be initiated against him/her (Section 56 II OWiG).[152]

Thus an admonition subject to a fine is considered to be an administrative act in response to an administrative offence that requires the violator's cooperation.[153]

Due to lack of space, this study dispenses with further details on other legal consequences. The following remarks are limited to the instrument having the most practical relevance in the law governing administrative offences, namely the administrative fine as the main legal consequence.[154]

Sanction character

An administrative fine pursues both repressive and preventive goals and thus has a dual function.

The repressive character is expressed by the fact that the violation of an administrative obligation per se is considered a wrong that requires sanctioning.[155] In this respect, an administrative fine means a disciplinary reaction to a contravention, even if the specific affected object of legal protection is largely ethically neutral.[156] This (repressive) concept is also to be found in the text of the law, which says that the specific contravention is to be 'paid for' by way of a 'fine', which amounts to 'punishment' as the legal consequence (Section 1 I OWiG).

III, §46, Rn. 198.

149 Maurach and Zipf, *Strafrecht Allgemeiner Teil*, Teilband 1, p. 18; Baumann, Weber and Mitsch, *Strafrecht Allgemeiner Teil*, §4, at para. 14.

150 Göhler and Gürtler, *Ordnungswidrigkeitengesetz*, §22, at para. 4.

151 BVerfGE 22, p. 132.

152 Rotberg, *Ordnungswidrigkeitengesetz*, 5th ed., 1975, §56, at para. 9; Lemke, *Ordnungswidrigkeitengesetz*, §56, at para. 17.

153 BVerfGE 22, p. 131; Lemke, *Ordnungswidrigkeitengesetz*, §56, at para. 3.

154 Baumann, Weber and Mitsch, *Strafrecht Allgemeiner Teil*, §4, at para. 14; Maurach and Zipf, *Strafrecht Allgemeiner Teil*, Teilband 1, p. 18.

155 Wolff, Bachof, Stober and Kluth, *Verwaltungsrecht 1*, §65, at para. 4.

156 Baumann, Weber and Mitsch, *Strafrecht Allgemeiner Teil*, §4, at para. 16.

However, the administrative fine simultaneously pursues the purpose of special and general prevention[157] in that this sanction presents itself as an 'emphatic reminder of one's duties',[158] much the same as a 'warning' or a 'lesson' to be learned.[159] Consequently, it has two intentions: the first is to urge the person concerned to behave properly (special prevention); and the second is to prevent contraventions by persons other than the person concerned (general prevention).[160] Accordingly, the administrative fine (also) pursues the goal of enforcing a certain order and, to this effect, is of preventive nature.[161]

In summary, you can say that the administrative fine is meant to punish a committed violation (repressive goal) and also acts as a deterrent to future violations (preventive goal).

Procedure

There is a special procedure for prosecuting and punishing administrative offences, a procedure that, as a matter of principle, is conducted by administrative authorities (Sections 35 *et seq.* OWiG).[162] Applicable to this procedure, unlike in criminal proceedings (*cf.* Section 152 II 2 StPO), is not the principle of mandatory prosecution but the principle of discretionary prosecution that is subject to a free decision after due assessment of the circumstances (Sections 47 I and 53 OWiG).[163] Consequently, the administrative authorities are not compelled to prosecute.

The procedure for prosecuting administrative offences is divided into two phases.

Phase one

Phase one includes the independent investigative activity by the competent administrative authority.[164] If an administrative offence is found to have been committed, the relevant administrative authority, in accordance with Section 35 II OWiG, is always responsible for prosecution.[165]

---

157 Waldhoff, in: Hofmann-Riehm, Schmidt-Aßmann and Voßkuhle, *Grundlagen des Verwaltungsrechts*, Bd. III, §46, Rn. 198.

158 BVerfGE 9, p. 167; Göhler and Gürtler, *Ordnungswidrigkeitengesetz*, vor §1, at para. 9.

159 BVerfGE 22, p. 132; Wolff, Bachof, Stober and Kluth, *Verwaltungsrecht 1*, §65, at para. 4.

160 Göhler and, Gürtler, *Ordnungswidrigkeitengesetz*, vor §1, at para. 9; Wolff, Bachof, Stober and Kluth, *Verwaltungsrecht 1*, §65, at para. 43.

161 Schall, *NStZ* 1986, p. 6; Göhler and Gürtler, *Ordnungswidrigkeitengesetz*, vor §1, at para. 9.

162 Rotberg, *Ordnungswidrigkeitengesetz*, §35, at para. 1; Jescheck and Weigend, *Strafrecht Allgemeiner Teil*, p. 60.

163 Bohnert, *Jura* 1984, p. 21; Jakobs, *Strafrecht Allgemeiner Teil*, p. 53.

164 Göhler and Gürtler, *Ordnungswidrigkeitengesetz*, §35, at para. 4; Lemke, *Ordnungswidrigkeitengesetz*, §35, at para. 7.

165 Lemke, *Ordnungswidrigkeitengesetz*, §35, at para. 10; Göhler and Gürtler, *Ordnungswidrigkeitengesetz*, §35, at para. 34.

Prosecution is usually effected by issuing an administrative order imposing a fine (Section 65 OWiG). However, this measure by the administrative authority is only provisional in nature in that the order imposing a fine does not become final and enforceable until the person concerned has submitted to it.[166]

On the other hand, if an appeal has been filed in accordance with Section 67 OWiG, the administrative authority reviews the correctness of its decision (Section 69 II OWiG). If the administrative order imposing a fine is not withdrawn, the imposing authority is obliged to hand the files over to the public prosecutor's office (Section 69 III OWiG).[167] It is only at this particular point that public prosecutors deal with administrative offences, otherwise they are not at all involved in this type of procedure.[168]

Phase two

Phase two is triggered by filing an appeal. This phase is similar to a 'usual' criminal trial (Section 71 I OWiG),[169] because by his/her appeal the person concerned establishes the jurisdiction of the court for prosecution (Sections 71 *et seq.* OWiG).[170]

Hence, the two phases of the procedure are only linked by the citizen's decision to file an appeal. Otherwise, both phases are completely independent of each other. Against the court order an appeal on a point of law can be filed with the *Oberlandesgericht*, or the State Court of Appeals (Sections 79 *et seq.* OWiG).[171]

Since proceedings for the imposition of administrative fines are not criminal proceedings, fines are not entered in the register of convictions (Sections 3 *et seq.* 11, *BZRG*, or Federal Repository Act). Moreover, fines cannot be converted into imprisonment for failure to pay a fine (Section 43 StGB), but they can be collected very well by an arrest to enforce a court order (Section 96 OWiG).[172] This arrest to enforce a court order is a mere coercive measure to enforce compliance.[173]

166 Wolff, Bachof, Stober and Kluth, *Verwaltungsrecht 1*, §65, at para. 27; Lemke, *Ordnungswidrigkeitengesetz*, §65, at para. 5.

167 Göhler and Seitz, *Ordnungswidrigkeitengesetz*, §69, at para. 35; Wolff, Bachof, Stober and Kluth, *Verwaltungsrecht 1*, §65, at para. 27.

168 Rotberg, *Ordnungswidrigkeitengesetz*, §35, at paras. 5 *et seq.*; Lemke, *Ordnungswidrigkeitengesetz*, §35, at paras. 1 *et seq.*

169 Lemke, *Ordnungswidrigkeitengesetz*, §71, at para. 3.

170 Göhler and Gürtler, *Ordnungswidrigkeitengesetz*, §35, at para. 10; Lemke, *Ordnungswidrigkeitengesetz*, §35, at para. 12.

171 Jescheck and Weigend, *Strafrecht Allgemeiner Teil*, p. 60; Lemke, *Ordnungswidrigkeitengesetz*, §79, at para. 1.

172 Jakobs, *Strafrecht Allgemeiner Teil*, p. 53.

173 Jescheck and Weigend, *Strafrecht Allgemeiner Teil*, p. 60.

4.2.2. *Judicial enforcement measures (Ordnungsmittel)*

General information

Administrative sanctions also include *Ordnungsmittel*,[174] or judicial enforcement measures. Such measures encompass all regulations that provide for a disciplinary fine or arrest for disobeying a court order as legal consequences[175] (Articles 6 *et seq.* EGStGB). The employment of *Ordnungsmittel* requires a violation of administrative rules.[176] This is why such standards are to be found mainly in procedural rules and in laws governing associations and institutions.[177]

Ordnungsmittel under procedural rules

The basis for imposing *Ordnungsmittel* under procedural rules is the legal obligation to observe procedural duties.[178] Among the more important types are *Ordnungsmittel* against witnesses for failing to appear in court or refusing to give evidence or to take the oath (Sections 51, 70 I, 77 StPO; Sections 380, 390, 409 *ZPO*, or German Code of Civil Procedure) as well as those measures that are imposed for contravening rules of civil law (Section 890 ZPO; Section 33, *FGG* or German Ex Parte Jurisdiction Act).[179] Finally, section 178 I 1 *GVG* (*German Judicature Act*) should be mentioned, which also allows the use of *Ordnungsmittel* for 'contempt of court'.[180]

Ordnungsmittel under the laws on associations and institutions

First of all, the use of *Ordnungsmittel* is also a measure within the scope of the laws governing associations and institutions. In this case, *Ordnungsmittel* are based on the autonomous jurisdiction of the administrative body to prosecute breaches of discipline on the part of association members and users of an

174 Göhler, *NJW* 1974, p. 825, 826; Baumann, Weber and Mitsch, *Strafrecht Allgemeiner Teil*, §4, at para. 18.

175 Wolff, Bachof, Stober and Kluth, *Verwaltungsrecht 1*, §65, at para. 46; Winter, *NStZ* 1990, p. 373.

176 Merk, *Deutsches Verwaltungsrecht*, 1962, p. 1011; Wolff, Bachof, Stober and Kluth, *Verwaltungsrecht 1*, §65, at para. 56 *et seq.*

177 Winter, *NStZ* 1990, p. 373; Wolff, Bachof, Stober and Kluth, *Verwaltungsrecht 1*, §65, at paras. 56 *et seq.*

178 Baumann, Weber and Mitsch, *Strafrecht Allgemeiner Teil*, §4, at paras. 18 *et seq.*; Wolff, Bachof, Stober and Kluth, *Verwaltungsrecht 1*, §65, at para. 56.

179 Jakobs, *Strafrecht Allgemeiner Teil*, p. 61; Jescheck and Weigend, *Strafrecht Allgemeiner Teil*, p. 14.

180 Fliedner, *AöR* 1974, p. 243; Winter, *NStZ* 1990, p. 373.

institution.[181] A typical regulation in this context is Article 20 IV *BayGO* (Bavarian Trade Law) which interferes when unsalaried co-workers violate their obligation of secrecy or fail to exercise proper care.[182]

Nature of sanctions

The nature of sanctions by the use of *Ordnungsmittel* is highly controversial. Some experts consider them to be purely repressive,[183] others argue that they are exclusively preventive in nature.[184] The probably prevailing opinion advocates a dual character,[185] which means that *Ordnungsmittel* are a quasi-penal measure (repressive legal nature) with the characteristics of a coercive measure (preventive legal nature).[186]

Adherents to this opinion argue that the repressive element is expressed by the fact that an administrative offence must have been committed before *Ordnungsmittel* are imposed.[187] This means that an already committed breach of duty is taken up to be sanctioned by way of the applied *Ordnungsmittel* (disciplinary fine or arrest for disobeying to a court order).[188] From that point of view it is a punitive measure[189] that aims 'at repression and retribution for an illegal behaviour' in that 'the perpetrator is blamed for an illegal act and reproached with it'.[190]

In addition, it is generally accepted that *Ordnungsmittel* also have a preventive effect.[191] After all, they are to enforce orderly (proper) behaviour (general preventive effect)[192] by deterring third parties from committing such an illegal act (negative general prevention) and strengthen the general public's confidence in the legal system (positive general prevention).[193]

Moreover, *Ordnungsmittel* are to deter the 'offender' himself from further wrongdoing[194] (preventive effect on a particular offender). In that respect they

181 Wolff, Bachof, Stober and Kluth, *Verwaltungsrecht 1*, §65, at para. 56; Widtmann and Grasser, *Bayerische Gemeindeordnung*, 2010, Article 20, at para. 8.

182 Widtmann and Grasser, *Bayerische Gemeindeordnung*, 2006, Article 20, at paras. 1 *et seq.*

183 Maurach and Zipf, *Strafrecht Allgemeiner Teil*, Teilband 1, p. 6; Wolff, Bachof, Stober and Kluth, *Verwaltungsrecht 1*, §65, at para. 56 *et seq.*

184 OLG Düsseldorf, *WRP* 1988, pp. 37–38.

185 BVerfGE 20, p. 331, 332; Zöller and Stöber, *Zivilprozessordnung Kommentar*, 29th ed., 2012, §890, at para. 5.

186 Zöller, Stöber, *Zivilprozessordnung Kommentar*, §890, at para. 5; Göhler and Gürtler, *Ordnungswidrigkeitengesetz*, vor §1, at para. 40.

187 BVerfGE 20, pp. 331–332; Göhler, *NJW* 1974, pp. 825–826.

188 Gaul and Schilken, *Zwangsvollstreckungsrecht*, 12th ed., 2010, §9, at para 27.

189 Maurach and Zipf, *Strafrecht Allgemeiner Teil*, Teilband 1, p. 6; Wolff, Bachof, Stober and Kluth, *Verwaltungsrecht 1*, §65, at para. 56.

190 BVerfGE 20, p. 331; Maurach and Zipf, *Strafrecht Allgemeiner Teil*, Teilband 1, p. 6.

191 BVerfGE 20, p. 331, 332; Baumann, Weber and Mitsch, *Strafrecht Allgemeiner Teil*, §4, at para. 19.

192 Brehm, *NJW* 1975, p. 250; Winter, *NStZ* 1990, p. 374.

193 Röhl, *Allgemeine Rechtslehre*, p. 218 *et seq*; Winter, *NStZ* 1990, p. 374.

194 Winter, *NStZ* 1990, p. 374.

are aimed at 'breaking the offender's will for the future by punishing him for something in the past'.[195] This shows the disciplinary nature of *Ordnungsmittel*.[196]

Procedure

Ordnungsmittel are fixed by way of an administrative act.[197] This is true even if, for example, a court (*cf.* Section 178 GVG) imposes the legal consequence because in this case the court acts as an administrative organ, not as a judicial organ.[198]

During the procedure, the OWiG does not apply because *Ordnungsmittel*, in particular those including a disciplinary fine, are not an administrative fine as defined by Section 1 I OWiG.[199] Instead, relevant special provisions apply, which means that decisions are normally (except as provided in special provisions concerning appeals such as, for example, Section 181 GVG) subject to objection and to action for rescission in an administrative court (*cf.* Section 42 I, 1st Alternative *VwGO*, or Rules of the Administrative Courts).[200]

The regulations for *Ordnungsmittel* are largely identical to those for the criminal fine and for imprisonment for failure to pay a fine (*cf.* Sections 459 *et seq.* StPO, Articles 7, 8 EGStGB). Unlike the means to enforce administrative acts[201] that will be discussed later, *Ordnungsmittel* in many cases are mandatory, not optional[202] (for example, Section 380 ZPO).[203] In other words, the principle of discretionary measures, as a rule, does not apply here.

---

195 Böhm, *NJW* 1974, pp. 443–444; Zöller and Stöber, *Zivilprozessordnung Kommentar*, §890, at para. 5.

196 OLG Düsseldorf, *Juristisches Büro* 1987, pp.1261, 1262; Rüping, in: Bonner *Kommentar zum Grundgesetz*, 2nd ed., 2011, Article 103 II, at para. 83.

197 Widtmann and Grasser, *Bayerische Gemeindeordnung*, 2007, Article 19, at para. 12; Wolff, Bachof, Stober and Kluth, *Verwaltungsrecht 1*, §65, at para. 65.

198 Kniestedt, *MDR* 1960, p. 197; Wolff, Bachof, Stober and Kluth, *Verwaltungsrecht 1*, §65, at para. 65.

199 LG Bremen, *NJW* 1970, pp. 1429–1430; Göhler and Gürtler, *Ordnungswidrigkeitengesetz*, vor §1, at para. 40.

200 Widtmann and Grasser, *Bayerische Gemeindeordnung*, Article 19, at para. 11; Wolff, Bachof, Stober and Kluth, *Verwaltungsrecht 1*, §65, at para. 65.

201 See 4.2.4.

202 Maurach and Zipf, *Strafrecht Allgemeiner Teil*, Teilband 1, p. 7; Kleinknecht and Meyer-Goßner, *Strafprozessordnung*, 54th ed., 2011, §51, at para. 16.

203 Zöller and Greger, *Zivilprozessordnung* Kommentar, §380, at paras. 1 *et seq.*

4.2.3. Withdrawal/denial of benefits/opportunities

General information

Other types of administrative sanctions[204] are the withdrawal[205] and the denial[206] of (legal) benefits or opportunities. The goal of both types (withdrawal and denial) is to make the persons concerned comply with their administrative duties.[207]

Examples of the withdrawal of benefits are the withdrawal or revocation of a once granted subsidy (*cf.* Sections 48, 49 VwVfG, or Administrative Procedural Law), the suspension of a driver's license (*cf.* Section 3 StVG), or the prohibition on trading for reasons of unreliability (*cf.* Section 35 I 1 GewO, or Industrial Code). Otherwise, denials of benefits include, for instance, disapproval (non-issuance) of a driving permit (Section 2 StVG), denial of a tax benefit as a result of abusive fictitious and evasive acts (*cf.* Section 42 AO, or Tax Code), or the annulment of a benefiting administrative act because it was brought about in an unethical manner (*cf.* Section 44 II No. 6 VwVfG).

Even these (few) examples show that this is a highly heterogeneous group of administrative sanctions that differ very much in terms of uses, the nature of the sanction, and the types of procedure. This is why the only case to be discussed here is what seems to be the most important case in practice, namely the annulment,[208] i.e., the withdrawal or revocation of a benefiting *Verwaltungsakt* (VA, or administrative act).

Withdrawal/revocation of a benefiting administrative act (VA)
The two public instruments (withdrawal and revocation) are special because they can be applied[209] even after the non-appealability of the (initial) VA (Sections 48 I 1 and 49 II VwVfG). Relevant provisions within the scope of the Administrative Procedural Law are Sections 48 and 49 VwVfG. However, what is to be borne in mind here is the subsidiarity principle according to Section 1 VwVfG. Thus, these two provisions are frequently replaced by special legal provisions (for example, by Section 15 I GastG, or German Licensing Act).[210] Nevertheless, in view of their fundamental and exemplary importance, these

204 Waldhoff, in: Hofmann-Riehm, Schmidt-Aßmann and Voßkuhle, *Grundlagen des Verwaltungsrechts*, Bd. III, §46, No. 212.

205 BVerfGE 27, p. 40 *et seq.*; Baumann, Weber and Mitsch, *Strafrecht Allgemeiner Teil*, §4, at para. 37.

206 BVerfGE 6, p. 221; BVerfGE 20, p. 369–370; Jarass and Pieroth, *Grundgesetz Kommentar*, Article 92, at para. 5.

207 Wolff, Bachof, Stober and Kluth, *Verwaltungsrecht 1*, §65, at paras. 3 *et seq.*

208 Maurer, *Allgemeines Verwaltungsrecht*, 18th ed., 2011, §11, at para. 11; Peine, *Allgemeines Verwaltungsrecht*, 10th ed., 2011, at para. 917.

209 Bull and Mehde, *Allgemeines Verwaltungsrecht*, 8th ed., 2009, at para. 789; Wolff, Bachof, Stober and Kluth, *Verwaltungsrecht 1*, §51, at paras. 31 *et seq.*

210 Peine, *Allgemeines Verwaltungsrecht*, at para. 924; Obermayer and Schäfer, *Kommentar zum Verwaltungsverfahrensgesetz*, 3rd ed., 1999, §48, at paras. 5 *et seq.*

basic standards (Sections 48 and 49 VwVfG) are to be the subject of the following discussion.

The withdrawal (Section 48 VwVfG) pertains to (originally) illegal administrative acts, whereas the revocation (Section 49 VwVfG) refers to (originally) legal administrative acts.[211] Consequently, typical of sanctioning laws, which always require illegal behaviour on the part of the person concerned,[212] are the two following constellations that can be distinguished by the reason for suspension, i.e., the type of misconduct by the beneficiary.

First, the beneficiary may already have illegally obtained a legal advantage (like having been granted a subsidy) such as by making false statements (Section 48 II 3 No. 2 VwVfG).[213] In such cases even the initial administrative act (the approval) is illegal, and the annulment is based on Section 48 VwVfG. In other words, the type of reaction is a withdrawal.

A different constellation would be a legally obtained advantage that is annulled as a result of a (subsequent) violation on the part of the beneficiary who has failed to comply with the attached obligations (Section 49 II 1 No. 2 VwVfG).[214] In such cases (misusing a subsidy, for example), the annulment is based on Section 49 VwVfG. In other words, the type of reaction is a revocation.

Nature of sanctions

An administrative agency can subsequently annul a (benefiting) illegal administrative decision by way of withdrawal. A withdrawal, thus, serves to restore[215] the legal condition that would have existed if the advantage had been denied. Consequently, this is a measure that is remedial in nature.

As for the result per se, the same holds true for the revocation in that this means is usually applied by an administrative agency if the factual and legal position which was the basis of the administrative decision has changed and the content of the (originally) legal administrative decision is no longer consistent with the applicable law.[216] Consequently, the revocation also serves to restore a legal condition.

Thus, the provisions to annul a benefiting administrative decision must be considered as remedial sanction provisions.

---

211 Stelkens, Bonk and Sachs, *Verwaltungsverfahrensgesetz*, §48, at para. 23; Maurer, *Allgemeines Verwaltungsrecht*, §11, at para. 11.

212 See 2.2.2.

213 Götz, *NVwZ* 1984, p. 480; Wolff, Bachof, Stober and Kluth, *Verwaltungsrecht I*, §51, at para. 57.

214 Peine, *Allgemeines Verwaltungsrecht*, at para. 967; Götz, *NVwZ* 1984, p. 480.

215 Stelkens, Bonk and Sachs, *Verwaltungsverfahrensgesetz*, 7th ed., 2008, §49, at para. 2; Bull and Mehde, *Allgemeines Verwaltungsrecht*, at para. 808.

216 Bull and Mehde, *Allgemeines Verwaltungsrecht*, at paras. 831 *et seq.*; Maurer, *Allgemeines Verwaltungsrecht*, §11, at para. 39.

Procedure

Both withdrawal and revocation, as has been said above, result in an administrative decision being annulled. Therefore, these two legal institutions, according to the 'Actus contrarius Theory', are to be characterised as administrative decision.[217]

Consequently, they are also subject to the rules pertaining to VA and, as a result, have to satisfy the formal and material criteria of a VA.[218] Furthermore, it follows that even an illegal annulment remains effective according to Section 43 II VwVfG, and may (eventually) become final.[219]

In principle, according to the wording of the law ('may'), the annulment of a VA is at the discretion of the agency (Sections 48 I and 49 I VwVfG); however, these provisions in the following paragraphs include numerous restrictions for the annulment of benefiting VA that can actually be reduced to two essential principles.[220]

For one thing, the principle applying here is the lawfulness of the administrative body which demands the restoration of the (original) legal condition.[221] In addition, the principle of legal protection of public confidence must be observed which requires due consideration for the beneficiary's confidence in the continued validity of the VA issued by the administrative agency.[222]

In the case of withdrawal as well as in the constellations of revocation mentioned above, these two principles are in conflict with each other.[223] While withdrawals always require careful consideration to determine which principle is dominant in any specific case,[224] a revocation according to Section 49 II VwVfG, always requires a special reason for revocation.[225] Therefore, in contrast to the withdrawal, a revocation is more narrowly defined by the law.

---

217 Stelkens, Bonk and, Sachs, *Verwaltungsverfahrensgesetz*, §48, at para. 1; Wolff, Bachof, Stober and Kluth, *Verwaltungsrecht 1*, §51, at paras. 51.

218 Maurer, *Allgemeines Verwaltungsrecht*, §11, at para. 20; Peine, *Allgemeines Verwaltungsrecht*, at para. 922.

219 Peine, *Allgemeines Verwaltungsrecht*, at para. 922.

220 Bull and Mehde, *Allgemeines Verwaltungsrecht*, at paras. 809 *et seq.*; Maurer, *Allgemeines Verwaltungsrecht*, §11, at paras. 22 *et seq.*

221 Götz, *NVwZ* 1984, p. 480; Stelkens, Bonk and Sachs, Sachs, *Verwaltungsverfahrensgesetz*, §48, at paras. 37 *et seq.*

222 Wolff, Bachof, Stober and Kluth, *Verwaltungsrecht 1*, §51, at paras. 3 *et seq.*; Götz, *NVwZ* 1984, p. 480.

223 Maurer, *Allgemeines Verwaltungsrecht*, §11, at para. 39; Bull and Mehde, *Allgemeines Verwaltungsrecht*, at paras. 810 *et seq.*

224 Kopp and Ramsauer, *Verwaltungsverfahrensgesetz*, 9th ed., 2005, §48, at paras. 57 *et seq.*; Peine, *Allgemeines Verwaltungsrecht*, at paras. 929 *et seq.*

225 Obermayer, Schäfer, *Kommentar zum Verwaltungsverfahrensgesetz*, §49, at paras. 18 *et seq.*; Bull and Mehde, *Allgemeines Verwaltungsrecht*, at paras. 664 *et seq.*

It should be mentioned that the period of one year, according to Section 48 IV VwVfG, must be observed (Section 49 II 2 VwVfG). It is generally held that this period is a time-limit for making a decision, not for processing, and it is based on the idea of forfeiture.[226]

4.2.4. Means to enforce administrative acts

General information

The following text explains by which means administrative acts can be enforced. Such means are not limited to administrative law. They are found in almost all branches of law as measures of law enforcement.[227] It is sufficient to refer to two examples: Section 888 ZPO, which serves to enforce non-delegable acts and Section 96 OWiG, which is aimed at enforcing the payment of fines imposed in conjunction with administrative offences.[228] Also of practical importance are the provisions covering the enforcement of certain acts by coercive police measures under *Land* (state) law[229] (*cf.* Article 54 BayPAG, or Bavarian Police Functions Act).

Of course, this study is limited to those measures of coercion that are imposed by administrative authorities, i.e., to measures that are administrative sanctions. Such sanctions are part of the enforcement under administrative law,[230] which includes compulsory enforcement of claims arising from administrative law.[231] In this respect, the nature of the sanction does not only extend to coercive measures, but to the entire range of enforcement under administrative law. In view of their exemplary importance, however, only coercive measures are to be introduced here.[232]

The law defines three different types of coercive measures: substitute performance, *Zwangsgeld* (coercive enforcement fine) with subsidiary coercive detention, and immediate coercion[233] (Section 9 I *Verwaltungsvollstreckungsgesetz* – VwVG, or Administration Enforcement Law). The essential rules pertaining

226 Kopp and Ramsauer, *Verwaltungsverfahrensgesetz*, §48, at paras. 145 *et seq.*; Stelkens, Bonk and Sachs, *Verwaltungsverfahrensgesetz*, §48, at para. 210.

227 Baumann, Weber and Mitsch, *Strafrecht Allgemeiner Teil*, §4, at para. 20; Maurach and Zipf, *Strafrecht Allgemeiner Teil*, Teilband 1, p. 7.

228 Jakobs, *Strafrecht Allgemeiner Teil*, p. 61 *et seq.*; Göhler and, Seitz, *Ordnungswidrigkeitengesetz*, §96, at paras. 1 *et seq.*

229 Maurach and Zipf, *Strafrecht Allgemeiner Teil*, Teilband 1, p. 7; Götz, *Allgemeines Polizei- und Ordnungsrecht*, p. 110 *et seq.*

230 Götz, *Allgemeines Polizei- und Ordnungsrecht*, p. 110 *et seq.*; Wolff, Bachof, Stober and Kluth, *Verwaltungsrecht 1*, §64, at paras. 53 *et seq.*

231 Bull and Mehde, *Allgemeines Verwaltungsrecht*, at para. 962; Peine, *Allgemeines Verwaltungsrecht*, at para. 1274.

232 Wolff, Bachof, Stober and Kluth, *Verwaltungsrecht 1*, §64, at para. 61 *et seq.*

233 Peine, *Allgemeines Verwaltungsrecht*, at para. 1297; Maurer, *Allgemeines Verwaltungsrecht*, §20, at paras. 17 *et seq.*

hereto are found in the laws governing law enforcement and public order, in the VwVG, in the respective state laws and in the *Gesetz über den unmittelbaren Zwang* (UZwG, or Immediate Coercion Act).[234]

Substitute performance

Substitute performance according to Section 10 VwVG is applicable when the obligated person fails to perform an act imposed on him/her. Substitute performance, to be precise, means the performance (by the authority or a third party) of a delegable act (such as towing a motor vehicle from a no-stopping zone) ordered by a VA.[235] In this context, an act is 'delegable' if someone other than the obligated person can perform it.[236]

In these cases the person concerned must tolerate any action linked with the performance and bear the resulting costs (Section 10 VwVG).[237] Beyond that, however, the obligated person remains unaffected by this coercive measure. Consequently, substitute performance, by its very nature, is the weakest type of intervention.[238]

Coercive enforcement fine/coercive detention

Moreover, according to Section 11, VwVG, a coercive enforcement fine can be imposed on an obligated person.[239] This type of measure is primarily considered in cases of non-delegable acts, acts of toleration, and failures to act because they cannot be enforced by way of substitute performance (for example, selling a noxious medical drug).[240]

Moreover, if the enforcement penalty cannot be collected, *Ersatzzwangshaft* (substitute coercive detention) can be ordered as a subsidiary measure (Section 16 VwVG).[241]

234 Maurer, *Allgemeines Verwaltungsrecht*, §20, at para. 4; Battis, *Allgemeines Verwaltungsrecht*, 3rd ed., 2003, p. 203.

235 Battis, *Allgemeines Verwaltungsrecht*, p. 205; Maurer, *Allgemeines Verwaltungsrecht*, §20, at para. 13.

236 Maurer, *Allgemeines Verwaltungsrecht*, §20, at para. 13; Bull and Mehde, *Allgemeines Verwaltungsrecht*, at para. 983.

237 Bull and Mehde, *Allgemeines Verwaltungsrecht*, at para. 886; Götz, *Allgemeines Polizei- und Ordnungsrecht*, p. 115 *et seq.*

238 Ipsen, *Allgemeines Verwaltungsrecht*, 7th ed., 2011, at para. 874; Bull and Mehde, *Allgemeines Verwaltungsrecht*, at para. 983.

239 Peine, *Allgemeines Verwaltungsrecht*, at para. 491; Bull and Mehde, *Allgemeines Verwaltungsrecht*, at para. 986.

240 Wolff, Bachof, Stober and Kluth, *Verwaltungsrecht 1*, §64, at paras. 73 *et seq.*; Peine, *Allgemeines Verwaltungsrecht*, at para. 1297.

241 Battis, *Allgemeines Verwaltungsrecht*, p. 205.

Hence, substitute coercive detention is not a means of coercion standing on its own. Instead, it is an aggravation of the enforcement fine.[242] Yet, it cannot be considered to be an administrative sanction, since – unlike the enforcement fine – substitute coercive detention is ordered by a judge, not by the administrative authority.[243]

Immediate coercion

We speak of immediate coercion according to Section 12 VwVG, if the enforcing authority directly forces the obligated person to perform an act, tolerate an act, or refrain from doing something, or if the enforcing authority itself performs the act.[244] Coercion is applied on persons or property by using physical force, auxiliary means, or weapons (Section 2 UZwG). Immediate coercion is thus the most stringent type of coercive measure and is therefore considered only as an ultima ratio, i.e., as a last resort,[245] when other coercive measures fail or are inexpedient (e.g., to detain a person).[246]

In borderline cases, it is difficult to draw a line between substitute performance and immediate coercion. In these cases, substitute performance is to be applied if the administrative authority itself performs the delegable act for the person obligated.[247] Otherwise, immediate coercion is applied if the authority's action is designed to attain a certain behaviour on the part of the person concerned.[248]

Nature of sanctions

Coercive measures do not serve to punish persons for a committed violation. Instead, they are designed to remedy a continuing illegal condition.[249] Their one and only goal is to counteract the continuation of an existing administrative injustice.[250]

---

242 Peine, *Allgemeines Verwaltungsrecht*, at para. 1297; Götz, *Allgemeines Polizei- und Ordnungsrecht*, at para. 401.

243 Bull and Mehde, *Allgemeines Verwaltungsrecht*, at para. 986; Berner and Köhler, *Polizeiaufgabengesetz*, 20th ed., 2010, Article 57, at para. 5.

244 Battis, *Allgemeines Verwaltungsrecht*, p. 205; Wolff, Bachof, Stober and Kluth, *Verwaltungsrecht 1*, §64, at para. 77.

245 Maurer, *Allgemeines Verwaltungsrecht*, §20, at para. 17; Battis, *Allgemeines Verwaltungsrecht*, p. 205.

246 Bull and Mehde, *Allgemeines Verwaltungsrecht*, at para. 987; Wolff, Bachof, Stober and Kluth, *Verwaltungsrecht 1*, §64, at paras. 64 *et seq*.

247 Maurer, *Allgemeines Verwaltungsrecht*, §20, at para. 18; Peine, *Allgemeines Verwaltungsrecht*, at para. 1299.

248 Peine, *Allgemeines Verwaltungsrecht*, at para. 1299; Maurer, *Allgemeines Verwaltungsrecht*, §20, at para. 18.

249 Winter, *NStZ* 1990, p. 374; Götz, *Allgemeines Polizei- und Ordnungsrecht*, p. 113 *et seq*.

250 Fliedner, *AöR* 1974, p. 243; Wolff, Bachof, Stober and Kluth, *Verwaltungsrecht 1*, §65, at para. 39.

This is also and particularly true for the coercive enforcement fine which is not considered a fine under the OWiG.[251] It is rather a mere enforcement measure, i.e., a means to enforce a person's future behaviour.[252]

Consequently, coercive measures are exclusively future-oriented and are therefore sanctions that are preventive in nature.

In addition, coercive measures have a remedial component in that they work towards the restoration of a legal condition.[253] This function is, however, of minor importance because the imposition of coercive measures, particularly the amount of the enforcement fine, is not directly connected with the harm which, for instance, is true of damages according to Sections 249 *et seq.* BGB.[254] Thus, the primary function of coercive measures is of preventive nature.

Procedure

According to Section 6 I VwVG, a prerequisite of the enforcement is that the enforceable administrative act is final or its immediate enforcement has been ordered (Section 80 II No. 4, III VwGO) or appeals have no suspensive effect (Section 80 II No. 1–3 VwGO).

In addition to these requirements, strict procedural provisions must be observed for the protection of the person concerned, before coercive measures can be taken.[255]

According to Sections 13 *et seq.* VwVG, the procedure itself can be divided into three phases: a warning, determining the type of measure, and applying the coercive measure.

Warning

According to Section 13 I VwVG, prior to a coercive measure being applied, a written warning must be given.[256] It must specify a certain period within which the person concerned can be reasonably expected to perform, and it must make reference to a certain coercive measure (Section 13 III VwVG), clearly identify it,

251 Sadler, *Verwaltungs-Vollstreckungsgesetz*, 8th ed., 2011, §9, at para. 15; Wolff, Bachof, Stober and Kluth, *Verwaltungsrecht 1*, §64, at para. 63.

252 Götz, *Allgemeines Polizei- und Ordnungsrecht*, at para. 397; Battis, *Allgemeines Verwaltungsrecht*, p. 205.

253 Wolff, Bachof, Stober and Kluth, Verwaltungsrecht 1, §64, at para. 63; Böse, *Strafen und Sanktionen im europäischen Gemeinschaftsrecht*, p. 48.

254 Böse, *Strafen und Sanktionen im europäischen Gemeinschaftsrecht*, p. 48; Wolff, Bachof, Stober and Kluth, *Verwaltungsrecht 1*, §64, at paras 64 *et seq.*

255 Götz, *Allgemeines Polizei- und Ordnungsrecht*, p. 118 *et seq.*; Maurer, *Allgemeines Verwaltungsrecht*, §20, at para. 20.

256 Ipsen, *Allgemeines Verwaltungsrecht*, at para. 885; Peine, *Allgemeines Verwaltungsrecht*, at para. 1301.

and – in the case of a substitute performance – include an estimate of the cost (Section 13 IV, V VwVG).[257]

Determining the type of measure

According to Section 14 VwVG, determining the type of coercive measure is the second phase of a coercive procedure. Such determination is done by the authority if the obligation is not met within the period specified in the warning.[258] The warning and determining the type of measure must correspond with each other in substance because otherwise the determination is unlawful.[259]

Applying the coercive measure

Finally, in the third phase of a coercive procedure, the coercive measure according to the preceding determination can be applied (Section 15 I VwVG). In the process of applying a coercive mesasure, any resistance offered by the obligated person – against a substitute performance or in the case of immediate coercion – can be countered by the use of force (Section 15 II 1 VwVG).

Enforcement must be immediately discontinued once its purpose has been achieved (Section 15 III VwVG). Their purpose being of a preventive nature, coercive measures become invalid and thus unenforceable at the moment the person obligated meets the obligation or the performance becomes impossible,[260] because the basis of the coercive measure no longer exists once the purpose of the measure is achieved.[261]

Legal Redress

Determining the coercive measure undoubtedly has the characteristics of a VA, the nature of the warning is controversial.[262] Nevertheless, this controversial issue can be left aside because Section 18 I 1 VwVG, clearly indicates that the hearing – at least with regard to legal redress – has to be treated like a VA. For this reason, the person concerned is not granted legal redress until afterwards –

257 Wolff, Bachof, Stober and Kluth, *Verwaltungsrecht 1*, §64, at paras 86 *et seq.*; Götz, *Allgemeines Polizei- und Ordnungsrecht*, p. 113.

258 Maurer, *Allgemeines Verwaltungsrecht*, §20, at para. 22; Ipsen, *Allgemeines Verwaltungsrecht*, at para. 888.

259 Peine, *Allgemeines Verwaltungsrecht*, at para. 1302; Maurer, *Allgemeines Verwaltungsrecht*, §20, at para. 22.

260 Wolff, Bachof, Stober and Kluth, *Verwaltungsrecht 1*, §64, at para. 85; Fliedner, *AöR* 1974, p. 261.

261 Fliedner, *AöR* 1974, p. 261.

262 BVerfGE 49, p. 170; Peine, *Allgemeines Verwaltungsrecht*, at para. 1304.

usually after an unsuccessful objection – by suing for rescission (Section 42 I, 1st Alternative VwGO).[263]

By contrast, the application of a coercive measure, according to the author's opinion, is a physical act that involves no further arrangements.[264] Consequently, it can only be attacked by way of an action for performance or by an action for a declaratory judgment.[265]

4.2.5. Disciplinary measures

General information

The last category of cases to be introduced at this point are disciplinary measures. As a rule, these measures are imposed by special courts or by special sections in courts of general jurisdiction.[266] Nevertheless, these reactions are also administrative sanctions because in reality their imposition by the courts is an administrative activity.[267]

Disciplinary measures have the closest affinity to criminal sanctions because – from a historical point of view – they have developed from criminal law.[268] Also attributed to this category are measures by professional associations and the disciplinary courts of the legal profession, the medical profession, and other professional groups that have disciplinary jurisdiction[269] because these measures are very similar to disciplinary measures[270] in that the main issues are a high degree of loyalty, obligation, and performance of a certain professional group.[271]

The most significant forms are the *Disziplinarrecht der Beamten* (BDG) (German Civil Service Disciplinary Act) and that pertaining to the military (*Wehrdisziplinarordnung*) (WDO) (German Military Disciplinary Code).[272] Also of importance are the disciplinary measures under criminal law relating to

263 Maurer, *Allgemeines Verwaltungsrecht*, §20, at para. 24; Peine, *Allgemeines Verwaltungsrecht*, at para. 1304.

264 Ipsen, *Allgemeines Verwaltungsrecht*, at para. 904; Maurer, *Allgemeines Verwaltungsrecht*, §20, at para. 24.

265 Peine, *Allgemeines Verwaltungsrecht*, at para. 1304; Ipsen, *Allgemeines Verwaltungsrecht*, at para. 904.

266 Tettinger, *Kammerrecht*, 1997, pp. 196–197; Wolff, Bachof, Stober and Kluth, *Verwaltungsrecht 1*, §65, at para. 32.

267 Fliedner, *Die Zumessung der Disziplinarmaßnahmen*, 1972, p. 29; Lochbrunner, *DVBl.* 1965, p. 309, 310.

268 Lambrecht, *Strafrecht und Disziplinarrecht*, 1997, pp. 24–25; Maurach and Zipf, *Strafrecht Allgemeiner Teil*, Teilband 1, p. 8.

269 Wolff, Bachof, Stober and Kluth, *Verwaltungsrecht 1*, §65, at para. 32; Baumann, Weber and Mitsch, *Strafrecht Allgemeiner Teil*, §4, at para. 29.

270 Fliedner, *AöR* 1974, p. 243; Maurach and Zipf, *Strafrecht Allgemeiner Teil*, Teilband 1, p. 11.

271 Tettinger, *Kammerrecht*, p. 195 *et seq.*; Wolff, Bachof, Stober and Kluth, *Verwaltungsrecht 1*, §65, at para. 32.

272 Jescheck and Weigend, *Strafrecht Allgemeiner Teil*, p. 14; Maurach and Zipf, *Strafrecht Allgemeiner Teil*, Teilband 1, pp. 9–10.

juvenile offenders which are disciplinary measures under juvenile law (Sections 13 *et seq.*, *Jugendgerichtsgesetz* – JGG, or Juvenile Court Act).[273] The individual system of possible reactions largely depends on the relationship between an organisation and its members.[274] Consequently, a clear line must be drawn between organisations that use compulsory recruitment (for instance, prisoners, Sections 102 *et seq.* *Strafvollzugsgesetz* – StVollzG, or German Penal Administration Act) and those that do not (civil servants, for instance; *cf.* Sections 1 *et seq.* BDG).[275] Analogously, the potential of sanctions differs greatly in the individual organisations. Typical examples in this context are a simple warning, a salary cut, or expulsion from the respective professional association.[276] In view of the great variety of forms of this category, the following discussion is limited to civil service disciplinary law to the extent which is deemed necessary.

Nature of sanctions

Disciplinary measures are designed to ensure discipline and integrity within the respective professional group and to avoid trouble by members of that profession.[277] In other words, their purpose is to encourage the allegiant to perform his/her duties correctly or to remove him/her from his/her position[278] if he/she is no longer tolerable for the ordinary conduct of business.

To this extent, at least, disciplinary measures are preventive in character. A controversial issue is whether such measures also have repressive elements.[279] The *Bundesverfassungsgericht* (BVerfG) (German Federal Constitutional Court) has consistently ruled in the affirmative,[280] explaining that a disciplinary measure is also at least 'a disapproving judicial reaction to culpable conduct'.[281]

Thus, according to the still prevailing opinion, disciplinary measures have both preventive and repressive characteristics.

---

273 Meier, Rössner and Schöch, *Jugendstrafrecht*, 2nd ed., 2007, §10, at paras. 1 *et seq.*

274 Jakobs, *Strafrecht Allgemeiner Teil*, p. 57; Häger, in: *Leipziger Kommentar zum Strafgesetzbuch*, vor §38, at paras. 77 *et seq.*

275 Müller-Dietz, *NJW* 1976, p. 919; Jakobs, *Strafrecht Allgemeiner Teil*, p. 57.

276 Häger, in: *Leipziger Kommentar zum Strafgesetzbuch*, vor §38, at paras. 78 *et seq.*; Baumann, Weber and Mitsch, *Strafrecht Allgemeiner Teil*, §4, at para. 29.

277 BVerfGE 21, p. 404; Taupitz, *NJW* 1986, p. 2852.

278 BVerfGE 21, p. 404; Tettinger, *Kammerrecht*, p. 196.

279 Baumann, Weber and Mitsch, *Strafrecht Allgemeiner Teil*, §4, at para. 30; Jakobs, *Strafrecht Allgemeiner Teil*, p. 57 *et seq.*

280 BVerfGE 26, p. 203, 204; BVerfGE 66, pp. 355–356; Appel, *Verfassung und Strafe*, p. 510 *et seq.*

281 BVerfGE 26, p. 204; Maunz, Dürig and Schmidt-Aßmann, *Grundgesetz Kommentar V*, 2006, Article 103, at para. 195; critical: Maurach and Zipf, *Strafrecht Allgemeiner Teil*, Teilband 1, pp. 10–11.

Procedure

The potential of sanctions against civil servants is conclusively laid down in Section 5 BDG.

Pertinent procedural rules are to be found in Sections 17 *et seq.* BDG.

According to these rules, the principle of mandatory prosecution applies to the institution of preliminary proceedings (Section 17 I 1, 2 BDG), while its implementation is subject to the principle of discretionary prosecution.[282] Thus, if a sufficiently clear indication is at hand, the institution of disciplinary proceedings is mandatory (the question being 'If'), whereas the implementation (the question being 'How') is determined by the disciplinary authority according to its best judgment.[283]

The principle of discretionary prosecution is defined in Section 13 I BDG. Consequently, it also applies to the decisions (Section 13 I 1 BDG) and assessments (Section 13 I 2 BDG) concerning disciplinary measures.[284]

If the proceedings are to be discontinued after preliminary proceedings have been conducted, a dismissal order will be issued (Section 32 BDG). On the other hand, if disciplinary action is to be taken, one or more of Sections 33 *et seq.* BDG, depending on the specific type of reaction, must be observed.

In conclusion, the possibilities of legal redress as provided by law are to be briefly discussed. As for legal redress, the BDG largely corresponds to the provisions of the VwGO. This is not at all surprising because, after all, disciplinary measures are VA.[285] So, as a first step, the person concerned must always make an objection in accordance with the rules (Section 41 I 1 BDG). It is not until such an objection has failed that legal action can be taken (Sections 45 *et seq.* BDG).[286]

4.3. APPLICABILITY OF CRIMINAL LAW PRINCIPLES TO ADMINISTRATIVE SANCTIONS

4.3.1. Introduction

The most important categories of administrative sanctions in the German legal system have just been discussed. The next step is to clarify to which extent

282 Köhler and Ratz, *Bundesdisziplinargesetz*, 3rd ed., 2003, §17, at paras. 3 *et seq.*; Gansen, *Disziplinarrecht*, 2005, §17, at paras. 1 *et seq.*

283 Fliedner, *Die Zumessung der Disziplinarmaßnahmen*, p. 22 *et seq*; Köhler and Ratz, *Bundesdisziplinargesetz*, §17, at paras. 3 *et seq.*

284 Gansen, *Disziplinarrecht*, 2005, §13, at paras. 1 *et seq.*; Köhler and Ratz, *Bundesdisziplinargesetz*, §13, at paras. 4 *et seq.*

285 Lochbrunner, *DVBl.* 1965, pp. 309–310; Fliedner, *Die Zumessung der Disziplinarmaßnahmen*, p. 32.

286 Köhler and Ratz, *Bundesdisziplinargesetz*, §13, at para. 3.

general legal principles, particularly criminal law principles, can be applied to administrative sanctions. In order to do so, as will be shown below, it is absolutely necessary to clarify the character of each individual sanction.

4.3.2. The principle of punishment determined by statutory law ('nullum crimen, nulla poena sine lege')

In the German legal system, the principle that punishment is determined by statutory law ('nullum crimen, nulla poena sine lege') is laid down in Article 103 II GG. It is one of the basic principles of (German) criminal law and, by emphasising the statutory prohibition of an arbitrary rule,[287] it substantiates the rule of law principle.[288] Thus, criminal law is, as Radbruch put it, 'not only the source, but also the limit to punishment'.[289]

Generally accepted are four forms of the principle of punishment determined by law:

The *Bestimmtheitsgebot* (their requirement of clarity and definiteness), the prohibition of analogy, the prohibition of retroactivity, and the exclusion of customary law.[290] In the course of this study, these principles will be discussed separately, followed by a clarification of the issue whether, or to what extent, Article 103 II GG, is applicable to the law on administrative sanctions.

Bestimmtheitsgebot ('*nulla poena sine lege certa*')

The *Bestimmtheitsgebot* (the requirement of clarity and definiteness) as defined in Article 103 II GG, is a special form of the general constitutional *Bestimmtheitsgebot* according to Article 20 III, 97 I GG, and sets even higher standards[291]; for, the more severe a threatened sanction is, the higher the demands on clarity and definiteness must be.[292] This requirement pertains to both the definition of the offence and the assessment of the sanction to be imposed.[293] The *Bestimmtheitsgebot* forces the legislator to define the conditions of criminal liability so clearly that the scope of application and the significance of criminal offences ensue from the wording or can be ascertained by way of interpretation.[294]

287 Wessels and Beulke, *Strafrecht Allgemeiner Teil*, at para. 44; Schmidt and Bleibtreu, Hofmann-Hopfauf and Schmahl, *Grundgesetz Kommentar*, Article 103, at para. 24.

288 Sachs and Degenhart, *Grundgesetz Kommentar*, Article 103, at para. 53; Pieroth and Schlink, *Grundrechte*, 27th ed., 2011, at paras. 1084 *et seq.*

289 Denninger and Wassermann, *Grundgesetz Kommentar II*, 3rd ed., 2001, Article 103, at para. 44.

290 Otto, *Allgemeine Strafrechtslehre*, §2, at paras. 1 *et seq.*; Denninger and Wassermann, *Grundgesetz Kommentar II*, Article 103, at paras. 44 *et seq.*

291 BVerfGE 78, pp. 381 *et seq.*; Jarass and Pieroth, *Grundgesetz Kommentar*, Article 103, at para.51.

292 BVerfGE 26, p. 43; Tiedemann, *Tatbestandsfunktion im Nebenstrafrecht*, 1996, pp. 197–198.

293 Jescheck and Weigend, *Strafrecht Allgemeiner Teil*, p. 137; Jarass and Pieroth, *Grundgesetz Kommentar*, Article 103, at paras. 52.

294 BVerfGE 92, p. 12; Appel, *Verfassung und Strafe*, p. 117.

This obligation serves two purposes.[295] Firstly, everyone must be put in a position to foresee what is prohibited under penal law and, in addition, what penalty can be imposed.[296] On the other hand, this obligation is to ensure that it is exclusively for the legislator to determine the conditions of criminal liability in advance.[297] To this extent, the *Bestimmtheitsgebot* from Article 103 II GG, contains a strict legal reservation that denies both the executive and the judiciary the power to make decisions as to the conditions for criminal liability.[298]

The prohibition of analogy ('*nulla poena sine lege stricta*')

The provision of Article 103 II GG, also defines a prohibition of analogous opinions by a court or the aggravation of a sentence.[299] This so-called prohibition of analogy protects the *Bestimmtheitsgebot* on the level of application of the law and is, therefore, primarily directed at judicial organs.[300] According to this prohibition, a person's conduct must not be brought under a particular rule of law unless the wording allows such an interpretation.[301] Consequently, the possible meaning of the law, as seen by a non-professional, marks the limit of the broadest interpretation.[302]

In other words, Article 103 II GG, specifies that any person subject to the law must be able to understand the wording of the law in terms of possible sanctions.[303] At the same time, this law supports the principle of the separation of powers (Article 20 II 2 GG) in that it is in the hands of the legislator, not of the judge, to declare an act as punishable.[304] Article 103 II GG, thus establishes a strict requirement for legislation by Parliament.[305]

---

295 BVerfGE 47, p. 120; Appel, *Verfassung und Strafe*, p. 117.
296 BVerfGE 92, p. 12; Jarass and Pieroth, *Grundgesetz Kommentar*, Article 103, at para. 51.
297 Dreier, Schulze-Fielitz, *Grundgesetz Kommentar III*, Article 103 II, at para. 38.
298 BVerfGE 92, p. 12; Appel, *Verfassung und Strafe*, p. 118.
299 Otto, *Allgemeine Strafrechtslehre*, §2, at para. 23; Jescheck and Weigend, *Strafrecht Allgemeiner Teil*, p. 134.
300 Von Mangoldt, Klein, Starck and Nolte, *Grundgesetz Kommentar III*, 6th ed., 2010, Article 103, at para. 155; Böse, *Strafen und Sanktionen im europäischen Gemeinschaftsrecht*, p. 393.
301 BVerfGE 75, p. 341; Von Mangoldt, Klein, Starck and Nolte, *Grundgesetz Kommentar III*, Article 103, at para. 155.
302 Wessels and Beulke, *Strafrecht Allgemeiner Teil*, at paras. 56 *et seq.*; Dreier and Schulze-Fielitz, *Grundgesetz Kommentar III*, Article 103 II, at para. 46.
303 Jarass and Pieroth, *Grundgesetz Kommentar*, Article 103, at para. 51; Appel, *Verfassung und Strafe*, p. 120.
304 Jescheck and Weigend, *Strafrecht Allgemeiner Teil*, p. 134; Schulze-Fielitz, *AöR* 1997, p. 6.
305 Appel, *Verfassung und Strafe*, p. 120 *et seq.*; Von Mangoldt, Klein, Starck and Nolte, *Grundgesetz Kommentar III*, Article 103, at para. 156.

Prohibition of retroactivity ('*nulla poena sine lege praevia*')

Another form of the principle of legality is the prohibition of retroactivity,[306] which, according to the prevailing opinion, puts the general rule of law principle into concrete terms.[307]

According to this prohibition, an offence can not be punished on the basis of a law that was created after the offence was committed.[308] The prohibition of retroactivity refers to both the 'If' and 'How' of criminal liability.[309] In other words, the legislator must not subsequently change the evaluation of the content of an offence committed in the past to the detriment of the perpetrator.[310]

This means that the prohibition of retroactivity gives an individual a reliable basis 'for adjusting his/her behaviour as he/she sees fit in order to avoid a punishable act'.[311]

Exclusion of customary law ('*nulla poena sine lege scripta*')

Finally, the prohibition of customary law ('nulla poena sine lege scripta') is to be attributed to the principle of legality.[312] According to this prohibition, it is not allowed to refer to customary law, i.e., to 'prevailing case law',[313] for the sole purpose of punishing a person or imposing a penalty higher than that provided by law.[314] Instead, it is exclusively statutory law that meets the requirements of Article 103 II GG.[315] In practice, the exclusion of customary law has largely lost its importance because its function has been taken over by the prohibition of analogy.[316] For this reason, this study abstains from a detailed discussion.

---

306 Degenhart, *Staatsrecht I*, 23rd ed., 2007, at para. 370; Jescheck and Weigend, *Strafrecht Allgemeiner Teil*, p. 137.

307 Dannecker, *Das intertemporale Strafrecht*, 1993, p. 250; Degenhart, *Staatsrecht I*, at para. 370.

308 Otto, *Allgemeine Strafrechtslehre*, §2, at para. 8; Appel, *Verfassung und Strafe*, p. 121.

309 Dannecker, *Das intertemporale Strafrecht*, p. 249; Wessels and Beulke, *Strafrecht Allgemeiner Teil*, at para. 48.

310 BVerfGE 95, pp. 131–132; Dreier and Schulze-Fielitz, *Grundgesetz Kommentar III*, Article 103 II, at para. 50.

311 Von Mangoldt, Klein, Starck and Nolte, *Grundgesetz Kommentar III*, Article 103, at para. 118; Appel, *Verfassung und Strafe*, p. 121.

312 BVerfGE 92, p. 12; Otto, *Allgemeine Strafrechtslehre*, §2, at paras. 27 *et seq.*

313 Schönke, Schröder, Eser and Hecker, *Strafgesetzbuch*, §1, at para. 9; Von Mangoldt, Klein, Starck and Nolte, *Grundgesetz Kommentar III*, Article 103, at para. 136.

314 Jescheck and Weigend, *Strafrecht Allgemeiner Teil*, p. 134; Wessels and Beulke, *Strafrecht Allgemeiner Teil*, at paras. 52 *et seq.*

315 Otto, *Allgemeine Strafrechtslehre*, §2, at para. 27; Schönke, Schröder, Eser and Hecker, *Strafgesetzbuch*, §1, at paras. 8 *et seq.*

316 Von Mangoldt, Klein, Starck and Nolte, *Grundgesetz Kommentar III*, Article 103, at para. 136; Schönke, Schröder, Eser and Hecker, *Strafgesetzbuch*, §1, at para. 9.

Applicability within the scope of administrative sanctions

In criminal law, the principle of legality and its four forms that have just been discussed is indisputably valid (Section 1 StGB).[317] By contrast, it is questionable whether the provision of Article 103 II GG, is also applied within the scope of administrative sanctions.

To answer this question, the widely prevailing opinion takes into account the purpose of the law.[318] According to that purpose, the provision protects against illegal punishment in terms of a 'disapproving judicial reaction to culpable conduct' by which 'an evil is imposed for illegal behaviour'.[319] Thus, a decisive factor for applicability – unlike in the merely preventive measure – is that the reaction also at least 'aims at repression and retribution for an illegal act'.[320]

The scope of applicability of Article 103 II GG, thus always extends to all forms of repressive sanctions.[321] Consequently, its protection is noticeable only in connection with those administrative sanctions that at least also pursue a repressive purpose.[322] In comparison, a broader applicability of Article 103 II GG, to other public measures, i.e., preventive or remedial measures, is rejected.[323]

Therefore, at least the *Ordnungswidrigkeiten* (administrative offences) from the range of administrative sanctions fall under the protection of Article 103 II GG[324] (*cf.* Section 3 OWiG) because they pursue repressive purposes (as well).

The same ought to be true for *Ordnungsmittel*, but in this case the BVerfG, very much like the prevailing opinion adopting the BVerfG's views, deviates from its own guidelines, i.e., from its own definition of the term punishment within the meaning of Article 103 II GG.[325] As explained above, *Ordnungsmittel*, as interpreted by the BVerfG, have a dual character and are also aimed at 'repression and retribution for an illegal act' because 'the offender is reproached with a violation of the law'.[326] Nevertheless, advocates of this opinion deny, without giving any supporting arguments, the protection of Article 103 II GG when it pertains to *Ordnungsmittel*.

317 Jarass and Pieroth, *Grundgesetz Kommentar*, Article 103, at para. 43; Schönke, Schröder, Eser and Hecker, *Strafgesetzbuch*, §1, at para. 3.

318 Umbach and Clemens, *Grundgesetz Kommentar II*, 2002, Article 103, at para. 117.

319 BVerfGE 42, pp. 262–263; Von Mangoldt, Klein, Starck and Nolte, *Grundgesetz Kommentar III*, Article 103, at para. 105.

320 BVerfGE 20, p. 331; Appel, *Verfassung und Strafe*, p. 124; critical: Denninger and Wassermann, *Grundgesetz Kommentar II*, Article 103, at para. 46.

321 Von Mangoldt, Klein, Starck and Nolte, *Grundgesetz Kommentar III*, Article 103, at paras. 105 *et seq.*; Dreier and Schulze-Fileitz, *Grundgesetz Kommentar III*, Article 103 II, at paras. 19 *et seq.*

322 See 4.2.1.

323 Von Mangoldt, Klein, Starck and Nolte, *Grundgesetz Kommentar III*, Article 103, at para.109.

324 BVerfGE 38, p. 371, 372; Von Mangoldt, Klein, Starck and Nolte, *Grundgesetz Kommentar III*, Article 103, at para. 10.6.

325 Volk, *ZStW* 83, p. 431, 432.

326 BVerfGE 20, p. 331; Maurach and Zipf, *Strafrecht Allgemeiner Teil*, Teilband 1, p. 6.

Yet, the person concerned is not totally without protection when *Ordnungsmittel* are imposed because they, very much like other non-repressive administrative sanctions, are subject to the general constitutional rules of *Bestimmtheit* and the protection of confidence.[327]

Similarly illogical is the prevailing opinion as far as disciplinary measures are concerned. Disciplinary measures, as has been shown above, also pursue repressive purposes.[328] For this reason, as a matter of principle, they also fall under the scope of applicability of Article 103 II GG.[329]

Nevertheless, the prevailing opinion also accepts blanket-clause-like statutory definitions as a sufficient jurisdictional basis for disciplinary measures.[330]

As a consequence, it seriously restricts the extent of warranties under Article 103 II GG, for disciplinary measures. In particular, the *Bestimmtheitsgebot* is practically not applied.[331]

As a result it can be said, that, in principle, Article 103 II GG protects against all repressive public measures, although there are certain exceptions in particular cases, which are not exactly comprehensible.

However, the person concerned is even in those exceptional cases not entirely unprotected. Here the general legal principles are applicable as in cases of other non-repressive administrative sanctions. Therefore, the *Rechtsstaatsprinzip* results in a *Bestimmtheitsgebot* for every kind of legislation[332] regardless of the specific moulding of Article 103 II GG.

Yet, the demands on the *Bestimmtheitsgebot* are not as high as in the case of Article 103 II GG.[333] In the same way, but less compelling, there is a prohibition of analogy in this area which results from Article 20 III 97 I GG.

Finally, a (common) prohibition of retroactivity has to be taken into consideration as well. This derives from the fundamental rights and the *Rechtsstaatsprinzip*.[334] However, it falls short of the scope of Article 103 II GG.[335]

In summary, the different shapes of Article 103 II GG as general legal guarantees are also valid for non-repressive administrative sanctions. In this

327 Maunz, Dürig and Schmidt-Aßmann, *Grundgesetz Kommentar V*, Article 103, at para. 196; Von Mangoldt, Klein, Starck and Nolte, *Grundgesetz Kommentar III*, Article 103, at para. 109.

328 See 4.2.5.

329 BVerfGE 26, p. 203; Dreier and Schulze-Fielitz, *Grundgesetz Kommentar III*, Article 103 II, at para. 19.

330 Sachs and Degenhart, *Grundgesetz Kommentar*, Article 103, at para. 59; Maurach and Zipf, *Strafrecht Allgemeiner Teil*, Teilband 1, p. 9.

331 BVerfGE 45, p. 351; Appel, *Verfassung und Strafe*, p. 125.

332 Maunz, Dürig and Schmidt-Aßmann, *Grundgesetz Kommentar V*, Article 103, at paras. 196 *et seq.*; Von Mangoldt, Klein, Starck and Nolte, *Grundgesetz Kommentar III*, Article 103, at para. 109.

333 BVerfGE 26, p. 43; Tiedemann, *Tatbestandsfunktion im Nebenstrafrecht*, pp. 197–198.

334 BVerfGE 72, p. 257.

335 BVerfGE 30, p. 385.

respect Article 103 II GG is the more specific guarantee, which restricts the normally higher demands to repressive reactions.

At last in German constitutional law the term penalty is used in a material sense.[336] This term has serious weaknesses and discrepancies, however.[337] Nevertheless, there has never been a discussion – except in the above stated exclusions – on which administrative reactions are included in this penalty term and which are not. A reason for this might be that there are no universal valid criteria.[338] Interpretations concerning the term are even functional and are made with regard to certain aims, i.e. the meaning of a term has to be set in relation to its usage.[339]

Therefore, it can only be decided in the particular case whether a sanction norm falls within criminal law or not. Since the results are convincing in contrast to the way they were found, the judgements of the *Bundesverfassungsgericht* have hardly been criticised by legal scholars so far, apart from the exceptions stated above.[340]

4.3.3. The principle of guilt ('nulla poena sine culpa')

The principle of guilt and responsibility ('*nulla poena sine culpa*')[341] also belongs to the classical warranties under penal law. Although this principle is not explicitly embodied in the German Constitution, it is generally recognised.[342] The principle of guilt is mainly derived from the state's obligation to protect human dignity (Article 1 I GG) and from the principle of the due course of the law (Articles 20 III and 28 I 1 GG).[343] As regards content, it states that a penalty must not be imposed unless the offence can be held against the perpetrator himself/herself.[344]

Consequently, an objectively criminal responsibility, in the absence of a charge against the person concerned, is excluded on the basis of the principle of guilt.[345] Accordingly, Section 15 StGB determines that the perpetrator can only be

336 Volk, *ZStW* 83, p. 433; Appel, *Verfassung und Strafe*, p. 236.

337 Appel, *Verfassung und Strafe*, p. 210.

338 Volk, *ZStW* 83, p. 433.

339 Appel, *Verfassung und Strafe*, pp. 210 *et seq.*

340 Volk, *ZStW* 83, p. 433.

341 Maurach and Zipf, *Strafrecht Allgemeiner Teil*, Teilband 1, p. 85; Wessels and Beulke, *Strafrecht Allgemeiner Teil*, at para. 396.

342 Jescheck and Weigend, *Strafrecht Allgemeiner Teil*, p. 23; Baumann, Weber and Mitsch, *Strafrecht Allgemeiner Teil*, §18, at para. 2.

343 BVerfGE 20, p. 331; Baumann, Weber and Mitsch, *Strafrecht Allgemeiner Teil*, §18, at para. 2; critical: Frister, *Schuldprinzip, Verbot der Verdachtsstrafe und Unschuldsvermutung*, 1988, pp. 28 *et seq.*

344 BVerfGE 95, p. 131; Baumann, Weber and Mitsch, *Strafrecht Allgemeiner Teil*, §18, at para. 1.

345 Baumann, Weber and Mitsch, *Strafrecht Allgemeiner Teil*, §18, at para. 2; Böse, *Strafen und Sanktionen im europäischen Gemeinschaftsrecht*, p. 155.

punished for an offence committed deliberately or negligently.[346] In other words, criminal liability without fault is not permissible.[347] Herein lays the function of the justifying criminal liability of the principle of guilt.[348]

In addition to that, however, it also includes a component limiting punishment[349] because another consequence of the principle of guilt is that punishment must be commensurate with guilt.[350] In other words, the extent of guilt determines the degree of the penalty.[351] This means that the preventive purpose[352] must not lead to the exceeding of a justified penalty.[353] This notion has also found its way into the law. After all, according to Section 46 I 1 StGB, the perpetrator's guilt is the basis for the degree of the penalty.[354]

In summary, the principle of guilt has both a justifying and a limiting effect on the penalty.

Now it is necessary to determine the scope of applicability of the principle of guilt. According to the prevailing opinion, this principle is not only used under criminal law[355] but also for all other repressive sanctions.[356] After all, these reactions by the state are also designed to 'confront a perpetrator with an illegal act and reproach him with it'.[357] A prerequisite for such a reproach is 'reproachability' or guilt.[358]

Thus, the principle of guilt is also applied to repressive administrative sanctions, specifically and above all to *Ordnungsmittel*,[359] to disciplinary measures,[360] and within the scope of administrative offences.[361]

---

346 Böse, *Strafen und Sanktionen im europäischen Gemeinschaftsrecht*, p. 149.

347 Tiedemann, *NJW* 1993, p. 28.

348 Appel, *Verfassung und Strafe*, p. 109; Maurach and Zipf, *Strafrecht Allgemeiner Teil*, Teilband 1, p. 85.

349 Roxin, *Strafrecht Allgemeiner Teil I*, §3, at paras. 51 *et seq.*; Jescheck and Weigend, *Strafrecht Allgemeiner Teil*, p. 25.

350 Wessels and Beulke, *Strafrecht Allgemeiner Teil*, at para. 398; Appel, *Verfassung und Strafe*, p. 111 *et seq.*

351 Maurach and Zipf, *Strafrecht Allgemeiner Teil*, Teilband 1, p. 85; Wessels and Beulke, *Strafrecht Allgemeiner Teil*, at para. 398.

352 See 3.4.5.

353 BGHSt 20, p. 267; Roxin, *Strafrecht Allgemeiner Teil I*, §3, at para. 51; Lackner and Kühl, *Strafgesetzbuch*, §46, at para. 23.

354 Fischer, *Strafgesetzbuch*, §46, at paras. 5 *et seq.*; Maurach and Zipf, *Strafrecht Allgemeiner Teil*, Teilband 1, p. 85 *et seq.*

355 Wessels and Beulke, *Strafrecht Allgemeiner Teil I*, at para. 396; Maurach and Zipf, *Strafrecht Allgemeiner Teil*, Teilband 1, p. 85.

356 BVerfGE 20, pp. 331 *et seq.*; Thomas and Putzo, *Zivilprozessordnung*, 32nd ed., 2011, §890, at para. 15.

357 BVerfGE 20, p. 331; Appel, *Verfassung und Strafe*, p. 113.

358 Hildebrandt, *Irrtum im Bußgeldrecht der Europäischen Gemeinschaften*, 1990, pp. 95 *et seq.*; Bohnert, *Ordnungswidrigkeitengesetz*, 3rd ed., 2010, §1, at para. 19.

359 BVerfGE 20, pp. 331 *et seq.*; Thomas and Putzo, *Zivilprozessordnung*, §890, at para. 15.

360 Claussen and Czapski, *Das förmliche Disziplinarverfahren*, 4th ed., 1998, p. 119; Maurach and Zipf, *Strafrecht Allgemeiner Teil*, Teilband 1, p. 9.

361 Maurach and Zipf, *Strafrecht Allgemeiner Teil*, Teilband 1, pp. 17–18; Lemke, *Ordnungswidrigkeitengesetz*, Einleitung, at para. 22.

Within the scope of OWiG, the term guilt is replaced by the term 'reproachability' (*Vorwerfbarkeit*), or blame (Section 12 OWiG). This choice of terminology is merely designed to link the reproach of an administrative offence 'with the element of socio-ethical disapproval'[362], an element that is not contained in the reproach itself.[363] In essence, the terms 'reproachable' and 'guilty' have the same meaning.[364] Consequently, the requirements for its mere presence are the same[365], although (in view of the lacking moral reproach) guilt in the case of an administrative offence is much less significant than in the case of a criminal offence. In this respect, criminal law rulings are also relevant to rulings under administrative law.

In summary, one can say that the principle of guilt serves to provide the perpetrator with the necessary protection against any excessively repressive measures by the state.[366]

4.3.4. *The principle of judicial power exercised by judges, Article 92 GG ('nulla poena sine judicio')*

Pursuant to Article 92 GG, judges are entrusted with judicial power ('*nulla poena sine judicio*'). This provision puts the principle of separation of powers from Article 20 II 2 GG[367] in concrete terms and thus formulates an objective constitutional rule.[368]

According to this rule, judicial power is exclusively in the hands of public courts and their judges, i.e., the organs of the legislature and executive are denied the exercise of jurisdiction by law.[369] This is designed to ensure effective legal protection.[370]

Criminal jurisdiction undoubtedly belongs to the main fields of jurisdiction because a criminal penalty has a particularly lasting effect on the legal status of the person concerned and is linked to serious ethical blame.[371] Consequently, the

362 Göhler and Gürtler, *Ordnungswidrigkeitengesetz*, vor §1, at para. 30.

363 3.4.4.

364 Bohnert, *Ordnungswidrigkeitengesetz*, §12, at para. 1; Göhler and Gürtler, *Ordnungswidrigkeitengesetz*, vor §1, at para. 30.

365 Hildebrandt, *Irrtum im Bußgeldrecht der Europäischen Gemeinschaften*, p. 93; Bohnert, *Ordnungswidrigkeitengesetz*, §1, at para. 19.

366 Lange, *Rätsel Kriminalität*, 1970, pp. 97 *et seq.*; Jescheck and Weigend, *Strafrecht Allgemeiner Teil*, p. 24.

367 BVerfGE 22, p. 76; Sachs, Detterbeck, *Grundgesetz Kommentar*, Article 92, at para. 1.

368 Jarass and Pieroth, *Grundgesetz Kommentar*, Article 92, at para.1; Dreier and Schulze-Fielitz, *Grundgesetz Kommentar III*, Article 92, at para. 17.

369 Dreier and Schulze-Fielitz, *Grundgesetz Kommentar III*, Article 92, at para. 17; Sachs and Detterbeck, *Grundgesetz Kommentar*, Article 92, at paras. 4 *et seq.*

370 BVerfGE 60, pp. 296–297.

371 BVerfGE 22, pp. 79–80; Dreier and Schulze-Fielitz, *Grundgesetz Kommentar III*, Article 92, at para. 33.

courts must not be deprived of their judicial power, nor must judicial power be transferred to an administrative body, not even for original (first instance) jurisdiction.[372] In this respect, it seems to be somewhat problematic that administrative sanctions, as the term indicates, are imposed by an administrative body, and not directly by a court.[373] Nevertheless, this can not be interpreted as a violation of Article 92 GG, in that administrative sanctions, contrary to criminal penalties, are the type of sanctions that are not linked to special socio-ethical disapproval. On the contrary, the person on whom such a sanction is imposed remains free from the stigma of a criminal penalty.[374]

On top of this is the fact that the imposition of administrative sanctions undoubtedly means public power within the meaning of Article 19 IV GG, and, therefore, is definitely subject to the possibility of judicial review.[375] Consequently, the person concerned, as has been shown above, can resort (by means of legal remedies) to a court.[376] The 'sanction procedure' by an administrative body is thus turned into preliminary proceedings, but this practice can not be seen as an infringement of the Constitution.[377]

Article 92 GG, thus lays down a requirement of judicial authority for criminal jurisdiction, but not for the imposition of administrative sanctions.[378]

5. SUMMARY

Summarising, it can be stated that administrative sanctions must be broken down into three categories of reactions: remedial, repressive, and preventive reactions. They greatly differ in terms of the requirements for application and also in terms of legal consequences.

The classical warranties under criminal law, particularly the principles of legality and guilt, also apply to measures that 'only' have a quasi-punitive effect in that they – regardless of the designation given by the legislator – also pursue repressive goals.[379] So, if the nature of a public measure is to punish someone for a committed offence, then the principles also applicable here are the principles of criminal law.[380]

Nevertheless, the person concerned is not totally unprotected when it comes to other types of sanctions. After all they must meet the general constitutional

372 BVerfGE 22, p. 49.
373 Jakobs, *Strafrecht Allgemeiner Teil*, p. 53.
374 BVerfGE 8, p. 207; Bohnert, *Jura* 1984, p. 20.
375 BVerfGE 8, p. 208; Wolff, Bachof, Stober and Kluth, *Verwaltungsrecht 1*, §65, at para. 13.
376 BVerfGE 12, p. 275; Appel, *Verfassung und Strafe*, p. 555 *et seq.*
377 Bohnert, *Jura* 1984, p. 20.
378 BVerfGE 22, p. 81; Wolff, Bachof, Stober and Kluth, *Verwaltungsrecht 1*, §65, at paras. 40 *et seq.*
379 Tiedemann, *NJW* 1993, p. 27.
380 BVerfGE 20, p. 332.

principles, too, like the principles of *Bestimmtheit* (certainty) and the protection of confidence.[381]

In conclusion, administrative sanctions have a considerable theoretical flaw: being less severe than criminal sanctions as defined by the Criminal Code, they are linked with a procedure that reduces the defendant's rights.[382]

381 Maunz, Dürig and Schmidt-Aßmann, *Grundgesetz Kommentar V*, Article 103, at para. 196; von Mangoldt, Klein, Starck and Nolte, *Grundgesetz Kommentar III*, Article 103, at para. 109.

382 BVerfGE 45, pp. 289–290.

VII. COUNTRY ANALYSIS – GREECE

George DELLIS*

1. THE GREEK LEGAL ORDER AND THE PUNITIVE POWERS OF THE ADMINISTRATION – GENERAL OVERVIEW

It is necessary to start with a brief overview of the national public law: constitutional[1], administrative[2] and criminal.[3] The fundamental norms of the Greek legal order are laid down by the Constitution of 1975 (as amended in 1986, 2001 and 2008). Greece (Hellas) is a member state of the European Union and has ratified the European Convention on Human Rights (ECHR).[4] Article 26 of the Hellenic Constitution (HC) lays down the principle of the separation of powers. While the executive power is exercised by the President of the Republic and the Government, the judicial power is exercised by the Courts which are

* Assistant Professor of Public Law at the Athens' Law Faculty, Docteur en Droit et habilité de diriger des recherches at the University of Paris II (Panthéon-Assas), ex référendaire at the European Court of Justice, author of the book *Droit Pénal et Droit Administratif, l'influence des principes du droit pénal sur le droit administratif répressif*, LGDJ, Paris 1997.

1 See Spyropoulos (F), Fortsakis (T), *Constitutional Law in Greece*, Sakkoulas eds. / Kluwer, 2009; Dagtoglou (P), *Die Griechishe Verfassung von 1975, JöR* 1983.355; Iliopoulos-Stragas (J), *Grundrechtsschutz in Griechenland, JöR*, 1983, 395.

2 Spiliotopoulos (E), *Greek Administrative Law*, Sakkoulas/Bruylant eds., 2004; Dagtoglou (P), *Constitutional and Administrative Law*, in Kerameus (K)/ Kozyris (P) *Introduction to Greek Law*, 3nd revised edition, Kluwer Law International / Ant. N. Sakkoulas Publishers, 2008, 23; Dellis (G*), Le citoyen, l'Administration et le droit communautaire*, rapport grec, FIDE, 1998. III.243.

3 Spinellis (D) and Spinellis (C), *Criminal justice systems in Europe and North America: Greece*, Helsinki, Finland: HEUNI, the European Institute for Crime Prevention and Control, 1999, 65 p; D. Spinellis, "Criminal Law and Procedure", in: Kerameus/Kozyris, eds., *Introduction to Greek Law*, op.cit., p. 459; "Recent Trends in the Greek Criminal Proceedings: Limiting or Expanding the Rights of the Accused?", (1989) 62 *Temple Law Review*1261; Anagnostopoulos (I), and Magliveras (K), *Criminal law In Greece*, The Hague: Kluwer Law International, 2000 and "National Monographs: Greece" in Lieven Dupont and Cyrille Fijnault, eds. *International Encyclopaedia of Laws, Criminal Law*, The Hague, London, Boston: Kluwer Law International, 2000; Mylonopoulos (K), "Greece", in: C. van den Wyngaert, C. Gane, H. Kühne and F. McAuleys, eds., *Criminal Procedure Systems in the European Community*, Butterworths, 1993.163;.

4 Legislative decree n. 53/1974.

independent vis-à-vis the other powers. (Public) Administration[5] is part of the executive, while criminal sanctioning is mainly a judicial task. From that point of view, sanctions imposed by (administrative) organs of the executive, must be regarded as being of an administrative and not a judicial nature.[6]

Greece is a unitary State organized on the basis of the decentralized model (Article 101 HC); its powers are divided between central (Ministries) and decentralized organs (Decentralized Administrations). "Local affairs" are

5 The term "administration" is used in the present study as being synonymous with "public administration".

6 For references to administrative sanctions in Greece in a language other than Greek see: Kroustalakis (E), 'Grèce – Le système des sanctions administratives', in: Commission of the European Communities, The System of administrative and penal sanctions in the member states of the European Communities, Luxembourg: Office for Official Publications of the European Communities, 1994, vol I, national reports, p. 118 *et seq.*; Spinellis (D), 'The Legal and Practical Problems Posed by the Difference Between Criminal Law and Administrative Penal Law', (1988) 59 *Revue internationale de droit pénal* 217–225; Pitsela (A), 'Greece: The current sanctions system', in: A.K. van Kalmthout and P.P. Tak (eds.), *Sanction Systems in the Member States of the Council of Europe*, Deventer ed., vol I., 1988.151; Anagnostopoulou (D) & Mouameletzi (E), *National Report* in F.I.D.E., *Berichte fur den 17. Kongress* (Berlin, 9–12 October 1996), "*Procedures and sanctions in economic administrative law / Procédures et sanctions en droit administratif économique / Verfahren und Sanktionen im Wirtschafts-verwaltungsrecht*" (Deutsche Wissenschaftliche Gesellschaft für Europarecht) 1996.76; DELLIS (G), *Droit pénal et droit administratif: l'influence des principes du droit pénal sur le droit administratif répressif*, Paris, LGDJ, 1997; Papakyriakou (Th), Das Griechische Verwaltungsstrafrecht in Kartellsachen – Zugleich ein Beitrag zur Lehre vom Verwaltungs- und Unternehmensstrafrecht (Schreiftenreihe: Studien zum Wirtschaftsstraftrecht, Bd 15), 2002; Papakyriakou (Th), ‚National Report', *in:* G. Dannecker and O. Jansen (eds.), *Competition Law Sanctioning in the European Union. The EU-Law Influence on the National Law System of Sanctions in the European Area*, Kluwer Law International, 2004.

In the Greek language see Lytras (S), Definition and basic distinction of sanctions in Greek law, Sakkoulas ed., 1984; Lytras (S) The notion of administrative fines and the constitutionality of their infliction, Sakkoulas, 1986; Lytras (S) The disciplinary phenomenon in modern Greek public law, Sakkoulas ed., 1989, Stassinopoulos (M), The real nature of administrative sanctions, Archeion Nomologias, 1950.89; Papadatos (S), The imposition of a disciplinary sanction and the "non bis in idem" principle, EDD, 1963.385; Rotis (V), The repetitive exercise of disciplinary coercion, Epitheorisi Dimosiou kai Dioikitikou Dikaiou, 1966.22; Hatzinikolaou-Vouzika (R), The implementation of the penal law principles on disciplinary infringements, DioikDik 1969.124; Papanikolaïdes (D), Definition and legal characteristics of Administrative Sanctions, Sakkoulas, Salonika, 1975, Darzentas (M), The autonomy of the disciplinary law of public servants, EDD 1989.5; Rotis (N), Reformatio in peius in disciplinary law, ToS 1979.45; Stavrou (S), The rights of the defendant in disciplinary procedures and Article 6 ECHR, EEEvrD, 1991.371; Symeonides (S), The expansion of the sanctioning functions of the public administration and the doubtfulness of its constitutionality, Dioikitiki Diki, 1992.495, Remelis (K), The legal nature of sports disciplinary litigation, Armenopoulos 1994.101; Vlahopoulos (S), The application of the principle "nullum crimen, nulla poena sine praevia lege" in the context of disciplinary administrative law, Dioikitiki Diki, 1999.564; Maniatis (A), Sanctions within the framework of the implementation of European Community law in Greece, Armenopoulos, 1999.457; Dellis (G), The specificity of the judicial review of administrative sanctions, Dioikitiki Diki, 2002.890; Dellis (G) Judicial review of the sanctioning functions of the independent authorities, Dike, 2003.1281; Kourakis (N), "The theory of the sanction: An introduction", ed. Sakkoulas, 2008.

endowed to self-governed local authorities, the Municipalities, and the Regions, which are established as separate public law legal persons.[7] Furthermore, there are many other public law bodies with special tasks (social security, education etc.). Since 1989, a new model of administrative organization, the independent authorities – organs actually established by the HC[8] or the legislator and totally exempted from the hierarchical control of the Government – is regularly used in Greece. All the above-mentioned bodies constitute the "Administration stricto sensu" according to a formal criterion (the legal personality of the authority is governed by public law). Nevertheless, the "Administration lato sensu", which includes all entities acting in pursuit of the public interest or the provision of public services (utilities etc.). is much broader; it encompasses, apart from the State and the other public law persons, public-owned companies and enterprises or other legal persons governed, at least in part, by private law and controlled by the State or other public law persons. The separation between stricto sensu and lato sensu Administration is important to Greek law since only the former is entrusted with the power to issue administrative acts that are subject to the special provisions of administrative law and judicially reviewed by the administrative courts. Therefore, only the sanctions imposed by bodies and organs belonging to the "Administration stricto sensu" are considered as "administrative", while similar acts imposed by entities and bodies belonging to the "Administration lato sensu" – also known under the term of the "broader public sector"[9] – constitute private measures not falling under the scope of public sanctioning.

According to the principle of the rule of law, HC establishes the hierarchy of norms and the duty of the Judiciary to review the constitutionality of laws (Article 93 para. 2 HC)[10] and the legality of the administrative action (Articles 94–95 HC). The right of access to the courts is also guaranteed. The basic principles of judicial organization are also laid down by the HC, according to the model of the duality of jurisdictions.[11] Civil and criminal justice is served by the same Order (civil and criminal courts), while administrative litigation is brought before the administrative courts, the latter being divided between the

7 L. 3852/2010.

8 Article 101A HC.

9 See among others, Article 9.1, L.1232/1982 (Article 9 para. 1), as amended by Article 51 L. 1892/1990.

10 Dagtoglou (P), "The Judicial Review of constitutionality of laws; some thoughts on the present state of constitutional law in Greece", Revue européenne de droit public, 1989.309; FLOGAÏTIS (S), "Judicial Review of legislative acts in Greece", in: Control in Constitutional Law, 1993, 145.

11 "Greece" in Council of Europe, Judicial organisation in Europe, Strasbourg: Council of Europe Publishing, 2000, 348 p. at pp. 151–169, Vegleris (F), "De la séparation des juridictions administratives et des juridictions judiciaires (particularités du système pratiqué en Grèce)", in: Ecrits Français I: Ecrits Juridiques, 1993.13; Efstratiou (P-M) and Sakellariou (N), "Greece", in: E. Spiliotopoulos (ed), Towards a Unified Judicial Protection of Citizens in Europe(?), Esperia Publications, London, 2000.341.

Council of State (Supreme Administrative Court)[12] and the Ordinary Administrative Courts of First Instance and of Appeal. Thus, administrative sanctions are, in principle, reviewed by the administrative courts.[13]

The principle of legality entails the obligation of the Administration to comply with the norms governing its actions in the sense that such actions must be according and not contrary to these norms. The Administration issues administrative acts that are of a regulatory or individual nature in relation to their content and scope ratione personae and ratione materiae. With respect to the presumption of the legality of the administrative acts, such acts have legal effect immediately after their entry into force, despite any potential flaw, if they are not duly contested and thereafter annulled or revoked. The individual administrative acts are not subject, in principle, to an incidental review of legality and they may not be challenged after the elapse of the period set for their judicial or non-judicial control and not by any authorities (judicial or administrative) other than those entrusted by law with the specific power to exert such control. Administrative sanctions are a special form of individual administrative acts and in particular a sub-category of onerous acts in the sense that they produce negative and unfavourable effects for their addressees.[14]

The protection of individuals and private law bodies vis-à-vis the State is guaranteed by the HC, which includes a list of basic rights and fundamental freedoms, some of which refer to the limits of criminal coercion.[15] It also relies on the general principles of administrative law[16] governing the actions of Public Authorities such as the principles of equal treatment, of reasonable and good administration and of due process. All these guarantees apply to administrative sanctions in their quality as onerous individual administrative acts.[17]

---

12 Poulitsas (M), „L'influence de l'institution du Conseil d'Etat français sur le Conseil d'Etat Hellénique", in Le Conseil d'Etat, livre Jubilaire, Paris, 1952.539; Gerontas (A), Die Griechische Verwaltungsrecht; eine Einführung unter besonderer Berücksichtigung der Rechtsprechung des Staatsrates, Enger Verlag, 1993.

13 See below, section 4.2.

14 See below, section 2.2.1.

15 Vouyoucas (C), "Le droit hellénique: principes constitutionnels et principes généraux applicables en droit pénal", Revue de sciences criminelles et de droit pénal comparé 1987.65; Tsourelli (L), "Human Rights in Pre-trial Procedure in Greece", in: J.A. Andrews, ed., Human rights in criminal procedure: a comparative study, M. Nijhoff eds, 1981.202, Spinellis (D), "Reform Movements in Criminal Procedure and the Protection of Human Rights in Greece", Revue internationale de droit pénal / International Review of Penal Law 1989.1127.

16 Spiliotopoulos (E), 'La transparence administrative en Grèce', in: La transparence administrative en Europe, 1990.95, M. Stassinopoulos, Le droit de la défense devant les autorités administratives, LGDJ 1976; Pavlopoulos (P), Calogeropoulos (A), Lytras (S), Procédure administrative non contentieuse et problèmes juridiques en Grèce, Annuaire européen d'administration publique, 1978.I.427; Chalazonitis (K), "Le droit de la défense devant l'administration en droit hellénique", Revue hellénique de droit international, 1984, 255.

17 See below, section 3.2.

Administrative law has, in part, been recently codified. Except for the relevant provisions of the HC, the main procedural rules and guarantees are included in the Administrative Procedure Code (APC – L. 2690/1999). The rules concerning the judicial review of the administrative action may be found in two texts, presidential decree (p.d.) 18/1989 regarding the Council of State and the Administrative Court Procedure Code (ACPC – L. 2717/1999) regarding the judicial recourse before the "ordinary" Administrative Courts. Such codification is far from exhaustive, however; except for special legislative provisions, case law norms in the field of administrative law are shaped and formulated by the decisions of the Council of State, even if, formally speaking, case law is not a source of legal norms within the Greek legal order. There is no special legislation governing the imposition and the regime of administrative punitive sanctions lato sensu except for the Public Revenue Collection Code (PRCC – l.d. 356/1974) that deals with the special enforcement proceedings for the collection of public bodies claims against their debtors (i.e., seizure of assets found in the possession of the debtor or of a third party, real property attachment, etc.).

2. ADMINISTRATIVE SANCTION AS A PARTICULAR FIELD OF PUBLIC ACTION

2.1. THE EVOLUTION OF SANCTIONING ADMINISTRATIVE FUNCTIONS

The imposition of sanctions as a means of administrative action is a legal method directly related to the evolution and the expansion of the administrative functions and the Administration itself. In the beginning, such public action was, if not inconceivable, at least not obviously compatible with the concepts of traditional liberalism: the State should limit itself to what is strictly necessary, while the monopoly of public repression should be entrusted to the Judiciary. Nevertheless, forms of non-criminal sanctions, such as disciplinary measures or tax penalties, already existed.

The liberal approach gave its place to the active involvement of the Public authorities in economic and social life following the concept of the welfare State. Such intervention, mainly through unilateral administrative prerogatives, produced specific restrictions in various sectors of human activity. Compliance with those restrictions could not rely exclusively on criminal sanctioning. The proliferation of criminally sanctioned offences[18] and the necessity to involve criminal courts or to improve the efficiency of public coercion called for

18 Courakis (N), "Financial Crime Today: Greece as a European Case Study", *European Journal of Criminal Policy and Research* 2001, 197.

extensive decriminalization and the imposition of non-criminal sanctions.[19] Despite the large-scale transfer of punishable offences from penal to administrative law, Greek law has not yet established an organized global system of decriminalization nor established any principle of the subsidiarity of criminal sanctioning in relation to other means of public reaction to illegal activities. In most cases, the same statute provides for administrative and criminal offences depending on the severity of the infringement.[20]

Finally, during the last 20 years, punitive administrative measures have considerably increased due to the evolution of the State's role in modern society. Public intervention mainly aims to *regulate* (and not to substitute) private activities and to organize public risk management for the benefit of the general interest. Such tasks are often undertaken by independent institutions that enjoy the power to impose severe administrative sanctions in order to ensure respect for public regulation and risk management. The fact that Greece joined the European Communities is also a factor that contributed to the appearance of new fields of regulation whose respect is entrusted to the mechanism of punitive administrative sanctioning due to the absence of criminal offences stemming directly from EC law.

2.2. DEFINITION AND TYPOLOGY OF ADMINISTRATIVE SANCTIONS

Neither the legislation in force nor the case law of the Council of State have formulated an "official" definition of administrative sanctions. Nevertheless, it seems that Greek law understands these sanctions in a narrow sense. Such legal category includes individual administrative acts inducing a punishment to their addressee, as a consequence of the violation of a norm or an obligation by that same person. From that point of view, they may not be identified with measures of a similar nature imposed by the courts (civil, criminal or administrative) on the one hand, and by bodies of the Administration *lato sensu*, but not governed by public law, on the other.

2.2.1. Administrative sanctions and onerous administrative acts

In addition, one should not assimilate administrative sanctions in Greece with the vast category of onerous administrative acts. Not every act producing unfavourable effects for individuals is an administrative sanction. Nevertheless,

---

19 Sykiotou-Androulakis (A), *Le mouvement de dépénalisation en France et en Grèce: l'alternative administrative*", Sakkoulas /Bruylant, 1995.

20 As an example, Mavris (K)., Spinellis (C), Zagoura (P), "Greece", in: N. Dorn (ed.), *Regulating European Drug Problems, Administrative Measures and Civil Law in the Control of Drug Trafficking, Nuisance and Use*, The Hague/London/Boston, 1999, 159–180.

such a separation is not an easy one. If unfavourable police measures – those used *a priori* in order to prevent a potential risk for the general interest – seem to be distinguishable from administrative sanctions, at least in many cases[21], it cannot be said that a separation between *a posteriori* onerous administrative acts and administrative sanctions is always obvious, at least when the unfavourable measure does rely on objective grounds.[22]

2.2.2. More or less "punitive" sanctions – stricto and lato sensu administrative sanctions

Moreover, the purely punitive character of the administrative sanction, in other words the fact that it aims to punish the offender as a form of retaliation for his behaviour, is often confused with other objectives, for instance those to redress the legal situation transgressed, to compensate the victims for such a violation or simply to safeguard the enforceability of the norms in force or of the (non-punitive) administrative actions already taken. From that point of view, it is possible to propose two definitions of administrative sanctions. On the one side, administrative sanctions *stricto sensu*, are those mainly having a punitive character. On the other side, administrative sanctions *lato sensu*, include rectification and execution measures as well. Such a division is not without practical value when the question relates to the special regime to be applied to those measures.[23]

---

21 This statement does not apply to every situation and to all "administrative police measures". If, for example, an operational licence for a coffeeshop is revoked due to the fact that the holder has failed to comply with fire safety regulations, such revocation is primarily aimed at the *a priori* protection of public safety but at the same time, it could be seen as a sanction *lato sensu* punishing the individual for the violation of the applicable legislation.

22 For instance, the withdrawal of an illegal administrative act that was beneficial to the addressee is an unfavourable act but not a sanction. The same holds true for the refusal to satisfy a request when the conditions are lacking under the law in order for such a request to be approved. On the contrary, if the administrative act relies on the behaviour of the individual concerned, such action, often, but not always, represents aspects of repression or reprehension.

23 For instance, if a taxpayer deliberately conceals a part of his revenue, the Tax Department may impose a fine (action A) due to his behaviour and an accrual on the tax to be paid (action B). Such an accrual is automatically imposed in all cases of incorrect revenue declarations even if the omission to declare was unintentional. The same authority also has the power to activate enforcement procedures (action C) if the tax payer refuses to pay, procedures that could even lead to the seizure of his assets (action C1) or, according to the previous legal *status quo*, to his imprisonment (action C2). Finally, it may request the criminal courts to prosecute and punish the taxpayer (action D). In this case-study, only action A constitutes an administrative sanction *stricto sensu* that aims to punish the individual, while actions B and C1 are unfavourable administrative acts whose objective is to compensate the losses of the State arising from the tax evasion (action B) and to enforce the payment of the taxes, fines and accruals by the taxpayer (action C1); they could be considered as non-punitive administrative sanctions in a broad sense although their quality as "sanctions" is contested in Greek law. Action C2 (imprisonment as a means of administrative enforcement and not as a form of

2.2.3. *Pecuniary and non-pecuniary sanctions*

Apart from the distinction between punitive, compensatory and "coercive compulsory" sanctions, another important division is between sanctions of a pecuniary and those of a non-pecuniary nature. Pecuniary sanctions are those that impose on their addressees the obligation to pay a sum of money (lump sums, fines, penalties). Non-pecuniary measures are measures that withdraw a certain benefit or produce harmful legal effects of any kind: deprivation of promotion as a disciplinary measure against a civil servant, the provisional or permanent withdrawal of an operational licence granted to an entity. Greek law also imposes sanctions with a moral tone, such as exerting blame on civil servants or the publication of the names of tax evaders (businessmen, actors, singers) in newspapers.[24]

2.2.4. *Disciplinary and non-disciplinary sanctions*

Furthermore, one could distinguish disciplinary from non-disciplinary measures. Despite the difficulty of making this distinction in some cases, disciplinary measures are those aimed at employees and members of an institution or persons affiliated to the latter; such sanctions reprehend behaviours in order to preserve the internal order of the institution on the basis of a written or tacit code of conduct or a general duty. Non-disciplinary sanctions are those imposed by administrative authorities against individuals (including legal persons) who are not linked to them through an "internal" legal relationship. The distinction is important for practical reasons: administrative courts have been more willing to apply additional guarantees originating from criminal law in the case of disciplinary action rather than in a non-disciplinary context.

It is useful to provide a non-exhaustive list of the principal domains and the typology of the administrative sanctions *lato sensu* within the ambit of the Greek legal order.

Disciplinary sanctions may be traced back to the legislation regarding the civil service, mainly the Code of Civil Servants[25], and the codes governing the exercise of various professions, such as lawyers, pharmacists and doctors, engineers,

punishment – judicially abolished in 2010 as contrary to the Constitution and the ECHR) is not an administrative sanction according to Greek law because it is imposed by the Administrative Courts of First Instance and not by the administrative authorities. If the taxpayer is sentenced to a criminal sanction (action D) by the criminal courts (a fine and/or imprisonment), such punishment exceeds the scope of administrative repression and is therefore governed by penal law.

24 Another form of "moral" sanction is the "*notice*" (warning) issued by the Authority for the Protection of Personal Data for minor offences under the relevant legislation (CS 2279/2001).

25 Article 106, L. 3528/2007.

architects, journalists etc.[26] Subject to disciplinary measures are also members of the armed forces, students, prisoners[27] and athletes[28] and any group of persons who are bound to follow a special – ethical, deontological or other – code of behaviour.

2.2.5. Sub-categories of non-disciplinary sanctions

Systems of non-disciplinary sanctions are provided for in almost every field of administrative action. Still, it is useful to distinguish between three different categories.

2.2.5.1. Taxation, customs and social security

This is one of the first and most common fields of punitive and severe administrative action. A vast range of pecuniary sanctions have been laid down by legislation.[29] For many years, such measures were not acknowledged as administrative sanctions, but as a means of compensation and civil liability.[30] In addition, they were not subject to review by the ECHR.[31] Actually, the situation is now changing and some of the fiscal and social security penalties are considered to be a specific category of administrative and even punitive sanctions.[32]

2.2.5.2. Protection of the public order *lato sensu*

Traditional police activities may lead to the imposition of administrative sanctions. Parking tickets, fines for traffic violations, even the suspension of driving licenses or the removal of car number plates are a common example.[33] The legislation on public hygiene and safety[34], applicable to bars[35], restaurants

---

26 For instance, for lawyers, l.d. 3026/1954, notaries, l. 2830/2000, hotel owners, Article 8, L. 1652/1986, undertakers of public works, p.d. 278/1999.

27 L. 2776/1999.

28 Remelis (K), The legal nature of sports disciplinary litigation, *op.cit.*, p. 101.

29 L.d 4/1968, art. 75 L. 2961/2001, arts 89 and 97 of the Customs Code.

30 CS 1562/1979, CS 2183/1965.

31 Nevertheless, it seems that the Court in Strasbourg is willing to extend the application of Article 6 para. 1 ECHR to the field of pecuniary fiscal penalties, like tax surcharges, see the judgment in *Janosevic v. Sweden*, 23 July 2002, case no. 34619/97.

32 Articles 30–33 L. 820/1978, L. 2523/1997.

33 Articles 34 and 107 Road traffic Code. This statute provides an interesting example of the combination of criminal and administrative sanctions. For instance, speeding tickets are issued by police officers; if they are not paid, the file is transferred to the judicial criminal authorities and may lead to the imposition of a minor criminal sanction. Furthermore, the law introduced a "points system" according to which road traffic violations will correspond to a number of penalty points. If the total penalty points within a certain period of time exceeds the threshold provided by the law, the driving licence is withdrawn.

34 Market Police Code, Legislative Decree no. 136/1946, art. 57A and L. 3668/2008. See also for safety in the workplace, p.d. 338–9/2001.

35 See also p.d. 180/1979 and p.d. 36/1994 for the protection of minors.

and many kinds of stores (groceries, supermarkets etc.) lays down administrative sanctions of a pecuniary or non-pecuniary nature. The same is true for labour law[36], education[37], social security[38] and trade legislation.[39] A "fertile" field for the imposition of administrative sanctions is the protection of the environment.[40] Any activity or omission that leads to negative effects for the environment (pollution, degradation etc.) and/ or is contrary to the legislation in force justifies the imposition of fines by the local authorities or the Minister for the Environment that may vary from 50 to 2,000,000 euro, the sealing of the premises in the case of unlawful land use or even the withdrawal of operational administrative licences.[41] Another common type of administrative sanction are the measures against unlicensed or unlawful building work by virtue of the town-planning legislation.[42] According to the dominant case-law, the fines imposed for such offences are regarded as administrative sanctions, while the compulsory demolition of a building, that follows these offences, is not qualified as an administrative sanction *stricto sensu* but as a non-punitive measure of administrative coercion.[43]

2.2.5.3. Public regulation

Administrative punitive action within the framework of the modern regulatory functions of the State, is by far the most crucial aspect of the present study and has to be examined separately for three reasons. First, in most cases it entails the imposition of purely punitive measures of considerable severity. Second, such sanctions are imposed by independent agencies that have extensive powers in rule-making, investigation and adjudication. Third, in the majority of cases, EU law is involved. Such administrative sanctions may be imposed when there has been a breach of the free competition legislation through agreements, concerted practices or an abuse of a dominant position[44], as a means to enforce respect for

---

36 L. 2874/2000, L. 2224/1994.

37 For private schools, c.l. 2545/1940, for music education, Article 5 L. 2557/1997.

38 L. 2084/1992.

39 Article 13 L. 396/76, the trade in wine, Article 2 L. 2538/1997 for pesticides.

40 Alexiadis (S), "Grèce [Greece]: Crimes against the Environment in Greece", *Revue internationale de droit pénal / International Review of Penal Law* 1994.959; Konstantinopoulos (G), "[Environmental Criminal Law] – Greece", in: Michael G. Faure and Günther Heine, *Criminal Penalties in EU Member States' Environmental Law*, Maastricht 2002.187.

41 Articles 22 and 30 L. 1650/86 for the protection of the environment in general, Article 13 L. 743/77 and p.d. 55/1998 for sea pollution, L. 2637/98 and l.d. 420/70 for illegal hunting and fishing.

42 Article 382 Code of basic town-planning legislation.

43 Article 382.5 Code of basic town-planning legislation.

44 L. 703/1977. See Papakyriakou (TH), *Das Griechische Verwaltungsstrafrecht... op.cit.*, *ibid.*, "National Report", in: G. Dannecker and Oswald Jansen (eds.), "*Competition Law Sanctioning in the European Union... op.cit.*, and Alexandridou (E), Das neue griechische Gesetz gegen Wettbewerbsbeschraenkungen, *GRUR Int*, 1978, pp. 238 *et seq.*; Christoforou (Th), "Greek Law on Competition: An Analysis of Twelve Years' Case Law", *World Competition*, 1990 vol.

the financial legislation regarding the provision of banking and insurance services and the functioning of the stock market[45] or in the field of Radio/Television broadcasting[46], Energy[47], Telecommunications[48] and Maritime[49] or Air Transport. Generally speaking, it has become common practice for the legislator to introduce a mechanism for administrative sanctions into new fields of public intervention.[50]

2.2.6. *Overall evaluation*

It is impossible to proceed to a global estimation of the total number of administrative sanctions imposed in Greece. Nevertheless, it would not be erroneous to confirm that a significant part of some public bodies' revenue stems from the fines or other pecuniary penalties received every year. In any case, the severity of the administrative sanctions is constantly increasing. Actually, most of the independent agencies acting as public regulators are entitled to impose fines up to 1.3 or 5 million euro or even 10% of the offender's annual gross income. Fiscal penalties are often calculated as a percentage of the non-declared revenue and, from that point of view, they may be unlimited. Compared to the pecuniary sanctions provided under criminal legislation and decided by the criminal courts[51] after respecting all the well known guarantees of penal law, administrative fines appear to present a much more significant risk for the individual's rights or interests. *Mutatis mutandis*, non-pecuniary administrative sanctions that deprive the individual of the right to exercise a certain activity, business or profession may lead to his financial ruin with all the self-evident personal and social effects of such a consequence. The permanent withdrawal of an operational administrative licence could be compared to an "administrative death sentence", given that it totally terminates the benefits for the individual stemming from his legal relationship with the public authority.

14, pp. 51 et seq.; Liakopoulos (Th), "New Rules of Competition in Greece", *World Competition*, 1992–3, p. 17; Oelher/Tzouganatos, "Zum neuen griechischen Kartellgesetz", *RIW/AWD* 1978, pp. 720 *et seq.*

45 L. 3556/2007, L. 3606/2007.

46 L. 2863/2000, 2644/1998 and 2328/1995.

47 L. 2773/1999.

48 L. 4001/2011, 4070/2012.

49 L. 2932/2001, as modified by Article 17 para. 6 L. 3260/2004.

50 L. 2472/1997 for the protection of personal data, L. 2639/1998 for labour and social insurance issues, L. 3023/2002 for financing of political and electoral campaigns, L. 3730/2008 for smoking ban, L. 3783/2009, for the identification of subscribers by mobile network operators, L. 3867/2010 for the supervision of private insurance, L. 3877/2010 for the protection and insurance of agricultural activity, L. 3896/2010 for issues regarding the equal treatment between men and women and many others.

51 Up to 15,000 euro pursuant to the general provisions of the Penal Code (Article 57).

2.3. THE INSTITUTIONAL ASPECTS OF PUNITIVE ADMINISTRATIVE ACTIONS

Almost every public authority may be endowed with the power to resort to administrative sanctions. Moreover, institutions entitled to decide individual regulatory measures are in principle authorized to impose sanctions. In that context, the involvement of a judge or a lawyer in the proceedings is not a prerequisite for imposing an administrative sanction.

In very few cases the punitive procedure is *structurally divided* into two phases, the investigative and the adjudicative one.[52] Only the final act in the procedure – in other words, the administrative sanction – is considered to be an administrative decision that produces legal effects and may be directly challenged before the courts. There is no established general rule stipulating that the investigating authorities, or at least the persons charged with the collection of evidence, must be different from those deciding upon the imposition and the determination of the sanction. From that point of view, the administrative regime offers less protection for the person being prosecuted when compared to criminal law. However, one could evoke the general obligation of impartiality that applies to administrative law and the case law of the European Court of Strasbourg, so as to contend that such a condition is not fulfilled when prosecuting, investigating and judicial powers are conferred on the same person.[53]

It is worth underlining that Greek law, following the example of the European Commission within the framework of competition law, has granted *extensive investigative powers* to the authorities in question, especially in the case of independent agencies. Many independent regulators currently enjoy the privileges attributed to the Free Competition Authority and, among them, the power to undertake inquiries, to have access to documents and to confiscate them, to visit premises even without a prior notification to the entities concerned (dawn raids), and to collect depositions under oath or unsworn.[54] In that context, the authorized personnel of the independent regulators have powers assigned to police officers in the field of criminal law to conduct preliminary interrogations.[55]

Another important aspect of punitive and severe administrative action is its *autonomy* vis-à-vis other administrative or criminal procedures.[56] This means that, in principle, every system of administrative sanctions is independent of other public law systems and may be activated and implemented separately from and

52 According to the Greek Competition Legislation, see L. 3959/2011.

53 See below, section 3.2.2.

54 See e.g. L. 4070/2012 concerning the National Telecommunication and Postal Authority.

55 The same holds true for public law bodies such as the "Stock Market Commission" and the "Food Safety Control Body" (EFET – L. 2741/1999), that are not organized as "independent agencies" properly speaking. It therefore seems that any authority entrusted with "modern regulation" tasks is also vested with extensive investigatory and sanctioning powers.

56 DARZENTAS (M), *The autonomy ..., op.cit.*, p. 668.

cumulatively therewith. An illegal behaviour may constitute several administrative and criminal offences that allow more than one authority to prosecute, investigate and decide upon the imposition of multiple sanctions in parallel. For instance, a TV programme that violates the privacy of an individual may lead to the imposition of an administrative sanction on the journalist concerned by the independent agency for a breach of personal data protection, another administrative sanction by the Radio and Television Authority and criminal sanctions by the ordinary courts.[57] The Council of State has recently stressed its commitment to the autonomous nature of the administrative sanctions towards criminal ones even in cases in which both procedures concern identical or extremely similar behaviours, despite the opposite approach of the ECHR.[58]

Furthermore, each authority is not in principle bound to follow the findings and the judgments that have resulted from other procedures and which were conducted by other authorities, administrative or criminal. For instance, the Administration may impose heavy fines for the smuggling of gas combustibles, even if the person concerned was acquitted by the criminal courts for the same offence.[59] Such autonomy may be limited in exceptional cases provided *expressis verbis* under the pertinent legislation. Tax legislation obliges the fiscal authorities to abide by criminal sentences imposed against tax evaders and to impose additional, administrative fines against the perpetrator.[60] On the other hand, the disciplinary authority must comply with a judgment of the criminal courts when a public servant has been acquitted, but only in relation to the facts ascertained by those courts.

Cooperation between the authorities concerning the carrying out of the investigation or the exchange of evidence is, as a general rule, neither compulsory nor prohibited. The pertinent acts occasionally refer to such collaboration, mainly between independent regulators.[61] In addition, there are situations where the investigative powers of the administrative law systems are used together with the investigative powers of the criminal courts and the information gathered by the criminal powers is used to impose administrative sanctions and *vice versa*. There are no specific provisions in Greek law to regulate mutual assistance between the administrative authorities on the European and international level, except for the duty arising under European law.[62]

---

57 CS 3545/2002.

58 See CS 2067/2011, CS 311/2012: The national Court directly refused to comply with the broad conception of the *ne bis in idem* principle that arises from the recent ECHR case law (judgments 10.2.2009 *Zolotukhin/Russia*, 16.6.2009, *Ruotsalainen/Finland*),.

59 CS 2950/1990 and CS (Plenum) 990/2004.

60 Article 21 par 3 L. 2523/1997 and the above-mentioned CS 2067/2011. Such cumulation of sanctions could, under specific circumstances, be in breach of Article 4 of Protocol no. 7 of the ECHR.

61 See L. 3959/2011 imposing cooperation between the regulators on telecoms and on free competition.

62 Directive 2002/94/EC (customs and excise), cooperation between the Greek Free Competition Authority or other national regulators and the European Commission according to Regulation (EC) 1/2003.

2.4. CONSTITUTIONALITY OF ADMINISTRATIVE SANCTIONS AS A FORM OF PUBLIC ACTION

It results from the analysis so far that punitive and severe administrative actions may not be ignored as a constitutional issue and some of the questions raised in that context cannot be easily bypassed. Yet, the only form of public punitive action referred to in the Constitution is the criminal one. There are no constitutional provisions referring expressis verbis to administrative sanctions. Only Article 96 para. 2 HC delegates to the legislator the discretion to assign minor cases – police offences punishable by a fine and petty offences relating to agrarian property – to non-judicial authorities such as those exercising police and agrarian duties, notwithstanding the fact that those decisions shall be subject to an appeal before the competent ordinary courts and such an appeal will suspend the execution of the sanction. This provision introduces a minor exception to Article 96 para. 1 HC by virtue of which the punishment of crimes and the imposition of all measures arising from criminal law belongs to the jurisdiction of the criminal courts. Therefore, it cannot be affirmed that the Hellenic legal order recognizes or rejects the phenomenon of administrative sanctions as a whole.[63]

Yet, the constitutionality of administrative sanctions stricto sensu has been contested in two ways.

Firstly, it has been argued that only judicial bodies are entitled to punish individuals and such power may not be transferred to administrative organs without violating the constitutional principles of the separation of powers (26 HC) and of the "natural judge" (Article 8 para. 1 HC). The courts have overruled that argument by denying the character of the administrative sanction as a means of retribution and punishment and by assimilating them to the other (non-punitive) means of administrative coercion.[64] This reasoning has been criticized by the literature[65] and does not correspond to the evolution of administrative sanctions for two reasons. On the one hand, there are many purely punitive sanctions imposed by the administrative authorities. On the other hand, the gravity of the sanction and the seriousness of its consequences vis-à-vis the individual's situation do not necessarily depend on the punitive character of such a measure. Thus the question remains: may the Administration be entrusted with the power to inflict such harm on the citizen on the basis of an a posteriori decision affirming that the latter has not complied with his obligations? Despite the fact that the conformity of the administration's punitive powers with the Hellenic constitutional order is certainly not crystal clear, the courts have given an affirmative answer to that question, but mainly for empirical and practical reasons (the efficiency of the administrative action, decriminalization).

63 Symeonides (S), The expansion..., op.cit., p. 495.

64 CS 538/1951, CS (Plen) 1825/1954, CS 2930/1974, CS 1396/1976, CS (Plen) 1854/1977.

65 Lytras (S) The notion of administrative fines..., op.cit.

Another argument was recently raised to contest the constitutionality of administrative sanctions imposed by independent regulatory agencies. These agencies have been given extensive authority to grant licences, to draft regulations, to exert administrative control and to carry out inspections as well as to reprehend any offences committed by persons or entities subject to their regulation. Such a compilation of prerogatives appears to be contrary to the separation of powers in the sense that the same organ acts as a legislator, a police authority and a judge. Although that opinion is not without foundation and, at the same time, it illustrates the important risk of arbitrary action in the functioning of a modern Administration due to the omnipotence of the independent agencies, the Council of State has consistently refused to adopt such a stance.[66] Therefore, it must be stated that the imposition of purely punitive and severe administrative sanctions is not considered to be in violation with the constitutional limits of public action. In principle and pursuant to the case law so far, the fact that such sanctions are imposed by authorities that enjoy also the power to formulate and implement the rules on the basis of which they are imposed, does not undermine their constitutionality.[67]

Nevertheless, punitive and severe administrative action is subject to a major constitutional limit regarding the nature of the measures to be imposed. Such severe and punitive action may not lead to restrictions on physical and individual liberty. According to Article 5 para. 3 HC "*personal liberty is inviolable; no one shall be prosecuted, arrested, imprisoned or otherwise confined except when and as the law provides*". In addition, Article 6 para. 1 HC requires a reasoned *judicial* warrant prior to any arrest or imprisonment. Moreover, Article 5 para. 4 HC – as amended in 2001 – stipulates that individual administrative measures imposing restrictions upon free movement or residence within and the right to enter and leave the Hellenic territory are prohibited, unless they are imposed as an additional penalty following a criminal court decision and then only in exceptional cases. Imprisonment as a means of compulsory execution of debts to the State was until very recently, provided for in some of the legislation despite its incompatibility with the ECHR. In year 2010, the Supreme Special Court (SSC) held that the legislation in question is invalid as contrary to the national Constitution.[68] Finally, since the administrative authorities are not entitled to

66 CS 3545/2002.

67 CS 96/2003: The Council of State pointed out that the establishment of the Authority for the Protection of Personal Data as an independent authority exempt from any form of administrative control and enjoying regulatory, normative, police and punitive powers, is not contrary to any provision of constitutional, EC and ECHR law. However, it is worth mentioning the dissenting opinion according to which the attribution of extensive powers to investigate of offences is not in conformity with the separation of powers.

68 SSC 1/2010. The issue was initially raised before the Plenary Session of the Council of State in order to examine whether compulsory incarceration for debts against the State is contrary to Articles 2 para. 1 and 5 para. 4 HC. Those provisions respectively establish the protection of human dignity and prohibit the imposition of individual administrative measures that

impose sanctions which restrict personal liberty and lead to the detention of a person[69] (*habeas corpus* limitation), they shall not be endowed with the competence to deal with serious crimes that should be punished by such measures. From that point of view, decriminalization is not an unlimited process that could marginalize the institutional role of the criminal courts.

To sum up, the Greek legal order considers nowadays administrative sanctions in conformity with constitutional norms, as a means to impose the respect of legality and the protection of values and rights established by the Constitution.[70] Nevertheless, since it often gives rise to the imposition of sanctions of a punitive nature and, sometimes, with extraordinary severity – even if they do not lead to the restriction of personal liberty – such administrative action is also a source of potential violations of fundamental rights and freedoms of the concerned individuals. To face such a risk, the national legal order shall, therefore, establish an appropriate regime for the administrative sanctions.

3. AT THE BEHEST OF A *JUS PUNIENDI*: A SPECIAL REGIME FOR ADMINISTRATIVE SANCTIONS?

3.1. GENERAL REMARKS

Given the acceptance of the constitutionality of punitive administrative actions, on the one hand, and the risks of arbitrariness that arise from the use of punitive powers by non-judicial bodies, on the other, the only way to safeguard individual fundamental rights is to submit such actions to an effective system of institutional, procedural and substantial checks and balances. In other words, to elaborate a series of norms that will neutralize the potential misuse of that form of public intervention.

A general overview of the legislation in force and of the dominant case law shows that, in Greece, administrative sanctions are *not* considered to be a field that should be clearly separated from other administrative actions. They are not,

---

restrict free movement. According to the preliminary judgement of the Section that submitted the case to the Plenum of the Council of State (CS 2611/2004), such restrictive measures seem not to be in harmony with the fundamental values prevailing in a modern legal system. Finally, the Plenary Session upheld the judgement of the Section and such position was also upheld by the Supreme Special Court.

69 Article 5 para. 4 HC.

70 From that point of view, the legislator may not exempt from punitive and severe administrative actions some categories of illegal land use, if such exemptions concerning the scope of sanctions and the responsibility of offenders are not justified by objective grounds. The Council of State has upheld that such a legislative provision is contrary to Article 24 HC for the protection of the environment, since it invalidates land protection established by law: CS 1440/1997.

at least not to a significant and sufficient extent, subject to a special regime which is based on a criminal rather than an administrative inspiration and origins, but are in principle governed by the general provisions of administrative law. Although a number of additional and exceptional guarantees have in many cases been given to individuals who may be subjected to punitive administrative action, it cannot be stated that this protection is extended to all kinds of sanctions or covers all. In other words, the Hellenic legal order has not yet fully admitted the necessity of a *ius puniendi commune* that will "transplant" the most important part of the traditional and unanimously acknowledged principles of criminal law to administrative sanctions.

Nevertheless, the internal law on administrative sanctions is bound to evolve under the influence of, if not pressure from European law.

On the one hand, administrative measures imposed against citizens as a means to safeguard the implementation of EU provisions, must comply with the fundamental principles and guarantees of the European legal order.[71] In the *Louloudakis* case, the Hellenic authorities had imposed a fine due to a violation of EC legislation on tax exemptions. With its judgment, the European Court of Justice (ECJ, Court of European Union after the Treaty of Lisbon) pointed out that, even with the absence of a harmonized system of penalties, the Member States must exercise their power to choose the appropriate sanctions in accordance with the general principles of Community law. Consequently, "*the administrative measures or penalties must not go beyond what is strictly necessary for the objectives pursued and a penalty must not be so disproportionate to the gravity of the infringement*".[72]

On the other hand, administrative sanctions, at least some of them, constitute "*criminal charges*" in the sense of Article 6 para. 1 of the ECHR. Following the *Garyfallou* judgment of the European Court in Strasbourg[73], a fine of 1,500 euro (1,500,000 drachmas at the time) imposed by the Minister of Commerce for a violation of national rules concerning imports and exports was "*sufficiently severe*" to be considered as a criminal charge for the purposes of the Convention. In that case, the Court reaffirmed[74] that any sanction pronounced by a public authority may be qualified as "criminal", although it is not defined as such by the

71 MANIATIS (A), *The sanctions…*, *op.cit.*, p. 458.

72 ECJ, *Louloudakis*, judgment of 12 July 2001, case no. C-262/99, point no. 67. In that judgment, the Court indirectly raised important questions such as the cumulation of sanctions *vis-à-vis* the principle of *non bis in idem* and the conformity of penalties which are predetermined by law with the principle of proportionality.

73 *Garyfallou AEBE* v. *Greece*, judgment of 24 September 1997 case no. 18996/91, *Mamidakis* v. Greece, judgment of 11 January 2007, case no. 35533/04.

74 Judgments in the cases of *Engel and others v. the Netherlands*, 8 June 1976, Series A no. 22; *Oztürk* v. *Germany*, 21 February 1984, Series A no. 73, *Campbell and Fell* v. *the United Kingdom*, 28 June 1984, Series A no. 80; *Weber* v. *Switzerland*, 22 May 1990, Series A. no. 177; *Lauko* v. *Slovakia*, 2 September 1998, case no. 26136/95; *Malige* v. *France*, 23 September 1998, case no. 27812/95; *Baischer* v. *Austria*, 20 December 2001, case no. 32381/96.

national legislation that establishes it, if such a qualification relies on the nature of the offence or the severity of the repressive measures taken. Therefore, guarantees offered by the Convention to any person facing "criminal charges" should be respected in that context as well. The "ECHR dimension" of punitive and severe administrative actions is becoming apparent in the case law of the Hellenic administrative courts[75], notwithstanding the fact that administrative sanctions are still mainly considered to be a specific category of administrative acts mainly subject to the principles and provisions of general administrative law.

3.2. THE GENERAL RULES OF ADMINISTRATIVE LAW IN THE FIELD OF ADMINISTRATIVE SANCTIONS

3.2.1. Legality – Competence

By virtue of the principle of legality, the use of sanctioning powers is not inherent in administrative functions, but has to be attributed *expressis verbis* by a legal provision to a specific administrative authority. The latter is empowered to use such powers only to the extent that the norms governing its actions acknowledge this specific competence. For instance, an administrative authority is not entitled to impose a fine exceeding the threshold set by the legislation.

Moreover, a law delegating to the administration a broad power to establish, by regulatory measures, a system of administrative sanctions would be contrary to Article 43 para. 2 HC; such measures (decrees or others provisions) would be *ultra vires,* since such a delegation would be considered insufficiently described by the legislator.

The courts review *ex officio* the legality and competence of sanctions even if the issue is not raised by the applicant.

3.2.2. Impartiality

According to Article 7 APC, all members of administrative authorities entrusted with decision-making powers must provide guarantees of impartiality. In the case of an existing or presumed risk of bias, the administrative sanction will be flawed on grounds of procedural *ultra vires.*[76]

---

75 CS (Plenum) 3319/2010, CS (Plenum) 990/2004, CS (Plenum) 2152/2000, Adm. Court of Volos, 53/1999. Stavrou (S), "The rights of the defendant in disciplinary procedures and Article 6 ECHR", *EEEvrD*, 1991, 371.

76 CS 664/2006, CS 3859/2002, 3411/2003.

3.2.3. *Right to a prior hearing*

Given the fact that administrative sanctions are unfavourable administrative acts, they may not be legally imposed if the right of the individual concerned to express his preliminary views, was not properly respected. The right to a prior hearing is a fundamental guarantee established by Article 20.2 HC and by Article 6 APC.[77]

First, the holder of the right has to be duly summoned to attend the hearing. The summons must specify the place, date, time and the subject-matter of the hearing and must be served at least five days in advance. In addition, the individual is entitled to be informed of the factual (but not necessarily the legal) elements that may constitute the basis of the sanction to be imposed against him and is also entitled to have access to the administrative file.[78] The hearing is not necessarily oral and may be limited to the submission of written documents and pleading. The individual can adduce counter-evidence and arguments that the repressive authority is obliged to take into account. Respect for all those procedural guarantees must be evident in the content of the decision which imposes the sanction and especially in its reasoning.[79]

3.2.4. *Reasoning*

According to Article 17 APC, the Administration has the duty to provide clear, specific and sufficient reasons for all individual administrative acts.[80] Such grounds should not necessarily be contained in the text of the decision itself, if such an obligation does not arise from the relevant provisions[81], but may be found in the administrative file. Nevertheless, pursuant to the dominant approach in the Hellenic legal order, sanctioning measures should include the most important aspects of their reasoning in the text of the measure itself.

A punitive measure shall be duly reasoned in two respects. Firstly, it shall contain the factual and legal elements that prove the perpetration of the infringement. Secondly, it shall present the grounds that justify the adjudication of the sanction.

3.2.5. *Notification*

The sanction will not have legal effect if it has not been served on its addressee. Nevertheless, according to general administrative law, if there has been no notification the administrative act itself is not invalid but remains idle.

---

77 CS 129, 673, 1399, 3272, 3816/2009, CS 1880–1, 2283, 2289–93, 3446, 4037/2008, CS 337, 405, 2042, 2408–13/2007, CS 103, 1213–15, 2861–62/2006, CS 4597/2005, CS 1022/2003.

78 Article 5 APC.

79 See also below, section 3.3.1, regarding the rights of defence.

80 CS 299/2006.

81 CS 1213/2010, CS 2532/2009, CS 43/2007.

3.2.6. *Stay of execution*

In principle, administrative sanctions have immediate effect automatically after their notification unless a stay of execution has been decided either by the administration itself or by the administrative courts as a means of interim relief. Exceptionally, the time-limit for initiating judicial proceedings against the measure and the lodging of the petition automatically suspend the execution of some punitive measures.[82]

3.2.7. *Use of discretion*

Despite the fact that, in some exceptional cases, the legislation determines the sanctions to be imposed for each particular offence, in general, there is a degree of discretion inherent in the power to impose an administrative sanction, since the imposing authority is normally in a position to choose between a variety of measures, as well as to determine the severity of the chosen measures. Such discretion may not be used arbitrarily but in harmony with the legal and relevant regulatory provisions.

Moreover, this discretion shall not exceed the limits set by the principles of *equality, good administration* and *proportionality.*

According to the principle of *equality* the Administration must "evaluate, on equal terms, the same legal and factual situations"[83]; the imposition of sanctions of different severity for the same prohibited actions must be considered contrary to the principle of equality. Similarly, the principle of *good administration* prevents administrative bodies from imposing sanctions that violate the legitimate expectations of the individual concerned or constitute a breach of the principle of *estoppel*. For instance, if the authority's acts or omissions have convinced the individual that his behaviour would not be punished, that authority is not entitled to change its policy after a "reasonable time" and then to prosecute the same individual. Yet, one should stress that the courts do not impose to the sanctioning authority the respect of a highly consistent and coherent sanctioning policy; sanctions may vary considerably from case to case.[84]

More important in practice is the principle of *proportionality* that has recently[85] been established *expressis verbis* in Greek administrative law, although some of its aspects were for a long time already being implemented as corollaries of the "good and reasonable administration" principle. Actually, proportionality

---

82 See below section 4.3.

83 Spiliotopoulos (E), *Greek Administrative Law, op.cit.*, pp. 352 *et seq.*

84 Nevertheless, the administrative authority may self-restrict its discretion through soft law: see below, section 3.3.2.1.

85 CS 2112/1984, CS 1426/1989, CS 1424/1990, CS (Plenum) 990/2004; Kontoyorgas-Theoharopoulos (D), *The principle of proportionality in internal public law*, Sakkoulas ed., Salonica, 1989.

is used to review the use of administrative discretion when appraising the determination and the severity of the administrative sanction in the sense that the sanction itself must be adequate and proportionate to the administrative offence committed.[86]

3.3. THE (LIMITED) TRANSFER OF CRIMINAL LAW PRINCIPLES IN THE FIELD OF ADMINISTRATIVE SANCTIONS

3.3.1. *"Repressive due process"*

Granting the person concerned a series of special procedural guarantees prior to the imposition of the sanction, known under the term of the *rights of defence*, is fundamental in almost every modern legal order.[87] Such rights aim to convert an administrative process into a "trial" similar to that under criminal law. In European law, they rely on a dual basis, the principles of EU law as formulated by the Court of the European Union on the one hand[88], and Article 6 ECHR on the other.[89] The idea is simple. Since an important part of the prerogatives of public punitive sanctions has been transferred from the judicial and criminal authorities to the non-judicial and administrative authorities through a vast process of decriminalization or the creation of new sanctions, additional to the criminal ones, the principles of legal certainty, of the rule of law and of the protection of the fundamental freedoms the individuals require a parallel transfer of the guarantees established by criminal law to the field of punitive administrative measures. From that point of view, "repressive due process" has to be followed prior to implementing a punitive administrative action.

Unfortunately, Greek law has not fully adopted that approach. In most cases of administrative punitive actions, the competent authorities or the judges do not refer to the rights of defence of the prosecuted individual but rather to the right to a prior hearing, in the sense that this is recognised under general administrative law as a prerequisite imposing an unfavourable individual action.[90] Nevertheless, the rights of defence should go beyond the simple right to be heard (*audietur et alteram partem*), given that administrative sanctions – at

---

86 See below section 3.3.3.3.

87 Tsourelli (L), "Human Rights in Pre-trial Procedure...", *op.cit.*

88 CEU, *Orkem*, judgment of 18 October 1989, case no. 374/97, Rec. 1989, p. 3283.

89 See the following decisions of the ECHR: *Ringeisen* v. *Austria*, 16 July 1971, Series A 13, *König* v. *Federal Republic of Germany*, 28 June 1978, Series A. 27; *Belilos* v. *Switzerland*, 29 April 1988, Series A. 132; D.J. Harris, "The Application of Article 6 of the European Convention of Human Rights to Administrative Law", *The British Yearbook of International Law*, 1974, 47, pp. 157 *et seq.*; C. Jacq, *Vers un droit commun de la sanction: incidence de la Convention Européenne des Droits de l'Homme*, Thèse Paris IX, 1989.

90 See above section 3.2.3.

least, purely punitive ones – significantly differ from the remainder of unfavourable administrative actions.

The components of a fair defence in the sense of "due process" include, in addition to the right to be duly informed of the procedure, to have access to the file and to have access to the grounds for the accusation (such rights automatically arise from the provisions of general administrative law), additional guarantees such as the right:

- to choose the means of defence and to demand an oral hearing;
- to resort to legal assistance or representation[91];
- to avoid self-incrimination(the individual concerned does not have to testify or assist the prosecuting and investigation authorities in a way that facilitates the gathering of evidence against him)[92];
- to be heard at the end of the hearing;
- to be heard with regard to each accusation (regardless of whether the accusation in question was included in the indictment or not)[93];
- to raise all kinds of arguments that may be useful to his defence including legal argumentation.[94]

Moreover, it would be contrary to the above-mentioned fundamental freedoms to apply to the rights of defence the same restrictions as to the right to a preliminary hearing in the context of general administrative law. In particular, the Administration should not evoke the ground of urgency in order to avoid totally its obligation to respect the rights of defence.

Recent judgments of the Council of State reveal that the supreme administrative judges are becoming progressively familiar with the specific nature and legal basis of the rights of defence in the field of punitive administrative sanctions.[95] For instance, they have held that the accused is entitled, by virtue of Articles 20 HC and 6 para 1 ECHR, to be represented by counsel during a procedure that may lead to the imposition of a disciplinary sanction even if the pertinent legislation does not establish such right.[96] Nevertheless, the opposite tendency, that continues to disregard the "sensitivity" of the punitive administrative procedure, has not been totally abandoned.[97]

---

91 See below fn. 96.

92 CS 689/2009.

93 CS 1152/2008, CS 2721/2007.

94 Such a privilege is granted only in the ambit of administrative sanctions and is not covered by the general right to prior hearing (CS 5711/1995).

95 CS 2447/2012, CS 3319/2010, CS 2514, 2077/2009, CS 1728, 463/2008, CS 3319, 981/2006, CS 3709, 1203/2005, CS 2797/2004.

96 CS 2364/2004, CS 2754/2002, CS (Plenum) 2152/2000, CS 37/1992, Adm. Court of Appeal of Athens 3524/1997, 1952/1991, 41/1990.

97 As an example, one could quote a case in which a member of an independent authority acting as a "reporting judge" in a procedure that led to the imposition of an administrative sanction

Due process in the field of public sanctioning is not restricted to the rights of defence. It includes the *fairness of the process* as well. As has already been explained[98], punitive administrative action does not necessarily follow the criminal law model regarding the clear and absolute separation of three different stages: the investigation, the prosecution and the trial. These stages are often interwoven.[99] Thus, it is difficult to lay down the specific guarantees governing each stage, especially those prior to the "adjudication".[100] Furthermore, the *impartiality* of the persons that make up the authority in question relies on the general rules of administrative law[101] and not on specific and stricter provisions adapted to the necessities of public sanctioning. In that sense, that authority may not always be regarded as "independent", at least pursuant to the case law of the European Court of Strasbourg.[102] This gap regarding the protection of the accused renders imperative that a judicial review of the administrative sanctions *lato sensu* is always available.[103] Yet, one should stress some steps forward: recently, the national judge held that in cases where sanctions are imposed by collective administrative organs, the *general principle of transparency* dictates that the relevant decisions are taken only in *public sessions* of these organs, namely in sessions where the access to public is free. Deviations from this general principle are only allowed for specific reasons which relate to the protection of public order and security, national defence, privacy and/ or the interests of minors. The abovementioned reasons should be laid down in specific legislative provisions, by virtue of which the collective administrative organs may decide – providing the required justification – the *in camera* holding of the session.[104]

---

was absent from the hearing during which the accused presented his defence. The Council of State considered that the member in question could be informed *a posteriori* of the defendant's argumentation through the minutes of the hearing and it dismissed the petition for annulment based on a violation of the rights of the defence: CS 2543/1999.

98 See above section 2.3.

99 The national courts do not insist on issues of structural independence in the sense that they have not opted for a strict implementation of the ECHR case-law. Therefore, the involvement of a person in more than one stages of the procedure leading to the imposition of an administrative sanction (for instance, at the phases of the investigation and of the adjudication) does not necessarily constitute a ground for annulment of the sanction in question. This issue is actually pending before the supreme administrative jurisdiction, regarding the role of the President of the Competition Commission in his quality as a) supervisor of the investigation, b) authority deciding on leniency issues and c) person presiding the collegium that takes the final decision whether there is a violation to be punished or not.

100 A good example of a case law insisting on the formalities to be followed at the "investigation phase" of the procedure is provided by judgments of the lower courts annulling sanctions imposed for environmental offences due to the absence of a duly drafted and signed investigation report (Adm. Court of Thessaloniki, 1/2000, Adm. Court of Athens 9765/1997).

101 See above section 3.2.2.

102 ECHR, *Procola v. Luxembourg*, 28 September 1995.

103 See below section 4.2.

104 CS 3319/2010.

3.3.2. *Legality in the context of punitive actions*

3.3.2.1. *Nullum crimen nulla poena sine lege*

Article 7 para. 1 HC lays down a fundamental guarantee that "*there shall be no crime nor shall punishment be imposed unless specified by the law in force prior to the perpetration of the act...*". It is not clear in Hellenic law whether this constitutional provision applies in the same way to non-criminal public sanctioning. The Hellenic Courts prefer not to refer expressly to Article 7 para. 1 HC in the case of administrative sanctions and in the past they have denied its application in the context of non-criminal sanctioning.[105] On the contrary, a large part of the literature has advocated the transposition of the Article 7 para. 1 HC guarantees to all kinds of public sanctions[106] or at least to those of a purely punitive nature[107], irrespective of their criminal or administrative character.

In the light of the above, it must be stressed that the principle of *nulla poena sine lege*, at least as an aspect of the legality principle, is indeed transposed to administrative sanctions. A provision delegating to the administration the general and unlimited powers to impose sanctions only according to its own discretion would be contrary to that principle. But in various contexts, the pertinent legislation gives the public authorities a particularly broad choice of sanctions (i.e., the imposition of fines from 1,500 to 1,500,000 euro) and this practice has never been considered contrary to a constitutional provision. In these cases the sanctioning authority may introduce restrictions to its discretion by announcing *ex ante* the criteria used for evaluating the severity of the offence.[108]

The principle of *nullum crimen sine lege* is respected even less restrictively.[109] On many occasions, the legislation establishing administrative sanctions refers somewhat vaguely to the violation of the legislation in force and not to specific infringements.[110]

3.3.2.2. Retroactivity

Pursuant to the general principle under administrative law, individual administrative actions do not normally have retroactive effect and do not extend

105 CS 2322/1983, in the case of an administrative sanction in the context of sporting regulations.

106 Manessis (A), *Constitutional Rights*, A., *Constitutional Freedoms*, 1981, pp. 196 *et seq.*

107 Dagtoglou (P), *Individual Rights*, A, 1991, pp. 267 et seq., Kourakis (N), "*Introduction..., op.cit.*, p. 20.

108 This practice has been successfully followed by the Greek Competition Commission; the courts held that the sanctioning authority is in principle bound to abide by the criteria set by itself.

109 See, Vlachopoulos (S), *op.cit.*, p. 565.

110 CS 3083/2000: a broad definition of the offence (illegal avulsion of forested land) in order to cover any form of afforested degradation.

back to a time prior to their notification. The same rule applies to administrative sanctions. Moreover, according to another general principle, the content of an individual administrative action is determined according to the factual and legal situation which exists at the time when it is imposed. As for the retroactivity of the norms in question, statutes may have retroactive force, apart from that introduce crimes or forms of punishment (Article 7 para. 1 HC), while regulatory measures cannot have retroactive effect.

Two questions arise: *Firstly*, what happens if, between the performance of the illegal behaviour and the imposition of the sanction, the law has in the meantime been modified in the sense that the administrative sanctions for that behaviour have become harsher? Does the prohibition of retroactivity extend even to non-penal crimes and punishments? This seems to be the dominant position, even without directly referring to Article 7 para. 1 HC. *Secondly*, in the case of normative amendments after the commission of the administrative offence or after the imposition of the administrative sanction that have the effect of reprehending that offence less severely, do such norms then have retroactive effect? The *retroactivity in mitius* of the norms imposing sanctions is well established in criminal law. The same approach may be found in specific legislation that determines a system of administrative sanctions[111] or in some diverse judgments of the administrative courts.[112]

3.3.2.3. Statutes of limitation for the offence. Amnesty. Clemency

In some cases the law provides for specific statutes of limitation for administrative offences. After the elapsing of such time-limits the administrative measure may not be activated. As for the rest, there is not a general and pre established limit *ratione temporis* for the imposition of the sanction.[113] Nevertheless, if the administrative prosecution or the imposition of the sanction will take place after a certain length of time, such use of public oppressive measures may be challenged as being contrary to the principle of "good and reasonable administration".[114]

An amnesty granted by certain statutes does not cover administrative offences, at least in principle. Measures of clemency may apply to administrative sanctions, for instance the restitution of car number plates (removed because of

111 For instance, Article 10 L. 2753/1999 introduces the principle of the retroactivity *in mitius* for a vast category of tax penalties. Moreover, the independent regulator on telecoms follows that principle even without any express referral in the relevant legislation.

112 CS 2233/2009, CS 2859/2003 (Plenum), CS 886/2000, CS 4973/1998, CS 2462/1981.

113 CS 1100/1995, "*the statutes of limitation which apply to criminal offences cannot be applied to administrative sanctions*".

114 CS (plenum) 602/2003. Recently, the Athens' Administrative Court of Appeals "created" a 5 year statute of limitation for stock market and competition law offences, despite the absence of such a provision in the relevant legislative texts (AACA 334/2009, 2017/2010).

parking violations) during holiday periods, or the partial reduction of some tax fines if the taxpayer decides to comply with the legislation in force.

3.3.3. *Responsibility*

3.3.3.1. Strict liability

In most cases, *strict liability* is sufficient. The sole infringement of a specific norm renders the offender automatically responsible for the violation and may lead to the imposition of the respective sanctions. Personal liability – in the sense of intent or negligence – is not a necessary condition for extra-criminal responsibility[115], although this is so in exceptional cases. Even then, the objective fact of non-compliance with the pertinent regulations constitutes a presumption of negligence. On the other hand, the absence of any negligence does not detract from the responsibility of the individual.[116]

3.3.3.2. Presumption of innocence

Speaking of presumptions, it is crucial to reiterate that, according to the ECHR, every person who is accused of an offence, even one of strict liability, must enjoy the *presumption of innocence*. The authority in question shall not depart from the preconceived notion that the prosecuted person is innocent; on the contrary, the authorities bear the burden of proof and any doubt should be for the benefit of the accused (*in dubio pro reo*).[117]

Those guarantees are followed in disciplinary cases, but are not officially established as a pillar of administrative sanctioning in Greece. Even worse, in many cases of administrative sanctioning, the pertinent legislation reverses the burden of proof as far as the defendant is concerned. It is not obvious whether such practice in all cases abides by the conditions laid down by the European Court of Strasbourg for establishing such presumptions against the accused.[118] The discussion is still open mainly in the context of severe sanctions imposed by independent regulators in the field of competition law. It seems that the courts are forced to recognize the fundamental guaranties in question but accept also broader restrictions regarding their implementation in the context of administrative sanctions.

---

115 The failure to duly notify a merger constitutes a ground for the imposition of an administrative fine by the Competition Commission despite the absence of negligence on the part of the undertaking concerned (CS 1732/2001). The same holds true for sea pollution. This may give rise to the imposition of severe administrative sanctions even if the individual proves his diligence at the time of the incident in question (CS 4390/1990, 2301/2000).

116 CS 1562/1979, CS 1253/1992.

117 ECHR, *Barberà, Messegué and Jabardo v. Spain*, judgment of 6 December 1988, Series A, no. 146, and *Janosevic*, judgment of 23 July 2002, *op.cit.*

118 ECHR, *Salabiaku* v. *France*, judgment of 10.1988, case no. 10519/83.

3.3.3.3. Choice of the appropriate sanction

Another group of guarantees traditionally offered to persons subject to a criminal procedure, are guarantees concerning the *determination of the proper sanction*. The severity of the punitive measure shall correspond to the specific characteristics of the offence committed by the accused.

Such a correlation is mainly achieved by a rigorous and elaborate application of the principle of *proportionality* in the context of administrative sanctioning. As has already been stressed, this general principle is familiar to Hellenic administrative law and is actually laid down by Article 25 HC.[119] In order to define a sanction which is proportionate to the violation, an *ad hoc* adjudication is always necessary. Such a test provides room for the individualization of the sanction on the basis of the specific elements of the particular case. If the eventual mitigating circumstances will reduce the severity of the measure, then an even harsher treatment of continuous offenders is also conceivable.

In general, the regulatory or legislative norms establishing the punitive powers of the Administration set the criteria for determining the sanction as well. Nevertheless, in some cases, the legislator does not give the authorities any room for discretion and predetermines the exact amount of the penalty for each specific infringement.[120] In such a situation, the person in question may not evoke mitigating circumstances that limit his liability. However, it is doubtful whether such a method of preventing the authorities from having the possibility to examine every case on an *ad hoc* basis adheres to the fundamental principles of *jus puniendi*. Some lower administrative courts have confirmed that the imposition of such sanctions is contrary to the fundamental principle of proportionality arising from the Hellenic constitution and the European Union legal order[121] and to Article 6 para. 1 ECHR proclaiming the right to a fair trial.[122] Nevertheless, the Council of State has not yet adopted a clear (positive or negative) position regarding predetermined penalties.

3.3.3.4. *Non reformatio in peius – non bis in idem*

According to a fundamental principle under criminal law, the punishment initially imposed on a person may not be reviewed so as to increase its severity. That same principle also applies to some categories of administrative sanctioning, mainly disciplinary measures within the civil service[123], although

---

119 An example of the proportionality test in the context of administrative fines for the smuggling of gas combustibles, in CS (Plenum) 990/2004.

120 Such practice is common in tax law.

121 Adm. Court of Thessaloniki, 984/2003.

122 Adm. Court of Volos, 53/1999, *Dioikitiki Diki*, 2000, 196.

123 Rotis (N), "*Reformatio in peius* in disciplinary law", *ToS* 1979, 45.

this has not yet been established in the case law as a general rule that covers all administrative sanctions, or at least all administrative punitive sanctions.[124]

Moreover, the question arises whether the prohibition of cumulatively punishing the same behaviour by instigating more than one procedure and by the imposition of more than one sanction – a prohibition which is well established in criminal law under the principle of *non bis in idem*[125] – is also respected within the framework of administrative law. As has previously been stressed[126], administrative punitive procedures are independent of one another and also to potential criminal procedures, even if they concern the same facts. Consequently, a certain behaviour may be contrary to several provisions, the infringement of each one giving rise to several procedures and sanctions. Apart from certain rare occasions[127], the Council of State has systematically overruled the argument that cumulative penal and administrative sanctions are contrary to the principle of *non bis in idem*.[128] It has also denied the existence of a rule preventing an independent administrative authority from punishing forms of behaviour already subject to a sanction imposed by another independent authority.[129] Such a formalistic approach may lead to situations which hard comply with the recent developments in the Strasbourg case law.[130] Nevertheless, the same Court upheld the infliction of a unique sanction for several offences arising from the same legislation since the opposite could lead to "excessive inclemency" *vis-à-vis* the offenders.[131]

Last but not least, it is worth noting that some of the procedural and substantive guarantees arising from the *ius puniendi commune* are not always suitable for administrative sanctions *lato sensu* and they should only be applied in the context of administrative punitive measures. However, it is important to underline that, since the distinction between punitive and non-punitive sanctions is often blurred, such ambiguity should not lead to "shrinking" the protection offered to the individuals concerned. Given that the field of "administrative punitive sanctioning" is constantly increasing and may lead to the imposition of extremely damaging measures (the withdrawal of administrative licences, fines amounting to several million euro etc.) the

124 Thus, the administrative court of appeals has the power to impose a fine which is higher than the one imposed by the court of first instance (CS 702/1987).

125 Anagnostopoulos (I), "Greece: *Ne Bis In Idem*", *International Review of Penal Law* 2002.965; Papadatos (S), "The imposition of a disciplinary sanction and the "non bis in idem" principle", EDD, 1963, 385.

126 See above section 2.3.

127 CS 2167/1992.

128 CS (Plenum) 990/2004, with interesting dissenting opinions. More recently, CS 2067/2011, CS 311/2012.

129 CS 3545/2002, CS 1013/1999, Adm. Court of Athens, 4160/2002.

130 ECHR, *Gradinger* v *Austria*, judgment of 23 October 1995, case no. 15963/90, *Zolotukhin* v. *Russia*, judgment of 10 February 2009.

131 CS 2513/1999, 2847/2001.

teleological dimension of the punitive or non-punitive aspect of those measures is secondary compared to the necessity to assure a minimum protection for those persons whose fundamental rights and interests are at stake.

4. REMEDIES

4.1. ADMINISTRATIVE RECOURSE

Before appealing to the courts against an administrative sanction, the person concerned may or, exceptionally, is obliged, to make use of the forms of *administrative recourse* laid down by the APC.[132] In that context, the person in question is always at any time entitled to have recourse to the authority which is responsible for the action (recourse for redress) or to the hierarchically superior authority (hierarchical recourse) and to request a re-examination of his case on the basis of its legality and its substance by virtue of Article 24 APC. Furthermore, in some cases, special provisions lay down a special administrative recourse that may be exercised within required time limits and this permits only a review of the legality of the contested sanction. Exceptionally, legislation may establish a mechanism of quasi-judicial administrative recourse that is compulsory as it first has to be resorted to as a condition for bringing the case before the courts.[133] The application has to be made within a fixed time-limit to a special authority that is empowered to review the case completely (as to its legality and merits).

4.2. JUDICIAL REMEDIES

As is apparent from the present analysis, it is of primary importance that the fundamental right of full and effective judicial protection should be strictly respected within the framework of administrative sanctioning.[134] Every measure containing sanctions *lato sensu* must be open to a potential judicial review. Due to the organization of the Hellenic judicial system, roughly presented above[135],

---

132 Tachos (A), "Le contrôle interne de l'administration publique en Grèce", *Revue internationale du droit comparé*, 1990, 967.

133 Public authorities are bound to inform the addressee about the existence of and the time-limits for quasi-judicial recourse against the sanction notified to him (CS (Plenum) 2893/1993.

134 Dellis (G), *The originality…*, *op.cit.*, p. 895.

135 See above, section 4; Spiliotopoulos (E), *Greek Administrative Law*, Sakkoulas/Bruylant eds., 2004, 261; Spiliotopoulos (E), Grèce, l'organisation de la justice administrative, *RFDA* 1988.240; Efstratiou (P-M) and Sakellariou (N), "Greece", in: E. Spiliotopoulos (ed), *Towards a Unified Judicial Protection of Citizens in Europe* (?), Esperia Publications, London, 2000, 341.

administrative sanctions are challenged before the administrative courts, but there are some exceptions: measures imposed by the police and agrarian authorities according to Article 96 para. 2 HC and those laid down by Article 5 para. 4 HC are brought before the criminal courts, while all actions against private bodies controlled by the State or other public authorities are heard by the civil courts[136], punitive measures included.

There is no specific recourse in Greek law dedicated to a judicial challenge of administrative sanctions before the Administrative Courts. These sanctions may be contested according to their quality as administrative acts by using the ordinary judicial means provided under the law.

Since 2012, the judicial control of the administrative sanctions is expressly assigned as a rule to the ordinary administrative courts[137] by means of a *recourse in substance*[138]: such control consists in a full review of the administrative act. It includes the review on the merits and the power of the judge to modify the sanction on the basis of his own appraisal.[139].

On the contrary, specific categories of administrative sanctions[140] are challenged before the Council of State through an *application for annulment*.[141] In that procedure, the extent of the judicial control is limited to the legality test, including the review of formal vices, legal errors, obvious factual errors and for excess of the limits of discretion. If the administrative sanction is only subject to such a legality scrutiny, the review is limited to the investigation of an "*obvious disproportionality*" that constitutes an "*incorrect use of discretion*" and which is a ground for annulment.[142] Even in the context of such a narrow scrutiny, the Council of State has elaborated interesting case law according to which the authority that intends to impose the most severe sanction allowed by law has the obligation to justify that choice by proving that any other, more lenient, decision would be inadequate and ineffective.[143] Nevertheless, since controlling the merits is not allowed, the question arises whether such a restriction, especially in the field of administrative punitive sanctioning, is compatible with the requirements of the European Court of Strasbourg.[144]

---

136 But there are some exceptions: measures imposed by the police and agrarian authorities according to Article 96 para. 2 HC and those laid down by Article 5 para. 4 HC are brought before the criminal courts, while all actions against private bodies controlled by the State or other public authorities are heard by the civil courts, punitive measures included.

137 And in some cases, before the Administrative Courts of Appeal,.

138 For instance, a full review of the sanction is established in case of severe disciplinary measures against civil servants.

139 Article 66 L. 4055/2012.

140 Mainly, those.

141 See Article 95, para. 1(a) HC.

142 For the application of the "obvious proportionality test" within the ambit of tax penalties, see CS 3129/2002. See also CS 477/2002.

143 Regarding the permanent withdrawal of an operational licence: CS 780/1999, CS 276/2000.

144 ECHR, *Albert and Le Compte v. Belgium*, 10 February 1983, *Fischer v. Austria*, 26 April 1995, *Umlauft v. Austria*, 23 October 1995. The answer to that question seems not to be in favour of

4.3. INTERIM RELIEF

In principle, administrative acts (including sanctions) come into force immediately after they are imposed and notified to the addressee, and they maintain their enforceable nature even if they are challenged before the courts.[145] In these cases, the party interested in suspending the execution of the sanction must lodge a separate *application for a stay of execution* before the judge who will hear the application for an annulment or the recourse in substance against such a sanction. The main judicial remedies shall have already been exercised when the application for a stay of execution is lodged. It must be stressed that, in Greece, the decision concerning such a suspension depends mainly on the nature and the gravity of the damage caused by the execution of the sanction. The applicant has to prove "*irreversible*" damage in order to achieve the necessary stay of execution.[146] Exceptionally, the application is upheld if the main application for annulment is "obviously well grounded" and is rejected when the main law suits are "obviously inadmissible or unfounded". Except for the stay of execution[147], the legislation does not lay down any other procedures for the judge to grant provisional measures.[148]

---

the Hellenic judicial system. The administrative courts when hearing an application for an annulment are not empowered to establish and assess the facts of the case. They are not entitled to substitute their own decision for that of the authority concerned, but always have to remit the case to that authority. Their review is confined exclusively to questions of law and therefore they could not be regarded as being equivalent to a body with "*full jurisdiction*". Despite its inherent weaknesses, the legality test in the application for an annulment has not been clearly criticized by the European Court of Strasbourg –until now, at least – as being insufficient in relation to the standards in Article 6 ECHR. The case was recently raised by the Plenary Session of the Council of State in its 3319/2010 judgment. It seems that the Council of State considers that if the administrative sanction falls under a limited judicial scrutiny, the fundamental rights of defence arising from the ECHR shall be more severely respected by the sanctioning authority.

145 See above section 3.2.6. Except for some specific cases where the legislation provides that the sanction is not enforceable during the time-limit for its judicial review and if such a review is requested, as long as the case is pending. Such a benefit is given to civil servants who have been subjected to severe disciplinary sanctions and also in the field of tax litigation.

146 Until the entry into force of L. 3900/2010, the applicant might also prove "*hardly reversible damage*", according to Article 202 L. 2717/1999 (Administrative Court Procedure Code).

147 Interim relief has been narrowed after L. 3900/2010 especially in cases concerning fiscal sanctions and fines.

148 Yet, in the context of the procedure under review, the judge may pronounce, apart from the suspension of the challenged act, any other appropriate measure for interim relief.

SELECTED BIBLIOGRAPHY

HELLENIC PUBLIC LAW (IN LANGUAGES OTHER THAN GREEK)

Chalazonitis (K), "Le droit de la défense devant l'administration en droit hellénique", *Revue hellénique de droit international,* 1984.255.

Dagtoglou (P), "Constitutional and Administrative Law", in: K. Kerameus/ P. Kozyris *Introduction to Greek Law,* 3nd revised edition, Kluwer Law International / Ant. N. Sakkoulas Publishers, 2008, 23.

Dagtoglou (P), "Die Griechische Verfassung von 1975", *JöR* 1983, 355.

Dagtoglou (P), "The Judicial Review of constitutionality of laws; some thoughts on the present state of constitutional law in Greece", *Revue européenne de droit public,* 1989, 309.

Dellis (G), Le citoyen, l'Administration et le droit communautaire, rapport grec, FIDE, 1998, III, 243.

Efstratiou (P-M) and Sakellariou (N), Greece, in E. Spiliotopoulos(ed), *Towards a Unified Judicial Protection of Citizens in Europe*(?), Esperia Publications, London, 2000, 341.

Flogaïτιs (S), "Judicial Review of legislative acts in Greece", in *Control in Constitutional Law,* 1993, 145.

Gerontas (A), *Die Griechische Verwaltungsrecht; eine Einführung unter besonderer Berücksichtigung der Recthsprechung des Staatsrates,* Enger Verlag, 1993.

Iliopoulos-Stragas (J), *Grundrechtsschutz in Griechenland, JöR,* 1983, 395.

Pavlopoulos (P), Calogeropoulos (A), Lytras (S), Procédure administrative non contentieuse et problèmes juridiques en Grèce, *Annuaire européen d'administration publique,* 1978, I, 427.

Spiliotopoulos (E), "Grèce, l'organisation de la justice administrative", *RFDA* 1988, 240.

Spiliotopoulos (E), *Greek Administrative Law,* Sakkoulas/Bruylant eds., 2004.

Spiliotopoulos (E), "La transparence administrative en Grèce", in: *La transparence administrative en Europe,* 1990, 95.

Spyropoulos (F), Fortsakis (T), *Constitutional Law in Greece,* Sakkoulas eds. / Kluwer, 2009.

Stassinopoulos (M), *Le droit de la défense devant les autorités administratives,* LGDJ 1976.

Tachos (A), "Le contrôle interne de l'administration publique en Grèce", *Revue internationale du droit comparé,* 1990, 967.

HELLENIC CRIMINAL LAW (IN LANGUAGES OTHER THAN GREEK)

Anagnostopoulos (I), "Greece: *Ne Bis In Idem*", *International Review of Penal Law* 2002, 965.

Anagnostopoulos (I), and MAGLIVERAS (K), *Criminal law in Greece,* The Hague: Kluwer Law International, 2000 and "National Monographs: Greece", in: Lieven

Dupont and Cyrille Fijnaut, eds. *International Encyclopaedia of Laws, Criminal Law*, The Hague, London, Boston: Kluwer Law International, 2000.

Courakis (N), "Financial Crime Today: Greece as a European Case Study", *European Journal of Criminal Policy and Research* 2001, 197.

Mylonopoulos (K), "Greece", in: C. van den Wyngaert, C. Gane, H. Kühne and F. McAuleys, eds., *Criminal Procedure Systems in the European Community*, Butterworths, 1993, 163.

Spinellis (D) "Recent Trends in the Greek Criminal Proceedings: Limiting or Expanding the Rights of the Accused?", (1989) 62 *Temple Law Review* 1261.

Spinellis (D), "Criminal Law and Procedure", in: K. KERAMEUS and P. KOZYRIS, eds., *Introduction to Greek Law, op.cit.*, p. 459.

Spinellis (D), Reform Movements in Criminal Procedure and the Protection of Human Rights in Greece", *Revue internationale de droit pénal / International Review of Penal Law* 1989, 1127.

Spinellis (D), and Spinellis (C), *Criminal justice systems in Europe and North America: Greece*, Helsinki, Finland: HEUNI, the European Institute for Crime Prevention and Control, 1999, 65.

Tsourelli (L), "Human Rights in Pre-trial Procedure in Greece", in: J.A. Andrews, ed., *Human rights in criminal procedure: a comparative study*, M. Nijhoff eds, 1981, 202

Vouyoucas (C), "Le droit hellénique: principes constitutionnels et principes généraux applicables en droit pénal", *Revue de sciences criminelles et de droit pénal comparé* 1987, 65.

ADMINISTRATIVE SANCTIONS IN GREECE (IN LANGUAGES OTHER THAN GREEK)

Anagnostopoulou (D) & Mouameletzi (E), *National Report* in F.I.D.E., Berichte fur den 17. Kongress (Berlin, 9–12 October 1996), "*Procedures and sanctions in economic administrative law/Procedures et sanctions en droit administratif economique/ Verfahren und Sanktionen im Wirtschaftsverwaltungsrecht*" (Deutsche Wissenschaftliche Gesellschaft fur Europarecht) 1996, 76.

Dellis (G), *Droit pénal et droit administratif: l'influence des principes du droit pénal sur le droit administratif répressif*, Paris, LGDJ, 1997.

Kroustalakis (E), "Grèce – Le système des sanctions administratives", in: Commission Of The European Communities, *The System of administrative and penal sanctions in the member states of the European Communities*, Luxembourg: Office for Official Publications of the European Communities, 1994, vol I, national reports, pp. 118 et seq.

Papakyriakou (Th), *Das Griechische Verwaltungsstrafrecht in Kartellsachen- Zugleich ein Beitrag zur Lehre vom Verwaltungs- und Unternehmensstrafrecht* (Schreiftenreihe: Studien zum Wirtschaftsstraftrecht, Bd 15), 2002.

Papakyriakou (Th), "National Report", in: G. Dannecker and Oswald Jansen (eds.), "*Competition Law Sanctioning in the European Union. The EU-Law Influence on the National Law System of Sanctions in the European Area*", Kluwer Law International, 2004.

Pitsela (A), "Greece: The current sanctions system", in: A.K. van Kalmthout and P.P.Tak (eds.), Sanction Systems in the Member-States of the Council of Europe, Deventer ed., vol I., 1988, 151.

Spinellis (D), "The Legal and Practical Problems Posed by the Difference Between Criminal Law and Administrative Penal Law", (1988) 59 *Revue internationale de droit pénal* 217–225.

Sykiotou-Androulakis (A), *Le mouvement de dépénalisation en France et en Grèce: l'alternative administrative*", Sakkoulas /Bruylant, 1995.

ADMINISTRATIVE SANCTIONS IN GREECE (IN GREEK)

Darzentas (M), "The autonomy of the disciplinary law of public servants", in *Timitikos Tomos G Papahatzis*, Athens, 1989, 665.

Dellis (G), "Judicial review of the sanctioning functions of the independent authorities", *Dike*, 2003, 1281.

Dellis (G), "The specificity of the judicial review of administrative sanctions", *Dioikitiki Diki*, 2002, 890.

Hatzinikolaou-VOUZIKA (R), "The implementation of the penal law principles in disciplinary infringements", *DioikDik* 1969, 124.

Kourakis (N), *The theory of the sanction: An introduction*, ed. Sakkoulas, 2008.

Lytras (S) *The notion of administrative fines and the constitutionality of their imposition*, Sakkoulas, 1986.

Lytras (S), *Definition of and a basic distinction between sanctions in Greek law*, Sakkoulas ed., 1984.

Lytras (S) *The disciplinary phenomenon in modern Greek public law*, Sakkoulas ed., 1989

Maniatis (A), *Sanctions within the framework of the implementation of European Community law in Greece*, Armenopoulos, 1999, 457.

Papadatos (S), "The imposition of a disciplinary sanction and the "non bis in idem" principle", EDD, 1963, 385.

Papanikolaïdes (D), *Definition and legal characteristics of Administrative Sanctions*, Sakkoulas, Salonika, 1975.

Remelis (K), *The legal nature of sports disciplinary litigation*, Armenopoulos 1994, 101.

Rotis (N), "*Reformatio in peius* in disciplinary law", *ToS* 1979, 45.

Rotis (V), "The repetitive exercise of the disciplinary coercion", *Epitheorisi Dimosiou kai Dioikitikou Dikaiou*, 1966, 22.

Stassinopoulos (M), "The real nature of administrative sanctions", *Archeion Nomologias*, 1950, 89.

Stavrou (S), "The rights of the defendant in disciplinary procedures and Article 6 ECHR", *EEEvrD*, 1991, 371.

Symeonides (S), "The expansion of the sanctioning functions of the public administration and the doubs concerning its constitutionality", *Dioikitiki Diki*, 1992, 495.

Vlahopoulos (S), "The application of the principle "*nullum crimen, nulla poena sine praevia lege*" in the context of disciplinary administrative law", *Dioikitiki Diki*, 1999, 564.

VIII. COUNTRY ANALYSIS – ITALY

Alessandro BERNARDI*, Ciro GRANDI** and Ilaria ZODA***

1. THE ITALIAN ADMINISTRATIVE SANCTIONS SYSTEM: INTRODUCTORY REMARKS

The administrative sanction is an instrument available to the Public Administration (hereafter PA) for the protection of a public interest. The literature provides two notions of the administrative sanction.

According to the first notion (an administrative sanction in a broad sense), it is an order entailing negative consequences for its addressee and is imposed by the PA following the finding of a breach of a legal regulation. In line with this theory, the concept of a "sanction" includes any kind of *lato sensu* punitive measures that the PA can impose in pursuing the public interest in question.

Different types of administrative sanctions can be identified on the basis of their contents: compensatory sanctions, aimed at compensating the PA for the damage caused by the violation; reparatory sanctions, aimed at eliminating the consequences of the breach by means of a *reductio in pristino* of the situation as it was before the violation; punitive sanctions, aimed at punishing the offender and preventing the realization of further offences; disciplinary sanctions, also with a punitive intent, but specifically aimed at punishing violations concerning the relationship between the PA and a public employee.[1] The common feature of these types of sanctions is their capability to produce negative consequence for the addressee; in contrast, however, they differ with regard to their function and objective.

---

* Sections 1 and 8.

** Sections 2 and 3.

*** Sections 4, 5, 6 and 7.

1 This category includes pecuniary sanctions, suspending or disqualifying sanctions, but also mere moral sanctions. The disciplinary pecuniary sanctions, however, differ from the punitive pecuniary sanctions, because they do not impose the payment of a sum of money but rather entail a reduction in or the suspension of the perpetrator's salary, or the loss of pension benefits (see Dolcini, Giarda, Mucciarelli, Paliero, Riva Crugnola, *Commentario alle "Modifiche al sistema penale"*, Milan, 1982, *sub* Article 12, p. 82). An example of a disqualifying disciplinary sanction is suspension from work; an example of a moral sanction is a warning or reprimand. The source of disciplinary power is Article 55 legislative decree no. 165/2001. See Caringella, *Il Diritto amministrativo*, Naples, 2003, p. 339.

According to the second notion (administrative sanction *stricto sensu*), this concept exclusively includes general measures[2] with a punitive-repressive function. These measures can be: *pecuniary*, consisting of the payment of a sum of money to the PA competent for the sector in question; *disqualifying or suspending*[3] sanctions, which – imposed instead of the pecuniary primary sanction – prevent the offender from exercising certain activities that require administrative authorisation.

There are several kinds of pecuniary sanctions: rather seldom the law provides for a predetermined sanction, which does not allow the authority to have any discretion to adapt the sanction according to the particular characteristics of the offence.[4] More frequently the legislator lays down the minimum and the maximum punishment, and leaves it to the competent authority to determine the actual amount (in line with the general principles of administrative action, primarily the principle of rationality[5], and within the parameters of Article 11 law no. 689 of 24 November 1981). Finally, the administrative sanction could also be proportional: in this case the amount of the sanction is calculated by a compilation of two different factors, the first is determined by the legislator (usually a fixed amount)[6], and the second to the seriousness of the violation in question.[7]

---

2 Thus with the exclusion of disciplinary sanctions.

3 Examples of this kind of sanction are revocations and lapses of rights and facilities, which prevent the offender from the exercise of some activities having public relevance. The disqualifying or suspending sanctions (regulated under Articles 20–21 law no. 689/1981) usually do not affect the offender's patrimony, but they still have a deterrent effect. They include different types of measures such as the prohibition of the exercise of rights or facilities (e.g. the closing of an establishment under Article 39 law no. 426/1927), or the revocation of administrative orders granting benefits, facilities, rights (e.g. revocation of an authorisation for peddling under Article 11 law no. 398/1976; revocation of a gaming licence or a firearms certificate under Article 31 law no. 986/1977); see Paliero-Travi, *La sanzione amministrativa*, Milan, 1988, p. 113.

4 This is when a petition of constitutional consistency for fixed sanctions has been lodged, with reference to the principle of equality (Article 3 Cost.): the punishment cannot be made proportional to the subjective element of the offence. Nevertheless, this type of sanction is legitimate, as long as it is provided for offences whose seriousness may not be graduated (e.g. parking offences). See Paliero-Travi, *La sanzione amministrativa*, *op.cit.*, pp. 99 *et seq.*

5 Article 10 law no. 689/1981 lays down general minimum and maximum limits (respectively 6 euro and 10,329 euro): nonetheless, the Legislator can derogate from these thresholds in any sectoral law (certain administrative offences are punished with extremely high fines). Article 10 law no. 689/1981 also states that the maximum of each sanction cannot exceed ten times the minimum. The PA shall rationally proportion the sanction and shall provide the necessary grounds for the decision – under Article 18 law no. 689/1981 and Article 3 law no. 241/1990 – by indicating the factual and legal motives, in relation to the evidence.

6 The first parameter could be both a fixed amount (e.g. 50 euro) or a sum to be determined between two limits (e.g. from 5 to 50 euro).

7 E.g. the quantity of gravel unlawfully extracted from a river bed, the delay in discharging a certain duty, the number of employees left without social security provisions. This type of sanction is usually not provided with a maximum limit, since the amount depends on quantitative elements of the offence, a limit for which cannot be given in advance.

In line with the latter definition, then, the concept of an administrative sanction is close to that of a criminal sanction, as they share the same repressive-punitive function: with the use of both these sanctioning instruments the punitive system relies on a "double stream".[8] The main distinguishing element is the different punitive intensity, given that only the criminal sanction can affect (directly or indirectly) the fundamental right of personal freedom (criminal fines will be transposed into custodial sentences (or compulsory community service or probation if they are not paid). What is more, certain ancillary negative consequences will exclusively follow penal sanctions (recidivism, a criminal record, a declaration of being a persistent or professional offender)[9], as well as the social stigmatisation that could exclude the offender from the social community.[10]

The administrative sanction is subject to the general principles governing the activity of the PA.[11]

The Constitution lays down the main principles on the matter, which represent the parameters of legitimacy of any legal act. In particular, Article 97 Cost. refers to: the principle of legality, under which the administrative action and organization are subject to the law; the principle of impartiality, which prescribes that the individual rights and interests affected by the administrative activity must be taken into account even if the task of the PA is to pursue the public interest; the principle of good functioning, under which the PA shall achieve its objectives in the shortest possible time (celerity) and with the lowest costs (economy). All together, these principles concern the *efficiency* of the PA.

Besides being regulated in the Constitution, the *stricto sensu* administrative sanction was substantively and procedurally regulated with the enactment of law no. 689/1981, called "*Modifiche al sistema penale*", which finally filled the lacunae concerning the sanctions in question (even though this act does not apply to some forms of administrative punishment such as sanctions in the financial sector and disciplinary sanctions, as provided for under Article 12).

On the other hand, the law of 7 August 1990 no. 241 ("*Nuove norme in materia di procedimento amministrativo e diritto di accesso ai documenti amministrativi*") regulates administrative proceedings, which amounts to those

---

8 This expression means that the Legislator, in order to prevent and deter criminality, makes use of administrative or criminal sanctions according to the seriousness of the breach.

9 See Nuvolone, "Pena (dir. pen.)", in *Enciclopedia del diritto*, vol. XXXII, Milan, 1982, pp. 788 *et seq.*

10 From a moral-social point of view, the reputation of the offender is seriously at risk and this will amount to "secondary punishment"; Paliero-Travi, *La sanzione amministrativa*, *op.cit.*, p. 22. Furthermore, the state of mind of the investigated person during the preliminary investigation (therefore before the trial), or the state of mind of the defendant before a criminal court, often determines this stigmatisation effect.

11 The criminal sanction, on the other hand, is governed by autonomous principles laid down in the Constitution and also in the criminal code and the code of criminal procedure.

activities culminating in the adoption of an administrative order (including the sanctioning order).

Other relevant acts are: law no. 1034 of 6 December 1971 ("*Istituzione dei tribunali amministrativi regionali*"), which establishes the judicial authorities which are competent in cases involving PA activity, and law no. 205 of 21 July 2000 ("*Disposizioni in tema di giustizia amministrativa*"), which lays down a set of instruments for the protection of individual rights affected by an administrative decision.

In spite of the analogies between administrative and criminal sanctions (mostly the preventive-punitive function), there are several remarkable dissimilarities. Criminal offences and their sanctioning concern the most serious forms of conduct that deserve a rigorous punitive response capable of also affecting personal freedom. As a result, the procedures for the finding of such violations must be particularly strict as far as the defendant's guarantees are concerned. In contrast, the administrative offence and sanction concern, in principle, less serious forms of behaviour, for which the restriction of personal freedom would be too severe. As a consequence, the minor consequences of the sanction justify the adoption of a less complicated (thus quicker and cheaper) investigative procedure, although the essential guarantees must nevertheless be respected.

However, the differences between administrative and civil sanctions are even more significant. The Italian system does not provide for punitive civil sanctions such as *astreintes* provided for in France and in Belgium.[12] In general, civil sanctions have a compensatory or restitutionary function with respect to an individual causing unlawful damage to another: any strictly punitive aim is excluded.

2. GENERAL PRINCIPLES

The administrative sanction is regulated according to some fundamental principles laid down in a complex legislative framework.

Firstly, the Italian Constitution provides a set of fundamental principles and rights related to the PA, which pervade the entire body of legislation on the matter, including the field of sanctioning powers. These principles and rights are:

The principle of legality (Article 97 Italian Constitution, hereafter "Const."). The administrative activity has to take place according to the law. The subordination of the PA to the law is already apparent when certain powers are granted with a

12 However, civil sanctions with a punitive effect have recently been introduced in the Italian legal system. For instance, law no. 39/2002 has given the judiciary the power to impose pecuniary civil sanctions against entrepreneurs who do not comply with an injunction granted at the request of consumers' associations.

view to attaining a specific public interest (that is, in its turn, determined by law). Furthermore, this principle also applies to the subsequent phase: each administrative proceeding has to abide by certain procedural rules regulated by law and which can only come to a conclusion with the adoption or imposition of a certain measure as indicated by the law. In this respect, there is a significant parallel between administrative and criminal sanctions, the latter also being permeated by substantive and procedural legality. Nonetheless, while the principle of legality in criminal law is laid down in Article 25 Const. (which means that a Constitutional amendment is necessary to bring about any change), in the administrative field it is clearly laid down in Article 1 of law no. 689/1981, derogations from which can be achieved by means of a subsequent legislative act.

The principle of equality (Article 3 Const.) The administrative proceeding, and in particular the sanctioning proceeding, must be structured in such a way as to reduce the disparity between the public authority and the individuals who are subject to the legitimate use of the administrative power. For example, there is a procedural phase when private parties are allowed to access the file and to submit observations concerning their rights in order to persuade the authority to adopt a decision that entails the slightest degree of possible harm to the interests of the individuals in question.

The right of defence (Article 24 Const). According to an extensive interpretation[13], this right applies to proceedings not only before the judicial authorities but also before the administrative authorities, since the latter may also adopt a decision which affects individual interests. Just like the principle of legality, the right of defence also influences the whole Italian sanctioning system (both in criminal and administrative matters).

The right of judicial protection (Article 113 Const.). The addressee of an administrative action has the right to be heard before a court in order to have his rights and interests judicially protected; the method for exerting this right is regulated by law.[14]

The principle of impartiality (Article 97 Const.). In exercising its activities (namely sanctioning powers) the PA must remain impartial with reference to the

13 Under the Constitution the right of defence is exclusively laid down with regard to proceeding before the judiciary. According to a restrictive interpretation, this principle does not apply to sanctioning proceedings before the PA. Nonetheless, the majority of commentators share an extensive interpretation.

14 It must be pointed out that Article 103 para. I Const. provides a dualistic judicial system, where the civil courts and the administrative courts have different jurisdictions and functions. Article 125 Const. lays down the principle of double jurisdiction, according to which the addressee of a judicial order can, under certain circumstances, lodge an appeal before a higher court.

interests in the proceedings. Even if the PA is expected to pursue a public interest, it has to take the position of private parties into account. It is worth pointing out that the principle of impartiality on the part of the judging body also applies in criminal law, although this is a slightly different notion. Under Article 104 Const., the judicial authority is autonomous and independent from any other power, therefore it must apply the law according to a fair interpretation, without representing the stance of the government currently in power.

The principle of good administration (Article 97 Const.). The administrative functionaries shall perform their activities so as to accomplish the effectiveness, the efficiency, the expeditiousness and the economy of the administrative action, with the slightest possible harm to individual interests. Moreover, the administrative activity shall always respect the principle of visibility.[15]

Besides the aforementioned constitutional principles and rights, according to law no. 241/1990, as amended by law no. 205/2000, administrative proceedings must respect additional principles, namely:

The principle of a fair proceeding is aimed at striking a balance between the public interest pursued by the PA and the individual interest which potentially conflicts with the former. With particular reference to sanctioning proceedings, this principle entails the right of the affected individual to participate in the proceeding.[16] The consequences are the duty to notify the addressee of the instigation of a proceeding (Articles 7–8), the right to intervene the proceeding (Article 9), and the right to access the file and to submit observations and documents (Article 10).

The principle of transparency and visibility. This principle assures the possibility for individuals to be notified of the activities of the PA, since the process may lead to the adoption of decisions which affect private interests, especially when it concerns sanctioning proceedings. Corollaries of this principle are: the duty to close the proceeding with a visible and public decision (Article 2); the general duty of providing the necessary grounds for any administrative actions[17] taken (Article 3); the duty to designate the specific official charged with carrying out the proceeding[18] (Articles 4–6); and the right of interested individuals to have access to the file (Articles 22–28).

---

15 See Caringella, *Il Diritto amministrativo*, *op.cit.*, p. 562. On the notions of the effectiveness, efficiency, expeditiousness and economy of the administrative action see Mazzarolli, Pericu, Romano, Roversi Monaco, Scoca, *Diritto amministrativo*, Bologna, 1998, p. 411.

16 Chapter III of law no. 241/1990 specifically regulates participation in the proceeding.

17 The duty to provide the necessary grounds for the sanctioning order also applies to criminal law, where it is specifically laid down in the Constitutional (Article 111 Const.).

18 The official in charge of the proceeding is a PA officer with the duty to monitor the proceeding and to guarantee the position of private parties.

The principle of simplification entails, in particular, the principle of the economy and effectiveness of an administrative action and the prohibition of delaying the proceeding by means of activities that are not necessary for the adoption of the final decision.[19]

In addition, heading I of law no. 689/1981 also lays down some disciplinary principles and rules regarding administrative sanctions. The fundamental principles are:

The principle of legality (Article 1), subject to which no one shall be punished with an administrative sanction which is not provided for by the law and no one may be punished as a result of an interpretation which extends the scope of application of a punitive provision by means of analogy. Although this principle, as is well-known, also applies to criminal offences, it has a rather different meaning in criminal law: as regards criminal law, the principle of legality is laid down in the Constitution and it has a more rigorous meaning; in the field of administrative law, the principle is laid down under statutory law and there may be significant derogations therefrom as an administrative offence can be regulated by regional law.

The principle of mens rea (Articles 2–3). The application of an administrative sanction requires that the offender has reached the aged of majority (18 years old)[20] and had the necessary mental ability at the moment when the crime was committed.[21] Under the principle of *mens rea*, responsibility only exists when the offender has acted with intent or recklessness.[22]

The principle of concurrent responsibility (Article 5). In the case of participation in an illicit administrative act, each participant will be charged with the offence in its entirety. However, the principle of apportioning the penalty requires that the sanction should be proportionate to each transgressor's personal contribution.

The principle of solidarity (Article 6). Certain categories of individuals or legal persons who have not taken take part in the offence are nevertheless subject to a

19 Only at the end of the proceeding will it be possible to assess whether all the activities were in fact necessary in relation to the final decision, and, therefore, whether the prohibition of delaying the proceeding has been violated. If so, the PA shall be held responsible towards the private party who can then resort to the administrative court to request the annulment of the illegitimate order.

20 On the other hand, under Articles 97 *et seq.* of the criminal code, criminal responsibility starts at the age of 14.

21 Italian doctrine distinguishes between the ability to understand and the ability to act according to one's free will; see Mantovani, *Diritto penale, Parte generale*, Padova, 2001, p. 667.

22 The PA has the burden of proving mens rea. The subjective element can be intent or recklessness.

form of solidarity with the offender as far as the execution of the pecuniary administrative sanction is concerned. Nonetheless, should the fine be paid by one person only, he will have recourse against the author of the illicit act.

The responsibility of legal entities is somewhat peculiar in administrative law, since a criminal offence can only be committed by a natural person under Italian criminal law. This is therefore a unique situation which allows certain forms of conduct to be penalised that would otherwise go unpunished and to avoid an undesirable lack of protection with respect to the illegal behaviour of companies. In certain cases, a criminal court may fine legal entities. Nevertheless, this is a form of civil subsidiary liability that arises when a manager, an agent or an employee of a legal entity becomes insolvent with respect to a criminal pecuniary sanction that has been imposed for an offence committed in the running of (or on behalf of) the company (Article 197 Criminal Code, hereinafter "c.p.").

The principle of personal liability for the payment of an administrative sanction (Article 7). Unlike the duty to pay compensation in civil torts, the obligation to pay an administrative fine cannot be transferred to the heirs of a deceased person. Parallel to the criminal law system, the purpose of an administrative fine is to punish only the author of the illicit act, stressing the preventive-punitive function of the sanction instead of the generic compensatory function.[23]

Turning now to the disciplinary rules on administrative sanctions under law no. 689/1981, the following is worth noting:

Justified actions which exclude responsibility[24] (Article 4): the performance of a specific duty[25], the exercise of a legitimate power[26], the state of necessity[27], a legitimate defence.[28]

---

23 In contrast, fiscal obligations can be transferred to the heirs of a deceased person so as to satisfy the primary public interest in collecting taxes.

24 In the criminal field, other justified actions operate (the awful consent of the victim, Article 50, and the lawful use of a weapon, Article 53 penal code).

25 The performance of a specific duty applies when the conduct complies with the law or an order issued by the public authorities, provided there is a of subordination relationship determined by public law between the subject who gives and the subject who receives the order, and provided the order is lawful. In contrast, a subject who executes an unlawful order shall be held responsible, unless he believes that the order is lawful or unless the order could not be considered objectionable (but an order to commit a manifest crime is never an excuse).

26 The criminal code provides for an analogous provision (Article 51 penal code).

27 In parallel with criminal law (Article 54 para. I penal code), a state of necessity operates when the conduct is the result of "having had to act by the necessity of saving oneself or others from the present danger of bodily harm, a danger not voluntarily caused (...), not otherwise avoidable, (...) provided that the act is proportionate to that danger".

28 Under the criminal code (Article 52 penal code), legitimate defence operates when an act is committed "having been compelled to do so by the necessity of defending oneself or another

The principle of continuity (Article 8) under which whoever, by means of a single or multiple action(s) violates different norms thereby resulting in administrative sanctions shall be punished with the sanction which would be imposed for the most serious violation, increased by up to a multiple of three.[29]

The criteria for the imposition of a pecuniary administrative sanction and of facultative ancillary administrative sanctions. Under Article 11, in order to determine the extent of the sanction the following elements must be weighed: the objective element (the gravity, the duration, the means of committing the transgression) and the subjective element (intent or recklessness) of the illicit conduct, the steps taken by the offender to rectify or mitigate the consequences of the violation[30], the personality of the offender[31] and his economic situation.[32]

3. THE PRINCIPLE OF DEFENCE

The law provides individuals with the necessary instruments to defend their interests when they are affected by administrative sanctioning proceedings.

First, following the discovery of the illicit conduct, the PA has the obligation to immediately notify the person responsible or, when this is not possible, to notify the charge within 90 days (Article 14 law no. 689/1981). This provision is intended to allow the alleged offender to take part in the proceeding and to defend his interests. Several possibilities are provided:

In order to prevent the imposition of a sanction, the investigated person can admit his responsibility and pay a reduced amount within 60 days after the notification (Article 16 law no. 689/1981).[33]

If the alleged responsible person does not admit his responsibility, he can also intervene in the next phase. When the 60 days have elapsed, the authority that has discovered the violation must deliver to the office which is competent to impose the sanction a file proving that the accusations and the notifications have taken place (Article 17 law no. 689/1981). The following phase of the proceeding

person against the present danger of unlawful injury (…), provided the defence is proportionate to the injury".

29 This also applies in the criminal field (Article 81 penal code).

30 The spontaneity and the effectiveness of the *post factum* behaviour are not strictly necessary; the reparation can also be partial. The behaviour of the transgressor during the investigation and any degree of recidivism are also taken into consideration.

31 In particular, one may think of diminished responsibility.

32 This parameter is very significant concerning the objective of prevention attached to administrative pecuniary sanctions, which must be proportionate to the financial penalty imposed on each individual offender.

33 The sum is calculated by the investigative body as the lower amount between one-third of the maximum and double the minimum, plus the costs of the proceeding.

is devoted to the gathering of evidence with a view to reaching a final decision[34]: during this phase the individuals in question can submit observations and documents and can exercise the right to be heard. Therefore, participation in the proceeding is up to the individuals concerned; before the intervention of these individuals, the PA does not have a general duty to take private interests into consideration. If the decision is adopted and a private request to be heard has been ignored[35], the final decision can be challenged because of a violation of statutory rules. This is an expression of the principle of *audi altera parte* which is a corollary of the principle of defence. Besides the explicit legal basis provided under law no. 689/1981, which lays down the general principles concerning administrative sanctions, the principle of defence is also laid down under Articles 7–10 of the general act on administrative proceedings, law no. 241/1990.

The right to access the file is worthy of special consideration: it allows the person in question to examine and to copy the relevant documents, subject to a previous motivated request. This right is regulated by Articles 22 *et seq.* law no. 241/1990 and by regulation no. 352 of 27 June 1990 (which regulates the right of access in details); the legislation in question has been amended by laws nos. 205/2000 and 340/2000.

Access to the file is intended to implement the aforesaid principles of transparency and impartiality, by allowing individuals to monitor the legitimacy of administrative activities. The exercise of the right in question can only be limited by strict conditions determined by law; the refusal of the PA to allow a private request to access the file (as well as the limitation or the postponement of such access) must be justified and the grounds for this decision must be provided.[36]

If, after 30 days from the private request, the PA has still not come to a decision, a refusal is implicit. However, in this case, as in the case of an explicit negative response or a postponement, individuals have two options: first, a complaint can be lodged before a court; second, a different administrative authority, the ombudsman, can be asked to review the decision.

---

34 This investigative phase depends on the initiative of the private parties, who have the right (within 30 days after the notification) to submit documents and observations, and to be heard. The term of 30 days is not mandatory, but the private party's activities must not delay the proceeding. The submission of documents does not require any formal standards.

35 It must be underlined that the PA is not obliged to allow the requests made by a private party, but only to receive and consider the documents. The PA is free to evaluate and weigh the individual circumstances of the case and to use its administrative discretion accordingly.

36 More in detail, limitations to the right of access to the file will only be legitimate if they are justified by a public interest which prevails over a private interest: for example, in the case of classified documents, documents concerning the details of prosecution witnesses, and any documents concerning national security or defence, international relationships, financial and monetary policy, public order, the prevention of crime and personal or business privacy (Article 24 law no. 241/1990).

If the first option is made use of, the judicial authority shall adopt a decision within 30 days, and it must also take into consideration the observations submitted by both parties. If the private party's petition is allowed, the court will order the PA to allow access to the file with immediate effect.[37] It must be pointed out that the competent judicial authority is not the ordinary civil court, but the administrative court, which under the Italian legal system has jurisdiction to hear administrative activities that affect private interests not having the essence of individual rights.

If the second option is made use of, the ombudsman notifies the competent authority that it should allow access (evidently, only when the ombudsman believes that the PA has illegitimately denied access); within 30 days from the notification, the PA shall confirm the right of access, but if there is further non-compliance or a delay the individuals can directly access the file without waiting for the formal confirmation. This second option does not impede individuals from resorting to the courts, after the ombudsman's decision: as a matter of fact, this decision can be challenged before the judicial authorities.

Moreover, if the PA does not spontaneously comply with the judicial order, the individual can resort to another instrument for protection: the "*giudizio di ottemperanza*" (compliance proceeding). Under Article 21*bis* law no. 1034/1971, when the complaint is partially or totally successful, the individual can ask the court to entrust an official ("*commissario ad acta*") with the duty of adopting the relevant administrative order; before doing so, however, the official shall verify that the PA has not already provided this of it own accord.

In conclusion, Article 328 paragraph 2 Italian Criminal Code regulates the offence of an "Omission or Refusal to Perform Acts of Office": "The public official or person charged with a public service who does not perform an official act or service within 30 days from the legitimate request of the interested party and does not account for the delay shall be punished by a term of imprisonment of up to one year or by a fine not exceeding 1032 euro". This criminal offence is an instrument by which to implement indirectly the right of access to the file.[38]

4. THE ORGANIZATION OF THE SANCTIONING POWERS OF THE PUBLIC ADMINISTRATION

The power to sanction is just one single expression of the general power to protect the public interest. Under Article 97 Const., the PA is entrusted with protecting such an interest according to the law. Since there are a number of different public interests deserving adequate protection, the Public Administration therefore divides them into several branches.

[37] The first instance decision may be challenged before a superior court.

[38] See Caringella, *Il Diritto amministrativo*, *op.cit.*, p. 780.

When the law provides for an administrative penalty for the violation of a given norm, the PA is the sole body which has competence to impose that penalty. Nevertheless, there are different offices within the public administration that are competent to impose the pertinent sanction, depending on the kind of interest that has to be safeguarded.

Ultimately, each branch of the Public Administration, being part of the complex administrative machinery of the State, has a power to sanction which is a crystallised form of the power/duty to protect the public interest. Evidently, single administrative actions must be carried out by a natural person. Therefore, the legal literature has developed the concept of "*rapporto organico*" (the organic relationship between the administrative body and the individual person who acts on behalf of the PA): in other words, the single official becomes "a part of the complex body of the PA", and each act by the former is directly ascribed to the latter. For that reason, the concrete exercise of sanctioning powers is delegated to officials.[39]

The commencing of the sanctioning proceeding is at the discretion of the PA, which commences an investigation on its own an initiative. The law prescribes that the investigative authority and the authority that has to assess the allegation must be different.

Consequently, the bodies involved in the proceeding are divided into monitoring and investigative bodies, and bodies having decisional powers: this distinction is aimed at safeguarding the impartiality of the final decision. The deciding body acknowledges the results of the investigation by means of the file being handed over by the investigative body. This file reflects the investigation and contains the evidence gathered in order to start the proceeding. The non-involvement of the ruling authority in the investigative activities guarantees its distance from the decision eventually taken. When it comes to a decision the competent body will finally examine both the evidence supporting the allegation and the documents submitted (if any) by the investigated person.

Where a decision is adopted in violation of the rules that allocate the internal competences of the PA, then it will be illegitimate due to a breach of the law. The addressee will then have the possibility to complain before the competent judicial authority (in this case an ordinary civil court) in order to obtain a declaration that the administrative decision is not lawful.

It is worth devoting particular attention to the *independent administrative authorities*: they differ from other public administrations due to their organizational, financial and accounting autonomy and most of all because they are not subjected to any political or governmental guidelines. While the main function of the PA is to strike a balance between conflicting public and private interests with a view to protecting public interest, the function of the

39 However, not all administrative bodies have the competence to sanction only those bodies specifically determined by the law and within the limits laid down by the law itself.

independent administrative authority is to monitor the enforcement of the law in particular sectors, keeping an equidistance from the public and private interests involved[40] in order to protect and regulate more general social interests.[41] Not all independent administrative authorities are provided with sanctioning powers.[42] Their scope of activity is more limited than the scope of other public administrations, which deal with individuals on a day to day basis.

5. THE ADMINISTRATIVE INVESTIGATION AND THE POWERS OF INQUIRY

The administrative decision imposing a sanction must be supported by solid evidence. The gathering of evidence is carried out by two categorises of subjects: PA bodies and external operators (Article 13 law no. 689/1981 provides for a detailed list of these subjects and defines their powers).

The first category comprises officials belonging to the administrative monitoring bodies; they can gather information, inspect objects and places except for private residences, undertake surveys, take photographs and carry out any technical experiment (Article 13, para. 1); they can order a precautionary seizure[43] (Article 13, paras. 2 and 3) in order to prevent the alteration or dispersion of evidence, in conformity with the Code of Criminal Procedure (hereafter the c.c.p.).

The second category comprises subjects not belonging to the PA; also officials and agents of the criminal investigation department, within their competence regarding administrative offences, can exercise the same authority as that granted to the PA officials. Furthermore, they have the exclusive power to carry out searches[44] under the provisions of the c.c.p. when there is no alternative way of discovering to find evidence (Article 13, para. 4).

40 Caringella, *Il Diritto amministrativo*, *op. cit.*, p. 428.

41 For example: the Antitrust Authority; the Authority for protecting the privacy of personal data; the Authority for electricity and gas supplies; the Authority for monitoring public works; the Authority for monitoring mass media communications; the Authority for public utility services.

42 For instance, the Authority for monitoring mass media communications can warn the publishing companies and radio/television networks not to keep violating the law.

43 A seizure requires a real and present danger of any alteration or dispersion of the object of a crime and of the evidence. Under Articles 13–14 Const., safeguarding personal freedom and private residences, the seizure (unless an inspection has been authorized) is only legitimate if it is carried out in places where the possessor has no right to exclude third parties.

44 The terms 'inspections' ("ispezioni") and 'searches' ("perquisizioni") mean in general the entering of places belonging to third parties' legal property. However, inspections can be carried out regardless of an offence having been committed and only in those places where a private entrepreneur carries out commercial or productive activities regulated by public sectorial law providing for administrative offences; in contrast, searches can also be carried out in different places (excluding private residences), but only after an offence has been

Therefore, for the exercise of sanctioning powers, the PA enjoys a number of instruments for gathering evidence and it is supported by the possible intervention of the criminal investigation department. Furthermore, the general provision laid down by law no. 689/1981 could also be complemented by other provisions granting supplementary powers.

Nevertheless, in order to be able to make use of the evidence when the PA must reach a decision, it is necessary to compile a report containing a description of the outcome of the investigation and an explanation for investigation undertaken: as a matter of fact, since the investigative bodies and the deciding bodies are different, the report is intended to inform the latter of the evidence gathered.

The duty to compile a written report is reminiscent of criminal proceedings: as a consequence Articles 136–137 c.c.p. (that indicate the fundamental elements of the report, such as the date, the criminal records of the persons concerned, the description of the operations carried out and the results thereof, transcriptions of oral declarations, personal statements *et cetera*) are also applicable here.[45]

The investigative bodies shall also respect a further obligation: when a violation has been detected, the person allegedly responsible should be immediately informed of the allegation; in the case of his absence or in a particularly complex investigation, a formal notification shall be made.[46] This duty is intended to acquaint the investigated person with the allegation and to make it possible, alternatively, for that person to immediately pay a reduced fine and thereby to end the proceeding (Article 16 law no. 689/1981) or for the formal proceeding to commence with the possibility for the private party to submit documents. The omission of the immediate notice or of the prescribed formal notification period (under Article 14 the notice shall be immediate, the notification must take place within 90 days after discovering the transgression) bars the proceeding and extinguishes the obligation to pay a fine.[47] The object of the immediate notice is a written report indicating the following elements: the *tempus* and *locus* of the discovered offence, the allegedly violated legal provisions, declarations (if any) by the defendant, the possibility to pay a reduced

---

committed. Inspections can only concern visible objects while searches look for hidden objects related to the offence. Only searches shall be allowed by the judicial authorities, which have to assess the necessity and usefulness of such a search.

45 Dolcini, Giarda, Mucciarelli, Paliero, Riva Crugnola, *Commentario alle "Modifiche al sistema penale"*, *op.cit.*, *sub* Article 13, p. 99.

46 The formal notification must indicate the same elements as they are included in the immediate notice, that is to say the results of the investigation and the possibility to end the procedure by paying a reduced fine.

47 In the case of participation in a violation by more than one person, this only applies to the person who has not received the notification. If the notification has not been complied with in relation to one offender, the proceeding in relation to the other(s) is not barred. Nevertheless, the person who benefits from this procedural error is obliged to compensate his accomplices.

fine, a statement by the official who drafted the notice and by the person who receives it, and a copy of the written report for the addressee.[48]

Concerning the possibility to make use of the evidence gathered during an administrative investigation in a criminal proceeding and *vice versa*, the very dissimilar features of the two procedural frameworks make this difficult: as a matter of fact, the procedures required for the imposition of an administrative sanction are far less rigorous than those required for the imposition of a criminal sanction; in parallel, the person allegedly responsible for an administrative offence enjoys a weaker set of guarantees. Therefore the evidence gathered within an administrative proceeding cannot in principle form a valid ground for a criminal conviction, which should be based on the evidence gathered within the criminal proceeding.[49] At most, if the evidence gathered in an administrative investigation discloses a crime, this evidence could constitute the starting point for a criminal investigation. In other words, if the criminal department becomes aware of certain elements possibly revealing the commission of a crime, it must duly inform the public prosecutor in order to continue the investigation and to instigate criminal proceedings.[50]

Generally speaking, the criminal courts have no competence to impose administrative sanctions. If the criminal investigation discloses an administrative illicit act, the imposition of an administrative sanction is not possible because the finding of administrative violations falls under the exclusive competence of the administrative bodies. In addition, the imposition of a criminal sanction and the imposition of an administrative sanction require the assessment of different kinds of liability, according to different sets of investigative criteria.

The law regulates one single connection between criminal and administrative offences: under Article 24 law no. 689/1981, if the finding of a crime is dependent on the finding of an administrative violation, competence over the latter then falls within the jurisdiction of the criminal court. However, if the judge determines that such a connection does not exist, he will return the file concerning the non-criminal violation to the competent administrative authority.[51]

48 The omission of one mandatory element renders the immediate notice void. See Dolcini, Giarda, Mucciarelli, Paliero, Riva Crugnola, *Commentario alle "Modifiche al sistema penale"*, *op.cit.*, *sub*. Article 14, p. 103.

49 As a matter of fact, if the evidence necessarily has to be gathered before the trial an appropriate procedural phase is introduced ("incidente probatorio") under the code of criminal procedure (Articles 392–404 c.p.p.) in order to safeguard the right of defence.

50 See Articles 330 (notice of a crime) and 347 (duty to notify) c.p.p.

51 If there is uncertainty as to the connection between the investigation of the two violations, the facts will in any event fall under the competence of the criminal court.

6. THE MEANS OF JUDICIAL PROTECTION FOR INDIVIDUALS AGAINST ADMINISTRATIVE ORDERS

Article 113 Const. grants any legal institution acknowledged under the law the right of judicial protection against jeopardizing administrative actions. This protection shall be enjoyed before the administrative courts or the ordinary civil court. In particular, the administrative judge has jurisdiction over any activity of the PA possibly affecting legal positions and interests which are different from individual rights, but still deserving protection; on the other hand, the ordinary judge has jurisdiction in civil and criminal matters when the PA embarks on an action which affects individual rights.

Articles 22–23 law no. 689/1981 regulate the right of interested persons to challenge the administrative sanctioning order, in the light of the principles of procedural concentration and orality.[52] The system provides the claimant with a high degree of protection, as a complete review of the administrative decision will be carried out by a totally different authority. Moreover, while the PA may somehow act in favour of the public interest that must be pursued, the judicial authority is by definition supposed to be impartial towards the interests at stake. By means of a judicial review, the private party requests a re-evaluation of the evidence adduced during the administrative proceeding, and calls for the administrative decision to be overturned based on the abovementioned evidence (considered as sufficient to justify a sanction). The judge will undertake a new assessment, although it will, of necessity, be very similar to the assessment carried out by the administrative authority.

The reviewing judge is the ordinary judge determined *ratione loci commissi delicti* (Article 22 para. I) in order to facilitate the gathering of the evidence. Article 23 para. IV grants the judge broad investigative powers, which go beyond the specific private complaint and the allegations of the parties, given that the task of the inquiry is to assess the existence of a violation.[53] The review will concern any aspects related to the legitimacy of the administrative sanction, regardless of the specific observations submitted by the claimant.

The possibility to challenge the administrative decision will be barred after 30 days from the notification (60 days if the addressee resides abroad).[54] The

52 The principle of orality prescribes that the case must mainly be discussed orally, while the principle of concentration prescribes that the proceeding, as fast as possible, must be brief.

53 Certain types of evidence are incompatible with the objective of the trial (e.g. evidence under oath, the formal and informal examination of the parties) and are not allowed; on the other hand, oral evidence is allowed, and expert evidence is often used; the procedures for gathering evidence are regulated by Articles 202 ss. code of civil procedure. See Dolcini, Giarda, Mucciarelli, Paliero, Riva Crugnola, *Commentario delle "Modifiche al sistema penale"*, *op.cit.*, *sub.* Articles 22–23, pp. 153–154.

54 The legal literature has highlighted the analogy between the case instigated as a consequence of the opposition against an administrative sanctioning order, and a civil trial in labour law

application shall contain all the elements indicated under Article 22 law no. 689/1981 and it shall enclose the challenged decision. In order to meet the prerequisites under Article 414 code of civil procedure (c.civ.p.), the application shall also be submitted by the claimant (the appointment of a lawyer is not necessary) and it must indicate the court which is addressed, the parties, the object of the petition, the factual and legal elements supporting the claim and the evidence.[55] If the application does not meet these prerequisites, it can be considered void under the general rules of Article 156 c.civ.p.

The subjects endowed with the possibility to lodge the application are the addressee of the sanctioning decision and the subjects jointly liable for the payment of the fine; the opponent is the PA body that has adopted the order and asks for its confirmation.

After verifying the admissibility of the application, the judge will schedule the first hearing for the appearance of the parties, by means of an order that must be notified to the litigants.

The PA has to appear as a party in the proceeding by submitting a copy of the file with the results of the administrative investigation and decision in order to allow the court to assess the grounds for the sanction imposed.

The claimant has to appear in person at the first hearing (except when there is a lawful impediment preventing him from doing so)[56], otherwise the decision will be confirmed.[57]

Both parties can appear at the hearing personally, but the PA body can also be represented by specifically delegated functionaries.

As we have said, the proceeding is characterized by concentration and its oral nature: after an evaluation of the probative material produced by the parties, the judge will define the requests and (apart from deciding on a further period for the submission of observations and a further hearing) will move on to the discussion of the case before coming to a ruling.

The court enjoys limited adjudicatory powers: it shall either allow the complaint by the private party or dismiss it, but it can never change the administrative decision *in peius* (for the claimant). This limitation is intended to exclude any "intrusion" on the part of the judiciary in the exercise of the administrative discretion that only pertains to the PA; as a matter of fact, the

issues: they share certain features like the informality of the private parties' activities, the oral nature and the concentration of the proceedings, and the judge's broad power of inquiry. Nevertheless, hearing an appeal against administrative orders differs with regard to the burden of proof. See Così Dolcini, Giarda, Mucciarelli, Paliero, Riva Crugnola, *Commentario delle "Modifiche al sistema penale"*, *op. cit.*, *sub.* Articles 22–23, p. 150.

55 In its turn the PA can submit the results of the sanctioning proceeding.

56 According to the criminal case law, only an impediment that makes it absolutely impossible to appear before the court can excuse any absence: e.g. the necessity to satisfy fundamental human needs; see Cassazione penale, I sezione, 20 March 1952, *Giustizia penale* 1952, III, 500; Cassazione penale 11 April 1979, *Rivista penale* 1980, 283.

57 The judicial order of confirmation can be challenged before the Corte di Cassazione.

significant differences between the administrative and the judicial processes have repercussions on the kind of actions that can be adopted. The duty of the judiciary, as is well know, is the application of the law, regardless of any political issues. The Constitution states that judges are subjected to the law and form an autonomous and independent body (Article 104). For that reason, in exercising jurisdiction there is no room for any political evaluation of the interest in question; the judge must stick to the application of the law. In contrast, the task of the PA is to pursue the public interest with the least possible harm to private interests. Thus, the administrative decision is tendentiously discretionary and politically orientated.[58] In the end, judicial rulings and administrative orders are rather incommensurable, even if both are an expression of a sanctioning power.

The ruling is read at the hearing, while the grounds for the decision can be subsequently notified to the parties, so as to make it possible to challenge the judgement before the Supreme Court ("Corte di Cassazione").

A further issue concerns the enforcement of the sanctioning decision (Article 27 law no. 689/1981). In order to initiate the enforcement procedure, the term for voluntary payment[59] and the term for challenging the decision before a court[60] must have elapsed: after that, if none of the aforesaid activities have been undertaken, the administrative order is a legitimate title empowering the enforcement proceeding.[61]

7. COOPERATION WITH FOREIGN AUTHORITIES IN ADMINISTRATIVE MATTERS

For a number of years the Member States of the European Union have engaged in a process of reinforcing their national systems of justice also by means of strengthening international judicial cooperation: as a result of this process, several European and international instruments have been adopted.

58 In line with some of the literature (representing a minority of the authors, however) the sanctioning power can also be used with discretion. According to Zanobini (*Le sanzioni amministrative*, Turin, 1924), if the PA believes it necessary in terms of public interest, it can also discretionally decide not to impose the sanction provided for by the law. Nonetheless, once a violation has been found, the commencing of the sanctioning proceeding is mandatory. Therefore if the competent authority expressly refuses to commence an investigation, it would be held responsible for the crime laid down in Article 328 c.p. (omission to perform acts of office).

59 The payment must be made, within 30 days from the notification of the order, to the competent administrative office ("ufficio del registro"); this office must notify the execution of the payment to the sanctioning authority within 30 days from the payment itself. The sanctioning order becomes enforceable after these two terms have elapsed.

60 In both cases the term is 30 days after the notification of the sanctioning order.

61 A challenge to the sanctioning order does not suspend the duty to pay, unless a suspension is ordered by means of a judicial decision based on serious grounds.

This cooperation has been traditionally developed in criminal matters – through the implementation of reciprocal assistance measures in the fight against organised crime and in judicial activities generally, and in civil matters – through the implementation of the principle of the mutual recognition of civil proceedings, with a view to establishing a common legal space wherein the freedom of movement of persons can be developed. The functioning of such forms of cooperation is partially hampered by the differences which exist between national legal systems; however, in the aforesaid sectors, cooperation is deep-rooted, it concerns significant and wide-ranging legal sectors and enjoys a concrete commitment on the part of the national authorities in the enforcement of existing agreements.

The same path towards cooperation has also been recently undertaken in administrative matters, although several difficulties have arisen.

Firstly, international conventions on administrative matters only lay down the guidelines for exchanging information and for joint monitoring activities, without providing for concrete assistance measures in the execution of administrative sanctions.

In this perspective, by means of law no. 149 of 21 March 1983, Italy ratified the *European Convention on the Service Abroad of Documents relating to Administrative Matters*, signed in Strasbourg on 24 November 1977, and the *European Convention on the Obtaining Abroad of Information and Evidence in Administrative Matters*, signed in Strasbourg on 15 March 1978; under these conventions, the contracting parties must designate a national authority – in Italy, the Ministry of Foreign Affairs – which is competent concerning procedures of reciprocal assistance, e.g. for the notification of administrative documents, for requests for information between States concerning the law, regulations, and customs, as well as factual information and documents. In spite of the fact that these forms of cooperation could concern several administrative fields, their scope of application is limited by the conventions themselves as they do not apply to fiscal matters; moreover, the signatories, by means of a declaration addressed to the Secretary General of the Council of Europe, can indicate the administrative matters with regard to which they will not apply the conventions.

This marks a significant contrast between civil and criminal fields, where the agreements enjoy a much wider scope of application and also concern the mutual recognition and the execution of judicial decisions. As a matter of fact, administrative cooperation is not provided with a sufficient set of legal instruments for the phase of the proceeding subsequent to the finding of the violation (which is to say the sanctioning procedure). An exception is provided by the *Convention on Mutual Administrative Assistance in Tax Matters* (signed in Strasbourg on 25 January 1988), concerning taxes excluding customs duties; this instrument states that the administrative assistance shall comprise not only the exchange of information, including simultaneous tax investigations and participation in tax investigations abroad, but also assistance in the recovery procedure, including conservation measures and the service of documents. Notwithstanding this, the agreement allows the signatories to limit their participation to certain types of taxes only (by means of a complex framework of exclusion clauses); Italy has not ratified the Convention, so that the difficult process of approximation between national public administrations is made even more difficult.

The efficacy of cooperation in the field of the execution of administrative sanctions is therefore subject to the signing of bilateral agreements limited to specific sectors; in other words, due to the lack of general multilateral conventions, the effectiveness of sanctioning procedures depends on the existence of an agreement between the issuing State and the State where the author of the violation resides.

This is the case in fiscal matters: if an Italian citizen, who has committed an administrative fiscal violation, moves abroad without leaving any assets in Italy, an administrative proceeding is commenced and carried out in Italy, apart from the execution. The transgressor must be notified of the proceedings if the PA knows his new place of residence; his notification is necessary in order to ensure the transparency of administrative actions and the possibility to lodge a complaint against the decision. On the other hand, the Italian authorities will delegate to the competent foreign authorities the task of executing the decision, therefore the effectiveness of the sanctioning procedure is entirely devolved to the foreign authorities.

The mentioned lack of general conventions leads to, especially in certain sectors, a discouraging level of ineffectiveness concerning administrative sanctions, so that the activities of those organs which are competent to find a violation are significantly influenced: when there are no international agreements that could guarantee the execution of the sanction abroad, the national authorities often refrain from reporting violations carried out by foreigners.

Furthermore, the PA frequently takes the economic benefits/costs of the sanctioning proceeding into account: the execution of a sanction abroad leads to higher costs than benefits. As a result, the ratio of the effectiveness of administrative sanctions turns out to be increasingly lower.

The very pessimistic attitude towards workable cooperation with a foreign PA is a possible explanation for the rationale underlying the old Article 207 of the road traffic code (legislative decree no. 285 of 30 April 1992), which allowed the driver of a vehicle registered abroad to pay a reduced administrative fine directly to the police officer who had discovered the violation. If the violator had not been able to make use of this possibility, he would have had to pay half the maximum penalty in the form of a bond, or otherwise guarantee the payment by submitting the details on his personal identity card. In the case of refusal, the driving licence would have been withdrawn, or the vehicle seized, until one of the aforesaid obligations had been fulfilled (in any case for a period not longer than 60 days). This provision, as is evident, was aimed at the immediate ending of the sanctioning procedure with the payment of a lower amount, thereby preventing the need for execution proceedings abroad. Nevertheless, the European Court of Justice found it to be inconsistent with Article 12 TEC, because it amounted to the disproportionate treatment of violators on the basis of the place where the vehicle was registered. Therefore Article 207 of the road traffic code was first amended by Article 4 of law no. 214 of 1 August 2003, and then by Article 25 of law no. 14 of 3 February 2004. The new regulation excludes the possibility to submit a personal document as a guarantee for the payment and also the authority of the public officer to withdraw the driving licence. Furthermore, when the vehicle is registered in a EU Member State or in a State that is part of the Agreement on the European Economic Area (EEA), the amount to be paid in the form of a bond must be equivalent to the reduced amount which terminates the procedure. In addition, the scope of application has been also extended to vehicles registered in Italy, even though the driver has obtained his driving licence in a EU non-member State.

However, also in the field of traffic law European States have undertaken attempts to approximate national legislation by adopting guidelines on cooperation, their implementation being left to the goodwill and the discretion of the individual parties. In fact, Italy with the enactment of law no. 949 of 19 November 1984 has ratified the *European Convention on the International Effects of Deprivation of the Right to Drive a Motor Vehicle*, under which "the Contracting Party which has ordered a driving deprivation shall without delay notify the Contracting Party which delivered the driving licence and the Contracting Party in whose territory the offender is habitually resident" (Article 2). In this way, the receiving contracting party can adopt a driving deprivation order, according to its national law. Italy has designated the Ministry of Transport as the competent authority for procedures under this Convention.

As a result of this brief analysis, several weak points inherent in administrative cooperation stand out, with special concern as regards its excessively narrow field of development. On the other hand, the establishment of workable administrative assistance requires conventional instruments between individual countries, in order to take into consideration the peculiarities of each legal system. In conclusion, the principal objective is to extend the existing instrument of cooperation to the sectors falling outside their scope of application, in order to fill the gaps that result from international sanctioning and to prevent the creation of areas of illegality.

8. THE LONG-TERM DEPENALISATION PROCESS AND THE CURRENT PRACTICAL OCCURRENCE OF ADMINISTRATIVE SANCTIONS

The *stricto sensu* administrative sanction is used in order to attain diversification and other options within the national punitive system; it is normally provided for forms of conduct that are not sufficiently serious to deserve criminal punishment.

Starting in the 1990s the importance of administrative offences has increased: the use of administrative sanctions to replace traditional criminal punishment has been looked upon as a possible solution to the crises within the criminal system (both at the substantive and procedural level). In fact, since the outset of the 20th century an excessive proliferation of criminal offences had occurred, because of politico-historical reasons and with a view to granting individuals an adequate system of protection against possible abuses in the exercise of the punitive powers of the State.[62] Nonetheless, after several decades such legislative practice had led to the enlargement of the criminal system and to the consequent deterioration in the application and interpretation of the law[63] as well as, moreover, the uncontrolled multiplication of pending trials and the excessive average duration of the proceedings.[64]

As we have said, mechanisms for ameliorating and speeding up the criminal system have been adopted both at the procedural and substantive level.

At the procedural level the solutions have mainly concerned the criminal sector: on the one hand, a number of concentrated alternative procedures for the imposition of sanctions have been introduced; on the other, justices of the peace have also been provided with competence in criminal matters.

With reference to the first-mentioned aspect, Book VI of the code of criminal procedure regulates the "*riti speciali*" (special alternative procedures)[65], whose principal and common trait is the lack of one of the phases that form the ordinary procedure (the preliminary investigation, the preliminary hearing and, finally, the trial).

---

62 In fact, only the system of criminal sanctions was sufficiently clear to comply with the standards for a fair trial.

63 For instance, the overlapping of different normative sources and the lack of coordination between them amounted to difficulties in interpretation.

64 The excessive duration of a trial violates Article 111 Const. establishing the principle of the reasonable length of proceedings, in conformity with the ECHR (*fair and public hearing within a reasonable time*). The guarantees shall not be so strict that they will unreasonably delay the trial. Moreover, the excessive duration of a trial brings with it problems concerning the statute of limitations for the crime and the ending of pre-trial custody, even when the crime in question is very serious with implications for public safety.

65 Different types of summary trial (for example, without preliminary hearings, or before the judge of preliminary investigation); plea bargaining.

At a substantive level, the legislator has embarked on a depenalisation process, firstly by abolishing obsolete offences (decriminalisation) and, secondly, by replacing criminal sanctions with administrative sanctions (depenalisation *stricto sensu*), according to certain criteria like the seriousness of the offence, the significance of the interest to be protected, the necessity for a criminal sanction and the statistical frequency of the violation.

The latter process (depenalisation *stricto sensu*) was first undertaken in the 1960s[66], at first by means of sectoral acts[67] and then by means of wide-ranging reforms.[68]

Nonetheless, the most relevant changes occurred with the enactment of aforementioned law no. 689/1981, which solved the main problem inherent in the ongoing depenalisation process: the lack of a general regulation for administrative sanctions. As is evident, the necessary prerequisite for the effectiveness of such a process is the availability of a certain type of punishment – as an alternative to criminal sanctions – subject to a comprehensive regulation.[69]

After this act, other reforms followed: law no. 561/1993, which depenalised legislation in several sectors; legislative decree no. 480/1994 concerning public safety; in the field of labour law, legislative decree nos. 211/1994 on the non-payment of social security charges[70], 566/1994 concerning the employment of juveniles, women having children and outworkers,[71] and 758/1994, which depenalised *contravvenzioni* (minor offences) punished exclusively with a fine (*ammenda*), thereby introducing a peculiar mechanism for extinguishing minor offences concerning health and safety at work, by making the sanctions system harsher; in the field of banking and stockbroking, legislative decrees nos. 385/1993 on the monitoring and management of banks and 58/1998 on stockbroking.

Eventually, law no. 205/1999[72], by means of which Parliament has delegated to the Government the power to reform a number of sectors[73], is worthy of

66 See Bernardi, *Brevi note sulle linee evolutive della depenalizzazione in Italia*, in *Indice Penale*, 2001.

67 For example, law nos. 317/1960 and 950/1960 concerning, respectively, road traffic law and environmental forestry law.

68 For example, law no. 706/1975 that depenalised minor offences (contravvenzioni) punished with only a fine (ammenda), adopted formal criteria that allowed transversal intervention.

69 As it is obvious, however, the sanctioning instrument should also be effective in the practice.

70 This act established that the payment of late contributions within a certain term after the notification of the allegation precludes punishability.

71 This act made the sanctions system relating to safety at work somewhat harsher and it depenalised those offences concerning the monitoring of labour relations by the PA.

72 Law no. 205/1999 was implemented by legislative decrees nos. 507/1999 and 74/2000. It is worth pointing out that the principle of the retroactive effect of tax law under Article 20 of law no. 4/1929 has been abolished. Under this law tax acts, even if repealed, still had to be applied to the actions committed at the time they were in force.

73 Food law, maritime law, road traffic law, customs law, tax law, stockbroking and banking.

particular attention: besides the wide-ranging scope of its application, this act contains a remarkable set of criteria for deflating the criminal system, each of which fits the peculiarities of the sector concerned.

Such comprehensive intervention had to look at general principles for selecting those offences to be depenalised in order to avoid any possible incoherence; therefore, the legislator adopted the principles of proportionality and subsidiarity (at a theoretical level) and took into account the statistical frequency of the violation in question (at the empirical level) as guidelines for this reform.

Under the principle of proportionality, the use of a criminal sanction should meet two parameters: the importance of the interest to be protected and the seriousness of the offence. Since a criminal punishment will entail high degree of distress as it can affect personal freedom, its imposition must be limited to those forms of conduct that seriously harm significant interests. On the other hand, when the interest to be protected has no traditional importance and when the offence is not particularly serious, an administrative sanction should be preferred.

Under the principle of subsidiarity, criminal sanctions can only be used when there are no other instruments of social control with equivalent effect. As is evident, this principle assumes the availability of a set of alternative sanctioning instruments which are very effective; otherwise the depenalisation process could lead to a lack of protection in certain legal fields.

The policy of looking at the statistical frequency of the violations in question prescribes that the most recurrent offences should be depenalised in order to reduce the workload of the courts. Nevertheless, this policy just adopt a balanced approach so that the legal protection of those who are most vulnerable will not be weakened.

According to these guidelines, the legislator has adopted a number of different techniques. The formal policy of making a selection based on the type of sanction provided for the offence has often been adopted.[74] However, such a choice is not always satisfactory as it leaves aside any consideration of the seriousness and the characteristics of the violation; on the other hand, it allows for a very rapid intervention as it applies automatically to any offence punished with a given sanction.

However, substantive criteria have also been implemented, for example considering the significance of the interest to be protected or the seriousness of the harmful conduct. On the one hand, the complexity of these evaluations

[74] This criterion assumes that he type of sanction imposed is based on an assessment of the seriousness of the offence. Consequently, to depenalise a leniently punished offence – as has often occurred with offences punished with only a fine – would mean depenalising less serious offences generally.

exclude wide-ranging reform, but having said that, they also better fit the principle of proportionality since they take each offence more into consideration.

As we have said, the precondition for a workable depenalisation process is the availability of an alternative type of sanction which is legislatively regulated and has an equivalent practical effect. While the first task has been achieved with the enactment of law no. 689/1981, the second is still to be attained.

The degree of effectiveness of administrative sanctions – or, in other words, the percentage relating to the imposition and execution of the sentence – depends on a number of factors: most of all, on the set of human, material and financial sources for the functioning of the system and on the efficiency and capability of the competent authorities. More in particular, the effectiveness depends on the activities of the investigative bodies, which are often not sufficiently staffed to carry out widespread inspections; on the cooperation between the different authorities involved in the sanctioning proceeding, which are not always properly coordinated; and on the economic efficiency of the PA which, in most cases, is pursued by cost reductions and not by improving operational efficiency.

Some statistical studies have demonstrated the effectiveness of administrative fines in some significant sectors.

In the employment sector the competent body is the *Ispettorato del lavoro*.[75] According to a national survey the payment of reduced fines (following an admission of responsibility) amounts to more than 50% of the money collected. On the other hand, besides these voluntary payments, only 12.53% of the fines imposed by means of administrative orders are immediately collected. The information concerning the remainder of the money collected is unclear: from the research carried out at the competent PA there is uncertainty as to the destiny of those fines not immediately collected. The most striking data relate to the following: only 5.37% of enforced executions succeeds.

In the field of public health[76] the competent investigative bodies are the agencies of the *Aziende Sanitarie Locali* (ASL), the local branches of the national health care system. The person who has competence to impose the sanction is the *Major*, who is the head of the local administrative organization (at the municipality level). According to a survey carried out at the local level, 85% of the sanctions imposed are immediately executed, only 9% of the files alleging violations are annulled and only 6% of the violations discovered require an enforcement procedure. Information concerning the percentage of sanctions effectively gathered as a result of enforcement procedures is not available.

---

75 The hierarchical organization of the Ministry of Labour is made up of Regional Departments, then by Provincial Departments, under which the *Ispettorati del Lavoro* operate.

76 The activities at stake concern veterinary medicine especially with regard to the health of animals, the hygiene of foodstuffs of animal origin, the hygiene of animal husbandry.

In the field of road traffic violations, the investigative bodies are national police road patrols and the *Carabinieri* (responsible for public security and belonging to the army) on highways and major roads and the local police for urban traffic. The bodies with competence to impose the sanctions are the *Prefettura* (the local representative of the government) or the Municipality where the violation has been committed. In general, the majority of violations are discovered by the local police or the national road patrols, since this forms a major part of their activities. According to the pertinent statistics, around 64% of all sanctions are paid immediately and only 5% of administrative orders are challenged before the courts. Some 31% of fines require enforcement proceedings. No figures are available with regard to the success of enforcement proceedings.

In conclusion, it is evident that the effectiveness of administrative sanctions varies to a great extent in the different sectors and that it is necessary to strengthen and improve the sanctioning procedures of the PA so as to avoid that the depenalisation process which has taken place during the last few decades (but is still ongoing) will lead to new areas of illegality and the weakening of the punitive system.

From a different standpoint, if the depenalisation process is aimed at decreasing the case load of the criminal courts – as is evident from the selection policy based on the statistical frequency of offences – then it should not turn into a destabilizing factor with regard to case load of the administrative and civil courts. Having said this, this possibility is not very likely to occur.

Firstly, the sanction is imposed as a result of an administrative (and not a judicial) proceeding.

Consequently, the judicial phase[77] is merely an eventuality that only occurs when the addressee of the sanction wants to challenge the administrative order. In order to discourage this choice, the legislator has provided for a general possibility to pay a reduced fine and to extinguish the violation (as we have seen, according to Article 16 of law no. 689/1981).

Besides this general possibility, in some sectors certain provisions are applicable that are intended to reduce the number of litigations concerning the imposition of administrative sanctions; they can either apply before a judicial proceeding has been initiated (in order to preclude this eventuality), or with regard to an already pending case.

In the field of public health, for example, the recorded violation is made known to the alleged offender and is transmitted to the budget office of the local public health agency. Within 60 days, the offender can preclude further proceedings by paying a reduced amount; as a consequence, details of the

77 Except in peculiar fields – e.g. fiscal litigation – the judgment instigated by the challenging of the administrative sanctioning decision takes place before the civil courts and not before the administrative courts.

recorded violation will be filed. In addition, the *Major* also enjoys the power to annul the sanctioning decision by means of a purely discretionary decision. Only if these options do not occur will the addressee of the sanction appeal against the administrative order before a civil court.[78]

In fiscal matters, legislative decree no. 472/1997 has introduced several alternative ways to reduce the case load of the "Commissioni tributarie", the special courts with competence to decide on fiscal matters.[79] The legislator, with a view to pursuing that objective, has encouraged tax payers who have committed a violation to resort to alternative methods of settlement, by granting them substantial advantages, especially significant reduction in the sanction and the non-application of ancillary punishment.

The main alternative procedures are:

- "*Definizione in via breve*" (a form of speedy settlement): Article 16 para. 3 of legislative decree no. 472/97 allows the violator and others who may be jointly liable to pay a fine reduced to one quarter of the amount imposed (provided it is not less than a quarter of the minimum sentence provided for the most serious violation relating to the tax in question) within the term (60 days) for the lodging of a petition before the fiscal commissions. This option bars the imposition of ancillary punishment.
- "*Ravvedimento operoso*" (active repentance): Article 13 of legislative decree no. 472/97 extends the scope of application of this provision that was first limited to VAT and direct taxes. The taxpayer who is responsible for a violation can evade the eventual sanction by paying the tax owed plus the legal interest and the administrative fine reduced to one eighth (or to one sixth depending on the type of violation and on the delay) of the minimum before the violation has already been discovered and no inquiry, inspections or investigation have been initiated.
- "*Accertamento con adesione*" (negotiated assessment). The negotiated assessment was introduced by Article 2*bis* and 2*ter* of legislative decree no. 564/1994; it was then integrated into law no. 656/1994. Eventually legislative decree no. 218/1997 amended this provision, widening its scope of application. The core of this provision is the possibility to determine, together with the PA by means of negotiation, the eventual fiscal debt. This procedure

---

78 The regulation of the sanctioning proceeding in the field of public health is laid down in different acts, mainly enacted by the Regions. As a matter of fact, legislative decree no. 502/1992 grants the Regions the competence to regulate the activities of the ASL (local health agencies) in the field in question. However, the general principles of law no. 689/1981 still apply.

79 Due to the particular complexity of this subject, the competence concerning fiscal litigation belongs to special administrative courts: the *Commissioni Tributarie Provinciali* (tax court of first instance) and the *Commissioni Tributarie Provinciali* (tax court for appellate proceedings).

is applicable when the fiscal administrative bodies have already carried out an inquiry or an inspection. The initiative could come from both the taxpayer or the administration. If a violation is found and the taxpayer agrees to pay a certain amount, the sanction can be significantly reduced.

- "*Conciliazione giudiziale*" (judicial conciliation): this has been regulated in the fiscal sector by Article 14 of legislative decree no. 218/1997. This provision (first introduced in civil procedure) allows the taxpayer to resolve, by means of agreement those cases which are pending before the provincial fiscal commission (the first level of fiscal jurisdiction). The prerequisite is therefore a pending case (unlike the "*accertamento con adesione*"). Both parties can propose this form of conciliation with regard to the amount of taxes to be paid: if an agreement is achieved, the pecuniary sanction will be reduced to 1/3. This is a paradigmatic example of attempting to reduce the case load by means of encouraging alternative measures.
- "*Autotutela*" (self-recognition of irregularities by the PA). Article 68 of regulation no. 287/1992 provides the fiscal administration with the specific power to annul its actions when an irregularity is found and a judicial decision has not yet been taken. The annulment shall be supported by sufficient grounds and notified to the interested party. This provision allows the PA to correct irregularities that would otherwise lead to meaningless judicial litigation.

Ultimately, as a general rule, Article 22*bis* of law no. 689/1981 – as introduced by Article 98 of legislative decree no. 507/1999 – assigned to the Justices of the Peace the competence to hear petitions against administrative sanctioning decisions[80], except for a list of subjects which have particular relevance[81] and for the most severe sanctions.

This legislative option has avoided the risk that the depenalisation process could further aggravate the case load of the already overburdened civil courts; the average length of judicial proceedings is immediately reduced as such cases are heard in a simplified procedure before a Justice of the Peace.

---

80 This competence previously belonged to the civil court.

81 The protection of workers; social security charges; city planning and construction projects; environmental protection; the hygiene of foodstuffs; company law and stockbroking; taxes.

IX. COUNTRY ANALYSIS – THE NETHERLANDS

Oswald JANSEN

1. INTRODUCTION

One of the interesting features of Dutch legal scholarship is the ongoing discussion on law enforcement that has been conducted since the Eighties of the last century.[1] In comparison with the discussion on this subject in legal scholarship elsewhere in Europe, as far as I can see, the Dutch discussion is different in that it involves an approach which takes the different kinds of law enforcement systems into account. The legal discussion about law enforcement not only focuses on criminal law or administrative law, but also on private law and even disciplinary law (*tuchtrecht*), and examines not only each discipline in its own right but also the way in which they relate to each other. This contribution, however, will be restricted to administrative law.

One of the interesting features of Dutch administrative law is the availability of a recent codification of general administrative law, the General Administrative Law Act or GALA (*Algemene wet bestuursrecht*), which not only has general provisions on enforcement action (*last onder bestuursdwang*) and periodic penalty payments or *astreinte* (*last onder dwangsom*), which are considered to be sanctions, but also on administrative fines (*bestuurlijke boete*). The general provisions on administrative fines came into effect on 1 July 2009, and marked an important stage in the recognition and development of administrative fines.

The development of administrative fines in the Netherlands is closely related to another feature which is interesting from a comparative administrative law point of view. The Dutch legal system does not have constitutional courts, nor review of the constitutionality of the legislation enacted by national parliament. In

---

1 Important examples are Wetenschappelijke Raad voor het Regeringsbeleid (Scientific Council for Government Policy), *Rechtshandhaving* (Law Enforcement), Staatsuitgeverij, 's-Gravenhage 1988; G.J.M. Corstens, *Civielrechtelijke, Administratiefrechtelijke of Strafrechtelijke rechtshandhaving?*, preliminary advice Nederlandse Juristenvereniging, Kluwer, Deventer 1984.

short, the European Convention on Human Rights (ECHR) plays an important role, as national courts can review the conformity of legislation with the ECHR and, in many cases, the European Court of Human Rights (ECtHR) fulfils the role of a constitutional court. The Öztürk Judgment of the ECtHR has been highly influential in the development of administrative fines in Dutch administrative law.

For these reasons, administrative fines, or more generally punitive sanctions (*bestraffende sancties*), will play an important role in this contribution. As remedial sanctions (*herstelsancties)* are also important, they will be described here too.

2. THE DEFINITION OF SANCTION

Although law enforcement in administrative law was discussed as early as 1931,[2] and specific sanctions were discussed in 1942,[3] 1949,[4] 1954[5] and 1957,[6] the first serious attempt to define administrative sanctions would be the PhD thesis of Oostenbrink of 1967.[7] According to his definition, administrative sanctions are: 'sanctions that stem from the relationship authority-subject and that may be imposed directly by the administration itself (...) without third-party intervention and, in particular, without court authorization'.[8] These sanctions are imposed 'in a constitutive decision of an administrative body,

2 H. Vos, *Handhaving van het bestuursrecht, in Nederlands bestuursrecht*, first edition 1931.

3 J. van der Poel, *Rondom compositie en compromis*, 1942. See also his contribution "Een nieuw kleed voor het fiscaal strafrecht", *Tijdschrift van Strafrecht* LX (1951). His contributions focus mainly on tax law. Nevertheless, his ideas about administrative fines and his statement that this sanction is suitable for a broad number of legal areas outside tax law has often been quoted in more recent literature. In his PhD thesis, he cited the findings of a commission named after its president: Commissie Van den Dries. This commission published a report in 1936 on the reform of criminal tax law in which this commission recommended the introduction of the administrative fine in tax law. A few examples of more recent literature: A. Mulder, *De verhouding van administratieve sancties en straffen*, in: A.D. Belinfante and A. Mulder, *De verhouding van administratieve sancties en straffen, preadviezen uitgebracht voor de algemene vergadering van de Vereniging voor administratief recht van 31 mei 1957*, H.D. Tjeenk Willink & Zoon N.V., Haarlem 1957, pp. 46–48, and Van Wijk/Konijnenbelt &Van Male, *Hoofdstukken van Bestuursrecht*, 15th edition, Amsterdam 2011, p. 467. Van der Poel illustrated the Dutch doctrine that criminal law was inspired by administrative law in the introduction of criminal law fines.

4 A. Mulder, *De handhaving van de sociaal-economische wetgeving*, doctoral thesis, Groningen 1949.

5 W.F. Prins, *Politiedwang, Geschriften VAR 1954.*

6 A.D. Belinfante and A. Mulder, *De verhouding van administratieve sancties en straffen, preadviezen uitgebracht voor de algemene vergadering van de Vereniging voor administratief recht van 31 mei 1957*, H.D. Tjeenk Willink & Zoon N.V., Haarlem 1957.

7 J.J. Oostenbrink, *Administratieve sancties*, VUGA-Boekerij, The Hague 1967.

8 J.J. Oostenbrink, *Administratieve sancties*, VUGA-Boekerij, The Hague 1967, p. 8.

taken in response to a specific infringement of a legal norm, which decision decreases some of the legal interests (in the broadest sense) to which the offender was rightly entitled to before the imposition of that sanction.'[9] In 1971 Van Angeren described sanctions as 'the means which the authority may use in accordance with the law, if the citizen fails to comply with administrative law, or threatens not to comply with it.'[10] In 1973 Duk wrote: 'Without the pretension of giving a definition, I generally class as 'sanction': reactions to wrongful conduct provided for by law (or at least allowed or required) – or consequences arising by operation of law – in so far as the interests of the offender are affected.[11] In 1988 Duk used a more concise definition: 'a response allowed (or required) by law to wrongful conduct, which is intended to directly affect the interests of the offender.'[12] In 1988 Konijnenbelt described sanctions as 'the public law weapons that the government may apply as a response to the failure to comply with obligations arising out of administrative law norms.'[13] In 1992 Rogier just used a more formal description: 'sanctions that are imposed by the administration (the government).'[14] After an analysis of all pre-existing definitions of 'administrative sanction', Hazewindus wrote in 1994 'Administrative sanctions are public law reactions on the part of an administrative authority to the failure to comply with obligations arising from administrative norms, as a result of which the interest of a person who fails to comply with such obligation is affected.'[15]

The definition of administrative sanction (*bestuurlijke sanctie*) used by the legislator in Article 5:2, first paragraph, under a, GALA is different from the usual definition in legal scholarship, as it uses 'imposed obligation or withheld entitlement' (*opgelegde verplichting of onthouden aanspraak)*', 'burdensome

9 J.J. Oostenbrink, *Administratieve sancties*, VUGA-Boekerij, The Hague 1967, p. 21.

10 J.A.M. van Angeren, "De sanctionering van het administratief recht", in: *Preadviezen uitgebracht voor de algemene vergadering van de Vereniging voor administratief recht van 29 oktober 1971*, H.D. Tjeenk Willink, Groningen 1971, p.1.

11 W. Duk, *Tanden van het recht. Oriënterende beschouwingen over sancties*, address given on the acceptance of the position of professor in a general introduction to law and comparative constitutional and administrative law at the University of Amsterdam on 1 October 1973, Tjeenk Willink, Zwolle 1973, p. 11.

12 W. Duk, "Handhaving van bestuursrecht", *NTB* 1988, pp. 105–110, esp. p. 105.

13 Van Wijk/ Konijnenbelt, *Hoofdstukken van administratief recht*, Lemma, The Hague 1988, p. 327. Since the 9th edition of this handbook, after the PhD thesis of Hazewindus of which the author was the supervisor, he changed his definition slightly into: 'the burdensome measures provided under public law that the government applies to a city as a response to non-compliance (...) with obligations arising from administrative norms'. See Van Wijk, Konijnenbelt and Van Male, *Hoofdstukken van Bestuursrecht*, 15th edition, Amsterdam 2011, p. 430.

14 L.J.J. Rogier, *Strafsancties, administratieve sancties en het una via-beginsel*, thesis EUR, Arnhem 1992, p. 17.

15 Pim (W.G.A) Hazewindus, *Administratieve sancties en vreemdelingenrecht*, thesis UvA, Gouda Quint, Arnhem 1994, p.13.

measure' (*belastende maatregel* (Konijnenbelt)) or in ' his interest is affected ('*in zijn belang getroffen*') (Hazewindus)). This is of importance for the position of the revocation of a beneficiary decision (*intrekking van een begunstigend besluit*) in this definition, as Michiels and De Waard argued in their criticism.[16]

In Dutch legal scholarship, it is generally accepted that administrative law measures as a reaction to a infringement *(overtreding)* are sanctions whether they have a punitive aim or not. If these sanctions have a punitive aim, they are called punitive sanction (*bestraffende sanctie*), if they have the aim of restoring the legal order they are called remedial sanction (*herstelsanctie*). I am following the names the legislator has chosen in Article 5:2 GALA, which reads as follows:

1. In this Act, the following definitions apply:
   a. administrative sanction: an obligation imposed or an entitlement withheld by an administrative authority on account of a violation;
   b. reparation sanction: an administrative sanction intended to fully or partially undo or terminate a violation, to prevent repetition of a violation or to eliminate or limit the consequences of a violation;
   c. punitive sanction: an administrative sanction intended to inflict harm on the offender.
2. An order to perform certain specific acts is not in itself an administrative sanction.

By choosing the element of the definition '*door een bestuursorgaan*' (by an administrative authority), the legislator explicitly excluded sanctions imposed by a judge, especially the criminal judge (*strafrechter*) and the disciplinary judge (*tuchtrechter*).[17] The Public Prosecution Service (*Openbaar Ministerie*), or more precisely the *public prosecutors* have the power to impose certain sanctions as well by imposing a punishment order (*strafbeschikking*) by way of an out-of-court settlement offered by the Public Prosecution Service (*OM-afdoening*).[18] GALA is not applicable to criminal proceedings (*strafvervolging*),[19] and this punishment order has explicitly been defined as an act of prosecution (*daad van vervolging)* to exclude the punishment order from GALA regulation. In the explanatory notes (*memorie van toelichting*), the legislator explains the definition of administrative sanctions as follows:

> 'In the second place, a sanction involves either an obligation imposed by an administrative authority or the full or partial withholding of an entitlement by an

---

16 F.C.M.A. Michiels and B.W.N. de Waard, *Rechterlijke toetsing van bestuurlijke punitieve sancties*, Boom Juridische uitgevers, The Hague 2007, pp. 9–10, pp. 24–25, p. 41.

17 Parliamentary documents II, 2003–2004, 29 702, no. 3, p. 82.

18 See Articles 74–74c DCC and 257a-257ba DCP. A translation of these provisions can be found at pp. 339–342.

19 Article 1:6 GALA.

> administrative authority. This obligation may be to pay a sum of money, as in the administrative fine, but it may also be an obligation to end a violation in combination with a conditional obligation to pay a sum of money, as in an astreinte. The words 'or entitlement withheld' have been included because there are sanctions in the setting of social security and subsidies that do not imply a new obligation on the offender so much as a reduction (possibly to nothing) of the (financial) entitlements that the offender would have had without the violation. In the third place, it is only a question of a sanction when an administrative authority imposes an obligation or withholds an entitlement as a response to a violation, in other words an act which violates a provision prescribed by or pursuant to law (Article 5:1, first paragraph). This element of the definition distinguishes administrative sanctions from obligations, such as levies, which administrative authorities can impose in response to acts that need not necessarily conflict with any administrative provision.'[20]

In (earlier) legal scholarship different terms have been and are sometimes still used, such as *punitieve sancties* and *retributieve sancties* to name punitive sanctions (*bestraffende sancties*), and *reparatoire sancties* or *situatieve sancties* to name remedial sanctions (*herstelsancties*). The most important examples of remedial sanctions are the astreinte (*last onder dwangsom*) and the enforcement action (*last onder bestuursdwang*).[21] The most important example of a punitive sanction (*bestraffende sanctie*) is the administrative fine (*bestuurlijke boete*).[22] All these sanctions have their own general set of rules in the General Administrative Law Act. As we will see the power to impose these sanctions, the competence of the administrative body to impose them and the infringements for which they can be imposed are all regulated in special acts; GALA just offers general rules and principles.

In addition to the astreinte and enforcement action, there are more remedial sanctions, such as the full or entire withdrawal of a subsidy or benefit (*gehele of gedeeltelijke intrekking van een subsidie of een uitkering*). Besides the administrative fine, other measures have been recognised as punitive sanction, such as the punitive revocation of a beneficiary decision (*bestraffende intrekking van een begunstigende beschikking*) or 'naming and shaming'.

---

20 Parliamentary documents II 2003–2004, 29 702, no. 3, p.83.

21 Both administrative sanctions are regulated in Title 5.4, Articles 5:21–5:39 GALA. The enforcement action (*last onder bestuursdwang)* is defined in Article 5:21 GALA where this is defined as a duty backed by enforcement action means: the remedial sanction, requiring: a. an order requiring full or partial reparation of the violation and b. empowering the administrative authority to carry out the order itself if it is not carried out or not carried out in time. The astreinte is defined in Article 5:31d GALA: a duty backed by an astreinte refers to the reparation sanction, requiring: a. full or partial reparation of the violation, and b. the obligation to pay a sum of money if the order is not carried out or not carried out in time.

22 The general rules on administrative fines are provided for in Title 5.1 and Title 5.4.

Depending on its aim, the revocation of a beneficiary decision (*intrekking van een begunstigende beschikking*) may be an administrative sanction or not; if it is considered to be an administrative sanction, depending on its aim once again, it may be considered a remedial sanction or a punitive sanction.[23] This means that it is difficult to categorise this measure, especially if the beneficiary decision (*begunstigende beschikking*) is a financial one.

To complete the image, I should add that the so called independent order (*zelfstandige last*) or single order (*enkelvoudige last*), which in many cases and especially in the area of economic and financial regulation is called an instruction (*aanwijzing*) in special acts, is sometimes considered to be an administrative sanction, as it is imposed on account of a violation.[24] Presumably to avoid problems, GALA has excluded this measure from the definition of administrative sanctions in Article 5:2, second paragraph. The explanatory notes read as follows:

> 'A number of administrative laws give an administrative authority the power to impose an obligation on a citizen or an enterprise to perform certain acts in order to comply with statutory provisions. It is then referred to as an independent or single order. (...) Administrative sanctions can often be applied against the failure to carry out such an order but, in many cases, the order can itself be imposed in response to a violation. The legislator thought that is was desirable in such cases that the authority first clearly defines which obligations ensue for the citizen from the violated norm before it is able to actually enforce compliance with those obligations. In this light, it is not desirable that the single order also be regarded as an administrative sanction. Now that the definition in the first paragraph could lead to some doubt on this matter, the second paragraph states specifically that the single order is not an administrative sanction.'[25]

Other punitive sanctions in case law and legal scholarship: the struggle for clarity

As the explanatory notes clearly show the legislator decided not to try to define punitive sanctions more clearly, which was probably a wise choice:

---

23 See on this revocation recently Willemien den Ouden, "De intrekking van begunstigende beschikkingen door bestuursorganen", in: T. Barkhuysen *et al.* (eds.), *Bestuursrecht harmoniseren: 15 jaar Awb*, Boom Juridische uitgevers, The Hague 2010, 689–715, K.J. de Graaf and A.T. Marseille, "Het intrekken en wijzigen van onjuiste besluiten: niet alles in een keer goed", in: M. Herweijer *et al.* (eds.), *Alles in een keer goed. Juridische kwaliteit van bestuurlijke besluitvorming*, Kluwer, Deventer 2004, pp. 305–323; M.A.M. Dieperink, "Omtrekken van een algemene regeling voor intrekken", in: *De vijfde tranche, Preadviezen Jonge VAR 2002*, Boom Juridische Uitgevers, The Hague 2003, p. 55 *et seq.*; C.L.G.F.H. Albers, "De intrekking van een begunstigende beschikking bij wijze van sanctie", *NTB* 2009. See more generally on the revocation of stable administrative decis-ions Rolf Ortlep, *De aantasting van stabiele bestuursrechtelijke rechtsvaststellingen in het licht van het Unierecht*, Kluwer, Deventer 2011.

24 O.J.D.M.L. Jansen, De zelfstandige last en de bindende aanwijzing, in: D. Doorenbos (*et al.*), Onderneming en Sanctierecht, Kluwer, Deventer 2013, p. 173-189.

25 Parliamentary documents II 2003–2004, pp. 84–85.

'Administrative sanctions that are not remedial sanctions are often called 'punitive' sanctions. They are referred to as punitive sanctions (*bestraffende sancties*) in the legislative proposal. Punitive sanctions are characterized by the fact that they are imposed with the intention of having a damaging effect on the offender.

There has been a great deal of case law and literature on the question when this criterion has been fulfilled. This can, however, be disregarded in this context now that the proposed provisions only apply to the administrative fine for the time being, whose character is in any case a punitive one, and to other punitive sanctions designated as such (see Articles 5:3 and 5:54).'[26]

The ECtHR case law on the definition of a criminal charge in Article 6 ECHR plays a crucial role in determining whether an administrative sanction should be considered punitive. Determining what sanctions are punitive according to the case law of the ECtHR is, however, rather complicated.[27] The criteria the ECtHR introduced with the Engel-case[28] in fact only amount to the question whether the ECtHR considers the aim of the sanction to be punitive or not. The Council of State seems to make a distinction between remedial and punitive sanctions by determining whether a sanction causes more disadvantage than the disadvantage a sanction only aimed at terminating or preventing a infringement would cause.[29]

In administrative case law so far, the punitive character of a few decisions to impose sanctions has been denied. Two administrative law measures, however, have caused difficulties in the determination of their punitive character: the temporary withdrawal of beneficiary decisions (*intrekking van een begunstigende beschikking*) and the publication of a decision to impose an administrative sanction ('naming and shaming').

Initially, the Council of State considered the temporary revocation of beneficiary decisions such as permits or the recognition as a MOT service provider for a short period as punitive but this case law has changed since the end of 2005.[30] The administrative courts now seldom regard the withdrawal or revocation of a beneficiary decision as punitive.

26 Parliamentary documents II 2003–2004, 29 702, no. 3, p. 84.

27 The latest analysis: R. Stijnen, *Rechtsbescherming tegen bestraffing in het strafrecht en het bestuursrecht*, Kluwer, Deventer 2011, p. 49–67. See also F.M.J. den Houdijker, *Rechtsbescherming bij bestuurlijke punitieve sancties: een bron van spanning?*, pp. 9–53, especially pp. 25–32.

28 ECtHR 8 June 1976.

29 See for example ABRvS 9 March 2011, *AB* 2011, 103. See on this discussion F.C.M.A. Michiels and B.W.N. de Waard, *Rechterlijke toetsing van bestuurlijke punitieve sancties*, Boom Juridische uitgevers, The Hague 2007, pp. 10–17.

30 Since ABRvS 2 November 2005, *JB* 2006/11. See R. Stijnen, *Rechtsbescherming tegen bestraffing in het strafrecht en het bestuursrecht*, Kluwer, Deventer 2011, pp. 60–63. See on this measure in general C.C.G.F.H. Albers, "De intrekking van een begunstigende beschikking bij

Due to the circumstance that the legislator in financial administrative law departed from its initial opinion that the publication of the discovery of a infringement, or the publication of a decision to impose an *astreinte* or a decision to impose an administrative fine is punitive, legal scholarship started to pay attention to the punitive character of such a decision.[31] Administrative courts have followed the aims the legislator gave to the publication and, for this reason, according to established case law, these decisions to publish are not considered to be punitive.[32]

3. THE DEVELOPMENT OF ENFORCEMENT ACTION (*LAST ONDER BESTUURSDWANG*) AND THE ASTREINTE (*LAST ONDER DWANGSOM*) IN THE NETHERLANDS

Enforcement action (*bestuursdwang*) is the oldest, most traditional and most widespread administrative sanction in Dutch administrative law. Since the Fourth Part of GALA was enacted, the official legal term changed into 'the order backed by enforcement action' (*last onder bestuursdwang*).[33] In older literature, this power to restore the legal order by actual act (*feitelijk handelen*) used to be named police enforcement (*politiedwang*). However, this name has nothing to do with the police, as *politie* is the early and now outdated term to refer to the 'administration'.[34] It is generally accepted that an explicit legal basis is required to implement this power. Many specific acts provide for this power.[35] As will be

wijze van sanctie", *NTB* 2009, pp. 173–184 and W. den Ouden, *De intrekking van begunstigende beschikkingen door bestuursorganen. Eens gegeven blijft gegeven?* In: T. Backhuysen (e.a.), *Bestuursrecht harmoniseren: 15 jaar Awb*, Boom Juridische uitgevers, Den Haag 2010, pp. 689–715; A.D.W. Duijkersloot, Maatregelen gericht op de vergunning, ontheffing of verklaring van geen bezwaar, in: D.R. Doorenbos (e.a.), *Onderneming en Sanctierecht*, Kluwer, Deventer 2013.

31 See for example F.C.M.A. Michiels, "Naming en shaming in het markttoezicht", *NTB* 2007, pp. 85-95; D.R. Doorenbos, *Naming & Shaming*, Kluwer, Deventer 2007, and C.A.H. van der Sanden, *De publieke schandpaal in het milieurecht, Milieu en Recht* 2011, pp. 438-444.

32 See R. Stijnen, *Rechtsbescherming tegen bestraffing in het strafrecht en het bestuursrecht*, Kluwer, Deventer 2011, pp. 65–66.

33 This alteration was criticised in legal scholarship, see for example P.J.J. van Buuren, G.T.J.M. Jurgens, F.C.M.A. Michiels, *Bestuursdwang en dwangsom*, Kluwer, Deventer 2011, pp. 8–9.

34 P.J.J. van Buuren, G.T.J.M. Jurgens, F.C.M.A. Michiels, *Bestuursdwang en dwangsom*, Kluwer, Deventer 2011, p. 10 and H.A.W. Snijders, *Gemeenten en bestuursdwang*, VUGA, The Hague 1982, pp. 17–19. See also Bernardo Sordi, Révolution, Rechtsstaat, and the Rule of Law: historical reflections on the emergence of administrative law in Europe, in: Susan Rose-Ackerman and Peter L. Lindseth (eds.), *Comparative Administrative Law*, Edward Elgar, Cheltenham 2010, pp. 23–36, especially p. 28.

35 See in addition to Article 125 of the Municipalities Act, Article 1:31 General Customs Act [*Algemene douanewet*], 28a Working Conditions Act [*Arbeidsomstandighedenwet*], 8:2 Working Hours Act [*Arbeidstijdenwet*], 24, 34 and 39 Public Records Act 1995 [*Archiefwet*

explained below, according to Article 5:32 GALA, the administrative authority is empowered to impose an *astreinte* instead of enforcement action. One should

1995], 44 Inland Navigation Act [*Binnenvaartwet*], 8 Agricultural Production Emergencies Act 1939 [*Bodemproductiewet 1939*], 17 Veterinary Medicines Act [*Diergeneesmiddelenwet*], 44 Licensing and Catering Act [*Drank- en horecawet*], 50 Drinking Water Act [*Drinkwaterwet*, 13, 22, Electricity Act 1998 [*Elektriciteitswet 1998*], 112 Flora and Fauna Act [*Flora- en faunawet*], 5, 9 Gas Act [*Gaswet*], 114 Medicines Act [*Geneesmiddelenwet*], 106 Health and Welfare of Animals Act [*Gezondheids- en welzijnswet voor dieren*], 6a Hoarding Act [*Hamsterwet*], 18 Port Security Act [*Havenbeveiligingswet*], 7 Ports (Emergencies) Act [*Havennoodwet*], 51, 52 Billeting Act [*Inkwartieringswet*], 30 Animal Feedstuff Framework Act [*Kaderwet diervoeders*], 22, 33, 66 Nuclear Energy Act [*Kernenergiewet*], 10 Care Institutions (Quality) Act [*Kwaliteitswet zorginstellingen*], 19 Agricultural Quality Act [*Landbouwkwaliteitswet*], 9 Local Rail and Tramway Act [*Locaalspoor- en tramwegwet*], 46 Pilotage Act [*Loodsenwet*], 37ae, 37u, 72, Aviation Act [*Luchtvaartwet*], 49 Fertilizers Act [*Meststoffenwet*], 35 Metrology Act [*Metrologiewet*], 47, 48, 132, Mining Act [*Mijnbouwwet*], 57, 67 Nature Conservation Act 1998 [*Natuurbeschermingswet 1998]*, 44 Labour Supply (Emergencies) Act [*Noodwet Arbeidsvoorziening*], 32 Medical Practitioners (Emergencies) Act [*Noodwet geneeskundigen*], 26 Emergency Food Supply Act [*Noodwet voedselvoorziening*], 60 War Act [*Oorlogswet voor Nederland*], 13b Opium Act [*Opiumwet*], 7, 12 Plant Diseases Act [*Plantenziektenwet*], 48 Postal Act 2009 [*Postwet 2009*], 24, 25, 37a Shipping Traffic Act [*Scheepvaartverkeerswet*], 76 Railways Act [*Spoorwegwet*], 15.2, 15.17 Telecommunications Act [*Telecommunicatiewet*], 18 EC Regulation on Territorial Cooperation (Implementation) Act [*Uitvoeringswet EGTS verordening*], 14 Transport (Emergencies) Act [*Vervoersnoodwet*], 54b Fisheries Act 1963 [*Visserijwet 1963*], 10, 22, 27 Requisition Act [*Vorderingswet*], 32 Commodities Act [*Warenwet*], 42b Public Works Act 1900 [*Waterstaatswet 1900*], 8.5, 8.7, Water Act [*Waterwet*], 169, 170 Road Traffic Act 1994 [*Wegenverkeerswet 1994*], 10 Local Rail and Tramway Building Act [*Wet aanleg locaalspoor- en tramwegen*], 26 Liability of Oil Tankers Act [*Wet aansprakelijkheid olietankschepen*], 4 Natural Gas Prices Act [*Wet aardgasprijzen*], 5.14, 5.15 Environmental Permitting (General Provisions) Act [*Wet algemene bepalingen omgevingsrecht*], 15 Ambulance Care Act [*Wet ambulancezorg*], 7 Public Works (Management of Engineering Structures) Act [*Wet beheer rijkswaterstaatswerken*], 27 Protection of Antartica Act [*Wet bescherming Antarctica*], 61, 65 Personal Data Protection Act [*Wet bescherming persoonsgegevens*], 8 Availability of Goods Act [*Wet beschikbaarheid goederen]*, 29 Civil Authority Special Powers Act [*Wet buitengewone bevoegdheden burgerlijk gezag*], 9 Capacity Management Inland Shipping Fleet Act [*Wet capaciteitsbeheersing binnenvaartvloot*], 8.5 Animals Act [*Wet dieren*], 8, 31 Explosives for Civil Uses Act [*Wet explosieven voor civiel gebruik*], 86, 87 Plant Protection Products and Biocides Act [*Wet gewasbeschermingsmiddelen en biociden*], 7 Approval and Implementation of Markham Field Agreement Act [*Wet goedkeuring en uitvoering Markham-overeenkomst*], 22 Swimming Pools and Baths (Hygiene and Safety) Act [*Wet hygiene en veiligheid badinrichtingen en zwemgelegenheden*], 25 Underground Grids (Information Exchange) Act [*Wet informative-uitwisseling ondergrondse netten*], 30 Cableway Installations Act [*Wet kabelbaaninstallaties*], 11.15, 11.21 Aviation Act [*Wet luchtvaart*], 80, 81, 82 Healthcare (Market Regulation) Act [*Wet marktordening gezondheidszorg*], 100a Individual Healthcare Professions Act [*Wet op de beroepen in de individuele gezondheidszorg*], 24 Experiment on Animals Act [*Wet op de dierproeven*], 16 Youth Care Act [*Wet op de jeugdzorg*], 35Betting and Gaming Act [*Wet op de kansspelen*], 12 Medical Appliances Act [*Wet op de medische hulpmiddelen*], 82c, 93, Passenger Transport Act 2000 [*Wet personenvervoer 2000*], 34, 56 Public Health Act [*Wet publieke gezondheid*], 14 Space Activities Act [*Wet ruimtevaartactiviteiten*], 37 Care Institutions (Accreditation) Act [*Wet toelating zorginstellingen*], 63 Security Regions Act [*Wet veiligheidsregio's*], 46 Carriage of Dangerous Goods Act [*Wet vervoer gevaarlijke stoffen*], 5.2

be aware that the *astreinte* is an administrative sanction that is used more often than enforcement action. Both enforcement action and *astreinte* assume that the person on whom the sanction is imposed will himself take action following the order. The enforcement action only has the attendant risk for the administrative authority that it must act if the order is not complied with by the transgressor.

The most common provision is Article 125 of the Municipalities Act [*Gemeentewet*], which reads as follows:[36]

1. The municipal administration is authorized to impose a duty backed by enforcement action.
2. The power to impose a duty backed by enforcement action is exercised by the municipal executive, if the action serves to enforce the rules carried out by the municipal administration.
3. The power to impose a duty backed by enforcement action is exercised by the mayor, if the action serves to enforce the rules that he carries out.
4. An administrative committee, a submunicipal council, the day-to-day administration of a submunicipality or the chairman of the day-to-day administration of a submunicipality to which the powers of the municipal council, the municipal executive or the mayor have been transferred has the power to impose a duty backed by enforcement action and the power to authorise entry into a dwelling only if this power is transferred explicitly.

General GALA regulation

GALA, however, only provides for a few general rules on this power (Article 5:21–5:31c GALA) and these provisions read as follows:

5:21 A duty backed by enforcement action means:

a. a duty to remedy the infringement partly or in a whole, and
b. the right of the administrative authority to take physical acts in order to execute the duty if the duty is not or not timely executed by the offender.

5:22 (does not exist)

5:23 This division does not apply if action is taken for the immediate enforcement of public order.

Road Haulage Act [*Wet wegvervoer goederen*], 5 Stray Current Act [*Wet zwerfstromen*, 15, 120b Housing Act [*Woningwet*] and 93 Seeds and Planting Materials Act [*Zaaizaad- en plantgoedwet*].

36 Administrative authorities at the provinces and Water boards (*waterschappen*) have a similar power according to Articles 122 Provinciewet and 61 (and 70) Water Boards Act [*Waterschapswet*].

5:24 1. The decision to impose a duty backed by enforcement action specifies the action to be taken to remedy the infringement.
2. The decision to impose a duty backed by enforcement action specifies the time limit within which the duty has to be executed.
3. It shall be notified to the offender, to the persons entitled to use the thing in respect of which the duty has been imposed and to the applicant.

5:25 1. An offender shall owe the costs incurred in connection with the taking of enforcement action, unless it would not be reasonable for these costs to be borne by him.
2. The administrative decision shall state to what extent the enforcement action is taken at the expense of the offender.
3. The costs of enforcement action shall include the costs connected with the preparation of enforcement action, in so far as these costs are incurred after the date on which the time limit expires within which the duty has to be executed.
4. The costs shall also be owed if the enforcement action is not taken or not taken in its entirety owing to the termination of the illegal situation.
5. The costs of enforcement action also include the costs resulting from the compensation for damage pursuant to article 5:27, paragraph 6.
6. The administrative authority determines by administrative decision the amount of the costs owed by the offender.

5:26 (does not exist)

5:27 1. In order to implement a decision to take enforcement action, persons designated for this purpose by the administrative authority taking enforcement actions shall have access to every place, in so far as this may reasonably be deemed necessary for the performance of their duties.
2. An administrative authority taking enforcement action shall be entitled to issue an authorization as referred in Article 2 of the Entry of Premises Act for gaining entry to a dwelling without the consent of the occupant.
3. A place which is not involved in the infringement shall not be entered until the administrative authority taking enforcement action has given the person entitled at least 48 hours' communication in writing.
4. Paragraph 3 shall not apply if timely communication is not possible because speed is of the essence. The communication shall then be given as quickly as possible.
5. The communication shall specify the way in which the entry will take place.
6. The administrative authority shall reimburse the damage which is caused by the entry of a place as referred to in paragraph 3, in so far as it would be reasonable for this to be borne by the person entitled, without prejudice to the right to recover this damage from the offender pursuant to Article 5:25, fifth paragraph.

5:28 The power to take enforcement action shall include the power to seal off buildings and sites and anything which may be in or on them.

5:29 1. The power to take enforcement action shall include the removal and storage of goods suitable for this purpose, in so far as the use of enforcement action requires this.
2. If goods have been removed and stored, the administrative authority that has taken enforcement action shall draw up an official report of this and supply a copy to the person who had the goods under his control.
3. The administrative authority shall arrange for the safekeeping of the stored goods and shall return such goods to the person lawfully entitled to them.
4. The administrative authority shall be entitled to defer such return until the costs owed pursuant to Article 5:25 have been paid.
5. If the person lawfully entitled is not also the offender, the administrative authority shall be entitled to defer the return until the costs of custody have been paid.

5:30 1. An administrative authority which has taken enforcement action shall be entitled, if goods removed and stored cannot be returned within thirteen weeks of the removal, to sell the same.
2. The administrative authority shall have a similar power within the same period, if the costs referred to in Article 5:25 together with the costs estimated for the sale are so high that they are out of proportion to the value of the goods.
3. Sale shall not take place within two weeks of the provision of the copy of the official report of the removal and storage, unless it relates to a dangerous substance or a substance likely to perish beforehand.
4. For a period of three years after the date of sale, the one who was the owner at that time shall be entitled to the proceeds of the goods less the costs owed pursuant to Article 5:25 and the costs of the sale. After the expiry of this period, any net proceeds of the sale shall pass to the legal entity to which the administrative authority belongs.
5. If the sale is not possible in the opinion of the administrative authority, it is entitled to transfer the ownership of the goods free of charge to a third party or to have them destroyed. Paragraphs 1 to 3 shall apply.

5:31 1. An administrative authority competent to impose a duty backed by enforcement action can decide to implement enforcement action without a previous duty.
   Article 5:24, paragraphs 1 and 3 shall apply.
2. If the situation is so urgent that the administrative authority cannot put the decision to take enforcement action in writing beforehand, the enforcement action can be taken immediately, but the authority shall take and notify a decision pursuant paragraph 1 as quickly as possible thereafter.

5:31a 1. The applicant of an administrative decision to impose a duty backed by enforcement action or another interested party affected by the infringement may request the administrative authority to implement enforcement action.
2. The request can be done after the time limit referred to in Article 5:24, paragraph 2 has expired.
3. The administrative authority shall decide on the request within four weeks. The decision is an administrative decision.

5:31b The administrative decision regarding the implementation expires, in so far as the decision to impose a duty backed by enforcement action is revoked or quashed.

5:31c 1. The objection, appeal or higher appeal against an administrative decision imposing a duty backed by enforcement action also relates to the administrative decision to implement enforcement action and to the administrative decision specifying the costs of enforcement action, in so far as the decisions are contested by the interested party.
2. The administrative court can refer the decision on the appeal or higher appeal regarding the administrative decision on the implementation or the administrative decisions on the costs of enforcement action to another authority, if the court deems it desirable that the administrative decision is heard by that authority.
3. If possible, the interested party shall produce in the appeal or higher appeal procedure a copy of the administrative decision he contests.
4. Paragraphs 1 to 3 apply to the procedure following a request for a provisional remedy.

These general provisions were added with the Third Part of GALA (*Derde tranche Awb*), which entered into force on 1 January 1998.[37] This general regulation was altered with the Fourth Part of GALA (*Vierde tranche Awb*), which entered into force on 1 July 2009.[38]

The changes brought about by the Fourth Part of GALA involved those resulting from the introduction of general provisions on administrative sanctions (Title 5.1 GALA) and those from the introduction of a general regulation in regard to provisions for money debts deriving from administrative law and this had consequences for the regulation of the way in which the costs incurred in connection with the taking of enforcement action are charged (current Article 5:25 GALA). The position of third interested parties was also improved by allowing them the possibility of requesting the administrative authority to implement enforcement action (Article 5:31a GALA). As a result of this alteration, the refusal of a request of this kind is now an administrative

37 Act of 25 June 2009, *Staatsblad* (Bulletin of Acts and Decrees) 2009, 264; see also *Staatsblad* 2009, 266.

38 Act of 20 June 1996, *Staatsblad* 1996, 333. See also *Staatsblad* 1997, 581.

decision (*besluit*) and opens access to legal protection in the administrative courts.

Astreinte

The *astreinte* was introduced in administrative law more recently. The introduction was inspired by the possibility of the civil courts' enforcing an order with periodic penalty payments. Enforcement action was considered to be ineffective in certain cases. Legal scholarship in the 1970s was evaluating the possibilities of whether civil preliminary relief proceedings (*civiel kort geding-procedure*) would achieve better results.[39] In a 1973 decision, the Netherlands Supreme Court [*Hoge Raad (abbreviated to HR*)] rejected this possibility. Since then, public law possibilities have been sought. In the 1980s a group of authors examined the possibilities of periodic penalty payments being imposed by the administrative courts. In the same period, another group considered an alternative: of entrusting administrative authorities with this power. The first and most important example of the power of an administrative authority to impose an astreinte was Article 28a Nuisance Act [*Hinderwet*] (since repealed*)*.[40] An important enlargement of this sanction's scope resulted from the alteration of the Environmental Protection (General Provisions) Act [*Wet algemene bepalingen milieuhygiëne*] or *Wabm* of 27 September 1990 with the Introduction of Penalty Payments Act [*Dwangsomwet*]. With this act, the provisions in the Nuisance Act were replaced by a provision in the *Wabm*, a law with a more general character than the Nuisance Act. As a result, this sanction could now be imposed for the infringement of many acts in the field of environmental law. On 1 March 1993, the Wabm was amended. One of the changes was its name: since then, this important act has been known as the Environmental Management Act [*Wet milieubeheer*] or *Wm*. The astreinte (*bestuurlijke dwangsom*) gained an even more general character when it was added to the new Municipalities Act, the Provinces Act (*Provinciewet*) and the Water Boards Act [*Waterschapswet*] on 1 January 1992 and 1 January 1994. And finally, the GALA provisions on this administrative sanction entered into force on 1 January 1998, and they were amended with the enactment of the Fourth Part of GALA on 1 July 2009.

The current provisions read as follows:

> **Article 5:31d**
> A duty backed by an astreinte means: the remedial sanction, containing:

[39] See J.H. Verweij, *De bestuurlijke dwangsom*, W.E.J. Tjeenk Willink, Zwolle 1997, pp. 11–18.

[40] Act of 4 June 1981, Bulletin of Acts and Decrees 1981, 409. Later this power was also added to the Spatial Planning Act [*Wet op de Ruimtelijke Ordening*] and the Soil Protection Act [*Wet bodembescherming*], but these powers were seldom used and have not been important for later developments.

a. a. a duty to remedy the infringement partly or completely, and
b. The obligation to pay a sum of money if the duty is not or not in time complied with.

Article 5:32

1. An administrative authority which is entitled to impose a duty backed by enforcement action may instead impose a duty backed by an astreinte.
2. The imposition of a duty backed by an astreinte shall not be chosen if this would be contrary to the interest intended to be protected by the regulation that has been infringed.

Article 5:32a

1. An administrative decision to impose a duty backed by an astreinte shall specify the measures to be taken in order to remedy the infringement.
2. An administrative decision imposing a duty backed by an astreinte which is intended to remedy an infringement or prevent a further infringement shall set a time limit within which the offender can perform the duty without the astreinte being forfeited.

Article 5:32b

1. The administrative authority shall fix the astreinte as a lump sum, as a sum payable by unit of time during which the duty is not performed, or as a sum per infringement of the duty.
2. The administrative authority shall also fix a sum above which no further penalty will be forfeited.
3. The fixed amount shall be in reasonable proportion to the importance of the interest that has been infringed and the intended effect of the imposition of the astreinte.

Article 5:33

A forfeited astreinte shall be paid within six weeks after it is forfeited.

Article 5:34

1. The administrative authority which has imposed a duty backed by an astreinte may, at the request of the offender, lift the astreinte, reduce it or stay its operation for a given period if it has become permanently or temporarily impossible for the offender to perform all or part of his obligations.
2. An administrative authority which has imposed a duty backed by an astreinte may, at the request of the offender, lift the astreinte if the administrative decision has been in effect for a year without the astreinte being forfeited.

Article 5:35

Contrary to Article 4:104 the power to collect forfeited sums shall be barred by prescription one year after the date on which they are forfeited.

Article 5:36 (Repealed as from 01-07-2009)

Article 5:37

1. The administrative authority takes an administrative decision concerning the collection of the forfeited sum, before it summons to pay the amount owed.
2. The administrative authority will also take an administrative decision concerning the collection of the forfeited sum if so requested by an interested party.
3. The administrative authority shall decide on the request within four weeks.

Article 5:38

1. If as a consequence of an administrative decision to revoke or change the decision to impose a duty backed by an astreinte an already existing administrative decision concerning the collection of the forfeited sum of that astreinte cannot be upheld, the latter will expire.
2. The administrative authority can take a new administrative decision which shall be in conformity with the altered administrative decision to impose a duty backed by an astreinte.

Article 5:39

1. The objection, appeal or higher appeal against an administrative decision imposing a duty backed by an astreinte also relates to the administrative decision to collect the forfeited astreinte, in so far as this decision is contested by the interested party.
2. The administrative court can refer the decision on the appeal or higher appeal regarding the administrative decision to collect the forfeited astreinte to another authority, if the court deems it desirable that the administrative decision is heard by that authority.
3. If possible the interested party shall produce in the appeal or higher appeal procedure a copy of the administrative decision he contests.
4. Paragraphs 1 to 3 apply to the procedure following a request to a provisional remedy.

4. DEVELOPMENT OF THE ADMINISTRATIVE FINE IN THE NETHERLANDS

For many years the administrative fine was rare in the Netherlands: traditionally, this sanction only existed in criminal tax law. For a long time, punitive sanctioning was regarded as a task exclusively for the courts. The evolution of the administrative fine was given an important stimulus in the Netherlands with the Öztürk judgment of the ECtHR dated 21 February 1984 and the case law of the Tax Division of the Netherlands Supreme Court resulting from this.

The ECHR has a direct effect on the Dutch legal system and every national court can apply the provisions of this treaty. Dutch courts are not authorised to check legislation against the Constitution and the Netherlands does not have a system of constitutional review. The Constitution has a minimal effect on the Dutch law on fines but, by contrast, Article 6 ECHR plays an extremely important role in the shaping of the Dutch law on fines. In the Öztürk judgment, the ECtHR ruled on a money fine imposed under German law because of an administrative offence (*Ordnungswidrigkeit*) in traffic law. In the Dutch debate, it was not just important that criteria were formulated in order to be able to determine which sanctions are punitive but also that Article 6 ECHR offers no opposition to the imposition of punitive sanctions by administrative authorities, provided that the plaintiff has access to an independent court after this and that certain guarantees apply. At the time of the Öztürk judgment, the administrative fine was a rarity in Dutch law: it only occurred in criminal tax law.[41]

1985

In 1985, the Supreme Court determined for the first time that the tax law surcharge was of a punitive nature and therefore Article 6 and the legal guarantees incorporated in it were applicable. This marked the beginning of a great deal of case law in which the legal system was fundamentally reshaped by this court along the lines set out in Article 6 ECHR. These developments led to the intention on the part of the legislature to have a thorough review of the regulation of tax penalties, which were still called increases at that time. Since then, this intention has resulted in legislation. The case law of the administrative courts in tax cases fulfilled and still fulfils an important exemplary function in sanction law. Neither are the other administrative courts completely inactive.

In 1989 the Traffic Regulations (Administrative Enforcement) Act [*Wet administratiefrechtelijke handhaving verkeersvoorschriften*] or Wet Mulder was published in the State Gazette. This made provisions for traffic fines and in 1992 came into force nationally. At the time, there was a great deal of discussion over this law, in particular among criminal lawyers. Before this, these lawyers had given little attention to all the other administrative fine provisions.

41 Apart from disciplinary law. An interesting conclusion: in the Netherlands the fine was at one time taken over from administrative law by criminal law, and now there are discussions, sometimes critical, about introducing fines into administrative law (J. van der Poel, *Rondom compositie en compromis*, Utrecht 1942, p. 265; F.C.M.A. Michiels, Bestuurlijke handhaving in ontwikkeling, in: J.T.K. Bos (e.a.), *Handhaving van het bestuursrecht*, Samsom H.D. Tjeenk Willink, Alphen aan den Rijn 1995, p. 86, and Van Wijk/Konijnenbelt/Van Male, *Hoofdstukken van bestuursrecht*, Reed Business, Amsterdam 2011, p. 467.

1994

On 12 January 1994 the recommendation of the Legislative Projects Review Committee (*Commissie voor de toetsing van wetgevingsprojecten*), which has since been disbanded, entitled Enforcement by administrative fines (*Handhaving door bestuurlijke boetes*), was published: it contained an important general recommendation that the administrative fine should be introduced on a large scale. The provisions for administrative fines in the Media Act [*Mediawet*], the Telecommunications Act [*Telecommunicatiewet*] (now repealed) and the Individual Rent Allowance Act [*Wet individuele huursubsidie*] came into force shortly before publication of this recommendation.

Using criteria drawn up by the Commission itself, the Commission examined legislation enforced as criminal offences under the Economic Offences Act [*Wet op de economische delicten (WED)*] and gave as advice that the provisions for a large number of these could soon be enforced by administrative fines. For a large number of other laws, as well as legislation outside the sphere of enforcement of the Economic Offences Act, further study would be required. In Model A, criminal law is entirely excluded in principle and the amount of the administrative fine is set down: the rates. In Model B, criminal or administrative steps may be taken and the administrative authority has the competence to determine the size of the fine. The government accepted many of the recommendations of this Commission.[42]

Since then, the amount of legislation containing a power of administrative fine has increased greatly and this fine now features in about 100 acts.[43] A brief description of many of them is given below.

1998

In 1998, the Michiels Commission published its report on Maintaining enforcement.[44] This Commission made some critical remarks about the position of the Cabinet, which was a result of the report on Enforcement by administrative fines, in favour of wide scale introduction of the administrative fine. In the eyes of this Commission, the government must not set too much store by the envisioned increase in efficiency. Adding the administrative fine to the instruments for enforcement available to government organisations allows them to act more credibly and more effectively, but use must be made of it. New instruments are not always what government organisations are waiting for.

---

42 In the Cabinet's position based on this report (Parliamentary Documents II 1993/94, 23 400 VI, no. 48).

43 See also Oswald Jansen, "Bestuurlijk en justitieel straffen in Nederland", in: R.C. van Houten (ed.), *Economisch strafrecht en bestuurlijke boete*, Wolf Legal Publishers, 2012, p. 21–79, 153–181.

44 Commissie bestuursrechtelijke en privaatrechtelijke handhaving, *Handhaven op niveau*, W.E.J. Tjeenk Willink, Zwolle 1998.

In the Cabinet's point of view of 18 April 2000,[45] drawn up as a result of this report, the government stated that the administrative fine is 'not a panacea for all enforcement miseries'. It is of great importance that the government brought the Cabinet's 1994 point of view up to date with this memorandum.

In the government's opinion, the application of an administrative fine allows expression of government organisations' own responsibility for enforcement. In this way, government organisations are being encouraged to give timely consideration to enforcement aspects when drawing up their policy proposals and regulations. Certainly, when administrative fines are introduced for activities that were not enforced when they fell solely within the criminal law system, the sanction will have a greater effect on compliance with regulations. Government organisations are more inclined towards enforcement in order to achieve their own policy objectives. Some increase in efficiency can be achieved for certain activities, although the effect of this must not be exaggerated according to the government. In the view of the government, administrative law is tailored more to decisions given on a widespread scale.[46]

Indications

The government then formulated a number of indications which need to be taken into account when considering the framework of a special law concerning the decision to introduce an administrative fine.

Indications concerning the norm

1. An administrative fine generally only has a slight normative value, which is the case if the offence causes no damage to persons or considerable damage to property;
2. The norm has been so clearly described that it is possible to develop a fixed course of action that guarantees simple and efficient execution. If a clear description is not possible, then the administrative fine can only be applied if it can be imposed by a specialised organization equipped to impose fines.

Indications concerning the enforcement practice

3. Transparency and consistency of the sanction system as a whole must be guaranteed.

   'A sanction system as a whole must be transparent. When norms can be enforced under both criminal and administrative law, then it is necessary to guarantee that

45 Parliamentary Documents II 1999–2000, 26 800, VI, no. 67.

46 Idem, p. 10.

the same 'rates' apply. It is necessary that this kind of transparency is maintained in the relevant policy area.'[47]

4. The offence is one for which fixed rates would be appropriate as punishment.
5. Documentation on re-offending is not necessary.
6. The offence is not carried out for criminal organizations or by them to any significant extent.
7. In the imposition of an administrative fine, coercive measures are only required to determine the identity of the perpetrator.

Indications concerning enforcement policy

8. The enforcing authority possesses enough expertise to put enforcement into practice sufficiently punitively.
9. The risk of a shifting of accent towards repression at the cost of prevention is manageable.
10. The risk of a shifting of accent towards repression at the cost of remedial sanctions is manageable.
11. Undesired consequences of monopoly positions due to the imposition of sanctions are manageable.
12. There is exchange of information between supervisory and enforcing agencies.

Finally, the government has stated that there will be no problems in enforcing a number of norms that are 'on the boundaries of the hard core of criminal law' by an administrative fine:

- secondary provisions which must make supervision by the authority possible;
- financial and administrative obligations for which a settlement under criminal law would have no added value;
- standardisation of conduct in markets regulated by the government, in which the legislator has made specialised organizations responsible for punitive enforcement.[48]

On 21 April 2004 the government sent the policy document on a practicable legal order (*Nota Bruikbare rechtsorde*) to Parliament.[49] Part of this document contains a regulatory model (*Reguleringsmodel*) on administrative fines. The 2004 document is based on the previous one of 18 April 2000 and in it the government continues to distinguish between two systems, viz. the A system

47 Idem, p. 11.
48 Idem, p. 12.
49 Parliamentary Documents 2003–2004, 29 279, no. 9.

(Model A) and the B system (Model B). In Model B, the administrative fine is an alternative in addition to the criminal law sanctioning system (infringements are both finable and punishable). Statutory delineations or agreements with the Public Prosecution Service determine whether infringements will be dealt with under administrative law or under criminal law. In Model A, infringements are only finable. Model A is a system of independent administrative fines and is thought to unburden the criminal law sanctioning system. In addition, according to the government, this structure offers greater possibilities for more effective enforcement since it will enable closer coordination and alignment of the enforcement organisation for the fine system in question. The Government's opinion only elaborates on an opinion on Model A and it presents the following conditions to introduce the administrative fine into legislation:

> 'a. The statutory norm has a slight moral connotation;
> b. The infringement of the statutory norm generally causes no injury to persons or damage to goods;
> c. The statutory norm is defined so clearly in the law or in further rules that a consistent course of action can be developed in practice on the basis of the statutory norms;
> d. The official or service charged with enforcement possesses sufficient expertise to give shape to this enforcement adequately;
> e. No deprivation of liberty or other drastic coercive measures are required for the enforcement of the norm.'

In addition to these conditions, the government presented indications (*indicaties*) to introduce the administrative fine in legislation, and made a few qualifying remarks.[50]

> 'Indications for the choice of this instrument are, in addition to the above:
> - it is easier to develop the specific expertise desired with regard to the subject matter with a specialised enforcement authority.
> - Other authorities can be assigned a function in the enforcement more specifically through the granting of an administrative power to fine to that authority and by giving them the means and possibilities to fulfil this task and in this way produce results therein.
> - If an actual supervisor (figuratively speaking) may seem far from the PPS, this is usually an indication of the low priority given to the criminal enforcement of the system of norms in question. Awarding an administrative power to fine may be a means of putting these neglected cases back on the enforcement map.

50 Parliamentary Documents 2003–2004, 29 279, no. 9, p. 25.

Qualifying remarks:
- The expected extent of the enforcement duties must justify the establishment and maintenance of a special enforcement system.
- Systems of administrative fines must be in balance with the required efforts outside the field involved in the area of enforcement: the costs and efforts on the part of the government to arrange a certain aspect of social life through the imposition of administrative fines must be proportional to the seriousness of the offences and the necessity to act, in the eyes of society.
- Where the lack of enforcement is in fact a symptom of insufficient administrative support for the norms in question, it is not desirable that an administrative fine is introduced to repair matters.'

The government policy documents of 2000 and 2004 show a position which allows administrative fines to be introduced into legislation on a larger scale. From 2005 until now, the position seems to have to changed somewhat due to a battle between the criminal law system and the administrative law system of law enforcement.

2005–2012 the battle between legal systems: the criminal law out-of-court settlement offered by the Public Prosecution Service (OM afdoening) versus the administrative law system of administrative fines

In approximately the same period, a few proposed bills were being discussed in parliament. In addition to the important general provisions on administrative fines in the Fourth Part of GALA (parliamentary paper number 29 702), an important proposal to change the criminal law system was being discussed, the Public Prosecution Service (Settlement) Act (*Wet OM-afdoening* (parliamentary paper no. 29 849). The latter proposed provisions to change the system of the out-of-court settlement (*transactie*) into the power of the public prosecutor, the police and some administrative authorities to impose a sanction by punishment order (*strafbeschikking*). Both regulations were enacted. The system of punishment orders will be introduced gradually and so the out-of-court settlement is still in use and the provisions on this are still of importance.

Out-of-court settlement offered by the Public Prosecution Service

A short introduction on the punishment order will be necessary in order to understand the differences between the system of the administrative fine and the system of the punishment order. These two systems fulfil a key role in the battle between the two systems of law enforcement.

The key provisions of the regulation on the out-of-court settlement can be found in the Dutch Criminal Code (DCC) and the Dutch Code of Criminal Procedure (DCP) and read as follows:

74 DCC

1. The Public Prosecutor, prior to the trial, may set one or more conditions in order to avoid criminal proceedings for serious offences – excluding serious offences for which the law prescribes sentences of imprisonment of more than six years – and for lesser offences. The right to prosecute lapses where the conditions set are met.
2. The following conditions may be set:
   a. the payment of a sum of money to the State, the amount being not less than €3 and not more than the maximum fine that can be imposed for the offence;
   b. renunciation of title to objects that have been seized and that are the subject to forfeiture or confiscation;
   c. the surrender of objects subject to forfeiture or confiscation, or payment to the State of their assessed value;
   d. the payment in full to the State of a sum of money or the transfer of objects seized as confiscation, in whole or in part, of the proceeds of crime subject to confiscation pursuant to Article 36e;
   e. full or partial compensation for the damage caused by the criminal offence;
   f. the performance of unpaid work or the following of a court-ordered course for a period not exceeding one hundred and twenty hours.
3. In the event of a criminal offence, a notice indicating the date on which the conditions set were complied with shall be sent without delay by the Public Prosecutor to the party concerned who is known to him.
4. The provisions laid down by or pursuant to Articles 22b, 22c, sections 1 and 4, 22e and 22k with regard to community punishment orders apply mutatis mutandis to the condition referred to in section 2f. The unpaid work or court-ordered course is to be completed within a period of six months after consent to the condition. The Public Prosecution Service can extend this period of time by one further period of six months. It will notify the person involved of this as quickly as possible.
5. By or pursuant to an Order in Council, rules can be set regarding fulfilment of the condition, referred to in section 2a. These rules will include, in any case, the place and the manner in which the sum of money is to be paid, the period of time within which this must take place and the responsibility for the sums of money received. By or pursuant to an Order in Council, rules can be given regarding compliance with the other conditions referred to in the second section.

74a DCC

Where, in the case of a criminal offence for which no principal penalty other than a fine is prescribed, the suspect or accused offers to pay the maximum fine within a period of time to be specified by the Public Prosecutor, and offers to comply with all other conditions to be set in accordance with Article 74, section 2, the Public Prosecutor may not refuse to set the conditions specified in Article 74.

(...)

74c DCC

1. The investigating officers who are assigned by Order in Council to specified matters pertaining to lesser offences committed by persons who have reached the age of twelve may in said order be given the authority granted to the Public Prosecutor under Article 74, section 1.
2. The payment of a specific sum of money may be set as a condition. By or pursuant to Order in Council instructions are to be laid down concerning the place and manner of payment and the term within which the payment has to be made.
3. Sections 1 and 2 are applicable mutatis mutandis in non-complex cases concerning the serious offences as referred to in Article 74, section 1, which have been committed by persons who have reached the age of eighteen, providing that the sum of money is not more than €350.
4. The officers in whom the authority specified in section 1 is vested shall exercise that authority according to guidelines to be issued by the Board of Procurators General.
5. By or pursuant to Order in Council, instructions are to be issued on the appointment of the investigating officers referred to in the first section, supervision of the way in which they may exercise the authority vested in them and instructions on the withdrawal of the appointment of an investigating officer.
6. By or pursuant to Order in Council, instructions are to be given concerning the accountability for sums of money paid pursuant to the provisions of sections 2 and 3.
7. Articles 74, section 3 and 74b apply mutatis mutandis in the setting of conditions by investigating officers.

The key provisions of the regulation on the punishment order (*strafbeschikking*) are the following:

257a DCP

1. The Public Prosecutor may issue a punishment order if he finds that a minor offence has been committed or a serious offence for which the law prescribes a term of imprisonment not exceeding six years.
2. The following punishments and measures can be imposed;
   a. a community punishment order not exceeding one hundred and eighty hours;
   b. a fine;
   c. confiscation;
   d. the obligation to pay a sum of money to the State for the victim;
   e. a disqualification from driving motor vehicles for a period not exceeding six months.
3. In addition, the punishment order may contain instructions with which the accused must comply. The instructions may not restrict the accused from professing his religion or personal beliefs, or reduce state security. They may include:
   a. renunciation of title to objects that have been seized and that are subject to forfeiture or confiscation;

b. the surrender of objects subject to forfeiture or confiscation, or payment to the State of their assessed value;
c. the payment in full to the State of a sum of money or the transfer of objects seized as confiscation, in whole or in part, of the proceeds of crime subject to confiscation pursuant to Article 36e of the Dutch Criminal Code;
d. payment of a set sum of money to the Criminal Injuries Compensation Fund or in favour of an institution whose mission is to represent the interests of crime victims, the amount of which may not exceed the maximum fine that can be imposed for the offence;
e. other instructions with regard to the accused's conduct, with which this person must comply during a period of probation to be set in the punishment order but not exceeding one year.

4. When a community punishment order is imposed and instructions as referred to in the third section, under e, are given, it is a condition that the accused cooperates in the taking of one or more fingerprints or offers an identity document for inspection as referred to in Article 1 of the Compulsory Identification Act [*Wet op de identificatieplicht*] in order to establish his identity.
5. The identity of the accused is to be established for the execution of the community punishment order and the guidance in complying with the instructions referred to in the third paragraph, under e.
6. The punishment order is to be in writing and to state:
   the name and known address of the accused;
   b. a description of the offence as referred to in Article 261, first and second paragraphs, or a short definition of the act for which the punishment order has been issued, as well as the time and the place where this act was committed;
   c. the criminal offence constituted by this act;
   d. the imposed punishments, measures and instructions;
   e. the date on which it is issued;
   f. the way in which an objection can be lodged;
   g. the way it will be executed.

257b DCP

1. By Order in Council, investigating officers to be appointed for this purpose in matters designated by that Order in Council regarding infringements can be given the power, until further notice, to issue a punishment order in which a fine is imposed.
2. Furthermore, by Order in Council, investigating officers appointed for this purpose in matters designated by that Order in Council regarding serious offences for which the law prescribes a term of imprisonment not exceeding six years, which are not complex, which have been committed by persons who have reached the age of eighteen can be granted the power, until further notice, to issue a punishment order in which a fine not exceeding €350 is imposed.
3. The officers in whom the authority specified in the first and second paragraphs is vested shall exercise that authority according to guidelines to be issued by the Board of Procurators General. By or pursuant to an Order in Council,

instructions are to be issued with regard to the appointment of the investigating officers, supervision of the way in which they exercise the powers vested in them as well as the termination of the appointment of an investigating officer.

257ba DCP

1. By Order in Council, the power of issuing a punishment order within the set limits can be given to bodies or persons to be designated for this purpose, who are charged with a public duty.
2. The officers in whom the authority specified in paragraph 1 is vested shall exercise that authority according to guidelines to be issued by the Board of Procurators General. By Order in Council, instructions are to be given with regard to the supervision of the way they exercise the power granted to them as well as the way in which the granted power is to be withdrawn by the Board of Procurators General.
3. The Board of Procurators General draws up guidelines as referred to in the second paragraph after consulting the bodies and persons charged with a public duty who are affected by the guideline in their exercise of the power to issue a punishment order, or with organs who represent these bodies.

One of the reasons for changing the criminal law system with this proposal was the protection of the criminal law system: it would be undermined by the administrative law system of administrative fines if criminal law failed to provide a similar system. Nowadays, about 100 acts provide for an administrative law system, and new ideas to broaden the possibility to impose administrative fines have to compete with the possibility of the same administrative authority being able to impose a criminal law punishment order. I will explain the criminal law system and the differences of that system with an administrative law system below.

The coexistence of these two competing sanctioning systems is complicated by the existence of two other sanctioning systems, the Traffic Regulations (Administrative Enforcement) Act [*Wet administratiefrechtelijke handhaving verkeersvoorschriften*], also called Wet Mulder,[51] which provides for an extremely efficient and effective system of imposing and collecting administrative fines for the infringement of traffic regulations on the one hand and the system of taxation of municipality parking regulations, on the other.

In the same period, in addition to the proposal of the Fourth Part GALA, three proposed Bills were being discussed in Parliament, which discussion influenced the debate on the design of the sanctioning systems in both criminal law and administrative law to a great extent. These three proposals were the proposed Public Prosecution Service (Settlement) Act [*Wet OM-Afdoening*], the Nuisance

[51] The common name Wet Mulder refers to its initiator, the late Prof. A. Mulder.

in Public Areas (Administrative Penalty) Act [*Wet bestuurlijke boete overlast in de openbare ruimte*] (30 101), and the Illegal Parking and Other Minor Traffic Offences Act [*Wet bestuurlijke boete fout parkeren en andere lichte verkeersovertredingen*](30 098).

On 8 November 2005 the Secretary for Justice sent a policy document on the relationship between administrative and criminal enforcement, as a consequence of an undertaking given to Parliament during legislative consultations with Parliament on the proposed Public Prosecution Service (Settlement) Act [*Wet OM-afdoening*] on 18 April 2005.[52] This policy document approached the question very much from a criminal law point of view. According to the government, the development of administrative fines outlined in this policy document would lead to a large variety of sanction systems, sanction modalities and authorities with the power to impose sanctions. This can put pressure on the 'coherence of enforcement.' The government pointed out that the criminal law system has a central authority, that of the Public Prosecution Service, whereas the administrative law system has no such body.

In the government's opinion, the introduction of the possibility of settlement by investigating officers under criminal law or by administrative bodies specifically designated for this purpose can represent a significant improvement in the enforcement possibilities. It also thinks it could lead to greater streamlining in enforcement. The government continued as follows: 'On the one hand, either all or part of the arsenal of criminal sanctions can be made available for enforcement as well as the range of powers offered by criminal-procedure investigations, which by their nature are often more far-reaching than the supervisory powers offered, for instance, under the General Administrative Law Act. On the other, the Public Prosecution Service is given the authority over the enforcement in such cases, while it can choose to leave the actual work and the associated setting of priorities to the officers or administrative bodies with the specific expertise, in proper consultation with the authorities involved. One effect of this approach could be that administrative sanctioning need no longer be chosen purely for reasons of efficiency. The implication of this is that – if the legislative proposal for the out-of-court settlement by the Public Prosecution Service is passed and comes into effect – the balance of arguments for one or another form of sanctioning could lead to different outcomes than at present. This could, in the end, lead to greater coherence within enforcement by making a more balanced and adequate complex of coercive measures available for the enforcement, for example, or by the creation of greater unity in the sanctions to

52 Parliamentary Documents 2005–2006, 29 849, no. 30. See also the report of this consultation: Parliamentary Documents 2004–2005, 29 849, no. 17, p. 39.

be imposed for related infringements.'[53] The government then formulated the following indicators in the choice of a certain system of enforcement.

Paragraph 1 – Private law or public law

Indicator 1

There can be an indication for private law enforcement if the following preconditions are complied with:

a. the norm is intended to protect the individual interest of the one natural person or juristic person in relation to the individual interest of another natural person or juristic person, and the choice whether enforcement is required in a specific case can, in principle, be decided by the parties (or their interest groups); and
b. there is, moreover, an adequate balance between the two parties, also in the sense that there is adequate access to justice.

The norms in contract law and liability law are examples of norms that could be enforced under private law. See Indicator 2 below for those cases in which precondition b is not complied with (no adequate balance between the two parties, for example no adequate access to justice).

Indicator 2

If there is not the necessary balance between the parties for enforcement under private law (Indicator 1, under b), it must first be considered whether the balance can be restored by private law means;

- Restoring the balance between parties by using private law means can be achieved by granting one party a stronger position than the other party, for example. The legislator can impose an extra obligation on the party that is in a better starting position, for example by intervening in the division of the burden of proof. Or the legislator can impose an obligation to provide information on the one party, failure to do so resulting in a loss of their advantageous position. Or the legislator can prescribe the engagement of an impartial third party, such as a civil-law notary or an accountant.
- If it is not possible to re-establish the balance in private law by private law means, then it must considered whether the balance can be achieved by public law means. The legislator can bring in a government body, such as the Public Prosecution Service in the investigation of the policy of a juristic person or by the enforcement of the regulations pertaining to annual accounts; the Prosecution Service then acts as the body to which the norm is in fact addressed. Or the legislator grants a supervisory body (think of the future Consumer Authority) the power to gather information from one party in order to strengthen the position of the other party.
- If access to justice is complicated for one of the parties, one possible option is to establish a special dispute-resolution agency to make access easier, as is the case for the rent assessment committee.

---

53 Parliamentary Documents 2005–2006, 29 849, no. 30, p. 3.

Indicator 3
If it cannot be left to the parties or their representatives (think of interest groups) to decide on enforcement in a specific case, this could be an indication for public-law regulation. Enforcement would become a government task.

Indicator 4
Preference should be given, in principle, to seeking a link with existing sanction systems that arrange for similar or related norms or sets of standards, as it would be rather cumbersome to impose different procedures for related violations, for example an administrative course for one violation and a criminal one for another closely connected violation. Something similar applies if it is desirable to apply a general tenet or a legal instrument that has been specifically elaborated for a certain field of law (in legislation and/or case law). This, too, is an indication that the sanctioning should address that field of law. Think here of such tenets as good faith in private law or types of participation in criminal law. One example of a legal instrument is international assistance in criminal cases. If there is a reason for public law enforcement of norms in which international cooperation is indispensable, this is an indication for regulation in criminal law.

Paragraph 2 – The desired sanctions

Indicator 5
Criminal law is the only option if the threat of a custodial punishment or one that restricts freedom or a measure for violation of the norm is desirable. Whether a penalty of this nature is desirable depends on many factors, including views in society on the seriousness of the violation, the deterrent effect that such a threat can have and such like.

Indicator 6
Initial consideration can be given to an arrangement in criminal law if new (possibly alternative) punitive sanctions are required.

Indicator 7
If new reparatory sanctions are desired, arrangement could be primarily in administrative law.
Exceptions are certainly possible in cases that are so interrelated with criminal law aspects that it would be appropriate to deal with them under criminal law: examples include the compensation order and the measure for confiscation of the proceeds of crime, which are both reparatory in character but are so closely connected with criminal law that concurrence with that law should be sought.

Indicator 8
If the violation of a norm under public law, in fact, always involves violence or inflicting injury on individuals, the application of criminal law is indicated. It may be important that a fully specified arrangement for damages is available in criminal law – as in private law as well but not in administrative law.

Paragraph 3 – The seriousness of the norm violation

Indicator 9
Criminal law enforcement is more likely to be eligible for enforcement than administrative law in the case of serious norm violations. This is a criterion that is strongly subjective but no less important: it appeals to the idea that those involved in certain violations of the norm must face justice in some way. The gravity of the norm violation can relate, first of all, to the nature of the offence (no one will argue in favour of an administrative settlement for a homicide) but it may also relate to perceived re-offending or the intention underlying the norm violation. It is also conceivable that the legislator wants to establish a new or more stringent norm as a fundamental value and, for this reason, opts for criminal sanctioning. Consider here the introduction of non-discrimination provisions and the criminal regulation of drunk driving.

Indicator 10
The more adjudication in public (in the sense of a hearing of the case in public during which the court does not have to decide on an administrative decision but one in which the natural or juristic person appears before the court and is 'tried' if need be) is required, the more criminal law will be the more appropriate option. With criminal enforcement, the agencies charged with enforcement always have the possibility, in principle, of presenting a case to a criminal court whereas, for administrative enforcement with administrative fines, the case is only presented in court if the person involved takes the initiative after an administrative authority has imposed a fine on this person, and the procedure is very often a closed one.

Indicator 11
There are counter-arguments to administrative enforcement by decentralized administrative authorities if local differences in enforcement are not desirable, if it is not desirable that the norm setter also acts as enforcer of the norm or if the local situation is irrelevant for enforcement.
If there are reasons for opting for administrative enforcement in such cases, then a nationally functioning body must apply it. In addition, criminal enforcement may also be chosen in a such a case, one in which the local situation may certainly be taken into account and the decentralized administrative authority may also be brought in but the role of the prosecution service is to ensure that no unacceptable differences in levels of enforcement can develop.

Paragraph 4 – the requirement of powers

Indicator 12
The application of criminal law is called for if far-reaching coercive measures or investigative powers are required to establish the truth and to impose a sanction. Criminal law must be the option in any case if new powers are needed that would signify a drastic infringement of fundamental rights, such as pre-trial detention, thorough searching of a dwelling, interception or recording of communications and

so forth. The application and use of far-reaching coercive means must be assessed by the body best equipped for this (partly in connection with a rational division of the review of questions of law) and this is the criminal judge. This also ensures the functional supervision by the public prosecutor or assistant public prosecutor in that case.

Indicator 13
If, in practice, it is expected that a sanction can only be effectively imposed by applying criminal-law means, this would not be consistent with an administrative sanction. Making the norm itself punishable under criminal law would be a more efficient way if, for example, the police and judicial authorities are expected to be called in frequently because Article 184 DCC (failure to comply with an official order) has to be invoked.

Indicator 14
An administrative fine is appropriate:
- to establish the facts, including the identity of the perpetrator of the offence, and if no far-reaching powers are required to apply the sanction (see Indicator 12 on this matter) and moreover
- if it is to be expected that no court judgment of the sanction and the applied powers will be generally called for in practice (in connection with the expected volume or for other reasons).

Paragraph 5 – Involvement of an administrative authority in sanctioning

Indicator 15
There are two principal approaches in giving an administrative authority a special involvement in public-law enforcement because of the expertise and manpower available there.
- Administrative enforcement can be chosen if the involvement of the Public Prosecution Service is not required and there are no indications for the application of criminal law.
- If the application of criminal law were to be the logical course, there are a number of options, included in Indicator 16, where it is always advisable to reach agreement with the PPS.

Indicator 16
If the criminal-law option is chosen, the following variations are available (assuming that the legislative proposal for an out-of-court settlement by the PPS will be passed into law and come into effect).
a. A logical step would be to designate officers working for an administrative authority as special investigating officers on the basis of Article 142 of the Dutch Code of Criminal Procedure [Wetboek van Strafvordering] (DCP), if there is reason to involve the PPS in an (extrajudicial) settlement in specific circumstances or if there are no reasons for allowing the administrative authority concerned a particular (limited) policy latitude. If need be, these officers can be

granted the power on the basis of Article 257b DCC to issue a police punishment order (the successor to the out-of-court settlement with the police in Article 74c DCC).

b. If an extrajudicial settlement on the part of the PPS is indicated but at the same time it is advisable that the administrative authority is given a restricted scope for policy-making, an Order in Council can award the administrative authority the power to issue a punishment order in the categories of criminal offences indicated therein. This advisability can result from the application of criminal law being interconnected with the responsibilities of the administrative authority concerned and a certain amount of policy latitude is allowed in their fulfilment.
c. If there are no indications for supervision of an extrajudicial settlement by the PPS, the administrative authority can be awarded an independent statutory power to impose a punishment order for the categories of criminal offences listed there. The quality safeguards intrinsic to the organization and operation of the administrative authority are important as well as the connection between the criminal offences allocated to the administrative authority and other forms of criminality, the standardization of the extrajudicial settlement and the degree to which the PPS can contribute to the quality of the extrajudicial settlement by the administrative authority.

Three years after the previous policy document, on 31 October 2008, the government sent the policy document on the choice of a sanction system (*Nota keuze sanctiestelsel*) to Parliament.[54] This policy document had been promised by the Secretary of Justice during the parliamentary discussions in the First Chamber (*Eerste Kamer)* about the bill concerning illegal parking and other minor traffic offences (*bestuurlijke boete fout parkeren en andere lichte verkeersovertredingen*), the bill concerning nuisances in public areas (administrative penalty) (*bestuurlijke boete in de openbare ruimte*)[55] and in the Memorandum in reply (*Memorie van antwoord*) to the bill on the Fourth Tranche of GALA (*Vierde tranche Algemene wet bestuursrecht*).[56] It was also necessary to present this policy document because the Secretary of Justice had promised to make an inventory of acts conferring a power to impose administrative fines during the parliamentary discussions about the proposed Public Prosecution Service (Settlement) Act [*Wet OM-afdoening*] and to present

---

54 Parliamentary Documents II 2008–2009, 31 700 VI no. 69 and Parliamentary Documents I 2008–2009 31 700 VI D. See, for example, on this. J.F.L. Roording, "Met beleid bestraffen. Verschuivingen tussen strafrecht en bestuurlijke boete bezien vanuit het handhavingsbeleid", in: R.C. van Houten (ed.), *Economisch strafrecht en bestuurlijke boete*, Wolf Legal Publishers, Nijmegen 2012, pp. 7–19. Roording points at the criticism on the development of the administrative fine by the president of the Supreme Court (*Hoge Raad*) in: G.J.M. Corstens and W.M. Limborgh, "Inperkingen van het rechterlijk domein", in: F.W. Bleichrodt et al. (eds.), *De rechter in het geding, Liber Amicorum J.P. Balkema*, Kluwer Deventer 2011.

55 Proceedings I 2007–2008, p. 13 477.

56 Parliamentary Documents I 2007–2008, 29 702, C, p. 23.

a list of those powers to be transferred to the criminal law system of punishment orders (*strafbeschikking*).

In this policy document the government chose, as its starting point in the introduction of the administrative fine, to entrust its enforcement to the administrative authorities with regard to laws that often create specific legal relationships between citizens or businesses and the authorities ('closed context'). 'Administrative fines are functional in this context and can reinforce the other enforcement tools, including those under public law.

Criminal law acts as the underlying principle behind the enforcement of general requirements that do not create a specific legal relationship ('closed context'). It is desirable that citizens and businesses need only deal with one distinct regime when general requirements are being enforced and are not confronted with a multiplicity of instruments on the part of the authorities. It is also important that public servants who are responsible for enforcement have access to a well-defined selection of sanctions whereby the distinction between the open and closed contexts acts as the guiding principle, although contradictory indications could lead to a different choice. This certainly applies to more serious issues where criminal law should be the predominant factor, but it is also relevant if international obligations, for example, prescribe a sanction system, or if the requirement of legal unity is less imperative and administrative bodies are at liberty to interpret effective enforcement in their own way. Accordingly, in the open context, the administrative fine may at times be eligible for use as an enforcement instrument, for example in enforcing rules drawn up by municipal authorities by virtue of their autonomous regulatory power: general municipal by-laws (known as APVs), for instance. The central authority is not eager to draw up compulsory regulations relating to the implementation of such matters by decentralized authorities. In the open context, there may nevertheless be some scope for administrative fines to promote the effectiveness of enforcement. Further examination will be carried out to clarify the extent to which a well-balanced system of fining under the two sectors of administrative and criminal law would promote unity in the enforcement system. In addition, it is only meaningful to opt for simultaneously applying different sanction systems if the situation is such that there are good and urgent reasons to do so and if this is workable in practice.'[57] In appendix II a translation can be found of the governmental decision model to choose between systems of administrative law enforcement.

57 Parliamentary Documents II 2008–2009, 31 700 VI no. 69, p. 15.

The administrative fine and the relationship between criminal and administrative law

Since 1994 discussions have been taking place about the relationship of administrative law to criminal law in the Netherlands and the administrative fine plays a significant role in this. In the Netherlands, every regulation on administrative fines is set down in administrative law.

Studies have proposed that regulation of comparable matters should be included in a separate law, or in the Criminal Code and in the Code of Criminal Procedure.[58] For applicability of the norms incorporated in Article 6 ECHR, it does not matter on the whole where regulation of the administrative fine is laid down. However, this does matter in principle for the applicability of the legal codification of administrative law and that of criminal law and of the law on criminal procedure.

Before the GALA general regulation of administrative fines in most of the regulations on administrative fines came into effect, the legislator included a number of provisions in order to fulfil the norms set out in Article 6 ECHR. This is also the case in current GALA regulation and it also includes a number of norms under criminal law.

In the delineation between criminal procedure law and administrative law, the legislator originally built in a formal legal blockade in the General Administrative Law Act in Article 1:6, preamble and under a, GALA. The inclusion of a chapter on the right of complaint in the General Administrative Law Act introduced a slight amelioration: the definition provisions and the provisions on the right of complaint also apply to criminal procedure (investigation, prosecution of criminal acts and the enforcement of decisions under criminal law). This blockade was only drawn up for practical reasons; the legislator had no underlying dogmatic intention. We can deduce this from the remarks made by the government in its explanatory documents in the draft proposal to the third tranche of GALA:

> 'Taking into account the separate position of criminal law, which is expressed in such things as separate legal codes and its own system of criminal judgments, it could thwart the system of criminal law, and therefore lead to confusion if GALA regulations were simply applicable besides the law codes. For this reason Article 1:6 has been included. This however does not detract from the fact that various aspects of the relationship between citizens and the administrative authorities that are charged with investigation, prosecution and enforcement in the sphere of criminal law are dominated by the same principles as those that play a role in administrative law. This applies not only to the consequences of policy rules but also to the effect of the

58 A summary of the proposals can be found in A.R. Hartmann and P.M. van Russen Groen, *Contouren van het bestuursstrafrecht*, Gouda Quint, Arnhem 1998.

principles of proper administration in general. In our view, it seems therefore correct that attempts are made to link criminal law with administrative law if aspects of the relationship between the administration and citizens are under discussion for which no specific provisions have been made in criminal law. This link can be clearly traced in case law, and in the same way this can be deduced from the approach in the guidelines of the Dutch Prosecution Service.

Article 1:6 does not intend such an exclusion of the application of administrative rules under criminal law. It does, however, indicate that direct and complete application of GALA within the sphere of criminal law is not yet a matter for consideration because the system of criminal law would then be thwarted too greatly. We do, however, trust that in the future criminal law will try to link up with administrative law where possible.'[59]

To be perfectly clear: Article 1:6, preamble and under a, GALA plays no part in the influence of criminal law and criminal procedure law on administrative law. It only has regard to the influence of the administrative law set down in the General Administrative Law Act on criminal procedure law and penitentiary administrative law.[60]

In the case of punitive sanctions, such as the administrative fine, the question arises whether criminal law or criminal procedure law should be applied. Norms under administrative law already affect criminal procedure law without provisions to that effect in legislation, but the interesting question which then arises is whether this also applies to the effect of norms under criminal law in punitive administrative law. Naturally, human rights norms under criminal law also apply to punitive sanctions outside criminal law. And this is also the case for the administrative fine. In the Netherlands, a great deal of case law has developed on Articles 6 and 7 of ECHR and Article 15 ICCPR. We have, however, seen judgments where the judge has not used this kind of stepping stone in order to allow the influence of a norm under criminal law and to apply it. We have, after all, seen that the administrative courts derive inspiration from the criminal courts to fill in an administrative norm. As I will elaborate later in this contribution, after the enactment of the general regulation on administrative fines, the GALA legislator expects practice to

59 Parliamentary Documents II 1994/95, 23 700, no. 5, pp. 28–29; PG Awb III, pp. 282–283.

60 I think exclusion of penitentiary administrative law outside the effective ambit of the General Administrative Law Act is incorrect. See O.J.D.M.L. Jansen, "De koude uitsluiting van het penitentiaire bestuursrecht", *NJB* 1995, pp. 1107–1114. The explanation included in the explanatory papers to the Penitentiary (Framework) Act are not at all convincing on this exclusion. See O.J.D.M.L. Jansen, *Commentary Article 1:6 GALA*, in: N.S.J. Koeman *et al.* (eds.), *Handboek Algemene wet bestuursrecht*. See also on this G. Knigge, "De verhouding van het strafrecht tot het bestuursrecht", in: M.S. Groenhuijsen and G. Knigge (ed.), *Het vooronderzoek in strafzaken. Tweede interimrapport Strafvordering 2001*, p. 106.

link as closely as possible to criminal law when applying the law on administrative fines.

Administrative criminal law

Many authors describe punitive administrative law as administrative criminal law. Although in the Netherlands, we may have a dispute as to the nomenclature between punitive administrative law (*punitief bestuursrecht*) and administrative criminal law (*bestuursstrafrecht*) in French this is the *droit administratif pénal* and the *droit pénal administratif*.[61] Hartmann and Van Russen Groen have described administrative criminal law as 'that part of law that can be differentiated from criminal law and administrative law in which administrative authorities under public law may impose sanctions of a punitive character without the intercession of the person involved or an independent judge'.[62] The two authors regard this as a separate area of law. 'If the imposition of punitive administrative sanctions is regarded as a special form of criminal law, then this should be standardized under criminal law. If the imposition of punitive administrative sanctions is regarded as a part of administrative law, then this should be standardized under administrative law. If administrative criminal law is regarded as a separate area of law and is defined as such, then a framework is established within which questions concerning standardization such as the furnishing of proof and the kind of legal protection needed to be offered can be given a more unambiguous answer'.[63] Finally, they conclude that the area of law falls neither under administrative law nor under criminal law.

Administrative criminal act

Hartmann, Van Russen Groen and Rogier argue in favour of an administrative criminal law.[64] The question of the desirability of this has also been brought up by the VAR working group on the fourth tranche of GALA.[65] Albers also argues

61 Franck Moderne, *Sanctions administratives et justice constitutionnelle. Contribution à l'étude du jus puniendi de l'Etat dans les démocraties contemporaines*, Economica, Paris 1993, pp. 43–55. Mireille Delmas-Marty and Catherine Teitgen-Colly, *Punir sans juger? De la répression administrative au droit administratif pénal*, Economica, Paris 1992.

62 A.R. Hartmann and P.M. van Russen Groen, *Contouren van het bestuursstrafrecht*, Gouda Quint, Arnhem 1998, p. 74. See also their *Bestuursstrafrecht* in: H. de Doelder and L.J.J. Rogier (ed.), *Opstellen over bestuursstrafrecht*, Gouda Quint, Arnhem 1994, pp. 48–49.

63 Hartmann and Van Russen Groen, p. 75.

64 See Hartmann and Van Russen Groen, pp. 115–133, in particular pp. 128–133, A.R. Hartmann, "De bestuurlijke boete. Naar een zelfstandige wettelijke regeling", *Trema* 1995, pp. 318–322 and his *De wettelijke regeling van de bestuurlijke boete naar vorm en inhoud*, pp. 42–46, L.J.J. Rogier, "Het boetestelsel van de Wet Mulder", in: W.G.A. Hazewindus and O.J.D.M.L. Jansen (eds.), *Van boeteatelier tot boetefabriek*, Kluwer, Deventer 1995, pp. 127–141, in particular p. 140 (proposal for a Dutch *Ordnungswidrigkeitengesetz*, a code on administrative criminal law).

65 VAR Working Group Vierde tranche Awb, *De vierde tranche Awb. Commentary vraagpunten*, Boom Juridische uitgevers, The Hague 2000, pp. 77–79.

in favour of a separate arrangement for administrative criminal law. In her opinion, this should be separated completely from administrative procedure law, whilst maintaining the guarantees of national criminal law and criminal procedure law. 'There is in fact no magic line but there is a clear demarcation between criminal law and administrative law and between the laws on criminal procedure and the laws on administrative procedure. The differences between criminal law and administrative law and between the laws on criminal procedure and administrative procedure are such that the imposition of a possibly originally criminal sanction by an administrative authority may not be without problems on the basis of present administrative law and the law on administrative procedure.'[66] Corstens has argued in favour of a general law on administrative fines, a kind of Economic Offences Act or *Wed* for administrative fines, which should not form a part of the General Administrative Law Act.[67]

Punitive sanctions should not be provided for in the General Administrative Law Act, since punitive sanctions do more than restore the legal order. A secondary legal relationship would develop. This would lead to all kinds of special demands coming into effect and a large number of provisions would be necessary in order to achieve sound regulation. The consequence of this would be an extremely extensive and somewhat obscure regulation. A separate law would not entail such disadvantages. A regulation with punitive sanctions would be a strange bedfellow in the General Administrative Law Act because this act presupposes reciprocal legal relationships, and punitive sanctions are one-sided: the inclusion of punitive sanctions in the General Administrative Law Act would alter its character. Punishment is a separate, clearly definable government activity. A system in which interpretation of criminal provisions is left to the four highest courts (Administrative Decisions Division, Central Appeals Court and the Industry and Trade Tribunal and the Supreme Court) should be rejected and the protection under law against all punitive sanctions, both criminal and administrative, should be placed in the hands of one judge: in the criminal court. It would be difficult to realise this with a regulation in the General Administrative Law Act.

---

66 C.L.G.F.H. Albers, "De bestuurlijke boete. Magische lijn of hellend vlak?", *JBPlus* 2000, pp. 138–152, in particular p. 152. See her latest *Rechtsbescherming bij bestuurlijke boeten. Balanceren op een magische lijn?*, dissertation Maastricht, Sdu, The Hague 2002, p. 430 and C.L.G.F.H. Albers, "De bestuurlijke boete in de gemeentelijke praktijk; straffen en gestraft worden", *De Gemeentestem* 2002 (issue 7178), pp. 637–647.

67 G.J.M. Corstens, *Een stille revolutie in het strafrecht*, Gouda Quint, Arnhem 1995, pp. 27–29.

5. RELATION TO GENERAL FIELDS OF LAW AND IMPORTANT GENERAL ACTS

5.1. INTRODUCTION: GALA AND ADMINISTRATIVE LAW

As a coherent and consistent whole, Dutch administrative law is still comparatively new. The first general codification of part of the general section of administrative law, the General Administrative Law Act, is still very recent: it only came into force on 1 January 1994. Numerous changes to Dutch legislation and regulations came into force in order to bring about the intended harmonisation of the general part of the administrative law, a matter that had been a subject of discussion for such a long time. One of the most important objectives of the General Administrative Law Act has therefore been the encouragement of uniformity in administrative law.

The official aims of GALA are:

a. promoting unity within administrative law legislation;
b. systematizing and, where possible, simplifying administrative law legislation;
c. codifying developments in existing administrative case law;
d. making provision for developments regarding matters whose nature makes them less suitable for arrangement in special legislation.

Although the aspiration of the General Administrative Law Act for harmonization may be described as high, this is certainly not the case for the desire for codification. The constitutional legislator's instructions on the subject of codification are confined to codification of the general rules on administrative law, in other words: to the general codification of part of the general section of administrative law. The government took the size of the project into consideration, when deciding to divide the General Administrative Law Act into sections, called 'tranches'. These tranches are like components in a building project, which was started in 1983. This has resulted in four tranches that have since come into force; the fourth, and most recent one, became effective as of 1 July 2009. Its introduction did not mark the end of the building project: an act providing for a general regulation of compensation for loss and damages for wrongful acts [*Wet nadeelcompensatie en schadevergoeding bij onrechtmatige besluiten*] has been published and it is expected that this bill will partly be enacted on 1 July 2013.[68] Another important example of the continuing building project is the Act on the modification of administrative procedural law [Wet aanpassing bestuursprocesrecht], *Staatsblad* 2012, 682. Also see *Staatsblad* 2012, 684. As well as these more comprehensive elements, there have been countless

68 Act of 31 January 2013, *Staatsblad* 2013, 50. Also see *Staatsblad* 2013, 162.

other minor amendments, draft bills on sections have been published and other additions to the General Administrative Law Act are either under consideration or are in preparation. It is often the case, as with so many construction projects, that additional work is required during actual construction. There are countless changes which are too small to be put into a tranche and which are added to the construction, the General Administrative Law Act. In addition, there are the changes arising from the evaluation of parts of the General Administrative Law Act and other incidental changes.

If numerous specific acts, rules and regulations differ from the general rule provided for in GALA by using different terms, systems or by providing for the same legal item or subject, the harmonizing effect aimed for will not be achieved. For this reason, together with the enactment of a part of GALA, bills and other regulations are enacted to bring acts, rules and regulations in conformity with GALA. In order to do justice to the desired harmonisation of Dutch administrative law, it is not sufficient to allow amending legislation to come into force at the same time that an amendment or alteration to General Administrative Law Act comes into force. After legislation has become effective, it will still have to be in principle in accordance with the relevant provisions of the General Administrative Law Act. In essence, the special legislator is not allowed on the basis of the Instructions for regulation (*Aanwijzingen voor de regelgeving)* to deviate from the General Administrative Law Act. In fact, to a certain extent, it is the case here that general law takes precedence over special law.

The picture just outlined must, however, be filled out. The latitude allowed to the special legislator and regulator to make their own regulations in the field of general administrative law depends on the degree to which any law set down in the General Administrative Law Act is compulsory. The greater the degree of compulsion the greater the harmonizing effect of the provision will be. The General Administrative Law Act has four kinds of provision in this respect: obligatory provisions, directory law (customary provisions), supplementary law (safety net provisions) and facultative law. The lower regulator may not deviate from an obligatory provision. Legislative policy has set down that the special legislator may not deviate from this, unless there are particular reasons for doing so. Moreover the special legislator must deviate explicitly and in a formulation as prescribed in the Instructions for regulation ('In afwijking van artikel … Awb …'). The structure of the General Administrative Law Act can be found in the appendices.

The General Administrative Law Act is built up in layers. In order, for example, to give an answer to the question whether an appeal can be lodged against a decision of an administrative body, the relevant provisions of Chapters 9, 7 and 1 of the General Administrative Law Act have to be consulted. For questions concerning which norms should be observed in a decision concerning an astreinte or an administrative fine from this administrative authority, the relevant provisions in Chapters 5, 4, 3, 2 and 1 from this act should be studied.

5.2. THE POSITION OF SPECIFIC LEGISLATION IN RELATION TO THE GALA REGULATION ON ADMINISTRATIVE FINES

Most rules in the general regulation of administrative sanctions in GALA are obligatory provisions (*dwingend recht*); only a few are of directory law (*regelend recht*). The enactment of this general regulation has removed the provisions in special laws (*bijzondere wetten*) that deviate from the general provision or the rules that provide for the same.

In addition, this general regulation contains directory law: one example is the 'customary provisions', which are provisions setting out a generally applicable ruling whereby the legislator has taken account of the necessity or desirability that a different rule should apply in a limited number of cases. This main rule may be deviated from in statutory provisions at each level. For the adjustment exercise this means that provisions that correspond with the main rule may lapse while, for deviating provisions, there must be an assessment each time as to whether there is sufficient reason to make an exception to the main rule. For such deviations, it is not necessary to specifically state in the special law that this is being done contrary to GALA.

In short, the legislator of specific acts has the choice to entrust a certain administrative agency with the power to sanction. By doing so, he has limited space to make his own choices. Applying this to the general regulation of administrative fines in GALA, the legislator has to determine the infringements for which an administrative fine can be imposed according to the principle of legality in article 5:4 GALA. He also has to fix the maximum fine which can be imposed. Furthermore, he has to choose between two systems of setting administrative fines: to give the administrative authority the liberty to choose its own fine within the statutory maximum (see Article 5:46, second paragraph, GALA) or to have administrative fine tariffs (*boetetarieven*) determined by a generally binding provision (*algemeen verbindend voorschrift*) (see Article 5:46, third paragraph, GALA). This choice determines the mechanism for imposing an administrative fine, and more importantly, the process of judicial review by administrative courts. It is possible that one specific act provides for both approaches depending on the infringements involved and/or whether the rule maker has used the power to fix administrative fine tariffs in generally binding rules. The last choice the specific legislator has to make according to article 5:53 GALA is whether the light procedure (*lichte procedure*) or the heavier procedure (*zware procedure*) applies to the imposition of administrative fines. As I will elaborate later in more detail in this contribution, the heavier procedure provides for more procedural guarantees and takes more defence rights into account in the preparatory phase of a decision to impose an administrative fine. In most if not almost all cases, the legislator provides for the heavier procedure *(zware procedure)*.[69]

Currently, there are almost 100 specific acts that provide for the power to impose administrative fines. It is not possible within this contribution to give a complete overview of those acts,[70] but it is possible to give a few characteristics.

Economic administrative law

The administrative fine is an important sanction in economic administrative law and, similarly to the situation in financial administrative law, has found common acceptance in a relatively short time.

The Media Act [*Mediawet*] was one of the first examples of an administrative fine in this legal domain; it was replaced by the Media Act 2008 on 1 January 2009.[71] Under this act, the Dutch Media Authority [*Commissariaat voor de Media*] has the authority to impose an administrative fine up to a maximum of €225,000 or, for certain infringements, ten per cent of the total sums of money that have been made available on average to the broadcasting organization for the provision of media services for the national public media service in the calendar years prior to the infringement during the current 'permission' period. The Authority is free to set the administrative fine within this fixed statutory bandwidth. The Authority has given greater substance to this competence through the adoption of policy rules, viz. the Policy Line on Sanctions 2007 [*Beleidslijn Sanctiemaatregelen 2007*],[72] which remain in force under the new law on the basis of the Policy Line on Sanctions under the Media Act 2008.[73] The Dutch Media Authority is also charged with implementing the Retail Price Maintenance (Books) Act [*Wet op de vaste boekenprijs*]. Under that law, maximum sums of €90,000 apply (Article 18) or of €4,500 (Article 22): the latter administrative fine applies to a infringement of the obligation to cooperate (Article 5:20, first paragraph, GALA). Here too, the Media Authority is free to set the administrative fine within the statutory limits. The Media Authority has

69 See Oswald Jansen, "Bestuurlijk en justitieel bestraffen in Nederland – op zoek naar (nog) meer eenheid", in: R.C. van Houten (ed.), *Economisch strafrecht en bestuurlijke boete*, Wolf Legal Publishers, Nijmegen 2012, pp. 21-79, 151-181.

70 An overview is provided for in: Oswald Jansen, "Bestuurlijk en justitieel bestraffen in Nederland", in: R.C. van Houten (ed.), *Economisch strafrecht en bestuurlijke boete*, Wolf Legal Publishers, Nijmegen 2012, pp. 21–79 and pp. 153–181.

71 Act of 29 December 2008, Bulletin of Acts and Decrees, (Staatsblad) 2008, 583.

72 Government Gazette (Staatscourant) 2006, 133.

73 Government Gazette (Staatscourant) 2009, 13. The Policy Line on Sanctions 1999 lapsed with the introduction of this policy line.

introduced policy regulations as a means of further regulating this power: these are the Policy Regulations for Sanctions on Retail Price Maintenance for Books 2009 [*Beleidslijn Sanctiemaatregelen Vaste Boekenprijs 2009].*[74] The Authority tends to apply bandwidths rather than fixed rates for almost all finable offences.

The penalty regulations applied by regulators and market authorities, such as the ACM (Authority for consumers and Makets)[75] represent an important group of penalty regimes. The ACM does not only apply the Dutch Competition Act [*Mededingingswet (Mw)*]: its Energy Department applies the Electricity Act 1998 [*Electriciteitswet 1998*], the Gas Act [*Gaswet*] and the Heating Supply Act [*Warmtewet*]; its Telecommunications, Transport and Postal Services Department applies the Passenger Transport Act 2000 [*Wet personenvervoer 2000*], the Railways Act [*Spoorwegwet*], Aviation Act [*Wet luchtvaart*] and the Pilotage Act [*Loodsenwet*]. The ACM also applies the Improving the Effectiveness of Review Procedures Act concerning the Award of Public Contracts Directive (Implementation) Act [*Wet implementatie rechtsbeschermingrichtlijnen aanbesteden (Wira)*].[76] All this legislation includes a penalty regulation. It will come as no surprise to discover that the penalty regulations imposed by the NMa share a strong likeness.[77]

I am going to restrict myself, in the context of this contribution, to a brief description of the Competition Act [*Mededingingswet (Mw)*]. On this basis, the following maximum fines can be imposed, depending on the finable offence: €450,000, or if that is higher, 10 per cent of the turnover (if the offender is the actual person in charge it remains €450,000) (under Articles 57 and 74, 75, 76a, Mw),[78] €450,000 or 1% of the turnover (including infringement of the obligation to cooperate in Article 5:20, first paragraph, GALA) (under Articles 69, 57a,

74 Government Gazette (Staatscourant) 2009, 75.

75 The Authority for consumers and Markets merged from the former NMa (Dutch Competition Authority), OPTA (Dutch Telecommunications Authority) and CA (Consumer Authority) – See Staatsblad 2013, 102 and 103. This legislation was enacted on 1 April 2013. I should also point at the legislative proposal to streamline the legislation applied by the new ACM: Parliamentary Documents (Kamerstukken) II, 2012–2013, 33 622, nos. 1–3.

76 Bulletin of Acts and Decrees (Staatsblad) 2010, 38.

77 Article 80 Railways Act provides deviating fine maximums (€10,000 and €50,000) for certain infringements and a procedural-law tariffs system. Improving the Effectiveness of Review Procedures concerning the Award of Public Contracts Directive (Implementation) Act (Wira) has a completely different fine maximum, viz. fifteen per cent of the estimated value of the public contract in question (Article 14 Wira).

78 See also Article 77i, first paragraph, preamble and under b, Electricity Act 1998 where 10% of turnover is set as the limit, not €450,000. See also Article 60ad, first paragraph, preamble and under b, Gas Act; Article 45f, second paragraph, Pilotage Act; Article 49, Postal Act 2009; Article 76, third paragraph, Railways Act; Article 15:4, second and third paragraph, Telecommunications Act.

70b,72, 73 Mw).[79] The ACM is at liberty to choose the size of the administrative fine up to the statutory maximum. For many years, the ACM (and the former NMa) was able to establish its own policy rules on determining administrative fines, which practice came to an end in 2009 with the Minister of Economic Affairs' Policy Regulations for the imposition of administrative fines by the NMa,[80] established by the Minister under Article 5d of the Competition Act. The policy rules relate not only to the imposition of fines under the Competition Act but also under the other legislation referred to above and applied by the ACM (former NMa).

The fine regulations imposed under the Competition Act have a number of particular aspects which are interesting for penalty law in general. In the first place, a distinction is made between supervision and examination in the preparation of fining decisions. This distinction is grafted onto the distinction drawn between supervision and investigation in economic criminal law. In the second place, there is the regulation of the commitment decision. The offender can apply to the ACM's Board for a certain commitment to be declared binding in order to avoid an administrative sanction. This is possible if it would prevent or bring to an end an infringement of a cartel ban or of the prohibition of abuse of a position of economic power (Article 49a et seq. Mw). In the third place, under the influence of European administrative law, the fine system has a broader *nemo tenetur* regulation, the legal privilege (Article 51 Mw). In the fourth place, lower maximum fines have often been included for the person actually in charge. To round off, mention should be made of the clemency arrangement and the 'click' fine. Under the clemency arrangement, participants in a cartel may receive full or partial immunity from the imposition of an administrative fine if they report a cartel to the ACM's clemency office. This has been set out in the Policy on Clemency.[81]

The Telecommunications, Transport and Postal Services Department of the ACM applies the Telecommunications Act [*Telecommunicatiewet*] and the Postal Act 2009 [*Postwet 2009*], which is legislation very similar to the Competition Act. The dominant system of legal protection falls under the competence of the Rotterdam District Court as court of first instance and the Trade and Industry

79 See also Article 77i, first paragraph, preamble and under a, Electricity Act 1998; Article 60ad, first paragraph, preamble and under a, Gas Act; Article 45g, third paragraph, 45h, first paragraph, Pilotage Act; Article 75, first paragraph, Railways Act; Article 15.4, fourth and fifth paragraph Telecommunications Act (unlike the Competitive Trading Act, for violations of the obligation to cooperate, the maximum of 1% of turnover is not applicable but only €450,000.

80 Government Gazette (Staatscourant) 2009, 14079.

81 Policy Rules of the Minister of Economic Affairs for the reduction of administrative fines concerning cartels (Government Gazette (Staatscourant) 2009, 14078).

Appeals Tribunal [*College van Beroep voor het bedrijfsleven (CBb)*] as appeal court.

The Underground Grids (Information Exchange) Act [*Wet informatie-uitwisseling ondergrondse netten (Wet ion)*] and the Space Activities Act [*Wet ruimtevaartactiviteiten (Wr)*] have a similar regime to the legislation just mentioned. These statutes also include a fine system (Article 26 *Wet ion* and Article 15 *Wr*, respectively) with two maximum fines: €450,000 and €100,000. Even so there are considerable differences between these two laws. The Wet ion has the lowest fine maximum (€100,000) for a infringement of the obligation to cooperate, whereas the *Wr* has the highest maximum fine for this infringement. The maximum fine in the latter act is not only €450,000 but is also related to the turnover of the offender (10%) in the relevant year. The Radiocommuncations Agency Netherlands of the Ministry of Economic Affairs is charged with the enforcement of this act, and the general administrative legal protection system district courts and the Administrative Jurisdiction Division) applies here.

Under Article 48 of the Inland Navigation Act [*Binnenvaartwet*], the Minister of Transport, Public Works and Water Management derives the power to impose an administrative fine of the fourth category according to Article 23 of the Dutch Criminal Code [*Wetboek van Strafrecht (DCC)*]. The fine maximum is raised by 50% if an offender re-offends. The fines are set by ministerial order in an annex to the Inland Navigation Regulations.

Personal data protection

The Dutch Data Protection Authority has the authority under Article 71 Personal Data Protection Act [*Wet bescherming persoonsgegevens (Wbp)*] to impose an administrative fine of €4,500. The Authority is at liberty to choose the value of the administrative fine up to that maximum. It seems to me, however, that this maximum fails to offer the Authority the necessary tools for effective enforcement. The Authority's power to impose fines is declared applicable by analogy in Article 35, third paragraph of the Police Data Act [*Wet politiegegevens*].[82]

Consumer protection

The ACM is the central authority here; it derives its power to impose administrative fines from the Consumer Protection (Enforcement) Act [*Wet handhaving consumentenbescherming (Whc)*]. A large number of traditional civil law provisions are enforced under this law. The ACM is not the only authority

82 This would have seemed an obvious step to me for the Municipal Database (Personal Records) Act [*Wet Gemeentelijke basisadministratie persoonsgegeven*] and the Judicial Data and Criminal Records Act [*Wet Justitiële en strafvorderlijke gegevens*].

charged with consumer protection. The same act provides for consumer protection by the Netherlands Authority for the Financial Markets [*AFM*] (Article 3.1 et seq. *Whc*), the Public Health Regulatory Service [*Staatstoezicht op de volksgezondheid*] (Article 3.5 *Whc*), the Media Authority (Article 3.7 *Whc*), the Transport and Water Management Inspectorate (Articles 3.9 and 3.10 *Whc*) and the Food and Consumer Product Safety Authority (Articles 3.11 and 3.12 *Whc*), each in their own specific field. *Whc* also provides for cooperation arrangements with other government agencies, viz. the Dutch Healthcare Authority [*Nederlandse Zorgautoriteit*], OPTA, the NMa and the Tax and Customs Administration/Fiscal Intelligence and Investigation Service and Economic Investigation Service [[*Belastingdienst*](*Fiscale inlichtingen- en opsporingsdienst en Economische controledienst (FIOD-ECD)]*. Other government agencies can also be designated under an order in council [*Algemene maatregel van bestuur (AMvB)*] but this has not happened yet, to my knowledge.

Legal protection is offered according to the economic model: the Rotterdam District Court as court of first instance and appeals are heard by the Trade and Industry Appeals Tribunal.

Financial administrative law

The Act on the Introduction of Penalty Payments and Administrative Fines (Financial Legislation) Act [*Wet introductie dwangsom en bestuurlijke boete (Wet Idbb)*] of 1 January 2000 marked the inclusion of the administrative fine in a wide range of legislation in financial administrative law.[83] A great deal of this legislation was included in the Financial Supervision Act [*Wet op het financieel toezicht (Wft)*].[84] The Act Implementing and Amending the Wft [*Invoerings- en aanpassingswet Wft*] harmonized the penalty regulations of a large number of statutes, such as the Sanctions Act 1977 [*Sanctiewet 1977*] and the Consumer Protection (Enforcement) Act (*Whc*) in so far as the powers of the AFM were concerned.[85] The fine system of the Pensions Act [*Pensioenwet*], which could traditionally be considered part of a different legislative regime, was harmonized with the regulation in the Wft. The introduction of the appurtenant Act Implementing and Amending the Pensions Act [*Invoerings- en aanpassingswet Pensioenwet*][86] brought about greater streamlining in a number of fine systems in special pension legislation. The Wft, the Pensions Act and the appurtenant amending legislation all came into force on 1 January 2007. The Penalty Scheme in

---

83 Bulletin of Acts and Decrees Act (Staatsblad) 1999, 509. The parliamentary history can be found at parliamentary paper number 25 821.

84 Act of 28 September 2006, Bulletin of Acts and Decrees Act (Staatsblad) 2006, 475. The parliamentary history can be found at parliamentary document number 29 708.

85 Act of 20 November 2006, Bulletin of Acts and Decrees Act (Staatsblad) 2006, 605. The parliamentary history can be found at parliamentary document number 30 658.

86 Act of 7 December 2006, Bulletin of Acts and Decrees Act (Staatsblad) 2006, 706. The parliamentary history can be found at parliamentary document number 30 413.

Financial Legislation (Amendment) Act [*Wet wijziging boetestelsel financiële wetgeving*][87] marked the adjustment of the entire range of legislation, and further harmonization was achieved through amendments to other legislation in the financial sector, such as the Sanctions Act 1977 (Sanctiewet 1977), the Foreign Financial Relations Act [*Wet financiële betrekkingen buitenland*] 1994, the Money Laundering and Terrorist Financing (Prevention) Act [*Wet ter voorkoming van witwassen en financieren van terrorisme*], the Audit Firms (Supervision) Act [*Wet toezicht accountantsorganisaties*] and the Trust Offices (Supervision) Act [*Wet toezicht trustkantoren*].

The dominant system of legal protection falls under the competence of the Rotterdam District Court as court of first instance and the Trade and Industry Appeals Tribunal [*College van Beroep voor het bedrijfsleven (CBb)*] as appeal court.

Fiscal administrative law

An administrative fine has long been part of this field of law. The case law handed down by the tax division of the Dutch Supreme Court shortly after the Özturk judgment by the European Court of Human Rights had a significant impact on the development of Dutch penalty law. Many of the choices that were made by the legislative body in the GALA fine system are directly attributable to this case law. Large numbers of administrative fines are imposed under fiscal administrative law.

The central fine system is, of course, outlined in the State Taxes Act [*Algemene wet inzake rijksbelastingen (Awr)*]. And it is important to be aware that this law has also been declared applicable by analogy in other legislation,[88] which means that the Awr fine system has a correspondingly large impact. It distinguishes between default surcharges and negligence penalties (in which an intentional act or gross negligence form part of the definition of the finable offence). The following maximum default charges can be imposed, depending on the finable offence: €123 (Article 67b, first paragraph, Awr), €1230 (Article 67b, second paragraph, Awr),[89] €4920 (Articles 67a, 67c and 67ca Awr).[90] The maximum fine

87 Act of 31 July 2009, Bulletin of Acts and Decrees Act (Staatsblad) 2009, 327. The parliamentary history can be found at parliamentary document number 31 458.

88 Important examples are Article 231, Municipalities Act, Article 227a Provinces Act and Article 123, second paragraph, Water Boards Act. In Article 234, fifth paragraph, Municipalities Act, a number of powers under the State Taxes Act are again excluded, viz. those in Article 67b, 67c and 67f, Awr. See also Article 13, second paragraph, Heavy Motor Vehicles Taxation Act [*Wet belasting zware motorrijtuigen*], Article 102a, second paragraph, Excise Duty Act [*Wet op de accijns*] and Article 13a, seventh paragraph, Private Motor Vehicle and Motorcycle Tax Act [*Wet op de belasting van personenauto's en motorrijwielen*].

89 This is also a fine maximum in Article 28b, 28c, Wages and Salaries Tax Act 1964.

90 This is also a fine maximum in Article 63b, Collection of State Taxes Act 1990 [*Invorderingswet 1990*], Article 13, first paragraph, Heavy Motor Vehicles Taxation Act [*Wet belasting zware*

for negligence penalties is 100% of the fine base (for example the amount of the tax assessment) (Article 67d, 67e and 67f Awr). Article 67pa and 67pb include a number of remarkable exceptions to the GALA fine system. First, the time limit of Article 5:45 GALA is declared inapplicable and, second, the option of a fine inspector, a fiscal fine nightmare, which could slip in by the backdoor under Article 10:3, fourth paragraph, GALA, is excluded.

The fiscal system of legal protection under administrative law applies to tax fines (District Court, Court of Appeal, Supreme Court).

The General Customs Act [*Algemene douanewet*] also has a fine system. Articles 9:1 et seq. include maximum fines of 100 per cent of the amount due by way of duties, €150 and €300.

The General Income-Dependent Schemes Act [*Algemene wet inkomensafhankelijke regelingen*] seeks to link up with the fiscal system. The fine system included in Articles 40 and 41 sets maximum fine amounts of €1,500 and €5,000. The dominant system of legal protection falls under the competence of the Rotterdam District Court as court of first instance and the Trade and Industry Appeals Tribunal [*College van Beroep voor het bedrijfsleven (CBb)*] as appeal court.

Administrative health law

With the Act Extending Administrative Law Enforcement of Public Health [*Wet uitbreiding bestuursrechtelijke handhaving volksgezondheid*],[91] numerous other fine regulations were added to already existent fine regulations, i.e. the Medicine Prices Act [*Wet op de geneesmiddelenprijzen*][92] and the Health Care (Market Regulation) Act [*Wet marktordening gezondheidszorg (Wgp)*].[93] The maximum amounts can vary enormously. The maximum fine in the Medical Appliances Act [*Wet op de medische hulpmiddelen*] and the Body Material (Safety and Quality) Act [*Wet veiligheid en kwaliteit lichaamsmateriaal*] is €900,000; in the Health Care (Market Regulation) Act [*Wet Marktordening gezondheidszorg*], it is €2,250, €100,000, €500,000 or €10,000,000; in the Medicines Act

motorrijtuigen], Article 102a, first paragraph, Excise Duty Act [*Wet op de accijns*]. In Article 13a, sixth paragraph, Private Motor Vehicle and Motorcycle Tax Act [*Wet op de belasting van personenauto's en motorrijwielen*], and in Article 37d, second paragraph, Motor Vehicle Tax Act [*Wet op de motorrijtuigenbelasting*], a fiscal fine maximum is again included, viz. €492.

91 Act of 15 April 2010, Bulletin of Acts and Decrees (Staatsblad) 2010, 191.

92 A power to fine had been included in this act from the beginning (see Act of 25 January 1996, Bulletin of Acts and Decrees (Staatsblad) 1996, 90. The parliamentary history can be found at parliamentary document number 24 266.

93 An administrative fine might have been expected in a number of statutory arrangements in this field of law, which could possibly have been included in this amendment, such as the Embryos Act [*Embryowet*] the Artificial Insemination (Donor Information) Act [*Wet donorgegevens kunstmatige bevruchting*] and the Public Health Act [*Wet publieke gezondheid*].

[*Geneesmiddelenwet*] a maximum fine of €450,000 applies; in the Care Institutions (Quality) Act [*Kwaliteitswet zorginstellingen*], the Termination of Pregnancy Act [*Wet afbreking zwangerschap*], the Blood Supply Act [*Wet inzake bloedvoorziening*] and the Opium Act [*Opiumwet*] it is €33,500; in the Psychiatric Hospitals (Compulsory Admissions) Act [*Wet Bijzondere opneming in psychiatrische ziekenhuizen*] it is €13,400 and in the Clients' Right of Complaint (Care Sector) Act [*Wet klachtrecht cliënten zorgsector*] and the Individual Healthcare Professions Act [*Wet beroepen in de individuele gezondheidszorg*] it is €6,700.

Only administrative fining powers are granted in this legal area, according to which the administrative body is free to determine the size of the administrative fine. An entire gamut of policy rules has been drawn up,[94] which provide further standardization of these powers and a model for the value of the fine(s).

The legal protection offered under the general administrative law system (appeal to the District Court and the Administrative Jurisdiction Division for appeal to a higher court) is the rule for this area of law. For the Healthcare (Market Regulation) Act, the Rotterdam District Court acts as the court of first instance and the Trade and Industry Appeals Tribunal as the court of appeal.

Licensing, Catering, Tobacco and Commodities Act

A maximum administrative fine of €100,000 can be imposed under the Licensing and Catering Act [*Drank- en Horecawet*]. The fines are set by an order declaring a collective agreement binding [*algemeen verbindend verklaring, (a.v.v.)*], according to the Administrative Fines (Licensing and Catering) Decree *[Besluit bestuurlijke boete Drank- en horecawet*] (see Article 44b, first paragraph, Licensing and Catering Act). The legal protection offered by the general

[94] The Policy Rules on administrative fines in the Medicines Act [*Geneesmiddelenwet*] (Government Gazette (Staatscourant) 2007, 123), the Policy Rules on administrative fines in the Care Institutions (Quality) Act (Government Gazette 2010, 9212), the Policy Rules on administrative fines in the Opium Act (Government Gazette 2010, 9189), the Policy rules in the Termination of Pregnancy Act [*Wet afbreking zwangerschap*] (Government Gazette 2010, 9187), the Policy Rules in the Psychiatric Hospitals (Compulsory Admissions) Act [*Wet bijzondere opnemingen in psychiatrische ziekenhuizen*] (Government Gazette 2010, 9176), the Policy Rules on administrative fines in the Blood Supply Act [*Wet inzake bloedvoorziening*] (Government Gazette 2010, 9179), the Policy Rules on administrative fines in the Clients' Right of Complaint (Care Sector) Act [*Wet klachtrecht cliënten zorgsector*](Government Gazette 2010, 9162), the Policy Rules on administrative fines in the Individual Healthcare Professions Act [*Wet beroepen in de individuele gezondheidszorg*] (Government Gazette 2010, 9177), the Policy Rules on administrative fines in the Medical Appliances Act [*Wet op de medische hulpmiddelen*] (Government Gazette 2010, 9147), the Policy Rules on administrative fines in the Body Material (Safety and Quality) Act [*Wet veiligheid en kwaliteit lichaamsmateriaal*] (Government Gazette 2010, 9145).

administrative law system also applies here: district courts as courts of first instance and the Administrative Jurisdiction Division as appeals court.

Under Article 11b of the Tobacco Act, the Minister can impose an administrative fine for violating provisions of that act. The maximum fines are €450,000 (advertising ban) and €4,500 (other infringements, such as the smoking ban). The fines are determined by statutory provision (the schedule to the act, which can be amended by an order in council). The Minister of Health, Welfare and Sport derives the power to impose a maximum administrative fine of €4,500 from Article 32a of the Commodities Act [*Warenwet*]. The economic system of legal protection applies to both fine systems: the Rotterdam District Court as court of first instance and Trade and Industry Appeals Tribunal for appeal to a higher court.

Planning and administrative environmental law (environmental law)
Administrative fines are only very rarely imposed in environmental law, in contrast to the situation in many other sectors. It would be only reasonable to expect a general regulation to impose fines for a large number of finable offences under the Spatial Planning Act [*Wet op de ruimtelijke ordening (WRO)*], Environmental Permitting (General Provisions) Act [*Wet algemene bepalingen omgevingsrecht (Wabo)*] and the Environmental Management Act *[Wet milieubeheer (Wm)*], but strangely enough this is not the case. A special fining power has been included in the Environmental Management Act, viz. the power for the Board of the Emissions Authority to impose an administrative fine under Article 18.16a *Wm*. The maximum fine is €450,000 or, if the turnover of the offender is more than €4,500,000, 10% of the offender's turnover (Article 18.16e *Wm*), and the administrative body is free to determine the actual size of the administrative fine. The legal protection system under administrative law (district courts and the Administrative Jurisdiction Division) also applies here. The government is working on a huge legislative project to merge 15 acts, to withdraw 2 acts and to change 25 other acts in order to achieve uniformity. The result of this project will be the Omgevingswet (See Parliamentary Documents II 2011–2012, 33, 118, no. 3). This Act will most probably introduce the power to impose administrative fines in the broad field of the environment in the broadest sense (spatial planning included).

The Fertilizers Act [*Meststoffenwet*] and the Plant Protection Products and Biocides Act [*Wet gewasbeschermingsmiddelen en biociden (WGB)*] have very similar fine regulations. In the Fertilizers Act, the maximum fines are rated partly according to the amount of nitrogen and phosphate (€7 or €11 per kilo, under Articles 57 and 58 Fertilizers Act), and partly in absolute terms (€11,250 or €45,000 for natural persons and €45,000 or €450,000 for juristic persons under Article 62 Fertilizers Act). For the application of the latter power to impose fines, the rates are defined in generally binding provisions set out in Schedule III of the Fertilizers Act (Implementation) Decree [*Uitvoeringsbesluit Meststoffenwet*] but I have found no statutory basis in the Fertilizers Act itself for this. The WGB has the same absolute maximum fines as the Fertilizers Act (Article 97).

Social administrative law

The introduction of the Social Security Benefits (Fines, Measures, Recovery and Collection) Act [*Wet boeten, maatregelen, en terug- en invordering sociale zekerheid (Wet BMTI)*] meant that a fine system was incorporated into a large number of social security laws. The administrative fine is still the usual sanction in this sector. The maximum fine is almost always €2,269.[95] In addition, the Sickness Benefits Act [*Ziektewet*] has maximum fines of €454 (Article 38, third paragraph and €455 (Article 38a, eighth paragraph).

The Work and Income (Implementation Structure) Act [*Wet structuur uitvoeringsorganisatie werk en inkomen*] has a fine system that includes two maximum amounts: €1,500 or, for an intentional act or gross negligence, €5,000 (Article 83c).

Articles 69, third paragraph and 96, third paragraph, of the Healthcare Insurance Act [*Zorgverzekeringswet*] provide for a power to impose a fine up to a maximum of 130% of a portion of the contribution or premium (to be determined by ministerial regulation) over a period of no more than five years.[96]

Working hours, working conditions and minimum wage

The Working Hours Act [*Arbeidstijdenwet*] contains two maximum fines – €11,250 for natural persons, and €45,000 for juristic persons (Article 10:7) – and the fines are increased by a maximum of 50% for re-offending. The administrative body is free to determine the size of the administrative fine within the given margins. There are two policy rules in which the standard amounts for fines are set out.[97] Strangely enough, Article 10:7, fourth paragraph,

---

95 See Article 17a General Child Benefit Act [*Algemene kinderbijslagwet*], 39 Surviving Dependants Act [*Algemene nabestaandenwet*], 17c General Old Age Pensions Act [*Algemene ouderdomswet*], 27a Unemployment Insurance Act, 48 Invalidity Insurance (Self-Employed Persons) Act [*Wet arbeidsongeschiktheidsverzekering zelfstandigen*], 21 Older Unemployed Persons Income Scheme Act [*Wet inkomensvoorziening oudere werklozen*], 29a Invalidity Insurance Act, 2:69 Work and Employment Support (Young Disabled Persons) Act [*Wet werk en arbeidsondersteuning jonggehandicapten*], 91 Work and Income (Capacity for Work) Act [*Wet werk en inkomen naar arbeidsvermogen*], 45a Sickness Benefits Act.

96 Article 117 of this Act has been wrongly kept, in view of Articles 8:28a and 8:72a GALA.

97 These are the Policy Rules on imposing fines in the Working Hours Act and the Working Hours Decree [*Arbeidstijdenbesluit*] (Government Gazette 2009, 14905) and the Policy Rules on imposing fines in the Working Hours Act and the Working Hours (Transport)(Road Transport) Decree [*Arbeidstijdenbesluit vervoer (wegvervoer)*] (Government Gazette 2007, 95).

still contains a 'hobby' issue of the Ministry of Social Affairs, which – fortunately – has no significance or importance in actual practice. 'Contrary to Article 8:69 of the General Administrative Law Act, the court can on appeal or on appeal to a higher court amend the size of the fine to the disadvantage of the person involved.'[98]

The fine system in the Working Conditions Act [*Arbeidsomstandighedenwet (Arbowet)*] distinguishes between two categories of fine: Category I at €9,000 and Category II at €22,500. If the offence is repeated the maximum is 50% higher (Articles 33 and 34 Arbowet). Policy rules with fine tariffs have been drawn up in accordance with the instructions in Article 34, fifth paragraph of the Arbowet.[99]

According to the fine system in the Minimum Wage and Minimum Holiday Allowance Act [*Wet minimumloon en minimumvakantiebijslag]*, the maximum fine is €6,700 and it is 50% higher if the offence is repeated. The competent administrative authority may determine the administrative fine up to this maximum. Fine tariffs are included in the Policy Rules for the Administrative enforcement of the Minimum Wage and Minimum Holiday Allowance Act [*Beleidsregels bestuurlijke handhaving Wet minimumloon en minimum-vakantietoeslag]*.

Aliens legislation

The Labour Inspectorate has the power to impose an administrative fine on behalf of the Minister under Article 19a of the Foreign Nationals (Employment) Act [*Wet arbeid vreemdelingen (Wav)*]. The maximum fine is €78,000 (Article 19d *Wav*). The fine maximum can be raised by 200% if an offence is repeated. Under Article 19d, sixth paragraph, *Wav*, the Minister has set out Policy Rules for the imposition of fines with regard to the *Wav*.[100]

The Modern Migration Policy Act [*Wet Modern migratiebeleid*][101] came into effect on 1 June 2013. According to this act, the Minister will have the power (Article 55a *Vw* 2000) to impose an administrative fine for certain infringements of the Aliens Act 2000 and the provisions regarding sponsors that are based upon it. The maximum fines are €1,500 for natural persons and €3,000 for juristic persons and if the offence is repeated, the maximum is raised by 50%.

---

98 See also Article 17f General Child Benefit Act [*Algemene kinderbijslagwet*], 44 Surviving Dependants Act [*Algemene nabestaandenwet*], 17h General Old Age Pensions Act [*Algemene ouderdomswet*], 27f Unemployment Insurance Act [*Werkloosheidswet*], 53 Invalidity Insurance (Self-Employed Persons) Act [*Wet arbeidsongeschiktheidsverzekering zelfstandigen*], 23 Invalidity Insurance (Self-Employed Persons) Act, 18f, fourth paragraph, Minimum Wage and Minimum Holiday Allowance Act, 29f Unemployment Insurance Act, 45f Sickness Benefits Act.

99 It concerns the Policy Rules on the Working Conditions Act (and policy rule 33 and schedule 1 to the policy rules there).

100 Government Gazette (Staatscourant) 2010, 2166.

101 Bulletin of Acts and Decrees (Staatsblad) 2010, 290.

Administrative fines for municipal authorities

A large number of fine systems have come into operation. Municipal authorities possess a reasonably large number of powers to impose fines. The Municipalities Act *[Gemeentewet (Gem.wet)]* includes a fine system (Article 154b-154n *Gem. wet*) that allows the Municipal Executive or the Mayor, if his executive functions are concerned, to impose an administrative fine of up to a maximum of €340 on natural persons and €2,250 on juristic persons if this has been set out by the municipal council in a municipal by-law. This fine system should, however, never have come into effect in its present form and, partly for that reason, it is not used at present. The fine system under the Municipalities Act is a bit of an odd man out and differs unnecessarily and extensively from the standard system. It will be sufficient for me to cite a few examples.

1. The Municipal Council has an autonomous power to create criminal offences (exclusively minor offences under Article 154, first paragraph, *Gem.wet)* but is restricted as to the maximum penalty it can set: three months detention or a second-category fine. In addition, the Municipal Council is bound, of course, by the General Section of the Dutch Criminal Code. A similar autonomous power might be expected in the creation of fineable offences but the wings of municipal autonomy are considerably clipped by the fact that the government can determine by order in council which infringements in the general municipal by-laws (APV) are fineable (Article 154b, first paragraph, *Gem.wet*) and, moreover, which tariffs – up to the statutory maximum – will apply. This power to restrict the autonomy of municipalities should be abolished and replaced by an arrangement in which the Council can decide for itself whether the sanction for a infringement is either punishable or fineable, and Councils could be obliged to choose between these two alternatives. The freedom of the Council to create administrative fines should be just as great as that to create punishable offences.
2. This fine system and that of the Traffic Regulations (Administrative Enforcement) Act (*Wahv*) are the only systems that stipulate that an administrative fine can only be imposed on persons over 12 years of ages, as set out in Article 154b, seventh paragraph, *Gem.wet.*[102] In the government's view, there is no requirement for such a stipulation in the general law on fines.[103]
3. Article 154c of the Municipalities Act should be repealed in its entirety for the following reasons. The administrative fine concerned is a minor one and generally simple to establish. The obligation to first draw up a fine report is required in serious fine procedures in which relatively large administrative

---

[102] This does not detract from the fact that an arrangement of this kind would not be amiss in the GALA penalty regime.

[103] Parliamentary Documents II 2003–2004, 29 702, no. 3, p. 125. Age does, in fact, play a role in the setting of fines. See, for example, District Court, Rotterdam 10 March 2011, *LJN* BP7350.

fines are concerned. There is no single fine system, not even in Article 3, first paragraph *Wahv*, in which it is prescribed that the regulator who discovers a infringement and takes the fine decision (even in less serious fine procedures) must also be a special investigating officer. Municipal councils should be free to determine how many regulators are required for their enforcement policy, how their enforcement teams are to be organized and how many of these regulators should be vested with special investigative authority. The legislative authority cannot foresee the number of cases in which this investigative authority will prove necessary.

4. There should be a repeal of the legal protection system defined in Article 154k, under which the subdistrict court is competent and the general law of administrative procedure does not apply. Legal protection in the administrative enforcement of all general municipal by-laws is provided under the general system of administrative procedure: district courts as courts of first instance and the Administrative Jurisdiction Division as appeal court. This system should be adhered to, not only if an astreinte is imposed for the infringement of a provision in the APV but also if an administrative fine is imposed for this infringement.[104]

In the interim period, the municipal administration has acquired a number of powers to impose fines which have been given a more customary structure. Article 85a of the Housing Allocation Act [*Huisvestingswet (Hw)*] allows the Council to impose an administrative fine for certain infringements of this law. The Municipal Executive is the competent body for this task. The second paragraph of Article 85a provides for three maximum amounts: €340, €7,500 and €18,500. The Council must determine the fine tariffs for this in a by-law. The legal protection offered by the general administrative law system applies here.

Article 18 of the Vacant Property Act [*Leegstandwet]* stipulates that the municipal council can determine in a by-law that an administrative fine can be imposed for certain infringements of this act. The maximum fine is €7,500 and the council must define the tariffs by by-law. The legal protection offered by the general administrative law system applies here as well. Article 64, second paragraph of the Security Regions Act [*Wet veiligheidsregio's*] determines that the municipal council can adopt a by-law in which breaches of fire-safety regulations are made liable to an administrative fine. The maximum fine is in line with the fine category in Article 34, fourth paragraph, under 1°, of the Working Conditions Act, viz. €9,000.

104 The system of legal protection under the general administrative law system is even followed for special public-law powers, such as exclusion orders (Articles 172a and 172b Municipalities Act and (with adjustments) administrative detention (Article 154a, eleventh paragraph, Municipalities Act).

Under Article 1.72, first paragraph, of the Childcare Provisions Act and Quality Requirements for Playschools *[Wet Kinderopvang en kwaliteitseisen peuterspeelzalen (Wkkp)]*, the municipal executive can impose administrative fines for the breach of the provisions of this law. There are three different maximum fines: €2,269, €5,000 and €45,000.

The municipal executive derives a power to impose an administrative fine under Article 29 ff. of the Civic Integration Act [*Wet inburgering*]. The maximum fines are €250, €500 or €1,000 (Article 34) and the rates have to be determined in a by-law.

It has already been mentioned during the discussion of tax penalty law that the municipal administration has the power under the State Taxes Act [*Algemene wet inzake rijksbelastingen*] to apply administrative fines in the enforcement of tax regulations imposed by the council.

In the following section, I will examine in greater detail the way in which the special legislator has chosen between making an infringement liable to a fine or making it punishable as an offence (par.3.2), the way in which the maximum fine is set (par. 3.3), the choice of a statutory fine tariff or a less regulated system (par. 3.4) and the choice between a lighter or heavier fine procedure (par. 3.5).

5.3. A PUNISHABLE OFFENCE OR A FINEABLE INFRINGEMENT

As I have written before almost 100 acts provide for the power to impose an administrative fine. As it is impossible to describe them all extensively, I shall confine myself to a few issues.

Injury or safety

In a number of fine systems, fineable offences become punishable offences if the infringement concerned has resulted in serious injury or death. The Traffic Regulations (Administrative Enforcement) Act [*Wet administratiefrechtelijke handhaving verkeersvoorschriften*] has a provision of this nature in Article 2, second paragraph, and Article 11:3, second paragraph of the Working Hours Act [*Arbeidstijdenwet*] has something similar in the case of certain infringements in which a child is involved. Article 33, fourth paragraph in conjunction with Article 32, first paragraph, of the Working Conditions Act [*Arbeidsomstandighedenwet*] turns a finable offence into a punishable offence if the offender knew, or could reasonably have known, that the fineable offence would cause, or could be expected to cause, danger to the lives or serious injury to the health of one or more employees. Under Article 32, second paragraph, this is an economic crime. Article 44a, third paragraph, preamble and under a of the Licensing and Catering Act rules that an infringement cannot be disposed of by an administrative fine if it resulted in immediate danger to the health or safety of a person. A large number of infringements in the Licensing and Catering Act are classed as economic crimes. Article 9, second paragraph, preamble and under b of the Care Institutions (Quality) Act states that deliberate or reckless conduct that results in immediate danger to the health or safety of persons is a punishable offence (breach).[105] Article 49, first paragraph, of the Inland Navigation Act provides that finable offences are punishable as violations if danger to public safety results or could result.

Punishable offence on the third time

The system of making an offence punishable when committed for the third time is laid down in a number of fine systems but there are various significant and important differences between them. Article 101, second paragraph of the Medicines Act [*Geneesmiddelenwet*] states that a finable offence that has not been designated an economic crime is a punishable offence (infringement) if an administrative fine has been imposed for the same offence in the previous 24 months. Another example is that of Article 19c of the Foreign Nationals (Employment) Act under which a finable offence is classed as a punishable offence if an administrative fine has been imposed, and has become irrevocable, for an infringement consisting of the failure to comply with the same statutory obligation on two occasions within a period of 48 months prior to the day on which the infringement was established, and these occasions were less than 24 months apart.[106]

Economic advantage

In Article 44a, third paragraph, preamble and sub b of the Licensing and Catering Act it is specified that a infringement cannot be disposed of with an administrative fine, if the economic advantage derived from the infringement would significantly exceed the statutory fine tariff.

Obligation to cooperate[107]

Traditionally, Article 184 of the Dutch Criminal Code (DCC) included a sanction for failure to comply with an order issued by a regulator. On this

105 Also Article 97 Individual Healthcare Professions Act.

106 Article 11:3, first paragraph, Working Hours Act is very similar. The finable act also becomes an economic offence under the third paragraph of this provision. Article 33, third paragraph, Working Conditions Act is very similar. Here too, a finable act becomes an economic offence in this way. Other examples are Article 9, second paragraph, preamble and under a, Care Institutions (Quality) Act and Article 97 Individual Healthcare Professions Act.

107 The administrative fine which will be discussed later is not the only administrative sanction for violation of Article 5:20, first paragraph, GALA. A power is very regularly given to impose a duty backed by an enforcement action and/or a duty backed by an astreinte and, occasionally, the power to withdraw a favourable decision, either entirely or partly. These will not be discussed in this paper.

ground, failure to cooperate is an offence, for which a term of imprisonment of not more than three months and a fine of the second category (€3,800) can be imposed. Articles 5:20, first paragraph of GALA and 184 of DCC are closely linked. In the explanatory notes to the third tranche of GALA, the government paid relatively great attention to the central role that Article 184 of DCC should play as a sanction for non-cooperation. Against this background, the assumption was that special penal provisions were to be scrapped, including those in the Economic Offences Act.[108] Failure to cooperate would only be disposed of with an administrative fine in exceptional cases.

Current legislation creates the impression that the way in which sanctions are imposed for non-cooperation can be extremely diverse. Article 34, first paragraph, preamble and under a *Wahv* still states that failure to cooperate is an infringement with the maximum sanction of a fine of the second category (€3,800). Infringements of the obligation to cooperate under the Economic Offences Act included there are classified as an economic offence and as a crime (Article 24a in conjunction with 26, Article 1, preamble and sub 5° and Article 2, fifth paragraph *Wed*). The maximum punishment is two years, a community punishment order, or a fine in the fourth category for natural persons (€19,000), or a fine in the fifth category (€76,000) for juristic persons. In a few cases, failure to cooperate with an order from a regulator is designated an economic offence under certain other special laws, such as the Trust Offices (Supervision) Act (as provided in Article 1, preamble and sub 2° Wed). Failure to cooperate under the Financial Supervision Act is an economic offence if the order is issued by an administrative authority (AFM or De Nederlandsche Bank N.V. (DNB)) but not if the same kind of order is given by a regulator appointed by this administrative authority, since only Article 1:74 *Wft* is listed in Wed.

Many fine systems designate non-cooperation as a finable offence and in incidental cases with the express exclusion of Article 184 of DCC.[109] The essential rule is that non-cooperation is both finable and punishable.[110] Not only are the maximum punishments diverse but the maximum fines vary widely as well.

---

108 See PG GALA III, pp. 353–354; Parliamentary Documents (Kamerstukken) II 1994–1995, 23 700 no. 5, pp. 89–90.

109 An important example is Article 69, second paragraph, Competition Act.

110 An overview: Article 77i, preamble and under a, Electricity Act €450,000 or 1%; Article 60ad, first paragraph, preamble and under a, Gas Act €450,000 or 1% turnover; Article 69 Competitive Trading Act: €450,000 or 1% turnover, Article 7.12, first paragraph, Media Act €225,000; Article 176, first paragraph, Pensions Act; Article 49, first paragraph, Postal Act 2009 €450,000 or 1% relevant net turnover; Article 75, Railways Act €450,000 or 1%; Article 15.4, first and fourth paragraph, Telecommunications Act: €450,000; Article 18, second paragraph, in conjunction with 19d Foreign Nationals (Employment) Act: natural persons €11,250 and juristic persons €45,000 (on a criminal offence for the third time); Article 26, second paragraph, Underground Grids (Information Exchange) Act [*Wet informatie-uitwisseling ondergrondse netten*] €100,000; Article 1.72, first paragraph, preamble and under a, and 2.28, first paragraph, Childcare Provisions and Quality Requirements for

5.4. THE MAXIMUM FINE

Under Article 5:46, first paragraph GALA, the special legislator must determine the maximum administrative fine that can be imposed for any particular infringement. The schedule includes a summary of all the maximum fines adopted by the special legislator to date and demonstrates how diverse the maximum fines are despite the fact that many similarities may be found within any specific legal area.[111] In some instances, the maximum fine in a special law seems to have been attuned to the maximum fine in criminal law that applied in the period between the introduction of the euro and 1 February 2006, whereas other legislation in the same field subsequently adopted the maximum fines set out in this 'pioneer' law. In the interim, the maximum fines in criminal law, on which the alignment was originally based, have been increased but, in much of the fine legislation, the maximum fines which applied from 1 January 2002 to 1 February 2006 are still in force: €2,250, €45,000, €450,000, and the following maximum fines which applied from 1 February 2006 to 1 January 2008: €6,700 and €670,000.

The special legislator has occasionally divided maximum fines into categories and, in some cases, a fine category from criminal law has been declared applicable by analogy. Examples include Article 120j of the Health and Welfare of Animals Act [*Gezondheids- en welzijnswet voor dieren*] in which the fifth category is declared applicable by analogy for natural persons, and the sixth category for juristic persons, and Article 48, second paragraph, of the Inland Navigation Act, under which the fourth fine category from criminal law is the maximum administrative fine. We can see a third variation in Article 64, second paragraph, of the Security Regions Act [*Wet veiligheidsregio's*] in which Article 34, fourth paragraph, of the Working

Playschools [*Wet kinderopvang en kwaliteitseisen peuterspeelzalen*]: €45,000; Article 1:80, first paragraph, preamble and under d, Financial Supervision Act (Violation of Article 5:20 GALA is not a finable offence in the Money Service Businesses Act [*Wet inzake de geldtransactiekantoren*]); Article 15, first paragraph, Space Activities Act [*Wet ruimtevaartactiviteiten*]: €450,000 or 10% turnover in the Netherlands; Article 27, first paragraph, Money Laundering and Terrorist Financing (Prevention) Act [*Wet ter voorkoming van witwassen en financiering van terrorisme*] (Wwft); Article 54, first paragraph, Audit Firms (Supervision) Act; Article 21, first paragraph, Trust Offices (Supervision) Act [*Wet toezicht trustkantoren*]; Article 171, first paragraph, Occupational Pension Scheme (Obligatory Membership) Act [*Wet verplichte beroepspensioenregeling*] (notable: violation of Article 5:20 GALA is not defined as a finable act in the Sectoral Pension Fund (Obligatory Membership) Act 2000 [*Wet verplichte deelneming in een bedrijfstakpensioenfonds 2000*] This seems to be an omission, just like the Money Service Businesses Act).

111 A remarkable variation of the fine maximum has recently been included in the Compulsory Education Act [*Leerplichtwet*], which is unique as far as I can see. Article 27, second paragraph, of that Act states that an administrative fine up to a maximum of €1,000 can be imposed for each infringement, and the total amount of the administrative fines may not exceed €100,000 in any school year.

Conditions Act is declared applicable by analogy, and in which the first category is set at €9,000.

Criminal law applies a higher category of fine for juristic persons than for natural persons. Under Article 23, seventh paragraph of DCC, a fine from the next higher category can also be applied. If a punishable offence relates to an economic offence, it can be put into a higher category under Article 6, first paragraph, of Wed if the value of the goods with which or in relation to which the economic offence was committed or which were obtained, either entirely or partially, by the economic offence is higher than one quarter of the fine that can be imposed for that offence.

A similar distinction is made in the fine maximums set in a number of fine systems. In incidental cases, a specific distinction is made between the maximum administrative fine that can be imposed on a juristic person and the maximum fine that can be imposed on the actual person (natural person) managing that juristic person.[112] A similar provision would not be out of place in both criminal and administrative law. Furthermore, incidental fine systems distinguish between types of juristic person and natural persons and a distinction is also made according to the size of the company or the juristic person. Recidivism usually increases the fine within the maximum statutory limit. In a number of cases, this means that the maximum fine is increased, usually by 50%,[113] but sometimes by 100%.[114] Recidivism can also convert a finable offence into a punishable offence.[115]

Under Article 23, ninth paragraph of DCC, the amounts in the fine categories can be adjusted every two years by an order in council. The provision reads as follows:

> 'The amounts set out in paragraph 4 will be adjusted by order in council every two years, to be effective as from 1 January of any year, according to developments in the consumer price index since the previous adjustment of these amounts. In this adjustment, the amount of the first category will be rounded down in multiples of €5, and the amounts in the second to sixth fine categories will be determined on the

---

112 See for example Article 57, first paragraph, and 75a of the Competition Act (Mededingingswet) and Article 60ad, second paragraph of the Gas Act.

113 As in Article 34, sixth paragraph, Working Conditions Act (Arbeidsomstandighedenwet), Article 10:7, second paragraph, Working Hours Act (Arbeidstijdenwet), Article 48, third paragraph, Inland Navigation Act (Binnenvaartwet) and Article 19d, second paragraph, Foreign Nationals (Employment) Act (Wet arbeid vreemdelingen).

114 As in Article 1:81, first paragraph, Wft.

115 Some examples: 33, third paragraph, Working Conditions Act (Arbeidsomstandighedenwet), 11:3 Working Hours Act (Arbeidstijdenwet), 101, second paragraph, Medicines Act (Geneesmiddelenwet), 19c Foreign Nationals (Employment) Act (Wet arbeid vreemdelingen).

basis of the amount of this first category, maintaining the mutual relationship between the amounts in the various fine categories.'

This option was introduced in a law dated 22 December 2005, which amended the Criminal Code and the Road Traffic Act [*Wegenverkeersweg 1994*] on 1 February 2006[116] in connection with the readjustment of several statutory maximum punishments (Bulletin of Acts and Decrees 2006, 11). Since then, the amounts – after adjustment on the basis of the aforementioned statutory amendment – have been altered a further three times: the first time as of 1 January 2008,[117] the second time as of 1 January 2010[118] and most recently as of 1 January 2012.[119]

	Before 1-1-2002[122]	**1-1-2002 to 1-2-2006**	**1-2-2006 to 1-1-2008**	**1-1-2008 to 1-1-2010**	**As of 1-1-2010**	**From 1-1-2012**
First category	NLG 500	€225	€335	€370	€380	€390
Second category	NLG 5,000	€2,250	€3,350	€3,700	€3,800	€3,900
Third category	NLG 10,000	€4,500	€6,700	€7,400	€7,600	€7,800
Fourth category	NLG 25,000	€11,250	€16,750	€18,500	€19,000	€19,500
Fifth category	NLG 100,000	€45,000	€67, 000	€74,000	€76,000	€78,000
Sixth category	NLG 1,000,000	€450,000	€670,000	€740,000	€760,000	€780,000

A similar system of fine categories could and should have been introduced when the fourth tranche of GALA came into effect.[121] It would have been possible at that time to include a general statutory basis for a two yearly adjustment of the maximum fines to coincide with the adjustment of maximum fines for criminal offences.[122] Currently, the maximum fines in administrative law are not adjusted

116 See Bulletin of Acts and Decrees (Staatsblad) 2006, 23.

117 By decree of 13 November 2007, Bulletin of Acts and Decrees (Staatsblad) 2007, 456.

118 By decree of 13 November 2009, Bulletin of Acts and Decrees (Staatsblad) 2009, 484.

119 By decree of 11 November 2011, Bulletin of Acts and Decrees (Staatsblad) 2011, 455.

120 Euro adjustment Act (Bulletin of Acts and Decrees (Staatsblad) 2001, 481) which came into force on 1 January 2002.

121 See O.J.D.M.L. Jansen, "De dynamiek van het publiekrechtelijke sanctierecht", NJV preliminary report, in: J. de Hullu *et al.*, *Herziening van het sanctiestelsel*, Kluwer, Deventer 2002, pp. 167–255, esp. pp. 197 and 230–232.

122 Adjusting the amounts of money is not unusual in administrative law and in GALA. Court fees are adjusted on the basis of Article 8:41, fifth paragraph, GALA and the penalties that are

except for the maximums in fiscal administrative law[123] and the maximum fines for which a fine category from criminal law has been declared to apply by analogy.

A similar situation threatens to develop as that which partly acted as an inducement to introduce fine categories in the Financial Penalties Act [*Wet vermogenssancties*] in 1983 from which the special legislator can choose the maximum.[124] The Explanatory Notes cite the first Interim Report from the Committee for Assets Transactions of 1969:

'If an overall view is taken, there can be no other conclusion but that the current regulation is chaotic, a patchwork, made up of hundreds of pieces, with new patches sewn on top. It is high time it was thrown on the scrapheap because no reasonable purpose is being served by this situation.'[125]

It is high time that the GALA fine regulation was supplemented. The new arrangement should follow Article 23 DCC as closely as possible, and that could well mean that the maximums in criminal law are found to be too low, especially for infringements committed by juristic persons and for offences under economic and financial administrative law, as well as those under tax law. The three highest fine categories in criminal law could be supplemented by a maximum which introduces a relationship with the offender's turnover, and that could possibly be restricted to juristic persons and equivalent entities. In this way, the fourth category fine could be €19,000 or – if this is greater – 1% of the turnover, the fifth category €76,000 or – if this is greater – 5% of the turnover, and the sixth category €760,000 or – if this is greater – 10% of the turnover. On the other hand, a logical step would be to increase the maximum fines that are based on a fine category before indexation to one related to a fine category after indexation. This might, for example, apply to the usual maximums of €45,000 and €450,000 in economic administrative law. There might be a requirement for a seventh category of €7,600,000 or – if that is greater – 10% of the turnover.

An addition to Article 5:46, first paragraph, GALA could be made which provides that the administrative fine is equal to the amount designated in the category for the infringement and that the categories defined in Article 23,

forfeit if an administrative authority fails to give a timely decision are adjusted on the basis of Article 4:17, 8th paragraph, GALA.

123 See Article 67cb Awr, which has been declared applicable for a number of other fiscal penalty regimes.

124 A recommendation from the Commission on Pecuniary Penalties in 1969 formed the basis for the introduction of fine categories. The government deviated from the Commission's recommendations in its legislative proposal to some extent by introducing a sixth category and setting higher values for the first categories.

125 Parliamentary Documents (Kamerstukken) II 1977–1978, 15 012, nos. 1–3, p. 25.

fourth paragraph, DCC apply by analogy. Furthermore – to avoid renumbering – it can be stipulated that the next higher fine category applies if a) the value of the goods in relation to which the infringement has been committed or acquired, either entirely or in part, by the infringement, is higher than one quarter of the fine which can be applied for that infringement, or b) if the offender is a juristic person as referred to in Article 5:1, third paragraph, GALA. The amending legislation will need to identify the correct fine category and this will necessitate changes to the associated maximum fines.

5.5. STATUTORY FINE TARIFF OR NOT

The special legislator can opt, up to the statutory fine maximum, for a system with fine tariffs set in a generally binding provision for each infringement or for a less regulated system in which the competent administrative authority can determine the amount of an appropriate fine up to the statutory maximum. GALA provides for a power of mitigation (Article 5:46, third paragraph, GALA) with regard to the statutory fine tariffs, and for a duty of coordination with regard to the discretionary powers: the amount of the administrative fine must be attuned to a number of circumstances including the seriousness of the offence, the degree of culpability, and the circumstances in which the infringement was committed (Article 5:46, third paragraph, GALA). In addition to this, the circumstances of the offender play a role although this important classification is not mentioned in the statutory provision. As I will now explain in greater detail, the chosen system also determines how the judicial review will take place. There is some tension between the circumstances taken into account by the legislator or determiner of policy rules in the general regulation of tariffs and the circumstances which might induce a court to apply a lower administrative fine.

There is some diversity in the way the fine tariffs are set by generally binding provisions. Some laws have an schedule attached in which the fine tariffs are set and which can be adjusted by order in council.[126] Other legislation includes the basis for arranging the fine tariffs by order in council[127] or by another generally binding provision, for instance by ministerial order[128] or by municipal by-law. In

---

126 See, for example, Article 11c of the Tobacco Act (Tabakswet).

127 See, for example, Administrative Fines (Licensing and Catering Act) Decree (Besluit bestuurlijke boete Drank- en Horecawet), Administrative Fines (Public Nuisance) Decree (Besluit bestuurlijke boete overlast in de openbare ruimte), Administrative Fines (Financial Sector) Decree (Besluit bestuurlijke boetes financiële sector), Administrative Fines (Commodities Act) Decree (Warenwetbesluit bestuurlijke boeten), Fining Decision Social Security Acts (Boetebesluit socialezekerheidswetten), Exemption and Administrative Fines (Sectoral Pension Fund Act 2000 Decree (Vrijstellings- en boetebesluit Wet Bpf 2000).

128 For instance, the GWWD Administrative Fines Arrangement under the Health and Welfare of Animals Act (Gezondsheids- en welzijnswet voor dieren, GWWD).

a number of systems, the regulator at a lower level can determine whether or not a discretionary fining power is applicable from the fact that fine tariffs can be determined by order in council. If no order in council is issued, then there is a discretionary fining power.

If there is a discretionary fining power, the administrative authority can arrange this coordination in policy rules, and this is a frequent occurrence.[129] The way in which the amount of the administrative fine is determined in policy rules varies. There are also differences in the way distinction is made in the circumstances allowing for lower fines and the way in which these are estimated. Very often, rates are included but quite often mention is only made of the circumstances that should be taken into account and the method of calculation to be applied. Sometimes, the legislator imposes the obligation on the administrative authority to publicize the policy rules.[130] The Minister determines these policy rules for a small number of independent administrative authorities.[131]

129 See, for example, the Policy Rules 2008 on the imposition of administrative fines for not timely registering for healthcare insurance, Policy Rules on administrative fines in the Medicines Act, Policy Rules on administrative fines in the Care Institutions (Quality) Act, Policy Rules on administrative fines in the Termination of Pregnancy Act, Policy Rules on Administrative Fines in the Psychiatric Hospitals (Compulsory Admissions) Act, Policy Rules on Administrative Fines in the Blood Supply Act, Policy Rules on Administrative Fines in the Clients' Right of Complaint (Care Sector) Act, Policy Rules on Administrative Fines in the Individual Healthcare Professions Act, Policy Rules on Administrative Fines in the Medical Appliances Act, Policy Rules on Administrative Fines in the Body Material (Safety and Quality) Act, Policy Rules on Administrative Fines for the Board of the Dutch Emissions Authority with regard to determining the size of the astreinte or an administrative fine in enforcing the rules for trading in emission rights. Policy Rules on Administrative Fines for R&D remittance reduction, Policy Rules on Administrative Enforcement in the Minimum Wage and Minimum Holiday Allowance Act 2010, the Administrative Fines (Inland Revenue) Decree, Administrative Fines (Inland Revenue/Customs) Decree, Policy Rule on Fine Imposition Working Hours Act and Working Hours Decree, Policy Rule on Fine Imposition in the Working Hours (Transport) Act and the Working Hours (Transport) Decree, Policy Rule on Sanctions in frequency use radio-broadcasting, Policy Rules in working conditions legislation, Policy Rules on Fine Imposition in the Foreign Nationals (Employment) Act 2010, Circular on Private Security Organizations and Detective Agencies, Administrative Fines (Inland Revenue and Allowances) Decree, Policy Rule on Employee Fine 2010.

130 As, for instance, in Article 19d, third paragraph, Foreign Nationals (Employment) Act.

131 See, for example, the Policy Rules of the Minister of Economic Affairs for the imposition of administrative fines by the ACM (Beleidsregels van de Minister van Economische Zaken voor het opleggen van bestuurlijke boetes door de ACM), Government Gazette (Staatscourant) 2013, 11214) under Article 21 Nondepartmental Public Bodies Framework Act [*Kaderwet zelfstandige bestuursorganen*]. A similar power has been included in Article 74 of the Personal Data Protection Act [*Wet bescherming persoonsgegevens*] but has not been used to my knowledge.

5.6. HEAVY OR LIGHT PROCEDURE

In the GALA fine procedure, an important distinction is made between the heavier-fine and the lighter-fine procedure (Article 5:53 GALA). As soon as this provision is applicable, the heavy-fine procedure applies. The essence of this procedure is that there is an obligation to issue a report regarding the fine before the decision on the fine is taken so that the offender is given the opportunity to produce a defence against the proposed imposition of a fine in good time (Article 5:53, second paragraph in conjunction with 5:48 GALA). The fine report is then the basis for the rights of the defence in the proceedings during the preparation of the fining decision. A number of safeguards have been built into the fining report and the heavy-fine procedure, such as the obligation to hear the defendant (Article 5:53, third paragraph in conjunction with Division 4.1.2. GALA in conjunction with 5:50 GALA), translation/interpretation and the assistance of an interpreter (Articles 5:49, second paragraph, and 5:50, first paragraph, preamble and under b GALA), a time limit of 13 weeks (Article 5:51, first paragraph, GALA) and the requirement for a separation of responsibilities (*functiescheiding*) (Article 10:3, fourth paragraph, GALA). A longer period of limitation applies for finable conduct that must be dealt with under the heavy fine procedure.

If the special legislator does not provide otherwise, the heavy fine procedure applies to all administrative fines of €340 or more. In a number of cases, the legislator has ordered that the heavy fine procedure also applies to lower administrative fines.[132] In a very limited number of other cases, the legislator has also guaranteed that the light procedure applies even to certain higher administrative fines.[133] Article 9b, third paragraph of the Healthcare Insurance Act provides that only a part of the safeguards of the heavy fine procedure apply: the obligation to draw up a report and the obligation to hear the defendant are not applicable but other safeguards such as the separation of responsibilities and the extension of the period of limitation do apply.

It seems as though the heavy procedure is almost always applicable and that makes one wonder whether a distinction should not be made between light,

---

132 See, for example, Article 34, third paragraph, Working Conditions Act (Arbeidsomstandighedenwet), Article 10:7, third paragraph, Working Hours Act (Arbeidstijdenwet), Article 154d Municipalities Act (Gemeentewet), Article 9d, third paragraph, Foreign Nationals (Employment) Act (Wet arbeid vreemdelingen), Article 36 Civic Integration Act (Wet inburgering), Article 18.16g, first paragraph, Environmental Management Act (Wet milieubeheer), Article 18f, third paragraph, Minimum Wage and Minimum Holiday Allowance Act (Wet minimumloon en minimumvakantietoeslag).

133 See, for example, Article 40, fourth paragraph, General Income-Dependent Schemes Act (Algemene wet inkomensafhankelijke regelingen), Article 67pa of the State Taxes Act (Algemene wet inzake rijksbelastingen).

medium and heavy procedures in the heavy procedure classification. All these procedures require a report, but in some cases it may be comparable to the simple record of a minor criminal case and in others to the voluminous master record that has been drawn up in a major criminal case.

In practice, the legislator has dramatically restricted the attraction of the fine system in a number of ways in the provisions of the Municipalities Act and prescribing the heavy fine procedure for low-value administrative fines is a good example of this. This could be classed as an example of the 'lighter' heavy fine procedure. On the other hand, the high administrative fines imposed under the Competitive Trading Act for violation of the cartel ban or for abuse of an economically dominant position, and the comparable administrative fines in other legislation such as financial legislation, the Telecommunications Act and the Consumer Protection (Enforcement) Act can be categorised as 'seriously' heavy. The administrative fines imposed on pirate broadcasters under the Telecommunications Act, the violations of the Foreign Nationals (Employment) Act and violation of the advertising ban in the Tobacco Act by smaller Dutch manufacturers could be included in the 'medium' category.

Generally speaking, offering safeguards in the imposition of fines seems to be a noble ambition but it does have a reverse side. A procedure which includes first a hearing of the fine report, an objection procedure, then an appeals procedure before the district court followed by appeal to a higher court entails serious expense for offenders that could possibly deny them the legal protection to which they are entitled.

The Foreign Nationals (Employment) Act (Wet arbeid vreemdelingen) demonstrates this. It is almost impossible for the average citizen to produce an effective defence in this fine law because such defence requirements are set that the average citizen is no match for the specialist legal adviser. The defendant's attempt to be proved right through a succession of courts means that the other party is more or less obliged to join battle before all these courts, at considerable cost. The costs that can be awarded to an offender who wins the case are not in proportion to the legal costs actually incurred. It must also be borne in mind that, under the Foreign Nationals (Employment) Act, all the employers in an employment chain linked to a foreign national who do not have a work permit for their employee are eligible for an administrative fine and are compelled in principle to incur similar legal costs. Of course, recovery actions among the parties are the order of the day and the employer at the end of the chain of liability is confronted with considerably higher costs.

5.7. THE CURRENT RELATION TO CRIMINAL LAW

It is generally accepted that the guarantees of Article 6 of the European Convention on Human Rights, as well as the similar guarantees of the International Covenant on Civil and Political Rights (ICCPR), that apply to criminal charges and procedures as defined by the ECHR, are applicable to administrative fines. According to standing case law, the applicability of the Article 6 guarantees does not mean that national criminal law or national criminal procedural law guarantees apply automatically. According to Article 1:6, GALA does not apply to criminal investigation and prosecution: in short, to decisions taken in the criminal procedure.

Nevertheless, the legislator has chosen to link the GALA regulation of administrative fines as closely to that of general criminal law as possible. As the following explanation of the legislator also shows, the enactment of the fourth part of GALA (*Vierde tranche Awb*), the most important parts of which are both the general regulation of administrative fines and the general regulation of money debts arising from administrative law (*bestuursrechtelijke geldschulden*) of the citizen on the government and vice versa which is not discussed in this contribution, marks an important stage in the development of general administrative law in the Netherlands. Therefore, it was important to explain the position of GALA in relation to the two other important codifications of criminal law and of civil law.

'The two most sizable parts of this legislative proposal, i.e. the regulation with regard to administrative debts and that to administrative fines, relate to subjects which were primarily arranged for in areas of law other than administrative law. Until fairly recently, the logical step for lawyers was to turn to the Civil Code in matters relating to the payment and further settlement of debts and the Criminal Code in matters relating to the punishment of norm violation. We now propose that rules be included in the General Administrative Law Act for both subjects, which would signify an important step in the development of general administrative law.

It is a regular occurrence that while administrative law makes no provisions for a certain phenomenon or a certain legal concept, the same or a very similar concept is provided for in private or criminal law. The reason for this is that general administrative law is a much younger branch of law and has therefore not evolved as far as the other two areas. Although special substantive administrative law has many rules, general administrative law regulates relatively few matters. This means that in relationships under administrative law, reference must often be made to the rules in other areas of law, especially in private law and, to a lesser extent, in criminal law. This is often not a problem but sometimes private law or criminal law rules are less suitable because they were not primarily drawn up for relationships under administrative law and they can sometimes fail to take sufficient account of the particular characteristics of that law, such as the imbalance of power between the citizen and the government. Adjusting the rules in question could be a solution. For instance, the Economic Offences Act can be seen as a supplement to criminal law and criminal procedural law in the light of the enforcement of administrative law regulatory legislation. But sometimes administrative law requires its own rules. In the past, they were often arranged for in special administrative law legislation. Taxation law, for instance, has long had its own rules, although they deviate to some extent from private law or criminal law with regard to the two topics arranged for in this legislative proposal – settlement of debts and punishment of violations. If the need for own rules under administrative law becomes apparent in more policy areas, nowadays it will more often be tempting to incorporate these rules into the General Administrative Law Act. From time to time, in the future, the question will be raised as to whether rules should be included in the General Administrative Law Act on an aspect for which rules have already been drawn up in private or criminal law. The aspect of compensation could be an issue worthy of consideration in the near future. Often the reason for allowing certain aspects to be arranged in GALA as well will lie in the fact that it is difficult to find a clear answer to the question of the extent to which the rules of other fields of law can be applied in administrative law. The very reason that administrative law, because of its specific character, may require different rules than those under criminal or private law, demands of the legislator that the utmost possible clarity be provided. This applies whether other areas of law can be followed or not. In the latter case, greater clarity could be achieved by explicitly stating that the relevant provisions of the Civil or Criminal Code apply by analogy to administrative-law relationships. The present legislative proposal offers a number of examples.

The starting point must be that unnecessary differences between the fields of law must be avoided. In those cases where private-law or criminal-law regulations are perfectly sufficient, then these should be followed. This is not only necessary but it is also possible: many of the legal principles that seem, at first glance, to be typically administrative, criminal or private prove on closer inspection to be an elaboration of the legal principles common to the various fields of law. The currently proposed regulation concerning the administrative fine is based on the principles of 'no punishment without guilt', the principle of no double jeopardy and no punishment without law. Punishment by an administrative authority instead of by a court requires a different interpretation at the level of the precise rules but the underlying principles are the same. In these cases, it is always a matter of finding a balance between giving administrative law its own different rules, where necessary, but following existing private or criminal law rules wherever possible. It is not a question of re-inventing the wheel but sometimes it has to be made to fit the measure of administrative-law.'[134]

The general principle that any unnecessary differences between the different areas of law have to be avoided as far as possible can be found again in the explicit rules in the general regulation of administrative fines and already plays an important role in case law about administrative fines. Hereinafter I will discuss the problem of legal unity.

5.8. THE PROBLEM OF LEGAL UNITY

5.8.1. Introduction: unity of what?

Together with criminal and criminal procedural law, fine law comprises part of sanctions law under public law. Both the general part of substantive criminal law and the general part of administrative law apply to the rules set out in generally binding provisions, non-compliance with which is punishable. The administrative courts uphold these provisions if, for instance, permits, licences or exemptions have been granted or refused, or sanction decisions taken on that basis. If non-compliance with these provisions results in a prosecution, the criminal court will apply the same provisions, and the same applies to the prosecution of public officials or for criminal offences, for example under Article 180 DCC (resistance) and Article 184 (intentional failure to cooperate). Civil courts in their turn apply the same provisions for an unlawful government act and the same counts for the public service tribunal and for other authorities such as the National Ombudsman.[135]

According to Article 1:6 GALA, the administrative law in GALA does not apply to criminal procedural law, but that does not mean that administrative law has no effect in that criminal procedural law.[136] The norms issuing from Article 6

---

134 Parliamentary Documents II 2003–2004, 29 702, no. 3, pp. 6–7.

135 During the discussion of sanction law for municipal executives, I have already criticized the deviating system of legal protection offered in the sanction law that is included in the Municipalities Act.

136 See inter alia: A. Hartmann and L.J.J. Rogier, "Verschillen en overeenkomsten tussen strafrecht en bestuursrecht", DD (23) 1993, pp. 1042–1058; O.J.D.M.L. Jansen, "Bestuursrecht en strafprocesrecht: doorwerken of afgrenzen?", in: T. Hoogenboom and L.J.A. Damen (eds.), *In de sfeer van administratief recht* (Essays offered to Professor Konijnenbelt), Lemma, Utrecht 1994, pp. 257–283; H.J.B. Sackers, "Strafrecht en bestuursrecht, twee geloven op één kussen?", in: H.Ph.J.A.M. Hennekens *et al.*, *Bestuursrecht aan de horizon*, W.E.J. Tjeenk Willink, Zwolle 1994, pp. 101–121 and his "De Algemene wet bestuursrecht in straf(proces) rechtelijk perspectief", *DD* 1994, pp. 802–813; O.J.D.M.L. Jansen, "De eindige toekomst van artikel 1:6 Awb", *NTB* 1999, pp. 150–156 and G. Knigge, "De verkalking voorbij: over de verhouding van het strafrecht tot het bestuursrecht", *RM Themis* 2000, pp. 83–96.

ECHR apply to all punitive public law but, according to established case law, the applicability of Article 6 ECHR does not mean that the norms of criminal and criminal procedure law are also automatically applicable.[137] For that matter, administrative courts applied norms for criminal and criminal procedure law in punitive administrative law *before* the fourth tranche of GALA came into effect, and when the draft bill and legislative proposal of the fourth tranche of GALA began to take shape, the court did so – where necessary – in implicit or specific anticipation of the penalty regime contained therein.

The legislator wishes to avoid any unnecessary discrepancies between the various fields of law. For our discussion of this subject, it implies that the starting point in the sanctions law is close alignment with criminal and criminal procedure law. In a number of cases, the legislator has given explicit expression to this aspect through the inclusion of concepts adopted from criminal law and through specific references to provisions in criminal law.[138] Where this has not been expressed by the legislator in so many words, it must be assumed that criminal law is followed as closely as possible in actual practice (by legal assistance providers, administrative bodies and the judiciary).[139] This fits in very closely with the administrative court's approach before the GALA penalty regime came into effect.

A number of topics will now consider the streamlining of criminal and criminal procedure law, on the one hand, and punitive administrative law, on the other, in the course of which there will be an examination of the unity within punitive public law.

5.8.2. Perpetration of an offence

In Dutch public-law sanctions law (at least in administrative and criminal sanctions law) the same concept of perpetrator (pleger) applies, where it concerns the perpetrator, co-perpetrator (medepleger), the author in an organizational context, with almost the same liability for juristic persons. The essence can be found in Article 5:1 GALA This provision reads as follows:

> In this Act, 'violation' means an act violating a rule laid down by or pursuant to law.

137 Supreme Court 7 September 1988, *BNB* 1988, 298.

138 See, for example, Article 5:1, second paragraph, (perpetrating and co-perpetrating), Article 5:1, third paragraph, (Article 51, second and third paragraph, DCC applicable by analogy), 5:5 (justification defences), 5:10a (examination (verhoor), 5:41 (absence of all guilt), 5:42 (in line with Article 69 DCC), 5:43 (in line with Article 68 DCC), 5:45 (in line with 70 DCC), 5:46, fourth paragraph (Article 1, second paragraph, DCC declared applicable by analogy).

139 There is one – probably small – exception to this exception: as is shown by the parliamentary history, the immunity of juristic persons who have been appointed in accordance with public law is almost entirely excluded in punitive administrative law, unlike the situation under criminal law.

2. 'Violator' means the person committing a violation or participating in its commission.
3. Violations can be committed by natural persons and by juristic persons. 51, second and third paragraphs, off the Criminal Code apply *mutatis mutandis.*

The government explained its choices about the way this provision has been attuned to criminal law as follows:

> 'Complicity (medeplichtigheid) in offences is therefore not punishable. In the light of this, there is no reason to introduce the concept of complicity in administrative sanctions law. Neither is there a real requirement for an administrative provision regarding soliciting the commission or incitement. (...). Soliciting the commission (...) is also a rare phenomenon in criminal law and very often the problems it is intended to address are dealt with under the doctrine of author in an organizational context. Incitement (uitlokking) – soliciting someone to commit a crime by means of gifts, promises, threats, etc – occurs equally rarely in less serious crimes and requires extensive investigation of the facts, which is something that administrative proceedings are less suited to.
> But there may be a requirement for the concept of co-perpetration. Co-perpetration is when two or more persons commit a crime together. For a co-perpetrator to be liable for punishment, it is not required that each perpetrator committed each separate component of the crime individually, provided that there is deliberate cooperation and joint execution. As in criminal law, in administrative law persons who are not the addressee of the violated norm because the necessary quality is lacking (for example, that of permit holder) can be designated as co-perpetrator and therefore as offender when they have committed an act which forms part of the offence description, provided that the addressee also takes part in the violation. This could mean that under certain circumstances an employee who violates a permit provision or a tax consultant who violates a norm addressed to the taxable person could, for example, be regarded as co-perpetrator and therefore as offender despite the fact that the violated norm was not actually addressed to them.'[140]

It should be emphasized here that this provision does not only provide for the liability in punitive sanctions but also in remedial sanctions (astreinte and enforcement action). The accessory is not an offender under administrative law, but the concept will certainly become an interesting factor in case law because of the defence argument that the transgressor may be linked to the violation, but only as an accessory.[141]

---

140 Parliamentary Papers II 2003–2004, 29 702, no. 3, pp. 79–80. The government refers inter alia to J.T.K. Bos, "De bestuurlijke boete, raakvlakken van bestuurs- en strafrecht, VAR-preadvies", in: J.T.K. Bos *et al., Handhaving van bestuursrecht*, Samsom H.D. Tjeenk Willink, Alphen aan den Rijn 1995, pp. 121–167, esp. p. 150 and A.B. Blomberg, *Integrale handhaving van milieurecht*, Boom Juridische uitgevers, The Hague 2000, pp. 50–51 and 417.

141 An example of this is: Chairman of the Trades and Industry Tribunal 8 April 2003, *AB* 2003, 247. See also my note at District Court Rotterdam, 15 July 2002, *AB* 2003, 343.

Co-perpetration (medeplegen)
According to some writers, the perpetration of a offence by a co-perpetrator (medepleger) signifies an extension of administrative liability. Only one judgment in administrative case law has been found in which this tenet has been explicitly applied. In its judgment of 22 December 2009, the Trade and Industry Appeals Tribunal (*CBb*) pronounced that an administrative fine can be imposed on two juristic persons, and on the actual manager of those two juristic persons, for a infringement of the Fertilizers Act involving 530 loads of manure. The two companies were registered at the same location. The District Court upheld the administrative fines (€450,000 for each juristic person, and two times €45,000 for the actual manager): the Tribunal reversed the contested judgment and considered as follows:

> 'The facts as demonstrated by the case documents and the arguments during the hearing have shown to the Tribunal that appellant 1 and appellant 2 were very closely connected as regards their business operations. The Tribunal pointed out, in this regard, that the appellant is the actual manager for both companies, that both companies are sited at the same location and that it concerns the same 530 loads of manure which were delivered to appellant 1's site and transported from there by appellant 2. For each load there is, therefore, in fact only one instance of not being or of not being able to be responsible for the removal of the amount of animal manure in question and therefore of just one infringement of Article 50, first paragraph under a of the Fertilizers Act (*Msw*). The conclusion is therefore that appellants 1 and 2 committed the infringement jointly as co-perpetrators. In such circumstances it would not be correct for the maximum fine to be imposed on both appellant 1 and appellant 2 with regard to the established infringement of 530 loads of manure and – by extension – on the appellant as the actual manager of both appellant 1 and appellant 2. Appellants 1 and 2 can, however, each be given a separate administrative fine with regard to this infringement since they can both be designated co-perpetrator of a infringement under Article 50, first paragraph, under b in conjunction with Article 51, first paragraph, *Msw*. Since no difference can be discerned in the contribution to the infringement by appellant 1 and appellant 2, on the basis of established facts and circumstances, the fine for both should be the same.'[142]

The CBb itself ruled in the case and imposed a fine of €225,000 on each juristic person and a one-off fine of €45,000 on the actual manager.

Perpetration of an offence by juristic persons (rechtspersonen)
Throughout sanctions law, as it pertains to public law, it is not only the juristic person (or equivalent entity) that can be held liable but also the actual manager or person giving the instruction.[143] The same way of attributing conduct to a juristic person must now be applied throughout the sanctions law pertaining to public law.

142 Trades and Industry Tribunal (CBb) 22 December 2009, *AB* 2010, 216.
143 It can be deduced from CBb 26 June 2008, *AB* 2009, 404 that a statutory basis is required to extend the liability of juristic persons to the actual manager or the commissioning party.

There is, in fact, very little case law from courts of appeal on such attributing under the GALA fine penalty regime. The only clear example is the judgement of the Trade and Industry Appeals Tribunal of 22 March 2011. Citing a casebook judgment of the Supreme Court dated 21 October 2003,[144] a pig dealer argued on appeal that the established infringements of the prescriptions for the transport of pigs had been wrongfully attributed to the juristic person. The infringements did not take place within the setting of the juristic person because the transport of sick or injured pigs is not allowed in the company and the company would do everything in its power to avoid any infringement. The Tribunal considered as follows:

> 'The appellant is of the opinion that it cannot be blamed as juristic person for the infringements since these are not part of its normal business activities. The [pig] dealer invoked the judgment of the Supreme Court of 21 October 2003 referred to earlier. In that judgment, the Supreme Court stated that the circumstance in which an act is part of the juristic person's normal business operations is an important circumstance in determining whether an act took place in the setting of the juristic person. If an act has taken place in that setting, that act can, in principle, be attributed to the juristic person and the juristic person can be designated as the perpetrator of the criminal offence.
> The Tribunal considered that the astreinte in question had been imposed because of the transport of pigs that were sick or injured. It has been established that the appellant's normal business operations involved the transport of pigs. Therefore it cannot be claimed that the infringements cannot be attributed to the appellant for the reasons given by it.'

Liability of juristic persons established under public law

Juristic persons established under public law are also offenders and their actual managers and/or persons giving instructions are liable. If it had been assumed in criminal law that, in certain cases, these juristic persons would be exempt from criminal prosecution, this line would not automatically follow for administrative law. This tenet is the only instance in which the legislator has addressed the possible divergence of criminal and administrative law. Initially, the Administrative Jurisdiction Division gave no opinion as to whether these juristic persons would be exempt under punitive administrative law,[145] but when Article 5:1, third paragraph, GALA had taken definite shape in parliamentary history, in a number of judgments handed down on 12 May 2010 on the imposition of fines on the State for infringements by various ministries, it renounced the immunity from sanctions for juristic persons established under public law.[146] The Division considered as follows:

Article 5:1, third paragraph GALA provides for this.

144 *AB* 2004, 310 note O.J.D.M.L. Jansen; *NJ* 2006, 328 note P.A.M. Mevis.

145 See Administrative Jurisdiction Division Supreme Court (ABRvS) 22 November 2006, AB 2007, 25 and ABRvS 23 April 2008, AB 2010, 180.

146 ABRvS 12 May 2010, AB 2010, 185, *LJN*MM4166 and *LJN*MM4167.

'The immunity that the State enjoys under criminal law on the basis of the above judgment from the Supreme Court dated 25 January 1994 places it in an exceptional position in criminal law. Neither the Wav nor the legislative history of this law offers reference points in accepting that the State may occupy a position of such a nature in the imposition of administrative fines under this law. According to the Explanatory Memorandum (*Parliamentary Papers II* 1993/1994, 23 754, no. 3. p. 14), the legislator intended, in Articles 1 and 2, to extend the scope of the *Wav* with regard to the – hitherto applicable – Foreign Workers (Employment) Act in the sense that appointment to a public service post also falls within the scope of the *Wav*. It cannot be inferred from the Explanatory Memorandum to the amendment to *Wav* in connection with the introduction of administrative enforcement (Aliens Employment (Administrative Penalty) Act, Parliamentary Papers II, 2003/2004, 29 253, no.3, p. 1) that the legislator subsequently wished to restrict the above scope once more by excluding the government from a fine imposition for any infringement of the *Wav*. The view that fines could be imposed on the State under the *Wav* is supported by the Division in the ruling of the Supreme Court on 3 March 1998 (VR 1998/130). In this ruling it is considered that, since there is no reason to approach public-law government authorities, including the State, differently from natural persons or private-law juristic persons with regard to sanctioning, it must be concluded that public-law juristic persons fall within the scope of that law in view of the administrative character of the sanctions for traffic offences provided for in the Traffic Regulations (Administrative Enforcement) Act.
The State's reference to the above ruling of the Division of 23 April 2008 points to no other conclusion. In that ruling, the Division has clearly left the general question whether criminal immunity also applies to the imposition of an administrative fine unanswered.'

5.8.3. *Concurrence and continuous act*

The criminal doctrines of two or more offences arising from the same act (*eendaadse samenloop*) and concurrence of offences (*meerdaadse samenloop*), and the continuous act (*voortgezette handeling*) are also important for punitive administrative law. They can all be regarded as elaborations of the principle of proportionality. In the draft for the fourth tranche of GALA, two or more offences arising from the same act were provided for but this topic had disappeared in the legislative proposal. The government included no text on the doctrine of a continuous act.[147] The government explained its arrangement of concurrence of offences (in Article 5:8 GALA)[148] as follows:

[147] Bos indicated in 1995 that not only should the doctrine of continued application not be applied in sanction law but that a statutory provision for this in sanction law would not be desirable. See J.T.K. Bos, "De bestuurlijke boete, raakvlakken van bestuurs- en strafrecht, VAR-preadvies", in: J.T.K Bos *et al.*, *Handhaving van het bestuursrecht*, Samsom H.D. Tjeenk Willink, Alphen aan den Rijn 1995, pp. 119–167, esp. pp. 157–159.

[148] This provision reads as follows: 'If one or more rules have been violated, a separate administrative sanction may be imposed for the violation of each separate rule.'

'Concurrence of offences is by far the most usual form of concurrence. Article 5.0.8 specifies that a separate administrative sanction may be imposed individually for each infringement. If an administrative fine can be imposed for both infringements, these fines can therefore accumulate. This is in line with the regulation in criminal law, where fines can also accumulate under Article 57, second paragraph, DCC. (...) Even so, this does not affect the fact that, in the case of the concurrence of offences, the total amount of the administrative sanctions imposed must adhere to the principle of proportionality. An administrative authority that imposes two or more administrative fines for infringements that are separate but connected will have to ask itself whether the total amount of the fines is still in accordance with the gravity of the infringement. An administrative authority that imposes a fine for an infringement that is related to one for which another administrative authority has already imposed a fine, or a penal sanction has been applied or a settlement penalty has taken place must consider the penalties that have been imposed previously by different authorities. Article 5:46 allows for this. Application of this article can therefore result in an administrative fine that is reasonable for the infringement in question but that may be regarded in a specific instance as unreasonable in respect of the punitive sanctions imposed by other administrative authorities or criminal-law authorities for related infringements.
The draft bill created an exception in the main rule of Article 5:8 for what is generally termed 'two or more offences arising from the same act' (*eendaadse samenloop*) in criminal law. This is the case when one act transgresses two or more provisions which, in their tenor, are so closely connected that in essence only one infringement ensues (cf. Art. 55, first paragraph, DCC). The reactions to this draft bill showed that there were certain questions as to the way in which this exception had been formulated and expounded on in the draft bill. From the standpoint of legislative simplicity, it would have been better to include no separate regulation on this point in administrative law now that two or more offences arising from the same act occur so rarely in practice – even in criminal-law practice. The aim envisaged by the drafters of the draft bill – that of preventing unreasonable cumulation of sanctions – could be achieved by applying the principle of proportionality. In the rare occurrences of two or more offences arising from the same act, it will always have to be said that the principle of proportionality is incompatible in concrete terms with the cumulation of sanctions that are allowed in theory under Article 5:8. Article 5:46, second and third paragraphs, gives the administrative authority the power and the obligation to set just one sanction when imposing administrative fines. It stands to reason that administrative courts will follow the jurisprudence of the Supreme Court with regard to Article 55, first paragraph, DCC in answering the question whether it is a matter of two or more offences arising from the same act. In that case, as already discussed, two or more offences arising from the same act will only occur very rarely.'[149]

Shortly after the legislative proposal for the fourth tranche of GALA was presented in the States General, the Tax Division of the Supreme Court issued a

[149] Parliamentary Papers II 2003–2004, 29 702, no. 3, p. 91.

ruling in which a rule consistent with the two or more offences arising from the same act in criminal law could be inferred from the principle of proportionality. The Supreme Court considered as follows:

> 'Article 67a *Awr* [State Taxes Act] relates to a discretionary power of the tax inspector. The inspector must exercise this power in accordance with written and unwritten legal principles, of which the principle of proportionality defined in Article 3:4, second paragraph, GALA is of specific relevance here. This principle implies that the penalty may not be disproportionate in relation to the seriousness of the conduct which was the reason for its imposition. In a case such as this, in which a tax payer who must supply information for more than one tax levy on *one* tax return as a result of which more than one omission is caused by the failure to submit or late submission of this form, this principle implies that the sanctions appropriate for these omissions may not be imposed cumulatively.
> As a rule, in such a case, the imposition of penalties to a total amount of the penalty that could be imposed under par. 21 of BBBB 1998 [Administrative Fines (Tax and Customs Administration) Decree 1988] for *one* omission – if the omissions do not occupy the same position in the series of omission: the heaviest omission to be fined – would lead to a result which justifies the circumstance that the omissions are a consequence of the failure to submit or the late submission of one and the same tax return. Special circumstances could be the reason for imposing a smaller or heavier fine in which Art. 4:84 GALA as well as paragraphs 44 and 45 of BBBB 1998 are important.'[150]

This ruling was adopted by the Administrative Jurisdiction Division in its ruling of 28 November 2007.[151] In this, the Division dismissed a ground for appeal based on the ruling that the Zutphen District Court had wrongly considered that there was no reason for mitigation of the imposed administrative fine because there was no question of two or more offences arising from the same act through the failure to apply for work permits for the work to be carried out by the two foreign nationals and also the failure to check the identity of the foreign nationals and include a copy of their identity documents in the records. It has become established case law of the Administrative Jurisdiction Division that infringements of Articles 2, 15, first and second paragraphs of the Foreign Nationals (Employment) Act (working without a work permit, providing identification document by one employer to the actual employer, and the obligation on the employer to check the documents and to include them in his own records, respectively) do not constitute two or more offences arising from the same act but should be regarded as two separate offences.[152]

---

150 HR 13 August 2004, *BNB* 2005/42 note Feteris; *AB* 2006, 25 note O.J.D.M.L. Jansen.

151 ABRvS 28 November 2007, *LJN* BB8945.

152 ABRvS 25 March 2009, *AB* 2009, 165 note O.J.D.M.L. Jansen, ABRvS 14 October 2009, *LJN* BK0138 (reference to ABRvS 28 November 2007), ABRvS 16 June 2010, *LJN* BM7746

Continuous act[153]

The argument that it concerns a continuous act constitutes an appeal to the principle of proportionality in the absence of such a provision as that of Article 56, first paragraph, DCC. In order for a deed to be classed as a continuous act, there must first be separate activities and not just one continuing activity. Moreover, there must be a certain connection between these activities and the acts: they must be the expression of *one* prohibited act of the will.[154] This implies that the acts have to be of a same kind and often that there has to be a short period of time between the acts. A number of rulings have since been pronounced in which this doctrine has been applied.

The concept of the continuous act was employed more often in the past in older jurisprudence on penalty law, in particular by the Central Appeals Tribunal (CRvB).[155]

In its ruling of 17 February 2010,[156] the Administrative Jurisdiction Division ruled that not having work permits for the work carried out by the twelve foreign nationals, and failing to check the identity of these foreign nationals and to include a copy of their identity document in the employer's administrative records are not to be regarded as similar offences and that there is therefore not a continuous act.

The Trade and Industry Appeals Tribunal (CBb) has also pronounced a number of rulings in which the doctrine played a part.[157] The doctrine was unsuccessfully appealed to in a violation of the advertising ban under the Tobacco Act. The CBb considered in its ruling of 4 May 2009:

> 'Regarding the position of C that there is a continuous act, so that the Minister – if there was a question of violation of Article 5, first paragraph, of the Tobacco Act on various occasions – would only be justified in imposing a fine one single time, the Tribunal is of the opinion that the fineable acts do not derive from the single, underlying decision referred to by C, that of introducing a new design for the company logo (and of the brand of cigarette), but from the decision, which was taken

(reference to parliamentary history 5:8 GALA). See also ABRvS 9 September 2009, *LJN* BJ7217, in which appeal was made to have the fine mitigated if there was concurrence of offences.

153 See also *inter alia* H.E. Bröring, *De bestuurlijke boete*, Deventer, Kluwer 2005, pp. 224–225.

154 See, for example, HR 11 June 1894, W 6516; HR 19 October 1931, *NJ* 1932, p. 1319; HR 23 September 1980, *NJ* 1981, 7 and HR 4 December 1990, *NJ* 1991, 345.

155 See for example CRvB 16 May 2001, AB 2003, 17 with note. HBr; CRvB 10 May 2000, AB 343 with note FP;JB 228 with note C.L.G.F.H. A (where there was, moreover, a question of continuing violation) and CRvB 7 February 2001, JB 2001, 116 with note C.L.G.F.H. A.

156 ABRvS 17 February 2010, *LJN* BL4163.

157 In addition to the case law discussed hereinafter, see also CBb 29 June 2006, *LJN* AZ3839 AB 2007, 248 (Commodities Act), and CBB 15 December 1981, AB 1982, 279 (disciplinary law).

again and again, to use this logo in the context of an event or activity or otherwise in such a way that its aim was to publicize or promote a tobacco product, either directly or indirectly.'[158]

The CBb ruled in its ruling of 16 November 2010 with regard to infringements of the Fertilizers Act, that several administrative fines had been wrongfully imposed since it had wrongfully not been assumed that it was a question of a continuous act. The CBb considered:

'However, in the opinion of the Tribunal, the infringements with regard to the incorrect sampling of a load of solid manure by the carrier and the failure to determine the nitrogen and phosphate levels (analysis) of the supplied and transported loads of animal manure must be considered to be one continuous act. Having a sample analysed can only be done if a sample has actually been taken. If there has been no sampling, a penalty can be imposed for that but, in that case, not for the failure to have the nitrogen and phosphate levels determined of a sample that has not been taken. So only one penalty can be imposed for these two infringements. The appeal is to that extent well-founded.'

6. GENERAL PRINCIPLES

6.1. INTRODUCTION

General principles of law exist in Dutch administrative law, criminal law and the law of criminal procedure. In addition to general principles like the principle of legal certainty and the principle of equality, administrative law distinguishes the general principles of proper administration [*Algemene beginselen van behoorlijk bestuur*].[159] Examples of these principles are the principle of legitimate expectations [*vertrouwensbeginsel*], the principle of due care [*zorgvuldigheidsbeginsel*], the principle of proportionality [*evenredigheidsbeginsel*] and the principle to state reasons [*motiveringsbeginsel*]. These principles are partly codified in GALA, and in so far as norms that are derived from these principles are not codified these norms will apply as unwritten law. Dutch literature as well as case law on general principles of proper administration is

158 See also CBb 28 May 2009, *LJN* BK4860, CBb 28 May 2009, *LJN*BK4874 and CBb 28 May 2009, *LJN* BK4968.This ruling is also interesting because one or more offences arising from the same act and the concurrence of offences also played a role in this case, not only the continued violation. See also CBb 28 May 2009, *LJN* BK4860, CBb 28 May 2009, *LJN* BK4874 and CBb 28 May 2009, *LJN*BK4968.

159 See for a extremely short description René Seerden and Frits Stroink, "Administrative Law in the Netherlands", in: Rene Seerden and Frits Stroink (eds.), *Administrative Law of the European Union, its Member States and the United States*, Intersentia, Antwerp 2002, pp. 145–197, especially pp. 168–171.

extensive.[160] It goes beyond the purpose of this report to elaborate on these aspects.

The principles in the law of criminal procedure [*Beginselen van een goede procesorde*] are the same as or at least comparable to a great extent to the general principles of proper administration (*algemene beginselen van behoorlijk bestuur*).[161]

In my analysis I will focus upon the principles that play a role in decisions to impose administrative sanctions, both remedial and deterrent sanctions. In Dutch legal scholarship a distinction is made between general principles of proper administration (*algemene beginselen van behoorlijk bestuur*) and general principles of proper procedure [*beginselen van behoorlijke rechtspleging*).[162] One of the principles of proper procedure is the principle of defence. As far as punitive sanctions are involved, this principle also applies in the pre-trial stage and, therefore, the principle of defence is also a principle of proper administration. In any case, the principle of defence is considered to be a regular principle of administrative law. Many rights of defence would be part of the general principles of defence. Some principles would have greater significance at the pre-trial stage than others and, as they should be considered to be general principles of proper administration, they should be discussed in chapter 6 of this analysis. Nevertheless, for comparative reasons the rights of defence, the principle of defence, will be discussed in chapter 7.

Besides the principles of defence, the most important legal principles concerning sanctions are the principle of legality (par. 6.2) and the principle of proportionality (par. 6.3). In paragraph 6.4, the principle of non-cumulation will be discussed. The principle of ne bis in idem/ una via which in Dutch law only applies to deterrent sanctions and in criminal law will be described in paragraph 6.5, and the principle of no fine on death in paragraph 6.6.

---

160 An impressive example is P. Nicolaï, *Beginselen van behoorlijk bestuur*, Kluwer, Deventer 1990. More general descriptions can be found in Van Wijk/Konijnenbelt & Van Male, *Hoofdstukken van bestuursrecht*, Reed Business, Amsterdam 2011, pp. 261–371; R.J.N. Schlössels and S.E. Zijlstra, *Bestuursrecht in de sociale rechtsstaat*, Kluwer, Deventer 2010, pp. 385–466; L.J.A. Damen *et al.*, *Bestuursrecht I*, Boom juridische uitgevers 2009, pp.295–435. The journal *Nederlands Tijdschrift voor bestuursrecht* regularly publishes an overview of case law and literature on these principles. The most recent ones are R.J.N. Schlössels, "Beginselen van behoorlijk bestuur", *NTB* 2012/22; R.J.N. Schlössels, "Beginselen van behoorlijk bestuur", *NTB* 2011/23; R.J.N. Schlössels, "Beginselen van behoorlijk bestuur", *NTB* 2010/33.

161 See C.P.M. Cleiren, *Beginselen van een goede procesorde*, Gouda Quint 1989.

162 See for example B.W.N. de Waard, *Beginselen van behoorlijke rechtspleging, met name in het administratief procesrecht*, W.E.J. Tjeenk Willink, Zwolle 1987; M. Schreuder-Vlasblom, *Rechtsbescherming en bestuurlijke voorprocedure*, fifth edition, Kluwer, Deventer 2013.

6.2. THE PRINCIPLE OF LEGALITY

Dutch criminal law also follows the principle of *nullum crimen sine praevia lege criminali, nulla poena sine preavia lege poenali* [no crime without previous criminal law, no punishment without previous law on punishment]. This is laid down in Article 16 of the Dutch Constitution and in Article 1 of the Dutch Criminal Code.[163] The principle of legality as laid down in Article 7 ECHR and Article 15 ICCPR is also applicable for punitive sanctions that do not come under criminal law.[164] These provisions play an important part in punitive administrative law, in particular for other punitive sanctions outside criminal law than the administrative fine. A considerably large number of judgments have developed in which these provisions play an important part. According to general interpretation,[165] the principle is equally applicable to remedial sanctions, in any case for enforcement action, the *astreinte* and the administrative fine. Article 5:4 GALA confirms the development in case law and legal scholarship and provides for the general requirement of a legal basis applicable to administrative fines, enforcement action and *astreinte*:

1. The authority to impose an administrative sanction only exists in as far as this is conferred by or in accordance with the law.
2. An administrative sanction will only be imposed on conduct which is contrary to the foregoing and which applies to conduct under or in accordance with any statutory provision.

Therefore it is the case for the stated administrative sanctions that the conduct for which they can be imposed must be laid down by statutory provision and the authority to impose them must be conferred by law. In addition, retrospective effect is not allowed. It is not set down explicitly in the proposed regulation, but the principle of *lex certa* is equally applicable: a provision enforced by administrative sanctions must be sufficiently clear, foreseeable and made known. This is derived from Article 7 ECHR[166] and is established case law for the national courts in punitive sanctions, but it also applies to remedial sanctions.[167]

---

163 The principle of legality in criminal procedure is set down in Article 1 of the Dutch Code of Criminal Procedure.

164 It is not clear yet which role Article 49 CFR will play.

165 Explanatory notes to the Bill (Memorie van Toelichting), Parliamentary Documents 2003–2004, 29 702, no. 3, p. 85.

166 ECtHR 25 May 1993, series A, vol. 260 *Kokkinakis/Greece* and ECtHR 27 September 1995, *NJ* 1996, 49 *G/France*. See recently Rogier Stijnen, *Rechtsbescherming tegen bestraffing in het strafrecht en het bestuursrecht*, Kluwer, Deventer 2011, pp. 107–121.

167 Thus the explanatory notes of the Bill, Parliamentary Documents 2003–2004, 29 702, no. 3, p. 85 and the Preliminary Draft p. 111.

In cases involving administrative fines, the infringer often invokes the *lex certa* principle, in most cases unsuccessfully. There are two situations in which this principle proves to be somewhat problematic: the infringement of duties of due care (*zorgplichten*)[168] and the infringement of provisions in the design of which the legislator made mistakes. Until recently the enforcement of duties of due care did not seem to be too problematic but a development seems to be taking place according to which one of the high administrative courts, the Administrative Jurisdiction Division of the Council of State, is setting a higher standard than in the past.[169] Interestingly enough, these cases involve remedial sanctions.

In addition, the codification of two other norms in the principle of legality also applies to administrative fines: the requirement that the law must set down the maximum sanction and the requirement of *lex mitior.* The latter is introduced by declaring that the *lex mitior* provision in criminal law is applicable.[170] Both have been set down in Article 5:46 GALA. This provision reads as follows:

1. The Act will determine the maximum administrative fine for a certain infringement.
2. Unless the amount of the administrative fine is determined by a statutory provision, the administrative authority will attune the administrative fine to the seriousness of the infringement and the degree of blame which may be attached to the infringer. The administrative authority will take into account the circumstances under which the infringement has been committed.

---

168 See for example F.J. van Ommeren, "Zorgplichten: wat zijn dat? Een poging tot het overbrugging van twee werelden", in: C.E.C. Jansen et al. (eds.), *Zorgplichten in publiek- en privaatrecht*, Boom Juridische uitgevers, The Hague 2011, pp. 23–45, and in the same book: S.E. Zijlstra, "Zorgplicht en algemeen wetgevingsbeleid", pp. 47–62; J. Struiksma and A.R. Neerhof, *Weinig kans voor zorgplichten in bestuursrechtelijke wetgeving*, pp. 63–77; Wim Timmer, *Het doel welgesteld. Een praktijkonderzoek naar de toepassing van doelregelgeving*, Boom Juridische uitgevers, The Hague 2011; B.J.V. Keupink, *Daderschap bij wettelijke strafrechtelijke zorgplichtbepalingen. Over het gedragingsbestanddeel 'zorgen'in het materiële strafrecht*, Wolf Legal Publishers, Nijmegen 2011; R. Stijnen, "De zorgplicht van artikel 4:23 Wft: geschikte financiële dienstverlening door financiële ondernemingen", in: R. Stijnen and R, Kruisdijk, *Zorgplicht en financieel toezicht*, pp. 15–41, and in the same book: A.B. Blomberg and L.J.J. Rogier, "De plaats van de aanwijzing bij de handhaving van de Wet op het financieel toezicht", p. 6783, and A.R. Hartmann and B.J.V. Keupink, "Enkele opmerkingen over de reikwijdte van de publiekrechtelijke aansprakelijkheid bij zorgplichten in de financiële toezichtswetgeving", pp. 85–109; P. Houweling. "Advisering over zorgplichtbepalingen", *RegelMaat* 2008/4; G.A. Biezeveld, "Zorgplichten in de milieuwetgeving", *RegelMaat* 2008/4, pp. 122–130; M.J.C. Visser, *Zorgplichtbepalingen in het strafrecht*, Gouda Quint, Arnhem 2001 and L.E.M. Hendriks, "De Hoge Raad en art. 14 Wbb. Zorgplichtbepalingen in het milieustrafrecht", *MenR* 1994/5, pp. 138–146.

169 ABRvS 10 August 2011, *LJN* BR4631 and ABRvS 21 December 2011, *LJN* BU8881; *AB* 2012, 210; *JB* 2012, 33.

170 Which can be found in Article 1, second paragraph, Criminal Code and reads as follows: 'Where a change has been made in the law subsequent to the time the offence was committed, the provisions of the law most favourable to the accused will be applied.'

3. If the amount of the administrative fine is determined by a statutory provision, the administrative authority will nevertheless impose a lesser administrative fine if the infringer puts forward a credible argument that, due to special circumstances, the administrative fine is too high.
4. Article 1, second paragraph, Criminal Code is accordingly applicable.

Recently, the Criminal Division of the Supreme Court took an important decision on the way the *lex mitior* principle [on the application of the more lenient penalty] should be applied.[171] In this decision, the Supreme Court placed the national codifications of this principle and existing case law in relation to the most important international law codifications of this principle: Article 7 ECHR, 15 ICCPR and 49 Charter. No less importantly, although the decision involved a criminal law case, the High Court also gave guidance as to the way in which the *lex mitior* principle has to be applied in administrative law. The Court here clearly stressed its role as the most important court to give guidance on the application of criminal law principles. In this case the Supreme Court's decision was evoked by an exceptionally thorough conclusion of the Advocate General *[advocaat-generaal]*, a prominent former professor in criminal law and a specialist on the subject: Geert Knigge.[172]

The main considerations of the Supreme Council are the following:

> 'The argument poses the question, in particular, whether the case law on the application of Article 1, second paragraph, DCC– that formed the basis for the Court's ruling – requires some adjustment as a consequence of the ECtHR's ruling of 17 September 2009 (Scoppola v. Italy), no. 10249/03, BK6009.
> (...)
> The case law of the Supreme Court on Article 1, second paragraph, DCC can be summarized in the following way.
> This provision, which refers to the "defendant", is confined to ongoing prosecutions.
> In the event that the offence description is altered to the advantage of the defendant after the offence has been committed, then Article 1, second paragraph, DCC applies if the change in the law ensues from a revision in the legislator's view with regard to the punishabiliity of the criminal offence committed before the change in the law (...).
> This criterion is also used in cases where the rules in applicable sanctions law have been changed, after the offence has been committed, in a way that is possibly favourable to the defendant (...).
> The Supreme Court was induced by these developments to refine its case law with regard to the changes in the rules of sanctions law. For those rules, which could relate to the specific maximum punishment as well as to more general rules concerning the

171 HR 12 July 2011, *AB* 2011, 312; *NJ* 2012, 78.

172 His exhaustive and excellent PhD was on this subject as well: G. Knigge, *Verandering van wetgeving*, Gouda Quint, Arnhem 1984.

> imposition of sanctions, it is from now on the case that a change that has been introduced since the offence was committed must be applied by a court with immediate effect – therefore without a review of the criterion of whether the criminal-law legislator's view has changed as to the punishability of criminal offences that were committed before the amendment of the law – if and to the extent that the change in the ongoing case is favourable to the defendant.
> In this connection, it should be noted that, in the light of the [above] developments, any transitional provisions formulated by the legislator will have to fit in with the international regulatory framework described above. If such is not the case, the courts will have to disregard these provisions.
> Even so, the Supreme Court still adheres to its consistent case law with regard to changes related to offence descriptions, such as changes in the components that instigate or negate the punishability of an offence, for example by the introduction of a different enforcement regime. The developments just outlined, which relate specifically to changes in the rules in sanctions law, do not prompt any changes to legal precedents in that particular field of law. The Supreme Court made the further remark that there is a firm basis for this case law, since liability under criminal law is principally determined by the rules that applied at the time the criminal offence was committed. An exception to this is, however, justified in the event that the legislator has revised its view of the punishability of the criminal offence that was committed before the law was amended.
> The legislator can set out this revised view in special transitional provisions, and this certainly provides greater clarity."

This case law of the Supreme Court is now followed by administrative courts applying Article 5:46, fourth paragraph, GALA.

6.3. THE PRINCIPLE OF PROPORTIONALITY[173]

According to Article 3:4, second paragraph, GALA the adverse effects of an administrative decision on one or more interested parties must not be disproportionate to the aims pursued by that decision. There should be a balanced weighing of the interests involved. 'Proportionality expresses the idea that a sledgehammer is not needed to crack a nut.'[174] This article is the codification of the principle of proportionality. According to some this principle

[173] See for example A.J.C. de Moor-van Vugt, *Maten en gewichten: het evenredigheidsbeginsel in Europees perspectief*, W.E.J. Tjeenk Willink, Zwolle 1995; Adrienne de Moor-van Vugt, "Proportionality in Dutch Administrative Law", *Tilburg Foreign Law Review* 7 (1998–1999), pp. 7 et seq. See also more general descriptions in: Van Wijk/Konijnenbelt & Van Male, *Hoofdstukken van bestuursrecht*, Reed Business, Amsterdam 2011, pp. 261–371; R.J.N. Schlössels and S.E. Zijlstra, *Bestuursrecht in de sociale rechtsstaat*, Kluwer, Deventer 2010, pp. 385–466; L.J.A. Damen *et al.*, Bestuursrecht I, Boom juridische uitgevers 2013, pp. 388–398 and 662–664.

[174] Peter Cane, *Administrative Law*, Oxford University Press, 2011, p. 191.

is an aspect of the principle of substantive due care (*materiële zorgvuldigheid*).[175] The review by Dutch courts of the conformity of administrative decisions with this principle is reluctant. It respects discretionary power [*beleidsvrijheid*).

An important application of the principle of proportionality relates to the proportionality of the deterrent sanction imposed. As we will see this principle is codified in Article 5:46. More importantly, this principle is also codified in Article 6 ECHR, and therefore courts have the possibility to declare legislation and statutes inapplicable due to a breach of international law. This possibility plays an important role in legislation where statutory law determines the tariffs according to which decisions to impose an administrative fine are imposed. One of the most important themes in the case law relating to punitive administrative law is the severity of the sanction; for administrative fines, the amount of the fine is, of course, important. There is substantial case law on the amount of the administrative fine: most of it refers to the law before the GALA penalty regime came into effect, but the arrangement in Article 5:46, second and third paragraphs GALA was clearly being anticipated and so I will take these provisions as my starting point. These two provisions read as follows:

2. Unless the amount of the administrative fine is determined by a statutory provision, the administrative authority will attune the administrative fine to the seriousness of the infringement and the degree of blame which may be attached to the infringer. The administrative authority will take into account the circumstances under which the infringement has been committed.
3. If the amount of the administrative fine is determined by a statutory provision, the administrative authority will nevertheless impose a lesser administrative fine if the infringer puts forward a credible argument that, due to special circumstances, the administrative fine is too high.

According to Article 5:46, second paragraph, the administrative fine should be attuned to three groups of circumstances: (1) the seriousness of the infringement, (2) the degree of blame which may be attached to the infringer, *and* (3) the circumstances under which the infringement has been committed. National case law applying Article 6 ECHR adds an important fourth group of circumstances: (4) the personal circumstances of the perpetrator.

The most interesting theme concerning the proportionality of administrative fines is the difference between the review of fine tariffs in policy rules and that in generally binding provisions.

175 See for example Van Wijk/Konijnenbelt & Van Male, *Hoofdstukken van bestuursrecht*, Reed Business, Amsterdam 2011, p. 325.

It is commonly accepted that a court's review of the proportionality of an administrative fine has to be 'full' or 'robust'. The legislator, literature, academic studies and jurisprudence wrestle with the question of the exact implications of this requirement – as it arises from Article 6 ECHR– for fine tariffs and for the application of Article 8:72a: the obligation of the court to deal with the case itself if it reverses a fine decision.[176]

If there is a complete absence of culpability, the administrative authority does not have the power to impose an administrative fine (Article 5:41 GALA). Only very rarely is this absence assumed. The Council of State deems that, in the case of infringements of the Foreign Nationals (Employment) Act [*Wet arbeid vreemdelingen (Wav)*] (an act which has provided this court with the most case law on fines over the years), the infringer has to make a plausible case that he has taken the greatest care that may be expected of him to prevent the infringement.[177] An appeal to an absence of all guilt to this end is almost always rejected[178] and the number of Wav cases in which the Administrative Jurisdiction Division has accepted that there was a complete absence of culpability can be counted on the fingers of one hand.[179]

If there is not a complete absence of culpability, the administrative authority has the power to apply an administrative fine. The court and the administrative authority have to ensure that the amount of the administrative fine is commensurate with the four sets of circumstances I mentioned before: the seriousness of the act, the degree of blame, the circumstances in which the infringement took place and the circumstances in which the infringer found himself.[180]If the legislator has not included fine tariffs in the generally binding provision (the 'free' power to fine), the alignment imposed in Article 5:46, second paragraph, GALA applies. This imposition seems to be restricted to the gravity

176 See on these subjects, recently: H.E. Bröring en H.K. Naves, "Waarborgen bij bestraffende bestuurlijke sancties: onvoltooid bestuursrecht", and B.W.N. de Waard, "De matigende rechter. Evenredigheid en bestuurlijke boeten", in: T. Barkhuysen *et al.*, *Bestuursrecht harmoniseren: 15 jaar Awb*, BJu, The Hague 2010, pp. 449–467 and 469–486, resp.

177 Standard judgments on this subject are ABRvS 11 July 2007, *AB* 2007, 311 and ABRvS 12 March 2008, *AB* 2009, 111. See also ABRvS 22 June 2011, *LJN* BQ8855; AB 2011, 263.

178 See, for example, recently ABRvS 6 April 2011, *LJN* BQ0302.

179 One example is ABRvS 23 September 2009, *AB* 2009, 401. The judgment of 17 December 2008, *LJN*BG7170 comes very close to the absence of culpability. The first judgment in which the Administrative Jurisdiction Division imposed a mitigation of 50% due to reduced culpability was that of ABRvS 26 September 2007, *AB* 2007, 401, to my knowledge.

180 On the basis of case law (compare the consideration of the Division in its judgment of 17 June 2009 referred to below with that of 27 January 2010) it could be argued that the court has to consider four groups of circumstances on the basis of Article 6 ECHR and the administrative authority only three. Article 5:46 GALA only mentions three groups of circumstances. Even so, the administrative authority must act in anticipation of the judgment of the court on this aspect.

of the infringement and the degree of blame. Consideration of the circumstances in which the infringement was committed seems only to occur 'if necessary', and no particular specifications regarding the personal circumstances of the infringer are given. In the Explanatory Memorandum, the government indicated that a person's ability-to-pay must be taken into account as well: that could be classed as personal circumstances. Case law also shows that personal circumstances have to be taken into consideration.[181] In principle, it relates to the circumstances that the infringer has to substantiate in his arguments. The criteria for this substantiation are strict in fine tariff systems, and most certainly in the Administrative Jurisdiction Division's case law.

Very often the administrative authority has laid down its applicable fine tariffs in a policy rule. Three judgments should be regarded as standard judgments in this respect: the judgments of the Administrative Jurisdiction Division of 17 June 2009 and 27 January 2010, and the judgment of the Central Appeals Tribunal of 27 May 2010.[182] The Administrative Jurisdiction Division considered as follows in its ruling of 17 June 2009:

> 'As opposed to the arguments of the Minister, the standard amounts for fines defined in the List of Tariffs may not be departed from solely in the event of the absence of culpability or a reduced degree of blame, or exceptional circumstances within the meaning of Article 4:84, GALA. Article 6 ECHR implies that the court has to review whether the administrative fine is commensurate with the seriousness of the infringement, the degree to which the infringer can be held accountable, and the circumstances in which the infringement was committed and in which the infringer found himself. The principle of proportionality set out in Article 3:4, second paragraph, GALA can also be an inducement to exclude the policy rules in a specific case and to apply a lower fine.'[183]

In the judgment of the Division dated 27 January 2010[184] and that of the Central Appeals Tribunal of 27 May 2010, a new standard consideration has been applied, one that anticipated the present GALA fine regime. The Administrative Jurisdiction Division considered as follows:

> 'The Minister has been able to reasonably establish the standard rates for fines adopted in policy rules so that he has to take these as his starting point in setting the amount of the fine. In view of the decision that is to be made, the Minister will also

181 Financial circumstances: ABRvS 11 March 2009, AB 2009, 143. Psychological circumstances: Rb. Rotterdam 10 March 2011, *LJN* BP7350.

182 AB 2010, 229 note Stijnen.

183 ABRvS 17 June 2009, *AB* 2009, 350. Criticism of this judgment came from H.E. Bröring and H.K. Naves in their contribution to *Waarborgen bij bestraffende bestuurlijke sancties: onvoltooid bestuursrecht*, just referred to. See also ABRvS 16 September 2009, *AB* 2009, 362.

184 See also ABRvS 21 July 2010, *LJN* BN1905.

> need to observe the principle of proportionality set out in Article 3:4 of the General Administrative Law Act during the decision-making process for specific cases. The implication of this is that the Minister, when setting the amount of a fine, must ask whether the fine arising from the standard rates for fines is proportionate to the aim of the legislator when all the circumstances of the case have been weighed carefully. These circumstances certainly include the nature and seriousness of the infringement, the degree to which the infringer can be blamed and the circumstances in which it was committed. When application of the standard fine tariff would not be proportional, mitigation is appropriate and fitting.
>
> Article 6 of the European Convention on Human Rights and Fundamental Freedoms, which applies to the imposition of a fine for the reasons now under discussion, entails that the court need not be too reserved in its review of whether the fine imposed by the minister in a specific case is consistent with the principle of proportionality.
> If the court is of the opinion that this is not the case and reverses the decision on that ground, it is to take the standard rate of fines as its point of departure in determining the size of the fine.'

Any fine tariffs that an administrative authority includes in policy rules are in principle binding.[185] Only in exceptional circumstances may these rates be deviated from under Article 4:84 GALA: these are circumstances which the policy regulator has not taken into consideration. In other words: if the administrative fine according to a tariff set out in a policy rule is disproportionate in a specific case, then it needs to be deviated from, under Article 4:84 GALA, if the disproportionality can be attributed to circumstances that the policy regulator has not taken into account. Should this disproportionality arise from other factors, then application of the policy rule has to be excluded in this specific instance.

When fine tariffs are set out in a generally binding provision, the power of mitigation in Article 5:46, third paragraph, GALA applies. The standard judgment is that of the Trade and Industry Appeals Tribunal [*CBb*] of 29 April 2004, in which the Tribunal considered, inter alia, as follows:

> 'The administrative fine in question can be regarded as a punitive sanction. Article 6 ECHR entails that the court needs to review whether the size of the imposed fine is in reasonable proportion to the seriousness and imputability of the infringement. This is not altered by the circumstance that Article 48d, first and second paragraphs, of the law prescribes that the amount of the fine is determined in the schedule to the statute. Furthermore, as considered by the Tribunal in its response to the arguments presented in the statement of defence on this matter, the Tribunal is of the opinion that the wording of the act – also for the regulator – does not exclude the fact that the review of proportionality just referred to should be carried out within the legal

185 See on this ABRvS 16 January 2008, *AB* 2008, 50.

framework established under Article 48d, fourth paragraph. Although the explanatory memorandum to this provision indicates a restricted approach on the part of the legislator where the latter only regards this paragraph as advisable 'by way of an exception in a special individual case' and where it lays the burden of proof of this exceptionality entirely with the infringer, the wording of the provision in itself presents no impediment to a full review of the proportionality. This implies that the administrative authority is always bound to use the power granted to it under Article 48d, fourth paragraph, as soon as there is any question of a disproportionality between the size of the fine on the one hand, and the seriousness and imputability of the infringement on the other.'[186]

In the explanatory notes, the explanation of the government with regard to the power of mitigation of Article 5:46, third paragraph, GALA is based on this judgment. This signifies that the basic assumption is that the court, if need be, 'stretches' the power of mitigation in order to comply with the stipulation of a full review in accordance with Article 6 ECHR. Administrative authorities and courts are even required to take steps to undertake a full review if special circumstances arise which the regulator has taken into account. In other words: unlike the situation in which rates are set out in policy rules, the regulation here is not declared inapplicable but the power of mitigation is extended. Article 4:84 GALA is not 'stretched' in policy rules but the policy rule is declared inapplicable as the occasion arises.

The most recent stage in the development of case law regarding the proportionality of administrative fines is the use of a new standard consideration resulting from mutual agreement of the three highest appeal courts in administrative law: the Administrative Law Division of the Council of State,[187] the Central Appeals Tribunal[188] and the Trade and Industry Appeals Tribunal.[189] The first two courts deal mainly with fine tariffs in policy rules, the latter with fine tariffs in generally binding provisions. The considerations of the Council of State:

---

186 CBb 29 April 2004, *AB* 2004, 317; JOR 2004, 173. See after that CBb 15 February 2005, *AB* 2006, 71; CBb 5 April 2005, *AB* 2006, 81 (Commodities Act), CBb 15 December 2006, *AB* 2007, 280 (Tobacco Act); CBb 1 April 2008, *LJN* BC. See for an explanation of Dutch criminal law on this point: Oswald Jansen, "Country Analysis – The Netherlands", in: Gerhard Dannecker and Oswald Jansen (eds.), *Competition Law Sanctioning in the European Union*, Kluwer Law International pp. 729–735, A. Klip and H.G. van der Wilt, *Country report on the Netherlands*, to be published by the AIDP (2003) and with a thorough law comparison J.A.W. Lensing, *Ne bis in idem in strafzaken – Een rechtsvergelijkende en internationaal strafrechtelijke orientatie*, Geschriften van de Nederlandse Vereniging voor Rechtsvergelijking, Kluwer, Deventer 2001, inst. 60, pp. 91–212.8271/BC8268; CBb 22 May 2008, *LJN* BD2542, CBb 11 December 2008, *LJN*BG8906; CBb 22 December 2008, *LJN* BG8819 and *LJN*BG8869 (Tobacco Act) and CBb 30 January 2009, *LJN*BH3320 and *LJN*BH3316; CBb 1 September 2011, AB 2011, 310.

187 Since ABRvS 21 July 2010, *AB* 2011, 264.

188 Since CRvB 27 May 2010, *AB* 2010, 229; *JB* 2010, 186.

189 Since CBb 1 September 2011, *AB* 2011, 310.

> 'In exercising this competence, the administrative authority must, pursuant to Article 5:46, second paragraph, GALA, attune the size of the fine to the seriousness of the infringement and the degree to which the infringer is to blame and consideration must also be given to the circumstances in which the infringement took place. For the sake of legal unity and certainty, the Minister may decide on and apply a policy as to the imposition of fines and the amounts involved. Even if the courts do not find that the policy as such is not unreasonable, when implementing this policy the Minister still needs to decide, where applicable, whether this would be in line with the requirements referred to above that have to be set out for the exercise of the power to impose a fine. If that is not the case, as an extension to or deviation from the adopted policy, the fine should be set at an amount that is appropriate and necessary. The court will not therefore be reticent in its review of whether the administration's decision regarding the fine complies with these requirements and whether the sanction is therefore proportionate.'

And the considerations of the Trade and Industry Appeals Tribunal:

> 'The administrative fine in question can be regarded as a punitive sanction. It ensures from Article 6 ECHR that the court needs to review whether the size of the imposed fine is in reasonable proportion to the seriousness and imputability of the violation.
> Under Article 22, first paragraph of the Trust Offices (Supervision) Act [*Wet toezicht trustkantoren, Wtt*], the value of the fine is determined by the provisions in the schedule to this act, with the proviso that the fine for an individual violation may not be more than EUR 900,000. The fine prescribed for these violations, as applicable to the trust offices that are referred to there, is EUR 87,125.
> The Nederlandse Bank imposed a fine on D in accordance with this set amount. The DNB is allowed a power of mitigation by virtue of Article 22, fourth paragraph, Wtt if the particular circumstances of a case make the fine disproportionately high in an individual case. As the Tribunal has already considered in previous judgments concerning almost identical provisions in the Securities Transactions (Supervision) Act 1995 [*Wet toezicht effectenverkeer 1995*], the Sectoral Pension Fund (Obligatory Membership) Act 2000 [*Wet verplichte deelneming in een bedrijfstakpensioenfonds 2000*] and the Tobacco Act [*Tabakswet*] – see on this the Tribunal's judgment of 30 January 2009 LJN BH3316; AB 2010/145, inter alia – the wording of this provision does not exclude a review of the proportionality being undertaken within the context of this paragraph of the Act. In the Tribunal's opinion, Article 22, fourth paragraph,Wtt forms the context within which, in specific cases, the fine imposed under the schedule to the Wtt could and should be assessed: in particular, is it proportionate to the nature and gravity of the violation, the degree to which the established violation can be imputed to the offender and, where necessary, the circumstances in which the violation was committed. The circumstances that could play a role here are not those that the legislator took into account when setting the size of the fine. In this way, serious consideration can generally be given to the requirement of true proportionality between the size of the fine and the nature and seriousness of the established violation.'

Finally, it is important to notice that although the court's review of the proportionality of an administrative fine has to be 'full' or 'robust' the extent of the review differs. This is best demonstrated by citing the considerations of two decisions:

In a decision of the Trade and Industry Appeals Tribunal of 15 December 2006 involving an administrative fine of €45,000 following a infringement of the Tobacco Act, this court wrote:

> 'Depending on whether or not the legislator took certain circumstances into account according to the legislative history, there will be greater or more limited scope for applying the power of mitigation because of those circumstances – in a similar way to a system of communicating vessels. In this way, serious consideration can generally be given to the requirement of true proportionality between the size of the fine and the nature and seriousness of the established transgression.'[190]

In its decision of the Council of State of 14 March 2012 we find the following consideration with regard to an administrative fine of €6,700 relating to an infringement of the Minimum Wage and Minimum Holiday Allowance Act [*Wet minimumloon en minimumvakantiebijslag*]. The tariffs here are fixed by policy rules:

> 'This fine will be imposed in the same way on every business, company or organization, regardless of their legal form and the number of their employees. The policy is therefore not differentiated. If a policy of this nature is being pursued, in each individual case there will have to be a stringent examination during its implementation of whether its application corresponds with the requirements that have to be set out for exercising the power to impose a fine.'[191]

6.4. CONCURRENCE OF ACTS AND NON-CUMULATION[192]

As I have explained above, the GALA regulation of administrative fines is closely attuned to the comparable criminal law provisions. Article 5:8 GALA provides for a regulation of concurrence of offences (*meerdaadse samenloop*). This provisions is closely attuned to the similar provision in Article 57, second paragraph, DCC. Two or more offences arising from the same act (*eendaadse samenloop*), which is considered to be a rare phenomenon in administrative law, is an unwritten rule in case law based upon the principle of proportionality. As far as administrative fines are concerned, case law follows Article 55, first

190 CBb 15 December 2006, *AB* 2007, 280; see also CBb 7 June 2007, *AB* 2007, 279 and CBb 1 September 2011, *AB* 2011, 310.

191 ABRvS 14 March 2012, *AB* 2012, 98.

192 See on this Aletta Blomberg, *Integrale handhaving van milieurecht*, Boom Juridische Uitgevers, The Hague 2000, pp. 203–219.

paragraph, DCC which provides for a regulation of *eendaadse samenloop*.[193] At the same time the general rule in administrative fines is that the number of fines can cumulate limitlessly if imposed on legally different punishable or fineable acts. Also, the aims of punitive sanctions (*bestraffende sancties*) and remedial sanctions (*herstelsancties*) are different, which according to Dutch legal scholarship, the legislator[194] and established case law[195] means that both sanctions can be imposed simultaneously.

6.5. *UNA VIA* AND *NE BIS IN IDEM*

The *ne bis in idem* principle is also recognized in the Netherlands but until 2009, the date of enactment of the GALA regulation of administrative fines, the principle only prevailed under criminal law. It did not apply to administrative sanctions, nor to punitive sanctions such as the administrative fine. However, this in no way meant that double punishment was possible or accepted in the Netherlands.[196]

The core section in criminal law is Article 68 DCC. This provision states:

1. Except in cases in which judgments are subject to revision, no person may be prosecuted twice for an act for which a final judgment has been rendered by a judge in the Netherlands, the Netherlands Antilles or Aruba.
2. Where a final judgment was rendered by another judge, the same person may not be prosecuted twice for the same act in cases in which:
   (1) that person has been acquitted or discharged in criminal proceedings;
   (2) that person has been convicted and sentenced and the sentence has been fully served, a pardon has been granted or the sentence has lapsed.
3. No person may be subjected to prosecution for an act that has been finally disposed of, so far as he is concerned, in a foreign country through his satisfying a condition set by the competent authorities in order to avoid criminal proceedings.[197]

193 See HR 13 August 2004, *AB* 2006, 25. Although this rule of *eendaadse samenloop* is invoked regularly it is seldom if ever granted.

194 Parliamentary Documents II 2003–2004, 29 702, nr. 3, pp. 90–92.

195 See for example ABRvS 16 January 1996, *AB* 1996, 409; ABRvS 11 February 2000, *AB* 2000, 185; HR 20 March 2007, *AB* 2007, 249.

196 See for an explanation of Dutch criminal law on this point: Oswald Jansen, "Country Analysis – The Netherlands", in: Gerhard Dannecker and Oswald Jansen (eds.), *Competition Law Sanctioning in the European Union*, Kluwer Law International, pp. 729–735, A. Klip and H.G. van der Wilt, *Country report on the Netherlands*, to be published by the AIDP (2003) and with a thorough law comparison J.A.W. Lensing, *Ne bis in idem in strafzaken – Een rechtsvergelijkende en internationaal strafrechtelijke orientatie*, Geschriften van de Nederlandse Vereniging voor Rechtsvergelijking, Kluwer, Deventer 2001, inst. 60, pp. 91–212.

197 Translation taken from Louise Rayar and Stafford Wadsworth, The American Series of Foreign Penal Codes, *The Dutch Penal Code*, Rothmann & Co, Littleton, Colorado 1997.

The *ne bis in idem* principle has also been set down in Article 14:7, ICCPR and in Article 4 of Protocol No. 7 of the ECHR. For both provisions, it is accepted in the Netherlands that they refer not only to criminal sanctions and prosecutions but also to punitive sanctions. The Netherlands has made a proviso to Article 14:7 ICCPR and has not ratified Protocol No. 7. This proviso runs as follows:

> 'The Kingdom of the Netherlands accepts this provision only in so far as no obligations arise from it further to those set out in article 68 of the Criminal Code of the Netherlands and article 70 of the Criminal Code of the Netherlands Antilles as they now apply.'[198]

The Netherlands has made this proviso because it was not certain whether Article 14:7 ICCPR excludes a second prosecution and punishment after judgment in a foreign country. With this proviso, the Netherlands wished to restrict the international effect of this proviso to the scope of Article 68 DCC.[199]

Before 2009 it was legal precedent for the criminal courts that the principle of *ne bis in idem* – considering the stated proviso and the circumstance that this principle is not contained in Article 6 ECHR[200] – does not apply when a person is prosecuted under criminal law, after this person has undergone a sanction for the same conduct as a punishment under administrative law.[201] According to prevailing administrative law, it is possible to impose a punitive sanction along-side a remedial sanction.[202]

In the literature on administrative law until 2009, there was the defence that, since there is no general equivalent of Article 68 DCC in administrative law, this norm could be inferred from the principle of proportionality.[203] The desirability of *Anrechnung* is also pointed out: in the severity of punishment, the criminal

198 Treaty Series 1978, 177.

199 M.W.C. Feteris, *Fiscale bestuurlijke boetes en het recht op een behoorlijk proces*, second edition, Kluwer, Deventer 2002, p. 435; C.L.G.F.H. Albers, *Rechtsbescherming bij bestuurlijke boeten*, thesis Maastricht, Sdu, The Hague 2002, p. 233; P.M. van Russen Groen, *Rechtsbescherming in het bestuursstrafrecht*, thesis Rotterdam, Gouda Quint, Arnhem 1998, pp. 294–310, particularly pp. 295–296. Parliamentary Documents II 1976/76, 13 932 (R1037), no. 3, p. 26 and 44, no. 4, p. 63 as well as the explanation to the provision (Treaty Series. 1978, 177, pp. 41–42).

200 ECtHR 12 December 1998, *R. vs. Luxembourg*, no. 12584/86; HR 21 May 1991, *NJ* 1991, 728. P.M. van Russen Groen, p. 294; Feteris 2002, p. 438.

201 HR 21 May 1991, *AB* 1992, 15; *NJ* 1991, 728; HR 5 February 1991, *NJ* 1991, 402/*AB* 1992, 38.

202 For criminal prosecution after a punitive administrative remedial sanction: HR 30 January 1996, *Gst.* 1996, pp. 589–592; Abr 16 January 1996, *AB* 1996, 409. For an administrative remedial sanction after a criminal conviction: AG 24 April 1992, *AB* 1992, 575; AG 15 May 1992, *AB* 1993, 386; Central Appeals Tribunal 21-12-1993, *RSV* 1994, 132 and HR 12 January 1999, *NJ* 1999, 289.

203 O.J.D.M.L. Jansen, "De dynamiek van het publiekrechtelijk sanctierecht", in: J. de Hullu, F.W. Bleichrodt and O.J.D.M.L. Jansen, *Herziening van het sanctiestelsel*, Kluwer, Deventer 2002, pp. 167–255, esp. 197–201; M.W.C. Feteris, *Fiscale bestuurlijke boetes en het recht op een behoorlijk proces*, second edition, Kluwer, Deventer 2002, p. 440.

court, the administrative authority empowered to impose administrative punishment and the administrative court should take previous sanctions into account.[204] In specific regulations on administrative sanctions, provisions were often made to prevent double punishment. Often this kind of provision is called a *una via* provision,[205] certainly when there is a choice between the application of criminal law and administrative law for the same conduct.

Since 2009, the General Administrative Law Act prohibits applying enforcement action as well as the duty backed by an astreinte for the same infringement. This regulation could be regarded as a *una via* regulation for remedial sanctions. There is also a ne bis in idem-provision against two administrative fines for the same infringements and a una via provision against a criminal sanction as well as an administrative fine for the same infringement.

The relevant provisions read as follows:

> 5:43 The administrative authority will not impose an administrative fine on an infringer if a previous administrative sanction has been imposed on that person for the same conduct, or otherwise if a notification under Art. 5:50.2.a has been made known.
>
> 5:44 1. The administrative authority will not impose an administrative fine if for the same conduct criminal proceedings have been instigated and the hearing has commenced, or a punishment order has been issued.
> 2. If the conduct also constitutes a criminal offence, then the matter will be referred to the Public Prosecution Service, unless it is determined by a statutory provision – and in such a case with the agreement of the Public Prosecution Service – that the matter may be dispensed with.
> 3. In the case of conduct which must be referred to the Public Prosecution Service, the administrative authority will only impose an administrative fine if:
>   a. the Public Prosecution Service has announced that it will not instigate criminal proceedings against the infringer, or

204 O.J.D.M.L. Jansen, *De dynamiek van het publiekrechtelijke sanctierecht*, pp. 200–201; P.M. van Russen Groen, *Rechtsbescherming in het bestuursstrafrecht*, Ph.D. thesis Rotterdam, Gouda Quint, Arnhem 1998, pp. 297–298; Hazewinkel-Suringa Remmelink, p. 603; G.J.M. Corstens, D. Doorenbos and J.F.L. Roording, "Samenloop van sancties op strafrechtelijk terrain", *NJB* 1992, p. 1344; A.C. 't Hart in his remarks at HR 9 October 1984, *NJ* 1985, 251 and HR 15 January 1985, *NJ* 1985, 450; E.F. Stamhuis, "*Ne bis in idem* en sanctiecumulatie bij fraudedelicten", *DD* 1991, pp. 465–473, esp. p. 472; J.F.L. Roording, Ph.D. thesis Nijmegen, Ars Aequi Libri, Nijmegen 1995, pp. 117, 238–240 and 243; See also HR10 March 1993, *BNB* 1993/198; ECJ 13 February 1969, case 14/68, *Jur.* 1969, p. 1 *et seq.* Walt Wilhelm.

205 L.J.J. Rogier, Strafsancties, administratieve sancties en het una via-beginsel, Gouda Quint, Arnhem 1992. There is also mention of a *una via*-principle, but that is not part of prevailing law: it is not a principle of law.

b. thirteen weeks have elapsed since the matter was referred to the Public Prosecution Service and no reaction has been received in that time.

Also Article 243 DCP was extended with a new second clause which reads as follows:

> 'If an administrative fine is imposed on the suspect in respect of the act, or if notification as defined in Article 5:50.2.a of the General Administrative Law Act has been sent, this has the same legal consequences as notification of non-continuation of prosecution provided that Article 245a is not applicable.'

Article 5:43 GALA is intended as codification of the principle of *ne bis in idem* in respect of administrative fines; Article 5:44 GALA as an *una via* regulation for the power to impose an administrative fine in addition to criminal proceedings.

The principle set down in 5:43 GALA means, according to the explanation in the Draft Proposal, that no one may be punished twice for the same infringement. The explanation continues:

> 'If someone commits two or more infringements at the same time, this person can be punished for both of these separately. Therefore, in this connection it is crucial whether an action in breach of two or more provisions should be regarded as one infringement or whether it can be interpreted as two or more independent infringements. In the first case, only one or more punitive sanctions may be imposed once for this infringement. If only one of the violated provisions forms the basis for this sanction, a second sanction is then no longer possible for breach of another provision. On the other hand, in the second case, a separate sanction can be imposed for each infringement.
> Case law from the Netherlands Supreme Court on Article 68 DCC is tantamount to that there is a question of 'the same act', if it 'appears that there is such a connection concerning the simultaneity of the acts of conduct and the actual relationship in acting and the guilt of the perpetrator that the tenor of the Article is such that they can be regarded as the same fact within the meaning of this provision (...).'[206] It is therefore reasonable that administrative authorities and administrative courts will refer to this criminal case law in their interpretation of the concept of 'the same infringement' in the proposed Article 5:43.'[207]

Unlike criminal law, the decision to prosecute and to sanction is in the hands of more than one administrative authority. In administrative law it is therefore possible that an act violates two provisions, and that two different administrative authorities are empowered to carry out enforcement. The explanation includes the following remarks:

206 HR 21 November 1961, *NJ* 1962, 89; HR 5 February 1963, *NJ* 1963, 320.

207 Parliamentary Documents II 2003–2004, 29 702, no. 3, p. 136; See also Draft Proposal pp. 122–123.

> 'This need not cause large problems in practice. The fact that the legislator has charged various administrative authorities with enforcement is in itself an indication that the aim of the violated provisions is to protect different interests. An act that is punishable under more than one penal provision is not likely to happen frequently. For this very reason, it will not often happen that the imposition of a sanction by one administrative authority will lead to another administrative authority imposing a sanction that would be in conflict with the prohibition of double punishment. (...) Of course this leaves unchanged the desirability of administrative authorities' aligning their sanction policies in related matters. Furthermore, Article 5:46 always provides enough scope for the mitigation of fines should the imposition of sanctions by various administrative authorities prove to be evidently unreasonable in a specific case.'[208]

Where a regulation has been set down in Article 5:43 GALA to prevent the repeated imposition of administrative fines for the same infringement, Article 5:44 GALA regulates the relationship between the imposition of administrative sanctions and prosecution under criminal law. In the Netherlands, acts can be exclusively punishable, exclusively liable to fine or both punishable as well as liable to fine. Article 5:44 codifies the principle of *ne bis in idem* in the relationship between sanctions under criminal law and under administrative law.[209]

According to the explanation with this provision, it does not just concern the fact that two punishments may not be imposed for the same infringement. 'There must also be prevention of someone being unnecessarily involved in sanction proceedings twice for the same infringement (*nemo debet bis vexari*).'[210] The choice between dealing with it under criminal law or under administrative law must become definite at a certain stage.

The framer of the explanation continues:

> 'it cannot be the case that, if the one course of action does not ultimately lead to the imposition of a sanction, the government can then simply try again by another route. Article 5:44 lays down this system of *una via* (...) in the case that the course under criminal law was initially chosen. Should the Public Prosecution Service decide to initiate prosecution under criminal law, then the course under administrative law is closed as soon as the case comes to court. Possible acquittal, a decision not to prosecute or non-admissibility of the Prosecution Service does not therefore resurrect the power to impose an administrative fine.
>
> The course under administrative law is also definitely closed when the Prosecution Service offers an out-of-court settlement and the infringer accepts this. A sanction

208 Parliamentary Documents II 2003–2004, 29 702, no. 3, p. 137; See also Draft Proposal pp. 123–124.

209 The norm could already be found in case law: HR 12 January 1999, *NJ* 1999, 289.

210 Parliamentary Documents II 2003–2004, 29 702, no. 3, p. 138; see also Draft Proposal p. 124.

has then in fact been imposed and then a second sanction for the same act should no longer be possible. However, should the Prosecution Service relinquish prosecution before the start of the hearing in court, other than because of an out-of-court settlement, then the administrative authority still has the opportunity to decide whether an administrative sanction is to be imposed.'[211]

From the explanatory notes it appears that the *Anrechnung* has also been introduced into administrative fines. This was derived from the principle of proportionality.

'An administrative authority that imposes two or more administrative fines for distinguishable but nevertheless connected infringements will have to decide whether the total amount of the fines is still in keeping with the seriousness of the infringement. Equally, an administrative authority that imposes a fine for an infringement that is connected with an infringement for which another administrative authority has already imposed a fine, or a punitive sanction has been imposed or a transaction under criminal law has taken place should take into account punishments imposed earlier by other authorities. Article 5:46 offers scope for this. Application of this Article can therefore lead to an administrative fine that is in general reasonable for the infringement in question but may be regarded as disproportionate in a specific case in connection with other punitive sanctions imposed by other administrative authorities or by authorities under criminal law for connected infringements.'[212]

If an act is both punishable under criminal law as well as liable to a fine, the competent administrative authority and the prosecution service should enter into consultations on the question whether the infringement should be dealt with under criminal or under administrative law. Article 5:44.2 GALA states that the administrative authority is in principle obliged to refer the infringement to the Public Prosecution Service. However, this is not very practical for large numbers of infringements.

'For large numbers of infringements it is not efficient (...) and it is not desirable from the point of view of consistency of policy that such consultations take place on each individual infringement. In practice for such cases, the Prosecution Service and the administration formulate criteria in mutual consultation for the choice between settlement under administrative law and under criminal law. These criteria are often set down in a covenant and/or in prosecution guidelines of the Public Prosecution Service. For this reason, the second paragraph provides that the infringement need not be referred to the Public Prosecution Service when the administration and the Prosecution Service have agreed on this. In addition, the possibility has been

211 Parliamentary Documents II 2003–2004, 29 702, no. 3, p. 138; see also Draft Proposal p. 124.
212 Parliamentary Documents II 2003–2004, 29 702, no. 3, p. 91; see also Draft Proposal p. 116.

> considered that the legislator himself formulates criteria for the choice between administrative law and criminal law.'[213]

Recently the Criminal Division of the Supreme Court published its important decision clarifying its approach to the *ne bis in idem* principle. It explicitly took all relevant provisions and treaties into account, including the GALA provisions.[214] The most relevant considerations are the following:

> 'The Supreme Court has seen that, in practice, there is a need for clarification of the criterion for the application of Articles 68 DCC and 313 DCP that has been developed in its case law with regard to "the same offence" (expressed succinctly), especially since recent statutory provisions rely to a greater or lesser extent on Article 68 DCC and/or Article 313 DCP and the relevant case law. Reference can be made here to Articles 255a and 257e, eighth paragraph, DCP with regard to the punishment order and to Articles 5:43 and 5:44 GALA with regard to the administrative fine. Moreover, recent European legal precedents on the *ne bis in idem* principle represent another underlying factor.
> All this has induced the Supreme Court to explain the applicable criterion but without the intention of introducing a substantive change. (…)
> The Supreme Court will clarify its assessment standard below, without intending to bring about any substantive change. The Supreme Court also sees no reason for any substantive alterations in the light of European case law since it cannot be said of the Dutch standard that it places too much emphasis on the review of legal elements (cf. legal ground 81 of the judgment of the ECtHR referred to elsewhere under 2.7.2 <niet te vinden?>) whereas this standard leaves sufficient leeway for what is referred to as the component relating to the offence itself. It should also be noted that the criteria applied in European case law – "inextricably linked" and "acts which are substantially the same" – cannot be solely regarded as referring to the offences, and that the Supreme Court deems that there were good reasons for the rejection of a criterion relating solely to the offence in Dutch case law because the adoption of a standard of this kind could lead to unacceptable outcomes (for example, see HR 27 June 1932, *NJ* 1932, p 1659 et seq.).
>
> In considering the question whether it is in fact "the same offence" in the situation covered by Article 68 DCC, the court needs to compare the accusation as described in the two indictments, and – in the situation covered by Article 313 DCP – the accusations described in the indictment and in the application for amendment of the indictment.
> This review needs to take the following relevant data into account as comparative factors.
> (A) The legal nature of the offences.

213 Parliamentary Documents II 2003–2004, 29 702, no. 3, p. 138; see also Draft Proposal p. 124.

214 HR 1 February 2011, *AB* 2011, 225; *JB* 2011, 56; *NJ* 2011, 394.

> If the charges do not fall within the same offence description, the degree to which the criminal offences differ may be important, especially in respect of (i) the legal interests which the respective crime definitions are aimed to protect, and
> (ii) the maximum punishments imposed for the respective offences, which maxima reflect, inter alia, the nature of the accusation and the classification as minor or serious offence.
>
> (B) The act(s) of the suspect.
>
> If the indictments or the indictment and the application for amendment of the indictment do not describe the same acts, the degree of difference between the acts may be of importance, both with regard to the nature and the apparent effect of the acts as to the time, place and circumstances under which they were committed.
>
> It should be remarked here that the wording of the concept of "the same offence" can in itself be taken to mean that the circumstances of the case partly determine the answer to the question of what this concept implies. As a rule, a significant difference in the legal character of the offences and/or in the acts can lead to the conclusion that there can be no question of "the same act" within the meaning of Article 68 DCC.'

This decision clearly shows the role the Supreme Court assumes in giving guidance not only to criminal law practice but also to administrative law practice in so far as it involves administrative fines in fields where it has no competence.

6.6. NO FINE ON DEATH[215]

Article 5:42 GALA provides that no administrative fine is applied or enforcement is continued if the infringer has died. This provision is in line with Article 69 DCC. In criminal law, Article 69 DCC also applies to juristic persons.[216] It is not apparent from the explanatory notes to the GALA penalty regime whether the legislator was aware of this.

In its judgments of 4 May 2010 and 16 June 2010,[217] the Administrative Jurisdiction Division seems to diverge unnecessarily from criminal law on this point. Both judgments of the Division relate to contested rulings of the District Court of Arnhem, in which the doctrine of the deceased juristic person was applied in penalty law; and for the first time as far as I can ascertain. The Division's judgment of 4 May 2010 relates to the contested ruling of 13 May

215 See on this theme, for example, R. Stijnen, *Rechtsbescherming tegen bestraffing in het strafrecht en het bestuursrecht*, Kluwer, Deventer 2011, pp. 549–550.

216 See *Handboek Strafzaken*, 108.5.3 and Rb. Rotterdam 7 December 1982, *NJ* 1983, 294; HR 8 March 1994, *NJ* 1994, 408; HR 24 September 2002, *NbSr* 2002, 239; *JM* 2003, 18; *NJ* 2004/186; HR 15 October 2002, *NJ* 2004, 187; HR 2 October 2007, *NJ* 2008, 550; HR 16 November 2010, *NJ* 2010, 625.

217 ABRvS 4 May2010, *AB* 2011, 14; 16 June 2010, *AB* 2011, 15.See also, more recently, ABRvS 29 June 2011, *LJN* BQ9676.

2009[218] and that of 16 June 2010 to the District Court of Arnhem's ruling of 14 May 2009.[219] The Division makes no specific mention of the doctrine of the juristic person that has ceased to exist, and so it is not known whether the Division thinks that this doctrine should also be applied in sanction law. The Division adopts the same approach as in its judgment dated 7 April 2010;[220] according to this, the legal form that is known to third parties on the day of the infringement is the determinative factor in answering the question as to the identity of the infringer, and it does not indicate whether it has to be assumed that this infringer can have died at a later date on the basis of the same information available to third parties (the inclusion in the trade registry) so that this person cannot be informed of the fine decision, or the collection of the administrative fine already imposed has to be abandoned.

7. RIGHTS OF DEFENCE[221]

7.1. INTRODUCTION

As I have stated above, the principle of defence is one of the principles of proper procedure in Dutch administrative law. As far as punitive sanctions are involved, this principle also applies in the pre-trial stage and, therefore, the principle of defence is also a principle of proper administration. For comparative reasons the right of defence, the principle of defence, is discussed in this chapter. The presumption of innocence will be discussed in par. 7.2, whereas the right to be informed will be described in par. 7.3, the right to legal representation in par. 7.4, the right against self-incrimination in par. 7.5, the right to access to the file in par. 7.6, the right to translation in par. 7.7, the right to be heard in par. 7.8, and the chapter will be closed with the description of the right to expeditious proceedings (par. 7.9), the right to an effective remedy (7.10) and the right to a reasoned decision (par. 7.11).

7.2. THE PRESUMPTION OF INNOCENCE[222]

The principle of innocence only plays a role in punitive procedures: these are procedures to which Article 6, second paragraph is applicable. The principle of

218 *LJN* BJ9058.

219 *LJN* BJ1228.

220 ABRvS 7 April 2010, *AB* 2011, 6.

221 See on this theme for example Oswald Jansen and Philip. M. Langbroek (eds.), *Defence Rights during Administrative Investigations*, Intersentia, Antwerp 2007.

222 See on this theme for example R. Stijnen, *Rechtsbescherming tegen bestraffing in het strafrecht en het bestuursrecht*, Kluwer, Deventer 2011, pp. 79–89 and 550–554.

'no punishment without guilt' is codified for the law on fines in Article 5:41 GALA.[223] The provision reads as follows:

> The administrative authority will not impose an administrative fine for the infringement if no blame can be attached to the infringer.

In infringements with a sanction under administrative law, guilt in the sense of culpability is generally not an element of the violation, and this is generally also true for violations under criminal law. In these cases also, the principle of 'no punishment without guilt' applies under criminal law, and Article 5:41 GALA provides for this in the law on fines.

> 'Similarly to criminal infringements, guilt in the sense of culpability is generally not an element of the crime in infringements with a sanction under administrative law. This means that the administrative authority need not prove culpability, but may assume this if perpetration has been definitely established. However, this leaves the principle of 'no punishment without guilt' intact even in these cases. (...) To avoid the imposition of a fine, the infringer will then have to appeal to the absence of all guilt, and make this absence convincing. This has been set down in Article [5:41].'[224]

This provision implies that the classic grounds for excluding culpability from criminal law apply here.

> 'Within the framework of this provision, it may then also be necessary to discuss the classic grounds for excluding culpability from criminal law – unreasonable use of force in self-defence, force majeure and an act in the execution of an incompetently given administrative order. In the actual practice of administrative enforcement, the last two are probably of primary importance. For the same reasons as for the grounds for justification (...) it was decided not to include a catalogue of written grounds for excluding culpability in GALA.'[225]

---

223 Perhaps it is unnecessary to say this: Dutch criminal law has no principle of law concerning punishment according to the degree of guilt, but this does seem to be the case for the law on fines. The reason for this is that the principle of proportionality implies that the severity of the sanction (usually the size of the fine) has to be tailored to the degree of culpability. According to the established case law of the Dutch Supreme Court, there is 'no foundation in law' for the argument that a punishment may not be imposed that is heavier than the guilt of the perpetrator would justify. (HR 12 November 1985, *NJ* 1986, 327 note T.W. van Veen; HR 10 September 1957, *NJ* 1958, 5). This case law has not generally been accepted as doctrine. See for example P.A.M. Mevis, *Hoofdlijnen van het strafrechtelijk sanctiestelsel*, W.E.J. Tjeenk Willink, Deventer 1997, p. 85.

224 Parliamentary Documents II 2003–2004, 29 702, no. 3, pp. 134–135; Preliminary Draft Proposal p. 121.

225 Parliamentary Documents II 2003–2004, 29 702, no. 3, p. 134; Preliminary Draft Proposal p. 121.

Even before the enactment of the Fourth Part of GALA (*Vierde tranche Awb*) the regulations on fines always provided that no administrative fine may be imposed if there is no culpability. This means that the accused can appeal on the grounds of absence of all guilt. In criminal law, this is a class of unwritten grounds for excluding culpability supplementing the grounds for excluding culpability set down in statute. In the law on fines, no single ground for excluding culpability is defined in further detail. The appeal to absence of all guilt there is comprised of the grounds for excluding culpability laid down in criminal law.

Following the ECtHR decision of 2 February 1996 in J. Murray, it is established case law in Dutch criminal law that the fact that a suspected person remains silent cannot be used as evidence. According to the same case law, this does not mean that the judge cannot value the fact that the suspected person did not give a clarifying or disculpatory explanation.[226] As far as I know this has not been decided on in administrative fine cases, but I really do not see why this rule would not be applicable there. It is not relevant in administrative law apart from administrative law relating to punitive decisions.

7.3. THE RIGHT TO BE INFORMED OF THE PROCEEDING AND ITS BASIS

The General Administrative Law Act does not provide for a general right to be informed about the results of a certain investigation. It can be argued that Dutch unwritten administrative law included the obligation to inform the citizen in certain cases about important issues touching upon his position. This is a requirement to be derived from the principle of due care (*zorgvuldigheidsbeginsel*). Specific laws provide for specific obligations to inform the citizen or the interested party.

In general the right to be informed is closely linked to the right to be heard (Article 6 ECHR). This right and some other defence rights are also applicable in the pretrial stage. Therefore and in order to ensure conformity with the demands of Article 6 ECHR, the Dutch legislator introduced some provisions in the general GALA regulation on administrative fines. These guarantees are linked to the fine report (*boeterapport*) and the announcement of the intention to impose an administrative fine (*voornemen tot het opleggen* van *een bestuurlijke boete*). These notifications that are provided for in Articles 5:48 and 5:50 GALA correspond with the right of the accused to be informed promptly, in a language which he understands and in detail, of the nature and cause of the accusation against him (Article 6, third paragraph (a), ECHR). As I have explained above,

226 HR 3 June 1997, *NJ* 584, HR 10 November 1998, *NJ* 1999, 139 and HR 1 June 2004, *NJ* 366.

the fine report is then the basis for the rights of the defence in the proceedings during the preparation of the fining decision. A number of safeguards have been built into the fining report and the heavy-fine procedure, such as the obligation to hear the defendant (Article 5:53, third paragraph in conjunction with Division 4.1.2. GALA in conjunction with 5:50 GALA), translation/interpretation and the assistance of an interpreter (Articles 5:49, second paragraph, and 5:50, first paragraph, preamble and under b GALA), a time limit of 13 weeks (Article 5:51, first paragraph, GALA) and the requirement for a separation of responsibilities (Article 10:3, fourth paragraph, GALA). A longer period of limitation applies for finable conduct that must be dealt with under the heavy-fine procedure. In short, the whole arrangement of the defence rights in the pre-trial stage hangs on the fine report.

Articles 5:48, 5:50 and 5:51 read as follows:

5:48
1. The administrative authority and the competent supervisor may draw up a report of the violation.
2. The report must be dated and state:
   a. the name of the violator;
   b. the violation and the rule infringed;
   c. if necessary, the date, time and place the violation was established.
3. A copy of the report will be sent or presented to the violator no later than the date of notification of the decision to impose the administrative fine.
4. If an investigating officer's report as referred to in Article 152 of the Code of Criminal Procedure has been drawn up of the violation, it will take the place of the report for the purposes of this part of the act.

5:50
1. If the violator has been given the opportunity to put forward his views concerning the intention to impose an administrative fine,
   a. at the same time as the invitation to express a view, the report will have been sent or distributed to the violator;
   b. the administrative authority will arrange the assistance of an interpreter, if it seems that this is reasonably required for the violator's defence.
2. If, after the violator has put forward his views, the administrative authority decides that:
   a. no administrative fine will be imposed for the violation in question, or
   b. the violation will still be laid before the Public Prosecution Service,

   the violator will be informed of this in writing.

5:51
1. If a report has been compiled, the administrative authority will reach a decision concerning the imposition of an administrative fine within 13 weeks after the report has been duly signed.

2. This period in which to reach such a decision will be suspended from the day on which the conduct has been laid before the Public Prosecution Service up to the day on which the administrative authority is competent to impose an administrative fine.

As I have explained above, according to Article 5:53 GALA the requirement to produce a report before taking and serving an administrative decision to impose an administrative fine only applies to administrative fines higher than €340, unless a specific provision states otherwise. This means that in almost all cases the heavier procedure where the production of a report is required before taking an administrative decision imposing an administrative fine applies. This also means that in most cases the defence rights attached to this report apply in this preparatory stage. As I have stated above, this makes one wonder whether a distinction should not be made between light, medium and serious procedures in the heavy procedure classification. All these procedures require a report, but in some cases it may be comparable to the simple record of a minor criminal case and in others to the voluminous master record that has been drawn up in a major criminal case.

In case law regarding the heavier procedures the following remarks of the government on the position of the fine report turned out to be rather important:

> 'The administrative report or investigating officer's report subsequently plays a significant role in the proceedings and very often serves as one of the most important items of evidence. It also provides the infringer with a substantial amount of information on the matters on which he will be required to put up a defence. The administrative report or investigating officer's report marks a demarcation line: the subsequent proceedings may only relate to those infringements on which an administrative report or investigating officer's report has been drawn up but need not, by any means, apply to all those infringements on which an administrative report or investigating officer's report has been drawn up.'[227]

Partly as a consequence of the requirements of Article 6 ECHR, the Trade and Industry Appeals Tribunal (*CBb*) made clear that the fine report must not leave any doubt in the mind of the infringer as to which infringement was committed according to the administrative authority and the basis on which these facts and circumstances were determined.[228] This means that an administrative decision imposing an administrative fine must not be based on facts and circumstances

---

227 Parliamentary Documents II 2003–2004, 29 702, no. 3, p. 151. See on this O.J.D.M.L. Jansen, De bestuurlijke boete in het financieel bestuursrecht – enkele opmerkingen, in: R.C.P. Haentjens and M. Jurgens (eds.), *Fraude op de financiële markten*, Kluwer, Deventer 2011, pp. 115–129, especially pp. 117–118.

228 CBb 2 February 2010, *AB* 2010, 317 with case note of O.J.D.M.L. Jansen. See also CBb 17 November 2004, *AB* 2005, 81 and CBb 6 November 2009, AB 2010, 215; CBb 22 January 2009, LJN BH 6932; CBb 2 July 2010, LJN BN 0534.

and other infringements than those taken into account in the fine report, not even if these facts could be found elsewhere in the dossier that the violator had enough time to study.

In some legislation in the economic field and the field of financial services, the fine report also marks the division between two phases in the preparatory stage: supervision *(toezicht)* and investigation (*onderzoek*). In this legislation, this division is also important for the way the right to remain silent and the design of the separation of responsibilities (*functiescheiding*) are arranged. This cocktail has recently brought about interesting case law.[229]

7.4. THE RIGHT TO LEGAL REPRESENTATION AND LEGAL AID

In Dutch administrative law, a guarantee is given that anyone may be assisted or represented by a legal representative in any dealings they may have with an administrative authority. If the legal representative is an attorney-at-law, administrative authorities do not have the possibility to refuse someone the right to be a legal representative in a certain dealing. The main provisions are Article 2:1 and 2:2 GALA.

2:1
1. In looking after his interests in dealings with administrative authorities, anyone may be assisted or represented by a legal representative.
2. An administrative authority may require a legal representative to produce a written authorization.

2:2
1. An administrative authority may refuse to allow assistance or representation by a person against whom there are serious objections.
2. The interested party and the person referred to in paragraph 1 shall be informed in writing of the refusal without delay.
3. Paragraph 1 shall not apply to attorneys-at-law and procurators.

In the procedure of objection against a decision, the same provisions apply as is the case with the procedure leading to a decision *in primo*. Articles 2:1 and 2:2 GALA do not apply to the procedure before an administrative court but they do have an equivalent in the regulation of this procedure The relevant provisions are Articles 8:24 and 8:25 GALA. These provisions apply both to procedures in first instance and in appeal (8:108 GALA).[230]

---

229 See CBb 6 November 2009, AB 2010, 215 and CBb 30 August 2011, LJN BR 6737 and Jansen 2011 (n. 229).

230 Before the enactment of the Act on the modification of administrative procedural law *[Wet aanpassing bestuursprocesrecht]* on 1 January 2013 the same provisions could be found in

The attorney-client privilege

According to Article 5:20.2, holders of confidential information such as attorneys are not obliged to produce information they hold on their clients. This paragraph reads as follows:

> Any person who is bound by a duty of secrecy by virtue of his office or profession or by statutory regulation may refuse to cooperate in so far as his duty of secrecy makes this necessary.

A 'legal privilege' does not generally exist in Dutch administrative law. As supplement to the provision in Division 5.2 GALA, Article 51 of the Competition Act provides for a 'legal privilege'. The government has illustrated this in the words of the Minister of Economic Affairs:

> 'Under Dutch law – both administrative law as well as criminal law – the obligation of secrecy applies only for documents that are in the possession of the holder of confidential information. I deem it desirable to make an exception to this rule in the present legislative proposal, with a view to alignment with the (...) case law of the European Court of Justice. In my opinion, it should not be the case that documents that are not allowed to play a part in an investigation instigated by the Commission might be brought in during supervision of compliance with Dutch prohibition norms. That would be thoroughly undesirable in the decentralized application of EC competition rulings.'[231]

On 1 April 2013 the Netherlands Competition Authority [*Nederlandse Mededingingsautoriteit (NMa)*], the Independent Post and Telecommunications Authority of the Netherlands [*Onafhankelijke Post en Telecommunicatieautoriteit (OPTA)*] and the Netherlands Consumer Authority [*Consumentenautoriteit (CA)*] merged into the Autoriteit Consument en Markt (ACM) (the Authority for Consumers and Markets).[232] On 15 May 2013 the governement published a legislative proposal in order to streamline the regulative powers of the new authority. According to this (Act on the ACM), the legislative proposal the *Instellingswet Autoriteit Consument en Markt* will be supplemented with a legal

---

Article 39, first paragraph, Act on the Council of State [*Wet op de Raad van State*], Article 21, first paragraph, Act on Appeals before the Central Appeals Tribunal [*Beroepswet*], Article 22, first paragraph, Act on Appeals before the Tribunal on Economic Affairs [*Wet bestuursrechtspraak bedrijfsorganisatie*] and Article 27j, first paragraph, and 29 General Act on Tax Procedure.

231 Parliamentary Documents II 1995–1996, 24 707, no. 3, p. 82. On 15 May 2013 the government presented a legislative proposal on the streamlining of the legislation applied by the new Authority for Consumers and Markets (ACM). Article 29 of this proposal provides for a legal privilege. See Parliamentary Documents II, 2012–2013, 33 622, nos. 1–3.

232 See Parliamentary Documents II 2011–2012, 33 186, no. 1–3. See also www.acm.nl and the proposed act on the streamlining of the legislation applied by the NCM (Parliamentary Documents II, 2012–2013, 33 622, nos. 1-3).

privilege (proposed Article 12g).[233] The proposed article is very similar to the previous provisions in Article 51 Competition Act [*Mededingingswet*] and 2.4, second paragraph, Consumer Protection (Enforcement) Act [*Wet handhaving consumenten bescherming*].

7.5. THE RIGHT AGAINST SELF-INCRIMINATION AND/OR THE RIGHT TO REMAIN SILENT[234]

7.5.1. Introduction

In Dutch criminal procedure law, the suspect has the right to remain silent when being questioned. The official who is putting questions to him that amount to an examination (verhoor) should point out the right to remain silent to the suspect beforehand (*caution*). This right has been defined in Articles 29 and 271 and 273 of the Dutch Code of Criminal Procedure (DCP). This arises from the principle of *nemo tenetur.* In the entirety of criminal procedure law that has been codified in the Code of Criminal Procedure, a number of other provisions have been made to do justice to this principle. Thus, it is regularly stipulated that certain demands for cooperation may not be directed at the suspect.

The right to remain silent and the caution only apply to questions that could be regarded as an examination (verhoor), in other words questions that concern the involvement of the suspect in a criminal act, and therefore the right to remain silent and the caution do not apply for other questions to the suspect. Moreover, this only applies to the suspect, i.e. the person against whom there is a reasonable suspicion, based on facts and circumstances, that he or she has committed a criminal act. Special criminal law complicates the picture even more. Obligations to cooperate which also apply to the suspect are set down here with great regularity. Yet these never infringe on the right not to incriminate oneself. It concerns other forms of cooperation, such as giving up items of property for seizure and the examination of business data and documents under criminal law.

The image of the right to remain silent is further complicated, if the distinction between supervision (*toezicht*) and investigation (*opsporing*) (the examination as a result of the reasonable suspicion that a criminal act has been committed) is included. Under administrative law, it is a principle rule that the person involved

233 See Amendment to the Act establishing the Netherlands Authority for Consumers and Markets and other acts relating to the streamlining of the market supervision to be held by the Authority for Consumers and Markets – Proposal of Act (31–5–2012), pp. 6 and 33 and the legislative proposal mentioned in the previous footnote.

234 See for example L. Stevens, *Het nemo-teneturbeginsel in strafzaken: van zwijgrecht naar containerbegrip*, Wolf Legal Publishers, Nijmegen 2005. Pages 123–143 focus on the *nemo tenetur* principle in administrative fine procedures.

should cooperate in the exercise of a power by a supervisory official (see art. 5:20 GALA). The right to remain silent derogates from the obligation to cooperate. This only applies to those questions concerning the involvement of the suspect in a criminal act. If the questions concern matters like the determination of a tax debt, the existence of the entitlement to benefit, or more generally, concern a non-punitive settlement under administrative law, then cooperation in answering the questions may not be successfully refused on the basis of an appeal to the right to remain silent. For the very reason that settlements under criminal and administrative law in regulatory law seldom follow entirely separate courses, the right to remain silent can be simply undermined. It is always a matter for the court to determine if this is so in the cases presented to it.

The picture becomes more complicated when ECtHR case law on the principle of *nemo tenetur* is considered. These complications concern the following elements. In the first place, the moment from which the principle of *nemo tenetur* enclosed in Article 6 ECHR applies is different from the moment that this is the case under Dutch law. According to Dutch law, this is from the moment that there is a reasonable suspicion that the person in question has committed a criminal act. In the case law of the ECtHR, this is a later moment; namely the moment that the State undertakes an action against the person concerned by which this person can derive the reasonable expectation that criminal proceedings are going to be instituted against him.

In the second place, the case law of the ECtHR on the scope of the principle of *nemo tenetur* is an important complicating factor. For it is a fact that this Court distinguishes between the right to remain silent and the right not to incriminate oneself. In particular, the question which forms of cooperation are protected by the *nemo tenetur* principle other than making a statement is one that is causing much thought for the practice of law. A great deal has been written about the scope of the right not to incriminate oneself but this has not yet led to a very clear consensus on the subject. One example concerns the question which arose in particular in connection with the Saunders judgment whether information that has been obtained by an administrative authority in a demand for information or inspection which falls within the obligation to cooperate (Articles 5:16, 5:17 and 5:20 GALA) may be used in a punitive procedure, i.e. a procedure which results in an administrative punitive sanction such as an administrative fine, or a procedure which can lead to a criminal sanction. Another question which has arisen, in particular after the judgment *J.B. v. Switzerland*,[235] is whether it is possible to compel cooperation for a demand for inspection with a duty backed by astreinte. This possibility occurs quite often.

235 ECtHR 3 May 2001, *AB* 2002, 343.

7.5.2. *The right to remain silent, the principle of nemo tenetur and the GALA regulation on administrative fines*

The right to remain silent and the obligation to give a caution are laid down in Article 5:10a GALA. It is a provision that holds for all punitive sanctions, not only administrative fines, and applies in both the primary decision-making phase and the objection procedure. Article 8:28a GALA sets out the judicial phase, and there the right to remain silent and the caution are restricted to the administrative fine. The right to remain silent and the caution are both linked to the oral examination and this signified a change in the penalty law for many penalty regimes, with the exception, for instance, of the examination in economic and fiscal law, as well as that in fiscal administrative law.

A logical step would be to turn to criminal case law for the interpretation of the concept 'examination' (*verhoor*): there examination is the asking of questions regarding a suspect's involvement in a criminal offence. The right to remain silent applies to questions from any official, not only from supervisors or personnel who are charged with preparing a fining decision.[236, 237]It would be incorrect to assume that only the latter group may ask questions as to the involvement of an infringer in a finable offence, although this is an attractive idea when setting up the fine investigation and the separation of functions.

If the questions concerning the involvement in a finable offence are posed at a comparatively late stage in a preparatory investigation, by presenting the infringer with already obtained evidence, for example, that questioning will often mark the start of a criminal charge. This idea is in line with the linking of the right to remain silent and the caution to the fine investigation, but such questions are, of course, often posed at an earlier stage in the investigation.

The government emphasizes that the oral examination (verhoor) is often a criminal charge and can be a starting point. The government wrote:

---

236 Parliamentary Papers II 2003–2004, 29 702, no. 3, pp. 94–95: 'The choice was to include this in title 5.1, because the right to remain silent derogates inter alia from the obligations defined in Article 5:16 in conjunction with 5:20 to provide supervisors with information. It must also be pointed out, to avoid any misunderstanding, that the meaning of the right to remain silent is not restricted to this. The right to remain silent also applies before administrative authorities and officials who are not supervisors within the meaning of Article 5:11.'

237 Some market authorities have made a link between a certain interpretation of the right to remain silent and the separation of functions. See inter alia: O.J.D.M.L. Jansen, "De bestuurlijke boete in het financieel bestuursrecht – enkele opmerkingen", in: R.C.P. Haentjens and M. Jurgens (eds.), *Fraude op de financiële markten*, Kluwer, Deventer 2011, pp. 115–129. See also the annotations under CBb 30 August 2011, *LJN* BR6737; CBb 6 November 2009, *AB* 2010,215 and CBb 9 February 2006, *AB* 2006, 292 and Jansen 2011 (*T&C Mededingingswet*), Art. 54a.

'In practice, the result will often be no different from a review against the existing wording. 'Oral examination' is, after all, an 'act from which the person involved can reasonably be expected to deduce that a fine is going to be imposed on him' and, in many cases, will be the first specific act by which the infringer is confronted with this fact.'

To my knowledge, the criminal court has only assumed that the examination (verhoor) can be a starting point, but never that this has been the case in any specific instance.[238] Recent case law on reasonable time limits has shown that the notification of an intention to impose an administrative fine is regarded, in principle, as the starting point in fine cases, and that an earlier moment can only be regarded as such in exceptional circumstances. This approach fits in with case law on criminal procedure.

In its judgment of 26 January 2011,[239] the Council of State gave its considerations on a defence of reasonable time limit, for instance:

'as a rule, the first act towards the fined person (is) [OJ] the notification of the fine defined in Article 19 *Wav* from which this person can derive the expectation that a fine will be imposed on him. In the vast majority of cases, the day this notification is given will count as the time at which the reasonable time limit referred to in Article 6, first paragraph, ECHR starts. As has been outlined in the history of the drafting of the *Wav* (Parliamentary Documents II 2003/04, 23 523, no. 3, p. 14), it cannot be ruled out that in any particular case the circumstances could arise, contrary to the basic principle given above, that before the fine notification is issued a specific act takes place with regard to the fined person by which he could reasonably foresee that a fine will be imposed on him. The mere act of giving the caution or sending a fine report is by its nature too indefinite to be classed as such an act in that context. Other than the [appellant] argues, neither the circumstance that the caution was given to [...] prior to the examination on 4 September 2007, nor the letter dated 16 June 2008 by which the fine report was sent to the [appellant], resulted in the commencement of the reasonable time limit at either of these moments.'

This approach by the Council of State and the criminal courts is also reflected in Trade and Industry Appeals Tribunal (*CBb*) case law. In its judgment dated 16 September 2010, the Tribunal considered as follows:

'The Tribunal fails to see that A reasonably formed the expectation that a fine was going to be imposed on it from the fact that it, or at least its representative, was examined concerning a violation of the Tobacco Act ascertained by an investigating

---

238 See also my annotation under Rb. Rotterdam 21 November 2005, *AB* 2006, 47.

239 ABRvS 26 January 2011 *LJN* BP2120. This is a standard finding. See, for example, before ABRvS 7 April 2010, *LJN* BM0221. In both judgments, the Division referred to the standard ruling in ABRvS 9 December 2009, *LJN* BK5859; *JB* 2010, 28; *JV* 2010, 37. See also for a comparable line CBb 16 September 2010, *LJN* BO5309.

officer, nor that it could reasonably have formed such an expectation. An examination is part of an investigation. To a person who is being examined in connection with a suspected violation of the Tobacco Act, and who is informed that he is not bound to answer the questions put to him in that connection, it will be clear that his activities are the subject of an investigation. But no conclusion as to whether the facts and circumstances that come to light during this investigation will eventually lead to the imposition of a fine can be drawn, in its generality, from the mere fact of an examination taking place. The Tribunal has found no indication that announcements were made by the investigating officer during the examination that could lead to this expectation on the part of A. Even so, even if could be assumed that pronouncements regarding the imposition of a fine were made by the investigating officer on that occasion, it is clear that the tasks and responsibilities within the Food and Consumer Product Safety Authority (VWA) are so allocated that such announcements cannot be regarded as coming from an official with the power to decide on the imposition of a fine. The investigation of which the examination, as already stated, is part results in a 'fine report'. The minister has stated, without challenge, that the report only includes a recommendation to impose a sanction; the decision of whether one will actually be imposed is taken at a different level in the organization.'[240]

In the meantime, a number of other interesting developments which are important for financial administrative law have been taking place concerning the interpretation of the right to remain silent and the caution. They relate in particular to the right to remain silent in written statements and the right to remain silent and the caution for juristic persons.

Oral or written examination: caution

The legislator has always assumed that the caution in punitive administrative law need not be given for written examinations, for example by a written demand for information.[241] In this, the legislator took HR 1 October 1985, *NJ* 1986, 405 as a point of departure, where it was considered:[242]

'According to the [legislative history], the legislator always regarded the concept of 'examination' as: an examination in which there is a confrontation between the questioner and the person questioned – and apart from the assistance of one or more interpreters – the contact between the questioned and the questioner is direct and in person, in which the questioner aims to bring about communication between him and the person being questioned during which it is expected that the former will immediately answer the questions put to him. The second full sentence of Article 29, first paragraph, DCP gives a clear, negative answer to the question which arises from this, i.e. whether – in the case of persons who can be classed as suspects within the

240 *LJN* BO5309.

241 See my annotation under CBb 2 February 2010, *AB* 2010, 317.

242 On this ruling see inter alia P.J. Wattèl, "Is een schriftelijk verhoor geen verhoor?", *NJB* 1986, p. 254.

meaning of Article 27 DCP – the person being questioned is obliged to answer the questions put to him: it reads: 'The suspect is not obliged to answer.' This provision is founded on the principle that a suspect cannot be obliged to cooperate actively in something that could lead to his conviction, except in the special cases provided for by the law. In order to prevent suspects from unintentionally cooperating in their own conviction because they do not know the statutory provision just mentioned or are not sufficiently aware of its existence during examination, a second paragraph has been added (…) which states: 'Before the examination, the suspect will be informed that he is not obliged to answer.'

[The above] leads to the view that sending questions to the suspect in writing, accompanied by a request to answer these questions – also in writing – cannot be deemed to be an examination within the meaning of Article 29 DCP since a sending of this nature falls outside the framework that the legislator had in mind for the concept of 'examination' and was a reason for adding the present second paragraph to Article 29 DCP. After all, there can be no question of a confrontation between the questioner and the questioned person (…) if questions in writing are sent and received by a person who is requested to answer those questions – also in writing. The latter is not required (…) to decide immediately, and under the psychological pressure inherent to an examination situation, whether or not he is going to answer the questions put to him but he can take some time to consider whether – and in the affirmative case how – he is going to answer the questions put to him in writing.

The last complete sentence of the third paragraph of Article 29 DCP confirms [this]: it reads: 'The information referred to in the second paragraph will be included in the official report', which provision fits within the framework of an examination as defined in 5.1.1 but does not fit within a request to answer questions that have been set out in writing and sent to the person concerned. The above considerations prompt the argument that the tenor of the second paragraph of Article 29 DCP entailing that the reply card sent to the suspect should have stated that the suspect was not obliged to give a (written) statement – cannot in fact be accepted.'

The GALA legislator also assumes that the caution should, in principle, be given only for oral examinations. The government considers in the explanatory notes as follows:

'The obligation to give a caution applies in the case of an examination. An examination is a oral questioning with a view to the imposition of a punitive sanction. The background to the obligation to give a caution may be inferred from the experience that an oral examination can exert a certain psychological pressure to answer. The caution is intended to prevent the person questioned from providing statements under this pressure which can no longer be said to have been given freely. Written questions exert much less pressure to answer because there is no direct confrontation with the questioner. It is not generally an examination if the questions are in writing and the caution is therefore not required. This is only otherwise if, in exceptional circumstances, a written question creates such pressure to answer that it is substantively an examination.'

The government assumes correctly that the right to remain silent applies in both oral and written examinations, and yet it has stated first and foremost that a caution need only be given for oral examinations, and only in special circumstances for written examinations.

Case law seems to have superseded this government view, and rightly so. In a number of rulings, the Criminal Division of the Supreme Court has determined that the right to remain silent (and therefore the caution as well) also applies to written demands.[243] In doing so, the Supreme Court has interpreted the concept of 'examination' with which the GALA legislator sought alignment.

The Trade and Industry Appeals Tribunal (*CBb*) recently went a step further by assuming that the obligation to give a caution also applies to written demands if the legislator has explicitly restricted these to oral statements. After the Tribunal had established that there was a suspicion at the time of the written demand, and the demand was directed at the punishment of the suspect, it considered as follows:

> 'In the opinion of the Tribunal, OPTA failed to inform Tele2 of this in the letter dated 7 May 2007 in violation of the provisions in the second complete sentence of Article 15.6 Telecommunications Act (*Tw*) (old). It is certainly true that this provision only prescribes that the caution should be given before requesting information orally but in the view of the Tribunal, this prescription should be understood to mean that the natural person or juristic person with regard to whom the situation referred in the first complete sentence of the above article applies under circumstances should also be informed of the right to remain silent before those concerned are asked for information in writing. The Tribunal is of the opinion that such circumstances apply here, since Tele2 was obliged, in accordance with Article 18.7, second paragraph, *Tw*, to give the information demanded by OPTA under Article 18.7, first paragraph, *Tw* in a letter dated 7 May 2010 and, consequently, it must be assumed that this demand put such great pressure on Tele2 to give a statement in writing that Tele2 found itself in a situation that could be compared substantively with an examination intended to acquire information orally.'[244]

I am not aware of any comparable judgments by other courts of appeal in administrative law and it will be a question of waiting and seeing whether case law will continue to develop along these lines.

---

243 HR 29 October 1996, *NJ* 1997, 232 and HR 21 October 1997, *NJ* 1998, 173. See also Schalken's annotation under HR 22 November 1994, *NJ* 1995/240, and also *Handboek Strafzaken*, 20.7, 20.9 and 108.7.5, as well as O.J.D.M.L. Jansen, 'Het zwijgrecht van ondernemingen in het Nederlandse boeterecht', *Tijdschrift voor onderneming en strafrecht* (TOS) 2004, pp. 67–77.

244 CBb 2 February 2010, *AB* 2010, 317.

Right to remain silent for juristic persons

The right to remain silent applies to both natural persons and juristic persons. This leads to the following particular question of law for juristic persons, one which seems to have received little attention in criminal procedural law: which natural person can invoke this right to remain silent on behalf of the juristic person.[245] The right to remain silent in competition law has not been brought in line with the GALA fine system on this point. It is still granted to the person who gives a statement 'on the part of the company' with regard to the infringement (Article 53 Competitive Trading Act (*Mw*)). On the basis of this, the Rotterdam court ruled that this right to remain silent can be invoked by any natural person appointed by the juristic person or ordered by the supervisor to give a statement on the part of the juristic person.[246]

With Article 5:10a GALA, the legislator has linked the right to remain silent to the examination and, by doing so, conferred a right to the juristic person under suspicion, but has not explicitly granted this – as in competition law – to every person who gives a statement on the part of the juristic person. In a number of recent rulings, the Council of State seems to grant the right to remain silent exclusively to the board of directors of a juristic person.[247]

An interesting question is whether the right of the juristic person to remain silent also applies to employees[248] to whom the demand for information has been directly addressed, and not by way of the juristic person. This concerns information about the involvement of the juristic person for whom the natural person is working.[249] If the employee involved is a director or works manager of

245 See inter alia my extensive annotation on this point under District Court Rotterdam 7 August 2003, *AB* 2004, 92; A.R. Hartmann and M.E. de Meijer '*De personele werkingssfeer van het zwijgrecht en de cautieverplichting bij de verdachte rechtspersoon*', *NJB* 1996, pp. 1768–1773; J.A.W. Lensing, *Het verhoor van de verdachte in strafzaken*, Gouda Quint, Arnhem 1988, p. 143; R.A. Torringa, *Strafbaarheid van rechtspersonen*, 1984, pp. 134–135, J. Wortel, *De onderneming in het strafrecht*, 1987, p. 96 and A.L.J. van Strien, *De rechtspersoon in het strafproces*, 1996, pp. 166–174 and 186–190.

246 Rb. Rotterdam 28 November 2003, *AB* 2004, 102; Rb. Rotterdam 7 August 2003, *AB* 2004, 92 and O.J.D.M.L. Jansen, 'Het zwijgrecht van ondernemingen in het Nederlandse boeterecht', *Tijdschrift voor onderneming en strafrecht* (TOS) 2004, pp. 67–77.See also Rb. Rotterdam 11 July 2006, *AB* 2007, 35 and ABRvS 3 May 2006, *AB* 317 (with note O.J.D.M.L. Jansen).

247 ABRvS 27 January 2010, *AB* 2010, 48 and ABRvS 9 December 2009, *LJN* BK5835; ABRvS 17 June 2009, *LJN* BI8490.

248 One variation on this is whether the claims may also be addressed to former employees. This question has led to two recent rulings by the Rotterdam District Court, in which the Court assumed that former employees are not entitled to remain silent. Rb. Rotterdam 9 June 2011, *LJN* BQ7658 and *LJN* BQ7633). See also the decisions of the Board of the NMa of 7 May 2010 in cases 6719 and 6622 (decisions on the objection of the primary decisions of 10 November 2009 in case 6719 and 9 July 2009 in case 6622. Meanwhile the CBb has decided that former employees have a right to remain silent, which is derived of the right of the suspected legal person they used to work for (CBb 21 December 2012, LJN BY 7031 and LJN BY 7026).

249 The supervisor has the power to demand information not only from juristic persons but also from employees and third parties, for example accountants. The principle of proportionality

the juristic person concerned, and is therefore authorized to decide on the question whether the juristic person is incriminated by his statement or not, this person is able to exercise the right to remain silent for the juristic person. But this is a relatively small circle of people. Other employees of the juristic person do not have the right to remain silent on behalf of the juristic person. They are 'witnesses'.[250]

As I have outlined above, three authorities have merged into the *Autoriteit Consument en Markt* (ACM).[251] The government published a legislative proposal in order to streamline the regulative powers of the new authority. According to this proposal the Act on the ACM (*Instellingswet Autoriteit Consument en Markt)* will be supplemented with an extension of the GALA provision on the right to remain silent (Article 5:10a). According to the proposed article 12i the right to remain silent will also be applicable to those making statements from the side of the company other than the legal representatives of the company.[252]

The nemo tenetur principle and forms of cooperation other than giving statements[253]

As we have seen above, the question resulting from ECtHR case law as to which forms of cooperation are protected by the *nemo tenetur* principle other than making a statement is one that is causing much thought for the practice of law. At the same time, case law shows that without an explicit legal provision Dutch criminal and administrative courts are reluctant to grant an appeal to the *nemo tenetur* principle where other forms of compulsory cooperation are involved than giving statements.[254] These cases involve, for example, the obligation to hand over objects for seizure by the police and the judicial authorities,[255] and the obligation to cooperate in the inspection of documents.[256] In a decision on a tax matter of 8 March 2002,[257] the Supreme Court ruled that the obligation to give

(Article 5:13 GALA) regulates the supervisor's choice of addressing the demand to employees. The consequences of a demand of this nature are of great importance for the position of those employees.

250 The apostrophes here indicate that witness refers only to those persons who have an obligation to appear as a witness before a judge (or before a parliamentary committee of inquiry).

251 See Parliamentary Documents II 2011–2012, 33 186, no. 1–3. See also www.acm.nl.

252 See Amendment to the Act establishing the Netherlands Authority for Consumers and Markets and other acts relating to the streamlining of the market supervision to be held by the Authority for Consumers and Markets – Proposal of Act (31–5–2012), pp. 7 and 35–36 and Parliamentary Documents II, 2012-2013, 33 622, nr. 2, p. 7 and nr. 3, p. 10-11.

253 See R. Stijnen, *Rechtsbescherming tegen bestraffing in het strafrecht en het bestuursrecht. Een rechtsvergelijking tussen het Nederlandse strafrecht en bestraffende bestuursrecht, mede in Europees perspectief*, Kluwer, Deventer, 2011, p. 83–89 and Albers, *Rechtsbescherming bij bestuurlijke boeten. Balanceren op een magische lijn?*, pp. 135–137.

254 This seems to be in line with ECtHR 29 June 2007, *NJ* 2008, 25, *O'Halloran en Francis vs. UK*.

255 HR 29 October 1996, *NJ* 1997, 232.

256 HR 21 October 1997, *NJ* 1998, 173.

257 HR 8 March 2002, *AB* 2002, 353.

grounds in an appeal against the decision to impose an administrative fine of an administrative authority is in itself not a breach of the *nemo tenetur* principle. If the grounds of the decision are short and vague, the grounds of the appeal can be short as well.

7.6. THE RIGHT OF ACCESS TO THE FILE

In order to better understand the right to access to a file, it is important to make a distinction between 'external openness' (*externe openbaarheid*) and 'internal openness' (*interne openbaarheid*). The Public Access Act [*Wet openbaarheid van bestuur*] provides for a regulation of external openness. The regulation of internal openness in administrative law is complicated. There is no general right of access to a file in the procedure preparing a decision in administrative law, except for the procedure to impose an administrative fine. Article 5:49 reads as follows:

1. On request, the administrative authority will allow the violator to inspect the information on which the fine or proposed fine is based and to take copies of this information.
2. In so far as reasonably required for the violator's defence, the administrative authority will ensure as far as possible that this information is communicated to the violator in a language which he understands.

Article 7:4 GALA obliges the administrative authority to deposit the notice of objection and all other documents relating to the case for inspection by interested parties for a period of not less than one week prior to the hearing in the procedure. According to the sixth paragraph of this Article, the administrative authority may refrain from depositing documents for inspection in so far as there are compelling reasons of secrecy. These reasons may involve privacy and company secrets.

Comparable provisions can be found in the regulation of the procedure before an administrative court. These provisions in Article 8:28–8:32 also apply to appeal procedures and, according to Article 8:108 GALA, to appeals to a higher court.

The translation of documents has barely been regulated in Dutch administrative law. Citizens have no general right to have full translations of these documents. In general, administrative authorities are not obliged to do more than a brief summary interpretation (*vertolking*) of the contents. The question has already been raised whether this practice is too limited in the light of Article 6 ECHR.

It is not possible to base a decision on information that has not been available to an interested party. This applies to administrative procedures involving both *civil rights and obligations* and *criminal charges* according to Article 6 ECHR.

7.7. THE RIGHT TO TRANSLATION DURING THE PROCEEDING

Written Dutch administrative law does not recognize a general right to translation (*vertaling*). The regulation of the procedure in administrative courts has a general provision on interpreters in Articles 8:35 and 8:36 GALA. This provision applies to higher appeal as well (Article 8:108 GALA).

Article 5:50 GALA provides for a general provision which applies in all procedures where the imposition of administrative fines is involved. This Article reads as follows:

1. If the violator is given the opportunity to express a view on the intention to impose an administrative fine,
   a. the report will be sent or presented to the violator at the same time as the invitation to express a view;
   b. the administrative authority will provide for the assistance of an interpreter if this is reasonably necessary for the violator's defence.
2. If, after the violator has expressed his views, the administrative authority decides:
   a. not to impose a fine for the violation, or
   b. to submit the violation to the public prosecutor after all, it will inform the violator of this in writing.

In an interesting competition law case the CBb decided that the Dutch Competition Authority had to provide for the full translation of the inventory list of documents that are part of the proceedings in order to enable the German speaking party to decide which documents they would like to have translated.[258]

7.8. THE RIGHT TO BE HEARD

The scope of the right to be heard in Dutch administrative law depends on the phase in the procedure and, at least in the procedure to prepare a decision, on the kind of decision. The right to be heard is rather limited in the procedure preparing a decision *in primo* (see Articles 4:7–4:12 GALA). This choice of the legislator is closely related to the broader right to be heard in the objection

[258] CBb 19 January 2009, LJN BH 0436.

procedure (*bezwaarschriftprocedure*) (see Article 7:5 and 7:13 GALA).[259] The idea is that the objection procedure will be used to repair mistakes made in the first phase. In the first phase, in particular, the function of the obligation to hear the citizen or the interested party is not primarily intended to act as a right of defence but its function is more that of the gathering of relevant facts.

In the decision-making procedure, administrative authorities have limited obligations to hear interested parties. The obligation is seen as a specific requirement deriving from the principle of due care (*zorgvuldigheidsbeginsel*). In other words, this obligation does not have the purpose of guaranteeing a defence right. The main provisions are Articles 3:2 and division 4.1.2 GALA.

If the administrative authority intends to impose a sanction or measure on someone, i.e. the interested party, it will in most cases be obliged to give him or her the opportunity to state his or her views. This obligation is related to the intention to make a decision, not on the outcome of some investigation. This means that this obligation only applies towards the end of a procedure. The citizen or the interested party has the right to choose whether he or she will be heard orally or in writing (Article 4:9 GALA). It is up to the administrative authority to decide what form the oral hearing will take. In some cases, a phone call may be sufficient. In others, a formal hearing would be more appropriate.

As administrative fines are financial decisions in the sense of Article 4:12 GALA, an exception is made to Division 4.1.2 in order to ensure that the interested party has a broader right to be heard in procedures involving administrative fines. The obligation of administrative authorities to hear an interested party when it intends to impose an administrative fine is no longer only to promote a careful preparation of decisions, but is now aimed at guaranteeing a defence right. This is to ensure that the procedure to impose administrative fines will be in conformity with the demands of Article 6 ECHR.

In the primary phase, a right to receive minutes of the hearing does not exist. In most cases, administrative authorities will refer to the hearing in the decision that has been taken after the hearing. In any case, the citizen does not have the right to approve the minutes as it is the administrative authority that is responsible for writing them. The letter of the interested party or his or her representative to comment on the minutes of the hearing will be added to the dossier. The administrative authority can, of course, change the minutes as a result of the comments of the citizen, but he or she just does not have the right to approve them.

As we have just seen, the right to be heard is broader and stronger in the objection procedure. Key provisions are Articles 7:2 and 7:3 GALA. It is

[259] See on this Philip M. Langbroek e.a., *Designing Administrative Pre-trial Proceedings*, Boom Juridische Uitgevers, Den Haag, 2013.

established case law that the exceptions of Article 7:3 shall be administered with reticence.[260]

7.9. THE RIGHT TO EXPEDITIOUS PROCEEDINGS

In Dutch administrative law a great deal of attention is currently being paid to prompt expedition of procedures. The right of a citizen to expeditious proceedings is generally recognized and there is also a legal framework of time limits arranged for in various laws. GALA also provides the possibility of addressing a judge to exhort the administration to make the decisions asked for within this time limit, and the like. This legal framework was changed rather dramatically recently with the introduction of an advanced and detailed legal system of time limits, including exceptions to these time limits (Article 4:13–4:15 GALA), a system of periodic penalty payments to be paid by the administrative authority to the applicant involved if this authority fails to decide in time (Articles 4:17–4:20 GALA), a regulation of the positive notional decision (*positieve fictieve beschikking*) (Articles 4:20a-4:20f GALA), and a fast and direct appeal to the administrative court without hearing (Article 8:55b-8:55f GALA) with the power of the court to impose periodic penalty payments on the administrative authority. In the light of the subject of this book, it is not possible to elaborate on this subject here.[261]

The requirement ensuing from Article 6 ECHR, both in procedures concerning criminal charges and civil rights and obligations, for a citizen to have his case dealt with within a reasonable time directly applies to almost all administrative law. There is detailed and complicated case law on this subject as well as the well-established and refined decision-making practice of the National Ombudsman and comparable complaints commissions. The administrative courts have developed established and detailed case law which sets out what should be considered the reasonable period of time for the most common administrative procedures according to Article 6 ECHR and the different stages within this procedure (complaints, appeal and higher appeal). If these time limits have not been complied with, the appellant [*appelant*] can claim damages to a fixed amount of €500 for

260 I should mention that the Act on the modification of administrative procedural law *[Wet aanpassing bestuursprocesrecht]* modified these rules. It is now possible not to organize a hearing session if the interested party has declared not to be interested in a hearing or if this party did not respond to the administrative authority's request to state his wishes in his respect. This act entered into force on 1 January 2013.

261 See on this Oswald Jansen (eds.), *Silence of the Administration in the EU*, Intersentia, Antwerp (forthcoming) and Oswald Jansen *et al.* (eds.), *Fictitious Decision Making in the EU*, Intersentia, Antwerp (forthcoming).

each period of six months that the reasonable time limit has been exceeded.[262] If the procedure involves an administrative fine instead of a sum in damages, the fine will be decreased by a fixed percentage up to a maximum amount.[263]

Comparable with many other regulations on decision-making procedures, the general GALA regulation on administrative fines prescribes a time limit for decisions on the imposition of an administrative fine. The relevant provision is article 5:51 GALA. This Article reads as follows.

1. If a report has been compiled, the administrative authority will reach a decision concerning the imposition of an administrative fine within 13 weeks after the report has been duly signed.
2. The period in which to reach such a decision will be suspended from the day on which the conduct has been laid before the Public Prosecution Service up to the day on which the administrative authority is competent to impose an administrative fine.

It is established case law that this time limit of 13 weeks is not a very hard limit, as exceeding this limit has no legal consequences.

7.10. THE RIGHT TO AN EFFECTIVE REMEDY

Under the Dutch written constitution, there is no general right to an effective remedy. Articles 6 ECHR and 47 CFR are the most important constitutional bases for this right. Although the definition of *civil rights and obligations* is rather complicated in administrative law, as not all administrative law can be considered as civil rights or obligations, it is generally recognized that the principle applies in all administrative law.

Generally speaking in administrative law, there are only remedies against orders defined in Article 1:3 GALA, which are not a generally binding regulation (*algemeen verbindend voorschrift*) or a policy rule.[264] The regular remedies apply to administrative decisions imposing administrative sanctions but remedies during the administrative investigations and against decisions or acts of inspectors are not easily available. It is almost generally accepted that written

262 I should mention that these damages do not limit the possibility of obtaining damages on the basis of the consequences for the person or company involved for having had to wait so long for a decision.

263 In a few cases concerning competition law fines the CBb applies a reduction of 10–15%, and a maximum amount of €10,000–15,000 (see CBb 25 March 2011, *LJN* BQ5977 and CBb 18 November 2010, *LJN* BO5193, and Jansen 2011, *T&C Mededingingswet*, p. 198).

264 This system becomes more and more contested in Dutch administrative law. See as a strong example F.J. van Ommeren *et al.*, *Het besluit voorbij*, Boom Juridische Uitgevers, Den Haag 2013.

requests from inspectors to provide information and to which citizens have to reply due to their duty to cooperate should be considered an order. The highest administrative court in economic affairs, the Trade and Industry Appeals Tribunal, has however decided that these requests are not orders,[265] and has been heavily criticized for this established case law. There is no established case law on the part of the other administrative courts.[266] In an increasing number of acts administrative authorities are given the power to impose administrative sanctions on the infringement of the duty to cooperate. The normal remedies against these administrative decisions apply, and there is an increasing body of case law on those kinds of decisions.

If administrative courts cannot offer an effective remedy, this does not mean that citizens cannot find a remedy elsewhere. In Dutch administrative law, the civil courts offer a general safety net. This possibility is often used in practice, and also in cases involving acts of inspectors in administrative investigations. Civil courts are reluctant to interfere in the interests of the administration to investigate a case for obvious reasons, but still offer an effective remedy. In so far as acts during administrative investigations are concerned, it should not be forgotten that the person concerned always has the possibility to use a remedy against an order to complain about acts during the investigation phase. This may possibly lead to an order being quashed due to a breach of the principles of due preparation (*zorgvuldigheidsbeginsel*) and of stating reasons (*motiveringsbeginsel*), for example.

In addition to the remedies offered by administrative courts and civil courts, the remedies offered by the *National Ombudsman* and comparable complaints commissions have some importance. Roughly speaking, a citizen can complain to the administrative authority to which the inspector or administrative investigator belongs and follow an *internal* complaints procedure. After that it is possible to address the *National Ombudsman*. Chapter 9 GALA contains a general regulation of the procedure at the *National Ombudsman* and at other *external* complaint commissions. The National Ombudsman and special complaints commissions do not have any competence to conduct a legal act in response to a complaint.

7.11. THE RIGHT TO A REASONED DECISION

One of the functions of administrative investigation is to prepare decisions, for example the decision to take measures or to impose sanctions. These decisions are orders (*besluiten*). According to Article 3:46 GALA, an order must be based upon sound reasons and, as a rule, these reasons should be stated when the order is notified. This article is part of a general regulation of stating the reasons for

265 CBb 21 July 1998, *AB* 1998, 437; *AB Klassiek* 32; CBb 2 March 1999, *AB* 1999, 168.

266 See Van Wijk/Konijnenbelt & Van Male 2011, p. 427.

decisions that is set out in Division 3.7 GALA, which consists of Articles 3:46 to 3:50 GALA.

The regulation for stating reasons in GALA is limited to decisions as defined in Article 1:3 GALA. It is generally assumed, though, that in addition to this regulation the unwritten form of the principle of stating reasons regulates other forms of administrative action. This may be found, for example, in reports of the National Ombudsman and of comparable complaints commissions.

Since the enactment of the fourth part GALA contains some specific rules for stating the reasons for decisions imposing sanctions, that is for imposing enforcement action (*last onder bestuursdwang*), periodic penalty payments or an *astreinte* (*last onder dwangsom*) and an administrative fine (*bestuurlijke boete*). These provisions apply in addition to the general provisions on stating reasons. The provisions are Articles 5:9 and 5:52 GALA. They read as follows:

> 5:9 The decision to impose an administrative sanction will state the following:
> a. the violation as well as the regulation violated;
> b. if necessary, an indication as to where and when the violation has taken place

> 5:52 The decision to impose an administrative fine will state:
> a. the name of the violator;
> b. the amount of the fine.

The report or the dossier resulting from an administrative investigation should enable administrative authorities to explain the facts and interests that have led to a decision. Therefore a breach of the principle of due preparation (*zorgvuldig onderzoek*) (Article 3.2 GALA) will also lead to a breach of the principle of stating reasons. The reasons stated in the decision are not only necessary to explain decisions to citizens and the persons concerned but also for citizens so that they can prepare their defence. Of course, administrative authorities are not allowed to withhold important facts and reasons.

8. ORGANIZATION OF SANCTIONING POWERS

According to Article 113, first paragraph, of the Dutch Constitution, the trial of criminal acts is entrusted to the judiciary. Few authors have discussed the question whether this provision means that administrative authorities are allowed to impose administrative sanctions with a deterrent aim.[267] It is generally understood that the imposition of sanctions by administrative authorities, the Office of the Public Prosecutor (OM) included, is not contrary to

267 See mainly P.A.M. Mevis, *Constitutioneel Strafrecht*, Deventer: Kluwer 1998, pp. 29–30 and L.J.J. Rogier, *Straffend bestuur*, Arnhem: Gouda Quint 2001, pp. 8–10.

this constitutional provision. As soon as sanctions that would deprive a person of their liberty are involved, they should be imposed by judges. As the constitution does not provide otherwise, these sanctions could also be imposed by other courts than the criminal courts. The *Öztürk* case brought the constitutional rule into the Dutch legal order that the imposition of deterrent sanctions by administrative authorities is possible as long as there are effective remedies against these decisions with independent courts and certain (criminal law) defence rights apply.

As we have seen above, the power to impose administrative fines is now entrusted to many different kinds of administrative authorities at the central state level, and to municipalities and independent authorities.

In order to achieve a separation of responsibilities (*functiescheiding*), Article 10:3, fourth paragraph, GALA limits the possibilities of granting a mandate (*mandaat*) to officials working at an administrative authority. This provision, that only applies if the heavy procedure applies (see Article 5:53 GALA), reads as follows:

> If Article 5:53 is applicable, a mandate to impose an administrative fine will not be given to the same person who drew up the administrative report or investigating officer's report.

In criminal procedures there is a separation of responsibilities between criminal investigation (police), prosecution (OM) and the imposition of a penal sanction by a court. When administrative authorities impose administrative fines, all these powers and responsibilities are combined within one authority. GALA provides for a limited separation as the provision cited above only results in a division between the investigation on the one hand and the imposition of the administrative sanction on the other hand.

The AFM and the ACM (the authority resulting from the merger of NMA, OPTA and the Consumer Authority) are examples of authorities that maintain a stricter separation, also referred to as *Chinese walls*. These authorities distinguish between inspection (*toezicht*), investigation (*onderzoek*) and the imposition of an administrative sanction, in most cases an administrative fine. This distinction is strengthened by the way in which incriminating statements are treated. If it is decided that there will be preparations for the imposition of an administrative sanction, any incriminating statements will be removed from the dossier and the remaining files will be transferred to the officers entrusted with the task of preparing the administrative decision.[268] In an important case, the Trade and Industry Appeals Tribunal (*CBb*) decided that these incriminating statements

---

268 This careful practice is based upon a risk analysis of the ECtHR *Saunders* case.

that have been removed from the file should be part of the dossier that administrative authorities have to send to the courts when an appeal is launched.[269]

9. INVESTIGATION/INSPECTION

Title 5.2 of GALA has general provisions on inspection. These provisions apply to any natural person appointed as supervisor (*toezichthouder*) according to Article 5:11 GALA. The power of an administrative authority to appoint a supervisor must be provided for by law (statutory regulation).

The supervisors appointed by any administrative authority will in principle have all the powers made available to them under this Title. The supervisors are therefore authorized to demand information (Article 5:16 GALA), as well as to inspect business information and documents (Article 5:17 GALA). They may enter premises, except for private homes, without permission from the occupant (Article 5:15 GALA) and may in principle examine goods (Article 5:18 GALA). Private homes are an exception to this. The supervisors must identify themselves on request on the basis of Article 5:12 GALA. Explicit authorization such as is required for officials of the Commission to enter premises is not required under Dutch law. Finally, they have several powers available to them concerning means of transport and their drivers (Article 5:19 GALA). Apart from those people entitled to remain silent (not obliged to give evidence) everyone is obliged to cooperate with the supervisor while he exercises his authority (Article 5:20, first paragraph, GALA). The supervisor can derive powers of requisition from the above obligation to cooperate in support of the other powers available to him.

The restrictions deriving from the principle of proportionality that is codified in Article 5:13 GALA for enforcement supervision apply to these powers. The provision fulfils an important role as a safeguard against restrictive infringements of the free legal sphere of the citizen. It replaces a large number of provisions which could previously be found in special legislation. Examples of this include recurrent passages such as 'in so far as it is reasonably necessary for the fulfilment of his function' or 'in so far as this is necessary to fulfil his function according to his reasonable judgment'. The principle of proportionality codified in Article 5:13 applies restrictions to the person subject to the power of supervision (the person involved, the third party), and to the modality of

---

269 CBb 6 November 2009, *AB* 2010, 215. See on this O.J.D.M.L. Jansen, "De bestuurlijke boete in het financieel bestuursrecht – enkele opmerkingen", in: R.C.P. Haentjens and M. Jurgens (eds.), *Fraude op de financiële markten*, Deventer: Kluwer 2011, pp. 115–129. For a moment (19 May 2005) the Ministry of Finance even had the intention to tighten the separation of responsibilities for financial authorities and to introduce a General Council within the authority that would be responsible for the decision to impose an administrative fine. See Parliamentary Documents II, 2004–2005, 30 125, no. 2.

execution (the supervisor must opt for the least damaging way of exercising authority). The principle can lead to general restrictions (certain powers may never be lawfully exercised) and special restrictions (the power can never be exercised lawfully in certain cases).[270]

The scope of the power to enter premises

The power of supervisors to enter premises without the permission of the occupant is restricted to premises other than private homes. The legislator must explicitly grant the power to enter private homes without the occupant's consent to the supervisor in order that he may exercise his powers. In the exercise of the power to enter premises, the supervisor may not go any further than looking around, possibly searchingly. The power may not have the implication of a thorough search. In established case law, the Supreme Court described 'house searching' (*huiszoeking*) as 'systematic and directed investigation'.[271] It involved such things as opening cupboards, drawers and clocks and breaking goods. Every investigation that amounts in fact to this is an investigation that goes further than just looking round, possibly searchingly; it is a thorough searching (*doorzoeking*). A thorough search (*doorzoeking*) requires an explicit formal legislative foundation. The legislator regards thorough searching as a power that should be reserved exclusively for criminal law.[272]

In criminal procedure law, a distinction is made between 'looking around searchingly' (*zoekend rondkijken)* and 'thorough searching' (*doorzoeking*).[273] The concept of 'house searching' that was included in the Code of Criminal Procedure was replaced by the concept of 'thorough searching' (*doorzoeking*) from 1 February 2000 onwards.

The difficult distinction between 'looking around searchingly' (*zoekend rondkijken*) and 'thorough searching' (*doorzoeking*) is made rather more complicated in the provision for enforcement supervision in Title 5.2 GALA. Title 5.2 GALA contains several 'quasi powers for thorough searching'. The premises to be entered are often ones that can be examined under the power of Article 5:18 GALA. In the government's view, examining the hygienic state of kitchen cupboards and the kitchen equipment in them is not thorough searching but only an investigation of goods within the meaning of Article 5:18 GALA. This opinion is wrong.[274] The powers in Article 5:19 GALA to examine a means

270 See for more detail: O.J.D.M.L. Jansen, *Het handhavingsonderzoek. Behoren het handhavingstoezicht, het boeteonderzoek en de opsporing verschillend te worden genormeerd? Een interne rechtsvergelijking*, PhD thesis, Ars Aequi Libri, PhD thesis, Nijmegen 1999, pp. 167–174.

271 Standard judgment is HR 28 May 1985, *NJ* 1985, 822.

272 Parliamentary Documents II 1995/96, 24 617, no. 3, p. 8. See for the act mentioned: M.M. Slotboom, *De wet uitvoering EG mededingingsverordeningen*, SEW 1998, pp. 96–100.

273 HR 28 May 1985, *NJ* 1985, 822.

274 This is an opinion I base on HR 21 December 2010, AB 2011,293, note O.J.D.M.L. Jansen.

of transport or the cargo looks very similar to a power to search thoroughly. The power to examine goods includes that of opening packaging.

Under Dutch law, only private homes are protected under the Constitution (Article 12 Constitution). These constitutional guarantees are elaborated on in the General Act on Entry into Private homes [*Algemene wet op het binnentreden (AWBi)*]. In this act, a number of other special premises are given protection, such as the meeting room of the representative body of the people during the meeting. Article 8 ECHR also protects certain other premises, such as premises that may be regarded as a 'home' or 'domicile'. From the judgments in *Niemetz* and *Chapell* it appeared that the ECHR also regards certain business premises as a 'home' in the sense of Article 8 ECHR. This line of approach was confirmed with the judgment in *Colas Est*[275] given in a French case on competition law. This judgment also contained the decision that the constitution applies not only to natural persons but also to juristic persons. In its judgment of 22 October 2002 in *Roquette Frères*, the European Court of Justice sought for connection with *Colas Est*.

In the Netherlands, particularly as a result of *Colas Est*, a number of questions have been raised that are of great importance for the power to enter under the Competition Act. One of these questions concerns the question whether supervisors and investigators are still entitled to enter business sites and premises without previous authorisation by a court. Another question is whether the same safeguards should be applicable for business premises as for private homes.

I am of the opinion that *Colas Est* does not necessitate a change of regulations.[276] There is almost always a legal base available to enter buildings and for every power to enter premises in enforcement supervision there is the principle of proportionality (Article 5:13 GALA). This principle should be applied by the courts and the supervisors involved in the same way as the principle of proportionality in Article 8, paragraph 2, ECHR. If this principle is applied strictly, previous authorization by the court is probably not required to enter business premises and property.

The scope of Title 5.2

Many laws entrust an administrative authority with the power to appoint supervisors. Title 5.2 does not apply to control activities in the field of taxation. The State Taxes Act [*Algemene wet inzake rijksbelastingen (AWR)*] explicitly exempts this section (Article 1, fourth paragraph) but this does not mean that the tax authorities have no monitoring powers. The State Taxes Act provides for them itself.

275 ECtHR 16 April 2002, AB 2002, 277 note O.J.D.M.L. Jansen.
276 O.J.D.M.L. Jansen in his note under this judgment AB 2002, 277.

The scope of Title 5.2 even extends the field of supervision and even of administrative law, as in many special laws, the powers provided for in this title have been made applicable to criminal investigation. The wording of the powers granted in the regulation of criminal investigation in the Economic Offences Act has been formulated almost identically to that of the comparable supervisory powers in Title 5.2 GALA.

10. LEGAL PROTECTION

10.1. INTRODUCTION: THE GENERAL SYSTEM

In the Dutch law on administrative procedure, it is the general pattern that someone who wants to take up arms against a decision must first lodge an objection (*bezwaar*) with the administrative authority that has taken the contested decision. After the decision on the objection (*beslissing op bezwaar*) has been taken by the administrative authority, appeal (*beroep*) can be lodged with the court. The regional courts of first instance are divided into a number of divisions, for example the criminal division and the administrative division. The administrative division is responsible for administering administrative law. The judges sitting on this bench are all independent of authorities and legislation and are members of the judiciary. Appeals against the judgment of one of these regional courts in the Netherlands can be lodged with one of the highest administrative judges: the Administrative Jurisdiction Division of the Council of State, the Central Appeals Tribunal or the Trade and Industry Appeals Tribunal.[277] The choice of which is the highest administrative judge with whom appeal can be lodged depends on the matter of the appeal. Since the enactment of the Act on the modification of administrative procedural law [*Wet aanpassing bestuursprocesrecht*] (on 1 January 2013), an appendix lists the acts that are within the competence of the Central Appeals Tribunal and the Trade and Industry Tribunal. The remaining acts automatically fall within the competence of the Council of State.[278] The Central Appeals Tribunal (*Centrale Raad van*

[277] It is sufficient here to mention the three most important administrative courts which fit in with the standard model described. Appeal in tax matters is entrusted to the tax chamber of the Courts of Appeal. The highest administrative court in tax matters is the tax division of the Netherlands Supreme Court. In the law on traffic fines, there is also a deviation from standard procedure: there is administrative appeal to the public prosecutor, appeal to the sub district court and appeal to the Court of Appeal in Leeuwarden. The system of legal protection against administrative fines imposed by municipalities following infringements relating to nuisance in public areas [*overlast in de openbare ruimte*] follows the system of traffic fines. Up until now these last provisions have no practical relevance at all, as municipalities do not use them.

[278] Article 9, 10 and 11 of Appendix 2. This Appendix is based upon the new Articles 8:5, 8:7, 8:7, 8:105 and 8:106 GALA.

Beroep) decides on social questions (benefits, pensions and civil service matters), the Trade and Industry Appeals Tribunal (*College van Beroep voor het bedrijfsleven)* on economic administrative matters and the Administrative Jurisdiction Division (*Afdeling bestuursrechtspraak*) often on environmental matters and environmental planning. In an appendix to this contribution a schedule is published on the organization of the Dutch system of legal protection since 1 January 2013. In the following paragraph I will discuss the latest important developments in Dutch administrative procedure law.

Chapters 6, 7 and 8 of the General Administrative Law Act contain the provisions for administrative procedure. Chapter 6 contains general provisions relating to objections, administrative appeals and appeals to the administrative courts. Chapter 7 contains provisions concerning objections and administrative appeals and Chapter 8 outlines appeal to the administrative courts.[279] Almost all of these provisions also apply to appeal to a higher court (8:108 GALA).

In economic administrative law – as in environmental law and environmental planning law – it is often the case that appeal may be lodged directly and in only one instance to the highest administrative court, contrary to the standard procedure just described. In the case of economic administrative law, this is the Trade and Industry Appeals Tribunal. The introduction of administrative fines in economic administrative law meant that the government wanted to introduce a system of legal protection with two bodies in order to comply with Article 15 ICCPR.[280] The Competition Act was the first law that brought this about. The court of first instance in competition law is the Rotterdam court Administrative Division) – in other words the other regional courts are not competent – the highest court is the Trade and Industry Appeals Tribunal.

Under Dutch law, it is the case that the administrative court and not the criminal court provides legal protection for sanction decisions, including the administrative fine, and it is this court that is obliged to apply laws of administrative procedure and not of criminal procedure. See on this in more detail above (paragraph 5.8) and below (paragraph 10.3).

10.2. RECENT REFORMS OF ADMINISTRATIVE PROCEDURE

Two acts have changed the system of legal protection and the law of administrative procedure considerably. These are the Act on the reform of the judicial map [*Wet*

279 This applies for the special procedures mentioned in the previous footnote.

280 Probably needless to say: this system applies for all decisions, not only decisions on fines.

herziening gerechtelijke kaart] and the Act on the modification of administrative procedural law [*Wet aanpassing bestuursprocesrecht*]. At the end of this paragraph I will briefly discuss the intention of the government to merge the three highest courts in administrative law cases and the discussion to leave the system of the appeal against an administrative act as entrance to the court.

Act on adjusting the judicial map

The Act on the reform of the judicial map changed the organisation of the courts on 1 January 2013 and 1 April 2013.[281] The 19 former regional courts (*rechtbanken*) are merged into ten regional courts (new Article 1 of the Judiciary (Territorial Division) Act). The five former appeal courts [*gerechtshoven*] have been reduced to 4 appeal courts. This act also changes the organization of the districts [*arrondissementen*] which determines the territorial competence [*relatieve competentie*] of the regional courts.[282] This also had consequences for the territorial competence of the appeal courts as the competence of these courts is based directly upon the competence of the regional courts.[283] The area of jurisdiction of the appeal courts [*ressort*] is based directly upon the district [*arrondissement*] of the regional courts. A diagram of the new organization is added as appendix to this contribution.

The Act on the modification of administrative procedural law [Wet aanpassing bestuursprocesrecht]

The Act on the alteration of administrative procedural law (*Wet aanpassing bestuursprocesrecht*) is the second important legislative change I should briefly discuss in this analysis. According to this act, four groups of alterations were made. The first group consists of changes that had the purpose of streamlining the existing law on administrative procedure [*bestuursprocesrecht*] and enhancing the effective and final resolution of administrative law disputes. The second group of changes have a more technical character. These changes will have the effect that the procedural law of the courts of appeal in administrative law will no longer be provided for in the respective institutional acts. Since 1 January 2013 GALA provides for the same procedural law for all administrative courts, both the courts of first instance and the courts of appeal and highest courts. The third group of changes redistributed the competences of Council of State (*Raad van State*), the Trade and Industrial Appeals Tribunal (*College van Beroep voor het bedrijfsleven*) and the Central Appeals Tribunal (*Centrale Raad van Beroep*). The fourth group of

---

281 Staatsblad 2012, 666 and 667.

282 The court districts [*arrondissementen*] are defined by referring to the territories of municipalities and provinces. See Articles 4 to 13 Judiciary (Territorial Division) Act [*Wet op de rechterlijke indeling*].

283 See Articles 14 to 17 Judiciary (Territorial Division) Act.

changes transferred the provisions required to implement Regulation 2003/1 from the Competition Act to GALA.[284]

The first group of changes have a more substantive character. As it will exceed the purpose of this analysis to discuss even these important changes to Dutch administrative procedural law, I will limit myself to a short list of these alterations:[285]

- The possibility of taking new or altered decisions into consideration in an existing administrative procedure will be streamlined;
- The possibility of passing over shortcomings of an administrative decision whenever interested parties are not affected is increased;
- The provisions on the hearing of interested parties in the procedures following an objection, an administrative appeal and a complaint is altered;
- The possibility of creating a grand chamber to take important guiding decisions in the highest administrative courts is introduced;
- The possibility of delivering independent opinions (*het nemen van onafhankelijke conclusies*) in important issues at the administrative courts of highest instance is introduced. The first advocaat-generaal bestuursrecht (advocate-general administrative law) prof. Rob Widdershoven was appointed on 1 January 2013;
- The possibility of cross-appeal [*incidenteel hoger beroep*] will be introduced. This part has not yet been enacted;
- The administrative courts of highest instance will be granted the power to determine that an administrative decision which has to be taken following its decision can only be challenged by appeal to itself (excluding the regular possibility of an appeal to the courts of first instance) (the 'judicial loop' ['*judiciële lus*'];

10.3. INSTITUTIONAL GUARANTEES IN THE APPLICATION OF CRIMINAL LAW ISSUES BY ADMINISTRATIVE AND CRIMINAL COURTS

Above we have seen that the legislator, legal precedents and legal assistance providers try to seek the greatest possible alignment with criminal law when applying penalty law. In this respect, it concerns the application of criminal procedural precedents in an administrative court. In the Netherlands, there are no institutional guarantees of uniformity in punitive public law just as, at the moment, no institutional guarantees of uniformity can be demanded within the highest

[284] See Parliamentary Documents II 2009–2010, 32 450 no. 3, pp. 2–3.
[285] See Parliamentary Documents II 2009–2010, 32 450 no. 3, pp. 2–3.

courts of administrative law (Central Appeals Tribunal, the Trade and Industry Appeals Tribunal, the Tax Division of the Supreme Court and the Administrative Jurisdiction Division of the Council of State) or – with regard to the interpretation of statutory provisions – between the administrative, criminal or civil courts.[286]

Courts are able to rule on certain questions in punitive administrative law – more concerned with generalities and principles – in a three-judge division, the necessary criminal law knowledge for which – in so far as necessary – can be drawn from the criminal division or be contributed by deputy judges.[287] Informal 'sanction chambers' could also be constituted in this way. If such chambers were to come into being solely for the harmonization of punitive penalty law and criminal law, I wonder whether a similar construction might also be necessary for other areas, such as the alignment between administrative and civil compensation law, tax law and administrative law, or between the application of regulations concerning the collection of administrative monetary claims, the collection of criminal monetary claims and civil law. I have the impression that the judiciary has some experience of putting such chambers together.[288] This also seems to be the case for the most senior judges: two justices were recently appointed as extraordinary justices to the Administrative Jurisdiction Division of the Council of State, and a number of State councillors and justices in the appeal court have been appointed deputy judges in one or other of the appeal courts. If I see things correctly, no appeal judges have been attached to the Council of State as justices.[289]

It can now be ascertained that the Supreme Court – or the Procurator General, at least – is using its powers to foster legal uniformity in punitive public law.[290]

286 The President of the Administrative Jurisdiction Division of the Council of State cited several examples of rulings which expressed the uniformity of the administration of justice in administrative law (*Rechtspraak als collectief goed*, *NJB* 2011, pp. 1602–1607, esp. p. 1607, note 2).

287 Where this would be opportune, criminal divisions of district courts could 'fly in' expertise in the field of administrative or fiscal law in a similar way, for example for economic criminal cases or fraud cases. I understand that this is fairly regular practice at some courts, but the picture differs from court to court.

288 It may be superfluous to mention here that the presidents of the higher courts of appeal deputize in each other's courts. The President of the Administrative Jurisdiction Division is not yet a deputy justice in another appeal court, but a number of State Councillors do deputize in other courts of appeal.

289 The unwitting outsider may surmise from this that the Administrative Jurisdiction Division sees itself as a higher court of appeal than the Central Appeals Tribunal and the Trade and Industry Appeals Tribunal, and the Supreme Court sees itself as a higher court than the Administrative Jurisdiction Division.

290 See the important conclusion of AG Knigge of 8 March 2011, *LJN* BP6878 followed by the important rulings HR 12 July 2011, *LJN* BP6878; AB 2011, 312 (Article 1, second paragraph, DCC) and HR 1 February 2011, *LJN* BM9102; *NJ* 2011, 394; *AB* 2011, 225 (*ne bis in idem*).

An important issue here is the Act on the modification of administrative procedural law I have just described, which includes the introduction of the option of one grand chamber (consisting of five judges) for appeals, as put forward in Article 8:10a, fourth paragraph, GALA, alongside the present options of single-judge and three-judge divisions. A chamber of this kind could be composed of members from each appeal court and a representative of the Supreme Court. Mention should also be made of the introduction (in Article 8:12a GALA) of the option of appointing a member of the administrative appeal courts on appeal to give an opinion in a certain case during a hearing before a three-judge division or grand chamber. A grand chamber of this nature could be appointed to rule on certain aspects in the field of punitive administrative law.

The most far-reaching alternative in creating institutional uniformity would be the abolition of the remnants of the French *dualité des jurisdictions* in the Netherlands and the ending of the dichotomy between the administrative system of legal protection and the 'normal' one (i.e. civil, criminal and fiscal). This would signify the creation of the possibility of an appeal in cassation before an administrative division of the Supreme Court, and this would establish not only the appeal in itself but it would also give shape to the appeal to a higher court within the ordinary judicature (administrative divisions of the appeal courts or a separate administrative court of appeal). This would mean that the Council of State would lose its law-dispensing function entirely, and the Central Appeals Tribunal and the Trade and Industry Appeals Tribunal would both cease to exist. Under this system, legal uniformity would eventually fall into the hands of the Supreme Court. This development would reflect the situation in a number of other EU countries, such as Spain, but it still seems very much a dream for the future.

In 2011 a majority in Parliament expressed its opinion that the judicial tasks should be taken away from the Council of State.[291] At first, the Government informed Parliament that it will not do so.[292] The new government, though, has the intention to merge the three highest administrative courts into a new administrative High Court. In May 2013 the Council for the Judiciary (Raad voor de rechtspraak) published a position paper expressed the Council's preference for a new administrative High Court apart from the current Council of State while transferring the judicial tasks from the Council of State to the new Highest Court.

In 2008, Van Ettekoven suggested that the office of the Procurator General at the Supreme Court be supplemented by a division of administrative-law oriented

291 Parliamentary Documents II 2011/2012,33 000 33 000 VII, no. 54.
292 Parliamentary Documents II 2011/2012, 32 450, no. 18.

advocates general.[293] They could then give their independent findings in any of the highest bodies.[294] To my mind, this is a much better arrangement than the one now proposed. Moreover, these advocates general could also serve in the Supreme Court and, in this way, make a real contribution to the greater legal uniformity that is necessary. These advocates general could also be recruited not only from the group of State councillors and justices in the appeal court but also from among practising lawyers and academics.[295]

Ettekoven also proposes that appeal in cassation to the Supreme Court be introduced for punitive administrative law, in order to ensure that the criminal-law concepts that have a role there are construed uniformly, and this would certainly go some way towards legal uniformity. The system of legal protection has, however, become so complicated and includes numerous one-off proceedings and separate courses of justice that, for this reason alone, this proposal should be rejected unless an administrative division of the Supreme Court is established, which would not only safeguard legal uniformity in applying criminal-law concepts, but also that of other sanctions law, and even the rest of administrative law such as, for example, the interpretation of the legislation and rules whose infringement leads to a finable act.

11. NATIONAL AND EUROPEAN/INTERNATIONAL MUTUAL ASSISTANCE OF ADMINISTRATIVE SANCTIONS

As seems the case in many EU Member States, the doctrine of private international law and of international criminal law is much more developed than a doctrine of international administrative law.[296] In Dutch law, very little

---

293 B.J. van Ettekoven, "Rechtseenheid en de advocaat-generaal in het bestuursrecht", *NJB* 2008, pp. 14–18. See also his "Rechtseenheid vanuit het perspectief van de rechtbanken. Over de toekomstige organisatie van de bestuursrechtspraak", in: T. Barkhuysen *et al.*, *Bestuursrecht harmoniseren: 15 jaar Awb*, BJu, The Hague 2010, pp. 281–297.On the proposal to have an administrative advocate general, see also M. Scheltema, "Nieuwe perspectieven voor rechtseenheid in het bestuursrecht", *NTB* 2010, pp. 219–220.

294 Scheltema points out of the possibility of appointing an advocate general as State Councillor Extraordinary, a post which could promote legal uniformity in the fields of the Supreme Court (Scheltema refers in particular to private law and criminal law). This is certainly a practical idea and therefore attractive, but preference should be given to a fundamental institutional division between decisions and eliciting decisions with conclusions from one or more independent advocates general.

295 These two groups could be established by appointing them as deputy justices or State Councillors Extraordinary, but this would be more difficult for the lawyers. The problem could be sidestepped by appointing them as advocate general and not as judge, justice or State Councillor at the same time.

296 And yet, in Germany and France, there are some closely connected recent developments. See Eberhard Scmidt-Aβmann, "Principles of an International Order of Information", in: Gordon

study is focused on the issue of mutual cooperation in administrative matters in legal scholarship on general administrative law,[297] nor is it discussed in the general handbooks on administrative law. A general regulation of mutual administrative assistance is lacking in GALA: in the parliamentary history of the Third Part of GALA (derde tranche Awb) the government wrote that the time is not ripe to have a general regulation on this issue. I estimate that the provisions in the Services Directive and the Dutch Services Act [Dienstenwet] on mutual administrative assistance could put this issue on the agenda of general administrative legal scholarship due to the broad range of these provisions.

Along the decision making spectrum, the substance of mutual administrative assistance could be divided into the exchange of information, cooperation in the service of documents such as administrative decisions, cooperation in the execution of administrative decisions and cooperation in sanctioning.[298]

Anthony et al. (eds.), Values in global administrative law, Hart Publishing, Oxford 2011, p. 124; Eberhard Schmidt-Aβmann, "Die Herausforderung der Verwaltungsrechtswissenschaft durch die Internationalisierung der Verwaltungsbeziehungen", Der Staat 2006, p. 327; Eberhard Schmidt-Aβmann, "The Internationalization of Administrative Relations as a Challenge for Administrative Law Scholarship", German Law Journal 2008, p. 2067; Markus Glaser, Internationale Verwaltungsbeziehungen, Mohr Siebeck 2010; Christoph Möllers et al. (eds.), Internationales Verwaltungsrecht, Mohr Siebeck, Tübingen 2007. As far as France is concerned I would like to point to the meetings Jean-Bernard Auby had organized on themes such as 'Problèmes d'extraterritorialité et de transnationalité en droit admnistratif comparé, européen et global', 'extraterritorialité et droit public' and 'A propos de situations de transnationalité intéressant le droit administratif.' Papers of these meetings can be collected via http://chairemadp.sciences-po.fr/fr/evenements/index.htm.

297 See Julian J.E. Schutte, "La coopération administrative", in: Mireille Delmas-Marty, Quelle Politique Pénale pour l'Europe, Paris: Economica 1993, pp. 194–210; J.A.E. Vervaele, "Horizontale, verticale en diagonale samenwerking tussen administratieve organen", in: J.W. van der Hulst (ed.), Administratieve bijstand in de EG, Arnhem: Gouda Quint 1995, pp. 5–17 and in the same book N. Verheij, "Internationale administratieve bijstand en Nederlands bestuursrecht", pp. 89–96; A.H. Klip and J.A.E. Vervaele, "Supranational rules governing cooperation in administrative and criminal matters", in: John Vervaele, André Klip (eds.), European Cooperation between Tax, Customs and Judicial Authorities, The Hague: Kluwer Law International 2001, pp. 7–47; P. Boswijk, O.J.D.M.L. Jansen and R.J.G.M. Widdershoven, *Transnationale samenwerking tussen toezichthouders in Europa*, Utrecht/Den Haag 2009; P. Boswijk e.a., "De wettelijke implementatie van administratieve samenwerking in de Europese Unie", *RegelMaat* 2009, pp. 322–339.

298 See on this, for example, Florian Wettner, "Das allgemeine Verfahrensrecht der gemeinschaftsrechtlichen Amtshilfe", in: Eberhard Schmidt-Aβmann and Bettina Schöndorf-Haubold, Der Europäische Verwaltungsverbund, Mohr Siebeck, Tübingen 2005, pp. 181–212; and his "The general law of procedure of EC mutual administrative assistance", in: Oswald Jansen and Bettina Schöndorf-Haubold (eds.), European Composite Administration, Intersentia, Antwerp 2011, pp. 307–333; O.J.D.M.L. Jansen, "108.15 Rechtshulp en wederzijdse administratieve bijstand", in: Handboek Strafzaken (loose-leaf) and Oswald Jansen, "The systems of International Cooperation in Administrative and Criminal Matters in relation to Regulation EC 1/2003", in: Gerhard Dannecker and Oswald Jansen (eds.), Competition Law Sanctioning in the European Union, Kluwer Law International, The Hague 2004, pp. 257–304.

Although cooperation in sanctioning could also be considered to be part of the other issues, I argue that sanctioning should form a category of its own.

Transnational cooperation on control[299]

EU law has many examples of obligations that are imposed on Member States to ensure the effectiveness of EU law by means of inspection. Many of these inspection or control activities need cooperation and mutual administrative assistance, both vertically with the European Commission and horizontally with the authorities of another Member State. Three kinds of control models can be distinguished in EU law:

- *national control*, according to which each Member State takes enforcement action on its own territory;
- *home state control*, according to which the Member State or country of origin takes enforcement action. This model requires mutual administrative assistance between the administrative authorities of the home state and other Member States;
- *network control*, according to which joint enforcement action is taken relevant Member States. This model requires a flexible division of competence of the administrative authorities of Member States.[300]

Sanctions

In theory both remedial sanctions and deterrent sanctions can have a transnational legal effect in three ways.[301] The decision imposing the sanction can have a legal effect abroad, the decision to impose the sanction can be addressed to someone who has his legal residence abroad and thirdly the decision imposing an administrative sanction can have transnational legal effect as a result of the fact that the administrative authority imposing the

299 See on this, for example, Oswald Jansen, "Het Europees en internationaal overheidscomposiet", in: H.R.B.M. Kummeling et al. (ed.), *De samengestelde Besselink. Bruggen bouwen tussen nationaal, Europees en internationaal recht*, Wolff Legal Publishers, Nijmegen 2012, pp.133–134; J.H. Jans et al., *Inleiding tot het Europees bestuursrecht*, Ars Aequi Libri, Nijmegen 2011, pp. 238–242 and Antje David, "Inspections as an instrument of control of implementation in the European composite administration", in: Oswald Jansen and Bettina Schöndorf-Haubold (eds.), *European Composite Administration*, Intersentia, Antwerp 2011, pp. 357–381; A.M. Keessen, *European Administrative Decisions*, Europa Law Publishing, Groningen 2009, pp.76–77; 86–88.

300 A.M. Keessen, *European Administrative Decisions*, Europa Law Publishing, Groningen 2009, p 77.

301 I am using here a distinction made by Matthias Ruffert, Der transnationale Verwaltungsakt, Die Verwaltung 2001, pp. 453–485 and Matthias Ruffert, "European Composite Administration: The transnational administrative act", in: Oswald Jansen and Bettina Schöndorf-Haubold (eds.), European Composite Administration, Intersentia, Antwerp 2011, pp. 277–306.

administrative sanction itself is in another jurisdiction than that of the home state.

Let me give an example. An administrative authority that discovers the import of waste into the European Union, and the subsequent transport of this waste through a number of EU Member States can impose an administrative sanction ordering the company that is responsible to take the waste back to the state of dispatch. According to Article 26 Regulation 259/93 on the supervision and control of shipments of waste within, into and out of the European Community, this waste should be taken back by the company or, if necessary, by the competent authority itself. In national legislation this could take the form of enforcement action or periodic penalty payments.

Enforcement action will have extraterritorial effect as it involves the transport from the state of discovery of the illegal traffic via one or more EU Member States to a State outside the EU. In order to make this transport possible, the assistance of the competent authorities of the transit states is necessary. Therefore, the Regulation I just mentioned obliges those states and authorities to cooperate with the transport. According to Article 26, second paragraph, Regulation 259/93, no Member State of dispatch or Member State of transit shall oppose to the return of this waste at the duly motivated request of the competent authority of destination and with an explanation of the reason.

The *astreinte* will also have extraterritorial effect, especially when the company involved will not follow up the order given by the administrative authority of destination. The result of this refusal is that a public law debt to pay the penalties arises that has to be recovered abroad.

As the other contributions in this book show, in many legal systems in the European Union, the Dutch one included, administrative authorities are entrusted with the power to impose administrative fines. In economic and tax matters, for example, as well as matters concerning financial services, administrative fines will be imposed on companies based abroad. Already, the servicing of the administrative decisions imposing the administrative fine have transnational legal effect. The recovery of the administrative fine abroad is only possible with sufficient basis in a EU regulation or international treaty.

The private international law possibilities of recovering sums of money transnationally, such as the Brussels II Convention,[302] do not apply, as debts deriving from periodic penalty payments, *astreintes* or administrative fines imposed are debts which arise from an act of a public authority and they are therefore not a civil and commercial matter. Thus, in order to recover *astreintes*

302 Regulation 44/2001 on jurisdiction and the recognition and enforcement of judgments in civil and commercial matters, OJ L 12, 16.1.2001, p. 1.

and fines transnationally, international or European public law provisions are needed.[303] Unfortunately, even in EU law an effective general system of the recovery of these kinds of public law debts is lacking. Only in a few specific areas has a system of recovery been provided for. An important example of such a specific system is provided for by Directive 2010/24/EU concerning mutual assistance for the recovery of claims relating to taxes, duties and other measures.[304] This directive is implemented in the Netherlands by the act concerning mutual assistance for the recovery of claims relating to taxes and several other claims in the European Union 2012 (*Wet wederzijdse bijstand in de Europese Unie bij de invordering van belastingschulden en enkele andere schuldvorderingen 2012*) which was enacted on 1 January 2012. Article 2, second paragraph, of this Directive explicitly defines the scope of the provisions on mutual assistance to administrative penalties, fines, fees and surcharges related to the claims the Directive is aimed at.[305]

Framework Decision 2005/214/JHA on the application of the principle of mutual recognition relating to financial penalties, implemented by the Dutch Act relating to the mutual recognition and enforcement of criminal sanctions 2008 (*Wet wederzijdse erkenning en tenuitvoerlegging strafrechtelijke sancties 2008*) shows the shortcomings of the available systems of mutual cooperation as far as administrative fines are concerned. These provisions on mutual assistance only apply to decisions issued by another authority than a court if the fine involves acts which are punishable under the national law of the issuing State by virtue of being infringements of the rules of law and if the person concerned has had an opportunity to have the case tried by a court having jurisdiction in particular in criminal matters. The exception is adjusted to the German system of *Ordnungswidrigkeiten* (translated as: 'punishable acts by virtue of being infringements of the rules of law'). Unfortunately, as the country analyses in this book show, in most cases legal protection against decisions to impose an administrative fine is offered by administrative courts. Therefore, the facilities offered by this framework decision cannot be used by most systems of administrative fining in the EU.[306]

303 See Oswald Jansen, The system of international cooperation in administrative and criminal matters, in: Gerhard Dannecker and Oswald Jansen (eds.), *Competition Law Sanctioning in the European Union*, Kluwer Law International, The Hague 2004, pp. 259–260.

304 This Directive repealed Directive 2008/55, which was a codification of the amendments of Directive 76/308.

305 See also Article 1, second paragraph (d) Wet wederzijdse bijstand in de Europese Unie bij de invordering van belastingschulden en enkele andere schuldvorderingen 2012.

306 See Oswald Jansen, "The system of international cooperation in administrative and criminal matters", in: Gerhard Dannecker and Oswald Jansen (eds.), *Competition Law Sanctioning in the European Union*, Kluwer Law International, The Hague 2004, p. 302.

The Framework decision I have just mentioned fits in the tradition of agreements on mutual assistance in criminal matters. Therefore, the imposition of deterrent sanctions by a criminal court is considered to be the general rule, whereas the imposition of these sanctions by administrative authorities is seen as an exception which should remain restricted.

At the same time, agreements on mutual assistance in administrative matters are lacking. As far as they do exist, they are scarcely ratified. Clearly the development of national sanctioning systems has advanced much more than the development in international and EU instruments required for the effective imposition of administrative sanctions.

The Dutch government has explicitly recognised this problem as well as a small number of administrative authorities such as the AFM and ACM.[307] Therefore, one of the criteria for the legislator in choosing between the criminal law system and the administrative law system to impose deterrent sanctions is the need for transnational recovery.

BIBLIOGRAPHY

C.L.G.F.H. Albers, *Rechtsbescherming bij bestuurlijke boeten*, The Hague: SDU 2002.

C.L.G.F.H. Albers, 'De bestuurlijke boete. Magische lijn of hellend vlak?', *JBPlus* 2000, pp. 138–152.

C.L.G.F.H. Albers, 'De bestuurlijke boete in de gemeentelijke praktijk; straffen en gestraft worden', *Gst.* 2002, 7178, pp. 637–647.

C.L.G.F.H. Albers en R.J.N. Schlössels, "De bestuurlijke boete: een koekoeksei in het bestuursprocesrecht?", *NTB* 2002/7.

C.L.G.F.H. Albers 'De 'beginselplicht' tot handhaving. Een stoelendans tussen bestuur en rechter?', *Gst.* 2004, 7206, pp. 233–244.

C.L.G.F.H. Albers, "De bestuurlijke boete en het bestuursprocesrecht. De verschraling van een goede strafvordering", *DD* 2006/2.

C.L.G.F.H. Albers, "De bestuurlijke boete onder het juk van het bestuursprocesrecht", *JBPlus* 2006/4, pp. 143–161.

C.L.G.F.H. Albers, 'De Wet OM-afdoening. Nagel aan de kist van de bestuurlijke boete?', *Gst.* 2008, 70, pp. 333–344.

C.L.G.F.H. Albers, 'De intrekking van de begunstigende beschikking bij wijze van sanctie', *NTB* 2009, pp. 173–184.

J.J. Bade en L.H. Waller, "Basic Instinct", in: T. Barkhuysen, W. den Ouden and J.E.M. Polak (ed.), *Bestuursrecht harmoniseren: 15 jaar Awb*, The Hague: Boom Juridische uitgevers 2010, pp. 503–518.

307 See Parliamentary Documents II 2005–2006, 30 699, no. 3, p. 5.

M. Bakker, J. Langeveld, M.G.J. Maas-Cooymans, H.F.T. Pennarts, C.N. van der Sluis, *Vierde tranche Algemene wet bestuursrecht (bestuurlijke handhaving). Praktische handreiking, parlementaire geschiedenis en strafrechtelijke jurisprudentie*, The Hague: Sdu 2010.

T. Barkhuysen, *Het EVRM als integraal onderdeel van het Nederlandse materiële bestuursrecht*, in *VAR-reeks* 132, The Hague 2004.

T. Barkhuysen, W. den Ouden, and J.E.M. Polak (ed.), *Bestuursrecht harmoniseren: 15 jaar Awb*, The Hague: BJu 2010.

T. Barkhuysen and A.W. Bos, "De betekenis van het Handvest van de Grondrechten van de Europese Unie voor het bestuursrecht", *JBPlus* 2011/1, pp. 3–34.

T. Barkhuysen and B.J. van Ettekoven, "De compensatie voor schending van de redelijke termijn van art. 6 EVRM door de bestuursrechter", *NTB* 2009/16, pp. 129–141.

G.J.M. van den Biggelaar, *De buitengerechtelijke afdoening van strafbare feiten door het openbaar ministerie*, Arnhem: Gouda Quint 1994.

A.B. Blomberg and F.C.M.A. Michiels, *Handhaven met effect*, The Hague: VUGA 1997.

A.B. Blomberg, *Integrale handhaving van milieurecht* (diss. VU), The Hague: BJu 2000.

A.B. Blomberg, G.T.J.M. Jurgens and F.C.M.A. Michiels, *Handhaving van het milieurecht onder de Vierde tranche Awb*, The Hague: Publicatiereeks Milieubeheer 2001, no. 11.

A.B. Blomberg, 'De gevolgen van de Vierde tranche Awb voor de handhavingspraktijk', *BR* 2005, 190.

A.B. Blomberg, 'Herstelsancties en hun effectuering onder de Awb', in: T. Backhuysen (e.a.), *Bestuursrecht harmoniseren: 15 jaar Awb*, The Hague: BJu 2010, pp. 487–502.

M.J. Blotwijk, "Compliance door publicatie", in: M. Jurgens en R. Stijnen (ed.), *Compliance in het financieel toezichtrecht*, Deventer: Kluwer 2008.

P.W.S. Boer and D.R.P. de Kok, 'Nieuwe keuzes tussen strafrechtelijke en bestuurlijke sancties', *NJB* 2009, 551.

P. Boer and Y. van Setten, 'Bestuurlijke boete en strafbeschikking: de oplossing voor de overlastproblematiek in uw gemeente?', *Gst.* 2008, 71.

A.J. Boorsma and K. Wilkeshuis, 'Actuele ontwikkelingen op het terrein van de bestuurlijke boete', *Tijdschrift voor Financieel Recht* 2011, no. 1/2, pp. 18–26.

J.T.K. Bos, *De bestuurlijke boete. Raakvlakken van bestuurs- en strafrecht, preadvies VAR 1995*, Alphen aan den Rijn 1995.

C.H. Brants and R. de Lange, *Strafvervolging van overheden*, Kluwer: Deventer 1996.

H.E. Bröring and H.K. Naves, 'Waarborgen bij bestraffende bestuurlijke sancties: onvoltooid bestuursrecht', in: T. Backhuysen (e.a.), *Bestuursrecht harmoniseren: 15 jaar Awb*, the Hague: Bju 2010, pp. 449–467.

H.E. Bröring and F.R. Vermeer, 'De functionele dader in het bestuurlijke sanctierecht', *JBPlus* 2003, pp. 124–139.

H.E. Bröring, Rationele "willekeur". Enkele opmerkingen over discretionaire boetebevoegdheden, inaugural speech Groningen 2005.

H.E. Bröring, *De bestuurlijke boete*, Deventer: Kluwer 2005.

H.E. Bröring and G.T.J.M. Jurgens, 'De bestuurlijke boete is zo gek nog niet!', *NTB* 2006, 48.

H.E. Bröring and N.K. Naves, "Waarborgen bij bestraffende bestuurlijke sancties: onvoltooid bestuursrecht", in: T. Barkhuysen, W. den Ouden, and J.E.M. Polak (ed.), *Bestuursrecht harmoniseren: 15 jaar Awb*, The Hague: BJu 2010, p.

Y. Buruma, *De strafrechtelijke handhaving van bestuurswetten*, Arnhem: Gouda Quint 1993.

P.J.J. van Buuren, G.T.J.M. Jurgens and F.C.M.A. Michiels, *Bestuursdwang en dwangsom*, Deventer: Kluwer 2005.

C.P.M. Cleiren, *De beginselen van een behoorlijke procesorde*, Arnhem: Gouda Quint 1989.

Commissie ter bestudering van de fiscale controlemiddelen (commissie Duk), *De controlemiddelen van de fiscus, Geschriften van de Vereniging voor Belastingwetenschap* no. 175, Deventer: Kluwer 1988.

Commissie bestuursrechtelijke en privaatrechtelijke handhaving, *Handhaven op niveau*, Deventer: W.E.J. Tjeenk Willink 1998.

Commissie heroverweging instrumentarium rechtshandhaving, *Het recht ten uitvoer gelegd*, The Hague 1995.

G.J.M. Corstens, *Een stille revolutie in het strafrecht*, Arnhem: Gouda Quint 1995.

G.J.M. Corstens, 'Bestuurlijke boeten in de vierde tranche Awb', *NJB* 2000, pp. 1185-1190.

J.H. Crijns, 'Rationaliteiten achter de Wet OM-afdoening' in: C.P.M. Cleiren *et al.*, *Op zoek naar samenhang; Het algemeen kader herziening strafvordering nader beschouwd*, Deventer: Kluwer 2006, pp. 51-70.

J.H. Crijns, 'Het wetsvoorstel OM-afdoening: een wolf in schaapskledij', *Sancties* 2004, 4.

J.H. Crijns, 'Een terugtocht van de politie uit de openbare ruimte? Over de consequenties van de bestuurlijke strafbeschikking en de bestuurlijke boete overlast in de openbare ruimte voor de taak en de positie van de politie', *Strafblad* 2010, 6, pp. 376-386.

L.J.A. Damen, Nicolaï, J.L. Boxum *et al.*, *Bestuursrecht. Deel 1*, The Hague: Centraal Boekhuis 2009.

G. Dannecker and O. Jansen (eds.), *Competition Law Sanctioning in the European Union. The EU-Law Influence on the National Law System of Sanctions in the European Area*, Kluwer Law International 2004.

A.E.A. Danopoulos & D. van Tilborg, 'Notenkraker: "Naming and Shaming" door de OPTA: kunnen nog niet onherroepelijk geworden boetes openbaar worden gemaakt?', *Tijdschrift voor Toezicht* 2011, 2.

H. de Doelder and L.J.J. Rogier (ed.), *Opstellen over bestuursstrafrecht*, Arnhem: Gouda Quint 1994.

H. de Doelder, M.E. de Meijer, D. Otto (ed.), *De bestuurlijke boete in perspectief*, Arnhem: Gouda Quint 1999.

H. de Doelder & L.J.J. Rogier (ed.), *Toezicht. Opstellen over veiligheidstoezicht en markttoezicht*, The Hague: BJu 2006.

F. de Vries, *De bestuurlijke boete in de douanewet* (dissertation EUR), Deventer: Kluwer 2005.

B.W.N. de Waard, 'De matigende rechter', in: T. Barkhuysen (e.a.), *Bestuursrecht harmoniseren: 15 jaar Awb*, the Hague, BJu 2010, pp. 469-486.

M. Delmas-Marty & C. Teitgen-Colly, *Punir sans juger? De la répression administrative au droit administratif pénal*, Paris: Economica 1992.

F.M.J. den Houdijker, S.K. Gabriël and J.A.M.A. Sluysmans, *Bestuurlijke punitieve sancties. Preadviezen Jonge VAR*, The Hague: BJu 2006.

W. den Ouden, 'De intrekking van begunstigende beschikkingen door bestuursorganen', in: T. Barkhuysen (e.a.), *Bestuursrecht harmoniseren: 15 jaar Awb*, Boom Juridische Uitgevers, Den Haag 2010, pp. 689–713.

C.A. Doets and A.J.P. Tillema, "Bestuursrechtelijke handhaving van de Wft", in: D. Busch et al. (ed.), *Onderneming en financieel toezicht*, Deventer: Kluwer 2010, pp. 859–915.

D.R. Doorenbos and M. Jurgens, "Specialisatie en concentratie van rechtspraak op het terrein van het financieel (bestuurs)strafrecht", in: J.W.M. Tromp, M. Jurgens, L.E. de Groot-van Leeuwen and P.P.T. Bovend'Eert (ed.), *Concentratie en specialisatie van rechtspraak: noodzaak of overbodig?* Deventer: Kluwer 2006.

D.R. Doorenbos, *Naming and shaming* (oration Radboud University Nijmegen), Deventer: Kluwer 2007.

D.R. Doorenbos and C.A. Doets, "Wijziging boetestelsel financiële wetgeving – Maximum overdrive", *Ondernemingsrecht* 2008/147, pp. 507–514.

D.R. Doorenbos, "Nieuw boetestelsel financiële wetgeving", *Ondernemingsrecht* 2009/13, pp. 538–545.

D.R. Doorenbos (e.a.), *Onderneming en sanctierecht*, Kluwer, Deventer, 2013.

A.P.W. Duijkersloot, 'Maatregelen gericht op de vergunning, ontheffing of verklaring van geen bezwaar', in: D.R. Doorenbos (e.a.), *Onderneming en sanctierecht*, Kluwer, Deventer, 2013.

M.C.D. Embregts, *Uitsluitsel over bewijsuitsluiting: een onderzoek naar de toelaatbaarheid van onrechtmatig verkregen bewijs in het strafrecht, het civiele recht en het bestuursrecht*, Deventer: Kluwer 2003.

M.W.C. Feteris, *Fiscale bestuurlijke boetes en het recht op een behoorlijk proces*, Deventer: Kluwer 2002.

E. Gras, 'De dwangsom als sanctie op tegenover de overheid verboden eigenrichting', *NJB* 2009, 1569.

B.J. van de Griend, *Het oogmerk als ijkpunt. Bestuurlijke sancties in bestuursrechtspraak en wetgevingsadvisering*, Raad van State, The Hague 2003.

E. Gritter, *Effectiviteit en aansprakelijkheid in het economisch ordeningsrecht* (diss. Groningen), The Hague: BJu 2003.

E. Gritter, 'Toerekening van opzet of schuld in het fiscale boeterecht: legitimatie en achtergronden', *DD* 2001, p. 353.

M.S. Groenhuijsen & F.G.H. Kristen, 'Het Bestimmtheitsgebot bepaald', *DD* 2001, pp. 330–346.

M.A. de Groote and R.M. van Bemmel, 'Invorderingsperikelen bij de bestuurlijke dwangsom', *Gst.* 2005, 82.

J. Gundelach and F.C.M.A. Michiels, *Ongegronde vrees. Een onderzoek naar de rechtspraak inzake handhavingsbesluiten*, Kluwer: Deventer 2003.

A.R. Hartmann, *Bewijs in het bestuursstrafrecht*, (diss. EUR), Arnhem: Gouda Quint 1998.

A.R. Hartmann and P.M. van Russen Groen, 'Bestuursstrafrecht' in: H. de Doelder & L.J.J. Rogier (ed.), *Opstellen over bestuursstrafrecht*, Arnhem: Gouda Quint 1994.

A.R. Hartmann, 'De bestuurlijke boete. Naar een zelfstandige regeling', *Trema. Tijdschrift voor de Rechterlijke Macht* 1995, 18(10), pp. 318–322.

A.R. Hartmann and P.M. van Russen Groen, *Contouren van het bestuursstrafrecht*, Arnhem: Gouda Quint 1998.

A.R. Hartmann, 'De wettelijke regeling van de bestuurlijke boete naar vorm en inhoud' in: H. de Doelder, M. de Meijer and D. Otto (ed.), *De bestuurlijke boete in perspectief* Deventer/Rotterdam: Gouda Quint/Sanders Instituut 1999, pp. 39–62.

A.R. Hartmann and L.J.J. Rogier, 'Bestuurlijke handhaving in het wetsvoorstel Vierde tranche Awb', *NJB* 2004, 36, pp. 1977–1882.

A.R. Hartmann, L.J.J. Rogier and C.J. Roon, 'Bestuurlijke boetebevoegdheden voor de gemeente', *NTB* 2005, 9.

A.R. Hartmann, 'Strafbeschikking en bestuurlijke boete: wildgroei in de handhaving?', *Justitiële Verkenningen* 2005, 6.

A.R. Hartmann, 'De bestuurlijke strafbeschikking: panacee voor de gemeentelijke handhaving', *Proces. Maandblad voor Berechting en Reclassering*, 2010, 2, pp. 64–75.

A.R. Hartmann, *Over de grenzen van de dogmatiek en into fuzzy law*, Apeldoorn/ Antwerpen: Maklu 2011.

A.R. Hartmann, 'De bestuurlijke boete', in: D.R. Doorenbos (e.a.), *Onderneming en sanctierecht*, Kluwer, Deventer, 2013.

W.G.A. Hazewindus, *Van boeteatelier tot boetefabriek*, Deventer: Kluwer 1995.

J.P. Heinrich & R.W. Veldhuis, 'Handhaving van bestuursrecht', *NTB* 2007, 31.

H.Ph.J.A.M. Hennekens, 'Sluiting van (drugs)panden door de burgemeester', *Gst.* 1997, 7055, pp. 317–325.

S. Heukelom-Verhage and M. Scheltema, 'Aanpassingswetgeving bij de vierde tranche; eenheidsstreven bereikt?', *NJB* 2008, 1322, pp. 1636–1642.

C.J. IJdema and U.T. Hoekstra, 'Overgangsperikelen vierde tranche Awb bij de invordering van verbeurde dwangsommen en kosten van bestuursdwang', *Gst.* 7329, 2009, 129, pp. 617–622.

O.J.D.M.L. Jansen, 'Commentaar artikel 1:6 Awb' in: N.S.J. Koeman *et al.*, *Handboek Algemene wet bestuursrecht*, Alphen aan den Rijn: Samsom H.D. Tjeenk Willink 1988.

O.J.D.M.L. Jansen, 'De koude uitsluiting van het penitentiaire bestuursrecht', *NJB* 1995, pp. 1107–1114.

O.J.D.M.L. Jansen, "De bestuurlijke boete in het wetsvoorstel mededingingswet", *NJB* 1996, pp. 1250–1254.

O.J.D.M.L. Jansen, *Het handhavingsonderzoek. Behoren het handhavingstoezicht, het boeteonderzoek en de opsporing verschillend te worden genormeerd? Een interne rechtsvergelijking* (diss. Nijmegen), Nijmegen: Ars Aequi Libri 1999.

O.J.D.M.L. Jansen, "De eindige toekomst van artikel 1:6 Awb", *NTB* 1999, p. 150–156.

O.J.D.M.L. Jansen, "Punitief en evenredig?", *JBplus* 2000, pp. 38–49.

O.J.D.M.L. Jansen, "Toezicht en onderzoek: een beperkt transnationale benadering", in: O.J.D.M.L. Jansen, B.M.J. van der Meulen and R.J.G.M. Widdershoven (ed.), *Handhaving van de Mededingingswet*, Kluwer 2001.

O.J.D.M.L. Jansen, 'De dynamiek van het publiekrechtelijke sanctiestelsel, NJV-preadvies', in: J. de Hullu, F.W. Bleichrodt and O.J.D.M.L. Jansen, *Herziening van het sanctiestelsel*, Deventer: Kluwer 2002, pp. 194–195.

O.J.D.M.L. Jansen, "Bestuurlijke leedtoevoeging, duivenhokken en lachen zonder voorwetenschap. Beschouwingen naar aanleiding van drie jaar boeten en dwangsommen in het financieel bestuursrecht", *Tijdschrift voor Onderneming en Strafrecht* 2003, pp. 63–76.

O.J.D.M.L. Jansen, 'Country analysis – the Netherlands', in: Gerhard Dannecker & Oswald Jansen (ed.), *Competition Law Sanctioning in the European Union*, Kluwer Law International 2004, pp. 729–735.

O. Jansen, "The Systems of International Cooperation in Administrative and Criminal Matters in Relation to Regulation EC 1/2003", in: Gerhard Dannecker, Oswald Jansen (ed.),*Competition Law Sanctioning in the European Union*, Kluwer Law International 2004, pp. 257–304.

O.J.D.M.L. Jansen, "Het zwijgrecht van ondernemingen", *Tijdschrift voor Onderneming en strafrecht*, 2004, pp. 67–77.

O.J.D.M.L. Jansen, 'De bestuurlijke boete' in: P.C. Vegter, A.M. van Woensel, P.A.M. Mevis, J. Boksem (ed.), *Handboek strafzaken* (Deventer, October 2007), chapter 108.

O.J.D.M.L. Jansen, 'De bestuurlijke boete in het financieel bestuursrecht – Enkele opmerkingen' in: R.C.P. Haentjens and M. Jurgens, *Fraude op de financiële markten*, Deventer: Kluwer 2011.

O.J.D.M.L. Jansen, "Commentaar hoofdstuk 6, 7 en 8 Mededingingswet", in: P.J. Slot et al. (ed.), *Tekst en Commentaar Mededingingswet*, Kluwer, Deventer 2011.

O.J.D.M.L. Jansen, "Bestuurlijk en justitieel bestraffen in Nederland – op zoek naar (nog) meer eenheid", in: R.C. van Houten (ed.), *Economisch strafrecht en bestuurlijke boete*, Nijmegen: Wolf Legal Publishers 2012, pp. 21–79, 153–181.

O.J.D.M.L. Jansen, De zelfstandige last en de bindende aanwijzing, in: D.R. Doorenbos (e.a.), *Onderneming en sanctierecht*, Kluwer, Deventer, 2013, pp. 173–189.

G.T.J.M. Jurgens, *Bestuurlijk gedogen* (diss.), Zwolle: H.E.J. Tjeenk Willink 1996.

G.T.J.M. Jurgens, 'De strafrechtelijke betekenis van bestuurlijk gedogen', *JBplus* 2002, pp. 106–117.

G.T.J.M. Jurgens & F.C.M.A. Michiels, 'Weg met de last onder bestuursdwang!', *NJB* 2005, pp. 1092–1093.

G.T.J.M. Jurgens, 'De Wet OM-afdoening: bestuurlijke beboeting in het strafrecht', *NTB* 2006, 46.

G.T.J.M. Jurgens, 'Harmoniseren of integreren? De strafbeschikking en de bestuurlijke boete vergeleken' in: L. Loeber (ed.), *Het wetsvoorstel OM-afdoening en de verhouding tussen strafrechtelijke en bestuursrechtelijke handhaving, Preadviezen voor de Vereniging voor wetgeving en wetgevingsbeleid*, Nijmegen: Wolf Legal Publishers 2007, pp. 21–70.

G.T.J.M. Jurgens, P.J.J. van Buuren, and F.C.M.A. Michiels, *Bestuursdwang en dwangsom*, Deventer: Kluwer 2011.

M. Jurgens & R. Stijnen (ed.), *Compliance in het financieel toezichtrecht*, Deventer: Kluwer 2008.

N. Keijzer, *The military duty to obey* (diss. VU), Amsterdam 1977.

B. Ketelaar, 'De burgemeester en de Wet Victoria', *APB* 1997, pp. 11–13.

A.P. Klap, 'Boeteoplegging in het economische bestuursrecht: afschrikking versus evenredigheid?', *SEW* 2012, pp. 322–335.

A.P. Klap, 'Prioriteringsbeleid in het kader van de bestuursrechtelijke handhaving', *JBplus* 2012, pp. 326–341.

G. Knigge, 'De verhouding van het strafrecht tot het bestuursrecht' in: M.S. Groenhuijsen and G. Knigge (ed.), *Het vooronderzoek in strafzaken. Tweede interimrapport Strafvordering 2001.*

N.J.M. Kwakman, 'De bestuurlijke boete: publiekrechtelijke eigenrichting', *NTB* 2006, 47, pp. 331–340.

N.J.M. Kwakman, 'Twee nieuwe sanctiestelsels ter bestrijding van overlast in de openbare ruimte op lokaal niveau', *NJB* 2009, 3.

T.E.P.A. Lam, 'Capita Selecta bestuursdwang en dwangsom', *BR* 2003,p. 278.

M.A.J. Leenders and O.J.D.M.L. Jansen, *De versterking van de bestuurlijke handhaving met de bestuurlijke boete in het kader van het integraal veiligheidsbeleid*, Ministry of Foreign Affairs, The Hague 15 May 2000, 125 p.

E.E.V. Lenos, *Bestuurlijke sanctietoepassing en strafrechtelijke waarborgen in de sociale zekerheid*, Lelystad: Koninklijke Vermande 1998.

M.E.G. Litjens, B.M.J. van der Meulen and A.A. Freriks, *Prorogatie in de AWB. Invoeringsevaluatie rechtstreeks beroep*, The Hague: BJu 2006.

M.E.G. Litjens, B.M.J. van der Meulen and A.A. Freriks, 'De werking van een controversiële rechtsgang. Invoeringsevaluatie rechtstreeks beroep in de AWB', *JBPlus* 2006, pp. 58–68.

H.J.H. van Meegen, 'Het huisverbod: bestuursrecht in handen van de familierechter', *JBplus* 2010, 1, pp. 2–15.

H.J.H. van Meegen, 'Huisverboden beoordeeld, maar hoe?', *FJR* 2010, 50.

P.A.M. Mevis, 'Bestuurlijke boete in Absurdistan', *Ars Aequi* 2005, 7–8, pp. 580–587.

F.C.M.A. Michiels, C.T. Nijenhuis and E. Niemeijer, 'De Wm-dwangsom in de praktijk van de handhaving', *M & R* 1995, pp. 113–117.

F.C.M.A. Michiels, 'Bestuurlijke handhaving in ontwikkeling', in: J.T.K. Bos (e.a.), *Handhaving van het bestuursrecht*, Samsom H.D. Tjeenk Willink, Alphen aan den Rijn 1995, pp. 7–118.

F.C.M.A. Michiels, 'Het handhavingstekort en de bestuurlijke boete', in: D. Otto et al. (ed.), *De bestuurlijke boete in perspectief*, Deventer: Gouda Quint 1999, pp. 63–75.

F.C.M.A. Michiels, 'Belangenafweging bij sanctiebesluiten', *Ars Aequi* 2000, pp. 111–117.

F.C.M.A. Michiels, 'Strafsancties in het bestuursrecht: een begaanbare weg', *Strafblad* 2005, 5.

F.C.M.A. Michiels and E.R. Muller (ed.), *Handhaving. Bestuurlijk handhaven in Nederland*, Deventer: Kluwer 2006.

F.C.M.A. Michiels, *Houdbaar handhavingsrecht*, Deventer: Kluwer 2006.

F.C.M.A. Michiels and B.W.N. de Waard, *Rechterlijke toetsing van bestuurlijke punitieve sancties*, The Hague: BJu 2007.

F.C.M.A. Michiels, 'Doorberekening en verhaal van handhavingskosten' in: A.B. Blomberg et al. (ed.),*Van Utrecht via Brussel naar Maastricht (Backes-bundel)*, Alphen aan den Rijn: Kluwer 2007, pp. 185–202.

F.C.M.A. Michiels, 'Naming and shaming in het markttoezicht', *NTB* 2007, pp. 85–95.

F.C.M.A. Michiels, 'Bestraffende bestuurlijke handhaving onder de Awb-IV', *Trema* 2009, pp. 282–288.

F.C.M.A. Michiels, 'Doorberekening van controlekosten: nieuw beleid noodzakelijk', *NTB* 2009, p. 25 ff.

F.C.M.A. Michiels and A.M.P.J.H. Sauvé, 'De praktijk van de last onder dwangsom in het milieurecht', *M & R* 2010, pp. 68–76.

F.C.M.A. Michiels, A.M.P.J.H. Sauvé, 'De praktijk van de last onder dwangsom in het milieurecht', *M &* R 2010, p. 68.

F.C.M.A. Michiels, *Hoofdzaken van het bestuursrecht*, Deventer: Kluwer 2011.

F.C.M.A.Michiels, 'Bewegingen in het handhavingsrecht', *JBplus* 2012, 8.

F. Moderne, *Sanctions administratives et justice constitutionnelle. Contribution à l'étude du jus puniendi de l'Etat dans les démocraties contemporaines*, Paris: Economica 1993.

P. Nieuwenburg and G.S.A. Dijkstra, 'Veiligheid, doelmatigheid en de rechtsstaat: De Wet OM-afdoening', *Filosofie & Praktijk* 2010, 1, pp. 72–80.

J.E.M. Polak, 'Bestuursrechtelijke handhaving: bevoegdheid of verplichting? Hebben juristen niets meer te bieden?' in: T. Barkhuysen, W. den Ouden and J.E.M. Polak (ed.), *Recht realiseren. Bijdragen rond het thema adequate naleving van rechtsregels*, Deventer: Kluwer 2005, pp. 201–214.

J.M. Polak, 'De strafbeschikking en de bestuurlijke boete vergeleken. Twee preadviezen met stellingen', *NJB* 2006, 24, pp. 1320–1321.

S. Pront-van Bommel, "Controle op de naleving van administratieve wetgeving", in: W. Konijnenbelt (ed.), *De derde tranche. Commentaar op het voorontwerp voor de derde tranche van de Algemene wet bestuursrecht*, Alphen aan den Rijn: Samsom H.D. Tjeenk Willink 1992.

D. Roef, *Strafbare overheden* (diss. Maastricht), Antwerpen-Groningen: Intersentia 2001.

D. Roef, 'De ommekeer in Pikmeer. Over de vervolgbaarheid van overheden na Pikmeer II', *JB* 1998, pp. 215–226.

L.J.J. Rogier, *Strafsancties, administratieve sancties en het una via-beginsel*, Arnhem 1992.

L.J.J. Rogier, 'Bestuursstrafrecht vanuit een bestuursrechtelijk perspectief', in: H. de Doelder en L.J.J. Rogier (red.), *Opstellen over bestuursstrafrecht*, Gouda Quint, Arnhem 1994, pp. 117–129.

L.J.J. Rogier, 'De bestuurlijke boeten in de algemene wet bestuursrecht?', in: H. de Doelder en L.J.J. Rogier (red.), *Opstellen over bestuursstrafrecht*, Gouda Quint, Arnhem 1994, pp. 157–172.

L.J.J. Rogier, *De algemene wet bestuursrecht en strafrecht*, Kluwer, Deventer 1995.

L.J.J. Rogier, 'Het boetestelsel van de Wet Mulder', in: W.G.A. Hazewindus and O.J.D.M.L. Jansen (ed.), *Van boeteatelier tot boetefabriek*, Deventer: Kluwer 1995, pp. 127–141.

L.J.J. Rogier, 'De Wet tijdelijk huisverbod', *Gst.* 2009, 128.

L.J.J. Rogier, 'De Vierde tranche Algemene wet bestuursrecht in werking. Twee magische lijnen verschoven', *NJB* 2009, 1198, pp. 1560–1566.

L.J.J. Rogier, 'Bestraffende sancties in de Awb', in: T. Barkhuysen (e.a.), *Bestuursrecht harmoniseren: 15 jaar Awb*, Boom Juridische Uitgevers, Den Haag, 2010, pp. 689–713.

L.J.J. Rogier, 'Nieuwe bevoegdheden van de burgemeester. Sancties, bevelen en andere maatregelen', *NTB* 2010, 45, pp. 309–314.

L.J.J. Rogier, 'De Afdeling Bestuursrechtspraak van de Raad van State over de Wet tijdelijk huisverbod', *Trema* 2012, 4.

G.P. Roth, 'Het effect van de Vierde tranche Awb op de handhaving van de Wet financieel toezicht', *Ondernemingsrecht* 2008, 14, pp. 500–507.

G.P. Roth, 'Publicatie van sancties', in: D.R. Doorenbos (e.a.), *Onderneming en sanctierecht*, Kluwer, Deventer, 2013.

J. Roording, *Sanctierecht in de belastingen en de sociale zekerheid*, Nijmegen: Ars Aequi Libri 1994.

L.D. Ruigrok, 'De dwangsom in nieuw perspectief. Over het voorkomen van ordeverstoringen', *Gst.* 2010/88.

I. Sluiter, F. de Vries, & R.P.A. Kraaijeveld, 'Het nieuwe boetestelsel in de financiële toezichtwetgeving; flexibel, afschrikwekkend én effectief?', *FR* 2009, 5–6, pp. 210–217.

H.A.W. Snijders, *Gemeenten en bestuursdwang* (diss. Nijmegen), The Hague: VUGA 1982.

R. Stijnen, *Rechtsbescherming tegen bestraffing in het strafrecht en het bestuursrecht*, Deventer: Kluwer 2011.

J.M.H.F. Teunissen, 'De strafbeschikking: geen noviteit', *Gst.* 2007, 27.

J.R. van Angeren, 'De last onder dwangsom', in: D.R. Doorenbos (e.a.), *Onderneming en sanctierecht*, Kluwer, Deventer 2013.

G.A.C.M. van Ballegooij and T. Barkhuysen, *Bestuursrecht in het Awb-Tijdperk*, Deventer: Kluwer 2012.

C.A.H. van de Sanden, 'De publieke schandpaal in het milieurecht', *M & R* 2011, 137.

VAR-werkgroep Vierde tranche AWB, *De vierde tranche AWB. Commentaar en vraagpunten*, The Hague: BJu 2000.

J.W. van der Hulst, 'De bijkomende kosten van een verkeersboete', *Jurisprudentie Wegenverkeersrecht* 2012, pp. 433–262.

G.A. van der Veen, 'Extra spoedeisende bestuursdwang en de Derde tranche: de bestuursrechter weer gepasseerd?', *NTB* 1994, pp. 271–272.

P. H. S. van Rest, *Het ambtelijk bevel als strafuitsluitingsgrond* (diss. Groningen), Arnhem: Gouda Quint 1991.

P.M. van Russen Groen, *Rechtsbescherming in het bestuursstrafrecht*, Deventer: Gouda Quint 1998.

F.R. Vermeer, 'Lang leve de dwangsom!', *Gst.* 2002, 7167, 1.

F.B. Vermeer, *Gedogen door bestuursorganen*, Deventer: Kluwer 2010.

F.R. Vermeer, 'De beginselplicht tot handhaving en de ruimte om te gedogen', *JBplus* 2001, pp. 76–85.

J.H. Verweij, *De bestuurlijke dwangsom*, Deventer: W.E.J. Tjeenk Willink 1997.

M.J. Vos, 'Alleengebruik echtelijke woning en tijdelijk huisverbod', *EB* 2010, 47.

J.P.A.F. Vriens, 'De strafbeschikking, bestuurlijke boete of…?', *JBA* 2009, 3, pp. 34–37.

P.G. Wiewel, *Rechtsbescherming tegen bestraffing*, Nijmegen: Ars Aequi Libri 2001.

APPENDIX I. THE STRUCTURE OF THE GENERAL ADMINISTRATIVE LAW ACT[308]

CHAPTER 1 INTRODUCTORY PROVISIONS
Title 1.1 Definitions and scope
Title 1.2 Implementation of binding decisions of authorities of the European Communities

CHAPTER 2 DEALINGS BETWEEN INDIVIDUALS AND ADMINISTRATIVE AUTHORITIES
Division 2.1 General provisions
Division 2.2 Use of Languages in Dealings with Administrative Authorities
Division 2.3 Dealings with Administrative Authorities in an electronic way

CHAPTER 3 GENERAL PROVISIONS CONCERNING ORDERS
Division 3.1 Introductory provisions
Division 3.2 The duty of care and the weighing of interests
Division 3.3 Provision of advice
Division 3.4 Public preparatory procedure
Division 3.5 Interrelated decisions
Paragraph 3.5.1 General provisions
Paragraph 3.5.2 Information
Paragraph 3.5.3 Coordination of decision-making and legal protection
Division 3.6 Notification and communication
Division 3.7 Reasons for orders

CHAPTER 4 SPECIAL PROVISIONS CONCERNING ORDERS
Title 4.1 Administrative decisions
Division 4.1.1 The application
Division 4.1.2 Preparation
Division 4.1.3 Time limit for decisions
Paragraph 4.1.3.1 Time limit for decisions
Paragraph 4.1.3.2 Penalty for failure to give a timely decision

308 This structure is based upon the version of GALA of 1 January 2013 and the changes resulting from the Act on the modification of administrative procedural law [*Wet aanpassing bestuursprocesrecht* (Staatsblad 2013, 50; Staatsblad 2013, 162) and the Act providing for a general regulation of compensation for loss and damages for wrongful acts [*Wet nadeelcompensatie en schadevergoeding*] (Staatsblad 2013, 50; Staatsblad 2013, 162).

Paragraph 4.1.3.3 Positive notional decision for failure to give a timely decision

Title 4.2 Subsidies

Division 4.2.1 Introductory provisions

Division 4.2.2 The subsidy ceiling

Division 4.2.3 The granting of subsidies

Division 4.2.4 Obligations of the subsidy recipient

Division 4.2.5 The fixing of the subsidy

Division 4.2.6 Repeal and alteration

Division 4.2.7 Payment and recovery

Division 4.2.8 Subsidies granted per financial year to juristic persons

Paragraph 4.2.8.1 Introductory provisions

Paragraph 4.2.8.2 The application

Paragraph 4.2.8.3 The granting of subsidies

Paragraph 4.2.8.4 Obligations of the subsidy recipient

Paragraph 4.2.8.5 The fixing of subsidy

Title 4.3 Policy rules

Title 4.4 Money debts arising from administrative law

Division 4.4.1 Setting and substance of the obligation to pay

Division 4.4.2 Default and statutory interest

Division 4.4.3 Statutory limitation

Division 4.4.4 Due notice and collection by writ of execution

Division 4.4.5 Objection and appeal

Title 4.5 Compensation

CHAPTER 5 ENFORCEMENT

Title 5.1 Introductory provisions

Title 5.2 Supervision of observance

Title 5.3 Remedial sanctions

Division 5.3.1 Enforcement action

Division 5.3.2 Astreinte

Title 5.4 Administrative fine

Division 5.4.1 General provisions

Division 5.4.2 The procedure

CHAPTER 6 GENERAL PROVISIONS CONCERNING OBJECTIONS AND APPEALS

Division 6.1 Introductory provisions

Division 6.2 Other general provisions

CHAPTER 7 SPECIAL PROVISIONS CONCERNING OBJECTIONS AND ADMINISTRATIVE APPEALS
Division 7.1 Notice of objection preceding appeal to an administrative court
Division 7.2 Special provisions on objections
Division 7.3 Special provisions on administrative appeals

CHAPTER 8 SPECIAL PROVISIONS CONCERNING THE PROCEDURE IN APPEAL TO THE DISTRICT COURT AND HIGHER APPEAL
Title 8.1 General provisions on appeals in first instance
Division 8.1.1 Jurisdiction
Division 8.1.2 Proceedings by a single-judge, a three-judge section or the grand chamber
Division 8.1.2A Opinion
Division 8.1.3 Referral, consolidation and separation
Division 8.1.4 Challenge and excusal
Division 8.1.5 The parties
Division 8.1.6 Witnesses, experts and interpreters
Division 8.1.7 Sending of documents
Title 8.2 The hearing of appeals in first instance
Division 8.2.1 Registry fee
Division 8.2.1a General provision
Division 8.2.2 Preliminary inquiry
Division 8.2.3 Expedited proceedings
Division 8.2.4 Simplified proceedings
Division 8.2.4a Appeal against failure to give a timely decision
Division 8.2.5 Hearing
Division 8.2.6 Judgment
Division 8.2.7 Interlocutory ruling
Title 8.3 Provisional remedies and immediate judgment in the proceedings on the merits
Title 8.4 Compensation in damages
Title 8.5 Higher appeal
Title 8.6 Review

CHAPTER 9 DEALING WITH COMPLAINTS
Title 9.1 Dealing with notifications of complaint by an administrative authority
Division 9.1.1 General provisions
Division 9.1.2 The dealing with notifications of complaint
Division 9.1.3 Additional provisions for a complaints procedure

Title 9.2 Dealing with notifications of complaint by an Ombudsman
- Division 9.2.1 General provisions
- Division 9.2.2 Competence
- Division 9.2.3 Procedure

CHAPTER 10 PROVISIONS ON ADMINISTRATIVE AUTHORITIES

Title 10.1 Mandate, delegation and attribution
- Division 10.1.1 Mandate
- Division 10.1.2 Delegation
- Division 10.1.3 Attribution

Title 10.2 Supervision of administrative authorities
- Division 10.2.1 Approval
- Division 10.2.2 Annulment
- Division 10.2.3 Stay

CHAPTER 11 FINAL PROVISIONS

Appendix 1: Regulation on direct appeal

Appendix 2: Regulation of jurisdiction of administrative courts
- Chapter 1: Order excluded from appeal
- Chapter 2: Appeal in first instance to a special administrative court
- Chapter 3: Appeal in first instance to another court
- Chapter 4: Higher Appeal

Appendix 3: Reduced registry fee arrangement

APPENDIX II. CHOICE BETWEEN ADMINISTRATIVE FINE AND CRIMINAL LAW SYSTEM

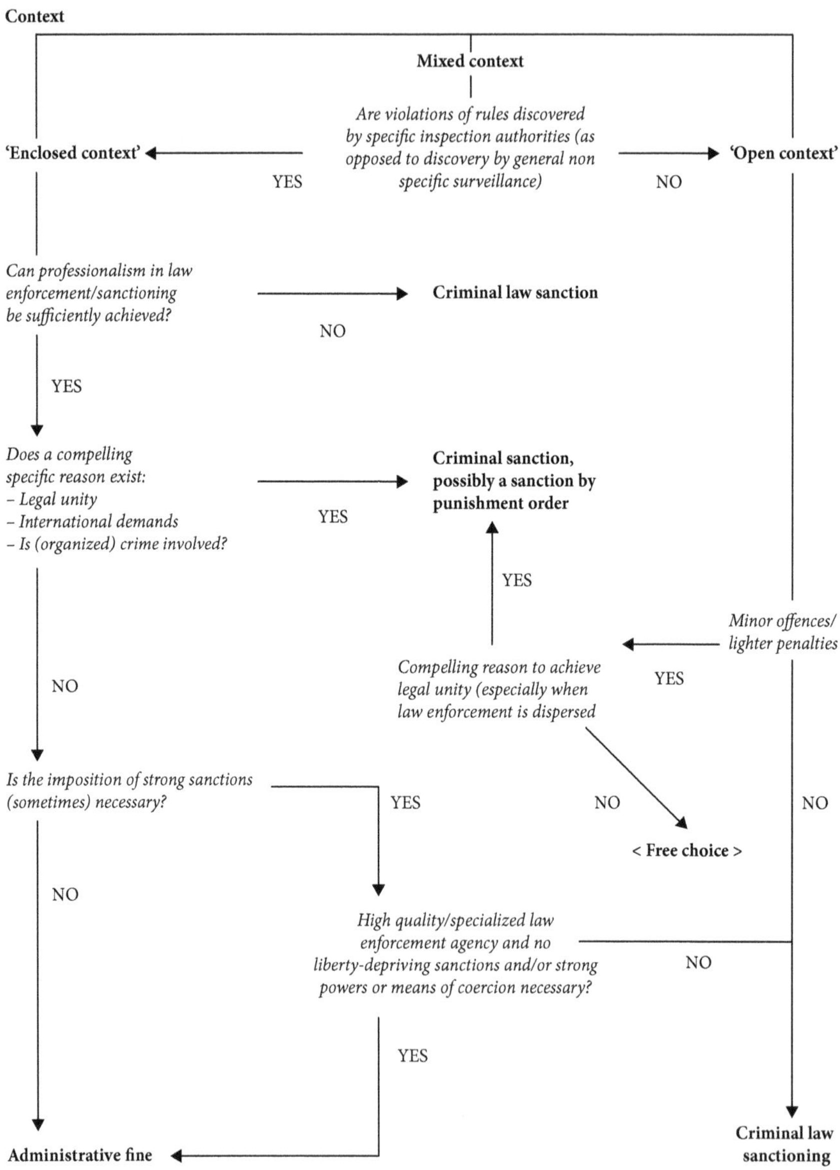

APPENDIX III. THE DUTCH SYSTEM OF LEGAL PROTECTION

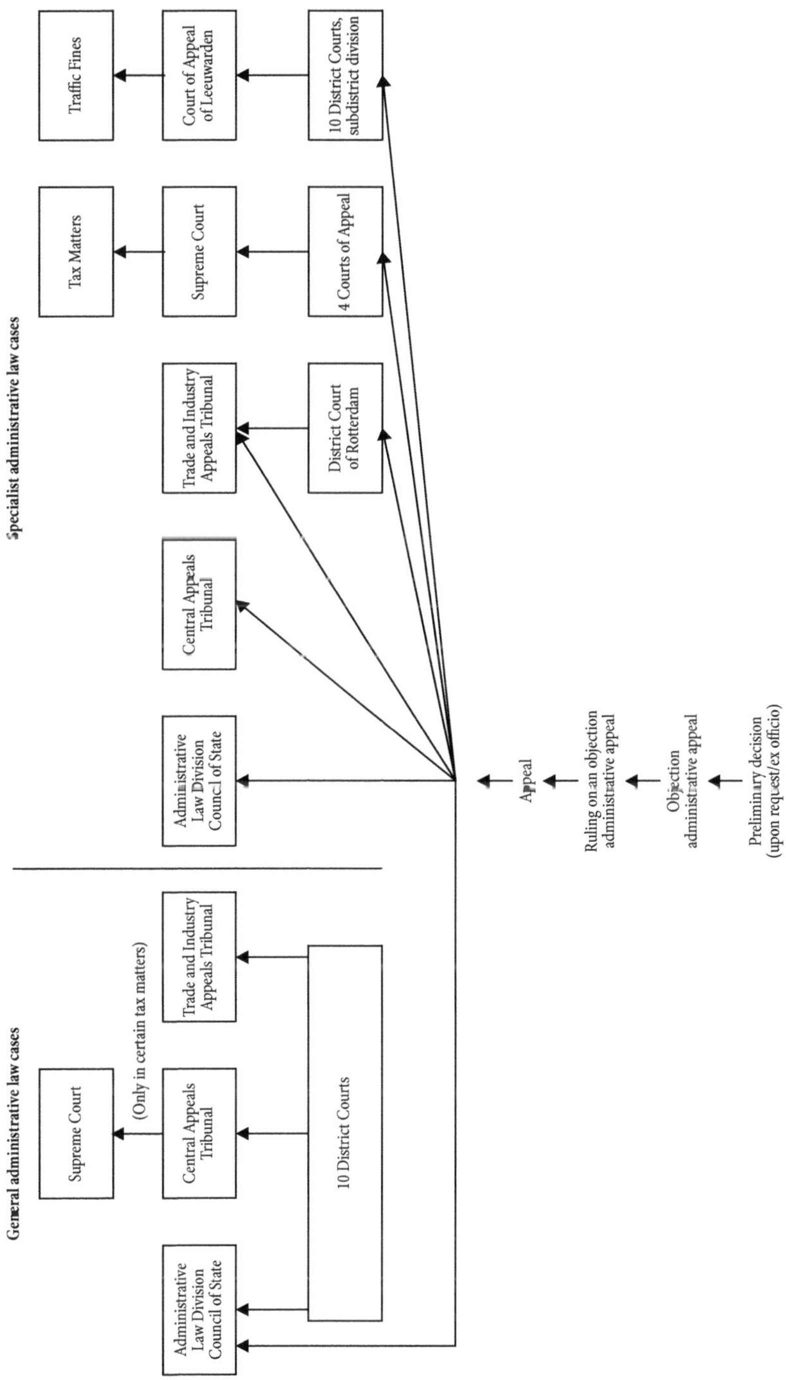

X. COUNTRY ANALYSIS – PORTUGAL*

Pedro Caeiro and Miguel Ângelo Lemos

1. INTRODUCTION

In the Portuguese system, there is no precise definition of the concept of *administrative sanctions*, either at a legislative level or in the literature. Therefore, we will start by proposing the following definition:

An administrative sanction is a measure imposed by the administration in order to punish a person or entity that has infringed a norm which protects administrative interests.

There are other administrative measures that affect directly the rights or interests of an individual in an unfavourable manner, although they do not qualify as sanctions.[1] However, as the questionnaire asks for a broad approach to administrative sanctions, our paper will address them as well.

2. ADMINISTRATIVE SANCTIONS

2.1. ELEMENTS AND TYPES

2.1.1. Elements

The proposed concept of administrative sanction encompasses three elements: the *teleological element* (the scope of the measure), the *material element* (the interests under protection) and the *institutional element* (the bodies that have the power to impose such measures).

---

* The authors wish to thank Mr. Neil R. Johnson for having kindly helped them with the revision of the English version of this paper.
The manuscript has been written and delivered to the editors in 2004, and partly revised in 2010 and 2013.

1 This assertion is also imposed by the Portuguese Constitution (CRP), at least in the interpretation of the *Tribunal Constitucional* (TC, Portuguese Constitutional Court).

Concerning the *teleological element*, it is important to stress the *punitive* purpose of administrative sanctions, which is to *prevent new infractions* through the punishment of an offender (general and individual deterrence).[2] Thus, they share some of the characteristics of criminal sanctions.

This is also the reason why these sanctions differ from the administrative measures related to the traditional administrative function of preventing risk. While unfavourable to those on whom they are imposed, the latter do not necessarily suppose individual responsibility: their primary aim is to safeguard the public interest, in general, against possible harm, even when no one can be held responsible for the hazardous situation.[3]

As for the *material element*, administrative sanctions intend to enforce the protection of administrative interests, i.e., interests whose preservation and promotion are primarily entrusted to the administrative function. It is well known that the new model of State born after the Second World War (the Welfare State) has widened the field in which the administration plays an important role.[4]

Indeed, the protection of those interests may sometimes require the use of criminal sanctions, when they are important enough to justify penal protection (*dignidade penal*, *Strafwürdigkeit*) and mere administrative sanctioning of the conduct would not be effective enough (*carência de tutela penal*, *Strafbedürftigkeit*). In some cases, the same legal interest (*bem jurídico*, *Rechtsgut*) may be under administrative *and* penal protection; the administrative *or* criminal nature of the offence will then depend on the seriousness of the conduct.[5]

The preceding considerations lead us to the conclusion that the first two elements are not sufficient to establish a clear distinction between penal and administrative sanctions. Therefore, in our view, only the *institutional element* gives full autonomy to the concept: administrative sanctions are imposed by the administration, whereas penal sanctions may only be imposed by the court.

2.1.2. Types

The Portuguese Constitutional Court (TC) interprets Article 165, no. 1, c and d of the CRP, as allowing *only* for three types of public law sanctions: a) criminal

---

2 See Rosendo Dias José, "Sanções administrativas", *Revista de Direito Público*, Ano IV (1991), p. 47.

3 See below B, I, 2.

4 See Jorge de Figueiredo Dias, "O movimento de descriminalização e o ilícito de mera ordenação social", in: Instituto de Direito Penal Económico e Europeu (ed.), *Direito Penal Económico e Europeu: Textos Doutrinários*, Vol. I, 1998, pp. 20 et seq.

5 For example: under Portuguese law, so-called "drunken driving" is an administrative offence (*contra-ordenação*: see below, A, II, 2 if the Blood Alcohol Concentration (BAC) is equal to or higher than 0.5 g/l; but it is considered to be a crime if the BAC is higher than 1.2 g/l (Article 292 of the Penal Code).

penalties; b) *coimas* and other sanctions imposed by the *Direito de Mera Ordenação Social* (Administrative Offences Law, hereafter DMOS); and c) disciplinary sanctions.[6] According to that interpretation, the Constitution provides for a *closed typology* of public law sanctions and, as a consequence, neither Parliament nor the Government can create *new* types of sanction.

Therefore, unfavourable administrative measures must comply with the following framework: if they do not qualify as proper sanctions, the legislator is relatively free to create them, as long as general constitutional principles are respected[7]; if they qualify as sanctions, they must belong either to DMOS or to disciplinary law - otherwise, they will violate the Constitution.[8]

Consequently, we may distinguish between three types of administrative sanctions:

First, and most important, the sanctions provided by the *Direito de Mera Ordenação Social* (DMOS): the infringement of those norms is called *contra-ordenação* (*Ordnungswidrigkeit*) and is punishable with a *coima* (*Geldbube*) and other accessory sanctions.

Secondly, there are disciplinary sanctions applicable to public officials and other persons who are in a special relationship with the administration (students of public schools, prisoners) and who have failed to meet their obligations.

Similar to disciplinary sanctions *stricto sensu*, there are also disciplinary sanctions imposed by the bodies that supervise the activities of professionals subject to public regulation (doctors, lawyers, etc.).

In the third place, there are sanctions in administrative contracts for instances where a (private) party fails to fulfil his/her duties. Article 302, d of the Code of Public Tenders confers upon the administration the power to apply the sanctions provided for in administrative contracts with private entities in the case of their non-execution.

Usually, those sanctions have a pecuniary nature, but they may also entail the inhibition of rights related to the contract (e.g., the administration may take over the contracted works or service).[9] Therefore, several authors discuss whether

6 See *Decisions* of the TC no. 155/91, no. 160/91, no. 294/91 and 336/91.

7 See below, B), III.

8 The *Decision* of the TC no. 430/91 considered that Articles 10 and 13 of DL no. 14/84, of 11 January were unconstitutional, because they provided for an *atypical* administrative measure (the inhibition of the right to use cheques). Disagreeing with the Decision, Rosendo Dias José, pp. 53 et seq.; and Marcelo Madureira Prates, *Sanção Administrativa Geral: Anatomia e Autonomia*, 2003, pp. 126 et seq.

9 Pedro Gonçalves, *A Concessão de Serviços Públicos (Uma Aplicação da Técnica Concessória)*, 1999, pp. 252 et seq.; Vital Moreira, *Sumários do Curso de Direito Administrativo*, policop., Coimbra, 2003(?), p. 17.

there should be a legal typology of the sanctions, or should the administration have the power to "create" the sanctions in the contracts.[10]

As the decision to apply these sanctions is seen as an "administrative act", the private entity on whom they are imposed can appeal to the administrative courts.

Arguably, the administration retains a position of superiority and authority that makes these sanctions different from simple contractual (civil) sanctions[11], and, thus, the general principles that guide the administrative activity apply.[12] However, their *contractual nature* introduces a specific difference that allows us to consider them, in this context, not as sanctions proper.

As this project aims at a comparative study between the various European countries, and as it is not possible, for reasons of space, to deal with all those sanctions, our paper will focus on the sanctions provided by DMOS, which are, by far, the most important ones, not only from a practical point of view, but also because of what may be their relative originality in the European space.

Moreover, DMOS sanctions are of general application, and, contrary to disciplinary and contractual sanctions, do not depend on the existence of a special relationship between the administration and the addressee of the norms.

2.2. COIMAS AND OTHER SANCTIONS PROVIDED BY THE DIREITO DE MERA ORDENAÇÃO SOCIAL

2.2.1. Historical background

DL no. 232/79 of 14 July 1979 created the *Direito de Mera Ordenação Social* as a new branch of repressive law, following a former proposal by Prof. Eduardo Correia (1963), largely inspired by the German *Ordnungswidrigkeitengesetz* (1952). Three years later, that Act was revoked by DL no. 433/82 of 27 October 1982 (hereafter, RGCO), which redefined the general rules applicable to *contra-ordenações*, and which has been, from then on, the basic legal framework of DMOS, as amended by DL no. 356/89 of 17 October 1989, DL no. 244/95 of 14 September 1995, DL no. 323/2001 of 17 December and L no. 109/2001 of 24 December. However, one should note that there is a multitude of special laws that often modify this general framework[13] – which is precisely one of the flaws of the present regulation of the DMOS.

---

10 Divergent opinions on the issue can be found in Pedro Gonçalves, pp. 251 et seq.; and M. Madureira Prates, p. 190.

11 M. Madureira Prates, p. 159.

12 See below, B, III.

13 Especially in what concerns the maximum limits of the applicable *coimas*, where the general legal framework plays an almost "residual" role, see Maria Fernanda Palma / Paulo Otero,

The introduction of the DMOS in our legal system, together with the enactment of the new Penal Code (1982), was part of a larger reform of Portuguese repressive law, intending to "cleanse" the criminal system by eliminating the category of *contravenções* (criminal offences against administrative interests[14]): serious offences against the economy, public health and the financial interests of the State should be considered as proper *crimes*, while less serious offences against administrative interests should be dealt with by the means of *mere administrative sanctioning*.[15]

Consequently, the new Penal Code punished (and still punishes) *only crimes*, and a large number of *contravenções* have been converted either into criminal offences or *contra-ordenações*.[16] The remaining *contravenções*, punished by legislative acts enacted before 1982, should go through the same process of conversion in the course of time. Nevertheless, the reform was not achieved: not only have some *contravenções* remained, subject to the general legal framework contained in the ancient Penal Code (1886)[17], but also a new category of administrative offences was created – the so-called *transgressões* It was not until 2006 that Parliament passed a law (L no. 30/2006 of 11 July) that finally converted the existing *contravenções* and *transgressões* into *contra-ordenações*.

2.2.2. Basic features of the Direito de Mera Ordenação Social

Presently, the DMOS is the most important branch of administrative sanctioning in the Portuguese repressive system.

According to Article 1 of the RGCO, *contra-ordenação* is the unlawful and censurable act punishable with a *coima*. Indeed, crimes can also be defined as "unlawful and censurable acts"; therefore, the (legal) distinction between a crime

"Revisão do regime legal do ilícito de mera ordenação social", *Revista da Faculdade de Direito da Universidade de Lisboa* 37 (1996), p. 559.

14 *Contravenções* have been part of the Portuguese (criminal) system since 1852 (the date of the first Portuguese Penal Code), due to the influence of the French *Code Pénal*.

15 On this issue, see the seminal study (1973) by Eduardo Correia, "Direito Penal e Direito de Mera Ordenação Social", (republished) in Instituto de Direito Penal Económico e Europeu (ed.), *Direito Penal Económico e Europeu: Textos Doutrinários*, Vol. I, 1998, pp. 3 et seq. Stressing the link between the movement for decriminalisation and the creation of DMOS, J. Figueiredo Dias, (fn. 4), pp. 19 et seq.

16 See, e.g., DL 28/84 of 20 January 1984 (Crimes against the economy and public health); see below, C, II. See also R. Dias José, pp. 52 et seq.

17 The majority of scholars rightly criticise the persistence of *contravenções* in the Portuguese legal system and the inadequate and unplanned creation of new ones by the legislator: see, e.g., J. Figueiredo Dias (fn. 4), p. 25; and Teresa Pizarro Beleza, *Direito Penal*, Vol. I, 1985, pp. 130 et seq.

Nevertheless, for a critical view of the penal reform of the 1980s, especially concerning the introduction of *contra-ordenações* in our punitive system (and the projected elimination of *contravenções*), see Manuel Cavaleiro de Ferreira, *Direito Penal Português*, I, 1980, pp. 15 et seq.; and Miguel Pedrosa Machado, "Elementos para o estudo da legislação portuguesa sobre contra-ordenações", in: Instituto de Direito Penal Económico e Europeu (ed.), *Direito Penal Económico e Europeu: Textos Doutrinários*, Vol. I, 1998, pp. 145 et seq.

and a *contra-ordenação* is a formal one, because the nature of the offence depends on the type of sanction provided for by the law: crimes are punished with penalties (namely, imprisonment and fines), *contra-ordenações* are punished with *coimas*.[18]

The formal nature of the legal distinction should not make us forget that there is also a *material* difference between crimes and *contra-ordenações*[19], in the sense that the legislator does not have *absolute* discretion in qualifying a given conduct as either one or the other.[20] Such a decision is subject to the fundamental (constitutional) principles that limit the power to criminalise a conduct[21], especially the principle of necessity in its three dimensions: the existence of a relevant social interest that needs protection; the proportionality of State reaction to undesired behaviour; and criminal law as *ultima ratio*. Also, there are other principles that limit legislative discretion in the qualification of offences; e.g., in a system that provides for the criminal liability of corporations and legal entities (such as the Portuguese), it would not be adequate to consider the *same* conduct as a crime, when committed by individuals, and as an administrative infraction, when committed by legal entities.

2.2.3. Coimas

According to Article 17 of the RGCO, *coimas* are pecuniary sanctions. Each *contra-ordenação* is punishable with a *coima* between a minimum and a maximum amount.

As a rule, the minimum amount should not be lower than €3.74 nor higher than €3,740.98 (individuals) or €44,891.81 (legal entities).[22] If the offence is committed by negligence, the maximum limits may not exceed €1,870.49 and €22,445.91, respectively. However, there are two exceptions to this rule:

---

18 See below, 3.

19 The original version of Article 1 of the RGCO contained a norm (no. 2), which stated that "the law shall determine the cases where a *contra-ordenação* may be imputed, irrespective of the censurable nature of the act". The content of this norm was an unequivocal sign that the legislator of 1982 intended to create a system clearly distinct from criminal law. However, no. 2 of Article 1 was removed from the RGCO in 1995, thus contributing for the undesirable approximation of DMOS and criminal law: see Frederico da Costa Pinto, "O ilícito de mera ordenação social e a erosão do princípio da subsidiariedade da intervenção penal", in: Instituto de Direito Penal Económico e Europeu (ed.), *Direito Penal Económico e Europeu: Textos Doutrinários*, Vol. I, 1998, pp. 209 et seq., *passim*.

20 Scholars agree on the conclusion, although there are some important differences between them concerning the possibility of using a qualitative criterion to distinguish crimes from *contra-ordenações*: see J. Figueiredo Dias (fn. 4), pp. 26 et seq.; Manuel da Costa Andrade, "Contributo para o conceito de contra-ordenação", in: Instituto de Direito Penal Económico e Europeu (ed.), *Direito Penal Económico e Europeu: Textos Doutrinários*, Vol. I, 1998, pp. 104 et seq.; M. Pedrosa Machado, pp. 145 et seq.; and José de Faria Costa, *O Perigo em Direito Penal*, pp. 462 et seq.

21 Arguing that this decision is (consequently) subject to the control of the Constitutional Court, see J. Figueiredo Dias (fn. 4), p. 27; and R. Dias José, p. 37.

22 Article 17 of the RGCO, as modified by DL no. 323/2001 of 17 December 2001.

a) The law may establish maximum limits higher than those indicated in Article 17 of the RGCO, as long as it is a Law by Parliament or a Decree-law by the Government authorised by Parliament[23], because those limits are considered to be part of the "general framework" of the DMOS and the competence to legislate on that matter is reserved for Parliament by the Constitution (Article 165, no. 1, d CRP).[24]

b) If the offence has brought an economic benefit to the offender that is higher than the maximum limit of the applicable *coima*, and if there is no other way to remove that benefit[25], the *coima* may be increased up to the amount of the benefit, although the increase cannot exceed 1/3 of the maximum limit established for that offence (Article 18, no. 2 RGCO). In these cases, it is possible that the general maximum limits indicated in Article 17 are exceeded.

The actual amount of the *coima* is determined by the competent authority within the applicable framework, taking into account "the seriousness of the offence, the guilt, the economic situation of the offender and the economic benefit that the offence has brought him" (Article 18, no. 1 of the RGCO).

Unlike the failure to pay (criminal) fines, the failure to pay a *coima* can never result in (surrogate) imprisonment. If the offender does not pay, the State may (only) levy execution on his property or, at his request, convert the *coima* to community service.[26]

2.2.4. Accessory sanctions

According to Article 21, no. 1 of the RGCO, the law may determine that a given *contra-ordenação* is punishable with *accessory sanctions*, to be applied together with the *coima*[27]:

---

23 See, e.g., Article 54, a of L no. 25/2008 of 5 June, where the violation of some duties concerning the prevention of money laundering is punishable with a *coima* of up to €1,250,000 (individuals) or €2,500,000 (legal entities).

24 In the same terms, see the *Decision* of TC no. 69/90 of 15 March 1990.

25 Differently from criminal law, the DMOS does not allow, *as a rule*, for the confiscation of *proceeds* and *benefits* from the offence, but only for the confiscation of objects, as an accessory sanction (Article 21, no. 1, a RGCO) and for the confiscation of dangerous objects, as a "side-effect" of the offence (Articles 22 et seq. RGCO). Nevertheless, confiscation of the proceeds is allowed in some special cases: see below, C, III.

26 Article 89-A RGCO.

27 Some authors criticise the legal rule according to which every *contra-ordenação must* be punished with a *coima*, because, in some cases, the deterrent effect is actually achieved by the accessory sanctions (see José António Veloso, "Questões hermenêuticas e de sucessão de leis nas sanções do regime geral das instituições de crédito – em especial, a inibição de direitos de voto por violação de deveres de revelar participações qualificadas", *Revista da Banca* 49 (2000), pp. 46 et seq.). Therefore, some propose that the law should provide for certain inhibitions of rights or a prohibition of activities as *main* sanctions, to which a *coima* could be added, if necessary, as a complement (M. Madureira Prates, pp. 124 et seq.).

a) confiscation of objects belonging to the offender;
b) prohibition from carrying out a profession or activity that requires a public title or authorisation;
c) deprivation of the right to subventions or benefits granted by public entities or services;
d) deprivation of the right to participate in fairs and markets;
e) deprivation of the right to participate in auctions and public competitions related to contract works or to the concession of public works, supply of goods and services, awarding of public services and awarding of licences or permits;
f) closing down of an enterprise whose functioning depends on an authorisation or licence issued by an administrative authority.

As a rule, sanctions referred to in b) to f) should be imposed for a maximum period of 2 years, although this period may be longer if the law is passed or authorised by Parliament.[28]

If the same act is both a crime and a *contra-ordenação* (concurrence of norms), the offender will be punished for the crime with the respective penal sanctions, but the judge may also apply, in addition thereto, the accessory sanctions provided for by the DMOS.

2.2.5. Fundamental principles of Direito de Mera Ordenação Social

2.2.5.1. Principle of legality

There is no *explicit* constitutional basis for a principle of legality in administrative sanctioning law, but authors tend to consider that the constitutional guarantees implied in the principle of legality of criminal law (Article 29 of the Constitution) are applicable, by analogy, to the DMOS.[29] Therefore, the principle of legality laid down in Article 2 of the RGCO ("*only conduct threatened with a coima by a previous law may be punished as a contra-ordenação*") should be seen as a *constitutional imposition* and not as a discretionary choice (subject to alteration) of the legislator.[30]

However, one should note that the principle of legality applicable in DMOS does not have to be *exactly coincident* with the one applicable in criminal law. Some adaptations may be required, either: a) because of their different constitutional framework; or b) for the sake of the coordination of both branches of law; or c) in order to ensure the efficiency of the DMOS.

Let us take a closer look at these adaptations:

---

28 See below, 5.1, a.

29 J.J. Gomes Canotilho / Vital Moreira, *Constituição da República Portuguesa Anotada*, 3rd ed., 1993, p. 195.

30 For a different opinion, arguing that the principle of legality in DMOS does not have constitutional, but mere legal grounds, see M. Fernanda Palma / Paulo Otero, p. 563.

(i) Competence to enact the DMOS (*nullum crimen, nulla poena sine lege scripta*)

As far as criminal law is concerned, Article 165, no. 1, c of the Portuguese Constitution states that only Parliament, or the Government authorised by Parliament, may legislate on the definition of crimes, penalties and criminal procedure.[31] The same framework applies to the definition of the *general rules* of DMOS (Article 165, no. 1, d), but the Government has an autonomous competence to create, alter and revoke the norms that define the *concrete offences* (*contra-ordenações*), with no need for authorisation by Parliament (Article 198, no. 1, a CRP), provided that the legal act respects those general rules.

(ii) Prohibition of unfavourable retroactivity (*nullum crimen, nulla poena sine lege praevia*)

As in criminal law, the principle of legality implies the prohibition of unfavourable retroactivity: the law creating a new *contra-ordenação* or determining heavier sanctions does not apply, *as a rule*, to acts committed prior to its enactment (Article 3, no. 1 RGCO).

Nevertheless, there is a particular problem that is not explicitly regulated by the law and does not gather a unanimous solution in the literature: the case where the law in force at the time of the offence considered the act as a *crime*, and the law in force at the moment of the trial considers the same act as a *contra-ordenação*.

Some authors argue that, the offence having been *decriminalised*, the law of the *tempus delicti* can no longer apply (Article 2, no. 2 of the Penal Code), and the new law is also inapplicable because it is not a *criminal* law and therefore does not fall under the provision of Article 2, no. 4 of the Penal Code (retroactive application of the milder *criminal* statute). Consequently, the retroactive application of the new law would be prohibited by the principle of legality of DMOS. These arguments lead inevitably to the *acquittal* of offenders who have committed crimes before the new law converts the offence into a contra-ordenação, as long as they are not definitively tried under the former law.[32]

Other authors argue that the former solution creates intolerable loopholes, because the legal system *continuously* considers the act as unlawful, and an acquittal due to the modification of the nature of the offence would be hardly understandable. Therefore, according to this line of reasoning, the new law should *always* be applied retroactively as the milder statute (by means of an analogy with Article 2, no. 4 Penal Code).[33]

---

31 In more detail, see Maria João Antunes / Pedro Caeiro, "Portugal", in: Kluwer Encyclopaedia of Criminal Law, suppl. 6 (May 1995), pp. 35 et seq.

32 Américo Taipa de Carvalho, *Sucessão de Leis Penais*, 2nd ed. 1997, pp. 120 et seq.

33 Jorge de Figueiredo Dias / Manuel da Costa Andrade, *Direito Penal. Questões Fundamentais. A Doutrina Geral do Crime*, 1996, §237.

In our opinion, the latter solution is not acceptable, because it is grounded on an unfavourable analogy, which is definitely forbidden by the principle of legality applicable in DMOS. Nevertheless, the legislator can avoid the undesirable consequences to which the former solution leads, by explicitly providing, each time that it is the case, for an *exceptional retroactive applicability* of the norms that *only* convert a crime into a *contra-ordenação*.

Indeed, this solution is easily acceptable for those who argue that the principle of legality in the DMOS does not have *constitutional* grounds, but only a *statutory* basis (Article 2 RGCO), which can be derogated by a statute with the same normative value.[34] But even if we do not share that point of view, we believe that the constitutional basis of the principle of legality in the DMOS does not necessarily mean that it must have the *same content* as it does in criminal law. Thus, it can be derogated, in exceptional cases, in order to protect other relevant interests. Furthermore, from a substantive point of view, and bearing in mind that the act was considered to be a crime at the moment when it was committed, we cannot say that the retroactive application of the law providing for the *contra-ordenação* will frustrate the offender's "legitimate expectations".

In sum, it is submitted that:

- the principle of legality in DMOS has constitutional grounds, but does not have to replicate the one applicable in criminal law;
- as a rule, the retroactive application of DMOS norms is forbidden by that principle and, therefore, should be considered as contrary to the Constitution;
- the latter proposition includes, in principle, those cases where the new law converts certain crimes into *contra-ordenações*: if the legislator does not provide for the retroactive application of the new law, the defendant must be acquitted;
- when the new law converts crimes into *contra-ordenações*, the legislator is exceptionally entitled to provide for the retroactive application of the new law, which does not violate the principle of legality of DMOS.

(iii) Definiteness (*nullum crimen, nulla poena sine lege certa*)

Whereas criminal law must be definite, so that individuals may fully understand the sense and the limits of the norms, it is accepted that the DMOS is more "porous", in the sense that its norms can have "blank spaces", which are to be completed by other norms or acts on the part of the authorities.[35] A good

34 See above, fn. 30.

35 On the issue of the admissible legislative techniques in the DMOS, see Frederico da Costa Pinto, *O Novo regime dos Crimes e Contra-Ordenações no Código dos Valores Mobiliários*, 2000, pp. 26 et seq. Arguing the admissibility of an (unfavourable) analogy in the DMOS, based on the silence of the law, M. Fernanda Palma / Paulo Otero, pp. 563 et seq.; see also above, fn. 30.

example is Article 68 of DL no. 28/84 of 20 January 1984, which punishes those who produce, sell, etc., goods or services "not complying with the rules set by the law for the undertaking of the respective activities".

2.2.5.2. Principle of favourable retroactivity (retroactive application of *lex mitior*)

The new law that revokes an existing *contra-ordenação* or sets milder sanctions must be applied retroactively (Article 3, no. 2 RGCO). This imposition is founded on the principle of necessity of repressive law (unnecessary sanctions are illegitimate) and not on the principle of legality.[36]

2.2.5.3. Principle of guilt (culpability)

This principle means that the sanctions can only be imposed on blameworthy offenders. Minors under 16, and people affected by a mental illness that prevents them from understanding the unlawfulness of their act, or from acting in accordance with the law, are not liable.

Guilt requires acting with intent or negligence, although the punishment of negligent offences requires a specific legal provision (Article 8, no. 1 RGCO). Thus, strict liability is not allowed.

2.2.5.4. *Societas delinquere potest*

Article 11, no. 1 of the Penal Code states that "only individuals are liable for criminal offences, except for what is established in the following number and in other specific cases foreseen in the law".[37]

Article 7 of the RGCO follows a different approach, stating that both individuals and legal entities are *always* held liable for *contra-ordenações*.

---

36 See Pedro Caeiro, "Aplicação da lei penal no tempo e prazos de suspensão da prescrição do procedimento criminal: um 'caso prático' ", in: *Estudos em Homenagem a Cunha Rodrigues*, vol. I, 2001, pp. 235 et seq.

37 Article 11, no. 2 establishes, under certain conditions, the criminal liability of legal persons for a wide range of crimes, including slavery, trafficking in human beings, sexual crimes (the victim being a minor), corruption, etc.
Legal persons are also held liable for criminal offences in a large number of economic, financial and tax crimes (see, e.g., Article 3 of DL no. 28/84 of 20 January 1984) and also for the crimes of terrorism and terrorist organisation (Article 6 of L no. 52/2003 of 22 August, which has transposed into Portuguese law the *Council Framework Decision of 13 June 2002 on combating terrorism*).

2.2.5.5. *Non bis in idem*

According to Article 79 of the RGCO, final decisions of the administrative authority concerning *contra-ordenações* and final judgments by the courts (irrespective of whether the case was tried as a *contra-ordenação* or a crime) prevent new charges for the same conduct as a *contra-ordenação* (no. 1).

The judicial decision or judgment, having the force of *res judicata*, that tries the case as a *contra-ordenação* prevents new charges for the same conduct as a crime (no. 2).

The conjugation of both norms means that, as a rule, final decisions in administrative *and* criminal procedures prevent the authorities from charging the offender for the same act *again* as a *contra-ordenação* or a crime, irrespective of whether the offender was acquitted or convicted.

However, there is an exception to the rule: if the final decision was taken by an administrative authority (in an administrative procedure), the judicial authorities may proceed against the offender in a criminal procedure. It is questionable whether this exception complies with the prohibition of double jeopardy enshrined in Article 29, no. 5 of the CRP, although this norm refers exclusively to "*the same crime*", especially in the case where the administrative decision has imposed sanctions on the offender.

Moreover, if, during the investigation, the administrative authorities consider that the offence can be qualified as a crime, they have a legal duty not to proceed and to remit the case to the Public Prosecutor.[38] This means that the criminal procedure for an act that has already been decided upon by administrative authorities is due to a wrongful appreciation of the case by the latter, and it would be rather awkward that such a mistake could cause unfavourable consequences for the offender.

2.2.5.6. Principle of subsidiary applicability of criminal (substantive) law

Article 32 of the RGCO states that the Penal Code is applicable as subsidiary law in as much as the RGCO does not provide for different solutions (as it is the case, e. g., in the rules concerning the punishment of concurrent *contra-ordenações*[39]).

This principle is consistent with the fact that most of the general rules of the RGCO have been copied from the Penal Code. Nevertheless, in some cases, the

---

38 See below, 6.5, ii.

39 According to Article 77 of the Penal Code, he who commits more than one crime is punishable by a single penalty, which cannot be lower than the highest of the penalties concretely applied to each crime, nor higher than the sum of all those (separate) penalties. Article 19 RGCO adopts these criteria as a basis (nos. 1 and 3), but adds a further limit, stating that the *coima* cannot exceed double the highest maximum limit applicable to the concurrent *contra-ordenações*. For a critical view on this issue, see F. Costa Pinto (fn. 19), pp. 248 et seq.

direct application of the principles and rules of criminal law, as subsidiary law, would mean a normative contradiction with the nature and the purpose of the DMOS.

For example: the rules that define authorship and participation in criminal law (the "*Tatherrschaft*" model) seem to be inadequate to frame a different kind of unlawfulness, where complex forms of interaction between individuals and legal entities are the rule, and where the offences are often mere infringements of duties (*delitos de dever, Pflichtdelikte*).[40]

That is also the case in the commission of a crime by omission: the RGCO does not have a rule similar to Article 10, no. 1 of the Penal Code, establishing the equivalence of action and omission for crimes that entail a material result. However, Articles 5 and 6 of the RGCO (definition of the moment and place of the act) make explicit reference to offences by omission, which means that omission is punishable under the DMOS. In this context, we could be led to "import" the rule stated in Article 10, no. 2 of the Penal Code, which limits the punishment of omission to cases where the offender has a special duty to safeguard the interest protected by the norm (*dever de garante, Garantenpflicht*) and, therefore, must act to avoid the undesired result. But, if we bear in mind the principle of legality (*lex certa*), such subsidiary application of a general rule of criminal law seems inadequate: whereas the failure to act by the guarantor, in the field of criminal law, can easily be seen as an offence against the protected interest – due to the ethical relevance of criminal norms – that general definition cannot apply to the DMOS, where the forbidden forms of conduct are, in most cases, ethically irrelevant. As a consequence, the law must identify the specific duties to act, and the persons that are bound by them, in each case where an omission is to be punished as a *contra-ordenação*.[41]

2.2.6. Procedure

2.2.6.1. A *sui generis* procedure: the RGCO and criminal procedural law

The procedure for *contra-ordenações* is somewhat peculiar, as the acts practised by administrative authorities are not subject to administrative law, but rather to the (few) rules contained in the RGCO and, as subsidiary law, in the Code of Penal Procedure (Article 41 RGCO). This framework is supposed to provide better protection for individual rights than common administrative law would.

The subsidiary application of criminal procedural law has to be carefully adapted to the DMOS.[42] Concerning, for instance, coercive measures, Article 42

40 For a thorough discussion, see F. Costa Pinto (fn. 19), pp. 218 et seq.

41 F. Costa Pinto (fn. 19), pp. 244 et seq.

42 Frederico da Costa Pinto, "Acesso de particulares a processos de contra-ordenação arquivados", in: *Estudos em Homenagem à Professora Doutora Isabel de Magalhães Collaço*, vol. II, 2000, pp. 616 et seq. See also above 5.6, concerning the subsidiary application of criminal substantive law.

does not provide explicitly for admissible coercive measures; instead – and rather awkwardly –, this provision only states that some of the coercive measures applicable in criminal procedure (remand in custody and interception of correspondence and communications) are *not* admissible in the DMOS. One could be led to the wrongful conclusion that other coercive measures (such as remand on bail, house arrest, prohibition of going to certain places, etc.) can be applied in the DMOS procedures. However, that is not the case. In the first place, because almost all of those measures can be applied only by a judge, and judges do not have any intervention in the administrative stage of these procedures.[43] In the second place, because the sole criminal coercive measure that can be applied by authorities other than the judge (*termo de identidade e residência*: Article 196 of the CPP) consists of the imposition of certain obligations that aim to ensure the presence of the defendant before the authorities whenever that may be necessary – and the presence of the offender in the DMOS procedural acts is voluntary.

Thus, we may conclude that coercive measures applicable in criminal procedure are not applicable in DMOS. This conclusion is consistent with the fact that Article 49 of the RGCO explicitly allows the administrative authorities and the police bodies to *identify* a person that is suspected of having committed a *contra-ordenação*, and Article 191, no. 2 of the CPP, explicitly states that identifying a suspect *is not* a coercive measure. Consequently, one has to interpret the prohibition contained in Article 42, no. 1, as a mere emphatic restatement regarding the gravest coercive measures.

2.2.6.2. Principle of legality

(i) According to Article 43 of the RGCO, the procedure is subject to the principle of legality. In procedural law, this principle has two consequences[44]:

- In the first place, the procedural acts must abide by the rules stated by the law. The administrative authorities do not have the power to undertake acts that are not legally typified, nor to create new forms of procedure.
- In the second place, the administrative authorities must investigate and proceed against *every contra-ordenação* that comes to their knowledge (mandatory prosecution), which means that they cannot file a case on the grounds of, e.g., the lack of a relevant public interest (discretionary prosecution).

---

43 In the judicial phase of the procedure, triggered by the appeal of the offender against the administrative decision (see below, 6.6), coercive measures are no longer necessary.

44 Frederico da Costa Pinto, *Direito Processual Penal*, AAFDL, 1998, pp. 195 et seq.

The original version of Article 51 of the RGCO (1982) allowed for a *warning procedure*, where the administrative authority, in cases of minor significance, could propose the payment of a symbolic amount (equivalent to €2.5) to the suspect, before the beginning of a formal inquiry; if the suspect accepted, the case would be filed, having the force of *res judicata*. This procedure had an important role in diverting petty administrative offences from formal prosecution. Nevertheless, DL 244/95 modified Article 51, replacing the warning procedure by the sanction of written admonishment, which is a final decision, and is subject, as such, to the ordinary procedure.

In spite of this surprising development (diversion procedures for petty offences are allowed even in criminal procedural law[45]) at the level of the *general* rules applicable to the DMOS, one should note that, recently, the Stock Market Code[46] has created a special *warning procedure* (*procedimento de advertência*) similar to the one contained in (former) Article 51 of the RGCO. According to Article 413 of the Stock Market Code, applicable to the *contra-ordenações* "if the offence consists of a reparable irregularity and has caused no damage to investors nor to the stock market, the Board of the Stock Market may warn the offender, and notify him to correct the irregularity" within a certain time. If the offender abides by this order, the case is filed and the warning is converted into a final conviction, having the force of *res judicata*.

Article 414 of the same Code also provides for an *abbreviated procedure* in cases of minor significance (*processo sumaríssimo*[47]): before presenting a formal charge, the Board notifies the offender of their decision to apply an admonishment, or a *coima* that cannot exceed triple the minimum amount set for that *contra-ordenação*, and orders the offender to adopt the conduct demanded by the law. If the offender abides by this order and pays the *coima*, the conviction becomes definitive, having the force of *res judicata*.

The failure to comply with the decision taken in terms of Article 413 and Article 414 results in the continuation of the common procedure.[48]

(ii) When the case reaches the judicial stage[49], the Public Prosecutor can withdraw the charges, with the defendant's consent, until the judge takes a final decision. The law does not provide for which criteria are to be used in the

---

45 See Manuel da Costa Andrade, "Consenso e oportunidade (reflexões a propósito da suspensão provisória do processo e do processo sumaríssimo)", in: *Jornadas de Direito Processual Penal. O novo Código de Processo Penal* (org. CEJ), 1988, pp. 317 et seq.; and Pedro Caeiro, "Legalidade e oportunidade: a perseguição penal entre o mito da 'justiça absoluta' e o fetiche da 'gestão eficiente' do sistema", in: *Legalidade* versus *Oportunidade*, (ed. Sindicato dos Magistrados do Ministério Público), 2002, pp. 45 et seq.

46 Enacted by DL no. 486/99 of 13 November, duly authorised by L no. 106/99 of 26 July.

47 This *processo sumaríssimo* is largely inspired in the homologous (and homonymous) procedure contained in Articles 392 et seq of the Code of Penal Procedure.

48 See F. Costa Pinto (fn. 35), pp. 28 et seq.

49 See below, 6.6.

decision to withdraw the charges, and criminal procedural law does not provide for a situation where the Public Prosecutor can withdraw the charges previously presented to the court.[50]

If we take into consideration the general principles of criminal procedural law and the rules that guide the activity of the Public Prosecutor, we see that there is no room for a decision based on discretionary grounds (like, e.g., the "lack of a relevant public interest"). But, in the Portuguese system, the Public Prosecutor's activity is subject to a *principle of objectivity* and therefore must not accuse at any price. In conclusion, we can say that the decision to withdraw the charges must obey the same criteria that apply to the decision not to accuse in a criminal procedure: either because there is not sufficient evidence that the suspect has committed the offence or because the act does not fulfil the necessary requirements to be sanctioned as a *contra-ordenação.*

2.2.6.3. Gathering of evidence

Article 42, no. 1 of the RGCO excludes "the utilization of evidence gathered in violation of professional secrecy". Indeed, this provision also means that such evidence cannot be *gathered* by the authorities.[51] Article 42, no. 2 states that the gathering of evidence which conflicts with privacy, as well as bodily examinations and blood tests, can only be carried out with the consent of the individual.

Article 48-A states that the authorities can seize the objects that served or were intended to serve for the commission of an offence, or were produced by an offence, as well as any other objects that may be used as evidence.[52]

Personal searches and searches in a given location must comply with the various legal acts that provide for the control and inspection powers of each competent authority.

2.2.6.4. Rights of the defence

(i) The suspect has the constitutional *right to be heard in the procedure and to present his / her defence* (Article 32, no. 10 CRP and Article 50 RGCO). If the administrative authorities apply a sanction without having given the offender the opportunity to exert this right, the decision is illegal and should be considered as such by the court at the appeal stage.

---

50 Article 280 CPP states that the Public Prosecutor can file a case, with no further consequences, in the case of petty offences for which the law explicitly admits the possibility of an exemption from punishment. But it is obvious that this mechanism of *diversion* does not apply in the DMOS, due to the very nature of this branch of the law.

51 On the relationship between exclusionary rules regarding the gathering of evidence and the ones concerning the evaluation of evidence (in *criminal* procedural law), see Manuel da Costa Andrade, *Sobre as Proibições de Prova em Processo Penal*, 1992.

52 Articles 178 et seq. CPP are applicable as subsidiary law.

This right includes:

- The right to be informed of orders and decisions taken by the authorities (Article 46, no. 1).
- The right to be informed of the right to appeal (namely concerning the applicable terms and forms) (Article 46, no. 2).
- The right to present evidence, including the right to have witnesses and experts heard by the authorities.

(ii) The suspect has the right to legal assistance (Article 53) and he can choose a lawyer to assist him at any stage of the procedure. The administrative authorities can appoint a designated lawyer to assist the suspect, at his request or *ex officio*, if that appears to be necessary or convenient, according to the circumstances of the case. There is a right to appeal to the court from the decision that overrules the offender's request to have a designated lawyer.

(iii) There is a right to appeal from the final decision of the administrative authorities to a court (judicial review), and from the court's decision to a superior court.[53]

2.2.6.5. Competence to proceed and to apply the sanctions

(i) In general, the competence to proceed against an offender and to apply the respective administrative sanctions belongs to the administrative authorities to whom the law entrusts that power, according to their functions and jurisdiction. This means that there is no central authority with concentrated sanctioning powers.

Usually, those authorities belong to the (central or local) administration (e.g., the Ministries and the Councils), but there are also independent authorities with specific competence to investigate *contra-ordenações* and to apply the respective sanctions, e.g, the *Comissão do Mercado de Valores Mobiliários* (General Board of the Stock Market). Some authors argue that, from the point of view of the protection of individual rights, it would be preferable not to entrust both investigative *and* sanctioning powers to the same authority.[54] However, this opinion seems to be far too influenced by criminal law principles. One should bear in mind that DMOS is intended to be a quick and efficient response to administrative infringements[55] and that offenders always have the right to challenge the administrative decision by appealing to a common court for judicial review.

---

53 See below, 6.6.

54 M. Madureira Prates, pp. 42 et seq.

55 See José de Faria Costa, "Les Problèmes Juridiques et Pratiques posés par la Différence entre le Droit Criminel et le Droit Administratif-Pénal", offprint of *Boletim da Faculdade de Direito da Universidade de Coimbra* LXII (1986), p. 27.

ii) In some cases, the *contra-ordenação* will be tried and sanctioned in first instance by the court. That is the case of (real) concurrence of crimes and *contra-ordenações*: the competence to proceed belongs to the public prosecutor and the sanctions will be applied by the court in the criminal procedure (Articles 38 and 77, no. 1).

2.2.6.6. Appeals

(i) If the offender is sanctioned by the administration, he has the right to appeal to a (common, not administrative) court, thus triggering the *judicial stage* of the procedure (Article 59). When the appeal is filed, the administrative authority has two options: either to revoke the decision that applied the sanctions – and the case will be closed–, or to remit the file to the Public Prosecutor, who will present it to the judge as a formal charge (Article 62).

(ii) The Public Prosecutor can withdraw the charges until the judge decides the case, provided that the defendant agrees to the withdrawal. As a rule, the Public Prosecutor should hear the administrative authority that applied the sanctions before taking that decision (Article 65-A).

(iii) If the judge considers the trial hearing to be unnecessary, he may simply record the decision, as long as the Public Prosecutor and the defendant do not oppose to that form of "abbreviated" trial (Article 64). Otherwise, a trial hearing must take place, in the terms and forms provided for the trial of *contravenções* and *transgressões*.[56]

The defendant has the right to be present at the hearing, but is not compelled to attend, unless the judge considers his presence to be necessary to resolve the case. If the judge has not ordered his presence, the defendant may choose to be represented by his lawyer (Article 67, no. 2). When the defendant is absent and does not have a lawyer, it seems that the judge must appoint him with a designated lawyer, on the strength of Article 11 of DL no. 17/91 of 10 January 1991 (Procedure and trial of *contravenções* and *transgressões*).

(iv) The decision must always contain the reasons why the administrative decision is maintained or modified, or why the defendant is acquitted (Article 64, no. 4 and no. 5).

(v) The decision of the court may be challenged by means of an appeal to a superior court (*Relação*), by the defendant or the Public Prosecutor, if one of the following conditions applies (Article 73):

- the defendant is convicted and ordered to pay a *coima* higher than €249.40;
- the defendant is convicted and accessory sanctions are imposed;

56 DL no. 17/91 of 10 January 1991.

- the defendant is acquitted, or the case is filed, in cases where the administrative authority had applied (or the Public Prosecutor had claimed for application of) a *coima* higher than €249.40;
- the court rejects the appeal from the administrative decision;
- the court decides the case without a formal trial hearing despite the defendant's opposition.

As a rule, the superior court may only control the interpretation and application of the law and has no power to re-evaluate the evidence presented.

vi) The appeal to the courts, both from the administrative and the judicial decision, is subject to the prohibition of *reformatio in pejus*, provided that only the defendant has appealed, or the Public Prosecutor has appealed in the defendant's interest (Article 72-A, no. 1).[57] However, the courts can increase the amount of the *coima* if the economic situation of the defendant has improved significantly in the meantime (Article 72-A, no. 2).[58]

2.3. OTHER UNFAVOURABLE ADMINISTRATIVE MEASURES (POLICE MEASURES *LATO SENSU*)

2.3.1. Definition

One of the most important functions of the administration is to protect public interest by controlling risk and preventing damage (police function *lato sensu*). This multiform capacity involves *activities* as disparate as street surveillance, the withdrawal of hunting licences, identifying suspects in a pub, removing a parked car, dispersing a violent demonstration, closing down a shop for sanitary reasons, etc., and a multitude of different *authorities*, like police bodies, of course, but also ministers, secretaries of State and general directors, civil governors (representatives of the Government in the administrative districts), mayors and other members of the council.[59]

The police function is carried out by taking measures that may entail a restriction of the rights of an individual or entity. These measures can consist of juridical acts (e.g., the withdrawal of licences) or material acts (e.g., the removal of cars from the public highway).[60]

57 This rule was introduced by DL 244/95, in 1995. For a convincing criticism of the "import" of this principle of criminal law to the DMOS, see F. Costa Pinto, (fn. 19) pp. 264 et seq.

58 See above, 3.2.

59 See Vital Moreira, pp. 1 et seq.

60 Vital Moreira, p. 5.

It is important to notice that these measures do not have a punitive aim and therefore cannot be qualified as sanctions.[61] In fact, even when they affect individual rights, their primary goal is to preserve the public interest against possible harm, irrespective of the allocation of responsibility for the undesired risk, whereas *coimas* and other administrative sanctions are aimed at the (general and individual) prevention of future offences through the repression of past infringements.

2.3.2. Examples of police measures

Considering the large variety of police measures, it is not easy to class them into a typology.[62] We will try to give some examples that could be mistaken for administrative sanctions.

2.3.2.1. Measures that are not necessarily connected with an imminent danger to the public interest

The administration has the general capacity to modify or withdraw licences and permits to exert certain rights, either because the individual no longer fulfils the required conditions, or because the legal framework has been modified in a way that the licence must be modified or withdrawn.[63]

Indeed, the capacity to *modify* or *withdraw* licences and permits is consistent with the capacity to *allow* them or to *refuse* their issuance: underlying the application of those measures is the idea that the undertaking of certain activities and the exercise of some rights is *potentially* dangerous to the public interest and, thus, must remain under the administration's scrutiny. Therefore, their application aims at avoiding abstract risks and does not *necessarily*[64] suppose an imminent danger to the public interest.

Such measures are taken as a result of continuous control of the persistence of the material and legal conditions of permissive administrative acts.[65] Examples: the restriction on the "opening hours" of bars in a given area by the Council, as a means of improving public security; the withdrawal of the driving

61 See J. J. Gomes Canotilho / Vital Moreira, p. 956. Although the authors refer this idea to the police function *stricto sensu* (see below, III, 2), it applies, *a fortiori*, to the measures taken by the administration in the context of the police function *lato sensu* (see below, III, 1). In the same sense proposed in the text, M. Madureira Prates, *passim*.

62 In detail, see M. Madureira Prates, pp. 136 et seq.

63 M. Madureira Prates, p. 147.

64 Although these measures may also be taken to avoid or remove an existing or imminent danger: see below, 2.2.

65 M. Madureira Prates, pag. 147.

licence possessed by an individual who has become blind; the withdrawal of a permit that allows the exercise of banking activities.[66]

2.3.2.2. Measures that are intended to avoid or remove an imminent or existing danger to the public interest

These measures may consist of *orders* directed at individuals, aiming at a modification of their conduct, so as to comply with the applicable legal rules, or of *direct action* by the authorities.

(i) Orders

In this group, we find the vast majority of the measures taken by administrative authorities aiming at avoiding risks or at removing present danger. They consist of commands for positive or negative behaviour.

Examples: Article 41, no. 4 of the Code of Publicity[67] provides that the authority that has the capacity to order cautionary measures (suspension, cancellation, prohibition, etc.) against publicity that may put at risk the health, safety, and rights of the addressees, minors or general public, may grant a delay to the advertiser, so that he can remove the unlawful elements from the advertisement.

An example of a duty of positive action are the conservation measures in buildings that can be ordered against the owner of the building, to avoid compulsory demolition (see Article 10 of DL no. 44258 of 31 March 1962).

(ii) Direct action by the administration

The purpose of these measures is also to safeguard the public interest from imminent danger or present offences.[68] However, the intensity of the risk, or the presence of an actual danger, are not compatible with orders to abide by the rules, requiring, instead, direct action by the authorities.

Examples: the demolition of a building at risk of collapse (Article 10 of DL no. 44258 of 31 March 1962); the slaughter of diseased animals (DL no. 28/96 of 2 April 1996); the withdrawal of an illegally possessed firearm (Article 107, no. 1, c of L no. 5/2006 of 23 February)[69]; the provisional closure of a restaurant or bar for safety reasons (Article 7, no. 1 of DL no. 101/2008 of 16 June); and the withdrawal of the permit of a bank that can no longer fulfil its obligations

66 In detail, see José António Veloso, "Sobre a natureza não-sancionatória da revogação da autorização das instituições de crédito e outras questões de fiscalização de actividades reservadas: algumas notas de justificação de decisões legislativas", *Direito e justiça – Revista da Faculdade de Direito da Universidade Católica Portuguesa*, vol. XIV, Tomo I, Porto, 2000, pp. 66 et seq.

67 Enacted by DL no. 330/90 of 23 October 1990.

68 M. Madureira Prates, p. 164.

69 M. Madureira Prates, p. 165.

(Article 178, f and d of DL no. 298/92 of 31 December 1992, amended the last time by L no. 36/2010 of 2 September).

2.3.3. Fundamental principles of police measures

2.3.3.1. Police measures *lato sensu*

In general, police measures are subject to the principles that define and limit the activity of the administration (Article 268 CRP): the pursuance of public interest, while respecting individual rights and interests guaranteed by the law; compliance on the part of the administration with the Constitution and the law; and respect for the principles of equality, proportionality, justice and impartiality. We will briefly describe those which are more relevant for our subject.

(i) Principle of pursuance of public interest while respecting individual rights

This principle means that the administration must always act in the benefit of public interest, even in the use of discretionary powers, thus prohibiting arbitrary measures.

The positive legitimacy given by the pursuance of public interest has its negative limit in the individual rights and interests protected by the law.

(ii) Principle of the administration's compliance with the Constitution and the law

The administration, as every public power, is subordinated to the Constitution (Article 2, no. 3 CRP). Although the administrative authorities, unlike the courts, do not have, as a rule, the power to refuse the application of a legal act on the grounds that it violates the Constitution (unless that violation is "*flagrant* and *notorious*"[70]), this principle prevents administrative authorities from autonomously violating the Constitution, obliges them to respect constitutional values when exerting discretionary powers, and imposes on them the duty to interpret and apply the law in a sense that corresponds more closely to constitutional principles and values. Moreover, the administrative acts that directly violate the CRP are null and void and should be declared as such by the administrative courts.[71]

70 J. J. Gomes Canotilho / Vital Moreira, p. 924.

71 See J. J. Gomes Canotilho / Vital Moreira, p. 922; and José C. Vieira de Andrade, *A Justiça Administrativa*, 4th ed., 2003, p. 199 (fn. 372).

The administrative authorities are also bound by the principle of the legality (*rectior*: "juridicity"[72]) of the administration, which entails two dimensions: the prevalence of the law and the precedence of a legal act. The first dimension prevents the administration from engaging in illegal acts; the second means that the administration may only act when a legal act has previously established that capacity. If the administrative measure has the effect of limiting a fundamental right, the principle of the legality of the administration is reinforced by Article 165, no. 1, b of the CRP, which states that only Parliament (or the Government authorised by Parliament) may enact laws that limit fundamental rights, liberties and guarantees.

(iii) Principle of proportionality

This principle is particularly important for our subject, stating that, "when the administration exerts discretionary powers, it is not sufficient to pursue the scope of the concession of those powers by the law: the public interest must be pursued by choosing, among the measures that are efficient to fulfil that scope, those who cause the least limitation or harm to the rights and interests of the administered".[73]

(iv) Principle of impartiality

Concerning our subject, this principle means that in the case where public interest conflicts with individual rights, the administration must consider with fairness whether the former shall prevail over the latter, so as not to cause unnecessary or disproportionate harm to the rights of the individual.

(v) Protection of individual rights against the administration

Article 268 of the CRP establishes several rights that protect individuals from illegal or abusive measures by the administration:

- the right to be informed of the proceedings that concern them and to know the definitive decisions taken in those proceedings (no. 1);
- the right to access administrative files and records, within the limits stated in the law for reasons of internal and external security, criminal investigation and privacy (no. 2);
- the right to be notified of administrative acts that concern them, which shall be properly justified when they affect individual rights (no. 3);

72 J. J. Gomes Canotilho / Vital Moreira, p. 923.
73 J. J. Canotilho / Vital Moreira, p. 924.

- the right to effective jurisdictional protection of their rights, which includes, namely, the right to challenge any administrative act (or an administrative norm with external effect) that affects their interests before a court, the right to a judicial decision ordering the practise of a due act by the administration or adopting preventive measures against the risk of an illegal or abusive act (no. 4 and no. 5).[74]

2.3.3.2. Police measures *stricto sensu*

Article 272 of the CRP deals specifically with the police function *stricto sensu*, i.e., the enforcement of democratic legality, of internal security and of the rights of individuals, entrusted to police bodies (namely, *Polícia de Segurança Pública* and *Guarda Nacional Republicana*).

Additionally to the principles described above, the police function *stricto sensu* is bound by other limitations: the principle of the legal typology of the admissible measures and the prohibition of excessive measures.

(i) Principle of the legal typology of admissible measures

Police measures *stricto sensu* and their contents must be specified by the law. Indeed, this principle is not as strict as the principle of legality in criminal law and it does not demand correspondence between each measure and the specific situations in which they can be applied[75]: the general description, in the law, of the admissible police measures is sufficient.[76]

(ii) Prohibition of excessive measures

This prohibition restates emphatically the principle of proportionality stated in Article 268, no. 2 of the CRP.[77] Considering the wording of Article 272, no. 2 of the CRP ("[the measures] cannot be used beyond what is strictly necessary") and, also, that this kind of administrative activity involves a higher risk of affecting individual rights, maybe we can speak of an *intensification* of the general principle of proportionality contained in the former norm.

---

74 These rights are regulated by L no. 13/2002 of 19 February 2002 (which approved the Statute of the Administrative and Tax Courts) and L no. 15/2002 of 22 February 2002 (which approved the Code of Procedure for the Administrative Courts). On this issue, explaining the evolution of the Portuguese system of administrative justice, see J.C. Vieira de Andrade, (fn. 71), pp. 27 et seq., *passim*.

75 Vital Moreira, p. 5.

76 Vital Moreira, p. 5.

77 See J.J. Gomes Canotilho / Vital Moreira, p. 956.

This principle means, for instance, that the police cannot use rubber bullets to disperse a crowd if water-cannons are sufficient for this purpose. Due to its direct applicability, a violation of the prohibition may entail the civil and criminal liability of the responsible officials and agents (Article 271 CRP).

(III) THE LIMITS OF THE FUNCTION OF PREVENTING CRIME

Article 272, no. 3 of the CRP states that "the prevention of crimes, including the crimes against the security of the State, may only be carried out in the respect for the general rules on police activity and the fundamental rights of individuals". Consequently, the prevention of crimes can only affect fundamental rights in the general cases admitted by the CRP (Articles 27 and 28).[78] In other words, this administrative function does not constitute an *autonomous and sufficient* ground for the law to establish restrictions on fundamental rights.

2.4. SOME EXAMPLES OF *CONTRA-ORDENAÇÕES* AND OTHER UNFAVOURABLE ADMINISTRATIVE MEASURES IN SPECIFIC LEGAL AREAS

2.4.1. Urban law (law on building)

DL no. 555/99 of 16 December 1999, amended the last time by L no. 36/2010 of 2 September), contains several *contra-ordenações*, like, e.g., building without a necessary licence, or the failure to previously communicate the works to the authorities, that are punished with *coimas* and three other accessory sanctions indicated in Article 99: the confiscation of objects used in the commission of the offence; the prohibition on carrying out the activities or professions connected with the offence in the council where it was committed, for a period of up to 2 years; and the deprivation of subventions granted by public authorities or services.

The competence to proceed to the inquiry and to impose sanctions belongs to the mayor (Article 98, no. 10), who also has the capacity to order a halt on works that are being undertaken without the necessary licences or permits, or that do not comply with the (approved) project or licence (Article 102, no. 1).

The proceeds from the *coimas* revert to the Council (Article 98, no. 11).

78 See J. J. Gomes Canotilho / Vital Moreira, pp. 956 et seq.

DL no. 12/2004 of 9 January 2004 regulates the contract works and lays down three types of *contra-ordenações* ("simple", "serious" and "very serious") for the infringement of the rules established therein.

"Simple" *contra-ordenações* are punishable with a *coima* from 500 up to €1,500 (individuals) or €3,000 up to €20,000 (legal entities and corporations).

"Serious" *contra-ordenações*, such as anti-competitive behaviour, are punishable with a *coima* from €1,000 up to €3,000 (individuals) or €5,000 up to €30,000 (legal entities and corporations).

"Very serious" *contra-ordenações*, such as contracting out services to a company that is not properly qualified, are punishable with a *coima* from €2,000 up to €3,740.98 (individuals) or €7,500 up to €44,800 (legal entities and corporations).

This statute also provides for some accessory sanctions, such as the prohibition on carrying out the activity connected with the offence, which implies a prohibition on completing the works and on participating in public or private contract rendering, and the prohibition on undertaking related activities.

The inspection and control of these activities, as well as the competence to investigate the alleged offences, is entrusted to the IMOPPI (*Instituto dos Mercados das Obras Públicas e Particulares do Imobiliário* – Institute for the Market of Public and Private Real Estate Works).

The capacity to impose the sanctions belongs to the Chairman of the Board of the IMOPPI.

2.4.2. Protection of the economy and public health

Anti-economic offences and offences against public health have their basic legal framework in DL no. 28/84 of 20 January 1984[79], which contains provisions concerning both crimes and *contra-ordenações*.

Some examples of *contra-ordenações* are: acts against the authenticity, quality or composition of foodstuff (e.g., the production of foodstuff that does not comply with the applicable legal rules or regulations on hygiene, the possession of substances or objects that can be used to falsify foodstuff); acts against consumers' rights (e.g., the failure to indicate the prices of the goods on display); and acts against retail reliability.

The authorities, taking into consideration the guilt and the economic situation of the offender, may also impose the following accessory sanctions: confiscation of goods; deprivation of subsidies or benefits granted by the administration; cancellation of supply of goods and services by the

[79] Amended by DL no. 347/89 of 12 October 1989, DL no. 6/95 of 17 January 1995, DL no. 48/95 of 15 March 1995, DL no. 20/99 of 28 January 1999, DL no. 162/99 of 13 May 1999, DL no. 143/2001, of 26 April 2001, L no. 13/2001 of 4 June 2001, L no. 108/01 of 28 November 2001, L no. 20/2008 of 21 April and L no. 70/2007 of 26 March.

administration or other public entities; deprivation of the right to participate in fairs and markets. These sanctions may be imposed for a period of 10 days up to 1 year (Article 56).

In addition to the general competence of the other administrative authorities and police bodies, the law confers upon the ASAE (Autoridade de Segurança Alimentar e Económica – *Authority for the Safety of Food and Economy) special* competence for the investigation and the procedure related to these *contra-ordenações*. The consumers' associations may intervene in the procedure through the presentation of memos and technical advice, and they may suggest carrying out tests and other forms of gathering evidence until the procedure is ready for a final decision (Article 73, no. 3).

The competence concerning the application of the *coimas* and accessory sanctions concerning the *contra-ordenações* established in Articles 57 to 60 belongs to the *Commission for the Application of Coimas in Economic Matters and Publicity* (Article 38, no. 1 of DL no. 237/2005 of 30 December).

Part of the proceeds of the *coimas* (20%) reverts to the IRS (*Instituto de Reinserção Social* – Institute for the Rehabilitation of Offenders) and the other part reverts to the State (Article 78, no. 1).

2.4.3. Banking law

DL no. 298/92 of 31 December approved the RGICSF (*Regime Geral das Instituições de Crédito e das Sociedades Financeiras* – General Legal Framework of Credit Institutions and Financial Corporations)

Article 210 punishes several *contra-ordenações*, such as the failure to comply with specific orders of the Banco de Portugal (Portuguese Central Bank) and the omission of certain mandatory communications to the same central body.

Article 211 punishes serious *contra-ordenações*, such as the unauthorised exercise of operations reserved for credit institutions and financial corporations; exercising functions, in a credit institution or financial corporation, against a legal prohibition or against the explicit opposition of the Banco de Portugal; disrespecting the prohibition on the exercise of the right to vote; engaging in intentional acts of ruinous management, to the detriment of the depositors, investors and other creditors; refusing (or obstructing) an inspection by the Banco de Portugal.

This legal act also provides for accessory sanctions, such as the confiscation of objects related to (as well as the proceeds of) the offence; a prohibition on carrying out certain functions in those institutions, for a period of 6 months to 3 years (Article 210) or 1 year to 10 years (Article 211); suspension of the right to vote, for a period of 1 to 10 years (Article 212).

The competence to proceed to the inquiry and to apply the sanctions belongs to the Banco de Portugal.

The proceeds of the *coimas* imposed on credit institutions revert to the FGD (*Fundo de Garantia dos Depósitos* – Fund for the Guarantee of Deposits). If the *coimas* are imposed on an investment enterprise that forms part of the SII (*Sistema de Indemnização aos Investidores* – System for the Compensation of Investors), the proceeds revert to that System. The proceeds of the remaining *coimas* revert to the State.

2.4.4. Environmental law

There are several legislative acts on this subject and we will refer solely to DL no. 78/2004 of 3 April 2004, which establishes the legal framework for the prevention and control of pollutant emissions into the atmosphere.

Article 34, no. 1, punishes with *coimas* from €250 to €1850 (individuals) and €2,500 to €22,400 (legal entities) several acts or omissions, such as the violation of the duty to ensure that the installation in question is designed and built in a way that reduces the emission of atmospheric pollutants by adopting the best available techniques applicable to the economic and technical conditions of the installation.

Article 34, no. 2, punishes with *coimas* from 500 to €3,700 (individuals) and 5,000 to €44,800 (legal entities) *contra-ordenações* that are more serious, such as the violation of the duty to expel pollutants into the atmosphere through a chimney and the failure to comply with the duty to monitor the emissions.

The competence to initiate and proceed with the inquiry belongs to the IGA (*Inspecção Geral do Ambiente* – General Inspectorate for the Environment) and the CCDRs (*Comissões de Coordenação e Desenvolvimento Regional* – Commissions of Coordination and Regional Development) in the area subject to their jurisdiction.

The competence to apply the sanctions belongs to the Director of the institution that has conducted the inquiry.

The proceeds of the payment of the *coimas* revert partly to the entity that has drawn up the notice (10%), partly to the authority that has proceeded with the inquiry (30%) and the remainder (60%) reverts to the State.

3. CONCLUSION

As a brief conclusion, we may say that, in the abstract, administrative offences law proves to be adequate to ensure the principle of criminal law as *ultima ratio*[80], without losing State control over activities that are subject to public law regulation.

[80] See Frederico da Costa Pinto, "As codificações sectoriais e o papel das contra-ordenações na organização do direito penal secundário", *Themis* III, no. 5 (2002), pp. 93 et seq.

However, the recent developments that have led to the approximation of the DMOS and criminal law (increasing the severity of the sanctions and strengthening the guarantees of the offenders) are not consistent with the purpose of the distinction. Further approximation should be avoided; otherwise, the autonomy of the DMOS and the goals it is meant to attain can be put at risk.

BIBLIOGRAPHY

Andrade, J. C. Vieira de, *A Justiça Administrativa*, 4th ed., 2003.

Andrade, Manuel da Costa, "Contributo para o conceito de contra-ordenação (A experiência alemã)", *Revista de Direito e Economia* (1980/1981), pp. 81 et seq.; republished in: Instituto de Direito Penal Económico e Europeu (ed.)., *Direito Penal Económico e Europeu: Textos Doutrinários*, Vol. I, 1998, pp. 75 et seq.*

Antunes, Maria João / **Caeiro**, Pedro, "Portugal", in: *Kluwer Encyclopedia of Criminal Law*, suppl. 6 (May 1995), pp. 35 et seq.

Beleza, Teresa Pizarro, *Direito Penal*, I, 1985.

Canotilho, J. J. Gomes / Moreira, Vital, *Constituição da República Portuguesa Anotada*, 3rd ed., 1993.

Correia, Eduardo, "Direito Penal e Direito de Mera Ordenação Social", *Boletim da Faculdade de Direito da Universidade de Coimbra* XLIX (1973), pp. 257 et seq.; republished in Instituto de Direito Penal Económico e Europeu (ed.)., *Direito Penal Económico e Europeu: Textos Doutrinários*, Vol. I, 1998, pp. 3 et seq.*

Costa, José de Faria, "A importância da recorrência no pensamento jurídico. Um exemplo: a distinção entre o ilícito penal e o ilícito de mera ordenação social", *Revista de Direito e Economia* 1983, pp. 3 et seq.; republished in Instituto de Direito Penal Económico e Europeu (ed.)., *Direito Penal Económico e Europeu: Textos Doutrinários*, Vol. I, 1998, pp. 109 et seq.*

–, "Les Problèmes Juridiques et Pratiques posés par la Différence entre le Droit Criminel et le Droit Administratif-Pénal", offprint of *Boletim da Faculdade de Direito da Universidade de Coimbra* LXII (1986).

–, *O Perigo em Direito Penal*, 1992.

Dias, Jorge de Figueiredo, "O movimento da descriminalização e o ilícito de mera ordenação social", in: Centro de Estudos Judiciários (ed.), *Jornadas de Direito Criminal: o Novo Código Penal Português e Legislação Complementar*, Vol. I, 1983, pp. 317 et seq.; republished in Instituto de Direito Penal Económico e Europeu (ed.), *Direito Penal Económico e Europeu: Textos Doutrinários*, Vol. I, 1998, pp. 19 et seq.*

–, "Para uma dogmática do direito penal secundário. Um contributo para a reforma do direito penal económico e social português", *Revista de Legislação e Jurisprudência* 116 (1984); republished in Instituto de Direito Penal Económico e Europeu (ed.), *Direito Penal Económico e Europeu: Textos Doutrinários*, Vol. I, 1998, pp. 35 et seq.*

Ferreira, Manuel Cavaleiro de, *Direito Penal Português*, I, 1980.

José, Rosendo Dias, "Sanções administrativas", *Revista de Direito Público*, Ano IV (1991), pp. 37 et seq.

Machado, Miguel Pedrosa, "Elementos para o estudo da legislação portuguesa sobre contra-ordenações", Scientia Iuridica (1986), pp. 59 et seq.; republished in Instituto de Direito Penal Económico e Europeu (ed.)., *Direito Penal Económico e Europeu: Textos Doutrinários*, Vol. I, 1998, pp. 145 et seq.*

Moreira, Vital, *Sumários do Curso de Direito Administrativo*, policop., Coimbra, 2003(?).

Palma, Maria Fernanda / Otero, Paulo, "Revisão do regime legal do ilícito de mera ordenação social", *Revista da Faculdade de Direito da Universidade de Lisboa* 37 (1996), pp. 557 et seq.

Pinto, Frederico da Costa, "O ilícito de mera ordenação social e a erosão do princípio da subsidiariedade da intervenção penal", Revista Portuguesa de Ciência Criminal 7 (1997), pp. 7 et seq.; republished in Instituto de Direito Penal Económico e Europeu (ed.)., *Direito Penal Económico e Europeu: Textos Doutrinários*, Vol. I, 1998, pp. 209 et seq.*

–, "Tendências da jurisprudência sobre contra-ordenações no âmbito dos Mercado de Valores Mobiliários", *Revista da Faculdade de Direito da Universidade de Lisboa*, 2000, pp. 299 et seq.

–, *O Novo regime dos Crimes e Contra-Ordenações no Código dos Valores Mobiliários*, 2000.

–, "Acesso de particulares a processos de contra-ordenação arquivados", in: *Estudos em Homenagem à Professora Doutora Isabel de Magalhães Collaço*, vol. II, 2000, pp. 601 et seq.

–, "A figura do assistente e o processo de contra-ordenação (anotação ao Acórdão da Relação de Lisboa de 20 de Maio de 1998), *Revista Portuguesa de Ciência Criminal* 12 (2002), pp. 105 et seq.

–, "As codificações sectoriais e o papel das contra-ordenações na organização do direito penal secundário", *Themis* III, no. 5 (2002), pp. 87 et seq.

Prates, Marcelo Madureira: *Sanção Administrativa Geral: Anatomia e Autonomia*, (Master's Dissertation at the Faculty of Law of the University of Coimbra; unpublished), 2003.

Veloso, José António, "Sobre a natureza não-sancionatória da revogação da autorização das instituições de crédito e outras questões de fiscalização de actividades reservadas: algumas notas de justificação de decisões legislativas", *Direito e justiça – Revista da Faculdade de Direito da Universidade Católica Portuguesa* XIV, tomo I (2000), pp. 61 et seq.

–,, "Questões hermenêuticas e de sucessão de leis nas sanções do regime geral das instituições de crédito – em especial, a inibição de direitos de voto por violação de deveres de revelar participações qualificadas", *Revista da Banca* 49 (2000).

* Quotations referring to these articles in the text use the second reference.

XI. COUNTRY ANALYSIS – ROMANIA

Elena Mihaela Fodor* and Corina Cristina Buzdugan**

1. INTRODUCTION: GENERAL DESCRIPTION OF SANCTIONS AND THE SANCTION SYSTEM

Romanian legal literature defines the sanction as a consequence of not observing a rule of conduct prescribed or sanctioned by the state. The definition is based on the Roman law notion of *sanctio*, which meant that a rule of conduct was prescribed with the authority of the emperor. All the measures taken for disobeying the law, having a punitive, preventive or remedial character are sanctions. Discussions have been taking place in the legal literature as to whether the term of "sanction" is appropriate for remedial or preventive measures (or should they merely be called "measures" or "consequences"?), but, so far, the general notion of "sanction" is still used.

The importance of the nature of a sanction lies mostly in the involvement of culpability and the personal character of the sanction. Punitive sanctions are only applied as a consequence of a culpable and illicit form of conduct (an intentional act or negligence) and have a personal character, which means that other persons, who were not involved in the infringement, cannot be held responsible for the purposes of the sanction.[1] Remedial sanctions are also applied against culpable illicit conduct, but in many situations they can also be applied against non-culpable illicit conduct, as long as prejudice has occurred. Remedial sanctions can be imposed against another person – a successor or another person designated or allowed by the law. Preventive sanctions are generally objective, which means that they may be applied even if there is no element of guilt or negligence in the illicit deed; they cannot be imposed against other persons, however, due to the purpose of such sanctions, which is to stop the person in question from pursuing certain conduct that is dangerous to

* Sections 2, 3 and 4.

** Section 1.

1 However, according to Article no. 25 of the Government Ordinance no. 92/2003 (The Fiscal Procedure Code) fiscal obligations may be transferred to the heirs. This would be correct in respect to the debt and the interest which have a remedial nature, but not the surcharges which have a punitive nature.

others. Under penal law, sanctions are grouped into main sanctions, complementary sanctions and accessory sanctions. Under administrative law, the contraventional sanctions are grouped into main sanctions and complementary sanctions. In both branches of law the main sanctions have a punitive character while the complementary and accessory sanctions have a predominantly preventive or remedial character and may be added to the main sanctions. For example, the Traffic Code demonstrates that the purpose of the complementary contraventional sanctions established thereunder (retaining, withdrawing or annulling driving licence, suspending the right to drive, immobilising the vehicle, etc.) have the purpose of averting danger and preventing other infringements.

Traditionally, under Romanian law, the sanctions are divided into civil sanctions, penal sanctions, administrative sanctions and disciplinary sanctions.[2]

Administrative sanctions can be divided into *contraventional sanctions*, considered to be the most important category, and *other administrative sanctions*.

Originally, the contravention ("contravenţia", "contravention" under French law) was a penal deed with the lesser social danger. The Romanian Penal Code enacted in 1865 replaced the French Penal Code of 1810, which divided penal deeds into felonies, offences and contraventions (the French "*crimes, delictes et contraventions*") according to the level of social danger. By Decree no. 184/1954, the provisions of the Romanian Penal Code or special laws establishing and sanctioning contraventions were annulled. This decree established that contraventions are administrative infringements and it determined a fine and a warning as sanctions for such deeds. By Law no. 32/1968, which defined and sanctioned the contraventions, the general legal framework was initially settled in the field of contravention responsibility. The main contraventional sanctions, according to this law, were a warning, fine and contraventional imprisonment. If the contraventional fine was not paid or it could not be executed on a compulsory basis because the offender was insolvent, the sanction of a fine could be transformed into contraventional imprisonment by the local (first instance) civil court. This law was later annulled by Government Ordinance no. 2/2001, which regulated the legal regime for contraventions, and this is the present framework act in this field. The latest legal act established the current contraventional sanctions and also the specific procedure as far as defining an illicit conduct as a contravention, establishing that a contravention has taken place, and sanctioning and executing the contraventional sanction are concerned. It also established

2 On this subject see G., Boboş, G., Vlădica-Raţiu, *Răspunderea, responsabilitatea şi constrângerea în domeniul dreptului,* Editura Argonaut, Cluj-Napoca, 1996, E.M., Fodor, *Sancţiunea normelor juridice în dreptul public şi dreptul privat,* in "Public şi privat în economie, învăţământ-cercetare şi drept", Editura Oscar Print, Bucureşti, 2002, pp. 293–308.

that the contravention report is suspended, if contested in court, until a final judgement is passed.[3]

Initially, a new sanction was added to the main sanctions established by Law no. 32/1968: obliging the offender to carry out community service. To the framework dispositions in Government Ordinance no. 2/2001, Government Ordinance no. 55/2002 added dispositions concerning the procedure for applying and executing the sanctions of contraventional imprisonment and obliging the offender to carry out community service. This latest legal act states that the possibility of changing the contraventional fine into contraventional imprisonment, if the fine has not been paid, was no longer possible. Both Government Ordinances were modified in 2003 and contraventional imprisonment has been excluded from the contraventional sanctions. Government Ordinance no. 2/2001 also states that contraventions that are sanctioned by obliging the offender to carry out community service can only be laid down in specific laws and must always have a fine as an alternative sanction.

Complementary sanctions have also been established, such as the confiscation of goods, closing down production or preventing a certain activity, suspending the activity, suspending or withdrawing a licence for developing an activity, blocking a bank account, halting certain works and restoring land to its original condition. These complementary sanctions are mostly of a preventing or reparatory nature. The Government Ordinance no. 2/2001states that other contraventional sanctions may be established by special laws. Such a complementary contraventional sanction may be, for example, suspending a driving licence for three months, as has been introduced under the Traffic Code.

The definition of a contravention provided by Law no. 32/1968 contained the proviso that a contravention was an illicit form of conduct with a lesser degree of social danger compared to a penal offence. However, the upper limit of the contraventional fine ("amenda contravenţională") was set at more than the upper limit of the penal fine ("amenda penală") and, due to the lack of the principle of proportionality (in comparing penal sanctions with their administrative equivalent), the fact that the fine and imprisonment were penal sanctions as well as administrative sanctions and due to the impossibility of suspending administrative sanctions, the possibility existed that a contravention could be punished more severely than a penal offence. Government Ordinance no. 2/2001 therefore excluded from the definition of contravention the proviso that it has a lesser degree of social danger compared to a penal offence.[4] Legal literature still

[3] Unfortunately, there are specific laws that mention administrative sanctions named "contravention" but also state that the general provisions of Government Ordinance no. 2/2001 do not apply. Thus, the procedure of issuing the sanctionatory act is the normal procedure for issuing any administrative act, and the procedure for contesting it is the one established by Law no. 554/2004 of the contentious administrative.

[4] I. Poenaru (I), I. Santai (II), *Noul regim al contravenþiilor, Ordonanța nr.2 din 2001*, Dreptul no. 12/2001, pp. 3–17.

agrees, however, that the reduced degree of social danger is a characteristic of the contravention as well as of any conduct that results in an administrative offence. But the upper limit of the contraventional fine is still twice as high as the highest penal fine for natural persons and there is no limit on other administrative fines. Government Ordinance no. 2/2001 did not set different framework limits for contraventional fines with respect to natural persons or legal persons. However, certain legal acts may set lower limits for natural persons and higher limits for legal persons. For example, Article no. 139^5 of the Law no. 8/1996, concerning copyright, states that for legal persons the limits for a fine are twice the limits set for natural persons. The inferior limit of contraventional fine, as set by Government Ordinance no. 2/2001 is 25 Ron (about 6 Euros) and the upper limits are 100.000 Ron (about 25.000 euro) for contraventions described and sanctioned by laws and Government Ordinances, 50.000 Ron (about 12.500 euro) for contraventions described and sanctioned by Government Decisions, 5000 Ron (about 1.250 euro) for contraventions described and sanctioned by County Councils and The General Council of Bucharest and 2.500 Ron (about 625 euro) for contraventions described and sanctioned by Local Councils and the Councils of the districts of Bucharest. For the obligation of the offender to carry out community service the limits are between 50 and 300 hours.

Features of contraventional sanctions that mirror their penal origin are the division of sanctions into main sanctions – having a punitive character – and complementary sanctions – having a predominantly preventive or reparatory character, and the legal nature of such sanctions according to the penal principles of *nullum crimen sine lege* and *nulla poena sine lege*. But, penal offences and their sanctions may only be established by law whereas contraventions and their sanctions may be established by law or supplementary provisions such as Government Decisions, and Decisions of Local and County Councils. Contraventions and their sanctions may be established by law and Government Decisions in all fields of activity. Local Councils and County Councils may lay down contraventions in those fields of activity where they have competence if laws or Government Decisions have not already determined contraventions in that field.

The Constitution adopted in 1992 stated that the law must not retroactivate, with the exception of penal law (the principle of *lex mitior*). Government Ordinance no. 2/2001 lays down in its Article 12, that illicit conduct will not be sanctioned as a contravention if, according to a new law, it is no longer a contravention, and, if a new legal act establishes a milder sanction than the legal act in force when the contravention was committed, the milder sanction will be applied. These provisions express the principle of *lex mitior* and may be regarded as a feature that mirrors the penal origin of contraventions.[5] When the

[5] V. Pătulea, *Aplicarea principiului legii mai favorabile în domeniul contravenţiilor*, "Dreptul" no. 3/1999, pp.139–141.

Constitution has been revised, in 2003, Article no. 15 that expressed the *lex mitior* principle for penal sanctions was modified, extending the application of the principle to contraventional sanctions. Decision no. 228/2007 of the Constitutional Court specified that the principle is also applied during the execution of the sanction.

The link between penal responsibility and contraventional responsibility can also be found in the fact that illicit forms of conduct of the same nature may be defined as being penal offences or contraventions depending on the specific conditions relating to the deed in question.[6] Usually, it is a difference in the degree of social danger. For example, the Traffic Code states that a person who drives while being under the influence of alcohol is committing the contravention of "driving under the influence of alcohol" if the alcohol concentration in his blood is up to 0.8‰ and is committing a penal offence if the alcohol concentration exceeds this limit. In other cases, special laws (in fields like forestry, environmental protection, taxes, business competition, the food industry etc.) state that contravening a certain legal regulation is sanctioned as a contravention if it is not committed in such circumstances as to be qualified as a penal offence. In such situations the principle of *non bis in idem* applies, one deed having to be qualified either as a contravention or a penal offence, but not both.

The main difference between contraventional sanctions and their penal equivalent is the authority that applies the sanction as contraventional sanctions are applied by an administrative authority, with the exception of obliging the offender to carry out community service, which can only be imposed by a court. Before 2006 contraventional sanctions could be imposed against both natural and legal persons, while penal sanctions could only be imposed against natural persons. This difference has disappeared when the Romanian Penal Code was modified by Law no. 278/2006, that introduced penal responsibility for legal persons. Still, a difference is made between legal persons and natural persons as legal persons may only be sanctioned with a contraventional sanction if a specific legal act contains such a provision. A recent amendment to the Romanian Penal Procedure Code states that there is a right of silence. No such right exists in the field of contraventional sanctioning.

The remainder of administrative sanctions, other than contraventional sanctions, also have to respect the principle of legality, as legality is considered to be a principle which is fundamental to the administration's activities. The sanctions, the infringements for which they are imposed, the competent authority and the procedure for applying the sanction and the possibility to contest the sanction in question have to be established by specific legal acts. Examples of other administrative sanctions are administrative fines, surcharges,

6 I. Poenaru, *Problemele legislatiei contravenționale*, in "Dreptul", no. 2/1998, pp. 46–57.

the removal of an illegally obtained advantage or an advantage obtained without fulfilling certain imposed conditions, halting the production of certain products, seizing vehicles, annulling firearms certificates etc. The administrative sanction is imposed by an administrative decision and the general administrative law principles regarding such decisions (legality, competence, procedure, form) will apply. Specific legal acts may contain detailed regulations. The procedure by which to contest the sanction is the one described by the Law on contentious administrative proceedings no. 554/2004 if not specifically stated otherwise.

Administrative sanctions may have a punitive character, such as a fine. Other measures are of a predominantly preventive nature. Examples are the contraventional complementary sanctions of confiscating goods which will be used to commit the contravention, the suspension of a licence for a certain activity or suspending the activity of the economic agent, other administrative sanctions such as compulsory medical treatment, applying customs seals etc. Administrative sanctions with a remedial character are considered to be, for example, surcharges or prohibiting certain works and restoring land to its original condition.

Recent case law took into account the decisions of the European Court for Human Rights that extended the notion of "criminal offence" to administrative sanctions, thus considering the application of some principles governing the criminal (penal) law in administrative sanctioning law.

2. GENERAL PRINCIPLES AND CODIFICATION

General legal principles concerning administrative sanctions are provided by the Constitution. Article 52 specifically refers to administrative acts, providing the right of a person who has suffered damage concerning a right or legal interest as a result of an administrative decision or when the public authority has not dealt with an application in due time, to obtain recognition of the claimed right, or an annulment of the decision and reparation of the damage. This, combined with the provisions of Article 21, which lays down the principle of free access to justice, results in *the right to contest administrative sanctions before a court of law.* The principle of *non-retroactivity* of contraventional law is stated in Article 15. Another constitutional principle is the principle of *equality* which means that all persons are equal before the law and before the administrative authorities, so equal treatment should be applied when sanctioning similar offences (Article 16).

The rights of the *inviolability of the home* and *the confidentiality of correspondence* are mentioned and they have to be respected by the investigative authorities (Articles 27 and 28).

In accordance with the *illegality of forced labour* (Article 42), Government Ordinance no. 2/2001 stated that the sanction of obliging the offender to engage in community service may only be applied by the court with the offender's consent. But, according to Article 9 in Government Ordinance no. 2/2001, if the offender does not pay the fine according to law, this sanction can be replaced with the sanction of obliging the offender to engage in community service by the court. The Constitutional Court has decided that in this case there is no need for the consent of the offender, as this would make impossible to apply a sanction to the offender (Decision no. 1354/2008).

Another constitutional principle that also applies in the field of administrative sanctions is the *right to a qualified defence before a court of law* (Article 24).

Article 23 of the Constitution establishes *the presumption of innocence* in the case of criminal offences. According to Article 20 of the Constitution, the dispositions concerning the rights and liberties of citizens "will be understood and applied in accordance with the Universal Declaration of Human Rights and other international conventions ratified by the Romanian Parliament. If there is a conflict between internal law and ratified international conventions, the latter will prevail". Thus, ratified international treaties and conventions, together with the Constitution form a "block of constitutionality", having equal value. In the case *Oztürk vs. Germany (1981)* the European Court of Human Rights stated that Article 6 of the European Convention of Human Rights applies if there is a "criminal accusation". In the view of the European Court for Human Rights the criteria to determine whether a "criminal accusation" has been made is not only the legal classification of the infringement, but also the nature of the infringement and the nature and severity of the sanction. In 1994 Romania has ratified the European Convention of Human Rights. Since the decision of the European Court of Human Rights in the case *Anghel vs. Romania (2008)*, where the Court decided that the contraventional sanction applied to the plaintiff meets the requirements for a "criminal accusation", the courts were asked to examine the legality of contraventional sanctions in accordance with the notion of "criminal accusation" as established by the European Court of Human Rights. The most disputed aspect in this context was the respect of the *presumption of innocence*. Some authors claimed that Government Ordinance no. 2/2001 does not provide the conditions for the presumption[7], mainly because examining the complaint against the contraventional sanction applied by administration is in the competence of civil courts. According to Article 47 of the Government Ordinance no.2/2001 its provisions are complimented with the ones of the Civil Procedure Code, which automatically makes the norms of the Civil Code incident. According to Article 1169 of the Civil Code, the one who makes a statement before the court has to prove it (*onus probandi incubit actori*). These

7 C.L. Popescu, *"Neconvenţionalitatea" şi neconstituţionalitatea procedurii contravenţionale judiciare de drept comun, în raport cu dreptul la respectarea prezumţiei de nevinovăţie*, in "Pandectele Române", nr. 6/2002, pp. 197–206.

legal provisions are combined with the principle which states that the administrative act is presumed correct. This way, the offender is not presumed innocent, but has to prove his innocence before the court. Some courts decided that the possibility of contesting the contraventional sanction to court, where one may bring proof of one's innocence, enacts the presumption of innocence.[8] They also argued that the sanctions are protecting important social values that could not be properly defended if the administration would have to prove the righteousness of the contravention report. Other courts gave more importance to the text of article no. 6 of the European Convention of Human Rights. For example, it was decided that in the contravention report drawn for speeding the finding agent has to mention the type and identification data of the device that registered the speed, the document of measurement control of the device and the plates number of the car where the device was fixed during the measurement. Presenting these data only in court would not be regarded as certain and thus the contravention report will be annulled.[9] It has also been decided that if the contravention report is not accompanied by the evidence to support the conclusions of the finding agent and the offender has no other proof for innocence, the presumption of truth for the contravention report is contradictory to article 6 of the European Convention of Human Rights and will not stand before it.[10] One court decided that the contravention report is proof enough if it contains the aspects observed personally by the finding agent.[11] *Per a contrario,* one may argue that if the contravention report is drawn upon the accounts of third parties (like in the case of a car accident without victims, or a complaint for disturbance of peace) it is the duty of the finding agent to prove the guilt of the offender. This requirement should be satisfied all the more considering the fact that the agent who applies the sanction is the same with the one who detects the infringement and the fact that in Government Ordinance no. 2/2001 there are no provisions for the possibility of the presumed perpetrator to administrate evidence before the sanction is applied.

General principles, concerning the sanctioning are to be found in Government Ordinance no. 2/2001.

The principle of *legality* can be deduced from the dispositions that state that certain legal acts can define contraventions, the appropriate sanctions and their limits (art.1). The general limits of the main contraventional sanctions are

---

8 Decision no. 186/R/2009, Tribunal of Bucharest, in N. Cristuş, *Răspunderea contravenţională. Practică judiciară 2007–2009,* Editura Hamangiu, Bucureşti, 2010, pp. 251–255.

9 The record of the Case-law Unification Committee of the Superior Council of Magistracy meeting, 19.11.2008, problem 17, at www.csm1909.ro/csm/linkuri/05_02_2009__20823_ro.doc, last consulted at 28.12.2012.

10 Sentence no. 2839/2008, First Instance Court Deva, in N. Cristuş, *op.cit.*,p. 258.

11 Sentence no. 1387/2009, First Instance Court of the 6th District Bucharest, in N. Cristuş, *op.cit.*, p. 246–250.

established in Articles 8 and 9. A warning may be applied as a sanction even if it is not especially provided as an alternative sanction, if the finding agent (see below) or competent authority believes that it is sufficient and if there is no legal disposition to prohibit this.

Quite often, in different particular laws, in the chapter destined to offences and sanctions, there are provisions stating that a certain infringement is a contravention, if it is not committed in such circumstances that qualifies it as a criminal offence. It has been argued that such a text is against the principle of legality. In fact, it is only a reflection of the connection between the criminal offences and contravention, as the circumstances show the social danger of the infringement. This latter interpretation is in accordance with article 18^1 of the Penal Code which states that it is not a criminal offence the infringement defined as such, if the social danger resulting from the circumstances of the deed is very low. In such a case, the prosecutor or the court may apply the sanction of administrative fee.

Another problem concerning the principle of legality is the clear distinction between the situations when the sanction is applied to the legal person and the situations when the sanction is applied to the representative of the legal person. When the legal text is not mentioning it clearly, it has been considered that the representative of the legal person, or the specialist of the legal person, will be responsible for infringements connected with organizing and conducting the accounts of the legal person, protection against fire or industrial safety activities, security or personnel measures, or other activities concerning the organisation and functioning of the legal person.[12] In other situations the responsibility will lie with the legal person. This interpretation is sustained by some case law. Thus, it has been decided that the sanction is to be applied to the legal person if it omitted to submit a financial report to the authorities[13], but in case of mistaken entries in the accounting books the sanction should be applied to the person in charge with accountability.[14]

Although generally it is considered that for the same infringement the sanction should be applied either to the legal person or to its representative, legislation presents dispositions contrary to this conclusion. In the Law no. 52/1994, regarding stocks and the stock exchange, Article 112 states that in case a contraventional sanction is applied to the legal person, the same sanction will be applied to its representatives or specialists that are guilty for the infringement because, although they might have stopped or prevented the infringement, they failed to do so.

12 F., Bradin, E., Popescu, *Raportul dintre răspunderea managerului şi cea a persoanei juridice în materie contravenţională,* in "Dreptul" nr. 10/2003, pp. 213–221.

13 Decision no. 85/R/2008, Tribunal of Brăila, in N. Cristuş, *op.cit.*, pp. 26–28.

14 Sentence no. 4888/2006, First Instance Court of Brăila, in N. Cristuş, *Răspunderea contravenţională. Practică judiciară 2007-2009,* Editura Hamangiu, Bucureşti, 2010, pp. 29–30.

There are no special mentions about the prohibition of analogy, but this is also the case in the criminal legislation. Nevertheless it is considered that both in criminal and contraventional law the prohibition of analogy is understood as a component of the principle of legality.[15]

Generally, in applying administrative sanctions the principle of *competence* has to be taken into consideration as a principle that governs the activity of the administration. According to Government Ordinance no. 2/2001 contraventional sanctions may only be applied by the following so-called finding agents (persons that have the necessary authority) as determined in Article 15: mayors, specially authorised officers and non-commissioned officers of the Ministry of Internal Affairs, persons authorised for this purpose by ministers and other leading figures from the central public administration authorities or by prefects, presidents of the county councils, as well as other persons stipulated by specific legislation (Article 15). If the specific legislation states that the finding agent is not competent to apply the sanction, he will forward the contravention report to the competent authority for the sanction to be applied. For example, according to the Traffic Code, in a case of driving under the influence of alcohol, the finding agent will apply the main contraventional sanction of a fine and will withhold the perpetrator's driving licence, but the complementary contraventional sanction of suspending the driver's licence will be applied by the chief of the County Police.

The sanction has to be supported by the necessary grounds for the decision. The finding agent has to draw up a contravention report containing, among other data, a complete description of the illicit conduct and the legal justification for the contraventional sanction (Articles 16 and 17).

There are also provisions referring to the *right of defence*. The finding agent is obliged to ask the offender if he wishes to say anything in his defence and is obliged to mention the allegations in the contravention report (Article 16). Also, the offender may refuse to sign the contravention report (for example, if he believes that its contents do not correspond to the truth) and in this case a certified witness has to sign it in order to verify the offender's refusal. If no witness can be found, the finding agent has to state this in the report (Article 19). Considering the incidence of Article 6 of the European Convention of Human Rights for a "criminal accusation", the courts decided that failing to provide translation to the offender, in order to inform him about the contraventional sanction that is being applied to him for speeding, is sanctioned with the absolute nullity of the contravention report signed by the perpetrator.

---

15 For this assumption in the criminal law see C. Mitrache, C. Mitrache, *Dreptul penal român. Partea generală*, Editura Universul Juridic, București, 2007, p. 44.

The contravention report must also contain the time within which the contraventional report may be contested and the authority where the submission has to be filed.

The principle of *proportionality* is mentioned, meaning that the sanction that is actually imposed has to be within the actual legal limits and proportional to the degree of social danger inherent in the illicit conduct (Articles 5 and 21). However, as mentioned above, the sanction is calculated within the range and limits of contraventional sanctions and a comparison is not made with penal sanctions for illicit conduct of the same nature.

The principle of *existing guilt* refers to the fact that in order to amount to a contravention, the illicit conduct must impute guilt (intention or even the slightest negligence – Article 1). Contraventional responsibility is not applicable to minors under the age of 14 years old (Article 11). For persons under 18 years old the contraventional fine is reduced by a half. Also, persons under the age of 16 cannot be sanctioned with being obliged to engage in community service. There are no special provisions on establishing the guilt of legal persons. Also, there are no special legal provisions on applying sanctions against legal persons or their representatives or both. Situations that exclude contraventional responsibility are a legitimate defence, state of necessity, physical or moral constraint, fortuitous situations, non-responsibility, involuntary complete drunkenness, error of fact, and infirmity that is connected with the deed (Article 11).[16] These situations may only be found to exclude contraventional responsibility by a court of law when the contraventional sanction is contested.

The principle of *personalising the contraventional sanction* refers to taking objective criteria (the seriousness of the social danger, specific circumstances, means and modality, purpose and effects) into account as well as personal circumstances (Article 21). The latter are not further described. This principle is less well defined compared to penal legislation where the criteria for personalising the sanction are more detailed as well as the effects of some of the existing circumstances. There is no record for contraventions, so one may not plead the fact that it is a first infringement.[17]

The principle of double jeopardy or *non bis in idem* has limited application in comparison with penal law. It refers to the situation when an illicit form of

16 Except for the latest, all other situations are identical with the ones that exclude criminal responsibility. As no definition or explanation is given in Government Ordinance no. 2/2001 for these circumstances, the ones from the Criminal Code will apply.

17 According to specific laws, previous offences may be taken into account. For example, Law no. 504/2002 for audio-video activities considers the criteria of the number of prior sanctions in the last year.

conduct against the same legally protected social value qualifies both as an administrative offence and a criminal offence and it may only be sanctioned as one or the other (Article 30). But, in addition to a main penal sanction, a complementary contraventional sanction may also be imposed. For example, according to the Traffic Code if a driver is convicted of serious bodily harm following a traffic accident, the main penal sanction of imprisonment will be applied together with the contraventional complementary sanction of suspending the driver's licence. If a person is guilty of different contraventions at the same time, a sanction will be applied for each contravention (Article 10). If multiple contraventions are sanctioned within the same contravention report, the sanctions will be added together, although they cannot exceed double the general upper limit for a contraventional fine (the upper limit is about 25,000 euro) or the general upper limit of obliging the offender to engage in 300 hours of community service. A contravention may be sanctioned with one of the main sanctions stipulated in the relevant legal act, to which one or more complementary sanctions may be added. This is due to the fact that only the main sanction is punitive, while those that are complementary are of a predominantly preventive or remedial nature.

According to the principle of *concurrent responsibility*, in the case of participation each person will be charged with the contravention separately (Article 10).

As mentioned before, the principle of *lex mitior* applies to contraventional sanctioning. The illicit conduct will not be sanctioned as a contravention if a specific legal act thereby allows such behaviour (Article 12).

The principle of *legal form* refers to the fact that the sanctioning administrative act (the contravention report) must be in a written form and has to contain all the information prescribed by law in order to be valid. The only exception is a warning that may be issued orally if the offender is present and the finding agent has the competence to issue such a warning.

There is no specific legislation in other administrative sanctions and not much literature either. If a special law does not mention any specific principles, the general principles of administrative law such as legality, competence, the right of defence and legal form are applied in the same way as for contraventional sanctions. Also the principles of proportionality and double jeopardy may apply in the same way. Providing sufficient grounds for the administrative decision is not the general rule in Romanian administrative law, but, even if specific legal provisions are lacking, the sanctioning administrative decision should provide the necessary grounds as, otherwise, it could not be reviewed by a court of law.

3. SANCTIONING PROCEDURE

The sanctioning procedure is not codified and is not very complex. However, taking into consideration the specific legal acts in different fields it may be concluded that, generally, the authority that discovers the infringement or is leading the investigation is also competent to apply the administrative sanction. Otherwise, the specific legal act has to indicate the authority which is competent. Generally, the administrative sanction is applied by a competent administrative authority. However, the Penal Code gives the public prosecutor and the judge the possibility to halt a criminal investigation, respectively to acquit the offender, and to apply the sanction of an administrative fine if the deed has all the elements of a penal offence, but is considered, due to the circumstances or consequences, to amount to a very slight social danger. Such a sanction will not give rise to a criminal record.

Inspections may only be carried out by designated competent persons or bodies, which are usually specialised persons or bodies. Local authorities also have specialist inspection bodies in different fields of public interest. Usually, specific legislation states that the inspection body may inspect objects and places (except for private residences) may take goods for analysis, may conduct technical experiments and are entitled to see all the documents relating to the activity in question. If an illicit conduct has been investigated as a penal offence and the public prosecutor or judge has decided that no penal offence has been committed but that it might amount to a contravention, the penal report together with a copy of the prosecutor's file or court decision will be sent to the administrative authority which has the competence to establish that a contravention has occurred. The administrative authority may use all this information.

The sanction is applied by means of an administrative decision in written form containing all the information required in the specific legislation. The decision has to be supported by sufficient grounds (description of the infringement and the legal grounds for the sanction) and it must indicate the time during which the decision may be contested and the authority which can decide thereon. In the case of contraventions, the decision is the contravention report.

A private party is protected by general constitutional principles such as the inviolability of one's private home and the confidentiality of correspondence and also by the right to contest the sanction before a court of law. In the contraventional field, the offender has the right to pay only half of the minimum fine fixed by the specific legislation for the particular contravention, if payment is made within 48 hours from the day on which the offender received the contravention report and if the specific legislation that defines and sanctions the contravention stipulates that this is possible. A private party is informed about this possibility through the contravention report. In these situations, if multiple contraventions are sanctioned with a fine within the same contravention report, the total sum paid by the offender within 48 hours must not exceed the maximum fine for the most serious contravention. Making use of this right does not preclude the offender from further contesting the sanction.

Some specific laws contain more detailed provisions. For example, the Fiscal Procedure Code describes the authorities which are competent to inspect the fiscal status of natural and legal persons and inspection procedure.[18]

Usually, the inspection has to be announced 15 or 30 days in advance. The date may be postponed following a justified request by the person to be inspected. The inspectors may see and take for inspection all kinds of documents belonging to the inspected person, they may carry out scientific tests, and may inspect property. Natural persons must be informed of their right to refuse entry to their domicile or residence. In such a case, the inspectors may enter if a court order has been obtained from the civil court. Fiscal inspectors may obtain assistance from the police in order to carry out the inspection. Other public authorities and public institutions are obliged to provide information to and to cooperate with the fiscal authorities. In the case of natural persons, one's spouse and close relatives may refuse to provide information. Persons who possess certain information due to their profession (priests, lawyers, experts etc.) are also exonerated from the obligation to provide information. The person inspected has the right to legal and professional assistance, the right to propose evidence and the right to be informed about the results during the inspection. The inspection will end with a meeting between the two parties to discuss the results of the fiscal inspection and the consequences. The person who is the subject of the investigation may present his point of view in writing. The results of the inspection will be included in a final report. If administrative infringements are found, the sanctions may be imposed through the final report or through a separate decision or contravention report. Contraventional sanctions may be contested according to the provisions of Government Ordinance no. 2/2001. Other administrative sanctions may be contested according to the law of contentious administrative proceedings no. 554/2004.

In the regulation concerning the organisation and functioning of the Financial Guard – a military body responsible for financial control within the Ministry of Finance – there are also provisions concerning the control procedure.[19] During the control procedure operations documents, registries and stocks may be verified, economic objectives may be surveyed and searches may be conducted. The personnel of the Financial Guard may enter any premises where goods are produced, stored or sold or where any activities subject to taxation are carried out. A search may be made of public or private areas

18 Title VII Chapter I form Government Ordinance no. 92/2003.

19 Articles 7 and 8 of the Emergency Government Ordinance no. 91/2003.

according to the rules of the Penal Procedure Code if there is evidence of fiscal fraud. The Financial Guard are entitled to confiscate goods according to the law, to take documents that may serve as evidence, to find contraventions and impose the proper sanctions, to report to the police or the Public Prosecutor's Office that a penal offence has been committed, to gather information about the situation subject to control and to use firearms according to specific legislation. A private party is protected by legal provisions that state that the control will end with a written report comprising the conclusions and respecting the requirement of impartiality. All information gathered during the control are confidential unless service obligations or justice determines otherwise. The personnel of the Financial Guard have to identify themselves during the control operations. The sanctions may be contested before a court of law.

In other fields, procedural requirements regarding control and sanctioning are not very detailed. Under construction law, for example, the regulations on the state control of building quality shows that inspectors are entitled to enter premises, to verify documentation and gather information and are obliged to respect the confidentiality of information obtained. They are also entitled to impose administrative sanctions.[20]

As mentioned before, the contraventional sanction of obliging the offender to carry out community service may only be imposed by the civil court. If, for the contravention committed, the sanction is a fine or, alternatively, a community service order and the finding agent believes that the sanction of a fine is insufficient, he will forward the contravention report to the local (first instance) civil court to decide the matter. The court will decide whether the sanction will be a fine or community service. In this case, the court will establish the existence of the infringement and the sanction.

4. LEGAL PROTECTION

As a general rule, administrative decisions which will harm a right or a legitimate interest may be contested before the competent contentious administrative court. The relevant legal provisions are to be found in Law no. 554/2004, complimented by the regulations of the Civil Procedure Code. The administrative decision has to be initially contested before the issuing authority or the hierarchically superior authority. This rule also applies to sanctioning administrative decisions, if specific legal provisions do not state otherwise. The fact that the investigative authority is also the one which is competent to impose the sanction means, however, that the possibility of the administrative authority changing its decision is very slight. The administrative authority usually has to

20 M. Duţu, G. Duţu, *Consideraþii asupra specificului contravenţiilor la regimul de autorizare a construcţiilor,*in "Dreptul" no. 10–11/1995, pp. 81–85.

be addressed within 30 days from the date when the sanctioning administrative decision was received (Article no. 7). If the answer from the administrative authority is not satisfactory, or if there is no answer at all, the sanction may be contested before a court of law. A copy of the contested decision must be attached to the petition to the court.

The court must be petitioned within 6 months starting from the day on which the person contesting the decision received an answer from the administrative authority or the last day of the term during which the administrative authority should have answered (which is usually also 30 days) (Article no. 11). For just cause, the term can be surpassed. After a duration of one year from the date when the person contesting the decision received the sanction it is then no longer possible to contest it.

The competent courts are the contentious administrative courts, which belong to the judiciary system and are organised within the Tribunals (county courts), the Courts of Appeal and as a separate section of the High Court of Cassation and Justice. Generally, for administrative decisions issued by central administrative authorities the first instance court is the contentious administrative court at the Court of Appeal and for administrative decisions issued by local administrative authorities the first instance court is the contentious administrative court within one of the Tribunals. If the contested administrative act is about taxes, contributions, custom duties and accessories of those, up to the sum of 500.000 Ron (about 125.000 euro) the competence belongs to the Tribunals and for higher sums to the Courts of Appeal (Article no. 10). According to the law for the organisation of the judiciary, Law no. 303/2004, specialised Administrative Tribunals can be organised in each county. The court procedure is based on the civil procedure principles like the necessity of an oral hearing, in pubic and the right to legal assistance or representation. Court actions are subject to taxation, but taxes are very low. Certain exemptions from taxation are stipulated by specific Acts.

Contesting the sanction does not automatically suspend the effects of the administrative sanctioning decision, unless specific legislation states otherwise. The judge has the power to suspend the effects of the sanctioning administrative decision for the duration of the trial if this avoids serious damage. The petition to suspend the administrative decision can be introduced to court immediately after it has been contested to the issuing authority (Article no. 14), or when the complaint is presented before the court (Article no. 15). In the first case, the court should be petitioned within 60 days since the suspension was granted. The court may completely re-evaluate the administrative decision, it may admit or order new evidence and can also control the legality of the sanctioning procedure. According to legal dispositions, the court can allow the petition contesting the sanction and annul the administrative decision, or it can dismiss the petition. This should mean that the court is not competent to change the sanction or reduce it. The court decision may be appealed to the superior contentious administrative court. The appeal will suspend the effect of the first instance sentence if the sanction has not already been levied. The court decision on appeal is final.

Sometimes specific legislation will give the offender the possibility to address the petition to an administrative authority with jurisdictional competence. Such an authority has the power to resolve a legal conflict using a procedure based on the principle of equality between the two parties. Generally, such a procedure differs from a judicial one as it is neither oral nor public. The decision (the jurisdictional act) is irrevocable. The jurisdictional act can be contested before the contentious administrative courts. According to the Constitution jurisdictional procedures are facultative and free from taxation (Article no. 21).

For contraventional sanctions, the rules on contesting a decision are laid down in Government Ordinance no. 2/2001. Contravention reports must be contested within 15 days from the date when they are received. According to article no. 32 the complaint is registered at the administrative authority to which the finding agent belongs, together with a copy of the contravention report. The administrative authority will immediately send the complaint, together with the whole administrative file, to the first instance civil court. The Constitutional Court has decided through Decision no. 953/2006 that this procedure is not in accordance with the Constitution, so that the complaint may be addressed directly to the competent court.

According to Article 34 of Government Ordinance no. 2/2001, the court will decide upon the sanction. This should mean that the court may control the legality of the procedure, may admit or order new evidence and may completely re-evaluate the sanctioning taking into account all the principles laid down in Government Ordinance no. 2/2001 and may annul, change or modify the sanction. The Ordinance specifically considers the possibility for the court to change a fine into a warning. The principle of *non reformatio in peius* is applied.

If the contravention report does not mention the name, surname and the capacity of the finding agent, the name and surname of the offender and for legal persons the name and corporate seat, the description of the facts and the date when they were committed or if the report is not signed by the finding agent, the court will find it affected by absolute nullity. This means that the court is capable to observe the deficiencies of the contravention report *ex officio.* For any other default, the contravention report is considered to be affected by relative nullity, which means that the petitioner has to mention the default and prove the injury.

A controversial issue is whether the court is competent to determine the infringement and the correct sanction, in the case of sanctions applied by the finding agent and contested in court, if it proves that the finding agent has mistaken the legal text and applied another sanction accordingly, or the report fails to mention the legal disposition that was breeched. Some courts decided that they are competent to establish the infringement according to the description of the deed contained in the report and apply the correct sanction, as article no. 34 states that if the contravention report is contested the court would decide on the sanction, whilst other courts decided that they are only competent to examine the legality of the report, and if the finding agent has mistaken the legal qualification of the infringement or failed to mention the legal disposition that was breached the report has to be annulled. The latter courts considered that in this way the principle of separation of state powers is respected.

The court decision may be appealed to the contentious administrative court of the Tribunals. The court decision on appeal is final.

A complaint against the contravention report before a court of law automatically suspends its effects until a final court decision is delivered and this is not subjected to taxation.

BIBLIOGRAPHY

G., Boboş, G., Vlădica-Raţiu, *Răspunderea, responsabilitatea şi constrângerea în domeniul dreptului,* Editura Argonaut, Cluj-Napoca, 1996.

F., Bradin, E., Popescu, "Raportul dintre răspunderea managerului şi cea a persoanei juridice în materie contravenţională", *Dreptul* no. 10–11/1995, pp. 213–221.

N., Cristuş, *Răspunderea contravenţională. Practică judiciară 2007–2009,* Editura Hamangiu, Bucureşti, 2010.

M. Duţu, G. Duţu, "Consideraţii a*supra* specificului contravenţiilor la regimul de autorizare a construcţiilor", *Dreptul* no. 10–11/1995, pp. 81–85.

E.M., Fodor, *Sancţiunea normelor juridice în dreptul public şi dreptul privat,* in "Public şi privat în economie, învăţământ-cercetare şi drept", Editura Oscar Print, Bucureşti, 2002, pp. 293–308.

C., Mitrache, C. Mitrache, *Dreptul penal român. Partea generală,* Editura Universul Juridic, Bucureşti, 2007.

V. Pătulea, "Aplicarea principiului legii mai favorabile în domeniul contravenţiilor", *Dreptul* no. 3/1999, pp. 139–141.

I. Poenaru (I), I. Santai (II), "Noul regim al contravenþiilor, Ordonanţa nr. 2 din 2001", *Dreptul* no. 12/2001, pp. 3–17.

C.L., Popescu, ""Neconvenţionalitatea" şi neconstituţionalitatea procedurii contravenţionale judiciare de drept comun, în raport cu dreptul la respectarea prezumţiei de nevinovăţie', *Pandectele Române* no. 6/2002, pp. 197–206.

XII. COUNTRY ANALYSIS – SPAIN

Manuel REBOLLO PUIG, Manuel IZQUIERDO CARRASCO,
Lucía ALARCÓN SOTOMAYOR and Antonio Mª. BUENO ARMIJO

1. RELATION TO GENERAL FIELDS OF LAW AND IMPORTANT GENERAL ACTS

1.1. INTRODUCTION

Administrative sanctions are governed by a special statutory regime within the Public Administration activities in Spain. This regime is necessary and is partly inspired by Criminal Law and Criminal Procedural Law. It offers citizens more guarantees than they would have under other administrative acts, that is, guarantees similar to those held by citizens when courts impose sentences.

It is generally accepted, in precedent and in legal literature, that the State's *ius puniendi* is exercised when the Administration imposes sanctions and when courts hand down sentences. It is assumed that the State's *ius puniendi* is exclusive and that it will be exercised, according to the law, either by the courts or by the administrative authorities. This is why some principles of Criminal Law, used with adjustments and caution, also apply to the sanctioning activity of the Administration. General principles from Criminal Law as well as principles specific to administrative sanctions in Administrative Law known as "Sanctioning Administrative Law" figure in the Spanish Constitution. Article 25 of the Spanish Constitution establishes some of the traditional principles of Criminal Law as being of application to criminal offences and administrative infractions, and also to punishments and administrative sanctions, as we shall see below.

1.2. THE CONCEPT OF ADMINISTRATIVE SANCTION

A definition of the administrative sanction is essential in order to specify the field of application of this singular juridical regime. The concept of administrative sanction should be a restrictive one, including only those administrative decisions that are similar to criminal sentences. A broader definition of administrative sanction would be useless or dangerous, as the field of application of these distinctive legal arrangements based on Criminal Law would be difficult to specify or would exceed justifiable limits, creating serious problems.

The laws do not provide a definition of administrative sanction, but the concept of sanction can be construed from precedent and legal authors have developed a theory aimed at providing such a definition. The underlying concept being that both administrative sanctions and criminal sentences are expressions of the same *ius puniendi*, then an administrative sanction could be defined as the punishment imposed by the Administration. From the above it must be deduced that:

- Administrative sanctions are imposed by administrative authorities (central government Ministers, regional and local representatives, other authorities subordinated to these, independent administrative authorities and so forth), but not by the courts.[1] This is the first and leading principle that substantiates a definition of sanction. The difference between administrative sanctions and criminal sentences is that the administrative authorities impose sanctions whereas the courts impose sentences. The other differences between criminal sentences and administrative sanctions derive from this essential distinction.
- Administrative sanctions must be punitive: they must affect or cause detriment to the sanctioned party; they must entail a either deprivation or a restriction of rights or of any advantage, or they must establish new obligations. If they are not punitive, they cannot be considered a punishment. However, there are many other administrative decisions which cause detriment but which are not punishments, nor can they have the juridical regime of administrative sanctions. Therefore, the last two elements prove necessary but not sufficient to define the administrative sanction.
- Sanctions must punish by causing detriment: the damage inflicted is intended as a direct and deliberate response to illegal conduct, and as a means of censure. Therefore, the detriment inflicted by the administrative sanction does not directly guarantee the protection of the general interest. This detriment is not imposed with a view to restoring legality or a modified physical reality or damaged values, or to compensate damage, or to compel proper conduct. All of these functions, in contrast, fall within the scope of other administrative decisions not considered administrative sanctions, and to which the statutory scheme of the latter cannot be applied.

---

1 See *infra*, IV *Organization of sanctioning powers.*

This is why the courts do not consider the following administrative measures, and others, as administrative sanctions: the return of investment grants if the beneficiary does not carry out the activity for which they were granted; the demolition of buildings constructed in contravention of town planning regulations or environmental standards; the closure of premises that do not comply with legislation or do not possess the required administrative authorisation; the withdrawal of potentially dangerous or unhealthy goods from the market; restraining sanctions; compensation paid by private individuals to the Administration for damage caused to public property; interest on delay, and so on.

Nevertheless, in practice the line between administrative sanctions and other administrative decisions detrimental to the public cannot be clearly drawn. In fact, whether administrative decisions with the same detrimental effect are to be considered administrative sanctions or not, depends on their intention to punish. For instance, the suspension of a driving licence may be considered either an administrative sanction or a means of guaranteeing road safety; surcharges for late tax payment is a sanction if the sum to be paid is very high; the expulsion of aliens may be either a sanction or a means of re-establishing legality; the revocation of favourable administrative acts could be considered a sanction or a means of guaranteeing the future general interest, and so on.

The power that laws confer on the Public Administration to impose administrative sanctions is called "*sanctioning power of the Public Administration*".

1.3. THE CONCEPT OF ADMINISTRATIVE INFRINGEMENT

An administrative sanction can only be imposed if an administrative infringement, in the strict sense of the term, has been committed. An administrative sanction is to a criminal sentence what an administrative infringement is to a crime. All types of non-compliance with the legal system are not to be considered administrative infringements. An administrative infringement is conduct violating the legal system (unlawful conduct), is typified by law as a violation, and is ascribed an administrative sanction under the same law. Guilt is also a requirement. Thus, an administrative infringement can be defined as an *unlawful action or omission, typified and culpable, and for which an administrative authority is conferred by law with the power to impose a sanction.*

1.4. UNFAVOURABLE ADMINISTRATIVE MEASURES THAT ARE NOT ADMINISTRATIVE SANCTIONS

This strict definition of administrative sanction makes it possible to isolate an useful juridical category, since it delimitates the scope of application of a particular juridical regime, different from those governing the remainder of administrative acts. Indeed, only such a strict notion can justify the application of that particular and differentiated juridical regime, whose principles and statutes are close to those used in Criminal Law. This can only make sense when considering the punitive nature of these administrative acts – or rather, administrative sanctions –, regardless of the detriment they cause or the infringement of the law by the citizens. It is useless to encompass administrative sanctions *stricto sensu* and the remainder of administrative acts unfavourable to the citizen in the same juridical category, for it does not make any sense to include different notions whose juridical regimes are opposite in the same category. Furthermore, it is dangerous to do so if the principles of Sanctioning Law – *ius puniendi* – were to be applied to all those non-punitive administrative acts.

Among the non-punitive administrative acts unfavourable to the citizen whose application stems from an initial infringement of the law by the citizen, we shall point to the following categories:

- Restraining sanctions.
- Measures to restore the infringed legality.
- Contractual penalties.
- The cancellation of an administrative concession.
- Reimbursements of aid and grants.
- Surcharges for late tax payments.
- Administrative fixation of compensation for damage caused by individuals to public property (rivers, roads, coasts, etc.)

Even though none of the above are administrative sanctions, the Administration cannot impose them without granting the appropriate guarantees for the citizen. Moreover, the Administration must, in contrast, be subject to the principles regulating every administrative activity, to the guarantees commonly laid down by the Law with regard to unfavourable administrative acts and to specific guarantees provided by general or sectoral statutory laws.

Among the general principles to which the administrative activity is subjected, we must underline the importance of the principle of legality, that of congruence and, finally, that of proportionality. In other words, the Administration can only apply these measures whenever there is a law expressly providing for them. Furthermore, this application may only be lawful when conducted in accordance with the conditions, proceedings, guarantees, etc., set out by that specific law, provided the law's established legality is preserved. The principle of congruence implies the suitability of the measure taken within the public interest-oriented purposes set by the law. And, finally, the principle of proportionality aims at the application of the less restrictive, best fact-related measures from all the legal and congruent ones.

Of all the checks and balances established by administrative activity laws, and more precisely, concerning unfavourable acts, we shall point to the following:

- the measure must be the result of an administrative procedure, in the course of which the citizen shall be heard. This safeguard notwithstanding, some of these measures may be temporarily taken until the procedure is completed. However, this procedure is practically non-existent in some instances (i.e., tax surcharges), or it ends up being part of a broader, differently-oriented procedure.
- all administrative acts, without exception, may be submitted to control by the "contentious-administrative" tribunals. This control is comprehensive.
- all these acts must include the means and grounds that justified them.

However, since they cannot be considered to be administrative sanctions, the particular juridical regime of administrative sanctions does not apply. Specifically, this kind of unfavourable act can be imposed together with administrative sanctions *stricto sensu*, without any infringement of the *non bis in idem* principle.

1.4.1. Restraining sanctions

First, it is necessary to remember that, despite its name, restraining sanctions are not true administrative sanctions. The explanations below concerning the enforcement of administrative sanctions will show that Public Administration has the authority to enforce administrative acts of its own volition if the citizen voluntarily fails to comply with them.

There are several means that the Public Administration can use to enforce its acts, namely "means of compulsory execution". We shall focus on one of them: the restraining sanction, which consists of requiring the citizen to pay a sum of money whenever he does not comply with an administrative act. This kind of "fine" can be periodically imposed within the time frame established by law – every week, every month, etc. – if the citizen continues his non-compliance. Although this sanction is included among the "means of compulsory execution", it is not a proper means to execute the administrative act, for this act can remain unfulfilled. It is, however, a means to overcome the citizen's reluctance to comply with the act.

1.4.2. Measures to restore the infringed legality

This category includes all those unfavourable administrative acts whose purpose is the re-establishment of the legality which has been infringed in order to protect public interest from being damaged. Thus, the withdrawal of an administrative authorization for a certain activity – or similar measures –, once the conditions required by law to exercise this activity are no longer respected. For example, to obtain a driver's licence it is necessary to comply with several requirements, one of them being the physical capability to drive. If, at some point, a citizen is not physically capable of driving, his driver's licence will be revoked. Likewise, to obtain the necessary authorization to open a nightclub it is required that the noise level does not exceed a certain volume. If, after a certain time, the noise surpasses those levels, the provisional suspension of the opening licence shall take place until those requirements are met.

1.4.3. The reimbursement of public grants

Public grants are payments that are conditional upon compliance with certain duties, and it is not required that their recipients provide equivalent compensation. Grants aim at the promotion of an useful public activity, and they can consist of the performance of a certain activity, the adoption of a particular behaviour or the existence of a particular situation.

Once the required duties have been completed, it is lawful to receive the grant. Therefore, whenever there is non-compliance, the right to receive the grant is either forfeited or withdrawn along with the interest thereon, depending on whether the payment had already been awarded or not. The obligation to restore a grant is called reimbursement.

1.4.4. Contractual penalties

These are punishments that the Administration can impose against its contracting parties because of non-compliance with the terms of the contract (i.e., a delay in the completion of public works). In some cases these penalties can be expressly contained in the Real Decreto Legislativo 3/2011, de 14 de noviembre, por el que se aprueba el texto refundido de la Ley de Contratos del Sector Publico. In other cases, the framework will be the one expressly provided by the terms of the contract, based on the principle of freedom of agreement.

1.5. GENERAL ADMINISTRATIVE SANCTIONS AND DISCIPLINARY ADMINISTRATIVE SANCTIONS

There is a distinction between administrative sanctions imposed against any person for his unlawful conduct, and those sanctions imposed against persons more closely linked to the Administration; the latter are considered more serious, as they involve an infringement of special duties. For instance, sanctions against civil servants, prisoners, students, and so on when they infringe their duties as such. This second category of sanctions is special in that there is a reduction of formal and material guarantees. The difference could be based on what is called "disciplinary administrative power" which is distinct from general administrative sanctioning power because it would not be an expression of the same *ius puniendi* of the State; it could also be related to the concept of "a special binding relationship" (*die besonderen Gewaltverhältlnisse*) with the Administration inherited from the German legal system. However, the distinction between both types of sanctions or the statutory regimes with which they conform is not clear. According to the precedents of the Constitutional Court, clear-cut distinctions cannot be established, only differences based on quantity or degree: for instance, both types of sanctions are bound to the principle of legality, although the interpretation of this concept is more flexible when dealing with disciplinary sanctions.

1.6. DIFFERENCES BETWEEN THE STATUTORY REGIME OF ADMINISTRATIVE SANCTIONS AND CRIMINAL SANCTIONS

Although criminal sentences and administrative sanctions are similar, and both Criminal Law and Criminal Procedural Law bear some resemblance to Sanctioning Administrative Law, many differences can also be found. The laws, the courts and the experts tend to highlight these differences, as they are far-reaching and comprehensive. We shall concentrate on three main differences:

- The rules of Criminal Law and Criminal Procedural Law do not apply to administrative sanctions, even when Administrative Law lacks a specific rule. Administrative Law accepts only some common principles, although these will be applied in different ways under Criminal Law and Sanctioning Administrative Law.
- Criminal Law is the exclusive competence of the State according to the division of powers between the State and the autonomous communities in Spain: only the Law of the State can establish offences, sentences and their legal regime. Moreover, in Spain Criminal Law is applied by criminal justice,

and the Judiciary falls within the competence of the State. On the other hand, Regional (autonomous) governments frequently enact laws that establish administrative violations and sanctions; it is equally frequent for the administrative authorities of the Regional governments to impose these sanctions insofar as such powers have been transferred to them. Consequently, if a Regional government has powers in the area of town planning or tourism, it will have jurisdiction to legislate on administrative violations and sanctions relative to town planning or tourism, and to apply that legislation.

- Criminal Law traditionally stated that only natural persons could commit offences and suffer penalties (*societas delinquere non potest*). In contrast, legal persons could commit administrative offences and be subject to the corresponding sanction. This was an advantage of Sanctioning Administrative Law over Criminal Law. However, Criminal Law has been recently ammended in order to accept, for the first time, that legal persons can commit offences and suffer penalties (*Ley Orgánica 5/2010, de 22 de junio, de Reforma del Código Penal*, entered into force on 23 December).

1.7. CONSTITUTIONAL AND LEGAL SYSTEM

The Spanish Constitution includes two Articles of vital importance on this matter: Article 25 establishes the most important material principles regarding infringements and sanctions; Article 24 refers exclusively to court proceedings, but applies to some extent to punitive administrative procedures. We shall deal with this matter in more detail, but it is essential to point out here that this constitutional basis has shaped the case law of the Constitutional Court, which in turn has an enormous influence on Sanctioning Administrative Law.

The European Convention on Human Rights forms a point of reference for Spanish domestic law, especially Article 6, which deals with administrative sanctions. Furthermore, Article 10(2) of the Spanish Constitution reads:

> "The Principles relating to the fundamental rights and liberties recognized by the Constitution shall be interpreted in conformity with the Universal Declaration of Human Rights and the international treaties and agreements thereon ratified by Spain".

Articles 24 and 25 of the Spanish Constitution, which deal with administrative sanctions, are among those fundamental rights; the European Convention on Human Rights, together with the case law of the European Court of Human Rights, is among those international treaties repeatedly cited by the Constitutional Court and the remainder of the Spanish courts.

However, with respect to administrative sanctions, the guarantees derived from the Spanish Constitution, the Constitutional Court's case law and domestic law go beyond those required by the European Convention on Human Rights.

The Act regulating Public Administration, Authorities and Procedures (*Ley de Régimen Jurídico de las Administraciones Públicas y del Procedimiento Administrativo Común* 30/1992, 26 November) (hereafter, LPA) is the domestic law that establishes the most important general rules on the statutory regime of Public Administration in Spain. Its title IX deals with "Sanctioning powers" in two chapters: Chapter I is entitled "Principles of sanctioning powers" (Articles 127 to 133) and deals with material aspects; Chapter II: "Principles of the punitive administrative procedure" (Articles 134 to 138) deals with formal and procedural aspects. This regulation focuses exclusively on principles. It reviews concisely the most salient general aspects, but does not establish general rules on sanctions, liability, aggravating or mitigating circumstances, nor does it classify infringements and sanctions. It provides no more than a framework for offences and sanctions.

The regulatory laws on each sector of administrative activity (health, public safety, pollution, commerce, consumer protection, roads, town planning, the protection of competition, and so on) are those which determine specific breaches, their corresponding sanctions, liable persons, aggravating or mitigating circumstances and so forth.

As stated above, these laws can be enacted either by the State or the Regional (autonomous) governments depending on which of them has jurisdiction in the matter. Therefore, if the State is competent in matters of public safety, the State will regulate infringements and sanctions in these matters, and where Regional governments are competent in town planning, then it is they who will determine breaches and sanctions in that area.

In conclusion, except for some limited general rules in the LPA, Sanctioning Administrative Law is spread throughout a vast number of statutory rules. Whereas Criminal Law has a code, Sanctioning Administrative Law does not.

1.8. CONTENT OF THE SANCTIONS

Article 25(3) of the Spanish Constitution establishes a limit regarding the content of sanctions:

> "The civil Administration may not impose penalties which directly or indirectly imply deprivation of freedom."

The military are not restricted by this prohibition, as it refers only to the "civil Administration".

Likewise, "inhuman or degrading punishment or treatment" is prohibited by Article 15 of the Spanish Constitution. *A fortiori,* inhuman or degrading administrative sanctions are considered to be prohibited.

The laws can provide for different administrative sanctions within the limits of the Constitution. There is no general legislation on the scope of administrative sanctions. Each specific regulatory law will determine infractions and duly establish sanctions. Due to the enormous number of laws that establish infractions and administrative sanctions over a wide range of areas, and because each law is permitted to impose those sanctions which it considers to be appropriate, it would be difficult to list each of the administrative sanctions in Spanish legislation. The most frequent ones are: fines; confiscation of goods, utensils or profits; the closure of premises for a certain period of time; a ban on certain activities for a certain period of time (prohibition on exercising a profession, managing credit institutions, driving motor vehicles, hunting and so on); limitation of the capacity to contract with the Administration or to obtain public aid for a certain period of time; admonition; publication of the infraction and the sanction imposed in the government or public press.

Without doubt, the most usual administrative sanction is a fine, when the offender is made to pay the Administration a sum of money. The sum may vary from a maximum of 1,000 euro under certain laws, to 6,000,000 euro or more under others. For administrative fines there is no constitutional limit to the amount, nor any legislation establishing that the sum for administrative sanctions should be lower than the amount established for crimes.[2] In fact, some laws lay down administrative fines which exceed those established for many offences under Criminal Law.

1.9. THE MATERIAL SCOPE OF SANCTIONING ADMINISTRATIVE LAW AND CRIMINAL LAW

In Spain, the Public Administration has always had wider sanctioning powers than most other European States. The Spanish Constitution acknowledges these powers in Article 25, explicitly mentioning administrative infractions and sanctions. The Constitution wanted to increase the guarantees that citizens had against administrative sanctions, not to reduce their range of application. This is

2 The Spanish *Código Penal* provides for the pecuniary sanctions for criminal offences, with a few exceptions, the maximum amount being €288,000.

why the constitutionality of the Administration's sanctioning power has never been brought into question even when it goes beyond the disciplinary context and special binding relationships with the Administration.

However, whether the laws are competent to define certain conduct as a crime or as an administrative offence is a moot point; that is to say, whether there are certain unlawful activities that should necessarily be sanctioned by the courts under Criminal Law, or whether there exists a specific, exclusive area for administrative sanctions.

It is assumed that certain serious forms of misconduct should be severely punished by the courts under Criminal Law – homicide, personal injury, sexual abuse and many more – especially because the deprivation of liberty can only be imposed as a punishment by the courts. Likewise, it is accepted that certain unlawful forms of conduct fall within the scope of administrative sanctions, especially disciplinary and other less serious breaches. However, there are activities that may be considered crimes on some occasions but administrative infringements on others. In fact, there are examples of forms of conduct that were once considered crimes, but are currently administrative infractions, and vice versa, administrative offences that became crimes. Likewise, the difference between administrative offences and crimes is frequently a quantitative one; for instance, tax fraud is normally considered to be an administrative offence up to a certain amount, whereby it then turns into a crime.

Summing up, the legislator cannot draw a definite line between what it must consider to be a crime or an administrative infraction or between what is punishable by a court or by administrative sanctions.[3]

There is a perceptible tendency to limit the ambit of crimes while increasing the field of administrative offences. Several factors confirm this trend: the assumption that Criminal Law should be the *ultima ratio* and respond to the "principle of minimum intervention"; the disproportionate number of cases in the criminal courts; the potential failure of criminal proceedings in defending the general interest; finally, the lack of preparation on the part of the judges of the criminal courts to decide on certain forms of conduct in certain fields. Some of these assumptions may be debatable, but there has been no move towards

[3] This has been admitted by the Spanish Constitutional Court in its decision 116/199 of 17 June, which resolved an appeal against the *Ley de Técnicas de Reproducción Asistida* (...). The applicants argued that some forms of behaviour against life and human dignity, considered administrative offences by this law, should be considered crimes. However, according to this decision, "*fuera de ciertos supuestos extremos, ninguna duda cabe acerca de la competencia del legislador para determinar cuál ha de ser la protección penal que deba dispensar a los bienes y derechos de los ciudadanos, máxime cuando en esa tarea ha de guiarse por el principio de mínima intervención*".

reducing the vast scope of the sanctioning power of the Public Administration. Rather, energies are being directed towards imposing strict limits on that power, so that citizens can benefit from similar guarantees, whether they suffer from criminal sanctions or administrative sanctions.

2. GENERAL PRINCIPLES

2.1. THE PRINCIPLE OF LEGALITY

Article 25(1) of the Spanish Constitution states:

> "No one may be convicted or sentenced for any act or omission which at the time it was committed did not constitute a felony, misdemeanour, or administrative offence according to the law in force at that time."

The term "legislation" refers to an Act (a law passed by Parliament, or other legislative decrees). The exclusivity of the law exists in both Criminal Law and Sanctioning Administrative Law. Exclusivity of the law applies mainly to the classification of offences (criminal or administrative) and the determination of the respective punishments (sentences or administrative sanctions); it also affects other important aspects of the statutory regime: persons liable for punishment, rules to determine the extent of the sanction, the cessation of liability and so on.

The exclusivity of the law does not forbid legislative decrees confined to punishing non-compliance with by-laws ("unrestricted sanctioning rules"). These non-legislative decrees are rules approved by the Administration and are termed "*reglamentos*".

Although the exclusivity of the law is established in identical terms for both Criminal Law and Sanctioning Administrative Law in Article 25(1) of the Spanish Constitution, case law has admitted a certain flexibility in the latter: by-laws may be legitimated to complete, detail and develop sanctioning laws. However, no Act can allow a regulation to establish offences and sanctions *ex novo*, as it would contravene the exclusivity of the law, and thus be unconstitutional. Likewise, by-laws cannot contain sanctioning rules without authorisation by the law, nor can they do more than develop it.

In all cases, the definition of an infraction and the establishment of the corresponding sanction can only be determined by a legislative decree. In conclusion, by-laws benefit from a broader function than under Criminal Law, albeit extremely limited. These ideas have been brought together in Article 129 of LPA:

> "1. Infringement of the legal system will be considered an administrative offence only *if a Law has established it as such…*
> 2. Only if an administrative offence has been committed can *sanctions* be imposed, and *of necessity these will be established by the law.*
> 3. By-laws are entitled to introduce specifications or degrees to the list of infractions and sanctions legally established, which, though not defining new offences or sanctions nor altering the nature and limits of those already determined by the law, will help to classify conducts or determine the corresponding sanctions more precisely".

In practice, it is difficult to gauge how far by-laws can develop; by-laws frequently develop sanctioning law provisions rather generously, without being overruled by the courts.

These general rules on the exclusivity of the law have been amended in certain areas:

- Breaches committed by civil servants. In this domain, the law appears to grant more leeway in the modification of by-laws. Sometimes the same status is applicable to infringements by and sanctions against other individuals subject to "a special binding relationship" (*das besondere Gewaltverhältnis*) with the Administration. However, it is not clear which situations can truly be considered to have a special binding relationship, and what effect this fine distinction might have on the exclusivity of the law.
- Violations committed by professionals (lawyers, doctors, architects, chemists and so on), which are penalised by professional associations. The Professional Bodies Act confers the professional associations with the power to punish any non-compliance with their respective rules of professional conduct. It is the professional association that approves the rules establishing offences, breaches and sanctions.
- Offences established in regulatory norms approved by local authorities ("municipal by-laws"). The Constitutional Court and the ordinary courts once annulled the municipal by-laws establishing new offences and sanctions that had not been provided for by the laws, as well as the sanctions imposed by such by-laws. Recently, however, there has been a major significant change in this matter. In order to boost local autonomy, the Constitutional Court has accepted[4] that Laws can establish certain matters concerning which local authorities may categorise offences and establish sanctions. On this basis,

4 See the Constitutional Court decision 132/2001, of 8 June.

municipal by-laws can establish offences and sanctions *ex novo,* within legal limits. Pursuant to this, the Municipal Code was recently modified[5], allowing local authorities to standardise violations relative to damage to local property, disturbance of local public services or breaches of the peace, and permitting the imposition of fines up to 3,000 euro. Other laws on specific matters of administrative activity are likely to develop the potential of municipal by-laws.[6]

2.2. THE PRINCIPLE OF TYPOLOGY RELATING TO OFFENCES AND ADMINISTRATIVE SANCTIONS

The law must define what is considered an infringement and establish the corresponding sanction (the *lex certa* requirement). According to the principle of typology, Laws cannot describe offences using indistinct or general statements, nor can they turn every non-compliance with the legal system into violations. On the contrary, they must specify and define as clearly as possible, the conduct liable to be considered an offence, and determine, within relatively restricted limits, the corresponding sanction. However, the requirements of the principle of typology are not absolute but relative:

- Insofar as they cannot be avoided, imprecise legal concepts may be used to determine what an offence is. However, an overly wide or generic formulation which classifies any conduct which transgresses the legal system as an offence cannot be admitted.
- The Administration is credited with a certain discretionary power to determine the corresponding sanction in each case, within the limits of the law and provided the sanction is not absolute.[7]

According to the principle of typology, making an analogy is likewise excluded. Article 129(4) of the LPA declares:

> "The rules governing offences and sanctions are not subject to analogous application".

2.3. THE PRINCIPLE OF THE PROPORTIONALITY OF SANCTIONS

A sanction must be proportional to the seriousness of the offence. This is the idea that sustains the principle of proportionality, which must be taken into account

---

5 *Ley 7/1985, de 2 de abril, Reguladora de las Bases del Régimen Local,* amended by *Ley 57/2003, de 16 de diciembre, de medidas para la modernización del gobierno local.*

6 *See Ley 37/2003, de 17 de noviembre, del Ruido.*

7 See *infra,* VI *Legal Protection,* §1.D).

by the legislator when it establishes the sanctioning framework: to decide what constitutes a breach; to establish what constitutes a minor breach, serious breach or gross misconduct; to determine the type or amount of the sanctions and so on. Likewise, this should be taken into account by the sanctioning body when imposing a specific sanction within the legal framework.

At this second stage, the legislator does not leave the administrative sanctioning body to define the sanction, but stipulates conditions to be taken into account when doing so. These indications are also an example of the principle of proportionality. Each law lists its specific conditions, although many of them appear in all of the laws: the profit obtained on committing the breach, the damage caused, the number of offences committed, negligence or premeditation on the part of the offender, the dominant position of the infractor in the market, and so on. The LPA has established various general conditions that must always be taken into account by the sanctioning body when determining the extent of the sanction: premeditation, the nature of the damage caused, and whether or not other infringements had previously been committed.

The principle of proportionality with respect to the imposition of sanctions does not constitute a fundamental right as such, and any contravention is reviewed by the courts, although not by the Constitutional Court.

2.4. THE PRINCIPLE OF NON-RETROACTIVITY OF ADVERSE SANCTIONING RULES AND RETROACTIVITY OF FAVOURABLE SANCTIONING RULES (*LEX MITIOR*)

Article 25(1) of the Spanish Constitution forbids the retroactivity of both criminal and administrative sanctioning rules. Therefore, no one can be punished for an action that was not considered to be an offence at the time it was committed, or be given a more severe sanction than the one established at that time. In brief, retroactivity *in malam partem* is forbidden.

However, although the Spanish Constitution neither prohibits nor imposes the retroactivity of favourable sanctioning rules, the laws have imposed retroactivity *in bonam partem*. This is provided for under Article 128 of the LPA[8]:

> "1. The sanctioning provisions in force at the time when the acts constituting the administrative offence took place shall apply.
> 2. Sanctioning provisions shall have a retroactive effect provided they are favourable to the presumptive offender".

8 Likewise, see Article 2 *Código Penal*.

2.5. THE PRINCIPLE OF GUILT

Administrative sanctions can only be imposed if the improper conduct is committed willingly and with culpability, that is to say, as a result of intent or fault, the same situation as under Criminal Law.

Although the requirement of guilt is not mentioned in the Spanish Constitution, the Constitutional Court has considered it to be an implicit and fundamental right, so that any law infringing this requirement would be unconstitutional.

Therefore, administrative sanctions cannot be imposed if some reason rules out guilt, for instance, in the case of a manifest error, or the principle of legitimate expectations. The duty to exercise due diligence, including a broad obligation to use prudence and judgement, is expected from many of the subjects liable to commit an administrative breach: credit institutions, manufacturers, and so on. Consequently, most not guilty pleas are finally sanctioned, as it is considered that the duty of due diligence was not sufficiently fulfilled.

Finally, the requirement of guilt does not rule out the sanctioning of legal persons, albeit tailored to their particular situation: generally, intent or fault must be proved in the natural persons responsible for the legal person.

2.6. THE PRINCIPLE OF *NON BIS IN IDEM*

The right not to be punished twice for the same offence (*non bis in idem*) is not established in the Spanish Constitution. Nevertheless, the Constitutional Court has declared that it is implicit in Article 25(1) of the Spanish Constitution and any infringement thereof is considered to be a violation of a fundamental right.

In fact, double punishment is not prohibited in all cases: the *non bis in idem* rule is considered to have been broken only if both penalties are imposed for the same facts, on the same person and on the same legal grounds. This is how the LPA reads:

> "Article 133. Concurrence of sanctions.
> Acts resulting in a criminal or administrative sanction cannot bring forth a second sanction when the subject, fact or legal grounds are the same."

Consequently, a person can receive two or more punishments for the same offence, provided they are founded on a different legal ground.[9]

9 I.e. If one of the sanctions has been imposed because human life was put in jeopardy, and the other has been imposed on the ground of a consumer campaign, there will not be any violation of the *non bis in idem* principle.

When several rules establish punishments for the same offence and are founded on the same legal ground, the right not to be punished twice raises the issue of choosing a single applicable rule:

- Providing that one of the rules falls under Criminal Law, and the other is a sanctioning administrative regulation, the criminal rule will always prevail. Consequently, whenever the Administration suspects that a certain act which constitutes an administrative offence can also constitute a crime, it should halt the punitive administrative procedure, transmit the case to the criminal courts and await the criminal judgement. If the criminal court decides that the act does not constitute a crime, the Administration can then resume the administrative procedure and impose a sanction, if appropriate.[10]
- If both are administrative rules, the *non bis in idem* rule imposes the right not to be punished with two administrative sanctions under the same legal ground.[11] However, a general rule on which of them should preferably be enforced has not been established, despite the fact that the corresponding sanctions may be quite different, depending on which of the administrative rules is applied.

The right not to be punished twice is especially significant in the case of persons with a special binding relationship with the Public Administration, especially in the case of civil servants. It is generally accepted that they can be punished with both the general penalty imposed on any person committing that crime, and the administrative sanction imposed to civil servants. However, there are exceptions and it is difficult to reach a general assumption based on case law.[12]

2.7. THE PRINCIPLE OF EQUALITY

Article 14 of the Spanish Constitution states: "Spanish people are equal before the law...". This principle of equality – which is also a fundamental right –

10 See *infra*, II *Rights of defence*, §1.D).

11 That is, if the same behaviour is considered to be an administrative offence under two different laws. E.g., Article 35.b).5º, *Ley 14/1986, de 25 de abril, General de Sanidad* establishes as an administrative offence "*La resistencia a suministrar datos, facilitar información o prestar colaboración a las autoridades sanitarias o a sus agentes*" whilst, almost identically, Article 101.2.a).1º, Ley 29/2006, de 26 de julio, de garantía y uso racional de los medicamentos, productos sanitarios, states an administrative offence whereby "*No aportar las entidades o personas responsables los datos, declaraciones así como cualesquiera información que estén obligados a suministrar por razones sanitarias, técnicas, económicas, administrativas y financieras*".

12 The same nuances apply to other cases, such as where administrative sanctions are imposed by the Professional Bodies on their members along with other conventional sanctions established for everybody.

governs administrative action in general and sanctioning action in particular. Consequently, it is unconstitutional to impose sanctions which infringe the principle of equality.

Alleging that the sanctioning power infringes the principle of equality is, however, generally rejected by the courts precisely in those cases where it may have the most practical importance: when sanctioned parties plead that the Administration has not imposed a sanction on other parties who have committed the same violation and that the principle of equality is therefore not being adhered to. The courts tend to pronounce that equality is not applicable in cases of illegality.

2.8. THE PRINCIPLE OF THE REQUIRED PROCEDURE

The Spanish Constitution forbids the imposition of sanctions without due process of law. The LPA lays down the following:

> "Article 134. Guarantee of procedure
> 1. Due process of law or legally established procedure is required to exercise sanctioning power.
> 2. …
> 3. On no account can sanctions be imposed without having followed the required procedure."

Consequently, no administrative sanction can be imposed prior to the corresponding procedure, as the punitive administrative procedure constitutes an essential guarantee for the accused: it ensures that his fundamental rights of defence are not denied.

The punitive administrative procedure features the following elements:

- The rights of defence held by the alleged offender during the procedure.
- The division of the procedure into two different stages: preliminary inquiries and resolution; these must be entrusted to different administrative bodies, so that the deciding body is not the same as the accusing body.[13] This is designed to guarantee the objectivity and impartiality of the competent body issuing a resolution.

---

13 Article 134.2 LPA states that: "Los procedimientos que regulen el ejercicio de la potestad sancionadora deberán establecer la debida separación entre la fase instructora y la sancionadora, encomendándolas a órganos distintos".

- Permanent access to the procedure, whereby the accused can be informed of each stage of the procedure, lodge pleadings, present documents and obtain copies of the existing documents at any point in the procedure, from the beginning to the end of the preliminary inquiries stage (Article 79(1) of LPA).

The first feature emanates directly from the Spanish Constitution. The other two elements guarantee, *ex novo* and in the interest of the defendant, two ordinary rights which respond to the express desire of the legislator, and have no constitutional foundation.

3. RIGHTS OF DEFENCE

3.1. ENUMERATION AND CONTENT OF THE RIGHTS OF DEFENCE

Article 24.2 paragraph 1 of the Spanish Constitution states:

> "… All persons have the right of access to the Ordinary Judge predetermined by law, to the defence and assistance of a lawyer, to be informed of the charges brought against them, to a public trial without undue delays and with full guarantees, to the use of the evidence pertinent to their defence, to not make self-incriminating statements, to not declare themselves guilty and to the presumption of innocence."

Contrary to what the Spanish Constitution sets out in Article 25, Article 24 refers exclusively to rights in criminal court actions, not to punitive administrative procedures. However, in the same way that the European Court of Human Rights has done with Article 6 of the European Convention on Human Rights, the Constitutional Court has transferred some of these rights, albeit with numerous adaptations and adjustments, to the punitive administrative procedure (not to other administrative procedures). Not all the rights in Article 24(2) of the Spanish Constitution are applicable to punitive administrative procedures; nor are the applicable rights necessarily in the same terms as in criminal procedures. Rather, they derive, both in part and in essence, from the rights laid down in Article 24(2) of the Spanish Constitution.

According to the Constitutional Court, also in the Punitive Administrative Procedure (PAP) the accused enjoys the following fundamental rights, guaranteed by Article 24(2) of the Spanish Constitution for the criminal procedure: to be informed of the charges; to use relevant means to prove his/her innocence; to refrain from self-incrimination and from pleading guilty; and the presumption of innocence.[14] We shall examine the essential contents of such rights:

3.1.1. *The right to be informed of the charge(s)*

In the punitive administrative procedure this entails the defendant's right to know the contents and charge(s) brought against him in order to be able to mount a defence, and also the resultant right that the acts for which the defendant is ultimately sanctioned are the same acts with which he/she was initially charged (a necessary correspondence between the charges and the final punitive resolution). As a result, the defendant must be notified of the charge and also of its legal categorisation, that is, he must be informed of the breach of the law in question, and of the sanction which might be imposed.[15]

3.1.2. *The right to use relevant means to prove one's innocence*

This confers on the accused:

- the right to adduce evidence, in due time and form.
- the right that the adduced evidence is duly accepted.
- the right that properly adduced evidence be supported by the relevant formal guarantees.

The rejection of any evidence must be explicitly justified. The putting forward of evidence must respect certain basic principles such as the principle of contradiction, the accused's right of access, and the presence of the investigating official.[16]

---

14 This Constitutional Court case law, along with some innovations introduced by the legislator, has been addressed in the LPA in these terms:
"Article 135. Derechos del presunto responsable
Los procedimientos sancionadores garantizan al presunto responsable los siguientes derechos:
A ser notificados de los hechos que se le imputen, de las infracciones que tales hechos puedan constituir y de las sanciones que, en su caso, se les pudieran imponer...
A formular alegaciones y utilizar los medios de defensa admitidos por el Ordenamiento Jurídico que resulten procedentes..."
"Article 137. Presunción de inocencia
1. Los procedimientos sancionadores respetarán la presunción de no existencia de responsabilidad administrativa mientras no se demuestre lo contrario...
4... se admitirán a propuesta del presunto responsable cuantas pruebas sean adecuadas..."

15 Case law has held that this right is usually met by notifying two essential documents to the accused: the agreement on the commencement of the procedure and, especially, the proposal of sanction.

16 However, the administrative sanction will only be annulled when the violation of the rights of defence has rendered the accused defenceless, that is, only if it has decisively affected the evidence adduced by the defence, when the latter has potential exculpatory relevance. Had this evidence been adduced, then it would have undeniably changed the outcome, thus benefiting the accused. Therefore, the right that is under scrutiny is not absolute, but is a

3.1.3. *The right to refrain from self-incrimination and from pleading guilty*

This right is applied with certain adaptations. In principle, the accused has the right to remain silent, is free to testify or refrain from doing so, and to decide on the content of any statement he/she may wish to make. However, this fundamental right is compatible with the duty of information and cooperation with the administrative inspectorate, even though the information supplied may ultimately be used to incriminate the accused.[17]

3.1.4. *The right to the presumption of innocence*

In the punitive administrative procedure this right applies in full. The most important consequences arising with respect to evidence[18] are as follows:

legally-conceived right that translates into the expectation of being allowed to adduce the decisive evidence.

17 That is, the administrative authorities cannot oblige the accused to incriminate him/herself or to declare his/her guilt. However, it does not mean that there are some practices which do not violate this right, i.e.,

– this right is not infringed when the accused is obliged to comply with an alcohol test (a breathalyser, or a blood or urine test). According to the Spanish Constitutional Court, this obligation is the result of a special kind of evidence, requiring the active cooperation of the accused. This having been said, it does not mean that the accused has to incriminate him/herself. Those who comply with these tests are not making a declaration that would imply an admission of guilt. (Constitutional Court decision 103/1985, 4 October; 107/1985, 7 October; y 161/1997, 2 October).

– when the accused is required to provide information to the inspection authorities (i.e., to provide tax returns to the Treasury), Constitutional Court decision 110/1984, 26 November.

– or, in the field of traffic sanctions, when the owner of a vehicle is required to identify the person who was driving when the offence was committed. "Este deber de colaboración del titular del vehículo con la Administración resulta inherente al hecho de ser propietario (…) que comporta ciertas obligaciones (…) debido al riesgo potencial que la utilización de un automóvil entraña para la vida, la salud y la integridad de las personas (…). De ahí que la carga impuesta (…) no se presente como excesiva o desproporcionada (…). Y aunque concurran en una misma persona las circunstancias de conductor y propietario del vehículo, a éste no se le impone el deber ni de efectuar declaración alguna sobre la infracción ni de autoinculparse de la misma sino únicamente de comunicar la identidad de quien realizaba la acción" (Constitutional Court decision 197/1995, 21 December).

All these examples represent legal obligations imposed on the accused by the Law. Compliance therewith, according to the Spanish Constitutional Court, does not infringe the fundamental right to not incriminate oneself or to declare one's guilt.

18 Along with the implications relating to the evidence, it is appropriate, to stress the fact that the presumption of innocence has implications regarding the punitive administrative procedure. This is especially so when it comes to the possibility of adopting provisional measures within the punititive administrative procedure, which, in the majority of cases, will result in prejudice to the accused (who must still be considered innocent). It is also the case when sanctions are to be enforced prior to being summoned before the courts, when this presumption has not yet been disproved.

- Evidence is necessary in order to take punitive measures. The prosecution must provide evidence in order to destroy the presumption of innocence and, subsequently, to punish. This must be prior to the sanction and must be sufficiently incriminating. Likewise, the evidence must be relevant to the acts that constitute the infringement and the guilt of the accused. Any deficiency or reservation in the evidence adduced will constitute grounds for acquittal.
- The proof must take the form of proper evidence in the strict sense of the term as used in Criminal Procedural Law. Not all verifications of evidence constitute proper evidence, which must of necessity fulfil two prerequisites: it must have been obtained with absolute respect for fundamental rights; and it must be adduced with the formal guarantees laid down by the law.
- The burden of proof rests with the administrative body which has brought the charges. The case law has held that it is the duty of the administrative body in question to prove the act that constitutes the administrative breach, the result emanating therefrom, the causality between both, and the involvement of the accused. However, the case law remains unclear when it comes to establishing whether there is an obligation on the accused to prove any exonerating and mitigating factors (the absence of guilt, self-defence, the exercise of a particular right, the statute of limitations), or whether it is the Administration that must prove the absence thereof.
- There should be a free evaluation of all the evidence adduced by the Administration. It must be considered as a whole, in accordance with "fair and reasonable criteria". This means that there is no rule obliging the Administration to give preference to some evidence over any other, but that it should evaluate all the evidence as a whole, using its good judgement and common sense (free evaluation of evidence). Thus the Administration can give more credence to any of the evidence adduced, be it for the prosecution or the defence (e.g. it may believe one witness but not another; or it may give more credence to documentary evidence than to a witness, or vice versa). In no case does the free evaluation of evidence allow arbitrary or irrational evaluations. Furthermore, the evaluation of evidence must be expressly reasoned in the judgment.

Finally, we should clarify that the evaluation of the evidence in the punitive administrative procedure does not bind the contentious administrative courts (litigation where the state is a party), which have full powers to entirely re-evaluate the evidence, not only any new evidence, but also any evidence adduced in the punitive administrative procedure.[19]

In conclusion, the presumption of innocence requires that the sanction eventually imposed should be grounded on prosecution evidence, however

19 See *infra*, paragraph 6 on legal protection.

minimal, which must be presented by the Administration, and which must have been obtained by valid means, formally adduced and fairly evaluated.

3.2. SPECIFIC RIGHTS OF DEFENCE IN THE PUNITIVE ADMINISTRATIVE PROCEDURE

From the commencement of the procedure, the accused is an interested party and is granted all the aforementioned fundamental rights:

- The decision which sets the punitive administrative procedure in motion constitutes a formal charge, and it must, of necessity, describe the wrongful act, its possible legal classification, i.e. the alleged violation, the punishment which it may incur, and the identity of the alleged guilty party. The defendant must be duly notified and be informed of the charges.
- Once this decision has been notified, the accused is given a certain amount of time to submit pleadings, present documents and adduce evidence. However, with some exceptions, the accused is neither obliged to plead nor to co-operate with the Administration in its enquiries into the facts. Notwithstanding his/her right to refrain from self-incrimination and confess guilt, the defendant can admit responsibility, without prejudicing his/her right to lodge an appeal at a later date.
- If the accused has requested the submission of certain evidence, the investigating official will necessarily admit any relevant evidence and will have the authority to reject any proof which he/she considers to be irrelevant. The dismissal of any evidence must be expressly reasoned. The decision as to the relevance of any evidence has important consequences, as the effectiveness of the fundamental right to evidence largely depends on the proper execution of this decision. The report confirming the relevance of the evidence must be reasoned and notified to the defendant. It will state what part of the requested evidence has been accepted and what has been rejected, as well as the evidence that the investigating officer has decided to submit on his/her own initiative.
- Subsequently, the evidence will be submitted, allowing the accused to be present and to take an active part in the process (testimony of a witness, on-site inspections, expert testimony). The accused is also guaranteed the possibility of presenting an oral argument.
- Having examined the evidence, the investigating official will draft the proposal to resolve the case, which will include either a penalty or a decision to acquit, according to whether he/she considers that the Administration has obtained sufficient evidence. In the former case, it will refer to the facts deemed to have been proved, the specific breach understood to have been committed, the precise sanction proposed and the identity of the party responsible.

- The accused must be informed of this proposal. Thus, the defendant's right to be informed of the charges is duly satisfied. Once the proposal has been delivered, the accused has a new time within which he/she should submit pleadings, present documents and examine the entire case. This formality is fundamental and is known as "the hearing stage" (*trámite de audiencia).*
- After being heard, the investigating official will submit the proposal to resolve the case and the entire file to the competent sanctioning body. Having reviewed all the proceedings, the competent body will deliver its decision, be it a sanction or an acquittal, which formally ends the administrative procedure, and will inform the defendant accordingly. The punitive resolution may coincide completely with the sanction proposed by the investigating official. However, the resolution may diverge from that proposed by the official (e.g. changing the violation into a more severe one, or aggravating the sanction), provided that the accused is given the opportunity of a new hearing. What it cannot do, however, and in accordance with the right of the accused to know the charge, is to accept as true any facts which are different from those which were proved in the investigating official's proposal to resolve the case. There is an exception to this: when the official deems that the investigation phase was defective and decides to carry out additional enquiries. In such cases, the accused will be given a new hearing.

3.3. THE PUNITIVE RESOLUTION. PROVIDING THE NECESSARY GROUNDS

The LPA states that any administrative resolution imposing a sanction must be reasoned. Therefore the logical process leading to the imposition of a specific sanction must be based on legal grounds. This motivation must deal with the following aspects:

- The determination of all the relevant facts. That is, the facts constituting the breach, those related to its cause and responsibility, and those which lead the Administration to impose a particular sanction within the punitive framework laid down in the law.
- An evaluation of the submitted evidence, particularly the evidence giving rise to the ruling.
- The person or persons held responsible.
- The breach or violations committed.
- The penalty or penalties to be imposed.

The LPA requires the punitive sanction to cover all the issues presented in the punitive administrative procedure, especially those articulated by the defendant.

Case law has linked the grounds for the sanctioning resolution with Article 24(1) of the Spanish Constitution, which proclaims the basic right to effective judicial protection and prohibits an insufficient defence. Therefore, not providing sufficient grounds for the decision or making effective legal control impossible is deemed to infringe this fundamental right. It should be noted that, in general terms, deficient reasoning in any other administrative decision does not breach Article 24(1) of the Spanish Constitution.

4. ORGANIZATION OF SANCTIONING POWERS

As indicated above, essential to the concept of the administrative sanction is the fact that the penalty is imposed by the administrative authorities; that is, by authorities that form part of the general government (Central, Regional, Local administrations, etc.).

Sanctioning powers belong to the ordinary administrative authorities, which exercise many other functions and powers. They are administrative authorities which do not specialize in imposing sanctions, which form part of the normal hierarchical structure of the Administration, and which have no legal status giving them greater independence or specialization.

Nonetheless, in Spain, as in many other States, certain so-called "independent administrative authorities"[20] are beginning to emerge in different sectors of administrative activity. The laws establishing these "independent administrative authorities" have given each of them the power to penalise violations occurring in their particular sector. Notwithstanding this, the administrative sanctions imposed by these "independent administrative authorities" are still uncommon. It cannot therefore be said that it is a constitutional prerequisite that sanctions be imposed by independent administrative authorities. The vast majority of administrative sanctions are imposed by the Central Government or regional Ministers, or by the Central Government representative or other Government subordinates in each province, and by Mayors, etc.[21]

---

20 Among others, the *Banco de España*, the *Comisión Nacional de la Competencia*, the *Comisión Nacional del Mercado de Valores*, the *Agencia de Protección de Datos*, etc.

21 The only specific provision to ensure the impartiality of the punitive administrative authorities is the distinction between the body imposing the sanction and the one which delivers the judgment. In practice, this is not a real guarantee because of several reasons, such as the existence of a hierarchy or dependence between these bodies. Nevertheless, in some sectors this is a real and effective guarantee.

5. INVESTIGATION/ INSPECTION

5.1. POWERS OF INVESTIGATION AND INSPECTION PRIOR TO THE INITIATION OF A PUNITIVE ADMINISTRATIVE PROCEDURE

In general, the laws which regulate the intervention of the Administration in a wide range of sectors, and which establish violations and administrative sanctions, tend to grant the Administration the powers of investigation and inspection so as to ensure compliance, and to detect any possible administrative breaches, should they arise. By and large, the powers given to the public Administrations are:

- The power to have access to all premises of interest for inspection purposes or to obtain evidence of any violations. If these premises are open to the public, no relevant legal problems arise. Greater difficulties arise when these premises are deemed to be "domestic homes", because the Spanish Constitution states that a private domicile cannot be entered or searched without the owner's consent or a court order. Furthermore, it should be noted that the Constitutional Court has established that this domicile protected by the Spanish Constitution refers to both natural persons and to legal persons. In conclusion, in all these cases, the Administration will have to obtain the consent of the interested party or to apply for a court order.
- The power to have access and to examine the documents of the inspected party and the power to request information thereon. The Constitutional Court has stated that these powers do not contravene the basic right to refrain from self-incrimination and from confessing guilt.
- The power to take samples and to carry out tests on these samples and to investigate the way in which certain services or activities are carried out.

The exercise of such powers is normally assigned to certain public bodies (inspectorates) specialising in these tasks. Liaison between the inspection bodies and the sanctioning authorities is extremely close. These actions are known as actions prior or preliminary to the punitive administrative procedure. In the performance of their activities the inspection bodies may detect irregularities that possibly constitute an administrative breach, and they will convey these facts to the sanctioning bodies. Alternatively, before instituting a punitive administrative procedure, the sanctioning bodies may ask the investigative authority to take the necessary steps to determine whether or not there are grounds to justify such a procedure, and to identify the alleged authors. The following are salient aspects of their legal regime:

- They do not form part of the punitive administrative procedure. They are therefore not taken into account when it comes to calculating the time which the Administration has for ruling on the case.
- They do not interrupt the statute of limitations as far as the breach is concerned.
- Persons subject to investigation enjoy none of the rights of defence which they have in the punitive administrative procedure.

The major legal debate surrounds the value of these preliminary actions with respect to the subsequent punitive administrative procedure. The LPA establishes that facts which are compiled by government officials (those in charge of investigation and inspection) and recorded in a public document shall carry the necessary weight and credibility. This provision has important consequences. It confers the necessary weight and credibility to acts which have been performed without the specific guarantees of the punitive administrative procedure. However, this weight and credibility

- Refers only to facts which have been directly observed by the official in question. It encompasses neither his legal opinions nor hearsay evidence.
- May mean that the said document, on its own and without repeating the inspection in the punitive administrative procedure, can destroy the presumption of innocence and justify the imposition of a sanction.
- Does not mean that this is evidence which the law values over all other evidence. It is simply another item to be added to the body of evidence that will be submitted in the punitive administrative procedure. However, in practice, the sanctioning bodies tend to give preference to this evidence, on the basis of the supposed neutrality and expertise of the official who carried out the inspection.

However, some laws go a step further and add that the information gathered will be deemed true and accurate. This means that these laws grant extra weight and credibility to this evidence. Although the case law fluctuates, we consider that the said presumption of truth would breach the presumption of innocence, as it would force the alleged offender to prove his/her innocence.

5.2. THE SANCTIONING ADMINISTRATIVE BODIES' POWERS OF INVESTIGATION AND INSPECTION

Now we will examine the powers possessed by the sanctioning administrative bodies to prove that the imputed infringement has in fact been committed. The Administration is obliged to carry out any activity which is considered necessary to reach an accurate final decision, irrespective of active or passive conduct by the accused in each procedure. The investigating official must therefore adduce evidence, however minor that may be:

- He will be able to opt for any type of evidence which is admissible under the law.[22]
- He/she can verify the relevant facts at any time during the procedure, even before its institution, as we have seen above.
- Facts declared to have been proven in a binding criminal judgement are binding on the Administration, and are consequently exempt from evidence in the punitive administrative procedure. This is not the case as regards facts that the criminal judge deems not to have been proved, although this does not rule out the possibility of their existence. In contrast, what is declared proven in a punitive administrative resolution does not bind the criminal courts[23], because the punitive administrative procedure offers fewer guarantees than the criminal process and admits evidence which is considered insufficient in the latter (inspectors' reports).

6. LEGAL PROTECTION

Administrative sanctions are imposed by means of an administrative act, against which one can resort to an "appeal", as in the case of any other administrative act. In this regard no special case is made for administrative sanctions.

6.1. JUDICIAL CONTROL OF CONTENTIOUS ADMINISTRATIVE JURISDICTION: A CONTENTIOUS ADMINISTRATIVE APPEAL AGAINST SANCTIONS

All administrative sanctions can be contested

This refers to the possibility of challenging *all administrative sanctions before* the courts, as is the case for any other administrative act. In Spain this task is assigned entirely to the magistrates' courts and the courts of contentious administrative jurisdiction. Consequently, *all administrative sanctions, without exception, can be challenged before the courts of contentious administrative jurisdiction.* Appeals

---

22 LPA enshrines the principle of free choice regarding evidence. But, what happens if a rule provides that some facts must be proved by using specific means of proof? For instance, noise or speed must be measured by homologated devices, or drunkenness must be determinated by a blood analysis, or the condition of food must be verified by a specific analysis. In those cases, it seems that the most appropriate solution to the principle of free choice concerning proof is to regard this means of proof provided for by the law as prevalent, but not exclusive. So, it would be possible for the administrative authorities to prove certain facts by using different means of proof, like testimony, field reports or visual inspections.

23 See Constitutional Court decision 2/2003 of 16 January.

against administrative acts lodged before the courts of contentious administrative jurisdiction[24] are termed "contentious administrative appeals" (*recursos contencioso-administrativos*).

As a result, those who have received an administrative sanction can contest it in the contentious administrative jurisdiction courts. These are true judicial bodies, entailing all the guarantees of neutrality and exclusive submission to the law. They specialize in reviewing the legality of the acts of public Administrations, and in applying Administrative Law. In Spain, the task of reviewing administrative sanctions has never been considered pertinent for the criminal courts. The criminal courts are not therefore competent to decide on administrative sanctions.

Extension of judicial control of administrative sanctions:
Contentious administrative appeals against administrative sanctions are the same as those lodged against any other administrative act: the process is no different, and the powers of the courts are no different from those used to control the legality of any non-sanctioning administrative act. There is *full judicial control* to verify whether or not the administrative sanction is in accordance with the law. It has to ensure:

- that the sanctioning administrative authority is competent to impose the sanction in question.
- that the punitive administrative procedure has been correctly observed, with particular attention to the rights of defence.
- the truth of the facts constituting the breach and the person responsible for that breach. The court can likewise adduce fresh evidence and re-evaluate the any other evidence.
- respect for the principles of legality, categorization, guilt, *non bis in idem*, etc.
- that the sanction imposed is within the necessary legal limits and that it respects the proportionality rule.

24 It is necessary to make some comments about the nature of Spanish contentious administrative jurisdiction, because of its differences from those with the same name in other States. Contrasted with the French model, the Spanish contentious administrative jurisdiction is an ordinary jurisdiction, composed of ordinary judges, exactly the same as civil and criminal judges. They all form part of the Judiciary. Having said this, however, in practice some specific judges specialize in Administrative law. But these judges that form part of the contentious administrative jurisdiction have the same status as the other judges: the same independence, the same process of selection, the same rights and duties... The same people who, during their professional careers, are civil or criminal judges, can become judges of the courts of contentious administrative jurisdiction. Civil, criminal and contentious administrative courts are subject to the same law (*Ley Orgánica del Poder Judicial*). However, the judicial proceedings that take place in each jurisdiction have their own principles and rules: the civil courts are regulated by the *Ley de Enjuiciamiento Civil*; the criminal courts by the *Ley de Enjuiciamiento Criminal*; and the courts for contentious administrative jurisdiction by the *Ley de la Jurisdicción Contencioso-administrativa (Ley 29/1998, 13 July)*.

- that the breach was committed within the statute of limitations.
- and any other aspect regarding strict compliance with the law.

If the contentious administrative court detects any illegality in the administrative sanction, it shall deliver a judgement to cancel the penalty. It may even award compensation to a person who has been given an unjust penalty if that penalty has resulted in damage. In some cases, the court may even modify the sanction imposed by the Administration[25], but it can only do so to diminish the sentence, not to increase it, even when it considers that the sanction imposed should have been greater (the prohibition of *reformatio in pejus*).

Judicial control of defects in the punitive administrative procedure

The contentious administrative court will only rescind the administrative sanction if infringements in the punitive administrative procedure resulted in a genuine limitation of the rights of defence, that is if they resulted in "defencelessness"[26].

Sometimes the courts will merely rescind penalties which are the result of procedural defects, while in other cases not only will the penalty be rescinded, but the Administration may also be ordered to repeat the punitive administrative procedure starting from the stage originating the process.

Judicial control in determining the category and the extent of the penalty

As described earlier, legal rules (laws and their by-laws) establish a penalty framework, but do not determine the specific sanction the Administration should impose for each violation. Generally, the penalty framework categorises infringements according to their severity (gross, severe and minor), indicating possible sanctions and their extent for each degree by category and establishing circumstances[27] to be taken into account by the Administration.

There is disagreement in the legal literature and in case law regarding how to classify the power held by the Administration to determine the exact penalty in each case. The majority opinion in case law maintains that this is a regulated power (the type and the exact amount of the penalty are of necessity derived

---

25 See *infra*, VI *Legal protection*, §1.D).

26 When the Spanish courts are faced with non-punitive administrative acts with procedural defects that result in "defencelessness", they do not revoke them if, afterwards, in another procedure, the citizen can resort to a complete defence. Sometimes the Spanish contentious administrative courts apply this solution to the administrative sanctions. But it seems that, little by little, another solution is increasingly preferred: the fundamental rights in Article 24 of the Constitution have to be respected in the punitive administrative procedure, so that, even if the citizen could have a complete defence in a later procedure, if his fundamental rights have been violated in the punitive administrative procedure, the sanction must be rescinded in any case. But, in this respect, there is still no determined answer.

27 See *supra*, II *General principles*, §3.

from that legal framework); another opinion, which we consider to be more accurate, maintains that it is a discretionary power (the Administration has some flexibility in determining the category and the exact amount of the penalty).

If discretion is admitted, judicial control would be limited to rectifying those cases where the penalty is clearly disproportionate. If discretion is not admitted, judicial control is absolute. In point of fact, the latter case is the one which currently prevails. The argument used by the courts is respect for the principle of proportionality. On this basis, they freely adjust the extent of the penalty imposed by the Administration. In this domain, administrative discretion often appears to have been overturned and replaced by judicial discretion.

Judicial control over the inaction of the sanctioning body

Greater problems are generated by judicial control over an administrative body that does not penalise forms of conduct which, according to the law, constitute an administrative infringement. Can a contentious administrative court impose the penalty which the Administration did not see fit to impose? Is it at least possible for a contentious administrative court to condemn the Administration? Could an individual who is prejudiced by the commission of an administrative breach actually achieve this? There are no clear answers to these questions. Only some laws relating to specific matters provide partial answers. This is a brief summary of the current situation in this area:

- There is a disparity of opinion in the legal literature as to whether the Administration is obliged to penalise the breaches it detects. There is an intermediate solution: the Administration does not have absolute freedom to refrain from penalising infringements in all cases, nor is it permanently obliged to punish them, depending on what is laid down in the regulating laws in each field. In default of specific rules, the Administration can be allowed a degree of discretion to decide which officials and means – limited and often insufficient – it will allocate to the administrative breaches it deems most vital to penalise. Of course, this discretionary power has its limits –arbitrariness or discrimination is not allowed – and it can be supervised by the courts.
- The contentious administrative courts recognise that there may be persons who have a right to require the Administration to penalise certain administrative breaches. Such persons can rightfully lodge a contentious administrative appeal against the Administration's refusal to sanction. Nevertheless, the courts seldom encounter an individual with a legitimate interest in seeing the Administration punishing another person.
- In no case whatsoever will the contentious administrative courts have the possibility to sanction a person directly, in place of the Administration: at most they can order the Administration to institute a punitive administrative procedure in order to verify whether or not a penalty should be imposed.

All things considered, this is unsatisfactory. In practice, if the Administration does not wish to punish a breach, it is extremely difficult, if not impossible, to compel it to take action.

The adoption of provisional measures by the courts

The Contentious Administrative Jurisdiction Act admits provisional measures with a wide scope. There is no special rule for administrative sanctions. Consequently, at the request of the interested party (who lodges an appeal against the penalty), the court, applying the general rules, will be able to order provisional measures. This usually results in suspending the execution of the penalty.

The Contentious Administrative Jurisdiction Act establishes that the provisional measure can only be ordered when the execution of the sanction could result in the appellant losing the legitimate purpose of the appeal. However, if this condition is fulfilled, the courts can still reject the provisional measure if its adoption prejudices the general interest or third parties.

With general rules like these, the case law is highly casuistic. With respect to fines, there is a tendency not to order suspension, whereas other types of penalties are generally more readily suspended.

In all cases, if the provisional measure gives rise to a certain detriment, the courts can order other measures to avoid or alleviate that detriment.

6.2. CHALLENGING A SANCTION BEFORE THE SAME PUBLIC ADMINISTRATION: ADMINISTRATIVE APPEALS AGAINST SANCTIONS

As well as appeals against the contentious administrative decision, Spanish law allows the possibility of impugning administrative acts before the Administration itself. Among these are the so-called "administrative appeals", by which an individual asks the Administration that performed an act to annul or amend it on the basis of its illegality. In this respect, administrative acts which impose sanctions are not a special case. Suffice it to say that it is sometimes necessary to interpose the administrative appeal before the contentious administrative appeal.

6.3. CONTROL BY THE CONSTITUTIONAL COURT: AN APPEAL FOR LEGAL PROTECTION AGAINST SANCTIONS AND APPEALS ON THE GROUND OF UNCONSTITUTIONALITY

As administrative sanctions may have been imposed in contravention of the fundamental rights laid down in Articles 24 and 25 of the Spanish Constitution, the so-called "appeal for legal protection" before the Constitutional Court may be possible if the sanctions have not been rescinded by the contentious administrative courts.

Furthermore, an appeal is possible on the ground that the Laws which regulate administrative infringements and sanctions are unconstitutional, especially with respect to Articles 24 and 25 of the Spanish Constitution.

6.4. ENFORCEMENT OF SANCTIONS

Here we refer to the moment when sanctions take effect. That is the moment when they become legally binding for the sanctioned party. In accordance with the LPA, there are two possibilities:

- If the sanctioned person does not lodge an administrative appeal in due time, the sanction can be executed once this period runs out.
- If the sanctioned person lodges an administrative appeal against the decision, it will only become enforceable after the competent administrative body has delivered its decision judgement on the appeal and confirmed the sanction.

In the area of judicial control, the lodging of an appeal against an administrative sanction before the contentious administrative courts, does not, in principle, prevent its enforcement. Nonetheless, case law has taken a progressive step by stating that if the sanctioned person has lodged an appeal before the courts, and in the appeal has requested, as a provisional measure, the suspension of the sanction, the Administration will not be able to demand its enforcement until the court rules on this provisional measure. To do so would contravene the fundamental right to effective judicial protection (if the Administration enforces the sanction, this will be useless if the court later decides to suspend the sanction as a provisional measure) as well as the presumption of innocence. In all cases, the enforcement of the sanction does not require the court to have passed the sentence that concludes the judicial process, but only requires the court to have ruled on the adoption of the requested provisional measure.

When the sanctioned party fails to comply with the sanction voluntarily, the Administration has the option of enforcing compliance by its own means. For example, if the sanctioned party does not pay a fine, the Administration can seize a bank account in order to enforce the sanction. To do so, the Administration need not go to court. However, for the Administration to enforce the sanction by its own means, it will have to initiate a non-sanctioning administrative procedure whereby the sanctioned party will be granted another opportunity to pay the penalty voluntarily.

7. NATIONAL AND EUROPEAN/INTERNATIONAL MUTUAL ASSISTANCE

7.1. MUTUAL ASSISTANCE BETWEEN THE DIFFERENT ORGANS AND PUBLIC ADMINISTRATIONS IN SPAIN

If the sanctioned party fails to pay the penalty voluntarily, the Administration is entitled to secure compliance using its own means. To do so it does not need to go to court, although in order to enforce the sanction the sanctioning administrative body generally needs the cooperation of another administrative body, either belonging to its own sector or to a different Public Administration.

Co-operation between bodies of the same Administration occurs due to the specialisation of some agencies in certain functions. For our purposes, this refers particularly to the use of force against people or things, a power which is conferred on the Police Force; and to the so-called "compulsory seizure" of the sanctioned party's property, a task which is assigned to the pertinent agencies of the Exchequer or the Public Treasury. This co-operation is governed by the same rules generally regulating relations between bodies within a single Administration.

Co-operation between two different public Administrations occurs:

- When such co-operation is a necessary consequence of the territorial distribution of public authority on Spanish territory.[28]

[28] In this respect, one should realize that in Spain there exist three levels of public Administration: the State Administration, the regional Administrations (17 Autonomous Communities and the Autonomous Cities of Ceuta and Melilla) and the local Administrations (more than 8,000 villages and towns). Each one can exercise, exclusively within their territory, the powers with which they have been assigned, the power to sanction being among them. Therefore an Autonomous Community (A) can sanction a firm whose factory is located in another Autonomous Community (B) on the ground of selling products that are harmful to

- When, despite having territorial competence to enforce the penalty, the sanctioning administrative body requests co-operation from another administrative body due to the lack of technical or material resources to perform this task. This is more common at the local level, as local authorities often request the co-operation of other Administrations for these purposes.

The Spanish Constitution does not explicitly mention any duty of co-operation between the different territorial public Administrations in the accomplishment of their objectives. However, the Constitutional Court has declared on numerous occasions that this duty of co-operation is implicit in the Spanish Constitution, and that it is of necessity a result of the territorial system of organisation laid down therein.

The LPA considers this duty of co-operation between all Public Administrations as a general obligation, and it therefore applies to the enforcement of sanctions in both the cases mentioned above. The LPA specifically develops this obligation in some of its more routine cases. Thus, in relation to the first point, it provides that the public Administrations "shall co-operate and give mutual assistance in the enforcement of their acts which have to be performed outside their respective territorial areas of competence". This is a true legal obligation which is not subject to the discretion of the Administration, despite the scarcity of legal proceedings in response to non-compliance by an administrative body. The obligation is such that the LPA has established that the requested co-operation can only be denied when certain specific situations concur.[29] The most usual legal instrument used in this co-operation is an agreement between public Administrations.

7.2. ASSISTANCE BETWEEN THE SPANISH AUTHORITIES AND OTHER MEMBER STATES OF THE EUROPEAN UNION OR OTHER STATES

Neither the LPA nor any other legislation of a general nature regulates the co-operation that the Spanish authorities must give to other States for the enforcement of the administrative sanctions that the latter may impose.

---

one's health. However, if the sanction consists of closing the factory, the Autonomous Community (A) is not allowed to send its staff to the territory of Autonomous Community (B) to enforce the closure.

29 Article 4.3 LPA: "La asistencia y cooperación requerida sólo podrá negarse cuando el ente del que se solicita no esté facultado para prestarla, no disponga de medios suficientes para ello o cuando, de hacerlo, causara un perjuicio grave a los intereses cuya tutela tiene encomendada o al cumplimiento de sus propias funciones".

Within the European Union there is general adherence to the provision in Article 4(3) of the Treaty on European Union, and to certain Regulations, Directives or Decisions which develop this principle of co-operation. In any case, this is part of Community law, not Spanish law.

With respect to the international domain, Spain abides by the International Treaties and Agreements to which it is a party.

In all cases, one consequence originates from the constitutional regime of the distribution of competences between the Central government, Regional (Autonomous) governments and Local Administrations, and the exclusive competence of the Central government in the field of international relations: no matter which Spanish Administration has imposed the sanction and requires international assistance, or whether international assistance is requested from the Spanish Administration, any mutual assistance will be channelled through the Central Administration.

8. ACTUAL IMPORTANCE IN PRACTICE

There are virtually no Laws regulating an Administration's intervention in specific sectors or areas which do not contain a corresponding administrative sanctioning regime.[30] Indeed, each sector generally has one or several regulatory Laws, either state or regional, containing numerous administrative breaches and sanctions. In addition, there are sanctions imposed by Professional Bodies and those provided by local Administrations.

---

30 We can point to the following:
Civil servants. Protection of public property: water, coasts, ports, roads, etc. Protection of public services or general interest services: transports postal services, electricity, telecommunications, gas, etc. Antitrust laws. Protection of forests, natural reservations and flora. Protection of wild fauna and domestic animals. Taxes. Contraband. Road traffic. Safety and health at work. Social security. Citizens' security. Private surveillance companies. Foreign affairs. Disturbing, unhealthy, fatal and dangerous activities. Public events and recreative activities. Bullfighting. Public intervention (credit entities: banks, insurances, etc.) Public intervention (commercial SMEs) Public intervention (industry) Public intervention (the stock market) Public intervention (agriculture and fisheries) Public intervention (tourism) Public intervention (real estate) Town planning. Protection of the atmospheric environment. Protection of historical heritage. Protection and promotion of the film industry. Public intervention (medicine) Public intervention (publicity) Control of jewelry and precious metals. Prevention of violence in sport. Public intervention (biotechnology) Protection against noise pollution. Protection of personal information. Aids and grants. Money laundering. Auditing. Health care. Defence of the consumer. e-signature regulation. Public intervention (wine and alcohol) Designations of origin. Public intervention (ordinary and toxic waste) Gambling.

The scale is wide-ranging and voluminous. So much so that the same forms of conduct are very often considered to be breaches under several different laws, and a number of administrative authorities have the power to sanction them.

Almost all administrative bodies of any importance have extensive sanctioning powers. Processing sanctioning procedures and imposing administrative sanctions takes up a large part of the public Administration's activity. These facts alone reveal the wide array of sanctioning powers available to the Spanish Administration. This is seen as an indispensable instrument for the Administration to safeguard and guarantee the objectives of public interest vested in it.

Furthermore, in many areas, the possible sanctions are extremely severe. Suffice it to say, for example, that the General Law on Telecommunications, for some very serious infringements, provides for a pecuniary sanction of up to 20 million euro. Furthermore, there are many other very severe sanctions, such as those consisting of the closure of premises for long periods or even permanently, or sanctions consisting of a prohibition on performing certain activities for long periods or indefinitely (for instance, a prohibition on acting as a credit company, on managing credit companies, or on carrying out mail-order activities etc.)

This has not given rise to any critical reaction. The constitutionality and convenience of the Administration's sanctioning power are not called into question, provided fundamental guarantees are respected. Not even academics specialising in Criminal Law oppose this extension of the Administration's punitive power, although it occurs to the detriment of the criminal courts' punitive power. Rather, they encourage this tendency by adhering to the principle of the "minimal intervention" of Criminal Law.

Although there is insufficient data to be able to make a categorical assertion, there may be no other State in the European Union where the sanctioning powers of the Administration are more far-reaching than in Spain.

XIII. COUNTRY ANALYSIS – SWEDEN

Patricia Blanc-Gonnet Jonason

1. DEFINITION AND TYPOLOGY OF SANCTIONS

1.1. DEFINITION OF SANCTIONS

Among the definitions of sanctions that are been found in Swedish doctrine, the definition proposed by Zila[1] has been chosen for the purpose of this report. According to Zila, sanctions are indirect constraints. An indirect constraint is constituted by a threat laid down in the law that a given inconvenience will be imposed upon a subject if this subject does not comply with the obligations he has according to the law. For this subject the inconvenience constitutes a new, secondary obligation (an obligation other than the one which the subject has not complied with), to do something, to omit or cease doing something or to endure some measure. In practice it means that this person (the subject) will have to pay damages or an amount of money which does not represent damages, will have to endure interference in his right to property or possession, to endure a limitation of his personal freedom of movement, to relinquish his right to practice an activity etc. If the subject does not submit to this inconvenience voluntarily, then the obligation can be forced by direct measures of constraint (by police measures, for instance).

This definition covers penal, civil and administrative sanctions.

1.2. TYPOLOGY OF SANCTIONS

After a brief survey of the penal and civil sanctions in the Swedish legal system the report will be devoted to a more in-depth description of the different administrative sanctions.

---

1 Zila is inspired by Ekelöf's definition, in *Straffet, skadeståndet och vitet*, Uppsala universitet. Uppsala 1942. p. 10, ibid. For an other example, see for instance the definition proposed by Ivar Agge, which includes measures like restitution, enforcement action and protection measures according to social law, Valda kapitel ur Den allmänna rättsläran. Efter föreläsningar av prof. Ivar Agge, Stokholms Högskolas juridiska Förening Förlag. Stockholm 1958, quoted by J. Zila in *I stället för straff – Sanktionsavgifter som kriminalpolitiskt medel mot bagatellbrottslighet*, Juristförlaget, 1992, pp. 88–89.

1.2.1. *Penal sanctions*

The Swedish Penal Code (*Brottsbalken* (1962:700), BrB) distinguishes between criminal sanctions and the "special legal effects of crime" (*särskild rättsverkan av brott*).

The criminal sanctions available in the Swedish Penal Code are the imposition of a fine, imprisonment, a conditional sentence, probation and committal for special care (care within the social welfare services, special care for addicts and psychiatric care). It should be noted that according to the Swedish legal terminology, only the imposition of a fine (böter) and imprisonment are designated as criminal punishments.

The measures called "special legal effects of crime" are especially the forfeiture and destruction of infringing goods as well as materials and implements used in carrying out the infringement and a special kind of fine which applies to legal persons (*företagsbot*). These sanctions are characterized by the fact that they are not independent sanctions, but instead complement criminal sanctions. Some of these sanctions are not criminal sanctions *stricto sensu* as they are also used as administrative sanctions. Among those "special legal effects of crime" the Penal Code explicitly designates the forfeiture of property and corporate fines (Chapter 36), but others sanctions like the revocation of a licence, the loss of authorization and expulsion of aliens are also included among those sanctions.

One of those special legal effects of crime, namely corporate fines (*företagsbot*), will now be described in more detail. This kind of measure may be interesting for this report – despite its criminal character – due to the problem which can emerge with the cumulative imposition of administrative sanctions and corporate fines.[2]

Although Swedish law does not recognise corporate criminal liability as such, a kind of criminal responsibility for legal persons and other entrepreneurs is providing through the institution of corporate fines, which is regulated in Chapter 36 of the Swedish Penal Code.

A corporate fine can be imposed when the entrepreneur has not done what could reasonably be required to prevent the crime, or the crime has been committed by a person who has a leading position on the grounds of his hability to represent the entrepreneur or because he is entitled to take decisions on behalf

2 This question has, moreover, been discussed in the frame of the preparatory works which preceded the amendment of Chapter 36 of the Penal Code towards an extension of the field of application of corporate fines. The proposal to suppress the reference to crimes committed in the exercise of business activities which had *to have "entailed gross disregard for the special obligations associated with the business activities or to be otherwise of a serious kind"* has been adopted, which enlarges the number of infringements where it may be possible to sanction with the help of a corporate fine and with the assistance of administrative, See Ds 2001:69, SOU 2002:50, p. 223 and Prop. 2005/06:59.

of the entrepreneur; he otherwise has a special responsibility of supervision or control of the business. The corporate fine shall amount to at least 5,000 Swedish kronor (€450) and, at most 10,000,000 Swedish kronor (€901,000).

Swedish penal sanctions will be illustrated by an example concerning an issue which is relevant to administrative sanctions, i.e. the environmental issue. Some environmental offences are subject to penalties[3] under the Swedish Environmental Code (Chapter 29), as for instance the *unlawful environmental activities*, committed when someone intentionally or with negligence commences or performs an activity without having obtained the necessary permit, in violation of the conditions for a permit. The act consisting of the commencement of an activity for which a permit must be obtained and such a permit has not been granted can also lead to the imposition of environmental sanction charges (miljösanktionsavgifter) by the supervisory authority. Nevertheless, the possibility to sanction twice for the same violation, both with penal sanctions and with administrative sanctions, has been excluded since 2006.[4]

1.2.2. Civil law sanctions

The most important civil law sanction is the sanction consisting of damages, a sum of money claimed by a plaintiff from a defendant as compensation for the harm which has occurred. An obligation to pay a damage can occur either within a contractual relationship (due to a breach of contract) or outside therof.[5] Besides, the general rules concerning damages laid down in the Tort Liability Act (1972:207), there are also special rules. For example the Environmental Code states that if an activity disturbs the environment (water pollution, air pollution, noise, vibration etc.) resulting in physical injury, material damage or pecuniary loss, the operator is under a duty to pay compensation.

Compensation in the form of damages is normally based on strict liability.

Civil law sanctions have, first and foremost, a reparative function and it is possible to combine a civil law sanction with another kind of sanction.

1.2.3. Administrative sanctions

There is no legal definition of an administrative sanction in the Swedish legal system; furthermore, such sanctions are not homogenous and the field lacks a common regulation. However, it is possible to provide a definition on the basis of certain criteria. Administrative sanctions can be defined as sanctions for

3 Penalties will normally range from fines up to two years imprisonment.

4 Prop. 2005/06: 182.

5 There are other types of civil law sanctions, for example interest on overdue payments.

infringements of *particular administrative regulations.* Furthermore, administrative sanctions are, in principle, imposed on a basis of *strict liability.* Accordingly, administrative sanctions are to be determined solely on objective grounds and will be imposed even when the sanctioned violation has not occurred intentionally or with negligence. Another criterion by which to define administrative sanctions relates to *the kind of instance* which is competent to impose such a sanction. Public authorities are in general competent to impose administrative sanctions while the courts are restricted to criminal sanctions.

The Swedish legal system recognises a large variety of administrative sanctions which are regulated in different ways. It is worth noting that the topic of administrative sanctions has not been subjected to general and in-depth studies in Sweden (as is the case in Spain or in France, for instance). There are a few monographs on the subject, but they tend to focus on a specific aspect, for example a specific kind of administrative sanction such as administrative fees.[6] Perhaps because of this lack of interest concerning the question of administrative sanctions, there is no commonly accepted method for classifying administrative sanctions in the Swedish legal literature.

One way in which to classify administrative sanctions is to divide them into four main groups:

- sanctions which constitute the negative side of the authorities' activities concerning authorization, i.e. the revocation of licences and the withdrawal of authorisation;
- public law fines;
- administrative fees;
- disciplinary sanctions.

A brief overview of each category of sanctions will be provided. They will be illustrated by concrete examples.

1.2.3.1. Revocation of licences and withdrawal of authorization

A large number of activities require the person concerned (a natural or legal person) to obtain specific authorization, a permit or a licence before embarking on the activities in question. For example, a serving licence is required in order to serve alcohol in a restaurant or bar, and a private individual or a company needs to obtain a building permit before construction can begin. Public

6 See W. Warnling-Nerep, *Sanktionsavgifter – särskilt vid olovligt byggande*, Juristförlaget, 1987. See also J. Zila, *I stället för straff- Sanktionsavgifter som kriminalpolitiskt medel mot bagatellbrottslighet*, Juristförlaget, 1992.

authorization is also required by Swedish law for those who wish to operate certain types of businesses, such as credit agencies and lotteries.

The necessary licence, authorization or permit is granted if the applicant complies with certain conditions determined by law. If the licensee etc. cannot continuously fulfil the requirements attached to the licence or fails to act as required by the conditions of the licence, then that licence may be revoked by the competent authority.

For example, it follows from the Lotteries Act that the authority which has granted the permit that is required to organize a lottery is empowered to revoke that permit (1994:1000) if the holder fails to comply with the provisions of the Lotteries Act or the directions, conditions or regulations issued pursuant to this Act (see Section 51 of the Lotteries Act).

In a similar manner the Alcohol Act (2010:1622) which requires a permit in order to serve spirits, wine or strong beer entities public authorities (municipal authorities) to revoke the serving licence. Such a permit may only be issued to persons who comply with certain conditions laid down in the Alcohol Act. The applicant has to be suitable to undertake this activity with respect to his personal and economic circumstances as well as other criteria (see the Alcohol Act (2010:1622), Chapter 8, Section 12). In addition to these preconditions relating to the applicant him/herself, the Alcohol Act lays down certain preconditions pertaining to the premises where the alcohol will be served.

A revocation of the serving licence may occur in the situations enumerated in Chapter 9, Section 18. For instance the licence may be revoked if the licensee fails to comply with the provisions of the Alcohol Act or if the licensee does not take measures against criminal activities to take place on the premises.

1.2.3.2. Administrative fees

Another kind of administrative sanction that has become commonly used, especially since the 1970s,[7] are administrative fees (*straffavgifter, sanktionsavgifter*). The legislator introduced this kind of sanction in order to decriminalize "what was regarded as mass offences with a low degree of blameworthiness"[8] and therefore to reduce the overload of the criminal courts. The reform was aimed at creating greater effectiveness in the application of the law insofar as in most cases it is the administrative authorities themselves and

7 In fact these sanctions appeared earlier. There is an example of this kind of sanction in the early 1910s. But it was only in the 1970s that such sanctions became extensively used and that the legal literature became interested therein. J. Zila, *I stället för straff- Sanktionsavgifter som kriminalpolitiskt medel mot bagatellbrottslighet*, Juristförlaget, 1992, p. 54.

8 M. Arnholm, M. Andersen, *The system of administrative and penal sanctions in Sweden*, Iutus, 1997, p. 19.

not the courts which impose these kinds of sanctions. The fees paid go to the Crown. Administrative fees tend to be repressive. In this way they are comparable to criminal fines.

Apart from the desire to diminish the workload of the courts, another reason put forward to justify the introduction of administrative fees was the possibility to impose sanctions on corporate bodies, i.e., to introduce corporate liability.[9]

Examples of legislation empowering the authorities to impose administrative fees are the Environmental Code (1998:808), the Parking Offences Act (1976:206), the Planning and Building Act (2010:900) and the Tax Procedure Act (2011:1244).

There is a large variety of administrative fees. The administrative fee is in fact a generic term to encompass different sanctions which have different and varying functions within the system of sanctions.[10]

Administrative fees can be classified in various ways.[11] The classification used in this report is the one which divides sanctions into two categories, depending on the relationship between the imposition of an administrative fee and the imposition of a criminal sanction.[12]

The first category contains administrative fees which are imposed as the sole sanction following an administrative offence.

The second category encompasses administrative fees which can be imposed cumulatively with a criminal sanction following a criminal act.

The first category of administrative fees can be illustrated by parking fees which are imposed due to a parking offence having been committed and the fees imposed due to transgressions of certain rules contained in the Planning and Building Act (2010:900).

Parking fines have to be paid by the owner of the vehicle which has been parked in such a way that it constitutes an infringement of the legislation concerning parking offences (i.e. the Parking Offences Act (1976:206) (*lag om felparkeringsavgift*) and the Parking Offences Ordinance (1976:1128). The general principle applied is strict liability as far as the owner of the vehicle is concerned,

---

9 Id. p. 19.

10 J. Zila, *I stället för straff- Sanktionsavgifter som kriminalpolitiskt medel mot bagatellbrottslighet*, Juristförlaget, 1992, p. 86.

11 Different kinds of fees can for instance be distinguished with reference to a variety of factors, e.g. the legislator's intention when introducing the fee or the way in which the legal rules regulate how a fee is to be determined, see M. Arnholm, M. Andersen, *The system of administrative and penal sanctions in Sweden*, Iutus, 1997, p. 17.

12 This classification constitutes the principal classification according to J. Zila, *I stället för straff- Sanktionsavgifter som kriminalpolitiskt medel mot bagatellbrottslighet Juristförlaget*, 1992, p. 100. The author mentions other classifications which can be combined with this principal classification.

regardless of who actually committed the offence. This kind of administrative sanction may not be prescribed where the offence is punishable according to criminal law (see the Parking Offences Act, Section 1). The combination of administrative fees and criminal sanctions is thereby forbidden. Parking fines are imposed either by a police officer or by a traffic warden. The municipal authorities decide on the amount of the fine within a scale fixed by the government.

Fines for breach of the planning and building legislation

Another example of fees which are imposed as the sole sanction following an administrative offence is the fine inflicted by a public authority to a person who has acted in breach of the planning and building legislation. It is for instance the case when a person, without the necessary permit, has carried out building or demolition work (Chap. 11 Section 52 of the Planning and Building Act).

Among the *second category* of fees, which comprises administrative fees in situations where those fees can be imposed cumulatively with a criminal sanction following a criminal act, the tax surcharge and environmental sanction charges can be mentioned.

Tax surcharges

Tax surcharges (*skattetillägg*) can either be imposed as the sole sanction for a minor tax offence or be combined with a criminal sanction which has been imposed because of a tax crime as laid down in the Tax Procedure Act (2011:1244).[13]

A tax surcharge is imposed on a taxpayer in three situations: if he or she has made an incorrect statement in a tax return or on the basis of a discretionary assessment, from the tax authority or when the tax payer has not complied with his duties concuring tax deductability.

This kind of fee was introduced into Swedish legislation in 1971 in order to create a more effective and fairer system of penalties than the old one, which was based entirely on criminal penalties. Tax surcharges are imposed by the local tax authority.

Environmental sanction charges

According to the Environmental Code (1998:808), Chapter 30, section 1, a special fee – the environmental sanction charge (*miljösanktionsavgifter*) – may be imposed if a legal or natural person has failed to comply with certain regulations issued pursuant to the Environmental Code. An example is where an activity, for which a permit must be obtained, is commenced without having

13 More about the combination between tax surcharges and criminal sanctions under *Topics currently discussed in Sweden.*

acquired such a permit or where an operation has not been reported to the authorities in accordance with the pertinent regulations.

The environmental sanction charges amount to between SEK 1,000 and 1,000,000 and are payable by operators pursuant to a decision by the supervisory authority.

The main objective of this administrative sanction is to strengthen the sanction system in the environmental field and to complement ordinary criminal sanctions.

The charge relies on strict liability; any form of criminal intent or negligence on the part of the business operator is therefore irrelevant. Furthermore, it is of no relevance whether the infringement has damaged the environment or human health or benefited the operator in any way. However, according to the Environmental Code, chap. 30, section 2, the charge does not need to be imposed where this is unreasonable, for instance when a criminal sanction has been inflicted for the same infringement.

A separate Ordinance (2012:259) specifies the infringements for which supervisory authorities can impose environmental penalty charges, as well as the respective amounts to be paid for various infringements.

1.2.3.3. Public law fines

The public authorities are often empowered to impose public law fines (vite) to compel an addressee to act in a certain way. These fines are a sum of money whose amount is fixed beforehand by a court or public authority and which is payable by someone who fails to fulfil, within a certain time-limit, a legal obligation as established by the court or public authority concerned. Fines that are collected go to the Crown.

This kind of administrative sanction may be illustrated by legislation concerning the working environment. In order to secure compliance with the Working Environment Act (1977:1160) – for example, in order to force an employer to fulfil the obligation to install safety equipment to avoid accidents – the competent public authority may issue the necessary injunctions and it may also impose a specified fine if the injunction is not complied with (Working Environment Act, Chapter 7, Section 7).

Public law fines are regulated by the Public Law Fine Act (1985:206). The rules contained in this Act are applicable to the public law fines that authorities are competent to impose under other statutes.

The Public Law Fine Act deals mainly with individual fines. They are fines which are imposed in a specific case in order to force a natural or legal person to act in a specified and prescribed way.[14]

---

[14] Besides individual fines there are also public law fines of a general nature. Those have significant similarities with criminal fines, are very rare in Swedish law.

There are two kinds of individual fines: procedural fines and substantive fines. Procedural fines may be used by the authority during the proceedings, for example in order to force a individual to deliver certain documents needed for the proceedings. Substantive fines, which are more interesting within the framework of this report, are fines which the decision-making authority may impose to compel an individual to obey a final decision, for example the decision to demolish a building which has been constructed without a permit.

The decision-making authority will set the amount of the fine in the order to pay. It can be a fixed sum which has to be paid if the individual has not complied with the injunction within the prescribed time-limit. It can also be a staggered sum which has to be progressively paid or on each occasion that the individual disobeys the authority.

There is no upper limit concerning the amount that can be fixed for a fine. The authority decides on an amount of money that can be expected to induce the addressee to obey the injunction, considering inter alia his economic situation.

The public authorities may only make use of a public fine if they are authorized to do so under the law. Such authorization is laid down in many statutes, for example concerning building legislation or health.

It is generally the county administrative court which *imposes* the fine subject to a demand from the authority which has issued the injunction to act (or to cease acting) in a certain way.

Like the underlying threat included in criminal fines, the threat included in public law fines works as a means of pressure. In fact, they oblige the individual to act in a certain way if he wants to escape the sanction. However, there are many differences between individual public law fines and criminal fines. Firstly, public law fines are determined beforehand (the authority establishes the amount of the public law fine which has to be paid if the addressee does not comply with the injunction), while criminal fines are determined *a posteriori*, after the offence has been committed, by the judge within the scale prescribed by the Penal Code.

Secondly, public law fines have an individual character. The decision-making authority itself decides if it wants to make use of such a sanction in relation to the individual. Criminal fines, on the other hand, have a general character insofar as each person who has committed a certain infringement risks having to pay a criminal fine (the same applies for administrative fees). A third difference concerns the addressees. Public law fines, as well as administrative fees, can be imposed both on individuals and on corporate bodies, while criminal fines only can be imposed on individuals.

The principal rule is the non-cumulative imposition of a criminal fine and a public law fine. A large number of administrative regulations explicitly lay down this principle, for example the Working Environment Act (1977:1160), Chapter 8, Section 1.

1.2.3.4. Disciplinary sanctions according to public law

The last category of administrative sanctions is disciplinary sanctions. According to the Public Employment Act (1994:260) a disciplinary sanction may be imposed on public servants (Section 14[15]). The liability of the employees of a public authority presupposes that they have intentionally, or by carelessness, neglected their employment duties. The disciplinary sanctions are in the form of a warning and a pay deduction (at most thirty days and up to a maximum amount of 25 per cent of the daily pay.)

Several disciplinary sanctions may not be imposed on an employee simultaneously; furthermore, the Public Employment Act contains rules preventing disciplinary sanctions from being imposed cumulatively with a criminal sanction.[16]

2. THE SWEDISH LEGAL FRAMEWORK REGARDING THE IMPOSITION OF ADMINISTRATIVE SANCTIONS

2.1. THE LEGISLATIVE POWER

According to the provisions of Chapter 8 of the Swedish Constitution (the Instrument of Government, *Regeringsformen*, hereinafter referred to as the RF[17]), chapter which regulates the legislative power, the *Riksdag* is empowered to enact or amend fundamental laws (like the Instrument of Government or the Freedom of the Press Act) and ordinary laws. Besides this elected body, it is only the Government which has a legislative power deriving directly from the Instrument of Government (Chapter 8, Section 1). The Government has a kind of residual competence, e.g., it has the power to enact regulations in all matters that the Instrument of Government has not pointed out in Chapter 8, Section 2 (or in

---

15 The liability of the employees of municipalities and county council is regulated by collective agreement.

16 An employee who has been subject to a disciplinary sanction may appeal against the decision in accordance with the Labour Disputes Act (1974:371).

17 The instrument of government has been subject to a reform entered in force in January 2011. For a comment of the changes in Swedish, see T. Bull, F. Sterzel, *Regerinformen – en kommentar*, SNS förlag, 2010 as well as the preparatory works SOU 2008:125 and Prop. 2009/10: 80 En reformerad grundlag (a reformed Instrument of Government).

other provisions laid down in the Instrument of Government or in other constitutional Act) as being included in the Riksdags own legislative power. Furthermore, the Government has the competence to enact rules for the implementation of the law. There is also, in some matters, a possibility for the *Riksdag* to delegate the legislative power to the government. A further delegation to central authorities and local authorities is also possible.

The answer to the question concerning which body has legislative power depends on the issues concerned (see *inter alia* RF Chapter 8, Section 2 and Chapter 8, Section 3).[18]

Matters like constitutional law, private law and penal law are within the competence of Parliament.

Concerning administrative law, a distinction has to be made between rules which are favourable to individuals or imply voluntary action on their behalf or are neutral as far as they are concerned on the one hand, and rules which impose a burden on individuals, on the other. The rules included in the first category belong to the Government's own legislative power. The rules in the latter category, for example the rules which empower an administrative authority *to impose a sanction*, belong to the rules that are included in the "field of the law", but not in the compulsory area of the law. It means that either Parliament itself takes the decision to empower public authorities to impose a sanction or it can delegate this power to the Government. There is also a possibility to further delegate the decision-making power to the central authorities or the local authorities For instance, the *Riksdag* has, through the Working Environment Act, proceeded to delegate the power to decide on the creation of sanction charges. According to Chapter 8, Section 5 of the Working Environment Act "The Government, or by the authority of the Government, the Working Environment Authority may prescribe the payment of a special charge" for the infringement of certain kinds of provisions.

2.2. PRINCIPLES GOVERNING THE DECISION-MAKING POWER OF PUBLIC AUTHORITIES

Some principles set limits on the competence of public authorities in relation to individuals and they therefore define the limits of these authorities when encroaching on individual freedoms, especially when these authorities impose sanctions.

The principles of legality, freedom from interference, objectivity as well as the principle of equality are regulated in the Instrument of Government. The

---

18 However, according to Swedish Constitutional law, the *Riksdag* always has the possibility to regulate an issue included in the Government's own legislative power, Chapter 8, Section 8.

principle of proportionality, which is not stated as such in the Instrument of Government, has emerged from case law due to the influence of European law.

2.2.1. The principle of legality

Chapter 1, Section 1 of the RF states that "all public power shall be exercised under the law". According to this provision, all public bodies, including agencies and municipal bodies, are bound by statutory law when carrying out their activities.

The term "law" as used by RF section 1:1 is to be interpreted extensively. It not only includes legislative statutes enacted by the *Riksdag* (Parliament), but also ordinances enacted by the Government or regulations enacted by the central authorities or local authorities.

2.2.2. Freedom from interference (the principle of the independence of public authorities)

A central concept in the Swedish administration is freedom from interference, which is laid down in RF Chapter 12, Section 2. According to this section, "Neither a public authority nor the Riksdag nor the decision-making body of a local authority may determine how an administrative authority shall decide in a particular case relating to the exercise of authority *vis-à-vis* a private subject or a local authority, or concerning the application of the law". It means that no authority, not even the Government or Parliament, may interfere in the decision-making process of a public authority. This independence is matched by individual responsibility for actions and decisions.[19] In practice, this provision forbids the Government or an agency from obliging another authority to take a decision concerning the imposition of an administrative sanction.

2.2.3. The principles of objectivity and equality

According to RF Chapter 1, section 9: "Courts of law, administrative authorities and others performing public administrative tasks shall have regard in their work to the equality of all persons before the law and shall observe objectivity and impartiality". Public authorities, while taking decisions, may not be influenced by interests other than those which have a direct bearing on the case at hand. Therefore, they may not base their decision on circumstances other than those which are laid down in the applicable statute. Some legal provisions guarantee the principle of objectivity, such as

19 L. Marcusson, *Condition of administrative procedure law in Comparative analysis of administrative law, European public law series, Bibliothèque de droit public européen*, vol. XXVI, Bruylant, 2002, p. 387.

the rules on bias, the rules prohibiting civil servants from engaging in certain forms of incidental employment or criminal provisions concerning misuse of office and bribery.

The principle of objectivity is closely connected to the principle of equality of all persons before the law in so far as unjustified special treatment for certain persons simultaneously implies that the principle of objectivity is not respected.[20]

2.2.4. The principle of proportionality

The principle of proportionality relating to unfavourable measures decided upon by the administration is based on case law.[21] It is a product of the influence of European law, both EC law and the COE law on Human Rights. An illustration of the reference to this principle by the Swedish courts is found in a case of judicial review of the Supreme Administrative Court[22] where the issue concerned an appeal against the decision of the Environmental Work Authority to impose public law fines, decision which had been confirmed by the government.[23] After hearing the case, the Supreme Administrative Court concluded that "the government has not exceeded the margin of appreciation given by the legislation" and stated that "the decision is not incompatible with the principle of proportionality".[24]

2.3. THE ADMINISTRATIVE PROCEDURE ACT AND THE ADMINISTRATIVE COURT PROCEDURE ACT

Two central pieces of legislation regulate the work of the administrative authorities and are therefore of great relevance for the issue of administrative sanctions. The Administrative Procedure Act (1986:223), *förvaltningslagen*, constitutes the general legal basis for the public administration's activities, and the Administrative Court Procedure Act (1971:291), *förvaltningsprocesslagen*, states the proceedings of the administrative courts.

These two Acts contain a large number of similar rules although the ones contained in the Administrative Court Procedure Act are somewhat stricter than those which are applied by the decision-making authorities. The difference is explained by the fact that the day-to-day work of the administration does not require such stringent procedural rules as the judicial procedure.

20 H. Strömberg, B. Lundell, *Allmän förvaltningsrätt*, Liber ekonomi, 2012, p. 671.

21 See below under "current issues", the proposal to state the principle of proportionality in the future reformed Administrative Procedure Act.

22 See the definition below.

23 In its role of hearing appeals from the Environmental Work Authority's decisions.

24 RÅ 2002 not 65.

2.3.1. General remarks concerning the Administrative Procedure Act

The Administrative Procedure Act (1986:223), which lays down the basic rules for the exercise of power by the state and municipal authorities, has the primary objective to protect the legal security of citizens in their contacts with the administrative authorities. Another important aim is a simple, fast and cheap procedure and to ensure that the authorities provide an efficient service to the public.

The Administrative Procedure Act applies to the handling of matters by the administrative authorities and the handling of administrative matters by the courts. However, some of the provisions of the Act do not apply to matters at the authorities of the municipalities and county councils where the decisions are subject to an appeal under Chapter 10 of the Local Government Act (1991:900).[25] However, in principle, the Administrative Procedure Act applies to matters that are subject to the ordinary appeal procedure, for example the majority of matters relating to building permits and permits to serve alcohol.

According to the principle *lex specialis derogat legi generali*, where an Act or an ordinance contains a provision that is inconsistent with the Administrative Procedure Act, that provision shall prevail. In practice, various administrative regulations (special regulations) contain rules of procedure. Some statutes, for example, state a different time-limit for lodging an appeal than the ordinary period of tree weeks laid down in the Administrative Procedure Act.[26]

Some rules contained in the Act are generally applicable to all the activities of the authorities. They are primarily those regarding the authorities' relation to the public, such as the duty to assist and inform the public, rules on disqualification, rules concerning the date when a document shall be considered to have been duly delivered to the authority concerned as well as the rules concerning the use of interpreters.

Other rules are of limited applicability. They are only to be applied in cases that are of importance for citizens' private rights, benefits or obligations, or for disciplinary punishments and comparable conditions. In other words, when there is a question of exercising public authority *(myndighetsutövning)*. Such cases of exercising public authority against a private subject place greater demands on the protection of the individual's rights. The Act lays down, for example, the party's right to the disclosure of pertinent documents and the right to be informed about the content of the decision. It further states that every authority shall, before delivering a decision, communicate to the parties all the

---

25 This means matters that are subject to an municipal appeal (*kommunalbesvär*).

26 For instance the Tax Procedure Act states specific time-limits for lodging an appeal against a decision by the tax authorities.

information which had been provided by third parties and it shall give the parties in question an opportunity to respond to this information. The situation where the public authority imposes an administrative sanction is a typical illustration of the exercise of public authority. The additional rules which are applicable in those cases are important guarantees for the private subject. Some of these rules are related to the individual rights of defence.

2.3.2. General remarks about the Administrative Courts Procedure Act

The main rules concerning proceedings in the administrative courts are to be found in the Administrative Courts Procedure Act (1971:291). This Act applies to the administration of justice by the administrative courts, that is, the Supreme Administrative Court (*Högsta förvaltningsdomstolen*[27]), the Administrative Courts of Appeal (*kammarrätterna*) and the county administrative courts (*förvaltningsrätterna*[28]). The rules contained in the Administrative Courts Procedure Act are inspired by the Code of Procedure which is applicable to the ordinary courts. Certain rules regarding the administrative courts and the procedure therein can also be found in specific Acts or ordinances within the field of administrative law. In cases of inconsistency between the rules contained in the Administrative Courts Procedure Act and the rules contained in other specific Acts, the latter provisions shall prevail.

The Administrative Courts Procedure Act very much resembles the Administrative Procedure Act, but the former, which applies to the courts themselves is more precise. It "demands more legal certainty and predictability".[29]

2.4. RIGHTS OF DEFENCE

The Administrative Procedure Act has as primary objective of guaranteeing the legal security of citizens in their contacts with the administrative authorities.

These contacts encompass proceedings which impose an administrative sanction. The Administrative Procedure Act contains some rules that could be regarded as contributing to the rights of defence.

They are providing for the rights of the party to have access to his dossier, to express his views before the authority takes a decision, as well as the right to be legally represented. These rules are complemented inter alia with the obligation

27 Called *Regeringsrätten* before 1 January 2011.

28 Called *länsrätterna* before 1 January 2011.

29 M. Arnholm, M. Andersen, *The system of administrative and penal sanctions in Sweden*, Iutus, 1997, p. 50.

of the administrative authorities to make use of an interpret if needed and with the obligation to state the reasons for any decisions which have been taken. Other guarantees are to be found in the rules regarding legal aid.

2.4.1. Right of access to the dossier/documents

In order to be able to safeguard their own interests during the administrative proceedings, it is crucial that the parties obtain knowledge concerning the investigation of their cases. In this way the parties have the possibility to oversee the regularity of the proceedings and to be able to consider the appropriateness of a possible appeal. And last, but not least, they then have the opportunity to argue for their case. This right is of fundamental character especially when it is a question of imposing sanctions.

Beside the traditional right of access to official documents which is laid down by the Freedom of the Press Act, the parties involved in an administrative procedure concerning the exercise of public authority have, first of all the right to obtain access to investigate material (disclosure); secondly, the right to be informed of any information which has been added to the case (communication). Both rights are stipulated in the Administrative Procedure Act.[30]

The right of access to official documents is regulated in the Freedom of Press Act (FPA), "which has constitutional standing". According to the second chapter of the FPA, citizens are entitled to view the documents held by the public authorities. However, this right only exists for those documents that are considered to be *official documents*. Concerning the documents created by a public authority, the principle is that a document becomes an official document when it obtains its final form.

Disclosure to the party. According to Section 16 of the Administrative Procedure Act, the party "is entitled to have access to the material that has been brought into the matter". It is a right which has to be claimed by the party. This kind of right of access, reserved to the party in a procedure concerning the exercise of public authority, is wider than the right of access stipulated in the FPA, e.g. it does not only cover documents that have reached a certain stage, but also documents that have not yet reached that stage of the process that permits them to be qualified as official documents.

Communication. According to section 17 of the Administrative Procedure Act, the public authority has the obligation to inform the party "about any information that has been brought into the matter by someone other than the party himself". The obligation to inform, which is the authority's responsibility,

30 As well as in the Administrative Courts Procedure Act.

is closely connected with the obligation to give the party in question an opportunity to respond thereto.

2.4.2. *The right of the party to express his views before the authority takes a decision*

The right of the party to express his views before the authority takes a decision is, within the framework of the Swedish administrative procedure, closely connected to the authority's obligation to inform the parties about any material that has been added to the dossier. These two rules taken together, both of which are regulated in Section 17 of the Administrative Procedure Act, are constituting the so called *principle of communication*. This principle provides a guarantee of legal security as well as essential means for the investigation insofar as the fulfilment of the rules leads to a continuous exchange of information and arguments between the parties in the proceedings and the authority in question.[31] Fundamental for the party is that no decision may be taken before the party has been given the opportunity to comment on the information that has been added to the matter.

Section 17 provides for exceptions with regard to the principle of communication, for instance, if it may be feared that the implementation of the decision on the matter would otherwise be rendered considerably more difficult, or if the determination cannot be postponed.

2.4.3. *Right of hearing*

The procedure by the administrative authorities is normally in writing. However, if the case concerns the exercise of public authority the party who wants to make an oral statement shall be afforded an opportunity to do so. This constitutes a specific guarantee especially for individuals who have difficulties in expressing themselves in written form.

All investigation material which is the result of an oral procedure must be laid down in writing if this information may be of importance for the outcome of the matter (this is referred to as the recording of information, Section 15 of the Administrative Procedure Act).

2.4.4. *Right of representation*

The basic idea of the Administrative Procedure Act is that the party, with the assistance of the authorities in question, is able to conduct the proceedings on his

---

[31] H. Ragnemalm, *Förvaltningsprocessrättens grunder*, Juristförlaget, 2012, p. 92.

own.[32] However, there are situations (illness, absence abroad or the complexity of the case) where the party wants or needs to make use of a lawyer or to be represented by an acquaintance or a parent, for example. Section 9 of the Administrative Procedure Act lays down the possibility for the party in question to make use of a representative (*ombud*) or counsel (*biträde*). However, the right of representation does not restrict the obligation for the party to take part in person if the authority so requests. The representative or counsel is bound by a general condition of suitability. And the authority may reject a representative or counsel if that person demonstrates a lack of ability or ignorance or is in some other way unsuitable.

2.4.5. Interpreter

Other rules which are of fundamental importance for the party, insofar as they guarantee the right to be heard and the possibility to defend oneself, are the rules which regulate the use of interpreters. According to Section 8 of the Administrative Procedure Act a public authority which is dealing with someone who does not have a sufficient command of the Swedish language or who has a severe hearing or speech impediment should make use of an interpreter when needed. The term "interpreter" refers both to the person who orally translates between two languages and to the written translation. The public authority has to make an objective appreciation of the need to use an interpreter. The authority will take the decision to use an interpreter with regard to the nature of the case, and the extent and character of the material which could be the object of translation. Furthermore, the authority has to consider the costs of the translation and set them in relation to the significance and the character of the case. In cases regarding coercive measures, the recourse to an interpreter may be especially important.[33] This should be the same concerning proceedings leading to the imposition of a sanction.

2.4.6. Stating the reasons for the decisions

Another rule which is essential for the legal security of individuals is the rule which determines that reasons have to be given for the decisions taken. This rule enables the party to control whether the decision is well-founded from a factual and legal point of view. According to Section 20 of the Administrative Procedure Act "a decision whereby a matter is determined by an authority shall contain the reasons that settled the outcome" if it is a matter regarding the exercise of public authority against individuals. This rule applies when it concerns final decisions (both deciding and dismissing the case). However, it is unclear how far the rule

32 B. Wennergren, *Offentlig förvaltning i arbete: om verksamheten och ärendehandläggningen i stat och kommun*, Norstedts juridik, 2008, p. 92.

33 Id., p. 91.

applies regarding the decisions taken in the proceedings. The authority decides of its own motion if the decision shall contain the necessary grounds or not.[34]

The rule of stating the reasons for decisions is accompanied by some exceptions. The reasons for the decision may be omitted wholly or in part, for example if "the decision is not adverse to any party or if for some other reason it is obviously unnecessary to state the reasons". The expression "the decision is not adverse to any party" is not very clear and its content may vary with regard to the circumstances. When the matter concerns an intervention by a public authority by means of an injunction to force an individual to take certain measures the decision is generally regarded as a decision which is adverse to a party.[35] This is also the case for decisions concerning the imposition of a sanction. The expression "or if for some other reason it is obviously unnecessary to state the reasons " also has to be defined. It encompasses the case when "no important interest has been neglected".[36] An example is when a higher instance declines to give the reasons for certain decisions because there is no need to amend the appealed decision which already contained satisfactory grounds.[37]

Another exception to the rule which requires reasons to be stated for a particular decision is when "the matter is of such urgency that there is no time to formulate the reasons for the decision". It is sometimes necessary for the authority to intervene so quickly that there is no time left for the authority to justify the decision. A possibility exists for the reasons to be drafted subsequently. According to Section 20, if the reasons for the decision are not given in the decision itself, the authority should, at the request of the party in question, include the reasons at a later date, if possible.

2.4.7. Legal aid

According to the Legal Aid Act (1996:1619) (*rättshjälpslagen*) legal aid can be granted to a party in a case. Legal aid is subsidiary to legal protection insurance and is only available to natural persons. The conditions for legal aid are the following: The person who request legal aid must have received at least an hour's legal advice, and the income of the applicant must not exceed a financial threshold. Furthermore, the applicant must need the assistance of a lawyer over and above the legal advice provided and it must not be possible to meet this need in any other way. However, Legal Aid can only be granted if, with regard to the nature and significance of the case and considering the value of the object in dispute and the overall circumstances, it may be considered reasonable for the state to contribute towards the costs. In practice, the parties in an administrative

---

34 Id., p. 129.

35 T. Hellners, B. Malmqvist, *Förvaltningslagen med kommentarer*, Norstedts juridik, 2010, p. 243.

36 Id., p. 245.

37 Id., p. 245.

matter seldom obtain legal aid. The reasons for this are that oral hearings are not so frequent and that it is, in principle, the public authority and not the party who bears responsibility for the investigation.

The Legal Aid Act also regulates legal advice. Everyone, natural persons and legal persons, can be granted legal advice in legal matters. Legal advice is provided by a lawyer or junior advocate at a lawyer's office. The party obtaining the advice has to pay a predetermined charge. The charge can be reduced when the person obtaining the advice has insufficient financial resources.

According to the Public Counsel Act (1996:1620) (*lagen om offentligt biträde*) a Public Counsel can be appointed for certain matters which are regulated in a special act such as The Care of Alcoholics, Drug Abusers and Abusers of Volatile Solvents Act (1988:870) or the Care of Young Persons Act (1990:52).

2.5. ORGANIZATION OF SANCTIONING POWERS

The question of organizing sanctioning powers has two aspects. The first concerns the kind of authorities which have such powers, the second aspect concerns the division of sanctioning powers within an administrative authority.

2.5.1. Which authorities have the power to impose administrative sanctions?

Some administrative sanctions are pronounced by *administrative authorities* themselves. These authorities exist at various levels. There are central authorities like the Work Environment Authority and the National Food Administration. There are also regional authorities like the County Administrative Board (*länsstyrelse*)[38] and, furthermore, there are local authorities, the different municipal committees, such as the building committee. Some other administrative sanctions are pronounced by *the courts* at the behest of an administrative authority.

The rules concerning the authority empowered to impose administrative sanctions are not homogenous. They vary not only between the different kinds of administrative sanctions but also within the same category of sanction. Administrative fees, for example (also called sanction charges), may in some cases be imposed by the decision-making/supervisory authority (for instance, concerning the application of the Environmental Code, Chapter 30, section 3). In some other cases the question of imposing charges is determined by the Court at the behest of the decision-making/supervisory authority (for example, concerning the application of the working environment legislation (Chapter 8,

[38] This authority represents the government to coordinate administration with national political objectives for the county, which is an administrative and political subdivision of the Kingdom of Sweden.

section 7 of the Working Environment Act). Information about the competent authority is to be found in the relevant administrative statutes.

However, the question regarding which authority should have sanctioning powers is the subject of discussions in Sweden within the framework of larger reform concerning supervision.[39] One of the topics being discussed is the supervision of administrative rules by the municipal authorities. The enforcement and the supervision of a large number of administrative statutes (such as the Environmental Code and the Alcohol Act[40]) are the duty of the municipal authorities. In those cases it is therefore the municipal authorities which have the necessary sanctioning powers.

Nevertheless, there is a proposal to transfer the task of supervision performed by the municipal agencies to the County Administrative Board. The arguments put forward in favour of such a proposal is the luck of equivalence and uniformity concerning the interpretation and application of the law in the country. The arguments which favour the *status quo* are, however, the local knowledge possessed by the municipal authorities and the proximity between the supervisory authorities and that which has to be supervised.

2.5.2. The division of sanctioning powers within an administrative authority

Concerning the division of decision-making powers – and especially sanctioning powers – within the *municipal authorities*, the pertinent rules are the following: According to the Local Government Act the council committees have the power to delegate the decision-making power, *inter alia*, to a member of the committee or to an employee of the municipality. The decision to impose an administrative sanction used to be taken by the head of the committee. This possibility to delegate does have some exceptions. One of those exceptions concerns the exercise of public power *vis-à-vis* individuals. Namely, the decision-making power may not be delegated regarding the exercise of public power *vis-à-vis* individuals where the cases are, in principle, of general importance or otherwise are of major importance (see the Local Government Act, Chapter 6, Sections 33 and 34).

The rules concerning the division of sanctioning powers within the *county administrative boards* are to be found in the Ordinance (2007:825) for County Administrative Board Regulations. Concerning the decisions taken by the county administrative boards when applying the Environmental Code, the general principle contained in the ordinance is the following: decisions (including decisions imposing sanctions) may be taken by the head of the board's

39 SOU 2004:100 "Tillsyn, Förslag om en tydligare och effektivare tillsyn".

40 These cases concern the situation in which a special duty has been entrusted to the municipalities by a special law. It does not concern the competence of the municipality according to the Local Government Act.

environmental section together with an expert on environmental issues. This head must be a lawyer with judicial experience.

The division of sanctioning powers by the *central authorities* is regulated by rules taken by the authority itself. Authorities' power to impose such rules is, in turn, based on rules laid down in the Agency Ordinance (*myndighetsförordning* (2007:515)) and in the specific ordinance containing instructions for the central authority concerned. For example, according to the rules of the Working Environment Authority, administrative sanctions have to be decided by the head of inspection (*tillsynschef*). But, in a case of emergency the inspector has the possibility to decide himself on immediate measure. The inspector cannot, however, impose a fine of his own accord.

2.6. INVESTIGATION/INSPECTION

The great expansion of the Swedish public sector – specially after the Second World War –, combined with the rapid increase of mass criminality (traffic violations, for instance) has led to a need to give several administrative authorities certain legal instruments in order to investigate violations of administrative statutes and, finally, to impose sanctions. Such powers cannot only be given to the courts, as they would soon become overloaded.

The decision-making authority endorses the responsibility for the investigation:[41] the authority has to lead the investigations and has to ensure that it gathers the material needed in order to create a solid basis for the decision to be taken.[42] The authority has, among other things, the duty to indicate what is required of the individuals concerned in order to collect sufficient material.

The responsibility to conduct the investigation involves an opportunity for the authority to ask other authorities for certain information or opinions. According to Section 7 of the Administrative Procedure Act the authority "shall avail itself of the opportunity of obtaining information from and the views of other authorities, if there is a need to do so".

The special administrative statutes can confer several investigative powers on administrative authorities. The supervisory authority may for instance be entitled:

- to access the locality where the activity is taking place (see, for instance, the Working Environment Act, Chapter 7, Section 5);

41 Ibid., p. 73.

42 This so called *official principle* is explicitly laid down in the Administrative Court Procedure Act but not in the Administrative Procedure Act. However, it is generally considered that this principle applies to public agencies as well.

- to access the information and documents needed for the investigation (see the Alcohol Act, Chapter 9, Section 13, the Working Environment Act, Chapter 7, Section 5 and the Environmental Code, Chapter 26, Section 21);
- to take samples of certain goods (see the Alcohol Act, Chapter 9, Section 13);
- to obtain assistance from the police (see the Environmental Code, Chapter 28, Section 8).

2.7. LEGAL PROTECTION

The most important form of administrative legal protection is the possibility to amend or cancel an incorrect decision.[43] The question of legal protection against administrative sanctions therefore concerns the right to appeal (2.7.2), but also the possibility for administrative authorities to correct themselves when their own decisions are patently erroneous (2.7.1).

2.7.1. Self-correction by the authority which has taken the decision

The Swedish legal system distinguishes between three situations.

- The authorities' statutory right to rectify any manifest written or calculation error or any other similar oversight,
- The authorities' statutory duty to reconsider their own decision when there have been errors of the most substantive kind
- The authorities' right, as developed in the case law, to take a new decision which may change a prior decision.

The institution of self-correction complements, in a certain way, the system of court appeals.

Thus, the basic idea behind the Swedish rules concerning administrative procedures is to avoid decisions taken by the authorities from being subjected to an appeal in the courts in order to keep process costs low. The Swedish system focuses therefore on first instance proceedings.

The Authorities' statutory right to rectify any manifest written or calculation error or any other similar oversight
According to Section 26 of the Administrative Procedure Act, a decision that contains a manifest error in writing, calculation or any other similar oversight by the authority or someone else has to be corrected by the authority which took the decision. When the matter concerns the exercise of public authority against individuals, Section 26 prescribes, moreover, that the authority shall give the parties an opportunity to express their opinion before a correction takes place.

---

43 See for example H. Strömberg and B. Lundell, *Allmän förvaltningsrätt*, 2012, p. 169.

The correction can be initiated by the authority itself or at the behest of the parties or other persons.

The Authorities' statutory duty to reconsider their own decision as a result of errors of the most substantive kind

In some cases concerning errors of the most substantive kind the decision-making authority has a *duty to rectify* which will take the form of reconsidering certain decisions. According to Section 27 of the Administrative Procedure Act "when an authority because of new circumstances or for some other reason finds that a decision that it has made at first instance is manifestly wrong, it shall correct the decision, provided that this can take place rapidly and simply and without detriment to any private party". The possibility of self-correction is bound to the rules which prescribe that an appeal against a decision is first handled by the authority that has taken the decision (Section 23). It opens an opportunity for this first instance to change its decision.

The duty of reconsideration also exists when the decision is appealed against, but only subject to the condition that the decision-making authority has not sent the case documents to a superior instance.

The authority will reconsider the decision either *ex officio* or on the request of the parties.

The Authorities' right, as developed in the case law, to take a new decision which may change a prior decision

Besides the cases laid down in Sections 26 and 27 of the Administrative Procedure Act, the decision-making bodies have the possibility to change their own decision according to the rules that have been developed in the case law. The rules are different depending on whether it is a case of unfavourable or favourable decisions. Both cases may be interesting for the purpose of administrative sanctions.

As far as *unfavourable decisions* are concerned, such as decisions containing a refusal to issue a permit for example, decisions containing injunctions compelling someone to act in a certain way or containing a prohibition, the decision-making authority is entitled to change the decision. This is also the case for decisions concerning sanctions. The authority can decide to make the decision more severe or to mitigate it if there are new, previously unknown circumstances or it has become evident that the first decision was incorrect.

Regarding *favourable decisions*, the possibility for the decision-making authority to change its own decision is closely connected to the question of protection *vis-à-vis* administrative sanctions and the question of the legal security of the individual. Thus, a change of decision can involve an administrative sanction for the individual in the form of a revocation of a licence or a loss of authorization. The principal rule concerning favourable decisions is that the decision cannot be changed. However there are three exceptions according to the case law. Firstly, if the favourable decision, for example the issuing of a permit, contains express provisions entitling the decision to be reversed. The second exception concerns the situation when serious safety reasons require an immediate cancellation of a decision (see, for example, a hunting permit which had been granted for a longer period than was intended and which had to be cancelled because of the risk which hunting would pose for mushroom or berry pickers[44]).The third exception concerns the situation in which the individual has obtained the decision by providing incorrect information to the authority or by keeping relevant information secret.

2.7.2. Right of appeal

There are no specific rules which apply to decisions imposing administrative sanctions. The general rules are applicable.

The provisions concerning which decisions may be the subject of an appeal to the administrative Courts are to be found in the special statutes which regulate administrative matters.

2.7.3. Where can the decision be appealed?

The main rule is that administrative decisions may be appealed to *higher administrative authorities or to administrative courts*.[45] The Swedish administrative court structure is comprised of three levels of general administrative courts: the county administrative courts, the Administrative Courts of Appeal and, finally, the Supreme Administrative Court.

According to Section 22a of the Administrative Procedure Act, a decision taken by an authority can be appealed to a general administrative court. This provision, included in the Administrative Procedure Act in 1998, crystallises the principle that the legal control of administrative decisions is carried out by the courts[46] and provides a possibility to refer to a competent court in those situations where the European Convention on Human Rights or EU law require the existence of a right to appeal and where the Swedish legislation does not

44 JO 1987/88 s. 258, quoted by H. Ragnemalm, *Förvaltningsprocessrättens grunder*, Juristförlaget, 2012, p. 128.

45 There are some exceptions. For example, according to the Environmental Code, decisions taken by County Administrative Boards may be appealed to the general courts in special session.

46 See, T. Hellners, B. Malmqvist, *Förvaltningslagen med kommentarer*, Norstedts juridik, 2010, p. 308.

provide for such a right. The origin of this new rule is to be found in two cases, the *Lassagård* case (RÅ 1997 ref 65) and the *Stallknecht* case (RÅ 1995 ref 58).[47]

The *Lassagård* case has had a big impact on Swedish law insofar as the Supreme Administrative Court has dismissed the traditional administrative principle according to which the decisions taken by an administrative authority could only be subject to an appeal if a legal provision provided for this.[48] The facts of the case were the following: The County Administrative Board had rejected an application by a company called Lassagård concerning area aid for 1995. The County Administrative Board referred to EC-Commission Regulation 3887/92[49] and argued that there was no right to this area aid because of the 20- day delay in the company's application. Lassagård appealed against the decision by the County Administrative Board to the Swedish Board of Agriculture (*Jordbruksverket*). This instance rejected the appeal arguing that the decision could not be appealed against, according to an ordinance (1994:1715). The County Administrative Court considered, in its turn, that the right to area aid constituted a "civil right" in accordance with Article 6 of the European Convention on Human Rights. However, the Court could not examine the action because of the application of Section 14 of the Administrative Court Act (1971:289) which stated that the administrative courts are only competent if they are designated as the competent courts. The Administrative Court of Appeal considered that the prohibition on an appeal against the decision taken by the Board of Agriculture constituted a violation of Article 6 of the European Convention and concluded that the Swedish rules may not be applied with reference to Chapter 11, Section 14 of the Instrument of Government.[50] In the frame of it's examination of the case the Supreme Administrative Court referred to the general principles of Community law and stated that the prohibition of an appeal against the decision taken by the Board of agriculture was not compatible with those principles.[51]

---

47 Furthermore, Section 22a aims to prevent a negative conflict of competence between the general courts and the administrative courts.

48 See J. Nergelius, *Förvaltningsprocess, normprövning och europarätt*, Norstedts Juridik, 2000, p. 77.

49 Regulation laying down detailed rules for applying the integrated administration and control system for certain Community aid schemes.

50 Which states that if a court finds that a provision conflicts with a rule of fundamental law or other superior statute, the provision may not be applied.

51 The second case mentioned, which preceded the *Lassagård* case, is the *Stallknecht* case. Miss Stallknecht claimed that the Board of Agriculture should pay her a sum of SK 665,000 (about 60,000 euro) as income support. But the payment had already been made to the wrong recipient. The district court rejected the action and stated that the decision concerning subsidies may not be appealed against. The Court of Appeal considered that article 6 of the European Convention on Human Rights as interpreted by the Strasbourg Court imposed the right to appeal against such a decision. The Supreme Court, which handled the case after the appeal instigated by the Board of Agriculture, used the same reasoning as the Court of Appeal regarding the existence of a right to appeal but concluded that the administrative courts and not the general courts had the competence to handle this kind of case. Both the

The rule laid down in Section 22a applies to the decisions taken by the central authorities and to County Administrative Boards.

Concerning the right to appeal against decisions taken by municipal agencies, the rules are not homogeneous. Some decisions may be appealed to the County Administrative Board (for example, the municipal agencies' decisions regarding building permits taken according to the Planning and Building Act). Other decisions may be appealed to the administrative courts. This is the case for decisions taken under the Alcohol Act.

The actual tendency in Swedish legislation is that more and more administrative decisions have to be appealed to the administrative courts.[52]

For instance the decisions by the Working Environment Authority containing an order to pay a fine, which were previously subject to appeal to the government, may since an amendment of the Working Environment Act, be appealed to the administrative court.[53, 54, 55]

2.74 *What kind of decisions may be appealed against?*

In some cases the special statutes specify the types of decisions which may be the subject of an appeal; in other cases not, however. In the latter cases, the general principles developed by case law serve to establish the distinction between those decisions in which it is possible to appeal and those in which it is not. According to these general principles, it is required that the decision is likely to affect someone's personal or economic situation to a not inconsiderable extent. Decisions concerning sanctions constitute, without doubt, such a decision.

In some cases the special statutes stipulate that certain kinds of decisions may not be appealed against, as for example, a decision containing an order to pay a fine when the addressee does not comply with the decision-making authority's injunction to act in a certain way. However, a prohibition on an

County Administrative Court and the Administrative Court of Appeal rejected the complaint because there was no statute providing for the right to appeal against such a decision. The Supreme Administrative Court considered that it was not clear whether the right to economic grants could be considered as "a civil right" and that it was therefore unclear whether Article 6 of the European Convention could be applied in the present case. The Supreme Administrative Court upheld the decision of the Administrative Court of Appeal. Stallknecht complained to the European Commission of Human Rights. The case finished with conciliation by the Swedish state.

52 *SOU* 2004:100, p. 137.

53 See Prop. 2007/08:62.

54 There was no right to be heard "by an independent and impartial tribunal".

55 The Act relating to Legal Review of Certain Administrative Decisions had been enacted in 1988.

appeal against a decision cannot be maintained if this infringes the requirements of the European Convention on Human Rights or EC law regarding the right to appeal to a court.

2.7.5. Leave to appeal

In most cases special leave to appeal is required in order to have a case heard by an Administrative Court of Appeal and, finally, by the Supreme Administrative Court.

The Supreme Administrative Court in principle only hears cases which are of interest from the point of view of possible precedents. However, leave to appeal is not required in all types of cases.

2.7.6. Judicial review

Concerning judicial review, the appellate court will hear the case from a legal and discretionary point of view. The court has the power not only to quash the decision but also to vary or supersede the decision with a completely new decision.[56]

2.7.7. Legal review

In the frame of the Act relating to the Legal Review of Certain Administrative Decisions (2006:304), the Supreme Administrative Court is empowered to examine whether the decision taken by the Government is compatible with certain legal provisions. However, the Court has only the power to quash the appealed decision. The system of legal preview was introduced[57] after Sweden had been condemned by the Strasbourg Court in the 1980s on the ground that the Swedish Administrative procedure, according to which the government was the last instance in many cases, did not comply with the standards laid down in the European Convention on Human Rights, and especially Article 6.[58]

The appeal has to be lodged within three weeks after the party has been notified of the decision of the lower instance. The plaintiff/transgressor has to send the appeal to the decision-making authority. This procedure is connected with the system of self-correction. The decision-making authority is given the

---

56 Besides the judicial review, called "*förvaltningsbesvär*", described above, the Swedish legal system provides for another kind of review, called "*kommunalbesvär*", which is applicable to decisions of local and regional municipal bodies taken under the Local Government Act (1991:900). However, if the municipal bodies take decisions under special statutes like the Alcohol Act and the Building Act, the ordinary judicial review will be applicable. The special kind of review is limited to a pure assessment of legality. Furthermore, the examination on appeal can only result, if the application is approved, in a reversal of the decision.

57 The Act relating to Legal Review of Certain Administrative Decisions had been enacted in 1988.

58 There was no right to be heard "by an independent and impartial tribunal".

possibility to change its decision. If the change corresponds to the one demanded by the plaintiff/transgressor, no appeal will be necessary. If the decision-making authority does not change the decision or at least does not do so in the way required by the transgressor, the appeal will be sent to the court.

2.7.8. Extraordinary remedies in the administrative procedure

A right to relief for substantive defects and a right to the restoration of lost time are laid down in the Instrument of Government, Chapter 11, Section 13. The grounds of relief have to be found in the Administrative Courts Procedure Act, Section 37 b and c. According to Section 37 b, relief for substantive defects may be granted where special circumstances exist that make it important to reconsider the case. Section 37 c states, furthermore, that the time lost during the period of the appeal may be restored if the person in question has a valid excuse for not appealing within the prescribed period for appeal.

2.7.9. The ombudsmen

The Parliamentary ombudsmen (JO) is another important legal institution that contributes to the protection of the rights of individuals in their contacts with the authorities. The task of the ombudsmen is to supervise all central and local government agencies. The ombudsmen have no power to interfere with the handling of or to re-examine individual cases, but have the possibility to make critical advisory comment, recommendation and serve as special prosecutors in cases of breach of duty within the public administration. The ombudsmen are also empowered to initiate a disciplinary proceeding.

2.8. CAN SANCTIONS BE EXECUTED IMMEDIATELY?

A large number of administrative statutes empower the administrative authorities to decide on the immediate execution of their decisions, decisions concerning sanctions included.

This power is conferred on the administrative authorities by for instance the Alcohol Act (Chapter 10, Section 1) and the Working Environment Act (Chapter 9, Section 5).

3. TOPICS CURRENTLY BEING DISCUSSED IN SWEDEN

Two topics having a connection with the question of administrative sanctions and currently being discussed in Sweden have drawn our attention:

1. One of the issues concerns Tax surcharges (*skattetillägg*) and the problematic of double sanctions and its compliance or no compliance with the European Convention on Human Rights and EU Law.
   Despite the decision of the Supreme Court arguing that the cumulative imposition of tax surcharges and penal sanctions for tax crimes does not contravene the prohibition for double sanctions contained in the European Convention on Human Rights[59], several inferior courts have defying the highest instance arguing that the precondition of "clear support" for giving the supremacy to the European Convention before national law, as advanced by the Supreme Court, is neither to be found in the Convention itself nor in the Case Law of the European Court for Human rights. Another argument raised against the reasoning of the Supreme Court is drawn from EU Law: the principle non bis in idem is also stated in the Charter of Fundamental Rights of The European Union which is included in the primary legislation of the EU and benefits consequently from the principle of supremacy.[60] Additionally, a request for a preliminary ruling has been lodged to the ECJ by a district court.
2. The second issue concerns the future reform of the Swedish Administrative Procedure Act.[61] The reform work, which can be seen as a part of the process of europeanisation of the Swedish law is in the meanwhile meant to lead to several changes in order to improve the legal protection of the individuals.[62] The proposed changes are inter alia the introduction of a provision on the principle of proportionality[63] as well as of an explicit duty of investigation for the public authorities.[64] Other changes are meant to render the public authorities' duty to state reasons for the decisions more concrete[65] as well as to improve and clarify the rules on self-correction.[66] Minor changes have also been proposed regarding the provision on the use of an interpreter[67] and

59 NJA 2010 s.168.
60 According to the legal opinion of Ulf Bernitz, 18-01-2011.
61 See the preparatory works SOU 2010:29.
62 SOU 2010:29, p. 22.
63 SOU 2010:29, p. 184.
64 SOU 2010:29, p. 417.
65 SOU 2010:29, p. 511.
66 SOU 2010:29, p.579 etc.
67 SOU 2010:29, p. 313.

concerning the provision on the right of representation.[68] The new Administrative Procedure Act was proposed to enter into force in January 2012.

BIBLIOGRAPHY

Arnholm, Maria and Andersen, Mattias, *The system of administrative and penal sanctions in Sweden*, Iutus, 1997.

Bull, Thomas and Sterzel, Fredrik, *Regerinformen - en kommentar*, SNS förlag, 2010.

Hellners, Trygge and Malmquist, Bo, *Förvaltningslagen med kommentarer*, Norstedts juridik, 2010.

Marcusson, Lena, "Condition of administrative procedure law", in: *Comparative analysis of administrative law, European public law series, Bibliothèque de droit public européen*, vol. XXVI, Bruylant, 2002. (Others articles are written by U. Björkman, A. Hellsten, A. Lidman and L. Lederwall).

Nergelius, Joakim, *Förvaltningsprocess, normprövning och europarätt*, Norstedts Juridik, 2000.

Ragnemalm, Hans, *Förvaltningsprocessrättens grunder*, Juristförlaget, 2012.

Strömberg, Håkan and Lundell, Bengt, *Allmän förvaltningsrätt*, Liber ekonomi, 2012.

Warnling Nerep, Wiweka, *Sanktionsavgifter, särskilt vid olovligt byggande*, Juristförlaget, 1987.

Wennergren, Bertil, *Offentlig förvaltning i arbete: om verksamheten och ärendehandläggningen i stat och kommun*, Norstedts juridik, 2008.

Zila, Jozef, *I stället för straff- Sanktionsavgifter som kriminalpolitiskt medel mot bagatellbrottslighet*, Juristförlaget, 1992.

PREPARATORY WORKS

Ds 2001: 69 Företagsbot (on corporate fines)

SOU 2002:50 Miljöbalken under utveckling, ett principbetänkande (Environmental Code under development)

SOU 2004:100 Tillsyn. Förslag om en tydligare och effektivare tillsyn (Supervision - proposal for a supervision that is more clear and efficient)

Prop. 2005/06:59 Företagsbot (on corporate fines)

Prop. 2005/06:182 Miljöbalkens sanktionssystem m.m. (on the sanctioning system within the Environmental Code)

Prop. 2007/08:62 Ny instansordning för arbetsmiljöärenden (new instance order in work environment issues)

SOU 2008:125 En reformerad grundlag (a reformed Instrument of Government)

SOU 2010:29 En ny förvaltningslag (a New Administrative Procedure Act)

Prop. 2009/10:80 En reformerad grundlag (a reformed Instrument of Government)

68 SOU 2010:29, p. 322.

XIV. COUNTRY ANALYSIS – UNITED KINGDOM

John McEldowney*

1. INTRODUCTION

The use of sanctions for a breach of administrative rules or legal duties is a developing field of study within the United Kingdom.[1] This chapter addresses how the United Kingdom system of sanctions developed and traces the major influences in that development. The approach to sanctions in the United Kingdom has changed remarkably over the past hundred years. It has been transformed from reliance on self-regulation and self-monitoring to areas of law where there are punitive criminal sanctions applicable to breaches of regulations or of administrative law. While in the past the use of the criminal law in terms of access to regulatory offences was relatively rare and confined to a discrete area of the law allowing the regulator to take prosecutions. However, in more recent times the scope or regulatory offences has expanded specifically in the financial services sector and permit a regulator to impose their own criminal sanction such as a fine or qualification as a director of a company. There is a new offence of corporate manslaughter under the Corporate Manslaughter and Corporate Homicide Act 2007 allowing companies and organisations to be found guilty of manslaughter.[2] In the area of environmental law, the Environment Agency has been proactive in prosecuting for breaches of environmental law, most notably for water contamination and water companies for failing to comply with their statutory obligations. There have been wide ranging changes introduced by the Hampton Review[3] in 2005 that favoured deregulation and cutting "red tape" and

* School of Law, University of Warwick.

1 See D. Oliver, T. Prosser and R. Rawlings ed., *The Regulatory State* Oxford: Oxford University Press, 2010; Simon Halliday, *Judicial review and Compliance with Administrative Law* Oxford: Hart Publishing 2004. For recent analysis see: Philip Hampton, Reducing Administrative Burdens: Effective Inspection and Enforcement Final Report London: HM Treasury, 2005, DTI, *Deregulation: Cutting Red Tape*, (1994), *Thinking About Regulation: A Guide to Good Regulation* (1994); *Getting a Good Deal in Europe* (1994).

2 See: *R. v P. Ltd.*, [2004] EWCA Crim. 1937.

3 Philip Hampton, Reducing Administrative Burdens: Effective Inspection and Enforcement Final Report London: HM Treasury, 2005. See: HM Treasury, *Implementing Hampton: From*

the MacRory Report[4] in 2006 recommending streamlining the penalty system and the adoption of civil sanctions. Following the MacRory Report, Part 3 of the Regulatory Enforcement and Sanctions Act 2008, introduce a range of civil sanctions as a more flexible way to impose penalties for regulatory breaches. In December, 2010 the Environment Agency has taken steps to introduced a range of civil sanctions under new revised *Guidance on Enforcement and Sanctions*[5] including fixed monetary penalties[6], variable monetary penalties, compliance notice, restoration and stop notices. The introduction of civil sanctions is intended to complement the existing system of criminal sanctions but with a more tailored and flexible approach to ensure effective regulation. MacRory argued that flexible risk based enforcement tools might achieve better regulatory outcomes.[7] The link between different styles of regulation and effective sanctions is slowly emerging in the aftermath of the financial crisis.

This paper will evaluate the range of sanctions available and their efficacy, but will mainly focus on the criminal law. Sanctions are a manifestation of different approaches to regulation. Civil sanctions are normally imposed by the relevant regulatory body, although there are doubts over the future of many regulatory bodies under the coalition government's proposals in the Public Bodies Bill, 2010 before Parliament. This leaves considerable uncertainty as to the future of regulation in the UK and opens up the question of the future effectiveness of sanctions if a "light touch" approach to regulation that emphasises the role of market forces rather than regulatory intervention dominates.

It should be remembered that there are a wide number of legal and economic instruments available to implement and enforce administrative decisions, ranging from the criminal prosecution of regulatory offences, to the use of licences and various financial and economic incentives[8]and civil sanctions. The chapter draws out the different characteristics of sanctions in various areas of the law. It questions whether or not there are any operating general principles. It also questions the values and justifications that may underpin the particular uses of sanctions in the United Kingdom. Sanctions that are linked to corporate regulation are distinct from environmental regulation or sanctions available to the courts in judicial review or civil proceedings. The traditional distinctions between civil and criminal procedures are blurred when considering the range

---

enforcement to compliance (2006).

4 See: R. Macrory, *Regulatory Justice: Sanctioning in a post-Hampton World: A Consultation Document* London: Cabinet Office, May, 2006 and *Regulatory Justice: Making Sanctions Effective* London: Cabinet Office, November, 2006.

5 Environment Agency, 4 January 2011.

6 Fixed Monetary Penalties vary from £300 for business and £100 for individuals.

7 Carolyn Talbot, "The Regulatory Enforcement and Sanctions Act 2008" (2009) *Environmental Law Review* 38.

8 J. Black, "Tensions in the regulatory state" (2007) *Public Law* 58 at p. 66.

of sanctions available. Sanctions available to courts and tribunals are distinguished from those available to the Government or policy makers. The range of government bodies that have administrative sanctions at their disposal has itself grown. This is partly the result of privatisation and partly the expansion of regulatory controls. There are also countervailing pressures in the development of de-regulation strategies intended to cut red tape and remove unnecessary procedures.[9]

The trend in the United Kingdom over recent years is to adopt more punitive measures to ensure enforcement. Correspondingly the range of legal sanctions that are available has increased to include various economic and fiscal instruments. Since the Human Rights Act 1998 has come into force there is a growing awareness of the human rights implications of administrative sanctions. There are recognisable shortcomings in sanctions that are purely punitive, especially as they are usually applied in an *ex post* way. Punitive sanctions invariably contain elements of deterrence as well as an imbedded system of command and control for their enforcement. Inevitably, however, to such strategies must be policed if deterrence is to work. The chapter explores how proactive strategies are needed that have a preventative character and may lead to sustainable regulatory strategies. The key issues surrounding administrative sanctions are devising appropriate responses to implement strategies that improve administrative decision-making in different sectors such as health, education, and environment and in the public and private sectors including financial organisations. However, locating the criminal law in sanctions raises questions about costs, deterrence and the proportionality of responses designed to prevent inappropriate behaviour or harm.

First, this paper examines constitutional history as an explanation of the context of administrative sanctions in the United Kingdom. Second, there is consideration of the main techniques, procedures and processes used in administrative sanctions. This provides a glimpse of the wide variety of sanctions including the use of the criminal law and civil sanctions under the Regulatory Enforcement and Sanctions Act 2008. The paper then addresses the question of the use of the criminal law in terms of companies and their liabilities. Corporate manslaughter under the Corporate Manslaughter and Corporate Homicide Act 2007 has not resulted in many prosecutions. Sanctions must also conform to the human rights implications of administrative sanctions and the requirements of fairness. Finally, there are conclusions that set out the main trends and findings in this developing area of the law.

9 Anthony Ogus, " Regulation revisited" (2009) *Public law* 332; John F. McEldowney, 'Defining the public interest: Public Law Perspectives on Regulating the Financial Crisis', in: John Raymond LaBrosse, Rodrigo Olivare-Caminal and Dalvinder Singh (eds.), *Financial Crisis Management and Bank Resolution* London: Informa, 2009 pp. 103–132.

2. THE CONSTITUTIONAL CONTEXT OF ADMINISTRATIVE SANCTIONS IN THE UNITED KINGDOM

In 1980 *Justice,* the British section of the International Commission of Jurists, published a path breaking report entitled Breaking *the Rules*.[10] The report identified the growing number of regulations needed to provide some degree of order in society; that in many instances this required the use of the criminal law, imposed in the normal way by the use of criminal prosecutions in the criminal courts; and that delegated powers to a wide variety of regulatory bodies provided for the utilisation of criminal sanctions and finally that in a complex and changing society this utilisation of the criminal law and the widespread use of criminal sanctions was *ad hoc* and random. The main concern identified in the Report is that overuse of the criminal law might bring the law into disrepute and this may result in a lack of public confidence in the system of law. The report noted:

But people simply do not regard many of the modern statutory offences as "crimes" in the same way as murder, robbery, rape and arson. They agree that there have to be rules and regulations – indeed there is often strong pressure for the Government to "ban" something or other – but they do not see the man who sells bananas off an unlicensed street barrow, or the motorist who forgets to sign his driving licence, or the firm that fails to make its statutory return to some public authority until after the due date as " criminals".

The increasing use of criminal sanctions and their proliferation was seen as a major challenge for the future. The Report took as its main aims to attempt to se if there might be a way to delineate those breaches of regulations or law that should be prosecuted as criminal offences and those that do not require a criminal sanction. The Report recommended a more systematic analysis of regulatory offences than in the past and that legislation should be adopted to draw a distinction between "crimes and contraventions" and that the future development of the law in this area should be monitored and that it should be possible to reduce the escalating number of potential criminal offences. Underlying the Report's analysis was the view that there may be a number of situations where decriminalisation of particular types of activity would be in the public interest. Despite the persuasive nature of the findings in the Report, it is clear that little has been achieved to implement its recommendations. In fact today in the United Kingdom, there is no general definition of what is an administrative sanction. There is no clear distinction between criminal offences

10 Justice Report, *Breaking the Rules* London: Justice, 1980, reprinted in 1987.

and administrative transgressions. Consequently there is no comprehensive list of the types of administrative breaches that theoretically may fall under the criminal law. There is the lack of any systematic prioritisation of penalty and broadly the United Kingdom has continued to deal with the problems posed in the Justice Report on an *ad hoc* basis.

Administrative sanctions that emerge from any review of the law of the United Kingdom are governed by the specific statutory arrangements that are applicable to a particular set of regulations or fall within the powers of a particular regulator. There is no specific statutory regime that applies to all public administration and there is no specific statutory code entitled administrative sanctions. The best that can be done is to fit the category of administrative decision-making into the applicable general law. This may be found both in general administrative law and also in the application of the general criminal law to administrative acts. As administrative law, in particular, and United Kingdom law in general is uncodified, it is necessary to explain how administrative sanctions have developed within the constitutional context of the United Kingdom. It will be apparent that administrative law in the United Kingdom provided a comprehensive system of remedies for breaches of administrative duties. These remedies emerge from the earliest foundations of the common law when a system of judicial remedies found in the medieval system of writs developed. From the early thirteenth century the writ system took root and from the fourteenth century it began to take its modern form. Its influence has endured in a way that is fundamental to the English legal system and Constitution. The most famous, the writ of *habeas corpus*, transcended all others in providing a remedy for unlawful imprisonment providing judicial authority to command the presence of the prisoner and where appropriate to release the defendant from custody.[11] *Habeas Corpus* illustrated many features of the English system. Remedies were often procedural in form. The writ in its early form rarely allowed the legality of imprisonment or custody to be questioned. The main focus was to ensure compliance with the writ namely that the person should be present in court on a stipulated time and day. The writ and the idea of command were synonymous with the order or authority of the court to require attendance. The process contained in the writ provided the command of the court and the compulsion on the Sheriff, as an officer of the court to compel attendance. Thus enforcement, command and sanction were rolled into the single process of the obtaining and granting of the writ of *habeas corpus*. There were many medieval writs and special procedures. It is impossible to provide an exhaustive list. The key points are that providing the courts assumed jurisdiction, the effect of the various remedies and the award of sanction were intrinsic to the

11 R.J. Sharpe, *The Law of Habeas Corpus* Oxford: Clarendon Press, 1976. Generally see M. Loughlin, *Foundations of Public Law* Oxford: Oxford University Press, 2010.

discretion of the courts and the particular sanctions and remedies that were available.

The hallmarks of the English attitudes to administrative sanctions are apparent: The use of the courts through procedural rules that require compliance with court orders; The jurisdiction of the courts determining the competence of the original decision-maker and the authority of law; The courts acting under Royal authority and determining matters according to the justice of the case; Finally, supporting court decisions through the rules linked to *stare decisis* entailing a system of binding precedent. The jurisdiction of the courts to rule on such matters was bound up with great rivalry that had been developed from the courts of common law and equity. It is apparent that the powers of the courts in terms of judicial review and oversight over procedural matters were very limited in scope. Often sanctions came about through remedies designed to test the procedures involved rather than the substance of each case. Judicial self-restraint was carefully shaped to avoid any direct conflicts between the courts and government. For example for many years the Crown was unable to be sued directly and Crown privilege or immunity provided a fetter on the rights of ordinary citizens.

In terms of settling the balance between judicial and administrative powers, it was parliamentary control over government that allowed the courts to develop their attitudes to judicial review. It was during the eighteenth and nineteenth centuries that statutory arrangements began to codify and elucidate the rules relating to administrative bodies charged with their own specific responsibilities. A hotchpotch of agencies, some statutory, some informal were created. A plethora of commissions, inquiries, inspectorates and regulators developed. The gradual expansion in the role of central government activities led to a gradual growth in the scale of government functions. Thus factory legislation, the regulation of mines, the poor law, the employment of children, public health and railways all contributed to regulatory systems involving different types of regulatory powers. One example of the multi-functional nature of such bodies is the use of public boards. Board members were appointed and nominated by government ministers. Their powers were broadly statutory but also included supervising standards of behaviour and performance. Over time the board system fell into disuse and because of their lack of appropriate accountability and direct answerability to parliament they diminished in popularity and acceptance. In contrast to the system of Boards, the role of inspectorates gathered strength. There were a whole series of inspectorates each with their own enforcement powers. The Prison Act 1835 established the prison inspectorate. A central inspectorate was formed for all alkali works under the Alkali Act 1863. A river inspectorate was established in 1876 under the Rivers Prevention of Pollution Act 1876 to ensure that pollution controls over rivers and waterways were effective. Similarly the device of an inspectorate was adopted for the system of railways under the Railways Act 1844. The industrial revolution created a series of regulatory structures, each with their own enforcement powers spanning the areas of mining, the poor law, the employment of children, public health and the regulation of licensing conditions for the sale of intoxicating drinks extended the range and variety of sanctions and enforcement powers. Government intervention into the market economy was used with a certain amount of suspicion, but it was welcomed when it was seen as an aid to industrial expansion. The Patents, Designs and Trade Marks Act 1883 set the standards of the period for the protection of industrial property and laid the foundations of the modern British patent system. Enforcement was provided by the courts and both civil and criminal law sanctions were available.

On the equity side, the relationship between trustee and the equitable trust that ranged from the development of the charitable trust to the private trust involved a whole raft of legal responsibilities and financial obligations. The operation of strict rules to protect funds and the longevity of the interests of the trust provided penalties for any breach of fiduciary duty. The influence of the fiduciary duty spilled over from the private branch of the law to the public sector involving local authorities and their councillors. This legacy endures today. Ratepayers are owed a duty of care by their councillors in respect of public money and to treat public funds in the same way as a trustee owes a duty to the beneficiaries of a trust. The sanction for the misuse of the public purse is that local authority councillors may be surcharged for any illicit spending or where the fiduciary relationship has been breached. The fiduciary relationship implies acting in good faith, avoiding conflicts of interest and securing fair dealing.[12]

Turning to more recent times, the range and variety of sanctions based on administrative law developed and expanded to meet the needs of the authorities to provide safe food, a safe place to work and to carry on industrial processes.

De Smith neatly summarises the range of possibilities[13]:

> It should be added that the exercise of many administrative enforcement powers (e.g. to abate a statutory nuisance, to destroy unwholesome food, to levy distress for rates, enter private premises for certain purposes) must be preceded by an application to a court or magistrate, and that liquor licensing – a jurisdiction that could have been entrusted to special statutory tribunals – is, and has been for over 400 years, a matter for local magistrates, who have also been made licensing authorities for various places of public entertainment, and have been empowered (in the last few years) to grant and revoke bookmakers' and betting agency permits and betting office licences.

---

12 P. Birks, "The Content of Fiduciary Obligation" (2002) 16(1) *TLI* 34. L.S. Sealy, "Fiduciary Obligations, Forty years on" (1995) 9 *JCL* 37.

13 De Smith, *Judicial Review of Administrative Action*, London: Stevens and Sons, 1968, p.17.

It will be readily apparent that in the United Kingdom judicial remedies provided an eclectic approach to administrative sanctions. Why is this so? Clearly the absence of a written constitution and the supremacy given to Parliament has given government a legal authority at a period in the formation of administrative sanctions that is quite different from most other countries. This is reflected in the way the law developed and in the various solutions provided to practical problems. It must be remembered that in the United Kingdom there has been no equivalent tradition to the system of *droit administrative* (administrative law) and no rigid distinction between public and private law, until relatively recently. The use of the criminal law was often used to underpin the practical working of the licensing system or in certain circumstances through the use of contempt of court powers, where appropriate, the courts had powers to use the criminal law to enforce civil wrongs.

It may be useful to summarise how the constitutional inheritance of the common law contributes to a wide range of sanctions. There are a wide variety of remedies available from the courts (today the administrative court) in respect of judicial review. It is possible to secure the performance of a public duty (mandamus), to have a decision quashed (certiorari) and to have a decision prohibited or prevented (prohibition). These are typical remedies available in public law. In addition there are wide ranges of private law remedies. Besides damages for unlawful administrative action, there is the use of an injunction or specific performance (in respect of contact).

Administrative sanctions may also arise from the use of collateral proceedings in an enforcement proceeding. The defence may raise the possibility in a criminal prosecution that the authorities acted outside the law (ultra *vires*). Civil proceedings to enforce some private wrong or for the non-payment of a fine or licence payment may also be questioned in collateral proceedings, raising issues about the legality of the action in the first place. Thus the system of administrative sanctions follows the nature of the complaint and the consequences of the proceedings that are used. The absence of too many rigid doctrinal distinctions between the rules governing public and private civil liability is maintained even today. Since the 1980s the exclusive jurisdiction of the Divisional Court (now the Administrative Court), over judicial review has provided a new categorisation for English lawyers. However, the inherent problem focus of the common law remains. Thus criminal proceedings may be used by public bodies such as local authorities to enforce by-laws or obligations. Indeed public authorities are themselves subject to criminal liability for any breach of their own regulations, for example in respect of food standards or in terms of Trade Descriptions Act liability.

Damages, restitution or private law remedies are available against a public authority, official or minister. There is a specific and occasionally used remedy of the tort of misfeasance in public office. The last few years has seen the general removal of special immunities enjoyed by a whole range of public officials including trade unions in respect of their civil liability arising out of trade disputes or carrying on their public duties. Public bodies are also subject to sanctions in tort or contract. Finally there is the operation of the jurisdiction of the courts in respect of infringements of human rights found under the newly enacted Human Rights Act 1998. The scope for legal challenge broadens considerably with the addition of a human rights perspective. This point is explored in more detail below.

There is the ordinary criminal law developed from its common law foundations. Thus the ordinary criminal law is applicable to administrative rule-breaking covering a range of offences from non-fatal offences against the person to manslaughter and murder. One of the areas of current discussion is the development of corporate liability, detailed below.

3. TECHNIQUES, PROCEDURES, AND PROCESSES IN ADMINISTRATIVE SANCTIONS

It is possible to consider and define administrative sanctions on an institutional basis and also based on techniques that are available to enforce sanctions. A distinction can be drawn between investigatory and inspectorate techniques, on the one hand and judicial review on the other. In the former a variety of agencies, bodies and organisations allow citizens to participate in decision-making. They also provide an opportunity for the resolution of disputes and, through this dispute resolution process, the application of administrative sanctions. The category of investigative bodies, enforcement includes inspectorates ranging from the Environment Agency, the Food Standards Agency. In the case of Food Standards, under the Food Standards Act 1999, the Agency is provided with monitoring powers for the setting of standards for food stuffs and enforcement powers to require compliance with food quality standards. A range of civil and criminal powers are available to the Agency. An important element in enforcement is publicity and generating advice through its publications provides an important forum for discussion and helps improve standards overall.

The Environment Agency, there are wide powers of enforcement. Sanctions include criminal prosecutions for environmental offences.[14] The Environment Agency is a good example of using criminal law in order to force compliance. There are a wide range of offences covering pollution including causing pollution, breaching licence conditions, or non-compliance with notices issued by the

14 For example, in 2002 there were over 29,000 confirmed pollution incidents in England and Wales. Out of this number there were 31 serious incidents that had a major impact on the environment. In 2002 there were 1,387 events that led to prosecutions and this resulted in 1,712 successful charges Environment Agency 2004.

regulator. There are also liabilities throughout the corporate chain of command up to senior managers and company directors. The penalties are substantial fines but fall short of imprisonment. The Environment Agency has powers of prosecution and provides a detailed list of their enforcement and prosecution policy.[15]

Part 3 of the Regulatory Enforcement and Sanctions Act 2008 provides for regulations to be approved by Parliament for flexible civil sanctions to be introduced and approval for the use of civil sanctions was given in March 2010. Although referred to as civil sanctions, a criminal standard of proof is required beyond a reasonable doubt before they are served, with the exception of the use of enforcement undertakings and stop notices that require the lesser civil standard of proof. Currently the powers under the Act are to be given to the Environment Agency but also extended to the Marine Conservation Organisation and may be in the future further extended to other regulators. There are five core civil sanctions applicable: Fixed Monetary Penalties, to be used for less serious offences and may be halved if paid earlier; Variable monetary penalties are to be used for more serious cases and intended to act as a deterrent through the application of variable financial penalties; Stop notices are applicable where the activity that is causing or threatening serious harm is to be halted. This is subject to compensation if the notice is withdrawn or later found to be unreasonable; Compliance notices are to be used for timely action to be taken and to ensure that an offence is prevented from being repeated. Finally, restoration notices are intended to be used where damage caused by an offence needs to be rectified. There is remarkable flexibility built into the system. There are various ways that offenders may volunteer to take action and also enter into voluntary agreements or undertakings. Only in the most serious cases will prosecutions be taken and there is an appeal to the newly created General Regulatory Chamber of the First-tier Tribunal with a further appeal on a point of law to the Upper Tribunal.

The flexibility of approach inherent in the new system is a major advance and is based on the belief that an over zealous approach to enforcement may be counter-productive. A subservient position, however, may result in the regulator not being taken seriously by the industry concerned. If the civil sanctions route fails then there is the possibility of formal criminal prosecutions in the courts. In such cases where there are criminal prosecutions, there is a need for consistency and also for the sentencing authorities, namely the courts, to adopt key

15 See www.environment-agency.gov.uk. S. Woolf and N. Stanley, *Environmental Law* London: Cavendish, 2004, p. 48. In 2001 the total penalties in fines amounted to £2.7 million. The average fine per prosecution was £6,410 for companies and £1,290 for individuals. Of the total number of pollution incidents, 13% involved waste management, 11% sewage and the water industry, 10% industry, 8% transport and 7% agriculture J. Black, *Managing the Financial Crisis-the Constitutional Dimension*, LSE (2010) Working Papers 12; R. Baldwin, "Is better regulation smarter regulation?" (2005) *Public Law* 485.

sentencing objectives[16] when considering the merits of each case. Given the variety of economic instruments that are available to regulators, it is clear that their choice should be governed by clearly published criteria and policy considerations. In the case of the Environment Agency this has proved difficult as public expectations and demands for action are an incessant pressure. In almost all case where a prosecution is thought to be successful in case involving companies, the Agency will consider criminal prosecution, unless there are very good reasons not to do so. More problematic are breaches of licence conditions[17] and the Agency has engaged in a public consultation process to consider the most appropriate policy. Despite this step there are concerns about a number of issues arising from the use of the criminal law to prevent environment pollution. There are limits on the financial resources including human resources that can be delegated to the task of investigation and prosecution. There are also media concerns if there are unsuccessful prosecutions and this may impact badly on the agency and its regulatory function in terms of morale and objectives.[18]

The privatised industries have also created a new generation of regulatory bodies all charged with responsibilities for the licensing of utilities, their regulation and performance and where appropriate the investigation of complaints. The Utilities Act 2000 provides for regulatory commissions for the energy sector. In respect of railways a commission on rail safety under the Railways and Transport Safety Act 2003 and in respect of water an office of water regulation under the Water Act 2003. Sanctions include reference powers to the Competition Commission (the former Monopolies and Mergers Commission). There are also powers to modify licences, set prices and regulate anti-competitive behaviour, as Prosser noted[19]:

> A number of licence conditions were included after telecommunications privatization aimed at prohibiting aimed at prohibiting particular customers or types of customer, or engaging in predatory behaviour or anti-competitive cross-subsidy. These, however, proved difficult to enforce, partly because it was not possible to obtain damages for their breach or to fine the companies.

It remains to be seen in the future as to the survival and role of such bodies under a more market led approach to regulation adopted by the coalition government.

---

16 *R. v F Howe & Son (Engineers) Ltd.*,[1999] 2 Cr App R 37, *R. v Yorkshire Water Services Ltd* (2001) *The Times* 12 December 2001, *R v Friskies Petcare UK Ltd* [2000] 2 Cr App R 401.

17 See www.environment-agency.gov.uk/commondata/105385/csguidance.pdf.

18 See House of Commons Select Committee on the Environment Transport and Regions, *Inquiry into the workings of the Environment Agency*, 6th Report HC 484 (1997–8).

19 T. Prosser, "Regulation, Markets and Legitimacy", in: Jowell and Oliver (eds.,) *The Changing Constitution* Oxford: Oxford University Press, 2004, p. 361.

There are lessons to be gained from the recent experience of the Financial Services Authority (FSA), which has considerable sanctions including levying fines under the Financial Services and Markets Act 2000. The Financial Services Authority has extensive regulatory powers to supervise the financial services sector, including powers to regulate insider dealing and fight financial crime or fraud. Section 401 – 403 of the Proceedings for Offences Act 2000 provides powers to prosecute for a variety of offences relating to insider dealing, money laundering, and fraud and market abuse there are specific statutory offences. Prosecution discretion includes taking cases to court or issuing a formal caution.[20]

In addition to the criminal jurisdiction of the FSA, the FSA has a large civil jurisdiction that imposes civil sanctions for market abuse under section 118 of the Financial Services and Markets Act 2000. This is enforced by the FSA through its own specialist tribunal. Insider dealing falls within this jurisdiction as set out in the Market Abuse Directive[21] under the Financial Services and Markets Act 2000 (Market Abuse) Regulations 2005.[22] The use of civil sanctions is consistent with the direction favoured by the European Union and it is also part of a wide-ranging debate on the use of civil sanctions and their application in the regulatory process in the United Kingdom.[23] On 3 August 2010, the FSA fined the Royal Bank of Scotland £5.6 million for failing to have adequate systems and screening procedures to prevent money laundering. The NAO noted how important[24] civil sanctions had become to the work of the FSA and this remains the case today.

Initially the FSA was not active in pursuing criminal prosecutions in the courts. Only in 2005, was the first criminal prosecution against market abuse taken[25] and this was successful. Even by 2007 there had been no insider dealing prosecutions under the Criminal Justice Act 1993taken by the FSA. This may have reflected a policy approach to use prosecutions sparingly or recognition of the high evidential burdens required to mount successful prosecutions. The need for jury trial and the complexity of financial instruments and markets may also have inhibited the use of prosecutions. Difficulties of detection are also evident

---

20 FSA Press Release 19 July 2004.

21 Directive 2003/6/EC.

22 SI 2005 No. 381.

23 R. Macrory (May 2006) *Regulatory Justice: Sanctioning in a post-Hampton World: A Consultation Document,* London: Cabinet Office and *Regulatory Justice: Making Sanctions Effective* London: Cabinet Office (November 2006).

24 NAO *The Financial Services Authority: A review under section 12 of the Financial Services and Markets Act 2000* HC 500 Session 2006–07 (27 April 2007) p. 49. noted that from 2001–02 there were an average of 200 cases each year dealing with money laundering and other breaches of the financial standards. At para. 4.63 2005–06, 17 cases involving financial penalties totalling £17.4 million, £14million of which was for one market protection case and £505,00 related specifically to financial crime.

25 *R. v Rigby, Bailey and Rowley* [2005] EWCA 3487.

in such cases. The fear of detection and the threat of criminal prosecutions may also act as a deterrent reducing the need for prosecutions. Certainly monitoring and surveillance are likely to be easier if the threat of criminal prosecutions is not aggressively pursued.

The banking crisis has changed the FSA's approach. Following the Turner Review[26], the FSA adopted a more intensive supervisory model in an attempt to redress past regulatory shortcomings. The use of fines and prosecutions was intensified. *The Economist* noted: 'That year (2009) saw a big change in the level and nature of fines imposed by the FSA: £34.9 million ($54.6 million) compared with £22.7 million in 2008 and just £5.3 million in 2007'.[27] Goldman Sachs was fined £17.5 million for weaknesses in failing to provide the FSA with appropriate financial information[28]and more recently, Royal Bank of Scotland and NatWest were fined £2.8 million for poor handling of customers' complaints.[29]

In fact the FSA is getting tougher and more vigilant. At the end of March 2010 a large investigation into insider dealing resulted in the arrest of six, amongst them employees of Deutsche Bank, BNP Paribas and Moore Capital, a large Hedge Fund. This accompanied large-scale penalties against a former interest rate trader at Merrill Lynch (a ban of at least five years) and the prosecution of a former stock broker at Cazenove. The FSA hired an additional 460 staff and the largest banks have been allocated 15 officials permanently stationed at the individual Bank's headquarters. No one can doubt that regulation is likely to be more intense as shown by criminal prosecutions such as *R. v Rollins* and *R. v McInerney*[30] where the Court of Appeal secured an important extension of prosecution powers for the FSA to prosecute beyond sections 401 and 402 of the Financial Services and Markets Act 2000 to include sections 327 and 328 under the Proceeds of Crime Act 2002.[31]

The FSA's own Business Plan 2010/11 is indicative of the robust approach planned by the FSA that includes deterrence, changing the current culture, and linking regulation and financial stability.[32] After the election of a new coalition government in May 2010 it was announced that the FSA's role and responsibilities will cease and be taken up by the Bank of England. The future of criminal prosecutions depends on the development of a network of information and adoption of strategies to combat market manipulation and abuse. General market misconduct needs to be addressed through the successful prosecution of

---

26 FSA, *The Turner Review: A regulatory response to the global banking crisis* London: March, 2009.

27 *The Economist* 27 March 2010, p. 81.

28 9 September 2010 see FSA reports.

29 11 January 2011 see FSA reports.

30 [2009] EWCA Crim 1941, [2010] 1 All ER 1183.

31 FSA *Decision Procedure and Penalties Manual and the Enforcement Guide* (PS07/12).

32 FSA's Annual Review for 2008–09 reported that the FSA imposed a record £27.3 million in financial penalties compared to an average of £14 million over the previous five years with an increase in FSA investigations and inquiries.

high profile hard cases and also through a public awareness and debate about strategy and how the public interest is to be protected. This debate is likely to be controversial especially in the face of issues such as the granting of immunities in return for evidence, whistle blowing within the city and even the use of 'supergrasses' for collecting evidence. There are dangers in malicious motives on the part of individuals that might give rise to unjust prosecutions. There are considerable doubts about the effectiveness of such strategies[33] in the light of human rights considerations and protections afforded to the accused. There is also a debate over whether civil or criminal sanctions are to be given priority and which is likely to be most cost effective and offer adequate deterrence.

Investigative techniques are a common way to provide sanctions. These are very much linked to the role of select committees in Parliament. Select Committees of both Houses have considerable powers to summon witnesses and hear evidence under the authority of Parliament and subject to contempt of court powers. Sanctions are very much linked to the judicial idea of command and control. A critical finding or censure of the government may lead to ministerial resignation or a disciplinary finding against a civil servant or department. This is increasingly rare as often the findings of select committees divide on party political lines, thus giving rise to very few modern instances where ministers resign because of a mistake or error of judgement.

Similarly, the National Audit Act 1983 provides the Comptroller and Auditor General, who is an Officer of the House of Commons, the power to inquire into the "economy, efficiency and effectiveness "of central government departments. This is very much couched in terms of a quasi-judicial role calling for the evaluation of value for money and standards of administration in respect of the duty to obtain best value for public spending. In this example, sanctions come in various forms. Criticism from the Comptroller and Auditor General may take the form of qualifying the department's accounts or in the case of a critical finding to make recommendations for improvements in financial scrutiny in the department's running of its accounts. This may give rise to sanctions such as having to appear before the Public Accounts Committee or as a result of the audit of a department's budget, the additional money having to be taken from existing resources that would otherwise fund some other activity.

Sanctions for maladministration in both local and central government are provided though the Office of the Ombudsman. At local government there are Local Commissioners, at central government the Parliamentary Commissioner for Administration (PCA) and also a Health Service Commissioner. This is very much a complaints driven system. It is also an example where sanctions may appear weak. There are no formal powers to award any remedy. Investigations

---

33 Wilson, G. and Wilson, S., 'Market misconduct, the Financial Services Authority and creating a system of "city grasses": blowing the whistle on whistle blowing' (2010) *Company Lawyer* 67, p. 80.

are undertaken and conclusions reached on the basis that a complaint may or may not be upheld. *Ex gratia* payments may be made when appropriate. In high profile cases with publicity and media attention this may add to the PCA's reach to obtain redress. However, this should not suggest that the PCA is without influence. There is a Select Committee on the PCA. This provides a forum in appropriate cases for his reports to be discussed. In the face of departmental reluctance to provide a remedy this may tip the balance in his favour. The most controversial is the Equitable Life affair leading to complex compensation schemes being set up to provide ex gratia compensation after considerable pressure from the PCA.[34]

For local government, there are Local Commissioners. Their remit is similar to the PCA and are complaints driven in terms of investigating cases of alleged maladministration. Again sanctions are practical in focus and remedial in action. Compensation is often used to put the complainant back in the position before the conduct complained about. The Local Commissioners in their role are linked to settling internal grievances. There is no equivalent of the Select Committee for the PCA to which the Local Commissioners may report. It has been suggested that one way forward is to have some kind of judicial enforcement of their decisions.[35] However, this view has not been supported by government legislation.

4. COMPANIES AND CRIMINAL LAW

The use of the criminal law[36] in the regulation of corporate and individual liability has developed as a result of recent accidents. These include the King's Cross Fire, various railway crashes, most notably at Southall and also the Zeebrugge Ferry disaster. Criminal sanctions involving companies include vicarious liability. This means that a company can be held responsible for the acts of its employees when acting within the terms of their employment contract. Historically there has been great reluctance to use manslaughter or other serious offences to penalise companies. This is partly because of the difficulty of finding evidence that meets the higher test of beyond reasonable doubt. There are also questions of public policy as to whether it is in the public interest to prosecute company directors. There is also the limitation that the main punishment for a company found guilty of some offence is a fine. The current law does not allow a company to be found guilty of murder which carries a mandatory life sentence[37]

34 See the Equitable Life Payments Bill 2010.

35 See: N. Lewis, and P. Birkinshaw, *When Citizens Complain, Reforming Justice and Administration* Open University, 1993.

36 See J. Coffee, "No soul to Damn: No Body to Kick: An Unscandalized Inquiry into the Problem of Corporate Punishment", (1981) 79 *Michigan LR* 386.

37 *IRC Haulage Ltd* [1944] KB 551. See Jonathan Herring, *Criminal Law Text Cases and Materials* Oxford; Oxford University Press, 2004.

The current law in the United Kingdom is drawn from the House of Lords decision in *Tesco v Nattrass*[38] and more recently settled in the Court of Appeal in the *Attorney-General's Reference (No. 2 of 1999)*[39] The Attorney-General's Reference arose out of the circumstances where a company charged with manslaughter following the Southall rail crash in 1997, could be guilty of manslaughter? The question was answered in the following way. If the company itself is to be convicted, it is necessary to show that there is a single person who has "the mind and will" of the company where the offence involves proving *mens rea*. The appropriate identification with a single responsible person within the company such as a senior manager appears to be a pre-requisite for a conviction. This is particularly relevant in terms of the wide variety of statutory offences that are applicable and where liability on the company would depend on identifying such a responsible person. The Court of Appeal rejected the idea that the most appropriate way to find company liability is to operate a principle of "aggregation" namely adding together the sum total of the states of mind of several senior managers to form a coherent whole. On the basis of "aggregated" guilt then the company might be liable.

In the House of Lords in *Tesco Stores Ltd., v Brent LBC*[40] Tesco was found guilty of supplying an 18 rated video to an under-age child. The video was supplied at the check-out by an employee. However, it was clear that the company had failed to provide a sufficient command and control system and that failure led to the company being liable. The status and responsibility of the individual employee is one of the most important determining factors in assessing corporate liability. Usually where there are strict liability crimes involved it is easier to find liability. However, in cases involving proving *mens rea* this is often problematic.[41] Thus the installation of a manger or assistant to deputise for senior management responsibility can be crucial when attributing liability.

This leaves room for considerable uncertainty. Unless the main subordinate is somehow linked to the senior management of the company there is difficulty in attributing guilt at the level that is sufficient to give rise to company liability. In terms of large companies, especially with complicated command and control systems, there is considerable difficulty and therefore doubt about finding company liability through the impossibility of finding a senior enough manager to take responsibility. In *P&O Ferries (Dover) Ltd.*,[42] a case arising from the Zeebrugge Ferry disaster, following the findings of an inquiry and then the prosecution of the it was not easy to find the Master of the Ship as part of the corporate structure of the company.

---

38 *Tesco v Nattrass* [1972] AC 153 (HL).

39 [2000] QB 796 Court of Appeal.

40 *Tesco v Brent* [1993] 2 All ER 718.

41 *Vane v Yiannopoullos* [1965] AC 486.

42 (1990) 93 Cr. App R. 72.

In contrast to large companies, small companies do not provide the same obstacles and therefore it may be easier to trace responsibility through to senior management.

Even though there is a new offence of corporate manslaughter there have been few successful prosecutions to date.[43] The Manslaughter and Corporate Homicide Act 2007 was passed is in response to public concerns about companies failing to exercise sufficient responsibility over their employees.[44] However there are a number of examples showing wide variation in the use of the criminal law and wide disparity in success.

The Health and Safety Executive is another good example of using prosecutions as a form of risk based regulation[45] Jonathan Herring[46] has pointed out a large proportion of workplace deaths were preventable (possibly between 70–85%) but under 20% of such cases is there a prosecution. Since 2003 there have been new guidelines covering the prosecution of deaths and also health and safety offences. In the case of the seven deaths from the Southall rail disaster a large fine of £1.5 million was paid. It is clear that public demand for penalties for perceived corporate failures comes from a number of concerns. First, there is the perception that the law is to readily used to penalise low paid employees who may be poorly educated and in unskilled jobs. Junior employees are seen as scapegoats leaving senior management and Directors free of liability when they may in fact be more to blame especially if there is a poor chain of command in place. Second there has been a public striving for greater safety given the variable track record in terms of food[47], health and medicine, rail safety and general social welfare including sporting events and activities. The public often feel that it is important to find fault and attribute blame as part of a general response to disaster.

This is a reflection of the shift in expectations that new technology and higher standards have given rise to in the public's mind and of the role of the media. Company activities have proliferated over the past two decades, often places them at the forefront of the relationship between the citizen and the particular

---

43 The background to the legislation see: *Law Commission Report* No. 237 (1996), *Home Office Report* (2000) and *Statement from Ten Downing Street* in 2003. The first case was in February 2010 against Cotswold Geotechnical Holdings Ltd. and after protracted investigations the case was dropped in December 2010.

44 See: S. Tombs and D. Whyte, " A deadly consensus: worker safety and regulatory degradation under New Labour", (2010) *British Journal of Criminology* 46.

45 The Health and Safety Executive reports for the year 2001–2 there were 249 fatal injuries to employees in the workplace, and 384 fatal injuries to members of the public (although 275 of these were acts of suicide or trespass onto railway systems).
In 35% of these there was a prosecution by the Health and Safety Executive, but a fine is the normal punishment Jonathan Herring, *Criminal Law Text Cases and Materials* Oxford; Oxford University Press, 2004, p. 729.

46 Jonathan Herring, *op.cit.*, p. 729.

47 The BSE crisis, the finding of salmonella in eggs, the development of a Food Agency in response to public concerns about food safety.

danger or activity. This has caused a trail of fault finding, often led by the media, directed at the prosecution authorities to react to blameworthy events. Very often the use of independent inquiries or reports has provided evidence in the public domain upon which blame may be attributed. When this does not result in criminal or civil liability, the public tend to loose confidence in the system and in regulation as a whole.

Lord Young's recent review of the Health and Safety[48] voiced concern about the growing compensation culture that was a product of excessive application of health and safety rules. His "no nonsense approach called for simplification, clarification and a" light touch" approach to regulation amidst mounting claims and costs. Administrative sanctions do not operate inside a political vacuum. It is clear that Lord Young's approach is influential, despite concerns that this might be moving towards a form of ineffective self regulation with little or no compliance. There is a potential over reliance on risk-based regulation that is linked to market regulation.[49]

It is important to understand that Richard MacRory's influential report, discussed above, in favour of extending civil liability rather than criminal law[50]is in reaction to the trend to criminalise many anti- social activities. The arguments in favour of strengthening civil liability fit with the civil status of companies and the use of corporate accountability mechanisms. Companies subject to criminal liability in the commercial world may only marginally change their behaviour to avoid breaches of the law when the limits of criminal law are in terms of fines and not imprisonment. The danger of using the criminal law is also bound up with the perception of using criminal sanctions for activities that are not really "criminal acts". Law breaking and rule-bending are not at a sufficient level to justify criminal sanctions. There are doubts that criminal law will be effective as in essence the blameworthiness calibrated in a fine or in some form of civil damages may be seen as no different. This appears to emerge from the Environment Agency's prosecution of environmental offences. The scale of fines has escalated but there appears to be no causal link to the diminution of environmental damage.[51]

Finally it is worth mentioning that the Human Rights Act 1998 which came into force in October 2000 brings the European Convention on Human Rights into the United Kingdom's domestic law. It also has potential to impact on how administrative sanctions should operate. In cases where the public body may act in breach of the Act, the courts have a duty to uphold rights and as far as it is

---

48 Lord Young of Graffham, *Common Sense – Common Safety*, Report to the Prime Minister October 2010.

49 See Steve Tombs and David Whyte, *op.cit.*

50 See: C.M.V. Clarkson, "Corporate Culpability" [1998] *Web Journal of Current Legal Issues.*

51 See ENDS Reports 2003–4 setting out the fines for different water companies each month but there appears to be no obvious change in the performance of the company in terms of environmental damage.

practicable to do so give account to rights. In respect of primary legislation the Act allows the court to grant a declaration of incompatibility. While this falls short of holding the Act unconstitutional or illegal, it permits the courts to give Parliament an opportunity to remedy the incompatibility between an Act of Parliament and convention rights. This may appear to concede judicial power to the political authority of the government of the day. In theory it is quite possible for Parliament to refuse to remedy the incompatibility identified the courts. In such instances there may be a request for the Strasbourg Court to consider whether UK law is compatible with convention rights. In cases where Parliament regards the incompatibility as sufficient, an order may be made amending primary legislation to render the legislation compatible with human rights. In this example the limits placed on administrative sanctions are very much linked to the traditional doctrine of Parliamentary sovereignty.[52] The question of whether the Human Rights Act applies may depend on whether or not the body in question is a public body.[53] The Act also brings into domestic law Article 6 (the right to a fair trial) of the European Convention on Human Rights in complementing the way that investigations and elements of proof are undertaken under the existing Police and Criminal Evidence Act legislation.

5. CONCLUSIONS

In drawing together some conclusions about the variety of administrative sanctions available in the United Kingdom it is important to emphasise how distinctive the United Kingdom's legal system and constitutional arrangements really are. In the absence of any fundamental legal code there it is clear that administrative sanctions are related to the type of complaint, the circumstances of how best to provide compliance and how effective sanctions are intended to be. For example persuading the administrative body to make a remedy may take the form of political and media pressure which may be just as effective as judicial or legal intervention. There is no classical typology of the regulatory body or the administrative decision-maker. The circumstances surrounding the creation of the agency or administrative decision-maker very often may determine the range of remedies that are available. Many administrative bodies utilise economic instruments or fiscal arrangements to implement their policies. The most recent example of such an approach is the use of congestion charging in parts of central London. The effectiveness of the charging regime has seen a diminution in traffic flows and a corresponding reduction in congestion.

There is no consistency in legal principles that give rise to regulatory or administrative compliance. The randomness of judicial review, the

52 *Marcic v Thames Water Utilities Ltd.* [2002] 2 All ER 55.
53 *Smartsource v Information Commissioner* [2010] UKUT 415.

unpredictability of legal challenges all provide uncertainty in the effectiveness of legal sanctions based on arguments before courts. As Halliday[54] has shown in his study of homelessness, the applicability of legal sanctions through judicial review depends on the awareness of the parties of their legal position as well as to eventual success in court. The importance of legal conscientiousness is a key component to the application of the law to administrative sanctions. The availability of legal aid and public funds is also an important consideration. Finally, there is evidence of an increasing popularity to rely on criminal sanctions or to adopt what Baldwin[55] refers to as a "punitive" approach to sanctions as part of an ongoing development in the field of regulation. The MacRory review[56] was path breaking by creating many flexible civil sanctions to provide a responsive and prudent approach to enforcement that is cost effective. It is too early to evaluate how the civil sanctions system will operate.

The most significant trend is that the criminal law is being used by a wide variety of regulatory bodies to provide fines for companies engaged in unsafe or environmentally harmful activities. The introduction of the Manslaughter and Corporate Homicide Act 2007 did not result in large scale prosecutions, but it might have an instrumental influence on the culture of many companies. At the end of 2012 there were 63 corporate manslaughter cases in the United Kingdom, but to date there have only been three convictions. The link between fines and improvements in company conduct, however, is not demonstrated. There are doubts about the effectiveness of fines unless they are linked to a sliding scale taking into account past behaviour and future improvement. The stigma attached to the criminal law is not always a guarantee of improvement in conduct. Sanctions are also a manifestation of different approaches to regulation and in the era of financial crisis and government spending cuts the role of sanctions and their effectiveness is at the top of the political agenda once more.[57] The form of regulation that is most effective is open to debate in the aftermath of the failures of financial regulation. Administrative sanctions are increasingly important and their success is linked to appropriate enforcement policy as part of regulatory governance. This is aimed at securing good behaviour and to ensure that the choice of sanction is part of enforcement policy.

---

54 Halliday *op.cit.*, p. 170. J. Black, M. Hopper, C. Band, "Making a success of Principles-based regulation", (2007) *Law and Financial Markets* 191–206.

55 R. Baldwin, "The New Punitive Regulation", (2004) 67(3) *Modern Law Review* 351. J. Black, "Tensions in the regulatory state", (2007) *Public Law* 58.

56 See R. MacRory, "Legislative Comment: Reforming regulatory sanctions- a personal perspective", (2009) *Environmental Law Review* 69.

57 C. Harlow and R. Rawlings, *Law and Administration Law in Context*, 3rd edition, Cambridge: Cambridge University Press, 2009. Also see D. Kershaw, "Evading Enron: Taking Principle Too seriously In Accounting Regulation", (2005) 68(4) *MLR* 594–625.

SELECT BIBLIOGRAPHY

Alan, TRS, *Law, Liberty and Justice: Legal Foundations of British Constitutionalism* Oxford: Clarendon Press, 1993.

Arndt, HW, "The Origins of Dicey's Concept of the Rule of Law", (1957) 31 *Australian Law Journal* 117.

Arthurs, H, *"Without the Law": Administrative Justice and Legal Pluralism in Nineteenth Century England* Toronto: University of Toronto Press, 1985.

Baldwin, R., "The New Punitive Regulation", (2004) 67(3) *Modern Law Review* 351–83.

Baldwin, R., "Is better regulation smarter regulation?", (2005) *Public Law*, 485.

Bergman, D., *The Case for Corporate Responsibility*, London: 2000.

Birks, P., "The Content of Fiduciary Obligation", (2002) 16(1) *TLI* 34.

Black, J. "Tensions in the regulatory state", (2007) *Public Law* 58, p. 66.

Black, J., *Managing the Financial Crisis-the Constitutional Dimension*, LSE (2010) Working Papers 12.

Black, J., Hopper,M., Band,C., "Making a success of Principles-based regulation", (2007) *Law and Financial Markets* 191–206.

Coffee, J, "No soul to Damn: No Body to Kick: An Unscandalized Inquiry into the Problem of Corporate Punishment", (1981) 79 *Michigan LR* 386.

Cosgrove, RA, *The Rule of Law: Albert Venn Dicey, Victorian Jurist*, London: Macmillan, 1980.

Craig, P.P., *Administrative Law*, 6th edition, London: Sweet and Maxwell, 2008.

Eddy, H., *Sanctions, Compliance Policy and Administrative Law*, Unpublished Law Reform Commission of Canada Paper, 1981).

Fisse, B., and Braithwaite, J., "The Allocation of Responsibility for Corporate Crime: Individualism, Collectivism and Accountability", (1988) 11 *Sydney L R* 468.

Fisse, B., *Corporations, Crime and Accountability*, Cambridge: Cambridge University Press, 1993.

Glazebrook,P., " A better way of Convicting Business of Avoiding Deaths and Injuries?", 2002 (61) *Cambridge Law Journal* 405.

Gobert, J, and Punch, M., *Rethinking Corporate Crime*, London: Butterworths, 2003.

Halliday, S., *Judicial Review and Compliance with Administrative Law*, Oxford: Hart Publishing, 2004.

Hampton, P., *Reducing Administrative Burdens: Effective Inspection and Enforcement Final Report*, London: HM Treasury, 2005.

Harlow,C., and Rawlings, R., *Law and Administration*, 3rd edition, Cambridge: Cambridge University Press, 2009.

Hawkins, K., *Law as Last resort: Prosecution Decision-making in a Regulatory Agency*, Oxford: Oxford University Press, 2002.

Herring,J., *Criminal Law Text Cases and Materials*, Oxford: Oxford University Press, 2004.

Hutter, B., *Compliance: Regulation and the Environment*, Oxford: Clarendon Press, 1997.

Jowell, J. and Oliver, D. (eds), *The Changing Constitution*, 7th edition, Oxford: Clarendon Press, 2011.

Judson, ML, *The Crisis of the Constitution 1603–1645*, New Brunswick NJ: Rutgers University Press, 1949.

Justice, *Breaking the Rules, British Section of the International Commission of Jurists* London: Justice, 1980, reprinted in 1987.

Keir, DL, *The Constitutional History of Modern Britain 1485–1937,* 3rd edn, London: Adam and Charles Black, 1948.

Kershaw, D., "Evading Enron: Taking Principle Too seriously In Accounting Regulation", (2005) 68(4) *MLR* 594–625.

Law Reform Commission of Canada, *Policy Implementation, Compliance and Administrative Law* Working Paper, 51 Ottawa: 1986.

Law Commission of Canada, *What is a Crime? Challenges and Alternatives Discussion Paper,* Canada: Law Commission, 2003.

Lederman, J., "Models for Imposing Corporate Criminal Liability: from adaptation and imitation towards aggregation and the search for self-identity", [2001] *Buffalo Crim LR* 642.

Lewis, N and Birkinshaw, P., *When Citizens Complain, Reforming Justice and Administration,* Open University, 1993.

Loughlin, M., *Foundations of Public Law,* Oxford: Oxford University Press, 2010.

MacRory, P., *Regulatory Justice: Sanctioning in a post-Hampton World: A Consultation Document,* London: Cabinet Office, May 2006.

MacRory, P., *Regulatory Justice: Making Sanctions Effective* London: Cabinet Office, November 2006.

McAuslan, JPWB, "Administrative Law, Collective Consumption and Judicial Policy", (1983) 46 *Modern Law Review* 1.

McAuslan, JPWB, "Dicey and His Influence on Public Law", [1985] *Public Law* 721.

McAuslan, JPWB, "Public Law and Public Choice", (1988) 51 *Modern Law Review* 681.

McEldowney, J.F., 'Defining the public interest: Public Law Perspectives on Regulating the Financial Crisis', in: John Raymond LaBrosse, Rodrigo Olivare-Caminal and Dalvinder Singh (eds.), *Financial Crisis Management and Bank Resolution,* London: Informa, 2009, pp. 103–132.

Ogus, A., "Regulation revisited", (2009) *Public law* 332.

Oliver, D., Prosser, T., Rawlings, R., *The Regulatory State,* Oxford: Oxford University Press, 2010.

Prosser, T., "Regulation, Markets and Legitimacy" in Jowell and Oliver (eds.), *The Changing Constitution,* Oxford: Oxford University Press, 2004, p. 361.

Sealy, L.S., "Fiduciary Obligations, Forty years on", (1995) 9 *JCL* 37.

Sullivan, G.R., "The Attribution of Culpability to Limited Companies", (1966) 55 *Cambridge Law Journal* 515.

Talbot, C., "The Regulatory Enforcement and Sanctions Act 2008", (2009) *Environmental Law Review* 38.

Tombs, S., and Whyte, D., "A deadly consensus: worker safety and regulatory degradation under New Labour", (2010) *British Journal of Criminology* 46.

Waldron, J, *The Law, Theory and Practice in British Politics,* London: Routledge, 1990.

Waldron, J, "A Rights-Based Critique of Constitutional Rights", (1993) 13 *Oxford Journal of Legal Studies* 18.

Wells, C., *Corporations and Criminal Responsibility,* 2nd edition, Oxford: Oxford University Press, 2001.

Wilson, G., and Wilson, S. (2010) 'Market misconduct, the Financial Services Authority and creating a system of "city grasses": blowing the whistle on whistle blowing', *Company Lawyer,* 67, p. 80.

XV. ADMINISTRATIVE SANCTIONS IN EU LAW

Adrienne de Moor-van Vugt*

1. INTRODUCTION

The European context has certainly been favourable to the development of administrative sanctions. EU law itself has stimulated the introduction of several kinds of administrative sanctions which Member States themselves did not have. And the European Court of Human Rights (ECtHR or Human Rights Court) has made it clear that states are allowed to use the instrument of administrative sanctions, as long as they observe the fundamental standards of Article 6 of the European Convention for the Protection of Human Rights and Fundamental Freedoms (ECHR), when the sanction is of a punitive nature.

Over time, both the European legal orders have adopted similar standards when it comes to imposing punitive sanctions. And not only that, but they have drawn nearer to each other; especially the EU has explicitly adopted the standards of the ECHR, after a period of time in which the Court of Justice developed its own EC standards on the basis of the principles that are common to the laws of the Member States.

When we look at the European framework for administrative sanctions, we see that Union law provides for several instruments to impose sanctions, whereas the ECHR ensures that the protection of the individual is taken care of. Of course, this is depicted too simply, and in reality both systems have each influenced national law in their own way, whereas the national systems in their turn have influenced both parts of the European framework.

In the following sections we will take a look at the European framework for administrative sanctioning from the perspective of Union law. Union law recognises different kinds of administrative sanctions, and it has also developed procedural guarantees for the offender. Since those guarantees have been

* This contribution was originally completed in September 2004. The text has been revised in October 2007 and (with the help of P.J. Krop LL.M) in January 2011. Currently, De Moor-van Vugt is professor of administrative law at the University of Amsterdam (The Netherlands). An elaborated version of this contribution has also been published in *Review of European Administrative Law* (REALaw) 2012–1.

inspired by the European Convention and refined by the ECtHR, the importance of the European Convention will be discussed as well.

2. ENFORCEMENT OF UNION LAW BY WAY OF ADMINISTRATIVE SANCTIONING

2.1. THE STARTING POINT

Traditionally, criminal law was considered to fall within the ambit of exclusive national sovereignty. The social, economic and cultural aspects related to criminal law were too different for Member States to be prepared to confer powers in that field to the E(E)C. From the outset it was clear that the Member States of the former EEC were not keen on handing over their sanctioning powers. Hence, jurisdiction in criminal matters was explicitly reserved for the Member States. However, the European Commission was given some powers in the field of the production of coal and steel and in the field of competition law. It was empowered to impose administrative fines directly on companies, which had acted in breach of the EEC and ECSC Regulations. Thus, the power to impose sanctions *and* to legislate them was concentrated on either the national level, or the Community level. This situation left more or less a vacuum with respect to the enforcement of E(E)C rules that needed to be implemented and executed by the Member States. The European Commission only had supervising powers to make sure that Member States lived up to their duties, but could not deal with infringements of E(E)C law; that needed to be done on the national level.

Over time, this became a serious flaw in the system. The European Commission found itself in a difficult situation when it concluded that the enforcement of Community law should be enhanced. It had virtually no instruments with which to do so.

Something needed to be done. The fraud against the EC budget was estimated to be up to 10 to 25% of the EC budget as a whole. This considerable amount was lost every budget year. Over time, not only the financial interests of the EC were an issue when it came to enforcement, but also the protection of the environment, the safeguarding of the free movement of goods, the rights of employees and other EC rights and freedoms. Much was done by the Commission in its supervising capacity by means of the action for failure to fulfil obligations. This was not sufficient though, because at that time the Commission had no means to enforce a Court's judgment that a Member State needed to fulfil it's obligations under EC law (now Article 260 TFEU).[1] When it comes to the topic of

1 References to articles in the EC treaties are adjusted to numbers in the Lisbon Treaty, unless it is functional to use the old numbers.

sanctioning, however, we can learn the most in the fields of the protection of the financial interests of the (former) EC (combating fraud against the EC budget) and competition law. The developments in the field of criminal law remain unmentioned, since the subject of this contribution pertains to administrative sanctioning.

2.2. FILLING THE GAP

We have just seen that the Commission did not have enough powers to make sure that Member States would react to infringements of EC law. The Commission started searching for ways to tackle this problem. It was found in the principle of loyal cooperation.

The principle of loyal cooperation, laid down in Article 4 §3 TFEU, is the most important basis for the duties of Member States to put an adequate sanctioning system into place. The Court of Justice decided that Member States are perfectly allowed to impose sanctions against infringements of Community law, even if the Treaty or secondary legislation do not provide for an explicit legal basis for them to do so.[2] And, not only that, in fact they have a *duty* to react to a breach of Community law under the rule of loyal cooperation. In the Greek Maize ruling the Court of Justice set this as a standard for future cases.[3] It added that, as a general rule, Member States are free to choose the way in which they wish to react: by means of civil, penal or administrative law. This freedom of choice is not unconditional: the sanctions must be effective, proportional and deterrent,[4] and it may be added that under circumstances this might mean that only criminal penalties are adequate in the eyes of the Court.[5] This stance in the case law was codified for fraud cases in (now) Article 325 TFEU. In following cases the Court ruled that Member States can be obliged to act upon infringements of Community law and start proceedings to enforce the rules. Not doing so can give rise to an action for failure to fulfil obligations.[6]

Over the years the freedom of choice has been limited by several regulations in which the EC prescribes which sanctions to use when Member State authorities detect an infringement of specific provisions. At first, this was done in regulations on a specific topic, for instance, premiums for sheep or cattle. Later on, the sanctions were clustered in sector regulations, applicable to all

2 Case 50/76, *Produktschap voor siergewassen* [1977] ECR 137; reiterated in case C-180/95, *Draehmpahl* [1997] ECR I- 2195.

3 Case 68/88, *Commission vs Greece* [1989] ECR 2965.

4 Case C-326/88, *Hansen and Son* [1990] ECR I-2911.

5 Case C-176/03, *Commission/Council* [2005] ECR I-7879.

6 Case C-265/95, *Commission/France* (Spanish strawberries) [1997] ECR I-6959; C-494/01, *Commission/Ireland* [2005] ECR I-3331; C-304/02 *Commission/France* [2005] ECR I-6263; C-119/04, *Commission/Italy* [2006] ECR I-6885, Case C-232/08, *Commission/The Netherlands* [2009] ECR I-166.

regulations in the sector of agriculture or fishery etc. The next step was to put all the sector regulations together and make one general regulation on the protection of the financial interests of the EC.[7] This Regulation 2988/95 prescribes several administrative sanctions in cases of irregularities against the rules and regulations of the Structural Funds of the EC. It is clear that these compulsory reactions to infringements are meant to fall within the scope of administrative law. The sanctions mentioned in the Regulation must be considered as possible reactions to infringements of Community law. The duty of Member States to impose them, stems from the more specific Regulations in the various sectors.[8] These Regulations can also provide for other sanctions, not mentioned in Regulation 2988/95.[9] Moreover, a Member State cannot lay down national penalties of a certain type (i.c. reductions and exclusions from the total amount of Community aid which can be claimed by a farmer who has applied for a slaughter premium), in case penalties of that type are already set out in detail in a Community Regulation.[10]

The Regulations and their sanctions were put into place after an extensive discussion within the institutions and with the Member States about the guarantees that should be available to the individual, when confronted with a possible sanction. Questions about the position of the individual in the preparatory stage of a sanction, the right to a fair hearing, the right to silence, the period of limitation, the guarantee of *ne bis in idem*, especially in cases when criminal penalties and administrative sanctions can be applied for the same offence, and access to justice played an important role in the discussions.

2.3. A QUESTION OF COMPETENCE

An important issue was dealt with by the Court of Justice in a case, which Germany started against one of the predecessors of Regulation 2988/95.[11] Germany was of the opinion that the EC did not have the competence to issue a Regulation in which it prescribed to the Member States that they had to use sanctions of a penal nature. Referring to the Member States' sovereignty in

7 Council Regulation (EC, Euratom) No. 2988/95 of 18 December 1995 on the protection of the European Communities financial interests, OJ L 312, 23.12.1995, pp. 1–4.

8 E.g. Commission Regulation (EC) No 2419/2001 of 11 December 2001 laying down detailed rules for applying the integrated administration and control system for certain Community aid schemes established by Council Regulation (EEC) No. 3508/92, OJ L 327, 12.12.2001, pp. 11–32, Article 33.

9 Article 5 para. 1, sub. g Regulation 2988/95; an example can be found in Council Regulation (EC) No 820/97 of 21 April 1997 establishing a system for the identification and registration of bovine animals and regarding the labelling of beef and beef products, OJ L 117, 7.5.1997, pp. 1–8, Article 21.

10 Case C-45/05, *Maatschap Schonewille-Prins* [2007] ECR I-3997.

11 Case C-240/90, *Germany/Commission* [1992] ECR I-5383.

criminal matters, Germany stated that punishment had always been the privilege of the Member States, and that this privilege had now been violated.

The sanctions Germany objected to were the surcharge and the exclusion. A surcharge can be imposed when a farmer is in default of his obligations stemming from an income support programme. Not only must he reimburse the support already paid, but, in addition, he is also required to pay an extra amount of money. Exclusion means that a farmer is excluded from a future subvention programme, because he has violated the rules of the current programme or of an earlier one. Both sanctions are meant to punish. It was Germany's contention that the EC Treaty did not provide a legal basis for such sanctions of a punitive nature.

The Court found the basis in the general rule that the EC has the power to determine what is necessary to attain the objectives of the common agricultural policy (CAP). Harmonization of the sanction system forms a part thereof, according to the Court. In that way, all reactions to irregularities be it of a punitive or a reparatory nature, could be based on the need to achieve the goals of the CAP.

The Court resisted the invitation made by the Germans to take a position on the Community's power in the 'penal sphere'.[12] The Court thus refrained from giving a clear view on the power to prescribe to Member States the imposition of punitive administrative sanctions; its judgment, however, is generally considered as allowing the EC to have full power to prescribe them in its legislation.

This view was supported by the case law of the Court in later years, stating that if necessary the Community can prescribe Member States to apply criminal penalties in certain cases. In a case about the Council Framework Decision on the protection of the environment through criminal law the Court ruled that as a general rule, neither criminal law nor the rules of criminal procedure fall within the Community's competence. However, this does not prevent the Community legislature from taking measures which relate to the criminal law of the Member States, when the application of effective, proportionate and dissuasive criminal penalties by the competent national authorities is an essential measure for combating serious environmental offences, and when it considers those measures to be necessary in order to ensure that the rules on environmental protection are fully effective.[13] However, the determination of the type and level of the criminal penalties to be applied does not fall within the Community's sphere of competence, the Court ruled in 2007. This case pertained to the Framework decision to strengthen the criminal-law framework for the enforcement of the law against ship-source pollution.[14]

12 Cons. 24.
13 See Case 176/03, *Commission/Council* [2005] ECR I-7879.
14 Case C-440/05, *Commission/Council* [2007] ECR I-9097.

In the Lisbon Treaty the views of the CJ have been codified. Article 83 §2 TFEU states: "If the approximation of criminal laws and regulations of the Member States proves essential to ensure the effective implementation of a Union policy in an area which has been subject to harmonisation measures, directives may establish minimum rules with regard to the definition of criminal offences and sanctions in the area concerned. Such directives shall be adopted by the same ordinary or special legislative procedure as was followed for the adoption of the harmonisation measures in question, without prejudice to Article 76."

3. ADMINISTRATIVE SANCTIONS

3.1. CRIMINAL CHARGE

As we have seen in the last section the discussion on administrative sanctions within the EC was fanned by the fear that the Community would take over the national power to impose criminal penalties. In order to obtain a clear view of the questions and problems stemming from the application of criminal penalties we must look at the ECHR. In Article 6 of that Convention, citizens are given fundamental rights when they are faced with a *criminal charge*. Article 6 of the Treaty on the European Union (TEU) stipulates that the EU shall respect fundamental rights, as guaranteed by the ECHR as general principles of Community law. Since the entry into force of the Lisbon Treaty, it is stipulated that these fundamental rights, guaranteed by the ECHR and as they result from the constitutional traditions common to the Member States, constitute general principles of the Union law. Also, the TEU now states that the Union shall accede to the ECHR (Article 6 §2 TEU).

In view of the guarantees that the Union must respect, we need to establish the scope of the notion of a *criminal charge*. The ECtHR has repeatedly stated that this notion must be construed autonomously, without taking into account the categories which national systems use. It considers several aspects in order to conclude the applicability of Article 6.

In the first place, it takes into account the scope of the rules that have been violated. If those provisions cover all citizens, be it in a certain capacity, e.g. as taxpayers, and not a given group with a particular status, this part of the test is satisfied. Secondly, the Court assesses the purpose of the sanction. If it is not intended as pecuniary compensation for damage but essentially as a punishment to deter others from committing an offence, the second stage is passed as well. Thirdly, the sanctions must be imposed under a general rule, the purpose of which is both deterrent and punitive. The last aspect to look at is the severity of the sanction. If that is very substantial, this factor also contributes to the conclusion that a criminal charge is at hand. For instance, the amount of a fine can be an indication for the severity of the sanction.[15] It is also of importance if a financial sanction can be replaced by imprisonment. If, having weighed the various aspects of the case, the Court notes the predominance of those aspects that have a criminal connotation, Article 6 is applicable. None of those factors are decisive on their own, but taken together and cumulatively they make the "charge" at issue a "criminal" one within the meaning of Article 6.[16] Thus, the Court has defined an administrative fine and a tax surcharge as a criminal charge. In 2009, the ECJ has adopted this definition of a criminal charge.[17]

3.2. DEFINITION OF SANCTIONS IN EC LAW

It seems that Union law does not prefer the term 'sanctions' as an umbrella term for labelling the state's reaction to unlawful behaviour. More often we find the terms 'penalty' and 'measure' in the English versions of EU rules. For that matter, the term 'penalty' as used in Regulation 2988/95 is translated in several language versions by an equivalent of the word sanction,[18] which points to the punitive character of a sanction. I have not found an overall term to cover reactions to an offence both of a reparatory and of a punitive nature. This does not seem to justify the use of the term 'sanction' as an umbrella label in my contribution to this book, but in the absence of a better one, it will make do.

The distinction between a penalty and a measure as such is meaningful. A measure is meant to be of a reparatory nature, while the purpose of the penalty is to punish the offender. In Regulation 2988/95 we can find the two types and a list of sanctions, which fall within their scope. These reflect the kinds of sanctions that are usual in Union law. The following reactions are considered to be measures (Article 4 Regulation 2988/1995):

- withdrawal of the wrongly obtained advantage:
- by an obligation to pay or repay the amounts due or wrongly received, or:
- by the total or partial loss of the security provided in support of the request for an advantage granted or at the time of the receipt of an advance.

---

15 ECtHR 23 March 1994, *Publ. ECHR*, Series A, No. 283-B *Ravnsborg*, in which case the imposed fine was considered to be so futile that the Court refused to define it as a criminal charge.

16 ECtHR 21 February 1984, *Öztürk*, Series A No. 73, p. 9, paragraph 50 with reference to the judgment of 8 June 1976 in *Engel and Others*, Series A No. 22, pp. 34–35, paragraph 82. ECtHR 24 February 1994, *Bendenoun* Series A No. 284, paragraph 47.

17 Case C-45/08, *Spector Photo Group* [2009] ECR I-12073.

18 French: *Mesures et sanctions administratives*, German: *Verwaltungsrechtliche Maßnahmen und Sanktionen*, Spanish: *Medidas y sanciones administrativas*, Italian: *Misure e sanzioni amministrative*, Dutch: *Administratieve maatregelen en sancties*.

To make sure that these reactions are taken for what they are meant to be, the Regulation states that these measures shall not be regarded as penalties. They can be imposed at all times, when an irregularity is found, without the need for culpability.

The penalties of Article 5 of Regulation 2988/1995 are listed here to show the large variation in types of penalties. They are:

a) payment of an administrative fine;
b) payment of an amount greater than the amounts wrongly received or evaded, plus interest where appropriate; this additional sum shall be determined in accordance with a percentage to be set in the specific rules, and may not exceed the level strictly necessary to constitute a deterrent;
c) total or partial removal of an advantage granted by Community rules, even if the operator wrongly benefited from only a part of that advantage;
d) exclusion from, or withdrawal of, the advantage for a period subsequent to that of the irregularity;
e) temporary withdrawal of the approval or recognition necessary for participation in a Community aid scheme;
f) the loss of a security or deposit provided for the purpose of complying with the conditions laid down by rules or the replenishment of the amount of a security wrongly released;
g) other penalties of a purely economic type, equivalent in nature and scope, provided for in the sector rules adopted by the Council in the light of the specific requirements of the sectors concerned and in compliance with the implementing powers conferred on the Commission by the Council.

These can only be imposed in cases of intent or negligence of the offender.

In 2002 the CJ was confronted with a fundamental question concerning the issue of subjective fault or culpability in relation to the character of a reaction to infringements of the rules.[19] The sanction in question was a reduction of an export refund, as a reaction to irregularities pertaining to the ingredients of the product that had been exported. This type of sanction is the reverse of the surcharge, as defined under sub b) of Article 5 cited above, and amounted to the same result: a financial loss on the part of the applicant. The plaintiff stated that the sanction in question constituted a punishment, and that for such a sanction the principle of subjective liability applies.

In her opinion AG Stix-Hackl paid ample attention to the character of the sanction.[20] She stated that the deterring nature of the sanction does not make it a

19 Case C-210/00 [2002] ECR I-6453.
20 Opinion of 27 November 2001.

punishment. To be considered as a criminal penalty, it must also include social or ethical disapproval. She also thought it significant that the sanction at issue could be passed on to a third party, if so agreed, by way of recovery or compensation.

The CJ found that the character of the measure or penalty must be defined on the basis of its purpose and its place in the system, and implicitly referred to the Article 6 case law of the ECtHR. The CJ stressed that in the CAP the objectives of a stable market, the combating of irregularities and the encouragement of compliance form an integral system, which seems to imply that it is not possible to single out the sanctions and assess them on their merits. But it does not seem to be the main reason for the Court not to consider them as punishment. The leading consideration seems to be the following:

> "41. In explaining the nature of the breaches complained of, the Court has emphasised on several occasions that the rules breached were aimed solely at traders who had freely chosen to take advantage of an agricultural aid scheme (see, to that effect, *Maizena*, paragraph 13, and *Germany v Commission*, paragraph 26). In the context of a Community aid scheme, in which the granting of the aid is necessarily subject to the condition that the beneficiary offers all guarantees of probity and trustworthiness, the penalty imposed in the event of non-compliance with those requirements constitutes a specific administrative instrument forming an integral part of the scheme of aid and intended to ensure the sound financial management of Community public funds."

It seems to be the idea of "contract" which defines the nature of the sanction: it cannot be a punishment, if one has agreed to it oneself. This seems to be in line with the ECtHR approach, where it states that if a rule covers only a given group, the connotation as 'criminal' is less convincing. However, the CJ's approach contradicts the other factors mentioned by the ECtHR and also the system that was adopted in Regulation 2988/95, which implies that certain sanctions, even if they are used in aid schemes that economic actors need to enter voluntarily, are indeed meant as punishment.

4. PRINCIPLE OF LEGALITY

For a long time, the principle of legality did not have a written basis in the treaties of the EU. Still, the principle has undoubtedly been part of the legal framework of the EU. In numerous cases the Court has stated that that a directive cannot, of itself and independently of national legislation adopted by a Member State for its implementation, have the effect of determining or increasing the criminal liability of those accused persons.[21] The Court demands a solid legal basis in national law, even if the conduct as such is prohibited by a Community Regulation. The CJ has emphasized that the principle of non-retroactivity of penalties, as enshrined in Article 7 ECHR, would prohibit the imposition of criminal penalties for conduct, that is not prohibited by national law, even if the national rule were contrary to Community law.[22]

With the adoption of the Charter of Fundamental Rights (Charter) the principle of legality is now underpinned with a thorough basis in the EU Treaties.[23] The Charter puts it as follows:

> "Article 49: Principles of legality and proportionality of criminal offences and penalties
>
> 1. No one shall be held guilty of any criminal offence on account of any act or omission, which did not constitute a criminal offence under national law or international law at the time when it was committed. Nor shall a heavier penalty be imposed than that which was applicable at the time the criminal offence was committed. If, subsequent to the commission of a criminal offence, the law provides for a lighter penalty, that penalty shall be applicable."

In Article 6 TEU the Charter is acknowledged to have the same legal value as the Treaties. Before the Lisbon Treaty the fundamental rights in the ECHR were categorized as general principles, common to the constitutional traditions of the Member States, as the TUE then stated. The Convention recognizes the principle of legality in Article 7:

> "1 No one shall be held guilty of any criminal offence on account of any act or omission which did not constitute a criminal offence under national or international law at the time when it was committed. Nor shall a heavier penalty be imposed than the one that was applicable at the time the criminal offence was committed.
>
> 2 This article shall not prejudice the trial and punishment of any person for any act or omission, which, at the time when it was committed, was criminal according to the general principles of law recognised by civilised nations."

The lack of a thorough basis in the TEU lead to the odd consequence that the principle was expressly mentioned in Article 2 of Regulation 2988/1995:

---

21 See for a recent judgment Joined Cases C-387/02, C-391/02 and C-403/02, *Berlusconi* [2005] ECR I-3565.

22 Case C-60/02, counterfeit and pirated goods [2004] ECR I-651.

23 Charter of Fundamental Rights of the European Union of 7 December 2000 [2000] OJ C 364.

"2. No administrative penalty may be imposed unless a Community act prior to the irregularity has made provision for it. In the event of a subsequent amendment of the provisions, which impose administrative penalties and are contained in Community rules, the less severe provisions shall apply retroactively."

This text might suggest that the principle of legality only applies to the penalties. In the *Kőnicke* case, however, the Court emphasized that a 'penalty, even of a non-criminal nature, cannot be imposed unless it rests on a clear and unambiguous legal basis'.[24] The phrase refers to the forfeiture of a deposit, which might be considered as a 'measure' in terms of Regulation 2988/95, and, as a general rule, is of a reparatory nature. It suggests that a legal basis is necessary for reparatory measures as well. However, the forfeiture of a deposit in combination with the recovery of sums paid, is in reality a penalty, and that was what the case was about. In conclusion, the principle of legality certainly applies to penalties in EU law; however, it is uncertain whether it applies to measures as well.

5. CULPABILITY

In the Charter the *presumptio innocentiae* is codified for offences of a criminal nature.

"Article 48: Presumption of innocence and right of defence

1. Everyone who has been charged shall be presumed innocent until proved guilty according to law.
2. Respect for the rights of the defence of anyone who has been charged shall be guaranteed."

This principle is not adhered to in EU law in the sense that an offender is always considered to be innocent until proven guilty before a court of law. Union law is for a large part administrative law, in which the standard of strict liability applies. Therefore, it is sufficient to establish that the offence has been committed and, regardless of culpability the offender is liable for the offence. There is no need to look at the circumstances of the case. However, administrative authorities must prove that an offence has taken place and that it was committed by the accused. In the process they may use information that they have gathered from the accused under the duty to cooperate. However, as we will see, the accused is not required to answer when he might incriminate himself and thus provide the authorities with the proof they needed in order to be able to establish an infringement and to impose a penalty. In case the authorities envisage a

24 Case 117/83 [1984] ECR 3291.

measure, this guarantee not to incriminate oneself does not need to be offered, as we will see when in Paragraph 6.2 the right to silence is discussed.

In the *Käserei Champignon Hoffmeister* case the AG concluded that the fault principle is not a general principle of Community law when it comes to administrative sanctions:

> "46. Firstly, a comparison of the legal systems of the Member States, as made by the plaintiff in its written observations, reveals, in particular, that the boundary between criminal and administrative penalties is a fluid one.
> 47. Thus, in the legal systems of the Member States the principles of criminal law, to which the fault principle undisputedly belongs, are variously applied. The narrower the range of purely administrative penalties – and hence the broader the range of criminal penalties – the clearer the distinction between criminal and administrative sanctions with respect to their legal treatment.
> 48. The scope of the fault principle also appears to vary. In the case of criminal penalties which give expression to minor social disapproval, the behavioural obligation may be so conceived that individual reprehensibility is induced merely by its not being fulfilled. Moreover, in its written observations the plaintiff itself acknowledges that where a sanction is based on objective criteria the possibilities of exemption could lead to more or less the same results as liability based on fault with reversal of the burden of proof.
> 49. It therefore appears that the general applicability of the fault principle to penalties of an administrative nature cannot be derived from the legal traditions of the Member States."[25]

As regards the case law of the Court, the Court explicitly found that the principle *nulla poena sine culpa* did not apply to measures such as the loss of security.[26] In *Germany vs. Commission*, which also involved a penalty imposed under the CAP, the Court reached the same conclusion, because administrative authorities had imposed the penalty in order to protect the CAP.[27] In the *Käserei Champignon Hofmeister* case the CJ found it to be of importance if a sanction can be qualified as being of a criminal nature. If this is not the case, as in *Käserei* with the penalty of a reduction of an export refund, the principle of *nulla poena sine culpa* does not apply, according to the Court.[28] In other areas, the Court has accepted that a system of strict criminal liability penalizing a breach of a Community Regulation is not in itself incompatible with Community law. These cases concerned national sanctioning systems of criminal law set up to enforce EC rules.[29] Thus,

---

25 Case C-210/00, opinion of Advocate General Stix-Hackl delivered on 27 November 2001.
26 Case 137/85, *Maizena* [1987] ECR 4587, para 14.
27 Case C-240/90, *Germany/Commission* [1992] ECR I-5383.
28 Case 210/00 [2002] ECR I-6453.
29 Case C-326/88 *Hansen & Son* [1990] ECR I-2911, paragraph 19; Case C-177/95 *Ebony Maritime and Loten Navigation* [1997] ECR I-1111, paragraph 36.

the Court stressed that the general principles of Community law do not preclude the application of national provisions under which an offender of Community Regulations may incur strict criminal liability. The Court's opinion, however, is without prejudice to the competence of the EU legislator to provide for rules as laid down in Article 5 of Regulation 2988/95, determining that in order to impose a penalty the offender must have shown intent or gross negligence.

6. PROTECTION OF THE INDIVIDUAL

The protection of the individual does not necessarily depend upon the qualification of the sanction as a penalty or a measure. The CJ has decided, for instance, that the rights of the defence must be respected in every case in which a decision is taken, that is unfavourable for an individual.[30] Moreover, the guarantees that are available to the individual are in most cases compatible with those stemming from the ECHR. The character of EC law as economic law brings about that the protection of the individual extends to legal persons (companies) as well.[31] This is not self-evident, since the ECHR was originally drafted for natural persons, and the CJ has tried to hook on to that Convention while developing specific guarantees in EU law. Still, the case law of both the CJ and the Human Rights Court has developed towards the recognition of guarantees for legal persons/companies, as we shall see from the following.

6.1. THE RIGHTS OF THE DEFENCE

The rights of the defence find their basis in the French '*droits de la défense*'. This is a body of rules, set up to protect an individual when he finds himself confronted with drastic decisions of public authorities.[32] The rights are acknowledged by the Court and must be respected in every case when a decision implies a sanction, even if the proceedings in question are merely administrative proceedings.[33] It is settled case law that respect for the rights of the defence is in fact a fundamental principle of Union law that must be guaranteed even in the absence of any rules governing the proceedings in question. They must be respected in all proceedings initiated against a person, which are liable to

30 Case 17/74, *Transocean Marine Paint* [1974] ECR 1063, case C- 32/95 P, *Lisretal* [1996] ECR I-5373.

31 Case 85/76, *Hofmann-LaRoche* [1979] ECR 461.

32 Conseil d'Etat 5 May 1944, *Dame veuve Trompier-Gravier, Rec.* p. 133. This case concerned the withdrawal of a permit as a consequence of the unbecoming behaviour of the permit holder.

33 Case 17/74, *Transocean Marine Paint* [1974] ECR 1063; and case 121/76, *Moli* [1977] ECR 1980; case 85/76, *Hofmann LaRoche* [1979] ECR 461.

culminate in a measure adversely affecting that person. The principle requires that the addressees of decisions, which significantly affect their interests, should be placed in a position in which they may effectively make known their views on the evidence on which the contested decision is based.[34] This entails that the addressee of such a decision must be given a sufficient period of time to prepare en make known his views.[35] The rights must be observed, not only by the courts, but also by national public authorities when they impose measures and penalties.[36]

In the Treaties and in Regulations rules are laid down on the right to a fair hearing and the rights of the defence. The TFEU provides for the right to a fair hearing for Member States before the Commission decides on the admissibility of state aid (Article 108), and before a procedure for a breach of Community law is introduced to the Court (Article 258). Furthermore, the right is provided for in competition law, for companies that are suspected of a breach of Article 101 TFEU. Regulation 1/2003 on competition law[37] states that the rights of defence of the parties concerned shall be fully respected in the proceedings (Article 27, §2).

In the Coal and Steel Treaty companies were given the right to be heard before a fine was to be imposed (Article 36). Although the right was laid down in some of the written law, it was considered to have a wider scope as a part of the general principles of Community law. This was due to the limited scope of the provisions in question. In 1991 the Court decided that the right to defend oneself against an accusation, which is guaranteed in Article 6 ECHR, is part of the Community legal order.[38] In later case law the Court acknowledged the same rights in all proceedings, which are initiated against a person and are liable to culminate in a measure adversely affecting that person.[39] In that leading case, *Listrestal*, it became clear that such measures not only include penalties, but also the withdrawal of a favourable decision such as a grant from the European Social Fund. Thus, the distinction between measures and penalties does not affect the protection of the rights of the defence.

In substance, the rights of the defence were developed in the context of competition law. The former Regulations 17/62 and 99/63 and the case law thereon defined in rather detail the elements of those rights. The new Regulation acknowledges the right to be heard by the Commission, the right of access to the file, and the protection of business secrets. The right to be heard is exercised,

---

[34] Case C- 32/95 P, *Lisretal*, [1996] ECR I-5373. See also Joint Cases C-402/05 P and C-415/05 P, *Kadi* [2008] ECR I-06351; Case C-510/06 P, *Archer Daniels Midland* [2009] ECR I-1843.

[35] Case C-349/07, *Sopropé*, pt. 37–38 [2008] ECR I-10369.

[36] See e.g. Case C-28/05 *Dokter* [2006] ECR I-5431.

[37] Council Regulation (EC) No. 1/2003 of 16 December 2002 on the implementation of the rules of competition laid down in Articles 81 and 82 of the Treaty, OJ L 2003, 1/1.

[38] Case C-49/88, *SAMAD* [1991] ECR I-3187.

[39] Case C-32/95P, *Lisretal et al.* [1996] ECR I-5373, cons. 21.

before the Commission declares that an infringement has taken place, and before it imposes fines or periodic penalty payments.

The rights of the defence have several aspects; the core is the right to express one's view on the matter, in short the right to a fair hearing. In the *Lisrestal* case the Court stated that the addressees of a decision should be placed in a position in which they may effectively make their views known. The possibility to do so depends on several conditions. These form the other elements of the rights of the defence.

One must be informed about the investigation, which may lead to a sanction (measure or penalty). This information must be timely, at such a moment that the decision has not yet been taken (*cf.* Article 27 Regulation 1/2003). This is an essential element, because the rights of the defence can be irreparably harmed in the preparatory phase.

The party involved must be informed about the allegation: the facts and the applicable rules that it has allegedly broken (Article 27, §1 Regulation 1/2003). He must have access to the files of the authorities in order to prepare a defence (Article 27, §2). In competition cases the Commission provides for a kind of summary, which is added to the letter of allegation.

The addressee can ask for the precise contents of the documents if he thinks that this is essential to his defence. However, there are some restrictions on access to files, especially in competition cases. Some parts of the file can be labelled as confidential, in order to protect a competitor's interests against another competitor (Article 27, §2). The company that has complained to the Commission of unlawful actions by his competitor also has procedural rights. He also has access to files, but not to the files containing delicate information about the company, such as business secrets. The Court is very precise in its examination of the necessity of confidentiality, because as the ECHR shows it is a fundamental aspect of the right to a fair trial that proceedings leading to a penalty should be adversarial and that there should be equality of arms between the authorities and the defence.[40] The right to an adversarial trial means that both sides must be given the opportunity to have knowledge of and to comment on the observations filed and the evidence adduced by the other party. Article 6 §1 ECHR requires that the authorities disclose to the defence all material evidence in their possession for or against the accused. However, the right of disclosure of relevant evidence is not an absolute right. In competition proceedings it is obvious that there may be competing interests, such as the protection of vital business information, which must be weighed against the rights of the accused. Thus, in some cases, it may be necessary to withhold certain evidence from the defence so as to preserve the fundamental rights of another individual or company. However, only such measures restricting the

[40] ECtHR 16 February 2000, *Rowe and Davis v. the United Kingdom*, Application no. 28901/95.

rights of the defence, which are strictly necessary, are permissible under Article 6 §1 ECHR.[41]

On several occasions the Court has stressed the importance of the right to express one's views on the evidence presented (now in Article 27 §1 Regulation 1/2003).[42] In the *Almini* case it stated that this right is all the more important when the EU authorities have wide discretionary powers.[43] The right to express a point of view pertains to the facts on which the decision shall be founded. The right has been given to the addressee of the envisaged decision.[44] In competition cases the plaintiff and interested third parties can be heard at their own request.[45] The interested parties must have sufficient time to prepare their defence.[46] The period needed is related to the complexity of the case and the volume of the files.

The parties concerned express their views in a written opinion. In general, there is no public hearing. Only in staff cases civil servants can express their views orally at a hearing. In competition cases sometimes an oral hearing takes place. In such cases, the EU uses special hearing officers, who are not involved in the actual decision-making process. The purpose of this rule is to avoid possible bias. The parties concerned can be represented by lawyers, who are also admitted to the bar of the Court of Justice, or by other suitable persons.

The right to be heard is an essential procedural requirement, which makes a decision susceptible to annulment when it is not adhered to. Regulation 1/2003 even states that the Commission shall base its decisions *only* on objections on which the parties concerned have been able to comment (Article 27, §1).

6.2. THE RIGHT TO SILENCE

In administrative law, it is quite usual that individuals or companies are required to cooperate with inspections and enquiries, answer questions, produce documents etc. In EU law this is not different. In fact, the EU adds rules about cooperation with inspections and enquiries in many rules.[47] Member States do

---

41 ECtHR 23 April 1997, *Van Mechelen and Others v. the Netherlands*, Reports 1997-III, p. 712, §58.

42 Council Regulation (EC) No 1/2003 of 16 December 2002 on the implementation of the rules on competition laid down in Articles 81 and 82 of the Treaty, OJ L 1, 4.1.2003, p. 1–25.

43 Case 19/70 *Almini* [1971] ECR 623.

44 *Lisrestal*: case cited above.

45 See Article 27 Regulation 1/2003: Complainants shall be closely associated with the proceedings.

46 Case C-349/07, *Sopropé* [2008] ECR I-10369.

47 E.g. Council Regulation (Euratom, EC) No 2185/96 of 11 November 1996 concerning on-the-spot checks and inspections carried out by the Commission in order to protect the European Communities' financial interests against fraud and other irregularities, OJ L 292, 15 November 1996, p. 2–5, Article 7.

the same in order to comply with the demands of the EU regarding the standard of enforcement. In view of the commitment of the EU to guarantee fundamental rights, enshrined in the Charter and the ECHR, the EU needs to set certain safeguards to protect the individual from incriminating himself. This raises the question whether information that was gathered under the duty to cooperate, may be used to underpin a decision to impose a penalty at all times. The rights of the defence can, of course, be impaired during preliminary inquiry proceedings, when the duty to cooperate with inspectors/investigators can cause undertakings to produce evidence of the unlawful nature of the conduct which the Commission will be sanctioning at a later stage.

To fully appreciate this matter we must first turn to the case law of the ECtHR. The Court has acknowledged that the right to silence is part of a fair trial, as guaranteed in Article 6 §1 ECHR. The question is in what kind of situations this right can be invoked. Article 6 ECHR does not recognize an absolute right not to give evidence against oneself, but only if and when necessary to protect the rights of the defence.[48] This means that, as a general rule, the parties involved are obliged to provide all the information requested, that is to say all factual information. In the *Saunders* case the Court established that it is a violation of the right to a fair trial when oral information obtained from the individual by tax inspectors during a normal inspection is used in a criminal trial. The violation can be found in the circumstance that the information is obtained under the exercise of compulsory powers, that is, under pressure of sanctions like a fine or imprisonment. In a later case the Court reiterated this judgment for the situation in which a public receiver had questioned someone under similar compulsory powers, and this information was used in a criminal trial as well.[49]

In the *Orkem* case the Court of Justice established that the right to silence had no foundation in written EC law.[50] This case was a competition case against a company, started by the European Commission. Up to that time national systems only recognized the right to silence for natural persons, in criminal proceedings, but the Court was clear in acknowledging the same right for undertakings.

The Court stated that the duty to cooperate in normal inspection procedures cannot be warded off easily. The duty to provide information ends when the authorities ask questions in order to establish an irregularity. In those situations there is no duty to answer questions.[51] As it was put in the *Orkem* case: the Commission may not compel an undertaking to provide it with answers, which

48 ECtHR 17 December 1996, *Saunders*. ECHR Report 1996-VI, p. 2044, para. 68.

49 ECtHR 27 April 2004, Application No. 21413/02, *Kansal v. The United Kingdom*.

50 Case 374/87, *Orkem* [1989] ECR 3283, cons. 28. See also case 27/88 Solvay [1989] ECR 3355 and T-34/93 *Société Générale* [1995] ECR II-545.

51 Cons. 34 and 5 *Orkem*, see also case T-112/98, *Mannesmannröhren-Werke* [2001] ECR II-729, cons. 67.

might involve an admission of an infringement, which the Commission should prove.[52] This seems to imply that even the answering of questions is not required in the inspection phase. We can find this in the competition Regulation 1/2003 when it says in the preamble that undertakings cannot be forced to admit that they have committed an infringement. In the next part of the sentence there is a 'but': undertakings are in any event obliged to answer factual questions and to provide documents, even if this information may be used to establish the existence of such an infringement. This formula of the right to silence is not repeated in the actual text of the Regulation. There, it only mentions the duty to answer questions on facts and to cooperate in the examination of books and other documents (Article 20).

6.3. PROTECTION AGAINST ENTERING BUSINESS PREMISES OR A HOME

Article 7 of the EU Charter protects the privacy of the home. The right is a codification of the fundamental right laid down in the ECHR, which has already been recognized in the Community legal order for a considerable length of time. Since the EU has declared that it shall abide by the fundamental rights laid down in the ECHR, this convention and its interpretation have become of importance. This has been problematic for the interpretation of Article 8 ECHR, because the ECtHR and the CJ took a different approach to the right of legal persons/companies to have their home protected.

In the *Chapell* case the Human Rights Court implied that undertakings are protected by article 8 ECHR, when authorities wish to enter their business premises.[53] The CJ, however, was of a different opinion at the time and stated that the protection of the home was guaranteed for natural persons only. However, it did recognize a certain degree of protection against arbitrary entrance to business premises.[54] In 2002 the two courts fine-tuned their case law, and both chose the same interpretation as to the rights of companies.

In the *Colas Est* case the ECtHR not only reiterated that Article 8 ECHR protects legal persons as well,[55] but also clarified the conditions for interference in the right under Article 8 §2. The leading thought in the case is that investigation powers must be proportionate to the (legitimate) aim that is pursued (necessary in a democratic society). Therefore, it is necessary that there is some form of previous judicial control available to prevent possible arbitrary action, in those cases where the investigative powers of the authorities are very wide, as was the

52 Cons. 35.
53 ECtHR 30 March 1989, no. 10461/83.
54 Cases 46/87 and 227/88 [1989] ECR 2859.
55 See cons. 41 ECtHR 16 April 2002, no. 37971/97, *Société Colas Est and others*.

case in *Colas Est.* In the *Roquettes* case the CJ adopted the line of reasoning of the Strasbourg court, and it added guidelines for national courts as to how to perform the task of judicial control.[56] Since the *Roquettes* case dealt with the problem of the scope of the investigative powers of the Commission in competition cases, the Court explained the standard of information that the courts should receive in order to be able to decide on the legality of the search. The Commission should be able to provide 'detailed information showing that the Commission possesses solid factual information and evidence providing grounds for suspecting such infringement on the part of the undertaking concerned.' This is more than the former Regulation 17/62 demanded; Article 14 solely obliged the Commission to state the subject-matter and the purpose of an investigation. Hence, it is clear that increasing the burden of proof can put the Commission in a difficult spot when third parties have an interest in confidentiality or when the investigation could be hampered because of the compulsory disclosure of certain information to the court. In an analysis of the case Waelbroeck and Leinemeyer state that the Commission needs to provide nearly a full description of the case, including an indication of the affected market and the nature of the suspected infringement, in order to enable the court to assess the use of investigative powers.[57]

The Roquettes rules have been incorporated in Regulation 1/2003, where it provides that the Commission is empowered to 'enter any premises, land and means of transport of undertakings and associations of undertakings' (Article 20, §2), but if, according to national law, judicial authorization for coercive measures is needed, it shall be applied for (§6 and 7). In that case the judicial authority 'shall control that the Commission decision is authentic and that the coercive measures envisaged are neither arbitrary nor excessive having regard to the subject matter of the inspection'.

It has now become clear that national courts are not competent to question the legality of an investigation, when initiated by the Commission, as is the case in competition law. Of course this is different when national authorities conduct an investigation or inspection in EU cases of their own motion. In that case the courts can rule on the legality thereof, provided that the rules on access to business premises or a home of the EU *and* the ECHR are taken into account.

This also means that, for the time being, under EU law different approaches are allowed. Waelbroeck and Leinemeyer indicated that only ten out of (at that time) fifteen Member States require a judicial search warrant.[58] This raises questions as to the compatibility of the Regulation and the case law with the Colas Est rule, which clearly requires prior judicial control for the use of

[56] *Roquettes* C-94/00 [2002] ECR I-9011, cons. 99.

[57] [2003] *CMLRev*, 1481–1497 (1490).

[58] *O.c.* p. 1494, only Austria, Finland, Ireland the Netherlands and Sweden do not require a search warrant for business premises. All states require one for the search of a private home.

extensive powers to search premises; all 27 Member States are now bound by this case law.[59]

7. JUDICIAL PROTECTION

As a general rule the judicial protection of the individual is a matter governed by national law.

This concept of the procedural autonomy of the Member States is limited by the principles of equivalence and effectiveness, well known from the *Rewe* and *Comet* cases.[60] In those cases the CJ laid down several minimum requirements for the system of judicial protection against the wrongful application of EC law as such. These minimum requirements pertain, among others things, to the right to have access to justice and to the right to have adequate procedures and remedies. The Court has put it as follows:

> "(I)t follows from the settled case-law of the Court that, in the absence of Community rules governing the matter, it is for the domestic legal system of each Member State to designate the courts and tribunals having jurisdiction and to lay down the detailed procedural rules governing actions for safeguarding rights which individuals derive directly from Community law, provided that such rules are not less favourable than those governing similar domestic actions (the principle of equivalence) and that they do not render practically impossible or excessively difficult the exercise of rights conferred by Community law (the principle of effectiveness) (see, inter alia, Case C-453/99 *Courage and Crehan* [2001] ECR I-6297, paragraph 29, and Case C-255/00 *Grundig Italiana* [2002] ECR I-8003, paragraph 33)."[61]

7.1. ACCESS TO JUSTICE

The right to have an effective remedy against violations of EU rights is an important part of the legal order of the EU. Both the Strasbourg and the Luxemburg court stress, that rights awarded by the respective treaties must be protected by an impartial and independent tribunal. The Court of Justice demands effective remedies in those cases when EU rights have been infringed.[62] The Court has set several conditions with which the national legal orders must comply in order to provide the right standard of protection. These

59 Case C-2/92, *Bostock* [1994] ECR I-995; compare also ECtHR 18 February 1999, no. 24833/94, *Matthews v. The UK*, where the Court established that Member States are bound by the Convention when they apply EC law.
60 Case 33/76, *Rewe* [1976] ECR 1989 and 45/76, Comet [1976] ECR 2043.
61 Case 276/01, *Steffensen* [2003] ECR I-3735.
62 Cases *Rewe* and *Comet*.

comprise access to a court, effective procedures to undo infringements, the duty to underpin decisions with adequate reasons, rules on standing and time-limits, the burden of proof and full jurisdiction of the courts. As a general rule, Member States enjoy procedural autonomy, provided that equivalent rules are applied to national and Union law cases, and that they are adequate to protect EU rights. The Court has limited this autonomy by setting the conditions mentioned above.

Every time a EU citizen is of the opinion that his/her Community rights have been violated, they must be able to address a court with a request for redress.[63] The Charter puts it as follows:

> "Article 47: Right to an effective remedy and to a fair trial
> Everyone whose rights and freedoms guaranteed by the law of the Union are violated has the right to an effective remedy before a tribunal in compliance with the conditions laid down in this Article.
> Everyone is entitled to a fair and public hearing within a reasonable time by an independent and impartial tribunal previously established by law. Everyone shall have the possibility of being advised, defended and represented.
> Legal aid shall be made available to those who lack sufficient resources insofar as such aid is necessary to ensure effective access to justice."

EU law does not determine *which* court or tribunal is competent, because this is a matter of procedural autonomy. Still, sometimes the Court needs to determine if a national institution qualifies as a court or tribunal that is allowed to ask a preliminary ruling of the Court.[64] This point, however, does not need discussion here.

EU law follows the case law of the ECtHR quite close. The Human Rights Court has allowed some limitations in the right of access to a court, such as time-limits, court registry fees and the obligation to have legal representation.[65] However, these limitations must serve a legitimate aim and may not be stricter than is necessary to achieve that aim.[66] The same holds true for the obligation to use preliminary proceedings, e.g. an action for objections, outside the courts. The Court sees to it that the limitations set in national law do not make it virtually impossible to make use of remedies that are available.

Some limitations are therefore not allowed, or must be compensated, as for instance the obligation to have legal representation. In complex cases or when legal representation is compulsory, the state must guarantee that citizens can have adequate counsel. In some cases this means that there needs to be a system of compensation for the costs of legal aid.[67] In criminal procedures even legal aid

63 Case 222/84, *Johnston* [1986] ECR 1651.
64 See e.g. case 246/80, *Broekmeulen* [1981] ECR 2311.
65 ECtHR 27 February 1975, *Golder*, Series A, vol. 18.
66 ECtHR 28 May 1985, *Ashingdane*, Series A, vol. 93.
67 ECtHR 9 October 1979, *Airey v. Ireland*, Series A, vol. 32.

without a fee must be available (Article 6 §3 ECHR). If national legal orders demand some form of security or a deposit in order to start court proceedings, this would not be in breach of Article 6, if it would serve a legitimate aim.[68] In EU cases it is allowed to demand a deposit or other security as well, as long as the principles of effectiveness and equivalence are not put into question. However, it is not allowed to require such a security solely from EU citizens that are non-nationals.[69] The condition of an effective remedy also entails that the system as such needs to be transparent and coherent.[70] Limitations to the right to access to justice that are allowed as such, can still be in breach of the Convention if they could lead to misunderstandings concerning the proper proceedings.[71]

7.2. PROCEDURAL RULES

The European Convention and its case law have set standards concerning the organization of the proceedings and the procedural rules. The Court of Justice has established similar rules in view of the principles of equivalence and effectiveness. Hereafter, they will be discussed with a slight emphasis on the rules developed by the ECtHR.

7.2.1. Public trial

Article 6 ECHR contains the provision that, as a general rule, a trial shall be public. The Convention leaves room for exceptions in the interests of morals, public order or national security in a democratic society, where the interests of juveniles or the protection of the private life of the parties so require, or to the extent strictly necessary in the opinion of the court in special circumstances where publicity would prejudice the interests of justice. In the *Pupino* case the CJ made such an exception for the hearing of the young children that had been abused by their teacher.[72] This is one of the rare EU cases on the principle of a public hearing in court.

The Human Rights Court has accepted several further exceptions to this rule, for instance when the case is complex and very technical. In such a situation the case may be better dealt with in a written form.[73] These exceptions could play a role in EU fraud cases. They could be necessary when biased publicity could hamper the course of justice, or in competition cases, when somehow confidential business information would become public and the interests of

68 ECtHR 13 July 1995, *Tolstoy Miloslavsky*, Series A, vol. 323.
69 Case C-29/95, *Pastoors* [1997] ECR I-285.
70 ECtHR 16 December 1992, *Geoffre de la Pradelle*, Series A, vol. 253-B.
71 ECtHR 4 December 1995, *Bellet*, Series A, vol. 333-B.
72 Case C-105/03. *Pupino* [2005] ECR I-5285.
73 ECtHR 24 June 1993, *Schuler-Zgraggen v. Switzerland*, Series A, vol. 263.

companies involved could subsequently be seriously damaged, or where the case is extremely complicated.

The rationale of a public trial is that the defendant can exercise his right to express his views about the facts and the allegations. An oral hearing is in order when the court is not clear as to the facts as they emerge from the files.[74]

In criminal charge cases the Human Rights Court accepts that a public hearing is refrained from on appeal when the case concerns a minor offence or when only mild penalties can be imposed. However, in each case in which the guilt of a defendant still has to be established, an oral and public hearing is obligatory.[75]

7.2.2. Standing

Both the Human Rights Court and the CJ accept limitations when it comes to standing in court proceedings.[76] The CJ stresses that these limitations may not make it practically impossible to exercise EU rights. The consequence of this case law is, that appeals against the imposition of a sanction (penalty or measure) should always be heard by a court, because unlawful sanction decisions as a general rule will infringe one's EU rights.[77]

The CJ case law about standing mostly concerns situations in which third parties seek redress before the courts, for instance when they have been discriminated against or when they claim protection of a directive.[78] Sometimes interest groups want to have access to a court, and the question whether they must be given that right depends on the scope of the rules involved.[79] In The Netherlands it is debated whether the CJ case law would allow for further restrictions by introducing the so called Schutznorm in future procedural rules. This rule only allows those people to have access to court, whose rights are actually protected by the rules they invoke before the courts. The general conclusion is that this rule would be a limitation that is acceptable to the CJ, provided that it is not applied too strictly.[80]

---

74 ECtHR 19 February 1998, *M. Jacobsson v. Sweden*, Rep. 1998-I.

75 ECtHR 12 February 1985, *Colozza*, no. 9024/80.

76 ECtHR 28 June 1990, Obermeier, Serie A, vol. 179.

77 Case C-13/01, Safalero [2003] ECR I-8679.

78 C-87/90 – C-89/90, Verholen e.a. [1991] ECR I-3757.

79 Case 361/88, TA luft [1991] ECR I-2607, in which the Court acknowledged that the scope of interested parties was very wide. Under the Arhus Convention members of the public all have access to justice, but it was unclear if the Convention allows for limitations of the legal grounds they want rely on. In case C-115/09, Trianel Kohlekraftwerk Lünen (nyr), the Court ruled that that non-governmental organizations promoting environmental protection have a right to rely before the courts on the infringement of the rules of national law flowing from Article 6 of the Habitats Directive, even where, on the ground that the rules relied on protect only the interests of the general public and not the interests of individuals, national procedural law does not permit this. In other words, the Court has dismissed the Schutznorm for interest groups in environmental cases.

80 G.T.J.M. Jurgens, "De bestuursrechtelijke relativiteitseis", in: De toegang tot de rechter beperkt, preadvies, VAR-reeks 144, p. 90–105.

The most important exception to limitations on standing in view of the subject of this article is the situation of the third party competitor who has an interest in the correct application of competition law. It is clear that he has access to court regarding decisions addressed to competitors, which may harm his interests on the market, e.g. consent to a merger.[81]

7.2.3. Time limits

As indicated above the ECHR does not forbid time limits to address a court, as long as they serve a legitimate aim and are necessary to attain that aim. However, they may not make the effective use of a remedy impossible, which may be the case when the time limit is very short. The CJ also allows time limits that are 'reasonable'. In exceptional circumstances time limits cannot be invoked to block access to justice. This may be the case when the authorities lead someone to believe that he has no (procedural) rights at all, or does not need to invoke them because the authorities will take care of the situation.[82] It is essential to know whether the persons involved were able to know their (procedural) rights when the time limit was running.[83] Such a situation may occur in sanctioning cases as well; however, such cases have not yet been brought before the CJ.

7.2.4. Legal assistance

As a general rule, everyone is entitled to defend himself. Many legal systems, however, demand legal representation by lawyers in private law cases and also in criminal cases. The Human Rights Court has accepted this.[84] Article 6 ECHR provides the right to free legal aid, if someone does not have sufficient means to pay and when the interests of justice so require.

This right does not seem to apply in preliminary proceedings, which are quite usual in administrative law. Often, before addressing a court, the party involved must raise objections before the administrative authorities. This can also be the case when the decision of the authorities entails a measure or a penalty. If in such a situation legal assistance seems necessary, in view of the complexity of the matter, these costs are often not reimbursed. This does not seem to be in violation of EU law or Article 6 ECHR, provided that it does not harm the right of effective judicial protection. It may be the case that the parties involved refrain from seeking judicial protection when they are confronted with the risk of incurring high costs which are not reimbursed. In criminal matters the Human Rights

81 See a Dutch case, President of the Trade and Industry Appeals Tribunal 4 January 1991, AB 1991, 185, Texaco.

82 Case C-321/96, *Edis* [1998] ECR I-4951.

83 Case C-208/90, *Emmott* [1991] ECR I-4269 and C-326/96, *Levez* [1998] ECR I-7835.

84 ECtHR 24 November 1986, *Gillow*, Series A, vol. 109, ECtHR 25 September 1992, *Croissant*, Series A, vol. 237-B.

Court demands free legal assistance in all criminal charge cases, which can lead to imprisonment.[85] In general, the seriousness of the offence and the possible penalty are indicators to answer the question whether legal aid must be free for those who need it.[86]

7.2.5. Burden of proof

When it comes to administrative measures and penalties it is the duty of the authorities to prove that an infringement of the rules has taken place. EU law does not have written procedural rules on evidence, albeit that some rules can be derived from the regulations in the several sectors. Furthermore, we can turn to the general principles of Union law, such as the rights of the defence and the principle of proportionality. In general, the rules on evidence must be assessed against the background of the principles of effectiveness and equivalence.[87] The procedural autonomy of the Member States constitutes the starting point after all.

The fact that the burden of proof lies with the authorities follows from the duty to underpin a decision with sufficient reasons.[88] The CJ has rejected the opinion of the Commission that it is solely up to the offender to provide evidence to the contrary. It follows from the principles of proper administration that the authorities must paint a full picture of the facts, including those that are in favour of the accused.[89] This does not mean that the accused does not need to bother to contradict the facts as presented by the authorities. The basic idea of a fair trial entails that parties can examine each other's propositions, evidence and witnesses, and offer proof to the contrary. For this purpose the rights of the defence have been developed. The principle of effectiveness brings about the need for the authorities to leave ample opportunity to come up with proof that the alleged offence must be put into a different perspective. Otherwise national law would render it practically impossible or excessively difficult to exercise rights conferred by Union law. It would also violate the right to a fair trial as enshrined in Article 6 ECHR. The adversarial principle brings about the right to challenge the evidence. Provisions that stand in the way of that right do not fulfil the demands of Article 6 and must be omitted.

In 2003 the CJ delivered a judgment in the *Steffensen* case, in which – contrary to the rules laid down in the applicable directive – it had not been possible to obtain a second opinion on analyses of samples of foodstuff.[90] The

85 ECtHR 24 May 1991, *Quaranta*, Series A vol. 205.
86 ECtHR 10 June 1996, *Benham*, Rep. 1996-III, p. 769.
87 Reiterated in case C-161/08, *Jan de Lely* [2009] ECR I-4075.
88 Cases 18 and 35/65, *Gutmann* [1966] ECR 150; cases 8–11/66, *Noordwijks Cementaccoord* [1967] ECR 91.
89 Cases 56 and 58/64, *Grundig/Consten* [1966] ECR 449.
90 Case C-276/01, *Steffensen* [2003] ECR 3735.

question was whether the results of those analyses were nevertheless admissible as evidence in an action brought before a national court against an administrative decision based exclusively, or at least for the most part, on those results. It was put to the Court that the admission of such evidence would be in breach of Article 6 ECHR. This case is interesting because, according to the Court, the right to have a second opinion does not only follow from the directive itself (in which that right was expressly provided for), but also from the adversarial principle of the ECHR.

Human Rights Court has held that, where the parties are entitled to submit to the court observations on a piece of evidence, they must be afforded a real opportunity to comment effectively on it in order for the proceedings to reach the standard of fairness required by Article 6(1) of the ECHR. That point must be examined, in particular, where the evidence pertains to a technical field of which the judges have no knowledge and is likely to have a preponderant influence on the assessment of the facts by the court.[91] In the *Steffensen* case, the Court relied on that case law and also held that, if the national court decides that the admission as evidence of the results of the analyses at issue in the main proceedings is likely to give rise to an infringement of the adversarial principle and, thus, of the right to a fair hearing, it must exclude those results as evidence in order to avoid such an infringement.

7.2.6. Full jurisdiction

The Convention states that a court must have *full jurisdiction*, the power to assess both facts (the merits of the matter) and the legal merits of the case.[92] Its scrutiny must not only pertain to legislation, but also to general principles of law.[93] The Human Rights Court has considered certain limitations to the jurisdiction of a court to be inadmissible, e.g. the limitation on rules of procedure when an administrative authority enjoys discretionary powers.[94] Especially in the case of a 'criminal charge', the courts must have full power to assess both questions of fact and questions of law.[95]

The Human Rights Court has allowed limitations as to questions of fact in very specific circumstances: the need for a very specialized examination of the facts can render it unfeasible for a court to perform the task. In that case it is allowed to have this done by experts. However, during this procedure the parties must be informed of the findings, and they must be able to comment on those findings. This follows from the adversarial principle that was discussed above.[96]

---

91 ECtHR 18 March 1997, *Mantovannelli, Rep.*1997-II, p. 425.

92 ECtHR 17 December 1996, *Terra woningen, Rep.* 1996, p. 2105.

93 ECtHR, 27 November 1991, *Oerlemans v. Netherlands*, Series A vol 219.

94 ECtHR 28 June 1990, *Obermeier v. Austria*, Series A, vol. 179.

95 ECtHR 2 March 1987, *Weeks vs. UK*, Series A, vol. 179.

96 ECtHR 18 March 1997, *Mantovannelli*, Rep. 1997-II, p. 425.

In the *Kadi* ruling the CJ overturned the ruling of the Court of First Instance, that the Community courts had no jurisdiction to review the internal lawfulness of a Community measure intended to give effect to a resolution of the Security Council. The Court held that the review of a Community measure, that is designed to give effect to resolutions adopted by the Security Council, doesn't entail any challenge to the primacy of the resolution itself. The Court must, in principle, review the lawfulness of all Community acts in the light of the fundamental rights forming an integral part of the general principles of Community law.[97]

The safeguard of full jurisdiction is of importance in relation to the assessment of the proportionality of a measure or penalty. In EC cases the Court has acknowledged the requirement of full jurisdiction. In competition cases it was even laid down in Regulation 17/62 (Article 17). In Regulation 1/2003 this is stated as follows:

> "Article 31
> The Court of Justice shall have unlimited jurisdiction to review decisions whereby the Commission has fixed a fine or a periodic penalty payment. It may cancel, reduce or increase the fine or periodic penalty payment involved."

Unlimited jurisdiction to assess a periodic penalty payment is remarkable when we realise that it is not generally accepted in the Member States that a court may change such a decision. This has to do with the margin of appreciation that is awarded to the administrative authorities when it comes to the use of discretionary powers. In Dutch law, for instance, a court may only annul a periodic penalty payment when it is of the opinion that the authorities have been acting ultra vires. In several Member States of the EU the scrutiny of a measure is less intense than that of a penalty.

In the (imaginary) situation that national law would not allow the court to fully assess the severity of a sanction, the instrument of ex officio examination could help. In the *Van Schijndel* case the Court held that the principle of effectiveness does not preclude a national provision which prevents national courts from raising of their own motion an issue as to whether the provisions of Community law have been infringed. This rule holds when examination of that issue would oblige the courts to abandon the passive role assigned to them by going beyond the ambit of the dispute defined by the parties themselves and relying on facts and circumstances other than those on which the party with an interest in application of those provisions has based his claim. The CJ has also declared that limitations in the jurisdiction of a national court must be justified by the basic principles of the domestic judicial system, such as the protection of the rights of the defence, the principle of legal certainty and the proper conduct

97 Joint Cases C-402/05 P and C-415/05 P, *Kadi* [2008] ECR I-06351.

of procedure.[98] If that is not the case, the national court is obliged to raise a plea of their own motion and assess ex officio whether the sanction is in compliance with imperative EU law, including the principle of proportionality.[99]

7.2.7. Reasonable time

The Human Rights Court has pronounced extensive case law on the condition in Article 6 ECHR, that a trial must take place within a reasonable time. It is important to stress, that preliminary proceedings, such as procedures for objections also count when it comes to determining the length of the procedure. This means that domestic law must guarantee that all the stages of a procedure concerning a sanction can be completed within a reasonable time. Moreover, the weight of the interests involved has an influence on the length of the procedure allowed. When, for instance, an administrative authority imposes a severe sanction, the proceedings of scrutiny must be short in view of the need to be quickly clear as to the legality of the sanction.[100]

This also implies that states are obliged to uphold an efficient system of procedures, and that they need to put an end to delays and backlogs. An overload of cases does not serve as a sufficient excuse, unless it is a temporary situation and adequate measures have been taken to resolve the problem.[101]

In Article 47 of the Charter the right to a fair and public hearing within a reasonable time is guaranteed. EU law does not have specific requirements as to the length of national procedures, although the principle of effectiveness does limit the time span of procedures. In competition cases on EU level the Court has stated that compliance with the reasonable time requirement in the conduct of administrative procedures relating to competition policy constitutes a general principle of Community law whose observance the Community judicature ensures.[102] The right to legal process within a reasonable period is applicable in the context of proceedings brought against a Commission decision imposing fines on an undertaking for infringement of competition law. The reasonableness of a period is to be appraised in the light of the circumstances specific to each case

---

98 Cases C-430/93 and C-431/93, *Van Schijndel and Van Veen* [1995] ECR I-4705.

99 Case C-312/93, *Peterbroeck* [1995] ECR I-4599. In the case *Van der Weerd* the CJ reiterated this approach, but also left ample room for national restrictions in this respect. Cases C-222/05 to C-225/05 [2007] ECR I-4233.

100 This can be derived from the case law in which the Human Rights Court considers the aspect of what is at stake for the applicant as an important criterion to assess breach of the requirement of reasonable time, e.g. ECtHR 8 July 1987, *H. v. UK*, Series A, vol. 120; 25 November 1992, *Abdoella*, Series A, vol. 248-A.

101 ECtHR 10 November 1969, *Stögmüller*, Series A, vo. 9; 13 July 1983, Zimmermann and Steiner, Series A, vol. 66.

102 Case C-282/95 P, *Guérin automobiles v Commission* [1997] ECR I-1503; Case C-105/04 P, *Nederlandse Federatieve Vereniging voor de Groothandel op Elektrotechnisch Gebied* [2006] ECR I-8725.

and, in particular, the importance of the case for the person concerned, its complexity and the conduct of the applicant and of the competent authorities.[103]

8. SEVERITY OF THE MEASURE OR PENALTY

8.1. PROPORTIONALITY

The principle of proportionality is a general principle of Union law, applicable to all Community actions, on the level of the EU as well as on the level of the Member States.[104] It is confirmed by Article 13 §2 TEU. The principle is an important tool for the CJ to review the use of discretionary powers. The Court determines the balancing of interests by applying the criteria of suitability and necessity to the measure taken. For criminal offences the Charter states in Article 49, §3 that the severity of penalties must not be disproportionate to the criminal offence.

The CJ sees to it that sanctions are in proportion to the offence. For those sanctions that can be directly imposed by EU organs, the Court has developed important case law with regard to the imposition of fines in competition law by handing down a catalogue of criteria to review their proportionality. A very important criterion is to what extent the offence has interfered with the goals of Community economic policy.[105]

The Commission and the Council have broad discretionary powers to take economic measures. The Court only applies a mild proportionality test in these cases.[106] The Court reviews measures involving financial support and assistance more strictly, focusing on the rights of the individual.[107] The most intensive proportionality test is applied when fundamental rights are at stake.[108]

The goals of the EU policy in question are very important in cases in which Member States impose EU measures and penalties. It is often argued that these measures and penalties, which are increasingly dictated by EU Regulations, are harsh and disproportionate. The Court reviews them in the light of an important aspect of EU policy: combating irregularities and fraud. If the measure or penalty is necessary to adequately execute an EU Regulation and to prevent fraud actions, even a severe penalty is considered to be proportional.[109]

---

103 Case C-185/95 P, *Baustahlgewebe* [1998] ECR I-8417, Joined Cases C-238/99 P, C-244/99 P, C-245/99 P, C-247/99 P, C-250/99 P to C-252/99 P and C-254/99 P, *Limburgse Vinyl Maatschappij and Others v Commission* [1999] ECR I-8375; and Case C-194/99 P *Thyssen Stahl v Commission* [2003] ECR I-10821.

104 See T. Tridimas, *The general principles of EU law*, Oxford, 2006.

105 For example, Cases 96–102, 104, 105, 108, 110/82, *IAZ* [1983] ECR 3369.

106 Case 316/86, *Krücken* [1988] ECR 2213.

107 See Case 199/87, *Jensen* [1988] ECR 5045.

108 For example, Case 44/79, *Hauer* [1979] ECR 3727.

109 See case 240/90, *Germany/Commission* [1992] ECR I-5383.

However, if the measure or penalty is of an administrative nature and the only aim of the obligation to which it is bound is to facilitate smooth management and control, the Court requires a differentiation between this kind of reaction to an offence and the measures or penalties that can be imposed when the primary duties in the Regulation are violated, as the *Otto Preisler Weingut* case illustrates.

> "The EC issued a Regulation on grants for distillation of wine; distillation of wine was promoted in order to diminish the quantity of wine in store in the EC. In this Regulation it was provided that those wine producers, who had not reported their production of that year in September, were excluded from the grants. Some German producers were affected by this exclusion. In the proceedings before the German courts they held that the Regulation was invalid, because it was disproportional in its sanctions. The Court examined the purpose of the obligation to report in September, and found that the aim was to ensure that the Commission would have enough data about the production of wine and the wine in stock in December. The Commission needs these data to make an estimate at the beginning of every sales year. The Court held that for this purpose the sanction as such would not be necessary, it was disproportional to provide for such a strict deadline in combination with such a severe penalty and declared the Regulation invalid to that respect."[110]

In competition law the case law on the proportionality of penalties is the best developed. The amount of the fine relates to the seriousness of the infringement and the consequences thereof for the market, the turnover of the companies involved, the period of time the infringement has lasted, and to the existence of aggravating circumstances such as being the initiator of or the leading player in the scheme, intent, recidivism etc.[111]

The Court of First Instance takes its task very seriously in this respect, and scrutinizes the decision to impose a fine very precisely. Although it does not very often use its power to diminish the fine, it does find reason to annul a decision partly or totally when the Commission has given insufficient reasons for the fine. This automatically results in the lowering of the fine, since the underpinning grounds are not present.[112]

Article 49, para 3 of the Charter states that the severity of penalties must not be disproportionate to the criminal offence. Up to certainly, the EU had only limited competence in criminal matters. However, with the Lisbon Treaty and recent case law of the Court about directives on criminal enforcement of environmental law, the powers of the EU have increased.[113] In the future Member

110 Case C-319/90, *Otto Pressler Weingut* [1992] ECR I-203.

111 See for an example Joined Cases T-109/02, T-118/02, T-122/02, T-125/02, T-126/02, T-128/02, T-129/02, T-132/02 en T-136/02, *Bolloré SA et al.* [2007] ECR II-947, cons. 480–484.

112 Joined cases T-236/01, T-239/01, T-244/01 to T-246/01, T-251/01 and T-252/01, *Tokai Carbon Co. Ltd* [2004] ECR II-01181.

113 Cases C-176/03 and C-440/05 and par. 2.

States will be confronted more and more with EU law, demanding that certain infringements shall be considered and punished as criminal offences. The case law on administrative sanctions will then gain importance for penal sanctions.

8.2. ACCUMULATION OF SANCTIONS

In the Charter the principle of *ne bis in idem* is laid down for criminal offences.

> "Article 50: Right not to be tried or punished twice in criminal proceedings for the same criminal offence
>
> No one shall be liable to be tried or punished again in criminal proceedings for an offence for which he or she has already been finally acquitted or convicted within the Union in accordance with the law."

An accumulation of penalties is generally seen as undesirable, because of the *ne bis in idem* principle. In some cases, national authorities can apply penalties for the same offence as described in Union regulations. In such a situation, EU law may oblige them to apply an administrative penalty, while at the same time national law may force the authorities to commence prosecution. This might happen when the public prosecutor has no discretionary power to decide on prosecution, and the expediency rule does not apply. However, it is also possible that the prosecutor considers the offence to be of such a nature that criminal proceedings are in order. EU law cannot prevent this.

Regulation no. 2988/95 offers a solution in a special provision (Article 6), which states that the imposition of financial penalties such as administrative fines may be suspended by a decision of the competent authority, if criminal proceedings have been initiated against the person concerned in connection with the same facts. When the criminal procedure is concluded, the administrative procedure shall be resumed. The administrative authority shall ensure that a penalty at least equivalent to that prescribed by EU rules is imposed, which may take into account any penalty imposed by the judicial authority on the same person in respect of the same facts (in German: the *Anrechnungsprinzip*). This provision has been added in case the criminal proceedings as well as the administrative procedure would lead to a financial penalty, especially a fine. Other kinds of financial repercussions, like the recovery of grants or the loss of a deposit are not covered by the article in question, because they qualify as a 'measure', and do not count with respect to protection against accumulation.

This provision shows that EU law recognizes the idea that the total of the penalties imposed may not be disproportionate to the offence. In 1969 the Court stated in the *Walt Wilhelm* case that the general principles of Community law require that in the decision to impose a sanction earlier penalties for the same fact are taken into account, not because the *ne bis in idem* principle was violated, but because the total of the sanctions should be proportionate to the offence.[114] The case concerned the accumulation of international and EC sanctions. The Court observed in a much later, similar case that any consideration concerning the existence of fines imposed by the authorities of a non-member State can be taken into account only under the Commission's discretion in setting fines for infringements of – in this case –Community competition law. Accordingly, although it cannot be ruled out that the Commission may take into account fines imposed previously by the authorities of non-member States, it cannot be required to do so.

It must be stressed that the Commission of course, in exercising its discretion, should also pay attention to the principle of proportionality. The Court of First Instance decided that national and Community sanctions in competition law can accumulate, provided that the Commission takes into account the national sanctions already imposed for the same fact when it decides on the amount of the fine.[115] By then, it had already been suggested that this case law should also be applied in case of accumulation of national sanctions with different sanctioning purposes. In that particular case a deposit was forfeited because of irregularities, and at the same time national authorities commenced criminal proceedings. The application of the principle of proportionality to the total of the two sanctions could make the application of the *ne bis in idem* rule obsolete.[116] The underlying idea has been adopted in Regulation 2988/95.

In competition law the problem is tackled in Regulation no. 1/2003 where it states that the competition authorities of the Member States are automatically relieved of their competence if the Commission initiates its own proceedings. If the authorities of two or more Member States have started proceedings the Regulation provides that it is sufficient that one authority handles the case; the others should suspend the procedure or reject the complaint in question (Article 13). However, the rule does not say which authority should withdraw from the case, those who started later, those who have a less solid case?

Article 50 of the Charter is also of importance in transnational cases. If a EU citizen is subject to a criminal charge for the same facts in several Member States, the CJ has ruled earlier in a Schengen case that the *ne bis in idem* rule applies.[117] As a consequence, offenders could be charged in one Member State with a minor offence and punished with a simple administrative sanction, whereas in the other Member State the same fact would be a criminal offence with severe criminal sanctions. This, of course, could lead to forum shopping.

---

114 Case 14/68, *Walt Wilhelm* [1969] ECR 1.

115 Case T-149/89, *Sotralenz* [1995] ECR II-1127.

116 See the conclusion in the *Könecke* case, 117/83 [1984] ECR 3291.

117 C-436/04, *Leopold Henri Van Esbroeck* [2006] ECR I-2333. This was a case about the Schengen agreement and the fact that Van Esbroeck had been subject to legal proceedings in different Contracting States for the same facts.

9. CONCLUSION

It is safe to say that the field of administrative sanctioning has been subject to an important influence of EU law. EU law has broadened the scope of administrative sanctioning by adding a variety of sanctions to the palette of sanctions in national law. The difference in approach between measures (of a reparatory nature) and penalties (of a punitive nature) is gradual. Most safeguards that have been implemented apply to both categories. The penalties, however, demand a more restrictive approach in the sense that the authorities need to respect the guarantees that have been set by the ECHR and the Charter, when it comes to a criminal charge. Although the CJ in the past adopted its own approach in the interpretation of the ECHR, which led to differences between the case law of the CJ and of the ECtHR, this has changed in recent years. Especially since the preparations for the Charter of Fundamental Rights, the case law of the CJ has followed the interpretations of the ECtHR more closely. Much work has been done to make the written law of the EU complete and to live up to the standards of the rule of law. The adoption of the Charter as part of the Lisbon Treaty certainly will help to further develop safeguards in administrative sanctioning procedures, as well as the upcoming accession of the EU to the ECHR.

LIST OF AUTHORS

Ken Andries, Professor at the University of Hasselt (Belgium) and research fellow at the University of Leuven. He is a lawyer at the Bar of Brussels.

Antonio Ma. Bueno Armijo, Assistant professor of administrative law at the University of Córdoba.

Alessandro Bernardi, Full Professor of Criminal Law at the University of Ferrara, Director of the International Doctoral School in Criminal Law and European Integration.

Emmanuel Breen, Attorney at Law, Paris Bar and Lecturer at Paris-Sorbonne University.

Corina Cristina Buzdugan, Lecturer, Head of the Public Law Department of the Faculty of Law from Cluj-Napoca, "Dimitrie Cantemir" Christian University Bucharest.

Pedro Caeiro, Assistant Professor at the University of Coimbra. He worked for the Portuguese Ministry of Justice in the area of legal reform and implementation of European criminal law. He also works as an independent consultant. He is a founding member and contact point for Portugal of the European Criminal Law Academic Network (ECLAN).

Manuel Izquierdo Carrasco, Professor of administrative law and director of the department of economic public law at the University of Córdoba.

Gerhard Dannecker, Director of the Institute for German, European and International Criminal Law and Law of Criminal Procedures at the University of Heidelberg, Chair for Criminal Law and Law of Criminal Procedures with concentration on European and international aspects.

Georges Dellis, Assistant Professor of Public Law at the University of Athens Law Faculty, a Lawyer at the Athens Bar Association and a former Référendaire at the Court of Justice of the European Union.

Elena Mihaela Fodor, Assistant professor, Dean of the Faculty of Law from Cluj-Napoca, "Dimitrie Cantemir" Christian University Bucharest. She is a member of The Institute for Administrative Sciences "Paul Negulescu" from Romania and of the Romanian Institute for Public Law and Administrative Sciences.

Ciro Grandi, Lawyer and Senior Researcher in Criminal Law at the University of Ferrara.

Frank Höpfl, Professor of criminal law at the University of Vienna.

Oswald Jansen, Lawyer and legal council of the municipality of The Hague and senior lecturer at the University of Utrecht.

Patricia Blanc-Gonnet Jonason, Assistant professor of public law at Södertörn University, Stockholm, Sweden and co-director of the International School of Transparency.

Robert Kert, Assistant professor of criminal law at the University of Vienna.

Mikael Koillinen, Senior Researcher of administrative law at the University of Turku.

Miguel Ângelo Lemos, Assistant at the university of Coimbra and senior-instructor at the university of Macau. He is currently preparing a Phd on the *nulum crimen sine lege* principle at the international, european and national levels.

Manuel Rebollo Puig, Professor of administrative law at the University of Córdoba.

John McEldowney, Professor of law at the University of Warwick.

Adrienne de Moor-van Vugt, Professor of administrative law at the University of Amsterdam.

Carlenrico Paliero, Lawyer and professor of criminal law at the University of Milan.

Johan Put, Professor at the Faculty of Law of the University of Leuven (Belgium), affiliated to as well the Institute of Social Law (ISR) as the Leuven Institute of Criminology (LINC). He is also assessor at the Belgian Council of State.

Lucía Alarcón Sotomayor, Assistant professor of administrative law at the University of Córdoba.

Ilaria Zoda, Assistant in Criminal Law at the University of Ferrara and officer at the *Agenzia delle Entrate* (Tax and Revenue Administration).

www.ingramcontent.com/pod-product-compliance
Ingram Content Group UK Ltd.
Pitfield, Milton Keynes, MK11 3LW, UK
UKHW051924100926
8556IPUK00022B/1362

9 781780 681